Middle Eastern and European Christianity, 16th–20th Century

Edinburgh Studies in Middle Eastern Christianity
Series Editors: Deanna Ferree Womack and Philip Michael Forness

Series Advisory Board: Dr Mary K. Farag, Dr John-Paul A. Ghobrial, Dr Fiona McCallum Guiney, Rev. Dr Mitri Raheb, Dr Heather J. Sharkey, Dr Jack Tannous

Published title

Middle Eastern and European Christianity, 16th–20th Century: Connected Histories
Bernard Heyberger; edited by Aurélien Girard, Cesare Santus, Vassa Kontouma and Karène Sanchez Summerer

edinburghuniversitypress.com/series/esmec

Middle Eastern and European Christianity, 16th–20th Century

Connected Histories

Essays by Bernard Heyberger

Edited by
Aurélien Girard, Cesare Santus, Vassa Kontouma and
Karène Sanchez Summerer

Translated by
M. Robitaille-Ibbett

EDINBURGH
University Press

Edinburgh University Press is one of the leading university presses in the UK. We publish academic books and journals in our selected subject areas across the humanities and social sciences, combining cutting-edge scholarship with high editorial and production values to produce academic works of lasting importance. For more information visit our website: edinburghuniversitypress.com

Edinburgh University Press Ltd
13 Infirmary Street,
Edinburgh, EH1 1LT

First published in hardback by Edinburgh University Press 2023

Typeset in 11/13 Adobe Garamond by
IDSUK (DataConnection) Ltd

A CIP record for this book is available from the British Library

ISBN 978 1 3995 0353 2 (hardback)
ISBN 978 1 3995 0354 9 (paperback)
ISBN 978 1 3995 0355 6 (webready PDF)
ISBN 978 1 3995 0356 3 (epub)

Contents

List of Figures vii
Acknowledgements viii
Notes on the Editors x
List of Abbreviations and Acronyms xii
Note on Transliteration xiii
Note on the Text xiv

Foreword 1
Heather J. Sharkey

Introduction: A New History of Middle Eastern Christians 10
Aurélien Girard, Cesare Santus and Karène Sanchez-Summerer

Part I Mobility, Networks and Protection

1. Eastern Christians in Seventeenth- and Eighteenth-century Catholic Europe 49
2. The Wasted Career of an Eastern Clergyman in Italy: Timothy Karnuk (Timoteo Agnellini), Syriac Catholic Archbishop of Mardin 90
3. Security and Insecurity: Syrian Christians in the Mediterranean (Seventeenth and Eighteenth Centuries) 105
4. A Border-crossing Ottoman Christian at the Beginning of the Eighteenth Century: Ḥannā Diyāb of Aleppo and his Account of his Travel to Paris 124
5. The Migration of Middle Eastern Christians and European Protection: A Long History 142

Part II Building Confessional Identities: Entangled Histories

6. The Westernisation and Confessionalisation of Christians in the Middle East: An 'Entangled History' ('*Histoire Croisée*') 163
7. Polemic Dialogues between Christians and Muslims in the Seventeenth Century 182
8. From Religious to Secular Imagery? The Rise of the Image among Christians in Syria and Lebanon in the Seventeenth to Nineteenth Centuries 199
9. Individualism and Political Modernity: Devout Catholic Women in Aleppo and Mount Lebanon between the Seventeenth and Nineteenth Centuries 225
10. Saint Charbel Makhlouf, or the Consecration of Maronite Identity 245

Epilogue: The Maestro and his Music 264
John-Paul Ghobrial

Complete Bibliography of Bernard Heyberger (December 2021) 271
Bibliography 292
Tabula Gratulatoria 323
Index 329

Figures

1.1	Area of circulation of Eastern Christians (seventeenth to eighteenth centuries)	53
1.2	Origin and destination of Eastern Christians on travel (seventeenth to eighteenth centuries)	54
8.1	Assumption of the Virgin Mary, Museum at Our Lady Monastery, Louaizeh (Luwayza), Zuk Mosbeh, Lebanon	203
8.2	Coronation of the Virgin Mary by the Holy Trinity (1690), fresco, Monastery of Qannūbīn, Lebanon	204
8.3	Evangelist Saint Luke, woodcut, in *Kitāb al-Injil al-sharīf al-ṭāhir* (Khunshāra: Monastery of Saint John of Shuwayr, Lebanon, 1776)	207
8.4	Woodcut in grotesque style, several times reproduced in *Kitāb al-Injil al-sharīf al-ṭāhir* (Khunshāra: Monastery of Saint John of Shuwayr, Lebanon, 1776)	207
8.5	Virgin Mary with the Child and Two Angels, woodcut in the style of a Byzantine icon, several times reproduced in *Kitāb al-Injil al-sharīf al-ṭāhir* (Khunshāra: monastery of Saint John of Shuwayr, Lebanon, 1776)	208
8.6	Sacred Heart of Jesus with Eucharist, door lintel, Monastery of Mār Yūsaf al-Ḥuṣn, Ghosta (Ghūsṭā), Lebanon	212
8.7	Portrait of ʿAbdallāh Qarāʿalī (1672–1742), first Superior of the Lebanese Monks of Saint Anthony, from 1716 onwards bishop of Beirut. Anonymous painting, undated (eighteenth century?). Museum at Our Lady Monastery, Louaizeh (Luwayza), Zuk Mosbeh, Lebanon	214

Acknowledgements

On 10 June 2020, the last session of Bernard Heyberger's seminar on Eastern Christianity was held online, at a time when Europe was just emerging from an initial phase of lock-down and when academic life was gradually discovering the convenience of video-conferencing. Listeners from Europe, North America and the Middle East, colleagues, students and former students, as well as members of a larger audience interested in this subject gathered virtually around Bernard Heyberger, who was taking stock of his teaching at the École Pratique des Hautes Études and the École des Hautes Études en Sciences Sociales (Paris) on the eve of his retirement as *directeur d'études* (full professor). Several listeners then took the floor to express their intellectual debt and gratitude. Once the cameras were switched off, former students and colleagues close to Heyberger discussed the possibility of a *Festschrift* to express this recognition in a publication. Remembering one of Bernard Heyberger's wishes, we decided to make his research better-known in English and to offer a comprehensive view of his work in the present volume.

We are grateful to EPHE (École Pratique des Hautes Études, PSL), NWO (The Dutch Research Council), IISMM (Institut d'études de l'Islam et des sociétés du monde musulman) and the research project *CrossRoads: European Cultural Diplomacy and Arab Christians in Palestine: A Connected History (1918–1948)*, CERHiC (Centre d'études et de recherche en histoire culturelle-Université de Reims Champagne-Ardenne) and CéSor (Centre d'études en sciences sociales du religieux-École des Hautes Études en Sciences Sociales / Centre national de la Recherche Scientifique) for financing part of this book project.

We would also like to thank Sarah Irving for her invaluable work in copy-editing the manuscript and the translators Mary Ibbett-Robitaille and Constance Bantman. We are grateful to the colleagues who allowed the republication of articles they had previously edited, Méropi Anastassiadou, Catherine Mayeur-Jaouen, Silvia Naef, Andreas Schmoller, Amira Sonbol and Chantal Verdeil, as well as the publishing houses. Heather Sharkey and John-Paul Ghobrial provided a foreword and an epilogue to this volume. We are very grateful to them. Finally, we thank the colleagues who contributed to the Tabula Gratulatoria.

Notes on the Editors

Aurélien Girard is Senior Lecturer at the University of Reims Champagne-Ardenne, in the Centre d'études et de recherche en histoire culturelle (CERHiC). Currently, he serves as a CNRS delegate to the Centre d'études en sciences sociales du religieux (Paris). He is a former Fellow of the École française de Rome. His work focuses on the history of Eastern Christians in the Arab provinces of the Ottoman Empire and on the history of Oriental studies in Europe in the seventeenth and eighteenth centuries. His most recent publications include the article 'Le Collège maronite de Rome et les langues au tournant des XVIe et XVIIe siècles: Éducation des chrétiens orientaux, science orientaliste et apologétique catholique', *Rivista Storica Italiana*, 132, 1 (2020), pp. 272–99, and the volume edited with Bernard Heyberger and Vassa Kontouma, *Livres et confessions chrétiennes orientales: Histoire connectée entre Empire ottoman, monde slave et Occident (XVIe–XVIIIe siècles)* (forthcoming).

Cesare Santus is Senior (Tenure Track) Assistant Professor at the University of Trieste and a former Postdoctoral Researcher of the National Fund for Scientific Research (FNRS, Belgium). In his book *Trasgressioni necessarie: Communicatio in sacris, coesistenza e conflitti tra le comunità cristiane orientali* (2019), he has studied the confessional dynamics within the Greek and Armenian communities of the Ottoman Empire, as well as their reaction to the Catholic apostolate in the seventeenth and eighteenth centuries. He is the author of several articles on the Muslim and Eastern Christian presence in early modern Italy (especially Rome), and he has recently published a second book, *Il «turco» a Livorno: Incontri con l'islam nella Toscana del Seicento* (2019). He is currently pursuing research on the role of the Roman Inquisition in examining the problems raised by the establishment of the Eastern Catholic Churches and more broadly by European missionary activity in the East ('L'adoration de Naaman: Pour une histoire croisée des querelles des rites', *Revue d'histoire ecclésiastique*, 116, 3–4 (2021), pp. 804–30).

Vassa Kontouma is Director of Studies and Dean of the Religious Sciences Department at the École pratique des hautes études (PSL, Paris), where she teaches *Orthodox Christianity, 15th–21th Centuries*. She is also president of the French Institute for Byzantine Studies (IFEB, Paris). Since 2019, she has co-directed the Villa Vigoni programme *Eastern Christians and the Republic of Letters between the 16th and 18th Centuries*. Her publications deal with Byzantine and post-Byzantine Greek theology. She co-edited the work *La Théologie byzantine et sa tradition* II (2002). She is also the author of *John of Damascus: New Studies on his Life and Works* (2015). Her most recent publication is 'The Archimandrite and the Astronomer: The Visit of Chrysanthos Notaras to Giovanni Domenico Cassini: A New Approach', in Kostas Sarris, Nikolas Pissis and Miltos Pechlivanos (eds), *Confessionalization and/as Knowledge Transfer in the Greek Orthodox Church* (2021), pp. 233–72.

Karène Sanchez Summerer is Professor and Chair of Middle Eastern studies at Groningen University. Her research considers the interactions between European linguistic and cultural policies and the Arab communities (1860–1948) in the Levant, Christian missionaries' impact during the formative years of the contemporary Middle East, and Arab Catholic communities in Ottoman and British Mandate Palestine. She is the PI of the research project *CrossRoads: European cultural Diplomacy and Arab Christians in Palestine: A Connected history (1920–1950)* (The Netherlands National Research Agency, 2018–22), as well as the co-editor of the series *Languages and Culture in History* (with Willem Frijhoff). Her recent publications include two volumes edited with Sary Zananiri, *Imaging and Imagining Palestine: Photography, Modernity and the Biblical Lens (1918–1948)* (2021) and *Europeans' Cultural Diplomacy and Arab Christianity in Mandate Palestine: Between Contention and Connection* (2021).

Abbreviations and Acronyms

AAV	Archivum Apostolicum Vaticanum, Vatican City
ACU	Archivio del Collegio Urbano, Vatican City
ADDF	Archivum Dicasterii pro Doctrina Fidei, Vatican City
ARSI	Archivum Romanum Societatis Iesu, Vatican City
AGC	Archivio Generale dell'Ordine dei Frati Minori Cappuccini, Rome
AN	Archives Nationales, Paris
AE	Affaires Étrangères
APF	Archivio Storico della Congregazione per l'Evangelizzazione dei Popoli (usually known as Archivio *de Propaganda Fide*), Vatican City
BAV	Bibliotheca Apostolica Vaticana, Vatican City
CP	Congregazioni Particolari
Registro	'Registro dei nomi, cognomi . . . degli alunni di Propaganda Fide raccolti dal Rettore Bonvicini, 1633–1753'
SOCG	Scritture Originali riferite nelle Congregazioni Generali
SC	Scritture riferite nei Congressi
SO	Sanctum Officium
St. St.	Stanza Storica
col./cols	column/columns
fol./fols	folio/folios
ms	manuscript
vol./vols	volume/volumes

Note on Transliteration

In transliterating Arabic, this volume generally follows the *International Journal of Middle East Studies* system, albeit maintaining the diacritical marks. There are, however, some exceptions to this rule. The ecclesiastical names of Melkite patriarchs are rendered according to the equivalent Anglicised form. Family names and all other personal names are transcribed according to scientific rules, except in cases where the original form is not known, or when demands for clarity and uniformity across the text require otherwise. In these cases, the names are given as they appear in the sources, mostly in Italian form, sometimes followed by the (hypothetical) original form in brackets. For the names of contemporary authors, we have adopted the spelling that was preferred and used by them, or that has become recognised as the norm over time. Proper names of places that have recognised English equivalents have been preferred. All Arabic terms that have entered the English dictionary have been used in their English form, without italics or transliteration. Bibliographic references respect the transliteration used in the title page of the cited works, even when in contrast with the system adopted here.

Note on the Text

The chapters of this volume were previously published in the following locations:

Chapter 1: 'Chrétiens orientaux dans l'Europe catholique (XVIIe–XVIIIe siècles)', in Bernard Heyberger and Chantal Verdeil (eds), *Hommes de l'entre-deux: Parcours individuels et portraits de groupe sur la frontière méditerranéenne* (Paris: Les Indes Savantes, 2009), pp. 61–94 (*translated*).

Chapter 2: 'La carrière manquée d'un ecclésiastique oriental en Italie: Timothée Karnûsh, archevêque syrien catholique de Mardîn', in Bernard Heyberger (ed.), *L'Italie vue par les étrangers, Bulletin de la Faculté des Lettres de Mulhouse*, 19 (1995), pp. 31–47 (*translated*).

Chapter 3: 'Sécurité et insécurité: Les chrétiens de Syrie dans l'espace méditerranéen (XVIIe–XVIIIe siècles)', in Méropi Anastassiadou and Bernard Heyberger (eds), *Figures anonymes, figures d'élite: Pour une anatomie de l'Homo ottomanicus* (Istanbul: Isis Press, 1999), pp. 147–63 (*translated*).

Chapter 4: 'A Border Crossing Ottoman Christian at the Beginning of the 18th Century: Hanna Dyâb of Aleppo and His Account of His Travel to Paris', in Serena Di Nepi and Felicita Tramontana (eds), *Contacts on the Move*, monographic section of *Studi e Materiali di Storia delle Religioni*, 84, 2 (2018), pp. 548–64.

Chapter 5: 'Migration of the Middle Eastern Christians and European Protection: A Long History', in Andreas Schmoller (ed.), *Middle Eastern Christians and Europe: Historical Legacies and Present Challenges* (Vienna: LIT, 2018), pp. 23–42.

Chapter 6: 'Pour une "histoire croisée" de l'occidentalisation et de la confessionnalisation chez les chrétiens du Proche-Orient', *The MIT-Electronic Journal of Middle Eastern Studies*, 3 (2003), pp. 36–49 (*translated*).

Chapter 7: 'Polemic Dialogues between Christians and Muslims in the Seventeenth Century', *Journal of the Economic and Social History of the Orient*, 55 (2012), pp. 495–516.

Chapter 8: 'De l'image religieuse à l'image profane? L'essor de l'image chez les chrétiens de Syrie et du Liban', in Bernard Heyberger and Silvia Naef (eds), *La multiplication des images en pays d'Islam: De l'estampe à la télévision (17e–21e siècle)* (Istanbul: Orient-Institut der DMG; Würzburg: Egon, 2003), pp. 31–56 (*translated*).

Chapter 9: 'Individualism and Political Modernity: Devout Catholic Women in Aleppo and Lebanon, between the Seventeenth and the Nineteenth Centuries', in Amira Sonbol (ed.), *Beyond the Exotic: Women's Histories in Islamic Societies* (New York: Syracuse University Press, 2005), pp. 71–85.

Chapter 10: 'Saint Charbel Makhlouf, ou la consécration de l'identité maronite', in Catherine Mayeur-Jaouen (ed.), *Saints et héros du Moyen-Orient contemporain* (Paris: Maisonneuve et Larose, 2002), pp. 139–59 (*translated*).

The author and the editors have in some cases decided to update the information provided by the original texts. Bibliographical additions and comments following the original publication are indicated in the notes using square brackets. The chapters already published in English have undergone a linguistic revision and editing process. Further minor changes were made to correct factual errors, or to ensure greater consistency between the chapters of the volume.

Foreword

CREATING COMMUNITIES IN THE STUDY OF MIDDLE EASTERN CHRISTIANITY

On 10 June 2020, a group of scholars navigated their way through the web conferencing system called BigBlueButton to reach the meeting of the seminar series on the 'Anthropologie historique des Chrétiens en Islam' (Historical Anthropology of Christians in Islam), or, as it was called before 2011, 'Histoire des Chrétiens d'Orient' (History of the Christians of the East). Over more than fifteen years, Bernard Heyberger had hosted this seminar in Paris, first from a room in the Sorbonne (2004–10); then from the Institut d'études de l'Islam et des sociétés du monde musulman (IISMM) in the beautiful sixth arrondissement (2011–18); and finally from Aubervilliers, the new campus site for parts of the University of Paris in the northeast of the city (2018–20).[1] At these sessions, he or a guest scholar would present research-in-progress on a topic pertaining to Middle Eastern Christian history in the Islamic world from the early modern period (sixteenth century) to the present. But this time was different: the series was ending because Bernard Heyberger was retiring.

Recall that in 2020, the COVID-19 pandemic was raging. Unable to welcome colleagues around a common table in Paris, Heyberger organised the meeting online. By this stage, academics were becoming more accustomed to online lectures and discussions, although many admitted that such meetings left them numb from staring into computer screens and dissatisfied by the lack of real contact. Many yearned for face-to-face encounters and struggled with lockdowns, quarantines and fears of the corona virus. And yet, this final meeting of the 'Anthropologie historique des Chrétiens en Islam' was a joyful affair, and its online format enabled many more to attend than as if the seminar had happened in Paris, in person. I connected from Philadelphia. Others came from Oxford, Leiden and Marseille; from Athens, Beirut and beyond.

As we recognised each other's names among the attendees on our screens and saw messages pop up in the 'chat' interface, expressing congratulations and gratitude, it struck me – as I am certain it struck others – that this seminar series had become more than the sum of its parts. It had become an intellectual arena, agora and laboratory, where a community of Middle Eastern Christian history *aficionados* was formed.

In his now famous book *Imagined Communities*, the anthropologist Benedict Anderson has made a case for the role of print capitalism and vernacular literacy in cultivating nationalism around what he has called 'imagined communities' of readers.[2] Through his scholarship and mentorship, Bernard Heyberger helped to forge a different kind of imagined community – an academic one, around a field of inquiry. Its members included an international mix of scholars working in several languages (French, Arabic, English, German, Italian, Turkish . . . the list goes on), on a spectrum of topics of mutual interest, often (but not exclusively) pertaining to Catholic cultures. More than merely sharing an interest in Middle Eastern Christian history, the members of this informal community – *our* community – evinced certain outlooks and approaches, which Bernard Heyberger modeled in his scholarship, welcomed in his seminar and encouraged among the students whom he advised.

Below I will attempt to consider what this volume achieves before surveying the salient characteristics of Bernard Heyberger's approach to the study of Middle Eastern Christian history from the early modern era to the present. I will then quickly survey his books, an awareness of which will enable readers of this volume to appreciate more fully the scope of his research.

CONNECTING MIDDLE EASTERN AND EUROPEAN CHRISTIAN HISTORIES

This volume promises to make Bernard Heyberger's scholarship accessible to a wider audience, by gathering ten articles that first appeared in disparate forums and by translating half of them from French into English. For scholars from the Anglophone world, the subjects covered here, mostly set in Greater Syria, may feel new and familiar at once. What may feel new is that the Eastern Mediterranean worlds he has described have centred on Roman Catholic, mainly French- and Italian-speaking missionaries and Eastern-rite Catholics, whereas Anglophone scholars have more often focused on Protestants and the Muslim, Christian, Jewish and other people with whom they interacted. What may feel familiar is that the institutional settings where many of these histories transpired (schools, churches and so on) are common to all historians of Christian missions in the region, not only Catholic and Protestant, but also, for example, Russian Orthodox.[3] Common, too, are certain kinds of interactions with Muslim authorities associated with the region's Ottoman and post-Ottoman states, debates over educational policies and priorities, and personality conflicts and forms of factional and sectarian in-fighting. There are also methodological parallels entailing the use of manuscript, print, visual and material sources. The bottom line is that this volume will aid in the comparative study of Christian organisations and people across lines of sect, language, region and nationality.

Bernard Heyberger's articles will also introduce some readers to the idea of 'connected history', in these cases between Western and Southern Europe and the region that we now call the Middle East. For the study of Middle Eastern Christian cultures, the phrase 'connected history' has important advantages over the phrase 'transnational history', which Anglophone scholars tend to use more frequently. Historians from self-consciously young countries – such as the United States, Canada and Australia – may be especially inclined to think transnationally.[4] (Consider that the first American Protestant missionaries reached the eastern Mediterranean lands in 1819, less than fifty years after the establishment of the US Republic). Those who write histories from the vantage points of young countries, as well as those who focus on the period from the late nineteenth century onward (by which time states such as Germany and Italy had unified and formed), may be more inclined to use a transnational paradigm, because the nation-state seems natural and self-evident, while referring to it does not risk anachronism. National and transnational paradigms are less relevant, however, and certainly less helpful, when we study old religious institutions such as the Catholic Church ('Rome') or organisations such as the Society of Jesus (the Jesuits), which drew members from many lands and which contributed to earlier forms of globalisation. The fact that much of Heyberger's research stretches back to the seventeenth century – when even the venerable France was still a work-in-progress! – suggests the limited relevance of nation-centred paradigms there, too. Think also about fluctuations in Ottoman lands and of the difference between, say, eighteenth-century Syria or Greater Syria (as a term applied to a general region) and the bounded republic of Syria that emerged after the First World War. In short, and for all these reasons, the 'connected histories' paradigm works much more effectively than national, transnational, or international alternatives when tracing long histories that link places, polities, religious institutions, people and times.

Many of the articles in this volume pivot between Syria and Rome. Heyberger has examined the careers of clerics and travellers who set out from Europe for Syria and conversely those who voyaged from Syria to Europe. He has included merchants who sailed Mediterranean waters and adventurers who succumbed to their wanderlust. Refreshingly, even while working on church-related histories that are often synonymous with patriarchy, he has investigated the history of women and not only of men. By seeing in this collection how he has traced the lives of people in motion, readers may come away with ideas for exploring other connected and mobile histories.

HISTORICAL ANTHROPOLOGY AND GLOBAL MICROHISTORY

There is more to Heyberger's distinctive approach than his attention to circulatory flows across the Eastern and Western Mediterranean worlds. Also salient is his approach to 'global microhistory', along with what Heyberger himself (in the name of his long-running seminar in Paris) called 'historical anthropology'. Both terms, global microhistory and historical anthropology, capture his style of examining details within broader landscapes, although the two terms do reflect different features of his work.

The phrase 'global microhistory', as elaborated by the historian Francesca Trivellato,[5] describes Bernard Heyberger's attention to social scales: his way of placing people in settings that range from households (perhaps the room where a woman sits reading) and churches (perhaps in the confessional, with an adherent and a listening priest), to schools, villages and cities, or to larger sectarian communities, such as the Maronite collective. Sometimes his scale reaches higher still, to cover diverse Catholics or Christians or trends that unfolded in Syria at large. One can see his global microhistory approach, with its different scales of inquiry, in the story of the 'wasted career' of Timothy Karnuk (see Chapter 2), a seventeenth-century Syriac Catholic archbishop who made his way to Rome and scraped by while dabbling in trade.

By contrast, the phrase 'historical anthropology' has the advantage of focusing on humans and their foibles, not theologies or doctrines. It captures another quality of Heyberger's scholarship: his ability to identify and assess quirky specimens of *Homo sapiens sapiens*. The title of one of his co-edited volumes, from which Chapter 3 in this collection derives, reflects this approach with its reference to the cultural 'anatomy' of '*Homo ottomanicus*' and to both elite and anonymous figures.[6] As a historian, Heyberger has drawn on rigorous archival research using both manuscript and printed works. But, like a physical and cultural anthropologist, he has examined his sources for social and material cues and then interpreted their significance. In one of my favorite examples, he has reflected in one of his books on the significance of a request that a monastery leader in Kisruwān sent to Rome in 1705, for a big church bell. Islamic state conventions, so he noted, had historically forbidden churches from ringing bells (allowing only the banging of the quieter semantron, or wooden clapper). But as the eighteenth century began, churches and monasteries in Syria were starting not just to hang bells, but also to ring them. This request was therefore a 'symbol', he suggested, 'of [growing] Christian liberty in Lebanon', in a period when Roman Catholic and European influence was on the rise.[7] The narratives he has constructed around details such as this one track much larger political shifts.

HUMOUR AND HUMANISATION

Those privileged to know Bernard Heyberger as a friend can attest that he has a sly sense of humour and strong sense of fun. These qualities have surfaced in his scholarship when he has cast his eye on his subjects' peccadilloes. The people whom he has studied rarely are saints, in either metaphorical or literal senses of the term. A notable exception appears in Chapter 10 in this volume, where he has studied an actual saint – Charbel Makhlouf (1828–98) – a Lebanese Maronite monk who was canonised in 1977! One gets the feeling that he has enjoyed writing about edgy or oddball figures, and that he has seen elements of comedy – or depending on the story, tragicomedy – when he has looked into the past.

One can also see a subtle comic dimension at work in his account of the Maronite adventurer Ḥannā Diyāb (see Chapter 4), who went to Paris in the eighteenth century. In Paris, Ḥannā Diyāb transmitted the stories of Aladdin and Ali Baba to Antoine Galland, who later recorded them in *Les Milles et une Nuits* – the version that informed all subsequent European editions of *The Arabian Nights*. Heyberger's article about devout Catholic women in Aleppo in the seventeenth through nineteenth centuries (Chapter 9) covers a very different subject, but humour glimmers there, too. It arises when he describes how some missionaries in their reports to Rome complained about pious Maronite ladies who were 'remaining too long in the confessional', talking the ears off priests about sinful things that they had thought about doing – but had seldom actually done.[8]

The humour in Bernard Heyberger's scholarship has a function: it humanises people, while making it easier to see Christian cultures as everyday lived experiences. His tolerance for human foibles confirms that what he has offered is not ecclesiastical history (focused on church institutions and their associated theologies or ideologies), but rather the social and cultural history of Christian communities that were made up of fallible, infinitely variable, flesh-and-blood people.

FOUR BOOKS

Two of Bernard Heyberger's books are well on their way to becoming classics in French-language studies of modern Middle Eastern Christianity, while two others appeal to wider audiences by using history to explain current affairs. Together they show his intellectual range. Since these four books are obviously not included in this collection, it makes good sense to survey them here.

His first book, which has become a touchstone in the field, developed from the research that he conducted for his doctoral degree. Titled *Les Chrétiens du Proche-Orient au temps de la Réforme Catholique (Syrie, Liban, Palestine, XVIIe–XVIIIe siècles)* (Christians in the Near East in the Time of Catholic Reform: Syria, Lebanon and Palestine in the Seventeenth and Eighteenth Centuries), it appeared in 1994. Drawing heavily on the Propaganda Fide archives in the Vatican, this book studied Middle Eastern Catholic and especially Maronite and Melkite communities, at a time when Rome was intensifying missionary overtures in Eastern Mediterranean lands. It presents a social history of church culture relative to European Catholics, on the one hand, and local Muslim society, on the other. The book has significantly contributed to women's history, too. Heyberger has argued that '[t]he [European Catholic] missionaries tended to valorise the place of the woman in society, to remove certain taboos regarding their impurity and ignorance [and to insist] among other things on the necessity of a girl's consent for her marriage'.[9] He has contended that the church in an age of growing Roman Catholic missionary influence became a vehicle for female emancipation.

His second book, also heading towards classic status, is *Hindiyya, mystique et criminelle, 1720–1798* (2001), which appeared in 2011 in English as *Hindiyya, Mystic and Criminal, 1720–1798*. In it, he has traced the life of Hindiyya 'Ujaymī, a Maronite nun who claimed to have visions of Mary and Christ and whose erratic behaviour and cult-like propensities eventually drew scrutiny from her former Jesuit supporters and from Rome. Reviewers have conveyed its drama and sweep by describing it as a study of the 'psychological aberrations of claimed religious experience' and as a history that has the quality of 'a good old-fashioned murder mystery'.[10] One scholar has even called it 'a real-life *The Name of the Rose*', referring to Umberto Eco's novel of intrigue.[11] Heyberger has used the scandalous story of Hindiyya to convey, again, what he has described as the 'feminisation' of Middle Eastern Christianity under the influence of Catholic missionaries, who encouraged new cultures of female devotion, as he constructed the biography of this powerful woman. At the same time, he has contributed to the political history of eighteenth-century Mount Lebanon more broadly.[12]

In two subsequent books, Heyberger has written for educated popular audiences and taken the story to present-day times. In *Les Chrétiens au Proche-Orient: De la compassion à la compréhension* (Christians in the Middle East: From Compassion to Understanding, published in 2011), he has discussed the demographic fluctuations of modern Middle Eastern Christian communities, their diminution relative to Muslim majorities and the complex reasons for these trends. He has made a case for the integral place of Christians in the region's Islamic society and for shared cultures among Christians and Muslims.

In 2017, he published *Les Chrétiens d'Orient*, a slim volume within a well-known French series of books called *Que sais-je?* (What Do I Know?). Begun in 1941, this series distills important topics for a general educated readership. In his contribution to the series, Bernard Heyberger has explained theological controversies and sectarian differences among Christians; patterns of tension and coexistence between Muslims and Christians; historic Islamic state policies towards Christians as protected subordinates, or *dhimmīs*; and the impact of modern Catholic, Protestant and Orthodox missionary movements. He has also considered the protracted demographic changes that reduced Christian communities over the centuries. The book makes its boldest contribution by analysing the modern and still ongoing history of Western imperial intervention in the name of and – as he has suggested, at the expense of – Middle Eastern Christian communities, with particular attention to France, the United Kingdom and Russia.[13] Just over a hundred pages long, this book, with its lucid appraisal of a complex history, will remain as valuable for experts as it will be for general readers.

CONCLUSION

In 2021, Heyberger wrote for the French journal *Annales* an article that assessed the upsurge of academic interest in modern Middle Eastern Christian history since the 1990s. He analysed reasons for this phenomenon and surveyed the scholarship from the 1960s (when the shift away from ecclesiastical history arguably began) to the present.[14] Citing dozens upon dozens of works, he has proven his point about the field's vitality while connecting it to the growth of interest in nineteenth-century Ottoman history and twentieth-century migration history more broadly. What may not be obvious from the footnotes of this article, however, is how many of the recent scholars whom he has cited are either former students or colleagues who have benefitted from his insights first-hand – scholars who have worked on a wide range of topics, across many geographic areas, from the eighteenth through the early twenty-first century. Bernard Heyberger has left his mark on the field not only through his own publications and his community-building seminar series, but also through mentoring and via the resulting publications.

One tell-tale sign of his influence is that many of the works of those he has mentored affirm the energy and resourcefulness of Christian people in historically Muslim-majority social contexts.[15] Bernard Heyberger has never presented Christians as passive victims; his articles and books are not sad. Like certain leading scholars of Middle Eastern Jewish history, he has rejected 'neo-lachrymose' interpretations of the history of non-Muslim minorities in Islamic societies.[16] Instead, he has insisted on the '*agentivité*' or agency of Christian actors as he has brought them into the light as integral members of Islamic societies.

In sum, this collection presents the substantive, diverse and creative works of Bernard Heyberger, who has achieved so much while setting examples for others to follow in research. From his base in Paris over many years, Bernard

Heyberger has helped build a small community around what in his seminar series he called the 'historical anthropology of Christians in Islam'. He did so while working with rigour, enthusiasm and his characteristically quiet but sharp sense of humour. Now a wider group of readers and scholars will be able to encounter and appreciate his works, many of which appear here in English for the first time, as they study topics ranging from migration and minorities to interconfessional dynamics and the relations between rulers and ruled. Perhaps these new readers may even join the imagined community of readers and thinkers who are *aficionados* of Middle Eastern Christian social and cultural history!

Heather J. Sharkey
University of Pennsylvania

NOTES

1. Still others joined this meeting because of their connection to another, continuing series that Bernard Heyberger had been co-organising since 2015, called 'Histoire connectée et comparée des christianismes en Orient', which has included scholars studying Eastern Christianity in the Middle East as well as in Ukraine, Russia, Romania and Greece.
2. Benedict Anderson, *Imagined Communities: Reflections on the Origin and Spread of Nationalism*, revised 2nd edition (London: Verso, 1991).
3. See Lora Gerd, *Russian Policy in the Orthodox East: The Patriarchate of Constantinople* (Warsaw: De Gruyter Open, 2014).
4. A prime example would be this work by an Australian scholar about US actors and transnational Christian missions and other activist organisations: Ian Tyrrell, *Reforming the World: The Creation of America's Moral Empire* (Princeton: Princeton University Press, 2010).
5. See, for example, Francesca Trivellato, 'Is There a Future for Italian Microhistory in the Age of Global History?' *California Italian Studies*, 2, 1 (2011), online: <http://dx.doi.org/10.5070/C321009025>
6. Meropi Anastassiadou and Bernard Heyberger (eds.), *Figures anonymes, figures d'élite: Pour une anatomie de l'Homo ottomanicus* (Istanbul: Isis, 1999).
7. Bernard Heyberger, *Les Chrétiens du Proche-Orient au temps de la Réforme Catholique (Syrie, Liban, Palestine, XVIIe–XVIIIe siècles)* (Rome: École française de Rome, 1994), pp. 58–59.
8. Bernard Heyberger, 'Individualism and Political Modernity: Devout Catholic Women in Aleppo and Lebanon between the Seventeenth and Nineteenth Centuries', in Amira El-Azhary Sonbol (ed.), *Beyond the Exotic: Women's Histories in Islamic Societies* (New York: Syracuse University Press, 2005), pp. 71–85. When I first read this article, the scene that Heyberger conjured struck me as something akin to a Woody Allen movie. I could imagine the loquacious, self-centred ladies of his tale

as eighteenth-century Maronite counterparts to the neurotic late-twentieth-century New Yorkers of Woody Allen's movies, who recount fantasies and hang-ups to their mid-town Manhattan therapists.

9. Heyberger, *Les Chrétiens du Proche-Orient au temps de la Réforme Catholique*, pp. 559–60.
10. Geoffrey Rowell, review of Bernard Heyberger, *Hindiyya, Mystic and Criminal (1720–1798)* (London: James Clarke & Co., 2013), in *Church Times*, 11 October 2013; Stefan Winter, review of Bernard Heyberger, *Hindiyya, mystique et criminelle (1720–1798)* (Paris: Aubier, 2001), in *MIT Electronic Journal of Middle East Studies*, 4 (2004), pp. 77–79.
11. Clement Grene, review of Bernard Heyberger, *Hindiyya, Mystic and Criminal (1720–1798)* (London: James Clarke & Co., 2013), in *The Expository Times*, 127, 6 (2016), pp. 303–4.
12. Bernard Heyberger, *Hindiyya, Mystic and Criminal, 1720–1798: A Political and Religious Crisis in Lebanon*, translated by Renée Champion (Cambridge: James Clarke & Co., 2013), p. viii.
13. Heather J. Sharkey, review of Bernard Heyberger, *Les Chrétiens d'Orient* (Paris: Presses universitaries de France, 2017), in *Islam and Christian-Muslim Relations*, 29, 1 (2018), pp. 111–13.
14. Bernard Heyberger, 'Le christianisme oriental à l'époque ottomane: Du postcolonial au global (1960–2020)', *Annales: Histoire, sciences sociales*, 76, 2 (2021), pp. 301–17.
15. On Middle Eastern Christian agency, see this article written with one of his former students, who is one of the editors of this collection: Bernard Heyberger and Aurélien Girard, 'Chrétiens au Proche-Orient: Les nouvelles conditions d'une presence', *Archives de sciences sociales des religions*, 171 (2015), pp. 11–35.
16. Mark R. Cohen, *Under Crescent and Cross: The Jews in the Middle Ages*, with a new introduction and foreword (Princeton: Princeton University Press, 2008). Strikingly, Cohen, who has challenged the 'neo-lachrymose' view of Middle Eastern Jewish history, first published his book in the same year as Heyberger's *Les Chrétiens du Proche-Orient*, in 1994 – suggesting important parallels in the development of the Middle Eastern Christian and Jewish historical fields.

Introduction: A New History of Middle Eastern Christians

Aurélien Girard, Cesare Santus and Karène Sanchez-Summerer[1]

Until the early 1990s, Eastern Christianity was virtually absent as an object of academic research, except for the history of its most ancient periods. Over the past two decades, however, a growing body of scholarship has been produced, on both the early modern and modern history of Middle Eastern Christians, with the social sciences investigating their contemporary features. Such an outburst of interest is due to a public opinion generally more informed about the social and political reality of the Middle East, in a period dramatically difficult for local Christians, as well as the interest of social scientists in minority studies. The first two sections of the Introduction will briefly sketch the origins of the current denominational diversity within Middle Eastern Christianity and the development of this 'new sub-field' of research, with a focus on the early modern age.[2] The third section will take into particular consideration the contribution made by the historian Bernard Heyberger to this renewal of studies and to the opening of new research paths on the connected history of Middle Eastern Christians between the seventeenth and nineteenth centuries. His ground-breaking work has spanned many disciplines (history, anthropology, art history), thanks to a method that has applied microhistorical analysis to the global mobility of people, texts and objects. Far from being limited to a single area study, his approach has produced many important contributions to the social and cultural history of early modern Catholicism *tout court*. In order to allow the international public to access his work, we will outline his intellectual path and discuss his most important publications, while also providing a comprehensive bibliography of his writings at the end of the volume.

1. MIDDLE EASTERN CHRISTIANITY: A BRIEF HISTORICAL OVERVIEW

To understand the living conditions of the Christian inhabitants of the Middle East in the Ottoman period, it is necessary to briefly present the various communities.

We are dealing with a plurality of different Churches, which are the result of a complex history marked by two main historical sequences. At first, between the fifth and seventh centuries, the faithful began to divide into groups along fracture lines that echoed political rivalries, linguistic and cultural differences, or divergent theological opinions, both within and outside of the eastern provinces of the Roman Empire. The Church of the East (also called 'East Syriac' or 'Assyrian' from the nineteenth century onwards) developed beyond the borders of the Roman Empire, in the context of the rivalries between the Persians and the Byzantines. The pre-eminence of the bishop of Seleucia-Ctesiphon (the capital of the Sassanian Empire), later called *catholicos*, was then proclaimed. At the end of the fifth century, this Church refused to ratify the Council of Ephesus (431) and opposed the title of 'Mother of God' attributed to the Virgin, preferring the formulation 'Mother of Christ' as laid down by the Constantinopolitan patriarch Nestorius: their detractors then called them 'Nestorians'. This Christianity spread eastwards, particularly into the Indian subcontinent, where the *catholicos* continued to ordain local bishops until the Portuguese conquest. The so-called 'Oriental Orthodox Churches' – a family that includes the Syriac Orthodox (formerly known as 'Jacobites'), the Armenian Apostolics (also known as 'Gregorians') and the Coptic Orthodox, on whom the Ethiopian Church has long depended – share miaphysite theses (that is, theses underlining the uniqueness of Christ's human and divine nature), a position that was rejected at the Council of Chalcedon (451) in favour of the recognition of two coexisting but distinct natures. The latter would become the confession of faith adopted by Greek Orthodoxy and the Catholic Church.

At the beginning of the seventh century, the Syriac Orthodox and East Syriac took advantage of the Persian occupation in the Roman East to install bishops there. The Byzantines, upon their return, tried to find a compromise around a Christological definition that would suit everyone ('monothelitism': two natures, but one will). But as the Muslim Arabs triumphed in the Middle East, the doctrine did not take hold and was eventually revoked at the Council of Constantinople in 680–81. From the 780s onwards, the Chalcedonian Christians of the emperor's party were called 'Melkites' (literally, 'followers of the emperor', from the Syriac word *Malka*, 'king'), although they were now living outside the Byzantine Empire. In the meantime, the Monothelite doctrine had gained some supporters around a monastery dedicated to Saint Maron, in Syria. They subsequently formed the Maronite Church, which was established in Mount Lebanon.

The denominations of these churches reflect the diversity of their languages and liturgical traditions. Characterised by a high degree of mobility and geographical dispersion, they occasionally share the same territories. While in medieval Europe there was a precise organisation into parishes and dioceses, with well-defined borders and a close link between each city and its bishop, in the East the prelates resided in monasteries and exercised their authority in a personal rather than territorial manner, since congregations and clergy belonging to different and rival communities lived together in the same regions. The best-known case is that of Antioch, a title claimed by the Melkite, Syriac Orthodox and Maronite Churches, even though the prelates who used that title resided in Damascus, southern Anatolia, or the Lebanese mountains, respectively.

By the middle of the sixteenth century, the main and most ancient Eastern Christian communities had come under Ottoman control. While the Christians of the Balkans and Anatolia had known Ottoman rule for almost two centuries – that is, long before Mehmed II made his triumphal entry into Constantinople in 1453 – the conquest of Mesopotamia, Syria and Egypt was relatively more recent, being the result of Selim I's military campaigns between 1512 and 1520. For the Christians of that region, however, subordination to an Islamic authority was an entirely habitual reality, as it had lasted since the time of the Arab expansion in the seventh century (except for the brief and limited experience under the Crusader kingdoms). This had not been without consequences: while on the Balkan peninsula and in the Aegean archipelago the Greek Church was clearly the majority among the population, in the Arab territories of the Levant the other Christian communities almost always found themselves experiencing a minority status.

The life of the non-Muslim subjects of the Ottoman Empire was governed by concepts and practices that went back (or claimed to go back) to the time of Islamic expansion in the Middle East or to the teachings of the Prophet himself, which had allowed the 'people of the Book' to remain in the territories of Islam upon payment of a personal tax. They were, however, subject to several restrictions which essentially concerned the public sphere, ranging from the adoption of some distinctive signs to the establishment of a fundamental inequality (a Muslim could marry a Christian woman and own a Christian slave, while the opposite was not possible) to the need to be discreet in worshipping (churches were devoid of bells and normally hidden from view). However, contrary to the idea of segregation between Christians, Jews and Muslims, which has long fuelled biased descriptions in which each group was presented independently of its environment and relations with the others, research has shown their interconnection and the existence of inter-confessional ties, or of intra-community rivalries.

The latter were particularly fomented by the arrival of Catholic and later Protestant missionaries. From the late sixteenth century onwards, the Latin Church engaged in the fight against the alleged 'abuses' and 'errors' of the Eastern Christians, leading to a certain 'Latinisation', while striving to bring the lost sheep back into the fold of Catholicism. It was especially from the nineteenth century onwards that Protestants of various denominations arrived with the aim of 'regenerating' the Christians of the Holy Land, especially through education. The Eastern Churches then underwent further fragmentation: apart from the Maronite Church, which had fully embraced Catholicism at the time of the Crusades, all the Eastern Churches split into two opposing parties, either accepting or rejecting the union with Rome. Indeed, Catholic propaganda provoked as a reaction the development of 'Orthodox identities' (the adjective then took on a confessional meaning) in the various Eastern churches.

The Arabic-speaking 'Greeks' of the Patriarchate of Antioch (Melkites) experienced a serious schism in 1724, with the establishment of two rival hierarchies throughout the Middle East. In the Church of the East, the Catholics, who took the name of 'Chaldeans', broke off definitively in 1830, although tensions had been apparent since the sixteenth century. The first approaches of the Syriac Church to Rome also date back to that century, but despite apparent missionary success under the patriarchate of Andreas Akhijan, it was only from 1781 onwards that an uninterrupted succession of Uniate patriarchs was established. The installation of a Catholic patriarch 'of Cilicia' in Lebanon in 1740 consecrated the birth of an Armenian Catholic Church. Finally, in 1895, the small Coptic Catholic Church also obtained the establishment of its own patriarchate in Cairo. The Catholic missionaries, notably the Franciscans of the Holy Land, also constituted a 'Latin' Church, while the Protestant missionaries established various churches from the nineteenth century onwards.

2. STUDYING MIDDLE EASTERN CHRISTIANITY

For more than twenty years now, the study of Middle Eastern Christianity has been experiencing what Heleen Murre-van den Berg has dubbed an 'unexpected popularity' and a real revival, not only in historical studies but also in other social sciences.[3] While this is probably linked to media exposure, the academic interest in them, however, has more ancient roots. In the following pages, we will try to give an account of the main historiographical turns in the field, based on some recent overall assessments. The best historiographical discussion is the one provided in a very recent article by the author whose essays are collected in this volume, Bernard Heyberger.[4] Inevitably, we will partly follow his approach to the matter in our survey. To avoid repetition, his works (which have participated in many of the historiographical turns discussed here) will be mentioned only in the third section of the Introduction.

2.1 From Confessional History to the Philological Approach

It was in the context of late Renaissance humanism and the Reformation that the study of Eastern Christianities made its appearance within the 'Republic of Letters'. At the time, the latter was torn apart by confessional dispute. Familiarity with Eastern Christian languages (Arabic, Armenian, Coptic, Gəʿəz, Greek and Syriac) was growing, while scholarly libraries endeavoured to collect Christian manuscripts across the East. From the seventeenth century on, Catholics and Protestants regarded Middle Eastern Christians as faithful heirs to the Holy Land's original Christianity: they searched these communities' written and oral testimonies for evidence of their own beliefs regarding the sacraments, the clergy's authority, or the content of the doctrine. The philological and historical method was sharpened in this context of confessional dispute.[5]

From the eighteenth century onwards, the secularisation of Orientalist studies went hand-in-hand with a lack of interest in Christians. Thus, Carl Brockelmann (1868–1956), defining Arabic literature as a manifestation of Islamic culture, left all texts written by Jewish and Christian authors for their co-religionists out of his monumental *Geschichte der arabischen Litteratur* (Berlin, 1898–1902).[6] Pushed out of the academic field, Eastern Christianity remained a topic of study for diplomats and clerics during the colonial period. Often adopting the positivist methods of contemporary historiography, they published documents and pieced back together a factual history. However, they isolated the Christian minority from the rest of Eastern society and fragmented it to the extreme, by emphasising the distinctions between confessional communities studied in isolation. With the nineteenth-century 'protection' policy, diplomats insisted on permanent ties between Catholic France and its 'Chrétiens d'Orient'.[7] As for historians from the clergy, from the East as well as the West, their gaze was shaped by their theological training, a generally apologetic intention and their defence of a given ecclesiology or tradition. Several writers, such as Joseph Nasrallah (1911–93) or Samir Khalil Samir (1938–), deeply influenced by the methods of philology, gave precedence to the manuscript as a source. Completing Brockelmann's omissions, the five indispensable volumes of the *Geschichte der christlichen arabischen Literatur* (Vatican City, 1944–53) by the Swabian priest Georg Graf (1875–1955) manifested the imprint of ecclesiastical history. In Lebanon, this historiography developed greatly, in an academic landscape organised along confessional lines.

Since this vast philological work rested on the search for manuscripts, their publication and cataloguing were not in vain. While the texts written in the communities' original languages (Armenian, Coptic, Greek, Syriac and so on) very quickly caught the attention of researchers and continue to be extensively studied,[8] Christian Arabic literature, in contrast, for a long time remained ignored by the Orientalists. Using Georg Graf's and Samir Khalil Samir's studies, Arabists first turned to authors from the medieval period and in particular to the Christian texts that offered an original theological answer to the religious challenge posed by Islam.[9] Arabic Christian literature in the early modern period has not been met with the same scholarly enthusiasm: it is usually claimed that this production was rather unoriginal, derived primarily from translations of Western works, therefore pointing to a process of Westernisation which drove Eastern Christians away from their original 'authenticity'. More generally, it has suffered the fate of Arabic literature between the sixteenth and eighteenth centuries, the age of 'decadence' (*inḥiṭāṭ)* preceding the 'Awakening' (*Nahḍa)* according to the established periodisation which, among others, the writer Jurjī Zaydān (1861–1914) has described. The same established narrative of decline and modernisation segments the history of the Church of the East's literary production.[10]

And yet, the mass digitisation of manuscripts in Eastern languages, especially by the Hill Museum & Manuscript Library (HMML), has made it possible to study more easily the vast collections owned by some ecclesiastical institutions in the Middle East, which can be hard to access. The numerous manuscripts which have been kept are evidence of the great cultural vitality of these communities and of their greater access to writing. The eruption of print in these churches was instrumental in transforming their relation to the written word.[11] Middle Arabic, a level of speech which for a long time was considered flawed and is often used in these texts, is now on the research agenda – from Jérôme Lentin's seminal works to the recent handbook by Esther-Miriam Wagner, both of which prominently feature non-Muslim authors.[12] The content of these collections is no longer reinterpreted according to a dualist East-West mode of thinking; instead, this literature is inscribed in a multipolar world, within the ongoing confessionalisation dynamics and the ideals of Humanism and Christian reforms.[13]

2.2 A Social History: New Problems, New Archives

An academic and secular historiography on Eastern Christians appeared first in Anglophone universities. The American University of Beirut trained historians who moved away from the apologetic perspective. Born into a Protestant family, Kamal Salibi (1929–2011), a student and then professor at AUB, criticised the confessionalisation of Maronite historiography in his work *Maronite Historians of Medieval Lebanon* (Beirut, 1959). This approach led him, like other historians at the time of the Lebanese Civil War, to deconstruct the ideological and identity determinants that have pervaded Lebanese historiographies in the context of confessional communitarianism.[14] Iliya F. Harik (1934–2007), also born in Lebanon and trained at AUB, then had an academic career in the United States; he defended a thesis on the political and social system of Mount Lebanon, in which he described the Maronite Church's functioning and its transformation in the eighteenth and nineteenth centuries. While it is true that, during the 1960s, Robert M. Haddad's works on the 1724 schism and then on Catholic Greeks focused on a single confession, as did Avedis K. Sanjian's research on Syrian Armenians, they built a social history which kept traditional ecclesiastical history at a distance.[15]

The advent of a secular approach to Eastern Christianity also benefitted from the fact that the *Annales* school's methodology was disseminated in Lebanon in the 1970s. The work and teaching of Dominique Chevallier (1928–2008) at the Sorbonne played a major part in how a generation of Lebanese social historians imported social history. In his thesis *La société du mont Liban à l'époque de la révolution industrielle en Europe* (The Society of Mount Lebanon at the Time of the Industrial Revolution in Europe), which was published in 1971, he left behind the confessional framework and described social structures and their transformations throughout the nineteenth century, through contacts with European expansion into the East. However, he did not bypass communitarianism, which he explored through a demographic approach.[16]

While the inspiration from Marxist historiography and the postcolonial context were conducive to these new orientations, this social turn benefitted especially from the opening up of the Ottoman Empire's central and provincial archives. Over the last two decades of the twentieth century, the empire's Arab provinces underwent an 'Ottoman turn' which rectified the claim that they had stagnated, or indeed receded.[17] These new archives comprise the empire's fiscal censuses, on which works of historical demography are founded;[18] the *sijillāt* (registers) of the Islamic courts, which include inventories following death, the defuncts' debts, *waqf* foundation deeds and other legal documents;[19] and the *awāmir sulṭāniyya*, the correspondence between Istanbul and its regional governors. André Raymond (1925–2011) and Abdul-Karim Rafeq (1931–) brought profound change to urban studies on the Ottoman Empire – first through their own work, then by training and inspiring so many researchers.[20] The functioning of urban societies appeared in a new light, which was very far from Orientalist stereotypes of the Islamic city. These sources offered the possibility of a 'history from below', which could not have been written based only on consular reports and travel narratives, as well as the opportunity of integrating gender-related issues[21] and promoting a 'spatial turn' in Ottoman urban studies. Thanks to these registers, historians have been able to reconstruct fragments of life stories.[22] In short, despite discriminatory measures, Christians benefitted from the authorities' tolerant attitude, which transpired in particular in their featuring prominently in court registers.[23] Christians played an active part in the prosperity of some sectors of activity and were present in guilds and craft corporations (*ṭawāʾif*), where they were not yet discriminated against for religious reasons.[24] Property-related transactions point to the expansion of Christian dwellings, which corresponded to their demographic increase in the Ottoman period. Christians were well integrated in Ottoman cities: court registers show how they coexisted with Muslims, although 'segregation – at least partial – [. . .], was accepted, if not desired, by the communities'.[25] The patterns varied significantly from one city to the next. Thus, the case of Aleppo, about which quite a lot is known thanks to the abundant sources, has attracted interest from historians such as Bruce Masters and Abraham Marcus, who have analysed European economic penetration in the Middle East.[26] André Raymond, who had started his research with a thesis on Cairo, showed that the social relations between Christians and the Muslim majority were 'more relaxed' in Aleppo than in Cairo – while nonetheless stressing the significant role of Syrian Christian traders living in the Egyptian city.[27]

Another document sometimes recorded by the qadi's courts was the creation of *waqf* (charitable endowment), a legal instrument skilfully used by minorities for the benefit of their monasteries and heirs. When examined alongside family and ecclesiastical archives, this type of source is very helpful in writing social histories, as evidenced by Richard van Leeuwen's work on the relations between the sheikhs of the Khāzin family and the Maronite Church, by Souad Slim's book on Greek Orthodox charitable endowments in Lebanon and by Sabine Mohasseb Saliba's studies on Maronite family monasticism.[28]

2.3 A Comparative Study of 'Minorities': Communities and the Role of Religion

Despite the criticisms made by some of the authors cited above, until the end of the 1970s the standard narrative about the non-Muslim subjects of the Ottoman Empire tended to present them as discrete bodies with respect to their context – in short, as autonomous communities, called *millets*, gathered around an ethnic-religious leader, the *milletbaşi*. This theory – embodied, for example, in the classic work of Hamilton A. R. Gibb and Harold Bowen – was in turn based on the alleged authority granted by Sultan Mehmed II to Christian and Jewish religious leaders in the aftermath of the conquest of Constantinople.[29] This model was radically undermined by the publication of a collective work coordinated by Benjamin Braude and Bernard Lewis, one of the first to take the various non-Muslim communities of the empire as a specific object of study. By criticising the value of the 'founding myths' of the various *millets*, Braude argued that it was untenable to retroactively project the organisation assumed by the non-Islamic communities of the Ottoman Empire in the eighteenth or even nineteenth century: both because a pyramidal and centralised ecclesiastical structure was something that belonged to the historical experience of the Catholic West, more so than to the tradition of the Eastern Churches, and because the Ottoman administration does not seem to have followed a predefined plan from the beginning, but rather a series of compromises and progressive concessions of autonomy based on different situations in time and space.[30] Even if in the following years some of Braude's more radical criticisms were partly mitigated,[31] further studies actually confirmed that even in the field of justice the Christian Ottoman subjects did not avail themselves so much of the ecclesiastical courts to which they were entitled, but resorted *en masse* to the courts of the qadi, especially when Islamic law turned out to be more advantageous than community law.[32]

The new focus on the religious communities involved a development of research in two directions. On the one hand, it fostered a study of the 'institutional' role that

Eastern Christian clergy played in Ottoman society and bureaucracy, something that led to a first exploration and employment of Ottoman documentation on the Orthodox Church.[33] Taxation, and in particular the issue of the collection of 'ecclesiastical taxes', soon appeared as a privileged place to study the link between the imperial administration and the Eastern clergy. It is in this context that the proposal appeared of considering the role of the Patriarch of Constantinople in a way similar to that of a *mültezim*, or 'tax farmer', a historiographical approach that has come to overturn the paradigm of patriarchs considered as autonomous ethnarchs or even rivals of the government, to place them instead within the Ottoman administrative system.[34] On the other hand, the dialogue with the social sciences promoted a more in-depth study of the religious life of Christians in the Middle East, hitherto neglected by social and economic history. This study, often conducted between history and historical anthropology, made it possible to highlight the existence of popular practices common to different religious groups, as well as shared devotions and mixed places of worship.[35]

These two perspectives finally blended in the work of some historians interested in studying the collaboration between Ottoman authorities and Eastern Christian hierarchies in the social disciplining of their subjects and in the imposition of religious uniformity, overcoming a previous condition of confessional ambiguity and interaction. An important push in this direction had come in the first place from Bernard Heyberger's pioneering work on the consequences of the Catholic apostolate in the territories of Ottoman Syria, followed by further studies on the building of a renewed Orthodox identity in reaction to it. Yet, the ideal context for the development of this line of research turned out to be the proposal to apply the European-born historiographical concept of 'confessionalisation' to the various religious groups of the Ottoman Empire. Although with due distinctions and cautions, more and more scholars have found it useful to study the simultaneous and entangled confession-building processes going on within the Eastern Christian communities in early modern times.[36]

2.4 Current Trends in Historiography and the 'Global Turn'

From the seminal work of Fernand Braudel onwards,[37] the Eastern Mediterranean has been an object of historiographical interest for its peculiar ability to keep different peoples and cultures in constant relation. While for a long time the main focus of scholars had been on trade, the last few decades have seen the appearance of more and more studies explicitly aimed at reconstructing the phenomena of cultural contact and hybridisation in the medieval and early modern age.[38] The interest in the plural, socially composite and transnational character of Eastern Christians' lives was also a late effect of the historiographical revolution promoted by the appearance of microhistory. During the 1970s and 1980s, some Italian scholars had in fact highlighted the importance of retracing the biographical paths of early modern 'normal/exceptional' people through a patient work of archival research, sometimes relying only on the occurrences of personal names. By reducing the scale of observation, they argued, it was paradoxically easier to illuminate the broader cultural, social and economic context in which these lives were embedded.[39] Since the 1990s, however, a generally widespread interest has risen towards global history, challenging old Eurocentric paradigms with the aim of connecting the histories of the different parts of the world in new ambitious macro-narratives, built on a large collection of secondary sources.

Despite the apparent diversity of these two approaches, the last decade has witnessed a collective effort to combine them, in an attempt to revitalise microhistory by proposing new questions and larger settings, while helping global historians 'to populate *their* models and theories with real people' (Andrade). The idea is to focus on 'individuals who embody geographical and cultural dislocation' (Trivellato), connecting with their own biographical wanderings and human relations different cultural and social contexts.[40] This description perfectly fits early modern Eastern Christians – transnational and transcultural subjects by definition; natural mediators between the Muslim World and Europe; able to circulate in a geographical space that stretches from Central Asia to America. This new approach has combined with the tradition of diaspora studies to illuminate the 'global lives' of Greek, Armenian, Aramaic and Arabic-speaking travellers, pushed to leave their countries of origin for economic, political and religious reasons; but it has also allowed historians to highlight previously little-known circuits of mobility.[41] To give just one example, while the commercial network of the Armenians of New Julfa is now well-known, the paths followed by the Eastern monks who travelled through Western Europe in search of alms still remain to be thoroughly studied, and the arrival of pilgrims and Catholic refugees fleeing sectarian clashes turned out to be a phenomenon of much greater dimensions than expected.[42]

The focus on the circulation and presence of Middle Eastern Christians in Europe eventually led to a renewal of the history of scholarship, too. Intellectual historians have developed a strong interest in the early modern Mediterranean circulation of cultural intermediaries and their impact on the knowledge transfer between Eastern and European scholarship. The most recent works have sought to shift attention from European Orientalists to the role played by Eastern Christians in guaranteeing them access to manuscripts and specialist knowledge. Far from being simple 'native informants' or subordinate collaborators of academic scholars, Maronites, Melkites and other Ottoman subjects are now properly recognised as the 'gatekeepers of Orientalism'. Still, the focus on manuscripts and libraries threatens to overshadow the fact that most Eastern Christians in the service of European courts were not there to exercise an intellectual or scientific activity, but essentially to perform administrative, bureaucratic, or even judiciary tasks, such as interpreting, performing doctrinal censorship or examining the authenticity of documents.[43]

From this short and inevitably non-exhaustive survey, it can be seen how studies on Eastern Christianity are currently thriving. Yet, there are still several aspects to be investigated and gaps to be filled. Although everyone now proclaims the need to overcome disciplinary barriers and to question traditional Eurocentric perspective, studies on Christian communities in the Middle East still risk remaining confined to area studies, without really dialoguing with the history of early modern European society and culture. As the following section will show, Bernard Heyberger is one of the few scholars who has always defended the need for a 'connected' approach of the history of Middle Eastern and European Christianities.

3. BERNARD HEYBERGER: AN INTELLECTUAL BIOGRAPHY

3.1 Background and Education: The History of Early Modern Catholicism and Interest in the Middle East (1973–86)

Bernard Heyberger was born in 1954 in Saint-Hippolyte, a small wine-making village in the Eastern French region of Alsace – an area which he never really left and to which he has remained deeply attached his entire life. While he has not written a great deal about it,[44] he has acknowledged that this experience has given him an 'obsession with social, cultural, confessional, linguistic and political borders'. These borders, so he has explained, 'generate inhibitions, but are also made to be transgressed, and constantly provide the opportunity to face others. Hence the comparatist passion which, I believe, is integral to my work'.[45]

During his studies at the University of Strasburg, he was trained in economic and social history and its quantitative methods, which reigned supreme in French academia at the time. He also discovered the 'history of mentalities' which was gaining ground during this period, by reading Emmanuel Leroy-Ladurie's *Montaillou, village occitan de 1294 à 1324* (Montaillou, an Occitan Village from 1294 to 1324, published in 1975), as well as Jean Delumeau's *La peur en Occident XIVe–XVIIIe siècles: Une cite assiégée* (Fear in the West, 14th–18th Centuries: A City under Siege, published in 1978). Among his tutors, he met Louis Châtellier (1935–2016),[46] a historian of Old Regime Western Catholicism, who introduced him to developing research projects in religious history which were opening up fresh perspectives on church history and which soon inspired his questionings on Middle Eastern Christians, exploring themes such as missions, pastoral visits, friaries, Jesuit congregations, devotions, pilgrimages, miracles, the construction of a Catholic *habitus*, confessional boundaries and so on.

Having passed the History *Agrégation* – France's highly competitive teaching qualification exam – in 1980 and having been appointed as a secondary school teacher in Alsace, he was certainly not predisposed to choose Eastern Christians in the Ottoman period as the topic of his doctorate. This topic held no academic legitimacy at the time, be it in the field of history or in Arabic studies. In those years, the 'East', shrouded with exotic charms, was for Bernard Heyberger connected to a family memory – his father had spent two days in Damascus during an adventure trip at the end of the Second World War and brought back a purse representing Marjeh Square – and with his earlier interest in Third-Worldist politics. The discovery of Syria during a trip filled him with wonder, leading him to embark on a BA in Arabic at Strasburg II University, which he completed in 1989: for the young secondary school teacher, studying the language and working on the Middle East became ways of not getting mired in provincial life and continuing to satisfy his intellectual curiosity. Not having a well-defined professional project, he started a doctoral thesis on the response of the Christian communities of Ottoman Syria to the Catholic apostolate, under the supervision of Louis Châtellier at Nancy II University. He was to experience this research – which took him to Syria, Lebanon and Italy – as a personal and, above all, an intellectual adventure in the face of a vast research area to explore.[47]

3.2 Between Syria and Italy (1986–93)

Encouraging Heyberger in his research, Châtellier oriented him first towards the vast documentary collections of Rome, notably the archives of missionary orders such as the Jesuits. During a scholarship at the École française de Rome (February 1986), Heyberger discovered the registers of the conversions obtained by the Discalced Carmelites of Aleppo in the seventeenth century – thanks to which he wrote his first academic article.[48] But it was above all the richness of the archives of the Congregation *de Propaganda Fide* which impressed him and which allowed him to come into contact with a researcher who was then in the process of applying the anthropological approach to the study of missionary sources: Serge Gruzinski. He thus participated in an issue of the *Mélanges de l'École française de Rome* which focused on what Roman sources can bring to the knowledge of non-European societies, with a programmatic contribution that condenses the salient points of his doctoral research and an appendix which was probably the first analytical description of the Propaganda documentary collection in French.[49]

The article was published in 1989, and in the same year Heyberger was awarded a scholarship at the French Institute for Arabic Studies in Damascus (IFEAD), to improve his knowledge of the language and strengthen his scientific curriculum. Under the guidance of Salim Barakat and Souheil Sbat, he trained in the translation of not only classical (al-Jāḥiẓ, al-Mutanabbī) and medieval authors (Usāma ibn Munqidh), but also Christian ones (documents published by Ferdinand Taoutel). He discovered the richness of the diary of the Syriac

Catholic teacher Naʿūm Bakhkhāsh (*Akhbār Ḥalab*, 1835–75), published a few years earlier by Yūsuf Qūshaqjī, which gave him his first glimpse of Aleppo's popular culture, a subject to which he would return several times. In his research he met members of the local clergy, such as Archimandrite Ignace Dick, author of a repertory of the archives of the Melkites of Aleppo, or the Salvatorian Father Faèz Freijate, who gave him a list of the documents of the Georges and Mathilde Salem Foundation, a collection of documents on which Heyberger spent a lot of time. Coming from a background very different from that of a traditional Orientalist, Heyberger perceived himself at IFEAD as an 'extraterrestrial';[50] moreover, at that time, the subject of Ottoman Christian communities had no academic legitimacy either in historical or in Arab studies, also because of post-colonial prejudices towards the concept of 'minorities'.[51] However, it is precisely this otherness that allowed him to understand the interest of subjects that had previously been completely ignored, such as the rules of the Melkite brotherhoods, which he found in the Salem Foundation.

Thanks also to his Syrian experience, in 1990 Heyberger was recruited as a scientific member of the École française de Rome. Over the next three years, his stay in the Eternal City proved to be extremely fruitful, allowing him daily access to the Propaganda archives in the historical headquarters of the Congregation (Piazza di Spagna). He allowed himself to be 'guided' by the archives themselves, browsing the series that keep the correspondence of the missionaries and Eastern faithful themselves alongside the decisions of the Congregation and taking detailed notes thanks to a system of files that would remain useful throughout his career and that he would continue to update over the years. In the archives he also had the opportunity to meet other Italian researchers who in the same years were interested in early modern Catholic missions, albeit in the New World: Luca Codignola, Matteo Sanfilippo and, above all, Giovanni Pizzorusso, with whom he developed a long-standing friendship, nourished by frequent intellectual exchanges on the attitude of the Roman Curia towards non-Catholics. They took part in the colloquium on the 'Frontiers of the Mission' that Heyberger organised in 1992 with Philippe Boutry, where he presented a paper on the limits of the information-gathering process of the Congregation of Propaganda.[52]

The training he had received in France enabled him to read the documents that he discovered in the Roman archives in the light of the history of mentality and historical anthropology, according to the teachings of Philippe Ariès, Roger Chartier and the above-mentioned Delumeau and Châtellier, without forgetting the phenomenological approach promoted by Alphonse Dupront. It was clear to him what his thesis did not want to be: 'I did not want to write a "history of the missions", nor a history of the "union" of the Eastern Churches with Rome', trying rather to 'grasp the effects of the Catholic Reformation from the point of view of the Eastern Christian themselves'. His aim was to bring the history of the Christian communities of the Middle East and their relationship with the Catholic West out of the 'ghetto of confessional and ecclesiastical history, in order to integrate it into the wider scientific debate'.[53] Reading an article by Lucette Valensi helped him to understand how to do this – namely, by reconstructing the life of Christians of the Middle East within their original context, without trying to demarcate them from the predominantly Islamic environment and without dividing them into discrete groups along lines of religious affiliation which, in fact, were often crossed by common social, economic or eating practices.[54] This implied not only a knowledge of the most recent works on the economic, urban and social history of the Arab provinces of the Ottoman Empire (Dominique Chevallier, André Raymond, Abraham Marcus, Thomas Philipp, Bruce Masters and Abdul Karim Rafeq), but also a clear distancing from those ecclesiastical and diplomatic historians who had been tempted to describe the various Eastern Christian communities as autonomous and isolated groups which had succeeded in preserving their 'authenticity' in the face of an hostile and oppressive Islamic environment, thanks to the protection of European nations, primarily France.[55] Against the narrow vision that belonged to the ecclesiastical, nationalist or diplomatic-colonial perspective, Heyberger advocated a broadening of the mental and geographical horizons through which the history of Eastern Christianity was usually described. It is no coincidence that, of the sixteen footnotes in the introduction, two were devoted to bibliographical references that apparently deal with very different historical and geographical contexts, such as *La colonisation de l'imaginaire* (The Colonisation of the Imaginary) by Serge Gruzinski (1988) and *Chine et christianisme* (China and Christianity) by Jacques Gernet (1982).[56]

Heyberger defended his PhD thesis in 1993 and published it in the following year. *Les chrétiens du Proche-Orient au temps de la Réforme catholique* (The Christians of the Near East at the Time of the Catholic Reformation) is a work that is now considered a 'classic' (it was republished in 2014 in the collection *Classiques de l'École française*), and it has truly opened up a new field of study.[57] The book was hailed by the reviewers as a 'social history of Eastern Christians',[58] but it is not only in this respect that it has left its mark. One of the most interesting aspects is that, while at the time Heyberger ignored the German historiography on confessionalisation[59] (and was indeed rather cautious in this respect, insisting on several occasions on the shared elements of a popular culture common to Christians and Muslims),[60] the results of his investigation are used today especially by those researchers who intend to underline the role of the Catholic apostolate in the construction of confessional identities in the Ottoman Middle East. One of the main conclusions of the book is precisely to stress the gradual emergence of a 'distinction' in behaviour and self-perception among those faithful who had been convinced by the Catholic apostolate. Moreover, 'the means used by Latin missionaries for the reform and education of Catholics, as well as for the conversion of "heretics" and "schismatics", are hardly different from those used in Europe in early modern times', relying essentially on confraternities, schools, catechism and spiritual direction, as well as – an important novelty in the Middle East – on the development of personal devotion by means of portable images, rosaries, or the practice of examination of conscience.[61]

3.3 From Mulhouse to Tours: Hindiyya *and a Broader Field of Research (1993–2004)*

Having been awarded his doctorate, Bernard Heyberger became a *maître de conférences* (senior lecturer) at the Université de Haute-Alsace in Mulhouse from 1993 to 2002. He taught modern history survey courses to BA and MA students, to those preparing for competitive entrance exams, as well as seminars on themes more closely linked to his research, such as Catholicism around the world, urban societies in the Ottoman Empire, or on connected and global history practices. He was affiliated with the Centre des recherches sur les études turques et ottomanes de Strasbourg (CERATO) and met researchers with whom he formed lasting intellectual bonds, such as Méropi Anastassiadou, Hans-Lukas Kieser, Silvia Naef, Johann Strauss, Christian Windler and others.

During this period, he started a new research project, which was the cornerstone of his *Habilitation à diriger les recherches* (2000) – the French qualification for university professors and research supervisors – which allowed him to be appointed as Professor of Modern History at François-Rabelais University in Tours (2002–11). In his *Habilitation* submission, which he called 'Pour une "nouvelle histoire" des Chrétiens d'Orient' (Towards a 'New History' of Eastern Christians), he presented a dissertation on the Maronite nun Hindiyya (1720–98), published in 2001. Born into Aleppo's bourgeoisie and under the spiritual guidance of Jesuit missionaries, Hindiyya founded an order dedicated to the Sacred Heart on Mount Lebanon, where she was regarded as a saint. From the very beginning, her order was the focus of a local power struggle between the mountain potentates, the missionaries and the Maronite hierarchs. It also sparked defiance from the papacy, which was ready to dissolve the order, to the great anger of the Maronite authorities. In the end, the sadistic violence inflicted on the sisters by the mother superior – always prompt to recognise the devil's work in all her opponents – caused the order to be banned by Rome, while Hindiyya was locked away in a monastery.[62]

This study was in continuity with Heyberger's previous work, through the sources mobilised and his intellectual project of a history of acculturation processes:

> It seemed to me that I had an example of 'the modern individual', shaped by the methods and themes of the post-Tridentine Catholicism I had previously analysed [. . .] Moreover, the story involved a woman. As

> I had already noted in my earlier research, Western influence had led to a feminisation of Christianity in the Middle East.[63]

Nonetheless, the work was also a turning point, on three different counts. First, it focused almost entirely on Lebanon, a country which was still difficult to access at the time of his doctorate due to the Civil War (1975–90). Secondly, thanks also to the influence of *microstoria*, Heyberger moved away from the structural analysis which had been such a distinctive feature of his first book, opting instead for a biographical study – a narrative form which does not appear congenial to historians trained in the *Annales* school. He concluded by noting:

> Yet the biographical form also implies making the figure of Hindiyya a 'globalising' subject, around which the entire field of research revolves. The advantage of this approach is that it allows the coherent reconstruction of networks of relationships as well as individual and collective strategies in relation to events.[64]

Those who were taught by him also know that Bernard Heyberger likes to tell stories, and this inclination later expressed itself through his studies on Abraham Ecchellensis and Ḥannā Diyāb.[65] Lastly, his book on Hindiyya also testified to his greater engagement with the social sciences. Reading Michel De Certeau and Michel Foucault allowed him to understand Hindiyya's bond with her spiritual advisor and the agency that she gained through mystical revelations: religious anthropology has also highlighted the specificities of female mysticism, on which there is a vast historiography on the West in the medieval and modern periods.[66] Heyberger mobilised tools from the anthropology and sociology of sectarian phenomena to analyse the 'criminal' part of Hindiyya's career. Conversely, it was also this book which brought Bernard Heyberger's research to the attention of anthropologists and ethnologists who at the time were starting to work on Eastern Christianity.[67]

And indeed, scholarly encounters have been at the heart of Bernard Heyberger's work, and he developed a marked taste for collaborative work. First, in 2003, for the book *Chrétiens du monde arabe*, he brought together several contributions, testifying to the nascent interest in conducting academic work on this topic.[68] The volume, which Bernard Heyberger and Silvia Naef co-edited, was the result of a conference held in Istanbul in 1999, on *La multiplication des images dans l'Orient musulman* (The Proliferation of Images in the Islamic East). It probed a paradox: while according to the prevailing interpretation Islam structured itself around the ban on images, Middle Eastern countries proved particularly welcoming towards images imported from the West from the mid-seventeenth century onwards. In his contribution, Heyberger demonstrated 'an explosion of consumption, importing and production of images amongst Eastern Christians'. Iconographic programmes became a power stake between and among rival confessions. Figurative representations were taken out of churches and fed into new forms of devotion in private homes (see Chapter 8).[69] This long-running investigation, begun in 1989 and revisited with an article in 2018, has also examined the influences at work in the production of local icons, characterised by a striving for local anchoring, combined with external inspirations: 'What stands out from this eclecticism is not a mere copy of the West, but a renewed tradition, a particular identity founded on this work on the self, through stimulation and competition'.[70]

In the same period, Heyberger organised a conference with Catherine Mayeur-Jaouen, called 'Le corps et le sacré en Orient musulman' (The Body and the Sacred in the Islamic East), the proceedings of which were published in 2006.[71] With this, he inaugurated an investigation into fasting: its paces and prescriptions clearly set Muslims and Christians apart in the Middle East, although the introduction of Latin Catholicism transformed the very meaning of fasting. Returning to the same line of inquiry later, he observed that the Roman authorities' attempt to clarify and normalise the rules in this field was in vain, which points to the 'Limits of Catholic Confessionalization in Eastern Christianity'.[72] Examining the flipside of the introduction of Catholic norms, he endeavoured to highlight resistance or indeed rejection: Aleppo's list of prohibitions (*ḥaramāt*), while testifying to the influence of the Western penance model, was still far from the values of modern Catholicism and might even have been a reaction to the missionaries' teaching.[73] Heyberger gave an overall theoretical framework to this reflection on Westernisation and confessionalisation, in a landmark article published in 2003, inspired by the connected history and '*histoire croisée*' approaches that were emerging at the time (Chapter 6).[74]

During the late 1990s and early 2000s, several of his works were aligned with and broadened his doctoral research and his *Habilitation*, such as his contributions on devout Catholic women (Chapter 9)[75] and on friaries.[76] Other publications were programmatic: venturing into historiographic *terrae incognitae*, he felt as if he were breaking new research ground, laying down milestones that he or others would subsequently explore in greater depth. In 1999, he undertook an investigation into 'books and reading practices', in which he showed that the dissemination of European printed material among Middle Eastern Christians also led to a local revival of manuscripts. Achieving higher literacy was also a target for missionaries, who considered that reading was essential in preparing for one's salvation. Reading gave access to edification literature, which was often translated from Western books, informed tastes and provided a practical morality.[77] Very recently, Heyberger has returned to the production of Arabic printed material for Christians, by evidencing the collaborative networks surrounding printing presses, as well as the power struggles crystallising around printing.[78]

With a seminal 1998 article, he contributed to opening the first research programme on sainthood, a highly prolific research area since the 2000s.[79] This publication opened several lines of investigation, not all of which have been explored subsequently. Calling for a systematic study of Christian Arabic hagiography from the sixteenth to the eighteenth century, he pointed out several ideological stakes attached to the cult of certain saints. Through an anthropological approach, he indicated that Christian sacredness was essentially a rural phenomenon. A 'modern' model of female sainthood was now added to the traditional figures of martyrs and ascetic individuals. It was only in the contemporary period that new saints were officially placed on altars in Eastern Catholicism. Heyberger devoted an article to the most famous of them, Saint Charbel Makhlouf (1828–98), who was canonised by the Catholic Church between the Second Vatican Council and the beginning of the Civil War (Chapter 10).[80]

3.4 The Research Seminar in Paris and Greater Visibility (2004–14)

From 2005 to 2010, Heyberger was a Senior Fellow at the Institut universitaire de France, a position that provided him with financial support and more time for research. In 2004, he was elected Professor-at-Large (*directeur d'études cumulant*) within the fifth section (specialised in religious sciences) of the École pratique des Hautes Études in Paris (EPHE), in a Chair called 'Histoire des chrétiens d'Orient (XVIe–XXIe siècles)' (History of Eastern Christians, sixteenth to twenty-first centuries). This was where, until his retirement in 2020, he delivered truly specialised teaching, in the context of a weekly seminar, which was eventually shared with another institution, the École des Hautes Études en Sciences Sociales (EHESS), following his appointment there as a full professor (*directeur d'études*) in 2011. For all his students and those who attended these sessions, the seminar was a real forum for education and scientific discussion, as well as a meeting place. Heyberger presented his own research at the seminar, returning to his earlier publications and discussing his ongoing work. Many guests, from postgraduate research students to experienced researchers from a wide range of disciplinary and geographical backgrounds, came to present and discuss their research on Eastern Christianities. This diversity contributed to making it a very unique place to advance and refine historical and social science research in the field. The interactions and discussions between participants – sometimes impassioned and always fascinating – went beyond the seminar's room and official hours.[81]

The progress of academic research on Christian minorities also coincided with the development of media interest in the topic. Heyberger, who through his institutional status now had a high public profile, often spoke in the French, Italian and Lebanese media, as the topic gained prominence in the French public opinion. As it came back to the fore in the media and in political debates, the issue of minorities and more specifically Christian ones went hand-in-hand with an alarmist rhetoric, justified by the disastrous consequences of the 2003 US intervention in Iraq and the jihadist militias' exactions in Iraq and Syria, which often targeted Christians. It was in that tragic context, where shedding light on different historical realities was sometimes arduous, that Heyberger in 2007 organised with Régis Debray an international conference called 'Chrétiens d'Orient: Quel avenir?' (What Future for Eastern Christians?). The event featured a new generation of researchers specialising on this topic, as well as representatives from the Eastern Churches, thus bringing testimonies and analyses into dialogue. Ten years later, he was on the scientific committee of the exhibition *Chrétiens du monde arabe* at the Institut du Monde Arabe in Paris, which met with great popular success: its display of many exceptional items emphasised the major role played by Christians in the history of the Middle East.[82]

From 2010 to 2014, Heyberger served as director of IISMM (Institut d'études de l'Islam et des sociétés du monde musulman; Institute of Islamic Studies and Societies of the Muslim World),[83] which consolidated his international network and his anchorage in more contemporary issues. Heyberger's approach through historical anthropology and the collaboration with Rémy Madinier, the co-director of IISMM who specialised on 'Islam of the margins', proved fruitful in the many initiatives undertaken at the head of IISMM to reflect on contemporary contexts in the MENA region. During Heyberger's seminar at EPHE, many questions from the participants had underlined their concerns about contemporary situations in the Middle East. This corresponded with Heyberger's desire, at this stage in his career and while the political situation particularly in Iraq and Syria was becoming bogged down, to situate his work in relation to contemporary perspectives – for example, through the analysis of Levantine figures.

His leadership of the institute brought him into greater contact with international academics, as well as actors from French civil society (this position has indeed placed him at the forefront of the IISMM's trademark, namely, continuing education activities).[84] This is partially explained by the very nature of the IISMM, not a research centre as such, but a coordination centre for research centres specialising in the societies of the Islamic world. Under his direction, the IISMM welcomed many national and international researchers, both tenured and non-tenured, ensuring a dynamism among the different research activities and conferences proposed. Heyberger for the first time proposed international doctoral schools, co-organised by the IISMM in association with the Netherlands and Germany in particular, as well as collaborative research projects between France and Germany,[85] confirming the international anchorage of the IISMM.

His activities with IISMM also corresponded with his investment in the publisher Karthala's IISMM collection[86] and the re-institution of the PhD prize on the Islamic world,[87] as well as numerous public conferences on current affairs, facilitated by the development of communication tools such as the *IISMM Digital Bulletin* and the regular feeding of social networks. After his directorship of the IISMM, the setting up of collective seminars animated with colleagues from EPHE and EHESS (described further below) enabled him to open up more contemporary issues while continuing to tackle questions concerning the Ottoman period.

Such chronological broadening did not prevent Heyberger from undertaking new research projects in early modern history. Thus, he worked on the construction of Orientalist knowledge – a topic which was only just beginning to be explored before the 2000s[88] and which has really gained ground over the past decade, as part of a new history of erudition.[89] While in the seventeenth century Orientalism had not yet risen to the status of a discipline, the 'Republic of letters', with its networks and methods, manifested a keen interest in the 'Orient', in particular in connection with confessional disputes. Historiography focuses now especially on the subalterns, intermediaries and collaborators who had sometimes been overlooked in previous studies but played a major role in the making of science. This was the case of traders, consuls, missionaries, or, once again, Eastern Christians. Running counter the long-prevailing claim that Western understandings of Islam hardly evolved during the modern period, a 2007 conference that Heyberger organised in Milan showed, on the contrary, how perceptions evolved throughout the seventeenth century, as the 'Turkish menace' tended to recede.[90] The sometimes ambivalent relationship between European missionaries, Eastern Christians and Muslims was also the focus of an article published in 2012, which concentrated on the literary *topos* of religious disputation between educated men belonging to different faiths (see Chapter 7).[91]

Above all, after *Hindiyya*, Bernard Heyberger started an intellectual companionship with another, equally fascinating figure who occupied him for several years: the Maronite Abraham Ecchellensis (1605–64). The 2006 conference at the Collège de France, the proceedings of which were published in 2010, started lifting the veil on the first, less academic part of Ecchellensis' life: in the early 1630s, having returned to Lebanon after his studies in Rome, he entered the service of the Druze Emir Fakhraddīn, sold silk in Tuscany and redeemed slaves. Subsequently, now a full-fledged member of the Republic of Letters, Ecchellensis moved around, especially between Paris and Rome, following the career opportunities offered to him. He published several works touching on subjects ranging from linguistics to sciences, in which he paid homage to his successive benefactors. An expert in 'Oriental languages', he taught Arabic and Syriac at Rome's Sapienza and at the Collège des lecteurs royaux in Paris, was extremely active with print shops, in particular the Polyglot typography of the Congregation *de Propaganda Fide*, and occasionally worked for the Roman dicasteries, overseeing their Oriental affairs. A particularly remarkable article, published in *al-Qantara*, has restored all the coherence of his thought in the context of the Orientalism of the first half of the seventeenth century: Ecchellensis endeavoured to deliver a synthesis between the expectations of learned circles, his dedication to the Catholic cause and his wish to present Arab, or indeed Muslim culture, by translating texts partaking in the humanist ideal.[92]

3.5 Research on Mediterranean Mobility and Works of Synthesis (2009–22)

After the mystic and the Orientalist scholar, the third Maronite to whom Heyberger devoted the work of several years was a young boy from Aleppo, Ḥannā Diyāb, not endowed with any particular virtues other than an exceptional narrative talent and a marked curiosity. It was because of the latter that in 1707 he agreed to accompany on his travels the French adventurer Paul Lucas, who needed an interpreter and help in his search for Oriental antiquities to take to the court of the Sun King. Following him, Ḥannā undertook a journey of more than three years across the Mediterranean, visiting Egyptian, Tunisian, Italian and French ports, until he reached Paris, where his hopes of becoming a royal librarian were finally frustrated. Returning to his homeland by another route, Ḥannā became a cloth merchant, and it was only in the last years of his life (1764) that he decided to write down his story. The manuscript, which arrived at the Vatican Library with part of the Sbath collection, was discovered in 1993 by Jérôme Lentin while he conducted linguistics research on Middle Arabic. Together with Bernard Heyberger, who had pointed out to him the unexplored potential of this documentary collection, they decided to prepare an edition and translation of the text, but due to the occupations of both this goal was not realised for a long time. It was thanks to the tenacity of one of Heyberger's students, Paule Fahmé-Thiery, that the project later came back to the fore, finally in 2015 leading to the publication of a French version, enriched by several commentaries.[93]

In his long introductory essay, Heyberger stressed the importance of Ḥannā's meeting during his stay in Paris with the Orientalist Antoine Galland, to whom he told various fantastic stories, including *Ali Baba* and *Aladdin and the Wonderful Lamp*. According to Heyberger, these tales, for which no Arabic or more generally Eastern sources have been found, but which bear structural resemblances to tales circulating around the Mediterranean, were probably reworked by Ḥannā Diyāb from his own imagination and personal experience and would later become the best-known and most emblematic episodes in the collection of the *Arabian Nights*. The discovery was of considerable importance, and in the following years several other editions, translations and studies were published on the subject.[94] However, the Arabic text provides many other reasons of interest, starting from Ḥannā's personal point of view, which appears not so much as representative of the encounter between different and opposing civilisations ('Christianity and Islam', 'East and West'), but rather of the porosity and ambiguity of the Mediterranean border (see Chapter 4).[95] Moreover, his detailed observations on the functioning of European society in the early eighteenth century should prove particularly useful to any kind of historian.[96]

In some respects, the publication of the travel account of an Eastern Christian who arrived in Catholic Europe in the hope of finding a job was also a revival of themes that Heyberger had already cultivated in the past. One of his very first articles, in fact, had reconstructed the 'wasted career' of the Syriac bishop Timothy Karnuk, better known in Italy as Timoteo Agnellini (see Chapter 2), and already in 1999 Heyberger had drawn up a first picture of the networks of solidarity that Eastern Christians tried to mobilise in order to deal with the dangers and difficulties encountered both in their countries of origin (confessional confrontations, economic and political rivalries) and on sea with European corsairs (see Chapter 3).[97] These investigations preceded the contemporary interest in life histories spanning different countries and cultures, which has been fuelled by the 'global turn' in historiography. Admittedly closer to microhistory than to global history,[98] if only because of the education he had received and his taste for 'in-depth' documentary exploration, Heyberger was following a path that crossed the two approaches – after him, many other scholars would place mobility studies even more explicitly at the intersection between 'the observation of individual strategies and trajectories, and the study of interdependence and integration processes at several scales, both local and global'.[99]

From this point of view, his 2009 study on 'Eastern Christians in Catholic Europe', if read with today's eyes, reveals itself as an example of 'global microhistory' *avant la lettre*, since it analysed both serial, quantitative data on the general phenomenon of Mediterranean circulations and qualitative elements from the biographical paths of certain otherwise unknown individuals (see Chapter 1).[100] In the case of the Christians of Syria and Lebanon, the interest in the phenomenon of migration was combined also with that of the 'protection' granted them by France, a phenomenon with strong ideological and political connotations, whose origins and more recent developments Heyberger has not neglected to investigate (see Chapter 5).[101]

The 2010s saw an intensification of his activity in organising seminars, not only the one he held at the EPHE and the EHESS, but also those conducted in collaboration with other academics, such as Wolfgang Kaiser, Gilles Pécout and Bernard Vincent (ENS, 2011–17), or, more recently, Elena Astafieva, Aurélien Girard, Vassa Kontouma, Radu Paun and Laurent Tatarenko, with whom he coordinated a series of sessions on the 'Comparative and Connected History of Eastern Christianities, Sixteenth to Nineteenth Centuries'. The talks and lectures by the different researchers who passed through the seminars, as well as the doctoral theses that he supervised,[102] became a fundamental stimulus to widen the field of thought and move towards comparison and generalisation. This was of great help to Heyberger when – thanks also to the new media visibility he had acquired after his directorship of the IISMM, which had made him known as a specialist in Eastern Christianity even outside the academic circuits – he received an invitation to write a short volume on Middle Eastern Christianity, intended for a general audience.

In 2013, *Les chrétiens au Proche-Orient: De la compassion à la compréhension* (Christians in the Near East: From Compassion to Understanding) was published by Payot. The aim of the book, which in the same year won the *Œuvre d'Orient* literary prize, was clear from the outset: to liberate the Christians of the Middle East from a perspective that saw them only as surviving traces of the 'original' Christianity, on the one hand, and as victims of the oppression of Islam, on the other. While it is true that Eastern Christians have long been of interest only to Western believers in search of 'a kind of projection of themselves in time and space [. . .] by ignoring what Eastern Christians may have that is authentically different, even disturbing, in relation to European Christianity', Heyberger instead focused on their contemporary specificities, by drawing a picture that also takes into consideration demographic and sociological data; while the clash of civilisations was on the lips of all commentators and Eastern Christians only made the headlines to evoke their misfortune, this historian decided to show their vitality and participation in the societies of the Arab world, of which they are actors in all effects.[103]

The work of historical and historiographical synthesis necessary for the realisation of such a book did not remain without fruit. Indeed, in 2017 Heyberger took up his notes for a work of a didactic and informative nature, published in the prestigious collection *Que sais-je?*[104] Aiming this time to break the impression of homogeneity or shared destinies underlying the label 'Eastern Christians', Heyberger performed a real *tour de force* to illustrate all the cultural, religious and political particularities of the Eastern faithful, through an account that covers almost two thousand years in a hundred pages. While always claiming that it is impossible to understand Eastern Christians without thinking of them within the predominantly Muslim societies in which they have lived for centuries, the author also underlined the role played by the West, . . .

> . . . which subjects them to interrogations about their identity and their tradition, to which they have to respond, constructing their own history and heritage under the gaze of missionaries, travellers, scholars and diplomats, Catholics and Protestants, who pretend to 'regenerate' them.[105]

Over the past few years, Heyberger has shifted his effort at synthesis to a more properly historiographical and academic level, by writing, one after the other, three articles which reconstruct the history of studies on Middle Eastern Christianity and take stock of the current state of research and its prospects.[106] All these recent publications have obviously also been an opportunity to reflect on his own intellectual journey and the most significant results of his work. From the start, Heyberger has never hidden what he calls . . .

> . . . a certain number of paradoxes in my itinerary: to be rooted in Alsace, but to be interested in a distant world; to study Arabic in order to take an interest in Christians (rather than Muslims); to go to Rome in order to work on Aleppo and Lebanon; to make use of the methods and hypotheses of Western religious history in order to write a history of Eastern Christianity . . . [107]

Like those travellers whose adventures in the Mediterranean he studied, Heyberger's career path did not follow a well-established plan, but was determined by chance encounters and human relationships: 'If you ask me about my intellectual journey, I will tell you personal stories'.[108] The network of colleagues, students and friends that he has built up over the years testifies not only to his human qualities, but also to the central role he has played in the renewal of studies on Eastern Christianity in the Ottoman period.

NOTES

1. Aurélien Girard is the author of sections 2.1, 2.2, 3.1, 3.3 and 3.4 (the latter together with Karène Sanchez Summerer). Cesare Santus is the author of sections 2.3, 2.4, 3.2 and 3.5. Paragraph 1 was co-written by Girard and Santus.
2. Fiona McCallum, 'Christians in the Middle East: A New Subfield?' *International Journal of Middle East Studies*, 42, 3 (2010), pp. 486–88. Some of the views expressed in these sections are also found in C. Santus, *Trasgressioni necessarie: Communicatio in sacris, coesistenza e conflitti tra le comunità cristiane orientali (Levante e Impero ottomano, XVII–XVIII secolo)* (Rome: École française de Rome, 2019).
3. Akram Khater (ed.), 'How Does New Scholarship on Christians and Christianity in the Middle East Shape How We View the History of the Region and its Current Issues?' *International Journal of Middle East Studies*, 42, 3 (2010), pp. 471–88; Laura Robson, 'Recent Perspectives on Christianity in the Modern Arab World', *History Compass*, 9, 4 (2011), pp. 312–25; Heleen Murre-van den Berg, 'The Unexpected Popularity of the Study of Middle Eastern Christianity', in Sidney Harrison Griffith and Sven Grebenstein (eds), *Christsein in der islamischen Welt: Festschrift für Martin Tamcke zum 60. Geburstag* (Wiesbaden: Harrassowitz, 2015), pp. 1–12; Bernard Heyberger, 'De l'histoire ecclésiastique à l'histoire connectée: Les chrétiens orientaux, l'Islam et l'Occident', in Noureddine Amara, Candice Raymond and Jihane Sfeir (eds), *Écritures historiennes du Maghreb et du Machrek: Approches critiques*, special issue of *NAQD*, Hors-série 3, 2 (2014), pp. 173–90; Bernard Heyberger, 'Préface: Un retour en scène des "Chrétiens

d'Orient" (1980–2020)', in Jérôme Bocquet (ed.), *La France et les 'chrétiens d'Orient': Écrire une histoire dépassionnée*, monographic issue of *Cahiers d'EMAM*, 32 (2020), online: <https://journals.openedition.org/emam/2364>; Deanna Womack, 'Christian Communities in the Contemporary Middle East: An Introduction', *Exchange*, 49 (2020), pp. 189–213.

4. Bernard Heyberger, 'Le christianisme oriental à l'époque ottomane: Du postcolonial au global (1960–2020)', *Annales: Histoire, sciences sociales*, 76, 2 (2021), pp. 301–37.
5. Alastair Hamilton, *The Copts and the West, 1439–1822: The European Discovery of the Egyptian Church* (Oxford: Oxford University Press, 2006); Aurélien Girard (ed.), *Connaître l'Orient en Europe au XVIIe siècle*, special issue of *XVIIe siècle*, 268 (2015), pp. 385–508; Jan Loop, Alastair Hamilton and Charles Burnett (eds), *The Learning and Teaching of Arabic in Early Modern Europe* (Leiden: Brill, 2017); Nicholas Hardy and Dmitri Levitin (eds), *Faith and History: Confessionalisation and Erudition in Early Modern Europe* (Oxford: Oxford University Press, 2019).
6. Hilary Kilpatrick, 'Brockelmann, Kaḥḥâla & Co: Reference Works on the Arabic Literature of Early Ottoman Syria', *Middle Eastern Literatures*, 7, 1 (2004), pp. 33–51; Johann Strauss, 'Is Karamanli Literature Part of a Christian-Turkish (Turco-Christian) Literature?' in Evangelia Balta and Matthias Kappler (eds), *Cries and Whispers in Karamanlidika Books* (Wiesbaden: Harrassowitz, 2010), pp. 153–200.
7. René Ristelhueber, *Les traditions françaises au Liban* (Paris: Felix Alcan, 1918); François Charles-Roux, *France et chrétiens d'Orient* (Paris: Flammarion, 1939); Pierre Rondot, *Les Chrétiens d'Orient* (Paris: Peyronnet, 1955); Jean-Pierre Valognes, *Vie et mort des chrétiens d'Orient: Des origines à nos jours* (Paris: Fayard, 1994).
8. See the proceedings from the conferences organised on a regular basis, such as those of the International Association of Armenian Studies (Association Internationale des Études Arméniennes), the Société d'études syriaques and the International Association of Coptic Studies.
9. Sidney Griffith, *The Church in the Shadow of the Mosque: Christians and Muslims in the World of Islam* (Princeton: Princeton University Press, 2008); David Thomas (ed.), *Christian-Muslim Relations: A Bibliographical History* (Leiden: Brill, 2009–), 20 vols, in progress; Samuel Noble and Alexander Treiger (eds), *The Orthodox Church in the Arab World, 700–1700: An Anthology of Sources* (DeKalb: NIU Press, 2014); J. Edward Walters, *Eastern Christianity: A Reader* (Grand Rapids: Eerdmans, 2021).
10. Heleen Murre-van den Berg, *Scribes and Scriptures: The Church of the East in the Eastern Ottoman Provinces (1500–1850)* (Leuven, Paris, Bristol: Peeters, 2015).
11. The research project *TYPARABIC: Early Arabic Printing for the Arab Christians: Cultural Transfers between Eastern Europe and the Ottoman Near-East in the 18th Century* (ERC AdG 2019), hosted by the Bucharest-based Institute for South-East European Studies and led by Ioana Feodorov, should return a host of new discoveries on this topic in the coming years.
12. Jérôme Lentin, *Recherches sur l'histoire de la langue arabe au Proche-Orient à l'époque moderne* (PhD dissertation, Université Paris 3, 1997); Esther-Miriam

Wagner (ed.), *A Handbook and Reader of Ottoman Arabic* (Cambridge: University of Cambridge, Open Book Publishers, 2021).

13. Febe Armanios, *Coptic Christianity in Ottoman Egypt* (Oxford: Oxford University Press, 2011), pp. 117–45; Aurélien Girard, Bernard Heyberger and Vassa Kontouma (eds), *Livres et confessions chrétiennes orientales: Histoire connectée entre Empire ottoman, monde slave et Occident (XVIe–XVIIIe siècles)* (Turnhout: Brepols, forthcoming).
14. Kamal Salibi, *A House of Many Mansions: The History of Lebanon Reconsidered* (London: I. B. Tauris, 1988); Candice Raymond, 'L'historiographie du Liban ottoman entre conflits idéologiques et renouveau disciplinaire', *NAQD*, Hors-série 3, 2 (2014), pp. 95–120.
15. Robert M. Haddad, *The Orthodox Patriarchate of Antioch and the Origins of the Melkite Schism* (PhD dissertation, Harvard University, 1965); Haddad, *Syrian Christians in Muslim Society: An Interpretation* (Princeton: Princeton University Press, 1970); Avedis K. Sanjian, *The Armenian Communities in Syria under the Ottoman Dominion* (Cambridge, MA: Harvard University Press, 1965); Iliya F. Harik, *Politics and Change in a Traditional Society: Lebanon 1711–1845* (Princeton: Princeton University Press, 1968).
16. Candice Raymond, 'Les Annales à Beyrouth: Circulations savantes et appropriations historiographiques entre la France et le Liban', *Revue d'histoire des sciences humaines*, 34 (2019), pp. 17–34; Raymond, 'Beyrouth avant Beyrouth: Historiographies contemporaines d'une "ville arabe ottoman" (XVIe–XVIIIe siècles)', *Revue des mondes musulmans et de la Méditerranée*, 148 (2020), pp. 131–48. Among the disciples of Dominique Chevallier, see Antoine Abdel Nour, *Introduction à l'histoire urbaine de la Syrie ottomane (XVIe–XVIIIe siècle)* (Beirut: Publications de l'Université libanaise, 1982); Souad Abou el-Rousse Slim, *Le métayage et l'impôt au Mont-Liban aux XVIIIe et XIXe siècles* (Beirut: Dar el-Machreq, 1993); May Davie, *Le millat grecque-orthodoxe de Beyrouth, 1800–1940: Structuration interne et rapport à la cité* (PhD dissertation, Université Paris 3, 1993).
17. Ghislaine Alleaume, 'Un "Ottoman Turn"? L'historiographie des provinces arabes de l'Empire ottoman', in Eberhard Kienle (ed.), *Les sciences sociales en voyage: L'Afrique du Nord et le Moyen-Orient vus d'Europe, d'Amérique et de l'Intérieur* (Aix-en-Provence: IREMAM, Karthala, 2010), pp. 23–39.
18. André Raymond, 'The Population of Aleppo in the Sixteenth and Seventeenth Centuries according to Ottoman Census Documents', *International Journal of Middle Eastern Studies*, 16, 4 (1984), pp. 447–60; Muhammad A. Bakhit, 'The Christian Population of the Province of Damascus in the Sixteenth Century', in Benjamin Braude and Bernard Lewis (eds), *Christians and Jews in the Ottoman Empire: The Functioning of a Plural* Society, vol. 2: *The Arabic-Speaking Lands* (New York, London: Holmes & Meier, 1982), pp. 19–66.
19. For a thoughtful presentation of the nature and use of these sources, see Elyse Semerdijan, *'Off the Straight Path': Illicit Sex, Law and Community* (Syracuse: Syracuse University Press, 2008), pp. 61–72.
20. Nelly Hanna and Raouf Abbas (eds), *Society and Economy in Egypt and the Eastern Mediterranean 1600–1900: Essays in Honor of André Raymond* (Cairo: The American University in Cairo Press, 2005); Peter Sluglett and Stefan Weber (eds), *Syria*

and Bilad al-Sham under Ottoman Rule: Essays in Honour of Abdul-Karim Rafeq (Leiden: Brill, 2010); Sylvie Denoix, 'Hommages à André Raymond (1925–2011): Un chercheur infatigable', *Revue des mondes musulmans et de la Méditerranée*, 131 (2012), online: <https://journals.openedition.org/remmm/7945>.

21. See in particular Elyse Semerdjian's works: 'Sinful Professions: Illegal Occupations of Women in Ottoman Aleppo, Syria', *Hawwa*, 1 (2003), pp. 60–85; 'Naked Anxiety: Bathhouses, Nudity, and the *Dhimmī* Woman in 18th-Century Aleppo', *International Journal of Middle East Studies*, 45 (2013), pp. 651–76; 'Women and the Politics of Conversion in Early Modern Ottoman Aleppo', *The Journal of Middle Eastern Women's Studies*, 12 (2016), pp. 2–30.
22. For example, Magdi Guirguis and then Julien Auber have used inheritance deeds and various contracts recorded at the Ottoman courts of Cairo to piece together the life and networks of Egyptian icon painter Yūḥannā al-Armanī. See Magdi Guirguis, *An Armenian Artist in Ottoman Egypt: Yuhanna al-Armani and His Coptic Icons* (Cairo: American University in Cairo Press, 2008); Julien Auber, *Yūḥannā al-Armanī et le renouveau de l'art de l'icône en Égypte ottomane* (PhD dissertation, Université de recherche Paris Sciences et Lettres, 2018).
23. About Damascus *sijill*, see Najwa Al-Qattan, 'Dhimmīs in the Muslim Court: Legal Autonomy and Religious Discrimination', *International Journal of Middle East Studies*, 31 (1999), pp. 429–44.
24. Abdul-Karim Rafeq, 'Craft Organizations and Religious Communities in Ottoman Syria (XVI–XIX Centuries)', in *La Shī'a nell'impero ottomano* (Rome: Accademia Nazionale Dei Lincei, 1993), pp. 25–55; Rafeq, 'Craft Organizations, Work Ethics, and the Strains of Change in Ottoman Syria', *Journal of the American Oriental Society*, 111 (1991), pp. 495–51.
25. André Raymond, 'Une communauté en expansion: Les chrétiens d'Alep à l'époque ottomane (XVIe–XVIIe siècles)', in *La ville arabe: Alep, à l'époque ottomane (XVIe–XVIIIe siècles)* (Damas: Institut français de Damas, 1998), p. 357. See Brigitte Marino, *Le faubourg de Mīdān à Damas à l'époque ottomane, 1742–1830* (Damascus: Institut français de Damas, 1997); Brigitte Marino, 'Le "Quartier des Chrétiens" (Maḥallat al-Naṣārā) de Damas au milieu du XVIIIe siècle (1150–1170/1737–1757)', *Revue des mondes musulmans et de la Méditerranée*, 107–10 (2005), pp. 323–51. About the Damascus case, see Najwa Al-Qattan, 'Across the Courtyard: Residential Space and Sectarian Boundaries in Ottoman Damascus', in Molly Greene (ed.), *Minorities in the Ottoman Empire* (Princeton: Markus Weiner, 2005), pp. 13–45.
26. Bruce Masters, *The Origins of Western Economic Dominance in the Middle East: Mercantilism and the Islamic Economy in Aleppo, 1600–1750* (New York: New York University Press, 1988); Abraham Marcus, *The Middle East on the Eve of Modernity: Aleppo in the Eighteenth Century* (New York: Columbia University Press, 1989).
27. André Raymond, *Artisans et commerçants au Caire au XVIIIe siècle* (Damascus: Institut français de Damas, 1973); Thomas Philipp, *The Syrians in Egypt, 1725–1975* (Stuttgart: Steiner, 1985).
28. Richard van Leeuwen, *Notables and Clergy in Mount Lebanon: The Khāzin Sheikhs and the Maronite Church, 1736–1840* (Leiden: Brill, 1994); Souad

Abou el-Rousse Slim, *The Greek Orthodox Waqf in Lebanon during the Ottoman Period* (Würzburg: Ergon Verlag, 2007); Sabine Mohasseb Saliba, *Les monastères maronites doubles du Liban: Entre Rome et l'Empire ottoman, XVIIe–XIXe siècles* (Paris: Geuthner; Jounieh: PUSEK, 2008); Sabine Mohasseb Saliba (ed.), *Les fondations pieuses waqfs chez les chrétiens et les juifs du Moyen Âge à nos jours* (Paris: Geuthner, 2016).

29. Cf. Hamilton A. R. Gibb and Harold Bowen, *Islamic Society and the West: A Study of the Impact of Western Civilization on Moslem Culture in the Near East* (London, New York, Toronto: Oxford University Press, 1957), vol. 1, part 2, pp. 207–61 (it should be noted that the authors issued a warning about their own conclusions, citing the scarcity of available documentary sources); Steven Runciman, *The Great Church in Captivity: A Study of the Patriarchate of Constantinople from the Eve of the Turkish Conquest to the Greek War of Independence* (Cambridge: Cambridge University Press, 1968).
30. See Benjamin Braude, 'Foundation Myths of the *Millet* System', in Benjamin Braude and Bernard Lewis (eds), *Christians and Jews in the Ottoman Empire*, vol. 1: *The Central Lands* (New York, London: Holmes & Meier, 1982), pp. 69–88; Kevork B. Bardakjian, 'The Rise of the Armenian Patriarchate', in ibid. pp. 89–100.
31. See, for example, Michael Ursinus, 'Millet', *Encyclopaedia of Islam*, second edition, vol. 7 (Leiden, New York: Brill, 1993), pp. 61–64.
32. Ronald C. Jennings, *Christians and Muslims in Ottoman Cyprus and the Mediterranean World, 1571–1640* (New York: New York University Press, 1993); Rossitsa Gradeva, 'Orthodox Christians in the Kadı Courts: The Practice of the Sofia Sheriat Court, Seventeenth Century', *Islamic Law and Society*, 4, 1 (1997), pp. 37–69; Sophia Laiou, 'Christian Women in an Ottoman World: Interpersonal and Family Cases Brought before the Shariʿa Courts during the Seventeenth and Eighteenth Centuries', in Amila Buturovic and Irvin C. Schick (eds), *Women in the Ottoman Balkans: Gender, Culture and History* (London: I. B. Tauris, 2007), pp. 243–71. For a general overview, see Antonis Anastasopoulos, 'Non-Muslims and Ottoman Justice(s?)', in Jeroen Duindam *et al.* (eds), *Law and Empire: Ideas, Practices, Actors* (Leiden, Boston: Brill, 2013), pp. 275–92.
33. Halil İnalcık, 'Ottoman Archival Materials on *Millets*', in Braude and Lewis (eds), *Christians and Jews in the Ottoman Empire*, vol. 1, pp. 69–88; Elisabeth A. Zachariadou, *Deka tourkika eggrafa gia tēn Megalē Ekklēsia* (Athens: Ethniko Idryma Erevnon, 1996); Paraskevas Konortas, *Othōmanikes theōrēseis gia to Oikoumeniko Patriarcheio: Beratia gia tous prokathēmenous tēs Megalēs Ekklēsias, 17os-arches tou 20ou aiōna* (Athens: Alexandreia, 1998); Bruce Masters, *Christians and Jews in the Ottoman Arab World: The Roots of Sectarianism* (Cambridge: Cambridge University Press, 2001). Only recently have some scholars begun to use Ottoman sources for the study of the internal issues of the Armenian Church; see, for example, Ensar Köse, 'İstanbul Ermeni Patrikliği'nin Osmanlı Hükümeti'yle Münasebetlerine Tesir Eden Dinamikler (18. Yüzyılın İlk Yarısı)', *Osmanlı Medeniyeti Arastırmaları Dergisi*, 3–5 (2017), pp. 1–24.
34. Halil İnalcık, 'The Status of the Greek Orthodox Patriarch under the Ottomans', *Turcica*, 21–23 (1991), pp. 407–36; Macit Kenanoğlu, *Osmanlı Millet Sistemi:*

Mit ve Gerçek (Istanbul: Klasik, 2004); Elif Bayraktar Tellan, *The Patriarch and the Sultan: The Struggle for Authority and the Quest for Order in the Eighteenth-Century Ottoman Empire* (PhD dissertation, Bilkent University, 2011); Tom Papademetriou, *Render unto the Sultan: Power, Authority, and the Greek Orthodox Church in the Early Ottoman Centuries* (Oxford: Oxford University Press, 2015); Hasan Çolak, *The Orthodox Church in the Early Modern Middle East: Relations between the Ottoman Central Administration and the Patriarchates of Antioch, Jerusalem and Alexandria* (Ankara: Türk Tarih Kurumu, 2015); Hasan Çolak and Elif Bayraktar Tellan, *The Orthodox Church as an Ottoman Institution: A Study of Early Modern Patriarchal Berats* (Istanbul: The Isis Press, 2019).

35. See, for example, Catherine Mayeur-Jaouen, *Pèlerinages d'Égypte: Histoire de la piété copte et musulmane, XVe–XXe siècles* (Paris: Éd. de l'EHESS, 2005); Dionigi Albera and Maria Couroucli (eds), *Religions traversées: Lieux saints partagés entre chrétiens, musulmans et juifs en Méditerranée* (Arles: Actes Sud, 2009); James Grehan, *Twilight of the Saints: Everyday Religion in Ottoman Syria and Palestine* (New York: Oxford University Press, 2014); Heather J. Sharkey, *A History of Muslims, Christians, and Jews in the Middle East* (Cambridge: Cambridge University Press, 2017).
36. For Heyberger's work, see below. In general, on the confessional dynamics linked to the Catholic apostolate in the Middle East, see Charles A. Frazee, *Catholics and Sultans: The Church and the Ottoman Empire (1453–1923)* (Cambridge: Cambridge University Press, 1983); George E. Demacopoulos and Aristotle Papanikolaou (eds), *Orthodox Constructions of the West* (New York: Fordham University Press, 2013); Cesare Santus, *Trasgressioni necessarie: Communicatio in sacris, coesistenza e conflitti tra le comunità cristiane orientali (Levante e Impero ottomano, XVII–XVIII secolo)* (Rome: École française de Rome, 2019); Lucy Parker, 'The Interconnected Histories of the Syriac Churches in the Sixteenth Century', *The Journal of Ecclesiastical History*, 72, 3 (2021), pp. 509–32. Particularly important are the introduction and the essays contained in Tijana Krstić and Derin Terzioğlu (eds), *Entangled Confessionalizations? Dialogic Perspectives on the Politics of Piety and Community Building in the Ottoman Empire, 15th–18th Centuries* (Piscataway: Gorgias Press, 2022).
37. Fernand Braudel, *La Méditerranée et le Monde méditerranéen à l'époque de Philippe II*, 3 vols. (Paris: A. Colin, 1949). The English translation by Sian Reynolds (London: Collins, 1973) is based on the second, revised edition.
38. Molly Greene, *A Shared World: Christians and Muslims in the Early Modern Mediterranean* (Princeton: Princeton University Press, 2000); Greene, *Catholic Pirates and Greek Merchants: A Maritime History of the Mediterranean* (Princeton: Princeton University Press, 2010); Eric R. Dursteler, *Venetians in Constantinople: Nation, Identity and Coexistence in the Early Modern Mediterranean* (Baltimore: Johns Hopkins University Press, 2006); E. Natalie Rothman, *Brokering Empire: Trans-Imperial Subjects between Venice and Istanbul* (Ithaca: Cornell University Press, 2011).
39. Edoardo Grendi, 'Micro-analisi e storia sociale', *Quaderni storici*, 35 (1977), pp. 506–20; Carlo Ginzburg and Carlo Poni, 'Il nome e il come: Scambio

ineguale e mercato storiografico', *Quaderni storici*, 40 (1979), pp. 181–90, English translation: 'The Name and the Game: Unequal Exchange and the Historiographical Marketplace', in Edward Muir and Guido Ruggiero (eds), *Microhistory and the Lost Peoples of Europe* (Baltimore: Johns Hopkins University Press, 1991).

40. Tonio Andrade, 'A Chinese Farmer, Two African Boys, and a Warlord: Toward a Global Microhistory', *Journal of World History*, 21, 4 (2010), pp. 573–91; Francesca Trivellato, 'Is There a Future for Italian Microhistory in the Age of Global History?' *California Italian Studies*, 2, 1 (2011), online: <http://dx.doi.org/10.5070/C321009025>; Romain Bertrand and Guillaume Calafat, 'La microhistoire globale: Affaire(s) à suivre', *Annales: Histoire, sciences sociales*, 73, 1 (2018), pp. 3–18; John-Paul A. Ghobrial (ed.), *Global History and Microhistory*, monographic issue of *Past & Present*, 242, suppl. 14 (2019).

41. John-Paul Ghobrial, 'The Secret Life of Elias of Babylon and the Uses of Global Microhistory', *Past & Present*, 222 (2014), pp. 51–93; Matteo Salvadore, '"I Was Not Born to Obey, But Rather to Command": The Self-Fashioning of Ṣägga Krəstos, an Ethiopian Traveller in Seventeenth-Century Europe', *Journal of Early Modern History*, 25, 2 (2021), pp. 1–33; Mathilde Monge and Natalia Muchnik (eds), *Early Modern Diasporas: A European History* (London: Routledge, 2022); Sebouh D. Aslanian, *Early Modernity and Mobility: Port Cities and Printers across the Armenian Diaspora, 1512–1800* (New Haven: Yale University Press, forthcoming). Middle Eastern Christians also circulated on the Balkans and in Eastern Europe: see Constantin Panchenko, *Arab Orthodox Christians under the Ottomans: 1516–1831* (Jordanville: Holy Trinity Seminary Press, 2016); Vera G. Tchentsova, 'Le premier voyage du patriarche d'Antioche Macaire III Ibn al-Zaʿîm à Moscou et dans les Pays roumains: 1652–1659', in Ioana Feodorov (ed.), *Relations entre les peuples de l'Europe Orientale et les chrétiens arabes au XVIIe siècle* (Bucarest: Bucureşti, Editura Academiei Române, 2012), pp. 69–122; and the Greek documents published by Tchentsova in a series of articles that appeared in *Orientalia Christiana Periodica* (2002–13).

42. Sebouh D. Aslanian, '"Many Have Come Here and Have Deceived Us": Some Notes on Asateur Vardapet (1644–1728), an Itinerant Armenian Monk in Europe,' *Handēs amsōreay*, 1–12 (2019), pp. 133–94; Feras Krimsti, 'Arsāniyūs Shukrī al-Ḥakīm's Account of his Journey to France, the Iberian Peninsula, and Italy (1748–1757) from Travel Journal to Edition', *Philological Encounters*, 4, 3–4 (2019), pp. 202–44; Sundar Henny, 'Nathanael of Leukas and the Hottinger Circle: The Wanderings of a Seventeenth-Century Greek Archbishop,' *International Journal of the Classical Tradition*, 27 (2020), pp. 449–72; Cesare Santus, 'Wandering Lives: Eastern Christian Pilgrims, Alms-Collectors and "Refugees" in Early Modern Rome', in Emily Michelson and Matthew Coneys Wainwright (eds), *A Companion to Religious Minorities in Early Modern Rome* (Leiden, Boston: Brill, 2021), pp. 237–71.

43. To give just a few recent examples, see John-Paul Ghobrial, 'The Archives of Orientalism and Its Keepers: Reimagining the Histories of Arabic Manuscripts in Early Modern Europe', *Past & Present*, 230, suppl. n° 11 (2016), pp. 90–111;

Aurélien Girard, 'Was an Eastern Scholar Necessarily a Cultural Broker in Early Modern Europe? Faustus Naironus (1628–1711), the Christian East, and Oriental Studies', in Nicholas Hardy and Dmitri Levitin (eds), *Confessionalisation and Erudition in Early Modern Europe*, pp. 240–63; Simon Mills, *A Commerce of Knowledge: Trade, Religion, and Scholarship between England and the Ottoman Empire, 1600–1760* (Oxford: Oxford University Press, 2020); E. Natalie Rothman, *The Dragoman Renaissance: Diplomatic Interpreters and the Routes of Orientalism* (Ithaca: Cornell University Press, 2021); Thomas Glesener, 'Gouverner la langue arabe: Miguel Casiri et les arabisants du roi d'Espagne au siècle des Lumières', *Annales: Histoire, sciences sociales*, 76, 2 (2021), pp. 227–67.

44. Bernard Heyberger, 'Le Gymnase de Strasbourg à travers ses commémorations: Quatre siècles et demi sur une frontière politique et culturelle (1538–1988)', *Histoire de l'éducation*, 97 (2003), pp. 3–36.
45. Bernard Heyberger, *Synthèse des travaux*, unpublished volume of the *Habilitation à diriger les recherches*, Université Nancy 2, 2000, Introduction.
46. Bernard Heyberger, 'Louis Châtellier (1935–2016)', *Annuaire de l'École pratique des hautes études (EPHE), Section des sciences religieuses*, 124 (2017), online: <http://asr.revues.org/1587>; Heyberger, 'De L'Europe des dévots à la Syrie des dévots: Un parcours', in *L'histoire en héritage: Louis Châtellier, François Roth: Hommages*, monographic issue of *Annales de l'Est*, 68, 1 (2018), pp. 17–29.
47. Bernard Heyberger, *Les chrétiens du Proche-Orient au temps de la Réforme catholique*, 2nd ed. (Rome: École française de Rome, 2014), 'Préface à la seconde édition', IX: 'À cette époque, je ne pouvais me projeter dans l'avenir, ni imaginer les retombées intellectuelles de mon travail. J'étais motivé par une mystérieuse impulsion qui me poussait à mener à bien une entreprise que je m'étais assignée à moi-même. Je ne savais pas exactement pourquoi je m'étais lancé dans cette aventure, mais je la trouvais exaltante [. . .] '
48. Bernard Heyberger, 'Les chrétiens d'Alep à travers les récits des conversions des missionnaires carmes déchaux (1657–81)', *Mélanges de l'École française de Rome: Moyen-Age, temps modernes*, 100, 1 (1988), pp. 461–99. He would come back often to the topic of conversions: Heyberger, 'Se convertir à l'Islam chez les chrétiens de Syrie', in Lucetta Scaraffia and Anna Foa (eds), *Conversioni nel Mediterraneo*, special issue of *Dimensioni e problemi della ricerca storica* 2 (1996), pp. 133–52; Heyberger, 'Frontières confessionnelles et conversions chez les chrétiens orientaux', in Mercedes García-Arenal (ed.), *Conversions islamiques: Identités religieuses en Islam méditerranéen/Islamic Conversions: Religious Identities in Mediterranean Islam* (Paris: Maisonneuve-Larose, 2001), pp. 245–58; Heyberger, 'Conversion et confesssionalisation au Proche-Orient (XVIe–XXIe siècles)', in Philippe Gelez and Gilles Grivaud (eds), *Les conversions en Asie mineure dans les Balkans et dans le monde musulman: Comparaisons et perspectives* (Athens: École française d'Athènes, 2016), pp. 191–210.
49. Serge Gruzinski, 'Christianisation ou occidentalisation? Les sources romaines d'une anthropologie historique', *Mélanges de l'École française de Rome: Italie et Méditerranée*, 101, 2 (1989), pp. 733–50; Bernard Heyberger, 'Le catholicisme tridentin au Levant (XVIIe–XVIIIe siècles)', ibid. pp. 897–909. See also the

general description of the Congregation of Propaganda in the encyclopaedic entry 'Missions (époque moderne)', in Philippe Levillain (ed.), *Dictionnaire Historique de la Papauté* (Paris: Fayard, 1994), pp. 1115–20.

50. Despite a certain isolation, the contacts made at this time with the other fellows (including Sabrina Mervin) and visiting researchers would later bear the fruits of a long-lasting collaboration. For example, after the publication of his thesis, Jean-Claude Garcin invited Heyberger to write the chapter on Christians in the collective volume *États, sociétés et cultures du monde musulman médiéval (Xe–XVe siècle)*, vol. 3 (Paris: PUF, 1999), pp. 145–63, which constituted an international recognition for Heyberger from the community of professional Arabists.
51. 'Pour la majorité des arabisants, travailler sur les "minorités" était tenu en suspicion de colonialisme, celui-ci étant accusé d'avoir multiplié les catégories et d'avoir instrumentalisé les "minorités" pour faire obstacle au nationalisme arabe' (Heyberger, 'De L'Europe des dévots à la Syrie des dévots', p. 20).
52. Bernard Heyberger, '*Pro nunc, nihil respondendum*: Recherche d'informations et prise de décision à la Propagande: L'exemple du Levant (XVIIIe siècle)', Proceedings of the conference *Les Frontières de la mission: Mélanges de l'Ecole française de Rome: Italie et Méditerranée*, 109, 2 (1997), pp. 539–54. Some articles of Pizzorusso are now collected in *Propaganda fide, I. La Congregazione pontificia e la giurisdizione sulle missioni* (Rome: Edizioni di Storia e Letteratura, 2022).
53. Heyberger, *Les chrétiens du Proche-Orient au temps de la Réforme catholique* (Rome: École française de Rome, 1994), 'Introduction'.
54. Lucette Valensi, 'La tour de Babel: Groupes et relations ethniques au Moyen-Orient et en Afrique du Nord', *Annales: Économies, sociétés, civilisation,* 41, 4 (1986), pp. 817–38.
55. The best example of this trend is a book that would be published at the same time as Heyberger's thesis, *Vie et mort des chrétiens d'Orient* by Jean-Pierre Valognes (Paris: Fayard, 1994), a work that is nevertheless rich from a data point of view.
56. Heyberger, *Les chrétiens du Proche-Orient*, 'Introduction'.
57. Ibid.
58. Lucette Valensi, 'Le choix des Annales', *Annales: Histoire, sciences sociales*, 50, 5 (1995), p. ii: 'Une étude admirablement conduite sur les chrétiens d'Orient, ceux d'Alep en particulier, entre 17e et 18e siècle. Non pas l'histoire des églises et des dogmes qui les séparent, non pas l'histoire des heurs et malheurs de la Croix sous la domination du Croissant, mais celle des fidèles d'une part; de leur première occidentalisation sous l'action des missionnaires envoyés de Rome de l'autre. Enfin, une histoire sociale des chrétiens d'Orient'. See also the review by Abdul-Karim Rafeq in the *Journal of the Economic and Social History of the Orient*, 42, 1 (1999), pp. 120–22.
59. 'Le concept allemand de *Konfessionalisierung* et les discussions à son sujet n'avaient pas encore franchi le Rhin quand je rédigeais ma thèse. C'est vers 1995 qu'ils se diffusèrent hors d'Allemagne, en particulier en France' (Heyberger, 'Préface: Un retour en scène des 'Chrétiens d'Orient').
60. He would later dedicate an article to this aspect: 'Pratiques religieuses et lieux de culte partagés entre islam et christianisme (autour de la Méditerranée)', *Archives des sciences sociales des religions*, 149 (2010), pp. 273–83. His work is often cited in

Grehan, *Twilight of the Saints*, with whom Heyberger feels to share an 'intellectual community', even if the two never met.

61. Heyberger, *Les chrétiens du Proche-Orient* (1994), p. 555.
62. Bernard Heyberger, *Hindiyya, mystique et criminelle (1720–1798)* (Paris: Aubier, 2001); Arabic version (Beirut: Dar al-Nahār, 2010); English version (Cambridge: James Clarke & Co., 2013).
63. Bernard Heyberger, *Hindiyya, Mystic and Criminal, 1720–1798: A Political and Religious Crisis in Lebanon*, translated by Renée Champion (Cambridge: James Clarke & Co., 2013), p. 220.
64. Heyberger, *Hindiyya*, p. 220.
65. See sections 3.4 and 3.5 below.
66. Jean-Pierre Albert, *Le Sang et le Ciel: Les saintes mystiques dans le monde chrétien* (Paris: Aubier, 1997).
67. Regarding the recent interest in Middle Eastern Christians on the part of social scientists, see Bernard Heyberger and Aurélien Girard, 'Chrétiens au Proche-Orient: Les nouvelles conditions d'une présence', *Archives de sciences sociales des religions*, 171 (2015), pp. 11–36.
68. Bernard Heyberger, *Chrétiens du monde arabe: Un archipel en terre d'Islam* (Paris: Autrement, 2003).
69. Bernard Heyberger, 'De l'image religieuse à l'image profane? L'essor de l'image chez les chrétiens de Syrie et du Liban', in Bernard Heyberger and Silvia Naef (eds), *La multiplication des images en pays d'Islam: De l'estampe à la télévision (17e–21e siècle)* (Istanbul: Orient-Institut der DMG; Würzburg: Ergon, 2003), p. 32 (see the English translation in Chapter 8 of this volume).
70. Bernard Heyberger, 'Entre Byzance et Rome: L'image et le sacré au Proche-Orient au XVIIe siècle', *Histoire, economie et société*, 4 (1989), pp. 527–50; Heyberger, 'Le renouveau de l'image de religion chez les chrétiens orientaux', *Archives des sciences sociales des religions,* 183 (2018), p. 201.
71. Catherine Mayeur-Jaouen and Bernard Heyberger (eds), 'Le corps et le sacré en Orient musulman', special issue of *Revue des mondes musulmans et de la Méditerranée*, 113–14 (2006).
72. Bernard Heyberger, 'Les transformations du jeûne chez les chrétiens orientaux', *Revue des mondes musulmans et de la Méditerranée*, 113–14 (2006), pp. 267–85; Heyberger, 'Fasting: The Limits of Catholic Confessionalization in Eastern Christianity in the Eighteenth Century', in Jan Loop and Jill Kraye (eds), *Scholarship between Europe and the Levant: Essays in Honour of Alastair Hamilton* (Leiden, Boston: Brill, 2020), pp. 217–35.
73. Bernard Heyberger, 'Morale et confession chez les melkites d'Alep d'après une liste de péchés (fin XVIIe siècle)', in Geneviève Gobillot and Marie-Thérèse Urvoy (eds), *L'Orient chrétien dans l'empire musulman: Hommage au professeur Gérard Troupeau* (Paris: Éditions de Paris, 2005), pp. 283–306.
74. Bernard Heyberger, 'Pour une "histoire croisée" de l'occidentalisation et de la confessionnalisation chez les chrétiens du Proche-Orient', *The MIT-Electronic Journal of Middle Eastern Studies* 3 (2003), pp. 36–49 (see the English translation in Chapter 6 of this volume).

75. Bernard Heyberger, 'Individualism and Political Modernity: Devout Catholic Women in Aleppo and Lebanon, between the Seventeenth and the Nineteenth centuries', in Amira Sonbol (ed.), *Beyond the Exotic: Women's Histories in Islamic Societies* (New York: Syracuse University Press, 2005), pp. 71–85 (see Chapter 9 in this volume). See also, more recently, 'Missionaries and Women: Domestic Catholicism in the Middle East', in Nadine Amsler, Andreea Badea, Bernard Heyberger and Christian Windler (eds), *Catholic Missionaries in Early Modern Asia: Patterns of Localization* (London, New York: Routledge, 2020), pp. 190–203.
76. Bernard Heyberger, 'Un nouveau modèle de conscience individuelle et de comportement social: Les confréries d'Alep (XVIIIe–XIXe siècle)', *Parole de l'Orient*, 21 (1996), pp. 271–83; Heyberger, 'Confréries, dévotions et société chez les chrétiens orientaux', in Bernard Dompnier and Paola Vismara (eds), *Confréries et dévotions dans la catholicité moderne (mi XVe–début XIXe siècle)* (Rome: École Française de Rome, 2008), pp. 225–41.
77. Bernard Heyberger, 'Livres et pratique de lecture chez les chrétiens (Syrie, Liban), XVIIe–XVIIIe siècles', *Revue des mondes musulmans et de la Méditerranée*, 87–88 (1999), pp. 209–23.
78. Bernard Heyberger, 'Réseaux de collaboration et enjeux de pouvoir autour de la production de livres imprimés en arabe chez les chrétiens (XVIIe–début XVIIIe siècle)', in Girard, Heyberger and Kontouma (eds), *Livres et confessions chrétiennes orientales*, forthcoming.
79. Bernard Heyberger, 'Sainteté et chemins de perfection chez les chrétiens du Proche-Orient', *Revue de l'histoire des religions*, 215 (1998), pp. 117–37; Nelly Amri and Denis Gril (eds), *Saint et sainteté dans le christianisme et l'Islam: Le regard des sciences de l'homme* (Paris, Aix-en-Provence: Maisonneuve et Larose, MMSH, 2007); Catherine Mayeur-Jaouen, 'Le saint, un modèle pour le croyant?' in Dionigi Albera and Katell Berthelot (eds), *Dieu, une enquête: Judaïsme, Christianisme, Islam* (Paris: Flammarion, 2013), pp. 637–702. For an overview of this historiography, see Heyberger, 'Le christianisme oriental à l'époque ottomane', pp. 315–20.
80. Bernard Heyberger, 'Saint Charbel Makhlouf, ou la consécration de l'identité maronite', in Catherine Mayeur-Jaouen (ed.), *Saints et héros du Moyen-Orient contemporain* (Paris: Maisonneuve et Larose, 2002), pp. 139–59 (see the English translation in Chapter 10 of this volume).
81. The yearly accounts of the seminars are published in the *Annuaire de l'École pratique des Hautes Études, section des sciences religieuses* (from 2006–7, available online: <https://journals.openedition.org/asr/>; for earlier issues, see: <https://www.persee.fr/collection/ephe>).
82. Bernard Heyberger, 'Transformations religieuses et culturelles à l'époque ottomane XVIe–XIXe siècle', in Raphaëlle Ziadé (ed.), *Chrétiens d'Orient: 2000 ans d'histoire, catalogue de l'exposition de l'IMA* (Paris: Gallimard, 2017), pp. 116–25.
83. Created in 1999 by the Ministry of National Education, Research and Technology, within the École des hautes études en sciences sociales (EHESS), the Institut d'études de l'Islam et des sociétés du monde musulman (IISMM) is a Research Support Unit (UAR CNRS/EHESS). Since the end of 2016, the

institute has also been under the supervision of the CNRS (Centre national de la Recherche scientifique) and is devoted to research activities and the dissemination of scientific knowledge on Islam and the Muslim world; see <http://iismm.ehess.fr>; <http://iismm.ehess.fr/index.php?2143>

84. For example, training activities for professionals in public administrations and companies (training programmes for prison wardens, the School of Magistrates and secondary school teachers, among others), see <http://iismm.ehess.fr/index.php?1104>
85. For example, 'Land and Landscapes in Mamluk and Ottoman Egypt (13th–18th centuries)', EGYLandscape Project ANR-DFG, <https://www.egylandscape.org/about/>; <https://prophet.hypotheses.org/about-prophet>
86. See <http://iismm.ehess.fr/index.php?1352>
87. See <http://iismm.ehess.fr/index.php?1189>
88. Alastair Hamilton, *William Bedwell the Arabist, 1563–1632* (Leiden: Brill, 1985); Alastair Hamilton and Francis Richard, *André Du Ryer and Oriental Studies in Seventeenth-Century France* (London, Oxford: The Arcadian Library, Oxford University Press, 2004); Alastair Hamilton, Maurits H. van den Boogert and Bart Westerweel (eds), *The Republic of Letters and the Levant* (Leiden: Brill, 2005).
89. For an overview of this historiography, see Alexander Bevilacqua, 'Beyond East and West', in Ann Blair and Nicholas Popper (eds), *New Horizons for Early Modern European Scholarship* (Baltimore: Johns Hopkins University Press, 2021), pp. 72–91; Heyberger, 'Le christianisme oriental à l'époque ottomane', pp. 328–32.
90. Bernard Heyberger, Mercedes García-Arenal, Emanuele Colombo and Paola Vismara (eds), *L'Islam visto da Occidente: Cultura e religione del Seicento europeo di fronte all'Islam: Atti del convegno internazionale, Milano, Università degli Studi, 17–18 ottobre 2007* (Milan: Marietti 1820, 2009).
91. Bernard Heyberger, 'Polemic Dialogues between Christians and Muslims in the Seventeenth Century', *Journal of the Economic and Social History of the Orient*, 55 (2012), pp. 495–516 (see Chapter 7 of this volume).
92. Bernard Heyberger (ed.), *Orientalisme, science et controverse: Abraham Ecchellensis (1605–1664)* (Turnhout: Brepols, 2010); Heyberger, 'L'Islam et les Arabes chez un érudit maronite au service de l'Église catholique (Abraham Ecchellensis)', *Al-Qantara*, 31, 2 (2010), pp. 481–512.
93. Hanna Dyâb, *D'Alep à Paris: Les pérégrinations d'un jeune Syrien au temps de Louis XIV*, translated and annotated by Paule Fahmé-Thiéry, Bernard Heyberger and Jérôme Lentin, with a preface by Bernard Heyberger (Arles: Actes Sud, 2015).
94. See, for example, Hanna Diyāb, *Von Aleppo nach Paris: Die Reise eines jungen Syrers bis an den Hof Ludwigs XIV*, translated from French by Gennaro Ghirardelli (Berlin: Die andere Bibliothek, 2016); Ḥannā Diyāb, *Min Ḥalab ilā Bārīs: Rihla ilā balāt Luwīs al-rābiʿ ʿashar*, edited by Muḥammad Muṣṭafā al-Jārūsh and Ṣafāʾ Abū Shahlā Jubrān (Beirut: Manshūrāt al-Jamal, 2017); Paulo Lemos Horta, *Marvellous Thieves: Secret Authors of the Arabian Nights* (Cambridge, MA: Harvard University Press, 2017); Ḥannā Diyāb, *The Book of Travels*, edited by Johannes Stephan, translated by Elias Muhanna, foreword by Yasmine Seale, 2 vols (New York: New York University Press, 2021).

95. 'A Border Crossing Ottoman Christian at the Beginning of the 18th Century: Hanna Dyâb of Aleppo and His Account of His Travel to Paris', *Studi e Materiali di Storia delle Religioni*, 84, 2 (2018), pp. 548–64 (see Chapter 4 of this volume).
96. A quote from Ḥannā's account opens the book of Nicolas Lyon-Caen and Raphaël Morera, *À vos poubelles citoyens! Environnement urbain, salubrité publique et investissement civique (Paris, XVIe–XVIIIe siècle)* (Paris: Champ Vallon, 2020).
97. Bernard Heyberger, 'La carrière manquée d'un ecclésiastique oriental en Italie: Timothée Karnûsh, archevêque syrien catholique de Mardin', in Bernard Heyberger (ed.), *L'Italie vue par les étrangers*, *Bulletin de la Faculté des Lettres de Mulhouse*, 19 (1995), pp. 31–47 (translated into English in Chapter 2 of this volume); Bernard Heyberger, 'Sécurité et insécurité: Les chrétiens de Syrie dans l'espace méditerranéen (XVIIe–XVIIIe siècles)', in Meropi Anastassiadou and Bernard Heyberger (eds), *Figures anonymes, figures d'élite: Pour une anatomie de l'Homo ottomanicus* (Istanbul: Isis Press, 1999), pp. 147–63 (see the English translation in Chapter 3 of this volume).
98. Despite his knowledge of Italian microhistory (especially Carlo Ginzburg and Giovanni Levi), Heyberger has always been more influenced by its French variant, which is interested in new interpretations produced by 'variations of scale' (Jacques Revel).
99. Heyberger, 'Le christianisme oriental à l'époque ottomane', p. 325.
100. Bernard Heyberger, 'Chrétiens orientaux dans l'Europe catholique (XVIIe–XVIIIe siècles)', in Bernard Heyberger and Chantal Verdeil (eds), *Hommes de l'entre-deux: Parcours individuels et portraits de groupe sur la frontière méditerranéenne* (Paris: Les Indes Savantes, 2009), pp. 61–94 (see the English translation in Chapter 1 of this volume). See also *supra* and the comments by Heather Sharkey in the preface of this volume.
101. Bernard Heyberger, 'Migration of the Middle Eastern Christians and European Protection: A Long History', in Andreas Schmoller (ed.), *Middle Eastern Christians and Europe: Historical Legacies and Present Challenges* (Vienna: LIT, 2018), pp. 23–42 (see Chapter 5 in this volume); Bernard Heyberger, 'La France et la protection des chrétiens maronites: Généalogie d'une représentation', *Relations Internationales,* 173 (2018), pp. 12–30; Bernard Heyberger, 'Pour une histoire des notions de "minorités" et de "protection"', in Valérie Assan, Bernard Heyberger and Jakob Vogel (eds), *Minorités en Méditerranée au XIXe siècle: Identités, identifications, circulations* (Rennes: Presses Universitaires de Rennes, 2019), pp. 243–62.
102. Charlotte Mus-Jelidi, Frédéric Pichon, Saloua Ouerghemmi, Aurélien Girard, Karène Sanchez Summerer, Cesare Santus, Maria Skordi, Mustafa Diktas, Julien Auber de Lapierre, Su Erol, Simon Najm, Anaïs Massot, Salim Dermarkar and Werner Gaboreau.
103. Bernard Heyberger, *Les chrétiens au Proche-Orient: De la compassion à la compréhension* (Paris: Payot, 2013), p. 8.
104. Bernard Heyberger, *Les chrétiens d'Orient* (Paris: PUF, 1st ed. 2017; 2nd ed. 2020).

105. Ibid. p. 122.
106. Bernard Heyberger, 'Préface: Un retour en scène des 'Chrétiens d'Orient' (1980–2020)', *Cahiers d'EMAM*, 32 (2020), <https://journals.openedition.org/emam/2364>; Bernard Heyberger, 'East and West: A Connected History of Eastern Christianity', in Ioana Feodorov, Bernard Heyberger and Samuel Noble (eds), *Arabic Christianity between the Ottoman Levant and Eastern Europe* (Leiden: Brill, 2021), pp. 12–33; Bernard Heyberger, 'Le christianisme oriental à l'époque ottomane: Du postcolonial au global (1960–2020)', *Annales: Histoire, sciences sociales*, 76, 2 (2021), pp. 301–17.
107. Bernard Heyberger, *Synthèse des travaux* (unpublished memoir for the *Habilitation à diriger les recherches*, Université Nancy 2, 2000), Introduction.
108. Personal interview with Cesare Santus, 17 September 2021.

PART I

Mobility, Networks and Protection

CHAPTER 1

Eastern Christians in Seventeenth- and Eighteenth-century Catholic Europe

Through the archives of the Roman Congregation *de Propaganda Fide*, one can attempt to reconstitute partially the careers of a certain number of Eastern Christians who travelled between the Middle East and Catholic Europe in the seventeenth and eighteenth centuries. The outcomes of this 'intensive technique for the reconstruction of biographical events'[1] can seem trifling, resulting in fragments of lives, picturesque indeed, but with little significance or representative value, revealing quite dissimilar individual lives of people of little importance, whether social, political, or cultural. It is also obvious that, limited in our documentation, we can only give a coherent image of the individuals at one moment in their lives and in precise circumstances. Through a close analysis and case comparison, however, it is possible to make sense of all the anecdotes collected from the Roman archives and to identify a few characteristic patterns in those lives.

This 'intensive technique' allows us to focus on people previously ignored and, beyond this, to reveal broader experiences of Eastern Christian migration with its routes and networks, much earlier than the great waves of the end of the nineteenth and twentieth centuries. The corpus of sources extracted from the archives of Propaganda Fide maps out a territory, that of the Mediterranean and its ports of call; a sea experienced according to the rhythm of wind-powered vessels and maritime conflicts; the Mediterranean as a political, military and religious border that adherence to the Catholic faith inspired or impelled people to cross. The most common reasons given by those who came to 'throw themselves at the feet of' the pope or of his cardinals were the persecutions suffered in the Ottoman Empire. In view of defending Christianity, the Church instigated these types of mobility, while at the same time trying to organise and control them.

But this Mediterranean border was also a space for mediation. The anonymous Christians of the Ottoman Empire mentioned here created links between people and places, forming the outline of all kinds of exchanges. As foreigners in Europe, they suffered the consequences of social instability inherent to their status, but they also benefitted from it, promoting their specific skills. By trying their luck on Christian shores, they became more or less conscious intermediaries between the Ottoman Empire and Catholic Europe, using money, networks and information as resources, sharing on both sides their knowledge or goods, even if these transfers were not very impressive or glamourous.

The nature of the sources, but also the present epistemological approach, leads me to reconstruct fragments of life stories by paying attention to the 'situated action' (*action située*) and relating 'the explanation of the phenomena to their actual sequence of events'.[2] The overall view that appears from these journeys into Catholic Europe is one of great uncertainty, of a succession of unpredictable events. In addition, from the perspective of these individuals, their actions appear guided less by any determinism or conscious strategy to realise their objectives than by a permanent desire to adapt to uncertainty and risk, to benefit from the personal connections and the incoherence and incompetence of bureaucracies, whether of church or state.

This does not prevent me from examining a few collective structures, or fields of interaction, that appear to determine the movements of certain individuals, who stand out in these archives, and their recourse to the authorities of the Catholic Church. For example, this study reconstitutes a modest 'market' of Orientalist linguistic skills in the Christian capital and in European ports. It highlights the link between church matters, maritime commerce and military conflict in the Mediterranean, as well as the importance of the Catholic missionary presence in the Levant for the establishment of networks of recommendation and protection. I also observe the tendency of Eastern Christians settled in the West to join forces in their travels and their business affairs, even if these associations sometimes ended in conflict.

TRAVELLERS AND MIGRANTS IN ROMAN ARCHIVES

Within the Roman Curia, the Congregation *de Propaganda Fide* was in charge of relations with the Christians of the Ottoman Empire. It is therefore not surprising to find mention of Eastern Christians passing through Rome in the historical archives of the Congregation. Not all those who passed through the Christian capital went to its offices, however. It is known that other Eastern Christians could be staying in Europe, including in Rome, the pope's city, without ever appearing in the archives of the Propaganda, their existence revealed indirectly through other sources.[3]

This chapter is not the result of a systematic recording of the information concerning Eastern Christians in Europe to be found in the archives of the

Propaganda. It is rather a purely empirical survey of the volumes consulted. It is towards the middle of the seventeenth century that more and more people appear to have undertaken the journey: our earliest reference only goes back to 1644.[4] This observation can also be explained by the fact that the recoding and preservation of documents only took place progressively after the foundation of the Congregation in 1622. The highest number of references falls between 1690 and 1735, and the most recent dates from 1779.[5] After this date, my browsing has been less systematic. But it is quite likely that, following a historical process common to all European states, the Church's offices from the middle of the eighteenth century onwards were less well-disposed to grant alms-collecting licences, which was the main reason for applying to them. Moreover, Roman endorsement in the Christian courts began to appear less necessary and less effective to the Eastern Christians who came to Europe in a period when the Church was generally losing influence in the Catholic States – a period that also witnessed the latter's development of repressive measures towards beggars and vagrants. In France, a text from 1753 specifically targets the 'Maronites or other Eastern Christians' and requires them to come to the country with certificates drawn up by the French consuls and validated by the aldermen and commercial deputies of Marseille, 'on pain of being imprisoned and treated like vagrants and vagabonds'.[6]

I have established a dossier of 178 names,[7] from which I have removed those who worked for the Vatican and the great figures of the Eastern presence in Europe, such as Giuseppe Simone Assemani (Yūsif al-Samʿānī), who often appears in affairs involving the lesser-known Eastern Christians with whom I am concerned here. An ex-pupil of the Maronite College of Rome and Scriptor in the Vatican Library from 1710, Assemani was its Prefect from 1739 until his death in 1768. He accomplished several missions in the Levant, in particular presiding over the 1736 Synod of Mount Lebanon, which adapted the Council of Trent for the Maronite Church.[8] Other alumni of the Maronite College, of whom 188 were listed between 1642 and 1788, appear in the files in question,[9] as well as a few of the seventy-eight Christians originally from Syria who figure in the list of students of the Collegio Urbano (directly dependent on the Propaganda) between 1641 and 1800. The College of Saint Athanasius, intended for Greeks, also welcomed fourteen Melkites between 1747 and its closure under Napoleon.[10]

As this research was largely focused on early modern 'Syria' (present-day Syria, Lebanon and Palestine), it is not surprising that most of the people noted therein originated from this region: thirty-six came from Aleppo, fifteen from Damascus, sixteen from the Lebanese mountains, four from Tripoli of Syria, four from Saida (Sidon), two from Beirut and two from Latakia. Palestine occupies a relatively large part, despite its small Christian population: eleven from

Jerusalem and three from Bethlehem, which is indicative of the existence of a Christian clientele for the Friars of the Holy Land, gravitating to its convents. Some came from Mesopotamia (eight from Mardin and Diyarbakir; one from Baghdad). It is interesting to note that two of the individuals listed belong to the second generation of immigrants: we learn from a Maronite, Michele Masbani, that he was born in Florence, where his father had settled, and from another, Giuseppe Gillal, a priest in Malta, that his father, originally from Jerusalem, had come to settle on the island.[11]

The individuals of our sample are principally Maronites (fifty-eight), then Melkites (fifty-one), Syriac Catholics (twenty-two), Armenians (twelve) and Chaldeans (five). This result is not surprising: Maronites and Melkites, who were the most numerous in the region, had closer links to the Holy See than others, such as the Armenians, who could use other networks for protection and recommendation in the West.[12] One must also take into account the bias due to the filing system of the archives: the first search involved the volumes and the entries entitled 'Maroniti' and 'Greci Melchiti'. Lastly, one must note a certain lack of precision in the descriptions: it sometimes happens that the religious affiliations attributed to an individual are not clear or are wrong.

Most of these people made themselves known to the Catholic authorities when in Rome (114 cases). But not only these: through the network of the Nunciatures in the Catholic countries, the Church could exercise control over those who moved around Europe, and so one also finds mention of Eastern Christians staying in Paris, Spain, Lisbon, Naples and even in Cologne or Vienna. We can piece together the wanderings of several of them around Catholic Europe (Figures 1.1 and 1.2). Without counting all those who manifested their desire to travel from the Christian capital to other towns or countries (as we do not know whether they were able to fulfill their wish), we can trace the presence of some of them outside Rome. Livorno, with its port, was a natural stopping point, sometimes permanent, along the route between the Levant and the papal city: twenty-one mentions, to which we must add incidences of Tuscany (one) and Florence (six). France appears as the secondmost common place to stay, with twenty-two mentions, including eight for Marseille and five for Paris. Nine people lived, at least for a while, in Malta. But we also find mentions of Venice (seven), Naples (five), Genoa (two), Madrid (three), Cologne (three), Vienna (two), Lisbon (two) and Algiers (three). The living space of these Eastern Christians was thus mainly Mediterranean, and the places where they settled were primarily ports. It is true that those who went to settle in Protestant countries, in London or in the Netherlands, had little chance of being recorded in the archives of the Catholic Church. But there were certainly fewer of them.[13]

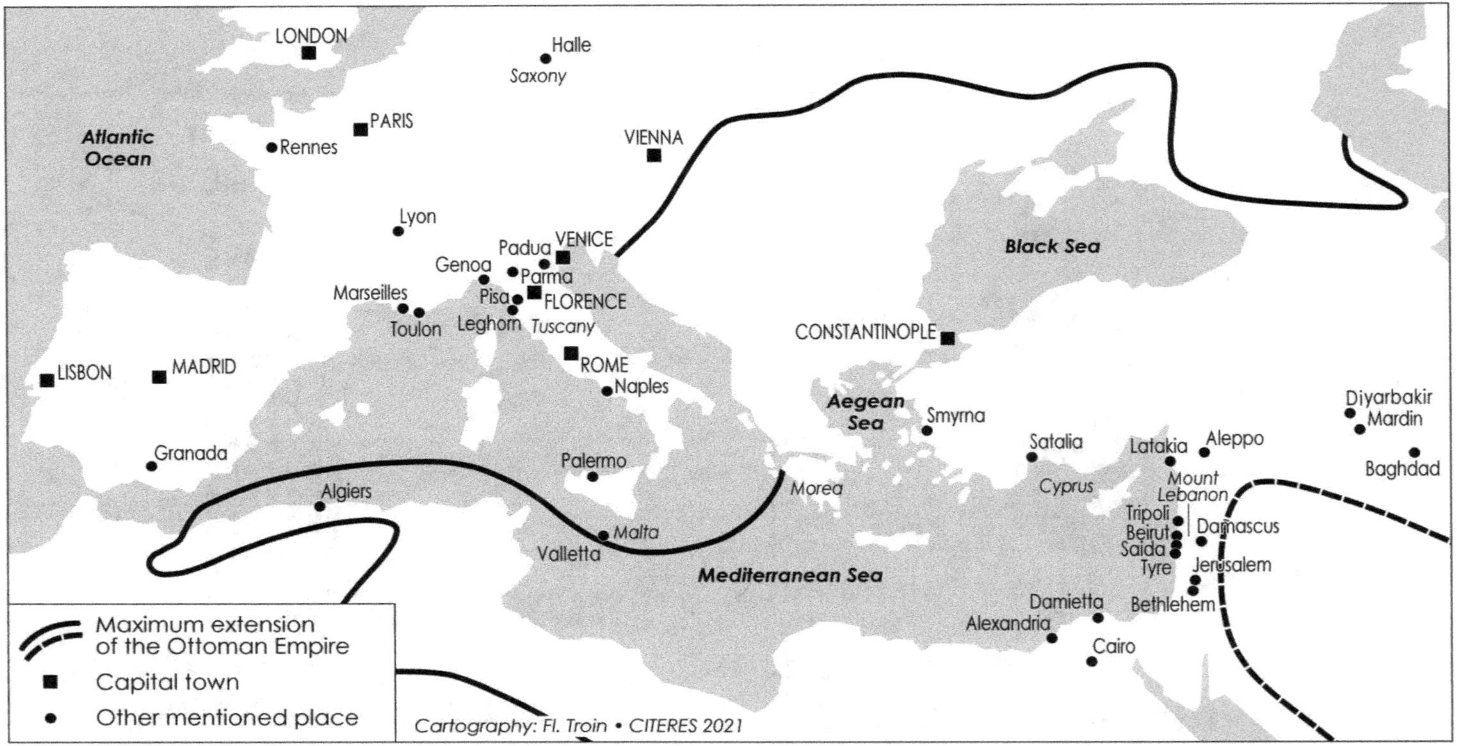

Figure 1.1 Area of circulation of Eastern Christians (seventeenth to eighteenth centuries).

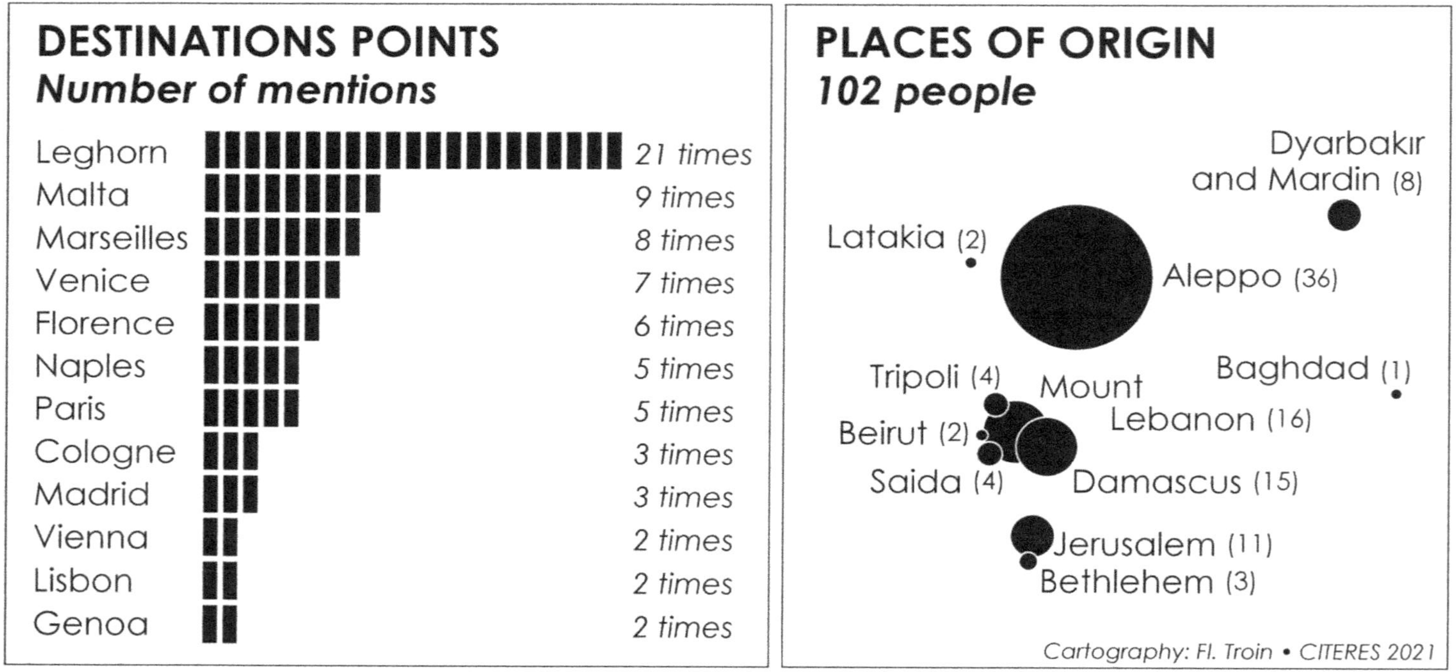

Figure 1.2 Origin and destination of Eastern Christians on travel (seventeenth to eighteenth centuries).

At least a third of them were ecclesiastics: fifty-seven were definitely priests or monks. The latter, who were often in pairs, generally came to Europe to collect money: I have noted eight of these pairs who travelled the length and breadth of the Catholic countries collecting alms.[14] Members of the Eastern clergy presented themselves as being commissioned by their bishop or their patriarch. In the present list, there are also three Eastern patriarchs and twelve bishops who came to the city of Saint Peter. Many (twenty-four) had been or were students, in particular at the Collegio Urbano, at the time they were writing to the Propaganda. Nine people said they were deacons, sub-deacons or 'clerics', which did not prevent them from practising another activity. One Syrian, living in Marseille, was listed as both 'cleric' and 'merchant'.[15] Eighteen were presented as 'merchants', of whom one was specified as 'a ship-owner' and another as 'broker'. Among those for whom the profession was not identifiable, several invested their money in trade in a speculative manner, often with setbacks.

Social status was not strictly determined. It was common, as we shall see, for ecclesiastics to be linked to commercial and financial business matters. Several lay people called themselves 'nobles', 'princes', or 'lords'. Thus, Lazzaro Aggiuri (Ajjūrī) from Aleppo presented himself as being 'of noble and ancient lineage'. In another petition, he asked for 'a patent of knight and count palatine', 'to be dignified in the eyes of his fellow countrymen, who hold this type of honour in high regard'.[16] Such titles also must have been used to open doors in Europe and to help obtain recommendations; the worst thing that could happen was to be 'unacknowledged'.[17] Several times it was necessary to clarify the fact that a Lebanese sheikh was not exactly what in Europe was called a 'prince' or a 'noble'. The medals of 'knight of Saint Lazarus', 'of the Golden Spur', or 'of Saint Peter' were equally very much sought after for the same reasons.[18]

THE CONTROL AND REPRESSION OF FOREIGNERS

In November 1695, a letter sent from Umbria informed the Propaganda that the Syriac priest Domenico Baroco (or Barocco) had indeed been transferred to the fortress of San Leo according to the instructions received from Rome. But the Papal Legate of Urbino drew attention to the fact that the priest was deprived of the sacraments as he knew neither Latin nor Italian, and that, at over seventy years of age, he risked dying without confession. The Congregation replied that they were sending him the clothes necessary to survive the winter and gave orders to look for someone in the region who spoke Syriac. It is surprising to learn that, less than two months later, in January 1696, an Arabic-speaking confessor was found in Rimini, and he gave the last rites to the poor priest in question, whose transport to Rome was already being considered so as not to let him die in sin. The confessor was undoubtedly a former Friar Minor from the Holy Land who knew Arabic. The pontifical legate added in his report that the prisoner said that he did not know the reasons for his detention, suspecting treachery on the part of his patriarch and that he would like to know what had become of the good clothes and the 150 *scudi* that he had had on him when he was arrested by the soldiers. In February 1698, the warden of the San Leo fortress again asked for a monthly pension for the poor old man who could not speak directly with anyone apart from his confessor, to whom he repeatedly said that he did not know the reasons for his imprisonment. In July 1699, a note stated that the same Domenico Baroco, detained in the prisons of the Capitol in Rome, had to be transferred to the Holy Office, where his life probably ended without the archives having revealed to us what he had come to do in Europe and why he ended up in the pontifical prisons.[19]

The line between travel and wandering is often a fine one, and a certain number of Eastern Christians demonstrably ended up falling into misery and vagrancy, thus becoming a major target of repression during the eighteenth century.[20] As a general rule, three reasons drove the Church to control and arrest itinerant monks: a suspicion of non-conformity to Catholic dogma and discipline; the risk of seeing them convert to Islam or Protestantism; or their improper handling of money received as alms. The Church was also concerned about avoiding complications with the states where they travelled. Sometimes, some of those who accused them did so to eliminate a rival or a trouble-maker and took it upon themselves to alert the authorities.[21] Eight people in our files received jail sentences, which mainly stemmed from such accusations. Timoteo Agnellini (Karnuk), the Syriac Catholic archbishop of Mardin, about whose troubled life I have written elsewhere, risked prison for the first time in 1678. François Picquet, former consul of France in Aleppo, had written an allegation that he had accumulated considerable sums in alms, that he was suspected of practising alchemy in Paris during the famous 'poison affairs' (he was using all his money for the purchase of coal and minerals), and that it was feared he would make his way to England if he felt threatened.[22] In 1700, he was summoned to Rome while living in Naples and this time was incarcerated for nearly three years on the orders of the Holy Office for having conferred ecclesiastical orders in return for money in Malta and for having collected alms without authorisation. The money raised was then used for disreputable activities, especially for loans with interest. Another prelate, the Armenian Archbishop Giacomo of Marash, was detained at the Castel Sant'Angelo in 1708 because it was feared that he would convert to Lutheranism. He was arrested through the intervention of the nuncio in Vienna and was still in prison in 1710. He had come to Rome at the age of twenty-three to study at the Collegio Urbano in 1696, but he had not been admitted. Back in Marash, he was dragged before the Muslim authorities by his co-religionists and put in prison, from where he was freed in return for money. He went through Tarsus and Cyprus on his way to find refuge in Lebanon with the Friars Minor of the Holy Land in Harissa;

then, after an argument with them, he turned to the Maronite patriarch Stefano Pietro (Isṭifān al-Duwayhī), who told the tale of his misfortune in a letter dated 26 September 1698.[23] In 1740, the inquisitor of Malta mentioned one Giorgio Amasi, a Melkite originally from Damascus, saying that he did not want to stay in Christian lands and desired only to deal with 'infidels'. As he was suspected of wanting to become a Muslim, the inquisitor had him locked up in the 'conservatorio detto dei Poveri', where he worked as a weaver. He wrote to his parents, asking them to send him help.[24]

Giovanni Sciain (Shahīn), a Melkite priest from Jerusalem, came to Rome in 1725. After having told all his troubles to the cardinals, he had his son accepted at the Collegio Urbano, while for himself he obtained written recommendations to go beg for money in Christian lands.[25] His passage was mentioned in 1727 by the nuncio in Venice, whose suspicions were raised by information concerning the alms he had previously collected in Genoa. After verification, the nuncio found him to be a good Catholic of respectable character.[26] In 1729, Giovanni Sciain wrote from Marseille to Giovanni Aminione, the envoy of the Melkite Catholic patriarch Cyril (Kīrillūs), declaring himself ready for any affairs concerning this patriarch but without wanting to reveal his intentions. Mosè (Mūsā), a Syrian cleric, merchant in Marseille, however, warned Aminione against Sciain. Apparently, the Melkite priest had left for Aix where he contacted a certain Madeleine, who sold everything to join him. Soon after, however, she was put in prison, and Sciain fled to Avignon. These letters were addressed to the Propaganda, whose secretary then sent a request for information about the individual to Avignon and to the nuncio in Seville.[27] In 1732, Sciain was identified in the prison of the Inquisition in Granada. The Inquisition suspected him of not really being a priest and of practising simony, especially by selling false blessings and indulgences. Moreover, he was also accused of having traded with the 'Moorish' and 'Turkish' slaves, to whom he had apparently promised that they would be redeemed. It is thought that he wanted to go to Gibraltar, which might imply that he wanted to reach the side of the English 'heretics' or of the Muslims. His partner Madeleine, of whom it was said that she was French and married and that she had followed him from Pistoia, was now in prison in Murcia. Sciain apparently carried with him forty-six patents, passports and various letters of recommendation, including one from the Cardinal Prefect of the Propaganda destined for the nuncio in Paris. The Inquisition also took interest in the books he owned: they were liturgical books in Arabic and Greek in which there was nothing to censure (except for one of them, the nature of which was unspecified, and which apparently belonged to one of his interpreters).[28]

At last, Sciain's financial affairs were cleared up and revealed a complex network of investments and circulation of money between Christian Europe and his hometown. In a report for the Propaganda in the same year, the commissioner of the Friars Minor of the Holy Land in Livorno lifted the veil on some of Giovanni

Sciain's travels in previous years. In fact, he had come to beg him for alms in 1726. He later returned, asking him to send 116 Venetian sequins to his wife Anastasia and to his children, still in Jerusalem. After a tour of Florence and Rome, Sciain gave the agent of the Friars Minor a further 60 Venetian sequins to be placed in trust with the Procuracy of the Holy Land in Jerusalem, before he went off to Marseille around June 1728. At the time, he wrote to his family in Jerusalem to tell them that they could go ask the Friars Minor of the Holy Land for all the money that they needed to pay off their debts and live in comfort, which put the Latin religious order in a difficult position and made the commissioner of Livorno declare that he would not again be caught being burdened with such people.[29] But Giovanni Sciain had also entrusted 48 sequins to the Franciscan Guardian of Damascus, Tommaso Campaja, summoned to Rome in 1725, and the considerable sum of 1,100 Venetian sequins to Lorenzo di San Lorenzo, Superior-General of the Franciscans and former Custos of the Holy Land, while waiting to go back to his country, taking the money with him or transferring it to his son at the Collegio Urbano, should anything happen to him. He was obviously integrated into a network of Eastern Christians settled in France and Italy: the Greek parish priest of Venice had intervened in his favour, and in Marseille Giovanni Aminione, the Melkite envoy of the patriarch and former student of the Collegio Urbano, had given him a certificate in 1728. In Livorno, he had entrusted money to Pietro Giallali, from Bethlehem, and to Nicola Fargialla (Farjallāh), a Melkite, both living in the town.[30] In Marseille, he had deposited 60 Venetian sequins with a certain Mūsā, an Armenian or Maronite merchant living there with one of his brothers, Yūsif. It is likely that this Mūsā was the one who denounced him. Later, it was also discovered that Sciain owed a Greek merchant the cost of some cloth that he had had sent to Jerusalem to decorate the church.[31] Eventually, the Inquisition of Granada absolved Sciain after reprimanding him and then decided to exile him for good from Spain, sentencing him to pay the legal costs and those of imprisonment. They seemed keen to get rid of him as fast as possible.[32] We hear of Giovanni Sciain again in May 1736, when the nuncio in Lisbon reported that he had been arrested while begging and that he had spent the money on spirits. He still had on him at least a hundred letters of recommendation and various kinds of authorisations, which made him a singular mediator between irreconcilable worlds: a certificate from the Greek and anti-Latin patriarch of Jerusalem, Chrysanthos, authorising him to hear confessions, was alongside a profession of faith given before the Roman Inquisition and a certificate of membership of the Roman fraternity of the Guardian Angel![33] On 22 July 1736, the Lisbon nuncio finally announced the death of Giovanni Sciain, after a long illness. He specified that, after having paid for the costs of his incarceration and his care, there remained hardly anything from the money he had collected.[34]

Giovanni Sciain's eleven years of peregrinations coincided exactly with the period during which Eastern Christians, begging on their own behalf or for their Church, were becoming increasingly numerous as travellers venturing the length and breadth of Europe, introducing themselves at the royal courts, to the point of worrying the authorities of the Catholic States as well as the Roman Curia, which had become more vigilant. A market in false certificates in favour of the numerous family members of the Maronite Habaisci (Ḥubaysh) sheikhs, who followed one another at a rapid pace through the European courts, was then revealed.[35] In Spain, in particular, the Levantine alms-collectors seemed to promptly end up in jail. In November 1753, Francesco Shediak (Shidyāq) wrote from Madrid that he had left his country behind and his family in great need because of the tyranny suffered at the hands of the infidels, that he had begged in Malta and in the kingdom of Naples but that, once in Spain, he had been thrown into jail where he had rotted for the last eight months 'without any fault or misconduct'. He had demonstrably failed to understand the hostility of the authorities towards begging and vagrancy, and he complained bitterly that having 'fled the tyranny of the infidels, enemies of our Holy Religion, I have fallen into that of the Catholics'. 'In our countries', he continued, 'we protect and accommodate the missionaries and Catholic laymen who come, and in their countries, we are thus mistreated'.[36]

THE REQUESTS ADDRESSED TO THE PROPAGANDA

We cannot always reconstitute the paths along which Eastern Christians travelled to Europe, nor can we find the reasons for which they were forced to seek help from the Propaganda. When Giuseppe Acchar from Aleppo said that he was in great need in Rome, on 23 November 1671, and asked for alms to return home, it is impossible to know how he had become stranded there and how long ago he had left his homeland. We do not know for what reasons the cardinals gave him 5 *scudi*.[37]

A few of these travellers seem to have gone to Rome for a short stay with a selfless motive, usually a pilgrimage, particularly in jubilee years. Thus, Dimitri Christoforo, a Maronite who said he had made the journey to satisfy his devotion in the Holy Year 1700, asked for free books before returning home. Lazzaro Naim, a Maronite sub-deacon, who had come for the Holy Year 1725, also wished to obtain certain publications before returning to Mount Lebanon, where he was to be ordained as priest.[38] But the surge of piety could merely have been an argument to seduce the cardinals, or it could have been mixed up with more prosaic reasons. Giovanni Aretin, an Armenian, said that he had come to Rome for his devotions and to visit the Holy Sites in 1677. He specified, however, that he had a Christian wife and two unbaptised daughters back home and asked for financial help for their upkeep and to bring them to Rome. The answer from the Congregation was negative.[39]

Like Giovanni Sciain, most of the Eastern Christians staying in Europe went to visit the offices of the Congregation to obtain direct help, to ask for an endorsement allowing them to beg in 'Christian countries', or to untangle some financial dispute. I have found twenty-two mentions of alms collections for churches and religious orders, as well as for individuals authorised and recommended by the cardinals.

Another way of asking for and obtaining aid from the Propaganda was to be accepted at the Collegio Urbano or another college in Rome: twenty-one such cases appear in the files. The desire to study was mixed with the the desire to flee poverty, which explains the scholastic failure of a great many of these students. Giorgio, son of Giovanni Sciain, entered the College at eleven years of age, at the start of his father's adventures and while two of his brothers were detained as hostages by Muslim money-lenders in Jerusalem, but unlike many he proved to be a brilliant student.[40]

Eastern Catholics also went to Italy to try and get back goods and ships confiscated by the corsairs of Malta or Livorno, as well as to obtain certificates of Catholicism that might shield them from future attacks: fourteen went to Rome, Malta and Livorno precisely for this purpose.[41] In one specific case, the supplicant Gabriele, a Melkite from Damascus, came to the Holy See to obtain certification of his Catholicism, which would allow him to reclaim his goods confiscated by the Venice magistrate: a fellow countryman from Damascus residing in the Republic had denounced him as non-Catholic.[42]

Among the motives put forward for coming to Europe, persecution was mentioned several times (thirteen cases). We know that conflicts within communities were in fact the main cause of the violence imposed on Christians by the Muslim authorities;[43] in several instances, the people really responsible for the persecutions were 'schismatic' or 'heretical' adversaries. A number of bishops and patriarchs arrived in Rome to escape the intrigues, threats and violence stirred up against them by their ecclesiastical opponents.[44] Several Melkites from Aleppo and Damascus arrived in Rome following tensions between the Catholic and the Orthodox within their community at the beginning of the eighteenth century. Neofito Giubair (Nāwufitūs ibn Jubayr al-Ḥalabī), in conflict with the patriarch of Damascus, Cyril al-Zaʿīm, concerning the election to the episcopal see of Beirut, was, according to his own testimony, handed over to the Turkish authorities of the town, having been denounced by his opponents. Sent on a ship from Saida to Damietta, he was robbed of his goods by corsairs at the mouth of the Nile. Having managed to live peacefully for some time in Damietta, a new conflict with the vicar of the Greek patriarch of Alexandria first forced him to flee to Cairo after a beating, then to embark for Malta in 1717. He hoped that he could count on the help of Giuseppe Assemani, whom he had known in Damascus and then in Cairo during the latter's missions for the Holy See.[45] Mosé and Benigno, sons of Nicola, Catholics from Aleppo, likewise said that they had suffered imprisonment, chains and beating at the hands of the Turks, and that they had been stripped of their goods following the persecutions against Catholics in 1724 by the Orthodox Patriarch Sylvester (Silfāstrūs al-Qubruṣī). They wished to obtain an endorsement to go to Vienna and around Germany. Meanwhile, during his mission to Constantinople, Lazzaro Aggiuri seems to have obtained from the Sublime Porte a ruling against the Orthodox patriarch, before coming to seek safety in Christendom.[46]

Other persecutions were sometimes blamed on the 'Turks' alone. Thus, in 1662, Francesco di Paolo, from Aleppo, had to flee to 'avoid the peril of losing either his life or his faith'. He carried with him a testimony from François Picquet, the French consul in the city, who had given him money to help him flee. Embarked on a Muslim ship, he was captured by a Maltese corsair and found himself on the island penniless, along with his two daughters, aged eighteen and fourteen years old. From there, he made his way to Rome where the Propaganda gave him alms of 10 *scudi*.[47] Fatallah Massaica, who described himself as a rich Chaldean merchant, said that he had fled Baghdad, then Diyarbakir. In the latter city, his son served the Capuchins. It was arguably because this boy was handsome ('*di qualche aspetto*') that the soldiers wanted to force him to become a Muslim. To buy the freedom of his son, the merchant had to spend his entire fortune, borrowing from Muslims, then flee into exile, leaving a large part of his family 'in the hands of the Turks'. He was given financial help, and his son was admitted to the Collegio Urbano.[48]

Such persecutions were usually due to debts owed to Muslim creditors, which could in turn have their origin in conflicts between Christians. Many of the latter engaged in maritime trade and transport, forming partnerships with Muslims who provided the funds. If this capital was lost, they or their children were held hostage and could be forced to convert in order to escape a trial in court. Thus, Giorgio Sasi, a Melkite from Damascus, borrowed the sum of 1,300 *pezzi* with interest from several Muslims in order to invest in a merchant voyage. But the boat and all its cargo fell into the hands of the English; Giorgio, having lost everything, left in the hands of his creditors two sons who risked apostasy if he did not find a way to pay back the money. This time, despite the recommendations that he presented, the Propaganda had no pity and sent him packing.[49]

If we are to believe his story, Elia Corbagi (Kurbājī), from Tripoli, seems to have fallen victim to his commitment to the Ottoman government in 1731. He declared that he was *commodo* (comfortable) engaging in his own trade, but that the pasha had forced him, seven years earlier, to look after the administration of the Customs. When, during the change of sultan and grand vezier in Istanbul, the pasha from Tripoli was imprisoned, Corbagi lost everything, and the new governor ordered him to pay large amounts of money and to take over the Customs once again. He preferred to flee, leaving his wife and children behind. He went to visit the Holy Places of Jerusalem, and from there he went on to Rome. When he petitioned the Propaganda, he still intended to return home: he wished to obtain from the Sublime Porte a *firman* designating him an honorary dragoman and placing him under the protection of France. He therefore requested an endorsement to travel to Paris.[50]

In 1740, a certain Abramo Cobbié from Damascus (Ibrahīm Khubiyya) asked for and obtained help from Saida to flee to 'Christendom'. He managed to find a clandestine passage on a boat belonging to a Maronite at the end of January 1741.[51] A later letter from Agostino Zarur (Zaʿrūr), abbot of the Melkite monks of Saint Saviour, claimed that he was a renegade who had converted to Islam for fear of death. After having occupied honourable functions as a Muslim, he was stricken with remorse, renounced his material goods and honours and sought refuge in the monastery above Saida, together with two slaves whom he brought back to Christianity. He embarked with one of these slaves and two other renegades. One of his protectors had prepared for him to be welcomed in Marseille or Livorno but had advised him to aim rather for the latter, as life was better there.[52] But a later biographical document in Arabic says that in 1728 he set off from Damascus to Cairo, where he married the daughter of a Melkite merchant, and that from there he settled in Venice in 1741, then in Rome in 1742. This text fails to mention his conversion to Islam.[53]

In two other cases, it was the close relatives of a 'martyr' – that is to say, of a Christian who after having converted to Islam had publicly returned to his original faith and therefore suffered capital punishment – who had to go into exile, either to avoid their own conversion by force, or to escape poverty after the confiscation of the goods from the house of the victim. Teodoro (ʿAbdallāh), the son of Dāwūd, a Melkite martyr from Aleppo executed on 28 July 1660, was sent to Rome in 1663, where, after brilliant studies at the Collegio Urbano and an attempt to return to Aleppo, he joined the Discalced Carmelites. He had a fine career under the name David di San Carlo, first in Rome in his order, then at the service of Vatican diplomacy during two long stays in Constantinople, before ending up as the apostolic vicar of Smyrna in 1713, at the age of sixty-three.[54] In January 1701, the Maronite patriarch gave his support to Yūsif Abū Rizq, brother of Yūnis, a sheikh (a term often wrongly translated in the archives as 'prince') and tax collector (*muqtaʿjī*) for the region of Tripoli, who had lived as Muslim for several years but returned to Christianity and was condemned for apostasy and burnt at the stake in May 1697.[55] In March 1702, the same Yūsif Abū Rizq once again asked for help, pointing out that he had fled to Christian Europe with about fifteen people. He had been staying in France and requesting the help of the monarchy in the meantime,[56] as confirmed by a denunciation to the Propaganda, dated 1704 at the earliest, which states that he had left Rome for France with Elia Assemani, an envoy of the patriarch, whose presence in Paris is attested in 1701. Jean de la Roque, who left a printed account of 'the history of the Maronite prince Junes', declared that he had learnt it from 'prince Joseph' (that is, the same Yūsif Abū Rizq), while the latter was staying in the French capital for several months. After that, Yūsif went to Florence, then to

Venice to obtain land in the Morea (Peloponnese), with a view to settling there with a colony of fifty people. From there he seems to have gone to Germany, then returned to Venice. We know this because of the testimony of a certain Bartolomeo De Marchis (himself a Maronite?), who was apparently employed to serve as his interpreter. Once in Rome, Bartolomeo was tried, and in order to defend himself, he talked with other Levantines of the capital, thus learning the details of the life of Yūsif Abū Rizq, and he testified against him. Yūsif was in turn imprisoned in 1704. Freed from prison through the intervention of Elia Assemani, he then went to Naples, where yet again he ended up in prison.[57]

TRAVELS OR IMMIGRATION

It is true that, after the drama of a close relative being sentenced to death for apostasy, or after one's own apostasy, Christians had no other alternative than to go into permanent exile in Catholic Europe, as was the case of the people mentioned above. One should note, however, that the fate of a Yūsif Abū Rizq or a Giovanni Shahīn did not seem to follow a predetermined trajectory, nor was it part of a conscious and coherent strategy of integration, which in the end proved inaccessible. It would be more correct to describe their careers as the result of a course of action that led them to an unforeseen point of no return.

A letter from Elia, the Armenian archbishop of Bethlehem, in this regard seems to signal an unanticipated sequence of circumstances and reveals to us the risks and dangers of the sea, mentioned in many testimonies. He reported that in 1687 about 210 Armenians were travelling from Constantinople to Jerusalem for Easter and that they were captured by three corsair ships under the Venetian flag – one French, one Maltese and one Greek. The corsairs stripped them of all their goods, including the clothes they were wearing, to a value estimated at 12,000 *scudi*. The victims decided to send him, Elia, together with some priests and servants, as an ambassador to the king of France. The latter received him with honours and gave him 250 *doublons*, to which were added the 2,000 *écus* offered by leading dignitaries and bishops. Arriving in Marseille, Elia sent his goods and the money to Livorno on a French ship, while he went to Toulon to meet the French corsair from whom he asked the payment of a third of the damage. But the corsair replied that he himself had been stripped of everything on the journey home and therefore did not have the means to repay him. At the same time, the French ship, having left Livorno, fell into the hands of the Spanish. Elia then decided to go to Tuscany, but once there, he learned that everything had already been sold and that the Spaniards had returned to Naples. He went to Rome, then, with some letters of recommendation, and to Naples, where he stayed for five months, to no avail. He returned to Rome, then to Madrid, where he stayed for two years. Finally, he received the answer that no merchandise taken from enemy ships would ever be restored, but he was given a letter of credit for 500 *scudi* to be paid by the viceroy of Naples. He waited in vain for fifteen months for the payment of this sum, then went to the Propaganda as a last resort, mentioning the reception that he would get from the Armenians if he returned to Jerusalem empty-handed. The Propaganda decided, ten years after the event, to recommend his cause to the viceroy of Naples.[58]

Permanent settlement in Christendom was not the aim of the majority of Eastern Christians who appear in the sources at hand. It is clear that many were considering short stays, which were eventually lengthened or repeated in order to establish contacts and conduct business. It was common to make a journey several times, making the most of the experience and the protections acquired on previous visits. The sheikh Taleb Habaisci (Ṭālib Ḥubaysh) – living clandestinely in Madrid after having fled Portugal and seemingly fearing the prisons of the Inquisition, just as Giovanni Sciain was imprisoned in Granada – wrote two desperate letters to Rome: we learn therein that he had already made the journey to Spain ten years previously.[59]

Those who came to the Roman authorities with a mission, sent by a patriarch, a bishop or a lay notable, generally went to see the Propaganda before taking their leave after a stay of a few weeks. Thus, Gabriele Tissan, envoy of the archbishop of Saydnaya, having professed his Catholic faith, asked for books and provisions to return home.[60] But it was never sure that the promise to return home, pledged in their petition to the Roman authorities, would indeed be acted upon. In 1681, the offices of the Propaganda pointed out that Timoteo Agnellini, after having spent several years at the Collegio Urbano, was meant to go back to his church with gifts and money, but he actually preferred to go to France to seek alms illegally.[61] In May 1700, Giovanni Battista del Giudice (Shidyāq Ḥannā al-Muḥāsīb), 'sent by a prince of his nation' (in fact, a member of the family of the Maronite Khāzin sheiks), requested books for his imminent return, for himself and for the churches of Beirut, listing them in a note. But we later find him in Paris, where he arrived in November 1700 and stayed until June 1701.[62]

On 10 May 1702, Giuseppe Michele, sent by the archbishop of Saida, Aftīmyūs (Euthymius) Ṣayfī, had asked for books before returning home. But he was still in Rome on 4 September of the same year, when he was begging for help to pay for his journey. Not having received enough money, he asked for an endorsement, which he obtained on 30 November 1702 and presented to the nuncio of Florence two years later. In 1705, he was mentioned in a denunciation by the commissioner of the Holy Land, accusing him of begging without an authorisation in the diocese of Naples.[63]

Alongside these more or less lengthy and improvised wanderings, there also exists evidence of more planned and organised migrations. This was the case of the family of Nicolas and Ḥabīb Mughaylaṣ, merchants for thirty years in Saida and Damietta, who in 1735 clandestinely embarked on a French ship to get to Marseille, according to a plan prepared in advance.[64] Their intention was probably to secure their own wealth and household against any confiscation, as was the case for Yūsif al-Qassīs in 1761. The latter, having amassed a considerable fortune as secretary and adviser of the emir of Galilee, Zāhir al-ʿUmar, attempted to smuggle it to Europe, before fleeing there with his family to enjoy it in safety. But his master could not tolerate that he escaped with his wealth. He had him arrested and his goods seized.[65]

Lazzaro Aggiuri arrived in Rome in 1729 and managed to enroll his brother Stefano Sciocrallah (Shukrallāh), aged twelve, at the Collegio Urbano, with the help of Giuseppe Assemani, who paid for his board and lodging for the first few months. He then asked for recommendations to the nuncios of France and Tuscany, with a view to preparing the transfer of his whole family to one of these two states, while at the same time applying to be granted the titles of knight and count, as mentioned above.[66] The choice of Tuscany may have been decided by the presence there of another brother. In September 1730, Aggiuri mentioned that he had obtained all the necessary certificates to settle there, but upon his project having become common knowledge in Aleppo, his family was arrested, and all his goods were confiscated. In 1733, he was back in the Christian capital where he drew a pension from the Church authorities. This time, he tried to obtain from the cardinals a recommendation to the French ambassador in Constantinople and to the consul in Aleppo in order to bring his entire family to Europe. The *chargé d'affaires* of the above-mentioned consulate gave a negative answer, invoking the feelings of the family, who were little disposed to this transfer.[67] In 1736, the same Lazzaro Aggiuri, with the title of 'count', pretended to want to go back to his town where his relatives were languishing in his absence. But he chose to go by road, which was a long and arbitrary route, as he asked for introductions to the court of Vienna and a passport for Constantinople. His brother left the College in 1739 and entered the Melkite monastery of Saint John of Shuwayr in modern-day Lebanon, citing the fact that he no longer had any family in Aleppo.[68]

LINGUISTIC ASSETS AND SPECIFIC ECCLESIASTICAL JOBS

To manage settling in Christian Europe, one needed a well-thought-out plan, a lot of patience and skills in handling people to obtain protection and be accepted. One of the principal assets that those exiled from the Arab provinces of the Ottoman Empire possessed consisted of their knowledge, sometimes approximate, of Middle Eastern languages. Experts in these languages were quite rare and sought-after in Europe, for scholarly work as well as tasks of interpretation and pastoral work in the ports where Christians and Muslims disembarked and stayed.

Teaching services, translations and library work allowed some of these migrants to have quite a comfortable career in various towns, but they were vulnerable to intrigues, especially if they lost their protector.[69] Timoteo Agnellini, having arrived in Rome from Marseille in 1671, had been recommended by the famous Jesuit scholar Athanasius Kircher, who said that he had checked the former's knowledge and had employed him as a copyist. It was at Kircher's suggestion that the Secretary of the Propaganda insisted on employing Carnuch at the rate of 6 *scudi* per month for three years. Several years later, the same man found employment in the Oriental printing house of Cardinal Barbarigo in Padua.[70] In 1710 the Damascene Solomon Negri, a scholar well-versed in several 'Oriental languages', was appointed to the chair of Arabic (and perhaps Syriac, too) at the Sapienza in Rome for 5 *scudi* a month. After negotiations, he saw his pay increased and was entrusted with additional teaching work at the Collegio Urbano, which gave him a monthly income of 15 *scudi*.[71] It is unlikely that he made the whole of his curriculum vitae, with his appointments in Protestant countries, known when he went to Rome for work. For, after having studied with the Jesuits in Damascus, he had stayed in Paris in the entourage of Louis Picques, the librarian of the Bibliothèque Mazarine, who had employed several Eastern people in his service and who had learned friends in England.[72] It was probably via this route that Solomon Negri then went to London, and from there he followed Heinrich Wilhelm Ludolf to Halle, where he founded the teaching of Arabic. Apparently, he made another trip to Constantinople to perfect his Turkish and Persian before being taken on in Rome.[73] In 1714, he went to the cardinals again to remind them that he had accepted both jobs at 15 *scudi* a month with a promise of accommodation and in the hope of a regular increase in earnings, when he could have continued his journey to the 'ultramontane countries', hoping for better luck there. However, his pay was reduced to 14 *scudi*, which provoked him to ask for leave.[74] Maybe he had already planned to go back to England, then to Halle. After two years in Saxony, he went back to London as an interpreter to the king and as editor for the Society for Promoting Christian Knowledge, a Protestant missionary institution.[75]

Several Eastern prelates, having no intention of returning home, tried to stay in Rome, obtaining a pension in exchange for their services. At the beginning of the eighteenth century, citing the obligation of residence for bishops, the Propaganda several times tried to force them to leave Rome and go back to their sees, but in vain.[76] Among them was one Gabriel Eva (Jibrāʾīl Ḥawwā), from Aleppo, founder of the Maronite order of the Lebanese monks, then archbishop of Cyprus. Having accomplished missions for the Vatican in Egypt in 1703 and in Syria in 1711 and following a dispute during a stay in Aleppo in 1724 that saw him sent to prison, he spent the rest of his life in Rome, being paid for various missions and serving the Maronite hospice of Santi Pietro e Marcellino, until his death in 1752. He also had his nephew, Tommaso Eva, brought to Rome where, after having studied at the Maronite College, he made a career, without going back home.[77] Athanasius Safar, the

Syriac archbishop of Mardin, after a mission in Persia and a stay in Paris, went to collect money in America, then settled down in Rome with the proceeds until the end of his life. He managed to get one of his nephews to join him, and on his uncle's advice the latter appealed to the Propaganda in 1734 to obtain an allowance from the money he had collected. Having tried to keep his three daughters with the 'art of silk weaving', the nephew said, he could not find any more work. The Congregation decided then to grant him 18 *scudi* annually, given via the intermediary of his parish priest. On his death in 1753, the allowance was transferred to his widow and then, in 1770, to one of his daughters.[78]

Administering the sacraments to Eastern Christians passing through Western Europe was a highly sought-after job that allowed such clergy to survive in modest but decent conditions. Timoteo Agnellini (Karnuk, Carnuch), during his long and adventurous life, zealously instructed the Eastern Christians in Naples, being employed in private capacity in the house of a local notable. Around 1710, he was teaching and hearing confessions for the Muslim catechumens in Rome, and he exercised similar functions at the Armenian church of Santa Maria Egiziaca.[79] Gabriel Eva, wanting to demonstrate the necessity for a Maronite presence in Rome, including a hospice, listed the services that they offered there: hearing confessions in Arabic and Turkish for the sick at the San Giovanni hospital; explaining to the doctors the symptoms of the sick who did not know Italian; catechising and converting Turks; and helping and instructing Arabic-speaking pilgrims.[80]

In 1688, a certain Giorgio di Grazia from Jerusalem claimed to have taught Arabic, Turkish and Greek in Naples for seven years, to have instructed slaves and renegades in the houses of 'private gentlemen'; eventually he asked for a recommendation to go to Spain to become a priest. In 1725, Paolo Isdrael, a Maronite Augustinian, begged the Propaganda to finance a college for the infidels that he had founded also in Naples.[81]

In 1682, a salaried priest was appointed to provide pastoral care to the Armenians of Marseille, as it already happened in Venice and Livorno. In the same town, Tommaso Herabied is mentioned as being active with the 'Turkish' slaves and supervising the printing of books in Armenian. He was later joined by the Syriac Grazia Nachet, a former student of the Collegio Urbano. The latter, captured by the Barbary pirates in 1669 as he was returning to Syria, was ransomed by the cardinals in 1670. Based later in Aleppo, he went to France with Athanasius Safar, sent on a mission by François Picquet concerning Persian affairs in 1685. He then decided to stay in Marseille to look after the 'Turks', justifying himself by the fact that in his twelve years in Aleppo he had not been very useful because of his lack of knowledge of Syriac. At the same time, he requested to be allowed to use the Latin rite. In 1687, he wrote to ask to have an Arabic-Latin Bible sent, which would be useful for the conversion of these same 'Turks'. By 1690, he had seemingly converted around a hundred Muslims. Another Syriac, Paolo Abdelnur, having arrived in Rome, in June 1706 asked to be helped or accepted at the Collegio Urbano. He was apparently not successful, as in December he asked for books from the Propaganda, this time with the intention of going to Marseille to give the sacraments and hear the confessions of Eastern Christians in Arabic and Turkish. Maybe he was thinking of succeeding Grazia Nachet. He wrote from Aleppo ten years later, mentioning the fact that he had spent all this time in France (in Paris) and that he had just returned home where his reception had been difficult.[82]

In 1663, an Armenian from Aleppo left the Collegio Urbano after only two years of mediocre studies and went to practise trade ('*mercatura*') in Livorno. The Propaganda dealt with the supervision and control of the Armenians in the Tuscan town in 1669, 1670 and 1674, when a conflict arose in relation to the Catholic profession of faith that was asked of them, as well as the question of the invocation of their patriarch in the liturgy.[83] The Greeks had been present in the town since the 1570s and had had a church there since 1606. As for the Melkites, they seem to have arrived in the second half of the seventeenth century, but their colony, composed mainly of people from Damascus, grew in the 1720s, during the persecutions of Catholics in Syria.[84] As early as 1706, a Friar Minor of the Observance, Giovanni Felice da Barga, former missionary in the Holy Land, was reported as holding religious services in Arabic in the town where he had retired in the house of his order.[85] In 1713, Name Facher (Niʿma Fakhr), from Tripoli, had a house in Livorno where he welcomed Eastern Christians passing through.[86] In 1726, a Melkite priest from Aleppo, Graziano Salemi, went to Rome to ask for assistance to spend the winter and to be housed at the ecclesiastical college of Ponte Sisto. He said that he had come to shelter in this '*alma città*', having been a victim of persecution by the Orthodox patriarch Sylvester. The following spring, the archbishop of Pisa informed the Propaganda that he had authorised the same Graziano Salemi to celebrate and administer the sacraments in Arabic for two months, serving the 'Arabs' of Livorno around Easter time.[87] But the same year, the 'Levantine, Greek, Melkite, Syriac traders' of the town petitioned the cardinals to point out that, not knowing any language other than Arabic, they had been deprived of the sacraments for months and sometimes years. They asked that the Maronite Giuseppe Giorgi, former student of the Maronite College and a long-time missionary in Aleppo, then on his way to France, be allowed to hear their confessions.[88] In 1735, Yūsif Buktī, Yuḥannā Buktī and Saʿāda Massara, merchants living in Livorno, made the same request in favour of the alms-collecting Maronite monk Girolamo from Aleppo, who had been in the Tuscan port for the previous two months and who knew Arabic, Armenian and Turkish. The latter managed to settle in the town until his death in 1768. At that time, he purportedly was receiving from the Grand Duke of Tuscany a stipend as a confessor. Taking advantage of the protection of the Eastern Christians of Livorno, he had freed himself from his religious order.[89] Tommaso Diab, also from Aleppo, probably succeeded him, as in 1773 he introduced himself as a Dominican and chaplain in Livorno, when he welcomed his cousin Arsenio Diab (Arsāniyūs Diyāb) who was passing through the town.[90]

The surveillance and education of Arabic-speaking Christians and captives from the Levant and North Africa in Malta can be comprehended by following the career of Michele Metoscita, chaplain to the slaves at the beginning of the eighteenth century. He left the Maronite College in June 1693, aged twenty-eight, after twelve years of robust studies, in order to return to his native country of Cyprus.[91] However, in 1695, he was in Rome as an envoy of the Maronite patriarch. He was back again in the same role in 1697.[92] In 1704, he had been settled in Malta for four years where he was supported by the Order of Saint John, which assigned to him the care of the slaves. The feedback on him was very complimentary, mentioning the several languages in which he taught and stating that he had led 300 'Turks' to the Catholic faith, thanks to his knowledge of their 'sect' and their language. His attendance to the galleys was useful, and the authorities used him as an interpreter. The patriarch summoned him to Mount Lebanon, but the Order of Malta did not want to let him go, despite repeated requests, and demanded that the Propaganda should decide whether he stay or leave. The latter responded that he should stay in Malta until a successor was found for him.[93] The following year, he was still on the island, with plans to develop his activities. The Discalced Carmelite Elia Giacinto di Santa Maria, passing there on his way from Lebanon to Rome, asked that a church be given to Metoscita, where he could better work at the conversion of the 'Turks' and start a printing business. In another request, the same person proposed that the breviary and missal of the Maronites be edited, while suggesting that, if that was impossible for the Propaganda's typography, the task should be entrusted to Metoscita. These projects encountered some difficulties, and the missionary came back on the offensive in favour of his protégé in June 1706. The Propaganda was favourable and granted him a church belonging to the Carmelites, but it refused him the right to print books.[94] This church, equipped with a few rooms 'situated on the dock of the galleys', was then the object of long-running disputes, as the bishop of Malta always opposed it being in Maronite hands, no doubt because of the kind of people who frequented it and the revenue it produced.

For several years, Michele Metoscita found himself at the centre of a conflict between the bishop of the island, who was perpetually hostile towards him, and the inquisitor, who upheld his cause. In 1708, a report from the convicts and the 'Turkish' galley slaves in favour of the 'Maronite priest' arrived at the Propaganda after having transited via the Secretary of State, but the bishop of Malta, justifying himself, replied negatively to a new demand for ownership of the church. In 1709, it was suggested that Metoscita be entrusted with the chair of Arabic teaching, founded in Malta by the inquisitor in 1637, which would take the post away from a canon of the cathedral, a friend of the bishop.[95] In 1711, the chaplain of the Order of Malta recommended Metoscita, and his dossier was once again examined by the cardinals. We learn that he had at his disposal in Valletta a recently built church in the slaves' prison, where he had lodgings for himself and his neophytes, who numbered a respectable ninety, while the catechumens counted six. For these activities he earned 10 *scudi* per month from the Order of Malta and other fees linked to the care of the converted. His insistence on obtaining the Carmelite church, far from his place of work, seems to have been motivated by a desire to be freer and not to live under the eye of the prison's commander. In so far as the chair of Arabic was concerned, we learn that it brought 200 *scudi* annually to its holder, canon Fabrizio Bonici, of whom it was said that he did not have the skills to fulfil the role, even though recruited after an exam. Thus, no one was teaching or acting as an interpreter for the Inquisition tribunal, and some went to take Arabic lessons with Metoscita at their own expense. Another project, to which the inquisitor was not favourable, but which had the support of the Grand Master and of the monks of Saint Jerome who catechised the Turkish slaves, was to establish a sort of foundation for the mission, of which the Maronite priest would be the main leader. This project does not seem to have progressed: in 1717, the teaching of Arabic in Malta, or at least the payments attached to it, still went to Fabrizio Bonici.[96] Around 1730, a priest and former student of the Maronite College, called Giuseppe Gillal, arrived, probably to try to take over from Michele Metoscita, who had died that year in Rome. He introduced himself at the Propaganda as the patriarch's envoy come to teach and catechise the slaves on the island. But the bishop seemed to have maintained the hostilities that he had previously shown towards Metoscita, as he also challenged the newcomer's right to practise.[97]

As mentioned above, Neofito Giubair (ibn Jubayr), originally from Aleppo, had arrived in Malta in 1717, fleeing persecution in Egypt.[98] With a recommendation to the inquisitor, he thought he would be able to find suitable employment or an annuity from the earnings of the Greek church in the town, but that was not possible. The Propaganda then wanted to send him with a stipend to the Greek Archipelago, but he turned down the offer. He stayed in Malta by living off the mass offerings, then went to Rome in 1725 to seek help and obtained an income from the Fabric of Saint Peter in return for hearing confessions of his 'nationals', catechising and converting the 'Turkish' slaves of the island. There had been a question of entrusting him the Greek parish in Malta, but knowing exclusively Arabic, he was not suitable for this role, which needed the knowledge of Greek. In 1729, the pension of 6 *scudi* having been suspended, he again petitioned the cardinals for help. He reappears in the archives in 1735, when the Greek parish priest of the island brought different charges against him: of 'latinising', thus not respecting the Greek rite, of sending the monthly 6 *scudi* back to his homeland and of being superfluous now that four priests from Jerusalem who knew Turkish and Arabic were looking after the slaves.[99]

THE RELATIONAL SPACE OF BUSINESS AND PROTECTION

Through the elliptical accounts of these lives, we can understand something of the network of relations to which Eastern Christians involved in travel or emigration belonged and from which they sought to benefit. This system does not appear as stable and fixed but rather as a set of resources to draw on, according to circumstances. Because of the very nature of the archival sources at hand, we generally learn of the individuals only when they have recourse to the Catholic network. This network, moreover, did not always act in favour of the individuals who belonged to it. On the contrary, it could become a space for conflict and, after having acted positively, could ask for favours in return from its members, trying to block their freedom of action: this was the case for all those who ended up in prison or were the object of a denunciation in Rome. One of the reasons, no doubt, that assured an income to certain Eastern Christians, especially in the ports, was the use that could be made of them for the surveillance or denunciation of Arabic- and Turkish-speaking foreigners, whether Christian or Muslim.

For most Ottoman Christians, the departure for 'Christendom' was motivated by a local situation that had become difficult for them, either because of their fellow believers or the Muslim authorities. Nonetheless, they did not usually leave without having taken the precaution of ensuring some support and letters of recommendation, as those who went to the cardinals without them were very rare.

One may also note that, in their original homeland, these departees had already been in touch with the 'Franks', who were able to help them find their place in Rome or one of the European capitals. François Picquet, consul of Aleppo, then bishop of Babylon after a stay in France and Rome, offered his protection to a significant number.[100] The recommendations from Latin missionaries in the East were also precious: mentioned above were the interventions of the Discalced Carmelite Elia Giacinto di Santa Maria in favour of Michele Metoscita. Jesuits and Capuchins were influential in France: Timoteo Agnellini had arrived from Diyarbakir in Marseille, accompanied by the Capuchin Jean François de Servin. Ilyās al-Mawṣilī, a Chaldean priest who was to leave a tale of his quest for alms in the New World, was received in Paris by the 'prince' de Saint-Aignan, nephew of the Capuchin of Aleppo Jean-Baptiste de Saint-Aignan. Filippo Gailan (Fīlībus Ghaylān), a Melkite priest from Damascus, came to Rome in 1700, after having suffered the persecutions of the patriarch Cyril al-Za'īm, as had Neofito Giubair. On his arrival, Gailan presented himself as a zealous Catholic, linked for some time to the Capuchins and Jesuits of Syria. He asked for help by showing his intention of attending the ceremonies for the Holy Year, of obtaining indulgences and then returning home. He received 20 *scudi* and a pile of books 'very valuable in those countries'.[101] But instead of returning to Syria, he went to Paris to obtain a grant from the king. The Capuchin Valérien, a missionary in Tripoli, in a note from 1707 recalled having visited his 'friend' Filippo Gailan in Rennes, who then wrote him letters from Paris, Lyon and Marseille.[102]

But it was in the entourage of the Friars Minor of the Holy Land that most candidates for departure were to be found. Indeed, the Franciscan province of '*Terra Santa*' represented an economic force not to be overlooked, maintaining a number of Christians in the households of its residences in the East; in several cases, it seems to meddle in the complex financial matters of its Oriental flock.[103] In addition, the information and protection network of the Friars of the Holy Land reached nearly all of Catholic Europe, where they had procuracies and were represented by commissioners whom we have seen in several episodes. Finally, the former missionaries to the Holy Land, once retired to their original religious houses, could be employed as Arabic speakers and experts in Oriental matters. The Propaganda preferred to recruit its apostolic delegates and envoys in the East in the 'breeding ground' of the Custody of the Holy Land. That is how an Eastern Christian could benefit from their help or their recommendation upon arrival in Europe; for example, Giovanni Sciain entrusted his savings to them. But this network of the Holy Land could also work against the Eastern Christians, notably when the latter, through their begging, encroached on the territory of alms collection that the Friars Minor intended to keep for themselves. Thus, Athanasius Safar on a begging trip to Mexico was once arrested at the request of the Friars of the Holy Land.[104]

Eastern Christians rarely set off at random. What emerges from our documentation is that they often travelled with interpreters, servants and travelling companions. They generally had family, friends or business links to fellow countrymen or co-religionists already settled in Europe. When Ilyās al-Mawṣilī went to Rome after his stay in France, he found his nephew Yunān there, a pupil at the Collegio Urbano. The latter then accompanied him to Naples and Palermo before going back to Aleppo. And when Grazia Zaccur, a Syriac from Aleppo, left the Collegio Urbano, expelled for being incompetent and insolent, he joined his coffee-selling uncle in Livorno.[105]

Giuseppe Assemani the 'Great', who had an exemplary career in Rome from 1710 to 1768, was able to help the Eastern Christians whom he took under his wing to benefit from his network of relationships. His recommendation was mentioned by a dozen of the claimants included here. In a letter written in Livorno in June 1715, Gabriele Ancari (Jibrāʾīl ibn al-Ankārī al-Ḥalabī al-Marūnī), a Maronite from Aleppo, tells how after a three-month wait in Rome he was received in a college thanks to the intervention (*bi-wāṣiṭa*) of the illustrious (*maʿrūf*) Yūsif al-Samʿānī, with whom he had studied theology and mathematics before falling out with him.[106] Assemani's influence came less from his position as Librarian at the Vatican than from his capacity to gather information and exploit it to his advantage, whether in favour of or against his countrymen. Thus, he was the author of a very persuasive report that denounced the 'so-called princes of Lebanon' from the Ḥubaysh family and their traffic of false certificates to gather funds illegally in Catholic Europe.[107] In another case, he drew the attention of the Propaganda to Gianbattista Baietto, a merchant from Aleppo but settled in Livorno, accused of stealing letters destined for Rome and of opening and reading them while they were disinfected at the Lazaret.[108] But he intervened positively several times in favour of Abramo Massad, a Maronite trader from Aleppo, settled in Cairo. He acted as intermediary specifically to obtain the restitution of the goods that Massad, with a colleague, had loaded onto two ships captured by Italian corsairs. On this occasion, he gave all the details on the quantity and value of the rice and coffee seized, on the people responsible for this confiscation and on the procedures in place in Malta.[109]

This last example draws our attention to the fact that the Eastern Christians settled in Europe did not generally break their ties with their homeland or with their families; on the contrary, they tried to enable their network to make the most of the businesses that spanned both sides of the Mediterranean. Michele Metoscita, like Assemani, busied himself in the service – surely more profitable than the care of slaves and Eastern Christians in Malta – of the Egyptian merchants who were victims of the Christian *corso*. He went to Rome for several stays, the duration of which is hard to estimate. In 1716, he appears as 'procurator' for the Cairo merchants in the Christian capital, with the task of obtaining reimbursement for merchandise and ships seized by the Maltese corsairs. Apparently, he was paid 130 *scudi* in advance for this mission. He recovered the value of the goods for those he represented. Nevertheless, Name Facher (Niʿma Fakhr), the Melkite from Livorno, claimed from him a bill of exchange for 700 *pezzi*, as a partial reimbursement of a payment of 1,000 *pezzi* which he pretended to have loaned to the traders of Cairo. The Propaganda, informed by the denunciation of Facher, reacted by asking Metoscita for an explanation and by warning him that 'such dealings are not compatible with the priestly ministry'.[110] In 1726, the same Name Facher who had left Livorno to settle in Satalia wrote to the Propaganda concerning two of his ships that had been seized by the Maltese corsairs Anastasio and Antonachi, between Egypt and the Aegean Sea. Unable to go to Malta himself, he chose the Melkite Neofito Giubair (whose arrival on the island was already examined above) as his representative before the local court.[111]

In 1724, other financial schemes involving Michele Metoscita were discovered, which reveal part of his network of relations. He appeared to be linked to two Maronites whom he may have met during his studies at the Maronite College in Rome. Pietro Benedetti (Buṭrus Mubārak), former student of the College, had settled in Florence in 1693, after a mission for the patriarch in the Catholic capital. He was given the job of 'putting order in the awful chaos of the fonts of nearly six Oriental languages . . .' This was in fact the Medici printing press, which had been established in 1590 and had stopped publishing in 1595.[112] He was then appointed professor of Arabic in Pisa in 1698. In 1707, at the age of forty-four, he decided to enter the Society of Jesus, renouncing his material wealth and donating part of it for the foundation of a seminary in Lebanon.[113] In 1719, Metoscita received an order to place 550 Roman *scudi*, belonging to a certain Gianbattista Ximenes and destined for this foundation, in Malta. But by 1724, he had neither reimbursed the capital nor paid the interest, and there was concern about the loss of this sum. In addition, the widow Ortola Cittadini had entrusted him with the sum of 26 *scudi* for the same purpose. In the end, Metoscita deposited in Malta, in the house of Balthazar Paci, the main body of a typography in Oriental languages, with crates of types, punches and matrices, financed in partnership by himself, the Maronite monk Abramo Gaziro (from Ghazīr)[114] and Pietro Benedetti, who contributed 300 *scudi*. Questioned by the tribunal of the Inquisition, the Maronite from Malta produced a notarised certificate from Rome, based on which he declared that he had entrusted the 500 *scudi* of Ximenes to three Levantines, Ḥabīb Bestros, Giorgio Galioparsi (or Calicocarsi) and a monk from Patmos, Meletio Chiarelli, in order to use them to pursue the litigation concerning the goods of Eastern Christians seized by the Maltese corsairs. As for the money destined for the typography, he contested the fact that these 300 *scudi* had belonged to Pietro Benedetti and said that the latter was indebted to him for 1,800 copies of three booklets printed by himself, worth 600 *scudi* (one *scudo* for three booklets). Furthermore, Benedetti owed a certain quantity of metal that Metoscita had sent to Livorno to have types cast.[115] There is no mention of the printing of these booklets anywhere, and we do not know if the printing material was partly that of the Medici typography. When Michele Metoscita died in Rome in 1730, Giuseppe Assemani immediately suggested writing to the inquisitor of Malta to lock away the types and the large quantity of books and goods that belonged to him. In fact, the inventory of his estate after his death listed paintings and numerous books, which were deposited at the Propaganda.[116]

The crossing of political and commercial borders between Christendom and the Ottoman Empire anticipated symbolic profits, such as the titles and medals coveted by some of the Eastern Christians discussed above, but mainly very material benefits. For example, Timoteo Agnellini sent Isaac, an Armenian from Naples, to negotiate in Venice, then in Aleppo, part of the alms that he had collected.[117] In 1709, Filippo Gailan, having left France, was reported to have been in Venice. He was then in possession of 400 Venetian ducats collected, so he said, as mass offerings. He converted them into fine clothes that he sent to the Capuchin Friar Valérien in Tripoli, to send them to Father Khalīl, a Melkite Catholic priest well-known in Damascus and closely linked to the missionaries. He specified that the package, worth 406 ducats in Venice, was worth 600 in Syria! The profit expected was meant to pay off the cost of printing the *Psalms of David* in Arabic at the Oriental press of Padua's seminary.[118] In the case of Filippo Gailan, it is very clear how the Catholic network made it possible to embrace both shores of the Mediterranean and two mutually hostile political and religious entities. However, as in the above-mentioned cases, this network could also work against him. Indeed, Father Jean Barse, a Jesuit from Damascus, wrote to his colleague, the provincial of Venice, to warn him against Gailan who enjoyed a good reputation in the Venetian Republic, despite rumours of scandals with women. He seemed to have taken advantage of Father Khalīl, asking him for excessive pay-offs, and to have endangered the former's reputation. A nephew of Gailan apparently dragged Khalīl in front of the qadi in Damascus, to make him reimburse the value of the fabric in question. Finally, the *Psalms* printed by the priest from Damascus in Padua were not offered freely to Christians in Syria but sold for a financial profit and with a small return from the point of view of the propagation of faith.[119]

CONCLUSION: WERE EASTERN CHRISTIANS MEDIATORS?

The fragments of the lives reconstituted here finally shed light on a fairly coherent group of people whose careers and pleas for help and support are directly linked to the policy of the Roman Church towards the Eastern Churches and, reciprocally, to the response of these Churches to Catholic invitations at a specific moment in their history. They do not highlight theological and ecclesiological debates, but rather very concrete issues relating to the movement of people and goods between 'Christendom' and the 'Turkish' East, through a system of networks and protections that one might call 'the Catholic connection'.

Most of the people mentioned here were, at least for some time, in the position of mediators – that is, of key persons linking men and goods. We observe in their way of working an attachment to the family network, to sectarian and geographic solidarity (between people of Aleppo or Damascus, or between Arabic speakers) on both sides of the Mediterranean. They were knowingly mediators when they dealt with negotiations for the return of Egyptian merchants' cargoes confiscated by Christian corsairs, when they visited every corner of Europe to beg for money (later sent to their family, their monastery, or their Church of origin), and when they transmitted information from one shore of the Mediterranean to the other. They were mediators, again in a professional capacity, when they were teaching or translating, or when they took it upon themselves to catechise the slaves in the ports.

They were less conscious mediators when, wandering around Europe, they portrayed a certain image of the 'Orient', partly in answering the expectations of the Westerners whom they met *en route*. Going to Rome or to a princely court, they claimed to be victims of a persecuting Islam. We have seen that, in some cases, this could be reality, but in general the difficulties that led them to 'Christendom' were more complex. Nevertheless, they referred to the image of an oppressive and hostile Islam in order to attract the attention and generosity of their listeners. Western representations of the 'Turk' thus became a narrative to which Eastern Christian supplicants could resort. They played on the existence of a 'culture of antagonism', but at the same time they contributed to maintaining and reinforcing it.[120]

The Roman observatory, with the correspondence that ended up there, was often too far away to grasp the concrete acts of mediation in detail. Thus, the number of conversions made in Marseille or Malta are not to be taken literally. They make us aware of proselytism towards captive Muslims, but few elements enable us to understand the reality of this activity.

We know that the monk Arsenio Diab, whose passage to Livorno in 1773 was mentioned earlier, not only worked in Lebanon and Aleppo after having studied painting in Rome, but also created for the cardinals of the Propaganda a geographical description of Mount Lebanon, accompanied by a magnificent coloured map.[121] Timoteo Agnellini, while in France in 1679, published in Arabic a *Hymn to the Virgin*, accompanied by the *Seven Penitentiary Psalms*, and later several other devotional works published in Padua.[122] Michele Metoscita and Filippo Gailan also published books, no doubt to distribute them among Arabic-speaking Christians, aiming to yield a profit. One would like to go further in the understanding of these activities of mediation by studying the painted or printed objects themselves and by finding details about their distribution and use. Sources other than the letters might reveal more directly the role of the exiles in spreading information. In his travelogue to America, Ilyās ibn Ḥannā al-Mawṣilī described the techniques for producing indigo and cochineal and mentioned having bought some of the latter for the impressive sum of 800 piasters.[123] The begging monks Yuḥannā Naqqāsh and Tūmā Kurbāj admired the Ducal printing press in Parma and made notes concerning the printing process and the machines used.[124]

These are clues about the role of travel and mobility in historical change and cultural transfer: perhaps most significantly, they show how openness to the Other was not the sole prerogative of literate elites.[125]

NOTES

1. Giovanni Levi, *Le pouvoir au village: Histoire d'un exorciste dans le Piémont du XVIIe siècle* (Paris: Gallimard, 1989), p. 12 [see also Chapter 2 below].
2. Bernard Lepetit, 'Histoire des pratiques, pratique de l'histoire', in Bernard Lepetit (ed.), *Les formes de l'expérience: Une autre histoire sociale* (Paris: Albin Michel), pp. 13–15.
3. Ilyās ibn Ḥannā al-Mawṣilī found fellow natives of the East like him in Saragossa, Madrid and Cadiz: *Il primo orientale nelle Americhe*, translated by Marina Montanaro (Mazara del Vallo: Liceo Ginnasio 'Gian Giacomo Adria', 1992), pp. 34–35, 37. The correspondence of the Lebanese monks in the eighteenth century shows a back-and-forth movement between Italy and the Middle East and discloses several details about the life of the Maronite colony in Rome.

One finds itinerant monks, living on charity, and Eastern merchants settled in Livorno: Butrus Fahd, *Taʾrīkh al-ruhbāniyya al-mārūniyya bi-farʿayhā al-Ḥalabī wa-l-Lubnānī*, 6 vols. (Jounieh: Matbaʿat al-Kraym, 1963–73), vol. 3, pp. 213, 303–4; vol. 4, pp. 168, 286, 356; vol. 5, pp. 96, 106, 124–25, 134, 159. The Melkite monks Yuḥannā Naqqāsh and Tūmā Kurbāj lived in Rome for around thirty years in the second half of the eighteenth century, interrupting their stay on two occasions to go collect alms in Spain, Portugal, Northern Italy and Hungary: Michel Abras, 'Le voyage de deux moines melkites en Italie du Nord en 1775', in Bernard Heyberger and Carsten Walbiner (eds), *Les Européens vus par les Libanais à l'époque ottomane* (Beirut: Orient-Institut der DMG; Würzburg: Ergon, 2002), pp. 59–65. The travelogue of Ḥannā ibn Antūn Diyāb from Aleppo, who accompanied Paul Lucas to North Africa and then to France after 1707 is preserved in BAV, ms. Sbath 254. [It has been recently published in French translation: Hanna Dyâb, *D'Alep à Paris: Les pérégrinations d'un jeune Syrien au temps de Louis XIV*, translated and edited by Paule Fahmé-Thiéry, Bernard Heyberger and Jérôme Lentin, with a preface by Bernard Heyberger (Arles: Actes Sud, 2015)]. René Ristelhueber, *Traditions françaises au Liban* (Paris: Felix Alcan, 1918), passim, mentions several Maronite missions and collections in France. [Since the publication of this article in French, a number of studies concerning Eastern individuals travelling through Europe in the seventeenth and eighteenth century have appeared: Monica Winet, 'Religious Education on the Road: An Anonymous Christian Arabic Diary', *Parole de l'Orient*, 39 (2014), pp. 297–312; John-Paul Ghobrial, 'The Secret Life of Elias of Babylon and the Uses of Global Microhistory', *Past & Present*, 222 (2014), pp. 51–93; John-Paul Ghobrial, 'Moving Stories and What They Tell Us: Early Modern Mobility between Microhistory and Global History', *Past & Present*, 242 (2019), supplement n° 14, pp. 243–80; Sebouh D. Aslanian, '"Many Have Come Here and Have Deceived Us": Some Notes on Asateur Vardapet (1644–1728), an Itinerant Armenian Monk in Europe,' *Handēs amsōreay*, 1–12 (2019), pp. 133–94; Sebouh D. Aslanian, 'The "Quintessential Locus of Brokerage": Letters of Recommendation, Networks, and Mobility in the Life of Thomas Vanandets'i, an Armenian Printer in Amsterdam, 1677–1707', *Journal of World History*, 31, 4 (2020), pp. 655–92; Sundar Henny, 'Nathanael of Leukas and the Hottinger Circle: The Wanderings of a Seventeenth-Century Greek Archbishop', *International Journal of the Classical Tradition*, 27 (2020), pp. 449–72; Stefano Saracino, 'Griechisch-orthodoxe Almosenfahrer im Heiligen Römischen Reich und ihre wissensgeschichtliche Bedeutung (1650–1750)', in Markus Friedrich and Jacob Schilling (eds), *Praktiken frühneuzeitlicher Historiographie* (Berlin, Boston: De Gruyter, 2019), pp. 141–73; Thomas Glesener, 'Gouverner la langue arabe: Miguel Casiri et les arabisants du roi d'Espagne au siècle des Lumières', *Annales: Histoire, sciences sociales*, 76, 2 (2021), pp. 227–67; Cesare Santus, 'Wandering Lives: Eastern Christian Pilgrims, Alms-Collectors, and "Refugees" in Early Modern Rome', in Emily Michelson and Matthew Coneys Wainwright (eds), *A Companion to Religious Minorities in Early Modern Rome* (Leiden: Brill, 2021), pp. 237–71; Cesare Santus, 'The Great Imposture: Eastern Christian Rogues and

Counterfeiters in Rome, c. 17th–19th centuries', in Cornel Zwierlein (ed.) *The Power of the Dispersed: Early Modern Global Travelers beyond Integration* (Leiden: Brill, 2022), pp. 98–130.]

4. APF, SOCG, vol. 62, fol. 92r, recommendation in favour of the Maronite deacon Chaedé (Shammās Shahāda) from Aleppo.
5. APF, SC, Greci Melchiti, vol. 10, fols 190rv, 192r, 129rv, 130rv, 196r, recommendations for Giovanni Agemi, a Melkite well-known in Rome, who had to leave Lebanon on account of his debts. Antje Stannek, 'Migration confessionnelle ou pèlerinage? Rapport sur le fonds d'un hospice pour les nouveaux convertis dans les Archives secrètes du Vatican', in Philippe Boutry, Pierre-Antoine Fabre and Dominique Julia (eds), *Rendre ses vœux: Les identités pèlerines dans l'Europe moderne (XVIe–XVIIIe siècle)* (Paris: Éditions de l'EHESS, 2000), p. 62, also estimates that the maximum number of guests in the Roman hospice for Protestant converts was reached during the first half of the eighteenth century.
6. Hélène Desmet-Grégoire, *Le divan magique: L'Orient turc en France au XVIIIe siècle*, 2nd ed. (Paris: L'Harmattan, 1994), pp. 48–49. See also the warning from the consul in Tripoli to the 'leaders of the Maronite nation' about 'rogues and vagabonds': Bernard Heyberger, 'Les nouveaux horizons méditerranéens des Chrétiens du *bilād al-šām* (XVIIe–XVIIIe siècle)', *Arabica*, 51 (2004), 4, p. 460. On the measures concerning the movement of foreigners that were put in place mostly after the period studied here, see Gilles Bertrand, 'Pour une approche comparée des modes de contrôle exercés aux frontières des anciens États italiens', in Claudia Moatti (ed.), *La mobilité des personnes en Méditerranée de l'Antiquité à l'époque moderne: Procédures de contrôle et documents d'identification* (Rome: École Française de Rome, 2004), pp. 253–303.
7. This number is not negligible when compared to the small number of Easterners found in France: Desmet-Grégoire, *Le divan magique*, pp. 17–53. But the author devoted himself only to Muslims. Eastern people seemed so few in France in the eighteenth century that they do not appear: Daniel Roche, *Humeurs vagabondes: De la circulation des hommes et de l'utilité des voyages* (Paris: Fayard, 2003), pp. 394–419. In the same way, the Arabic-speaking Christians seem elusive in studies on foreigners in Malta or Livorno. The Melkites were no doubt assimilated with the Greeks: Anne Brogini, 'Un cosmopolitisme de frontière: Les étrangers à Malte (fin XVIe–XVIIe siècles)', *Cahiers de la Méditerranée*, 67 (2003), pp. 15–32; Samuel Fettah, 'Le cosmopolitisme livournais: Représentations et institutions (XVIIe–XVIIIe s.)', ibid. pp. 51–60. [Yet, this remark in the original version of this article now has to be revised. There is no doubt that the lack of data in 2009 was also due to an historiographical bias: see the recent references quoted above, note 3, and especially Santus, 'Wandering Lives', pp. 140–41, who speaks about several thousand Eastern Christians having visited Rome between the end of the sixteenth and the beginning of the nineteenth century.]
8. Nasser Gemayel, *Les échanges culturels entre les Maronites et l'Europe*, 2 vols. (Beirut: Imprimerie Gemayel, 1984), vol. 1, pp. 420–34; Pierre Dib, *Joseph Simon Assémani et ses deux neveux: Leurs testaments* (Paris: G. P. Maisonneuve, 1939).

9. Gemayel, *Les échanges culturels*, vol. 1, pp. 95–143. From 1579 to 1788, 280 have been counted in all; Camille Aboussouan (ed.), *Le livre et le Liban jusqu'en 1900* (Paris: UNESCO, AGECOOP, 1982), pp. 159–280. [Aurélien Girard and Giovanni Pizzorusso, 'The Maronite College in Early Modern Rome: Between the Ottoman Empire and the Republic of Letters', in Liam Chambers and Thomas O'Connor (eds), *College Communities Abroad: Education, Migration and Catholicism in Early Modern Europe* (Manchester: Manchester University Press, 2017), pp. 174–97.]
10. Bernard Heyberger, *Les Chrétiens du Proche-Orient au temps de la Réforme Catholique* (Rome: École Française de Rome, 1994), p. 409. [Cesare Santus, 'Tra la chiesa di Sant'Atanasio e il Sant'Uffizio: Note sulla presenza greca a Roma in età moderna', in Antal Molnár, Giovanni Pizzorusso and Matteo Sanfilippo (eds), *Chiese e nationes a Roma: Dalla Scandinavia ai Balcani, secoli XVXVIII* (Rome: Viella, 2017), pp. 193–223.]
11. APF, Acta, vol. 102, 10 June 1732, 12, *Maroniti* (Florence); SC, Maroniti, vol. 4, fol. 170rv (Malta, undated). A certain Pietro Giallali, however, said to be from Bethlehem, was noted as resident of Livorno: SC, Greci Melchiti, vol. 2, fols 513r–514r (10 August 1732). [Here and elsewhere in the volume, the names of the individuals mentioned are quoted as they appear in the original documents, although the Italian transcription of a single name may vary. When possible, we also restore the Arabic version of the name.]
12. [This assertion in the original version of the article now has to be corrected: actually, a great number of Armenians visited Rome, but their presence was mainly recorded at the Holy Office, rather than at the Propaganda: Santus, 'Wandering Lives', 245–46.]
13. Gérald Duverdier, 'Propagande protestante en langues orientales aux XVIIe et XVIIIe siècles', in Gérald Duverdier, *Européens en Orient au XVIIIe siècle* (Paris: L'Harmattan, 1994), pp. 1–33. [Recent and ongoing research has attested that there were several Eastern Christians moving through Protestant states and that they often came to Rome first, as a pass from Catholic authority was useful for travelling in Protestant countries as well.]
14. APF, SC, Maroniti, vol. 1, fols 287rv, 285r, 345r. SC, Maroniti, vol. 3, fol. 305r (undated). SC, Maroniti, vol. 4, fols 65rv, 68rv (15 May 1729); fols 156rv, 157r (undated); fols 358r (1734). SC, Maroniti, vol. 8, fol. 388rv (1768). SC, Greci Melchiti, vol. 2, fols 223rv, 229r–230r, 231r–232v, 238rv, 240r, 242rv, 244r, 245r–246r, 247r, 251r, 271r (1730). SC, Greci Melchiti, vol. 10, fols 142r, 162r, 164rv, 172r (1779). See also Abras, 'Le voyage de deux moines melkites', and Fahd, *Ta'rīkh al-ruhbāniyya al-mārūniyya*, vol. 3, p. 213 (alms collection and prolonged stay in Florence and in Poland, 1744); vol. 5, pp. 96, 134 (alms collection in Spain and in Portugal, 1771).
15. APF, SC, Greci Melchiti, vol. 2, fol. 142r.
16. Ibid. fols 151r, 152rv, 168r (1729).
17. Roche, *Humeurs vagabondes*, p. 397 [in French, 'sans aveu'].
18. Letter from the superior of the Jesuit missionaries recommending Jean-Baptiste Judicy alias Giudice: Ristelhueber, *Traditions françaises au Liban*, pp. 159–60.

APF, SC, Maroniti, vol. 4, fols 69r–78r: 'Informazione alla SC circa i pretesi Principi del Monte Libano presentata da M.gre Assemani'. See also the case of 'prince Yūnis' and of his brother 'prince Yūsif' below, notes 54–56. Acta, vol. 69, 15 June 1699, 3: Francesco Heredi called himself a noble from Tripoli converted, baptised in Rome. Ibid. 16 November 1699, 11, *Maroniti*: a 'Maronite prince' asked for the title of Knight of the Golden Spur. Acta, vol. 78, 23 April 1708, 22, *Maroniti*: Prince Husn Khāzin said he was a descendant of the ancient kings of Damascus. Acta, vol. 89, 1719, fols 43v–44r: Abramo Massad asked for and obtained the title of Knight of the Golden Spur. SC, Maroniti, vol. 3, fol. 491rv (undated): the messenger of 'Prince' Hassan in Versailles obtained the title of Knight of Saint Lazarus.

19. APF, Acta, vol. 65, 20 December 1695, 1, *Soria*; Acta, vol. 66, 9 January 1696, 16, *Soria*; Acta, vol. 68, 17 February 1698, 18, *Soria*; Acta, vol. 69, 6 July 1699, 13, *Ungheria Soria*. [Cesare Santus recently spotted him in the archives of the Roman Inquisition (ADDF, SO, St. St., RR 3 d, fol. 151v, 20 August 1699) as 'D. Dominicus filius q. Baroghi'(?), having made a profession of faith and having been 'reconciled' after abjuring schism. He was said to be originally from Diyarbakir and eighty years old]. The Arabic-speaking confessor could be Francesco Antonio da Rimini, who after nineteen years in the Holy Land and two years in Constantinople asked to benefit from the privileges accorded to missionaries (Acta, vol. 54, 20 June 1684, 15, *Terra Santa*). Giovanni Ricci, *Ossessione turca: In una retrovia cristiana dell'Europa moderna* (Bologna: Il Mulino, 2002), has given an idea of the (rare) presence of the Orient and of Easterners in a provincial city on the Adriatic coast (Ferrara), but he remained quite superficial.
20. Roche, *Humeurs vagabondes*, pp. 937–45.
21. See the examples below, as well as that of the Copt Joseph Barbatus: Alastair Hamilton, 'An Egyptian Traveller in the Republic of Letters: Josephus Barbatus or Abudagnus the Copt', *Journal of the Warburg and Courtauld Institutes*, 57 (1994), p. 136. On the control of foreigners and the importance of denunciations in Malta, see Brogini, 'Un cosmopolitisme de frontière', pp. 26–28.
22. APF, SOCG, vol. 471, fol. 17r; fol. 18r, copy of a letter from François Picquet (6 January 1678.) [On Agnellini/Karnuk, see Chapter 2 in this volume.]
23. APF, Acta, vol. 78, 25 June 1708, 23, *Armeni*. [On Giacomo of Marash, see also the inquisitorial documents quoted by Santus, 'Wandering Lives', p. 259.]
24. APF, SC Melchiti, vol. 4, fols 111r–112v.
25. APF, Acta, vol. 95, 22 January 1725, 9, *Greci Melchiti*; 7 May 1725, 3, *Greci Melchiti*.
26. APF, SC, Greci Melchiti, vol. 2, fols 62r (17 May 1727), 64r–65r (7 June 1727), 66r (14 June 1727).
27. Ibid. fols 143r–144r (Arabic), 142r (Italian); fols 176r (3 September 1729), 402r (21 November 1731, Sevilla).
28. Ibid. fols 432rv, 464r–465v, 506r–507v, 510rv, 563r (letters from the nuncio of Seville and copies of letters and documents from the inquisitor in Grenada to the nuncio).
29. APF, SC, Greci Melchiti, vol. 2, fols 513r–514r (10 August 1732).

30. Cyrille Charon, 'L'Église grecque catholique de Livourne', *Échos d'Orient*, 11 (1908), pp. 227–37, has mentioned the presence in Livorno of Farjallāh Sakkakīnī, from Damascus, who arrived in 1666 and died in 1736, buried in the narthex of the Greek Catholic church. [On Sakkakīnī (Scacchini o Secaquini), see Guido Bellati Ceccoli, *Tra Toscana e Medioriente: La storia degli Arabi cattolici a Livorno (Sec. XVII–XX)* (Livorno: Editasca, 2008), pp. 238–40. 'Niccola Fargellà' (mentioned in ibid. p. 71, note 110) could have been a Sakkakīnī: there is a kinship between both family names. Another Niqūla Sakkakīnī appeared together with Farjallāh Sakkakīnī (ibid. p. 233, note 559). The family Fargialla/Fargellà appeared also under the name Fragela.]
31. APF, SC, Greci Melchiti, vol. 2, fols 513r–514r, 510rv; SC, Greci Melchiti, vol. 3, fols 357rv, 358r (22 May 1736).
32. APF, SC, Greci Melchiti, vol. 2, fols 507rv; 551rv (17 September 1732).
33. APF, SC, Greci Melchiti, vol. 3, fols 357r–360r (22 May 1736).
34. Ibid. fol. 365rv.
35. Heyberger, 'Les nouveaux horizons méditerranéens', pp. 455–61.
36. APF, SC, Maroniti, vol. 7, fol. 67r (Italian translation), 69v (Arabic original), November 1753. [This 'Francisco Chudiak' was arrested in 1769 in Santo Domingo (Caribbean) and sent to Madrid for trial: Glesener, 'Gouverner la langue arabe'.]
37. APF, Acta, vol. 41, 23 November 1671, fol. 2v. Acta, vol. 95, 31 July 1725, *Maroniti*, 9: Giuseppe di Pauoli, from Damascus, asked for books for teaching his three sons who were with him in Rome.
38. APF, SC, Maroniti, vol. 1, fol. 283r (17 August 1700). Acta, vol. 95, 16 April 1725, 3, *Stampa*. SOCG, vol. 454, fol. 193r: Abdal Messih, from Jerusalem, who had come to visit the Holy Places, wanted to return home. Acta, vol. 63, 3 September 1693, 7, *Elemosine*: Gabriele di Salomone, 'Greek' archpriest from Damascus, had letters certifying that he had abjured his errors and asked for help to return home; he obtained 4 *scudi*. SOCG, vol. 503, fol. 84r (8 February 1689): Father Daniele, a Basilian monk from Jerusalem, 'has come to Rome to see the tombs of the Holy Apostles and pay allegiance to the Holy Father'. Having made a profession of faith before the Holy Office, he asked for help for himself, his interpreter and a Greek companion. For the relationship between pilgrimage, conversion and alms, see Stannek, 'Migration confessionnelle ou pèlerinage?' and the whole of the volume. See also Philippe Boutry and Dominique Julia (eds), *Pèlerins et pèlerinages dans l'Europe moderne* (Rome: École Française de Rome, 2000).
39. APF, Acta, vol. 47, 6 September 1677, fol. 404r. Giovanni Scilhub or Scialup (Ḥannā Shalhūb Maʿūshī), asking for help for his four dependent children from Saida in 1704, recalled that he had been to Rome for the Holy Year (1700). In fact, his stay had been intended less for devotions than to free himself from an accusation of fraudulent bankruptcy which opposed him to the Friars of the Holy Land: SC, Maroniti, vol. 1, fols 340rv, 341rv (20 October 1704). The rest of the affair has been given in detail on fols 301r, 312r–314r (1702), 318r–320v (1704).
40. APF, Acta, vol. 95, 25 January 1725, 9, *Greci Melchiti*; 7 May 1725, 3, *Greci Melchiti*. He was a very good pupil but spit blood and died in 1734: ACU,

Registro dei nomi, cognomi [. . .] degli alunni di Propaganda Fide raccolti dal Rettore Bonvicini, 1633–1753, VII, 1. The Chaldean Fatah Allah (Fatḥallāh) Mesi, originally from Baghdad but having lived in Diyarbakir, received alms (APF, Acta, vol. 64, 4 May 1694, 8, *Elemosine*) and the admittance of his son at the Collegio Urbano (Acta, vol. 64, 29 November 1694, 10, *Collegio Urbano*, and vol. 65, 11 January 1695, 14, *Collegio Urbano*). Having lost everything, he asked for help to return home after a stay of at least two years in Rome (Acta, vol. 66, 27 February 1696, 6, *Soria*; 9 April 1696, 9, *Soria*). In 1645, Neeme di Kuri (Niʿma ibn al-Khūrī), a Syrian from Aleppo, aged only eleven, who had come to Rome with his father 'in order to persist in the faith', was admitted to the orphanage of Santa Maria in Aquiro. Now there was the question of having him enter the Collegio Urbano: SOCG, vol. 409, fols 29r, 46v (1645).

41. Bernard Heyberger, 'Sécurité et insécurité: Les Chrétiens de Syrie dans l'espace méditerranéen (XVIIe–XVIIIe siècles)', in Meropi Anastassiadou and Bernard Heyberger (eds), *Figures anonymes, figures d'élite: Pour une anatomie de l'homo ottomanicus* (Istanbul: Isis Press, 1999), pp. 147–68: 151–69 [see the translated version in Chapter 3 in this volume]. These questions concerning privateers went on for a long time: in 1738, an appeal by Rafaele Mogailes (Mughaylaṣ) concerned the heritage of his father, part of which consisted of money in dispute 'in the land of the Christians', following the confiscation of rice, linen, hemp and tobacco in Limassol and Latakia in 1718, 1720 and 1721: SC, Greci Melchiti, vol. 3, fols 616r–617r. [On the issue of Catholic privateers and the 'Greeks', see now Molly Greene, *Catholic Pirates and Greek Merchants: A Maritime History of the Mediterranean* (Princeton: Princeton University Press, 2010); Cornel Zwierlein, 'Interaction and Boundary Work: Western Merchant Colonies in the Levant and the Eastern Churches, 1660–1800', *Journal of Modern European History*, 18, 2 (2020), pp. 156–76.]
42. APF, SOCG, vol. 562, fol. 204rv (17 May 1707). He was sent to the Holy Office.
43. Bernard Heyberger, 'Se convertir à l'Islam chez les Chrétiens de Syrie', in *Conversioni nel Mediterraneo*, special issue of *Dimensioni e problemi della ricerca storica*, 2 (1996), pp. 133–52; Bernard Heyberger, 'Frontières confessionnelles et conversions chez les Chrétiens Orientaux', in Mercedes García-Arenal (ed.), *Conversions islamiques: Identités religieuses en Islam méditerranéen/Islamic Conversions: Religious Identities in Mediterranean Islam* (Paris: Maisonneuve-Larose, 2001), pp. 245–58.
44. APF, SC, Greci Melchiti, vol. 2, fol. 56r, report by Graziano Salemi, a priest from Aleppo, on the persecutions of Catholics in the town; fol. 586r, letter from Bishop Gerasimos (9 November 1732). See the *Vie de Néophytos, métropolite de Saïdnaya* published by Antoine Rabbath, *Documents inédits pour servir à l'histoire du christianisme en Orient*, 3 vols. (Paris: A. Picard, 1907–11), vol. 1, pp. 597–621 (Arabic text and French translation).
45. APF, SC, Greci Melchiti, vol. 1, fols 274r–278r, May 1717 (Arabic original: fols 280r–281v).
46. APF, SC, Greci Melchiti, vol. 2, fols 1r, 2v; fols 151r–152v (17 April 1729). Mosè Muchalla or Muhalac, from Damascus, reporting that he had to flee his

country following the persecutions by the Patriarch Sylvester, and having left his wife and children for debts, asked for help and a reference to leave to settle in Venice (around 1740?): SC, Greci Melchiti, vol. 4, fols 127r, 135rv. Giovanni of Jerusalem, a Syrian suffragan bishop, a convert to Catholicism in 1748 in Cairo where he lived under the protection of a Syrian merchant, was imprisoned on the death of the latter, then left for Rome: SC, Siri, vol. 1, fols 505r–506r, 508r.

47. APF, SOCG, vol. 235, fols 123r, 153v.
48. APF, SOCG, vol. 517, fols 346r. Acta, vol. 64, 29 November 1694, 10, *Collegio Urbano*. Acta, vol. 65, 11 January 1695, 14, *Collegio Urbano*. It is not certain that he remained there: he refused to take the oath required of the students.
49. Heyberger, 'Sécurité et insécurité', pp. 148–52. Géraud Poumarède, *Pour en finir avec la croisade: Mythes et réalités de la lutte contre les Turcs aux XVIe et XVIIe siècles* (Paris: PUF, 2004), pp. 475–527. APF, Acta, vol. 65, 12 March 1685, 4, *Elemosine*, and 7 May 1685, 5, *Elemosine*: Donato, a Maronite, said that he had left two children in the hands of the Turks. Acta, vol. 68, 5 July 1688, 18, *Elemosine*, and vol. 70, 19 December 1690, 4, *Elemosine*: Odoardo Atallah, a monk from Aleppo, stated that he had a sister who was a prisoner of the Turks. Acta, vol. 70, 12 June 1690, 9, *Elemosine*: Michele Giuseppe, from Bethlehem, said that his children were in prison in Jerusalem. SOCG, vol. 562, fol. 204rv (17 May 1707): a Greek from Damascus, seeking refuge in Venice, said his only income was a villa near Damascus, which had been taken from him by the Grand Mufti. SC, Maroniti, vol. 4, fol. 8rv (1727), 7r (1728): 'Prince' Elia Saleb from Mount Lebanon, recommended by the Duke of Lorraine and bearer of a letter for the nuncio of Poland, had left to the Turks his mother, his son and his brother, and he wanted to free them. SC, Greci Melchiti, vol. 2, fol. 21r (1725): Giorgio Abdallah, a Melkite from Cairo, accused of having forged money, was imprisoned for two years.
50. APF, SC, Maroniti, vol. 4, fols 222rv, 228r.
51. APF, SC, Greci Melchiti, vol. 4, fols 108rv (Italian), 109r (Arabic), 143r (Italian), 144r (Arabic), 146r–147r.
52. Ibid. fols 152r (Italian), 153r (Arabic).
53. Ḥabīb Zayyāt, 'Al-Akh Māryā Khubiyya al-Yasū'ī', *Al-Masarra*, 21 (1935), pp. 501–8.
54. ACU, *Registro*. APF, SC, Siri, vol. 1, fol. 232rv (20 December 1673). Acta, vol. 68, 27 May 1698, 13/14, *San Pancrazio*. Acta, vol. 83, 13 November 1713, 31, *Smirne*, fols 634v–638r, 643rv. For his father, see Heyberger, *Les Chrétiens du Proche-Orient*, p. 74, note 15, and Heyberger, 'Se convertir à l'Islam', pp. 135, 147, note 15.
55. APF, Acta, vol. 72, 13 March 1702, 4, *Maroniti*. The story of Yūnis Abū Rizq is well-known and quite well documented: Heyberger, *Les Chrétiens du Proche-Orient*, pp. 73–74.
56. APF, SOCG, vol. 541, fol. 208r. Ristelhueber, *Traditions françaises au Liban*, pp. 186–87, has noted certificates in his favour in the French archives dating from 1699 and 1700. SC, Maroniti, vol. 1, fol. 295r (27 June 1701): the nuncio from Paris indicated that it would be difficult to obtain help for 'the brother of the late Prince', because 'people from that same nation' asked too often for 'such help'.

57. Ristelhueber, *Traditions françaises au Liban*, pp. 188–92. Jean de la Roque, *Voyage de Syrie et du Mont-Liban* (Beirut: Dar Lahad Khater, 1981; 1st ed. 1722), pp. 219–20: letters from August 1701, attesting that Elia Assemani was about to leave France for Constantinople; p. 208: evocation of 'Prince Joseph'. For the denunciation of Bartolomeo De Marchis, see APF, SC, Maroniti, vol. 1, fols 371r–373v (undated); the confirmation of Yūsif's presence in Florence is on fol. 308r (25 January 1701), while his presence in and passage through Venice is mentioned on fol. 310r (20 May 1702).
58. APF, SOCG, vol. 527, fols 259r–260r (June 1697). SOCG, vol. 503, fol. 6, another request from him for help, after fifteen months in Rome (25 January 1689).
59. APF, SC, Maroniti, vol. 4, fols 230r, 240–241r. He had already drawn attention to himself in Rome in 1714: SC, Maroniti, vol. 2, fol. 485r.
60. APF, Acta, vol. 87, 7 June 1717, 8, *Stampa Greci*. SC, Maroniti, vol. 1, fol. 259rv: a certain Abram, Maronite, an envoy of the patriarch, asked for books before returning home (23 December 1699).
61. APF, Acta, vol. 51, 16 June 1681, 18, *Armeni* [See Chapter 2 in this volume]. I have identified this bishop from Mardin as Timoteo, although the document referred to him as Armenian. [His name was indeed Armenian, and it is possible that he came from a Syro-Armenian family: Raymond H. Kévorkian, *Catalogue des 'incunables' arméniens, 1511–1695 ou Chronique de l'imprimerie arménienne* (Geneva: Cramer, 1986), pp. 169–70; Santus, 'Wandering Lives', p. 269]. ACU, *Registro*, noted his departure for his residence with 150 *scudi*.
62. APF, SC, Maroniti, vol. 1, fol. 281rv (24 May 1700). Concerning his stay in France, see Ristelhueber, *Traditions françaises au Liban*, pp. 157–67, and the letters of the nuncio from Paris in SC, Maroniti, vol. 1, fols 285r (29 November 1700), 287rv (24 January 1701), 295r (27 June 1701).
63. APF, SC, Greci Melchiti, vol. 1, fols 36rv (10 May 1702), 54r (19 November 1704, the nuncio from Florence, quoting the reference letter dated 19 November 1702). Acta, vol. 72, 4 September 1702, 4, *Limosine Greci*: Stefano, deacon sent by the same Archbishop Ṣayfī, tried to obtain a pension to live in Rome. The answer was negative, but he was given a viaticum to pay his return journey to Saida: Acta, vol. 77, 28 March 1707. In 1711, he wrote from Malta: Acta, vol. 81, 12 May 1711, 3, *Greci*; 1 December, 8, *Greci Soria*.
64. Heyberger, 'Les nouveaux horizons méditerranéens', p. 454.
65. Thomas Philipp, *Acre: The Rise and Fall of a Palestinian City 1730–1831* (New York: Columbia University Press, 2001), p. 108.
66. APF, CP, Greci Melchiti, vol. 77, fol. 442rv. ACU, *Registro*. SC, Greci Melchiti, vol. 2, fols 151r–152v, 166r, 168r (1729).
67. APF, Acta, vol. 100, 26 September 1730, 19, *Melchiti*. SC, Greci Melchiti, vol. 2, fols 612r, 641r–644r (3 August 1733, Aleppo). The mention of a brother living in Tuscany appeared in a letter from the archbishop of Pavasso (?), in Florence: SC, Greci Melchiti, vol. 2, fol. 559r (16 September 1732).
68. APF, SC, Greci Melchiti, vol. 3, fol. 350r (undated); ACU, *Registro*. [Timothée Jock, *Jésuites et chouéirites ou la fondation des religieuses basiliennes chouéirites de*

Notre-Dame de l'Annonciation à Zouq-Mikaïl (Liban), 1730–1746 (Central Falls, USA: self-published, 1936), p. 112, note 1, has provided a biography of Aggiuri: born in Aleppo in 1688, he settled in Rome in 1725, becoming a gentleman of Cardinal Luigi Belluga, ambassador of Austria to the Holy See. He returned to Aleppo around 1739 in order to settle the conflicts around Melkite girls who had entered the Monastery of the Annunciation, where his sister Thecla was a nun under the direction of the Jesuits at Zūq Mikha'īl. Thecla later became the first Abbess of this monastery. In 1740, he definitively returned to Rome, where he lived at the church of the 'Navicella', belonging to the Melkite monks. He died there in 1773. About him, see also ibid. pp. 614, 622, 635. Unfortunately, Jock does not precisely quote the numerous documents to which he refers.]

69. See the tribulations of the Copt Josephus Barbatus in Hamilton, 'An Egyptian Traveller', those of Timoteo Agnellini in this volume and those of several others in Gemayel, *Les échanges culturels*, vol. 1, pp. 211–610. APF, Acta, vol. 68, 13 January 1698, 3, *Maroniti*. Abramo, a Maronite priest, former student of the college, worked on the printing of a lexicon in Padua, in the printing press founded by Cardinal Barbarigo, where Agnellini was employed for several years.
70. [70] APF, SOCG, vol. 429, fols 45r, 46r; Acta, vol. 41, July-August 1671, fol. 204rv [see Chapter 2 of this volume].
71. APF, Acta, vol. 80, 17 February 1710, 21, *Collegio Urbano*; 28 April 1710, 28, *Collegio Urbano*. [In recent years, many works on the life of Salomone Negri have appeared: see John-Paul Ghobrial, 'The Life and Hard Times of Solomon Negri: An Arabic Teacher in Early Modern Europe', in Alastair Hamilton, Jan Loop and Charles Burnett (eds), *The Teaching and Learning of Arabic in Early Modern Europe* (Leiden: Brill, 2017), pp. 310–31; Paula Manstetten, 'Kultureller Vermittler, *homme de lettres*, Vagabund? Zur Selbstdarstellung arabischer Christen in Europa am Beispiel Salomon Negris (1665–1727)', in Regina Toepfer *et al.* (eds), *Übersetzen in der Frühen Neuzeit: Konzepte und Methoden/Concepts and Practices of Translation in the Early Modern Period* (Stuttgart: Springer-Metzler, 2021), pp. 427–53.]
72. Francis Richard, 'Un érudit à la recherche de textes religieux venus d'Orient, le docteur Louis Picques (1637–1699)', in Emmanuel Bury and Bernard Meunier (eds), *Les Pères de l'Église au XVIIe siècle* (Paris: Cerf, 1993), pp. 253–76: the copyist Sulayman ibn Būlātiyya Shāmī copied a manuscript there in 1692 (p. 271). Joseph Nasrallah, *Histoire du mouvement littéraire dans l'Église melchite du Ve au XXe siècle*, vol. IV, 2 (Louvain: Peeters, 1989), p. 217, has reported a manuscript in the British Museum that he recopied in Paris in 1695. Both authors also referred to someone else from Damascus, Ḥannā ibn Qattā, who was active alongside Picques after a visit to Rome.
73. Duverdier, 'Propagande protestante en langues orientales', pp. 8–14.
74. APF, Acta, vol. 84, 24 July 1714, 9, *Collegio Urbano.*
75. Duverdier, 'Propagande protestante'. His biography in Latin was published in Halle in 1764.
76. Bernard Heyberger, 'La carrière manquée d'un ecclésiastique oriental en Italie: Timothée Karnūsh, archevêque syrien Catholic de Mardin', in Bernard Heyberger (ed.), *L'Italie vue par les étrangers, Bulletin of the Faculté des Lettres de Mulhouse,*

19 (1995), pp. 43–44 and note 37 [see the translated version in Chapter 2 in this volume]. APF, Acta, vol. 65, 14 June 1695, 3, *Caldei*: the Chaldean patriarch Joseph came to Rome to rest, after thirty years of service, after he had already been blind for two years. He came accompanied by a priest, ʿAbdallāh from Diyarbakir, whom he brought to stop him from creating divisions and to prevent him from going back home. Isaac, the archbishop of Niniveh, arrived in Rome in 1706 and was ordered to return to the Orient in 1714 and 1715, but always answered that it was not possible: Acta, vol. 76, 6 September 1706, 16, *Soria*; 20 December 1706, 8, *Soria*; Acta, vol. 83, 13 November 1713, fols 618r–619v; Acta, vol. 84, 24 September 1714, 17, *Soria*; Acta, vol. 85, 8 April 1715, fol. 163rv. Gregory Joshua, the Syrian archbishop of Jerusalem, ordered to leave, explained that he could not: Acta, vol. 81, 3 February 1711, 23, *Soria*; Acta, vol. 84, 17 December 1714, *Soria*; Acta, vol. 85, 14 January 1715, fol. 19rv.

77. Bernard Heyberger, *Hindiyya, Mystic and Criminal, 1720–1798: A Political and Religious Crisis in Lebanon*, English translation by Renée Champion (Cambridge: James Clarke & Co., 2013), pp. 4–5, 41, 158, 166. For an attempt to force him to return either to Cyprus or to Lebanon: APF, SC, Maroniti, vol. 3, fols 444rv, 450r–451r.
78. APF, SOCG, vol. 519, fols 174rv, 176r. Heyberger, 'La carrière manquée', pp. 38, 46. Richard, 'Un érudit à la recherche de textes religieux', p. 272: Safar copied out manuscripts for Picques in Paris in 1685. Acta, vol. 104, 1 March 1734, 44, *Soriani*: appeal by Giovanni Domenico Safar.
79. Heyberger, 'La carrière manquée'.
80. APF, SC, Maroniti, vol. 3, fol. 139rv; 141r: a similar certificate from the Prior of the hospital (30 August 1716).
81. APF, Acta, vol. 58, 16 November 1688, 21, *Elemosine*; SOCG, vol. 502, fol. 494r. Acta, vol. 95, 8 January 1725, 5, *Maroniti*.
82. APF, Acta, vol. 52, 25 February 1682, 3, *Armeni*. Acta, vol. 54, 20 March 1684, 15, *Armeni*. Acta, vol. 55, 17 December 1685, 22, *Francia* (Grazia Nachet); ibid. 26, *Varie*: long report on the activities among the galley-slaves of Marseille, indicating the role of Tommaso Herabied. [On the Armenians in Marseille, see Olivier Raveux, 'Entre réseau communautaire intercontinental et intégration locale: La colonie marseillaise des marchands arméniens de la Nouvelle-Djoulfa (Ispahan), 1669–1695', *Revue d'histoire moderne et contemporaine*, 59, 1 (2012), pp. 83–102]. Acta, vol. 57, 23 December 1687, 5, *Stampa*: Nachet asked for an Arabic-Latin Bible for the converted 'Turks'. SOCG, vol. 507, fols 237r, 235v, and Acta, vol. 60, 12 June 1690, 28, *Collegio Urbano – Soria*: having lived in Marseille for four years, he obtained absolution for having passed to the Latin rite without permission. On Grazia Nachet, see also ACU, *Registro*. On Paolo Abdelnur, see APF, Acta vol. 76, 14 June 1706, 7 *Soria*; SC, Siri, vol. 1, fol. 405rv; SC, Maroniti, vol. 3, fol. 126r.
83. ACU, *Registro*. Numerous references to the Armenians of Livorno in APF, Acta, vol. 38 (1669), and vol. 39 (1670). SOCG, vol. 447, fols 241r–255r, dossier on the Armenians of Livorno. Acta, vol. 54, 20 March 1684, 11, *Armeni*: the Armenian merchant Gregorio Gerach, 'schismatic Persian Armenian',

professed the Catholic faith at Livorno [on this individual, see now Sebouh D. Aslanian, '"A Ship with Two Rudders"? Gregorio di Girach-Mirman of Venice, Global Armenian Trade Networks, and Religious Ambiguity in the Age of Confessionalization', in Helen C. Evans (ed.), *Art and Religion in Medieval Armenia* (New York: Metropolitan Museum of Art, 2021), pp. 85–108].

84. Charon, 'L'Église grecque catholique de Livourne'.
85. APF, Acta, vol. 76, 20 December 1706, 2, *Missioni.*
86. APF, SC, Maroniti, vol. 2, fol. 262rv (26 June 1713). He reported the visit to Livorno of a Maronite Daud, whom he housed while waiting for a French boat to go to Alexandria, then from there to Saida.
87. APF, SC, Greci Melchiti, vol. 2, fol. 56r (undated) and 60r (19 April 1727).
88. Ibid. fol. 76r. Yūsif ibn Girgis al-ʿAskarī left the College in April 1704, was active in Aleppo, then catalogued manuscripts at the royal library in Paris (1734–35). He was the author of numerous translations into Arabic: Gemayel, *Les échanges culturels*, vol. 1, pp. 116, 293–96.
89. He was known as Girolamo Nonziata of Aleppo: APF, SC, Maroniti, vol. 9, fols 42rv, 44v. SC, Maroniti, vol. 4, fols 388r (Arabic), 386rv (Italian translation), 390r (opinion on Girolamo, doubting his capacity to celebrate in Latin and to hear confessions). Girolamo, a begging monk, appeared in Rome: ibid. fols 364r, 366r (14 August 1734), 445r. He was sent by the patriarch in 1729: ibid. fols 65rv, 68r. He left his Order and settled in Livorno where he founded a chapel: Fahd, *Taʾrīkh al-ruhbāniyya al-mārūniyya*, vol. 2, p. 260; he was reported as being in the company of two runaway monks: ibid. vol. 3, pp. 213–17. [A lot of evidence concerning the same, called 'Girûnimûs Nunziata' by the author, can be found in Bellati Ceccoli, *Tra Toscana e Medioriente,* pp. 70–80. The Buktī family settled in Livorno: ibid. passim, and Guillaume Calafat, 'Ramadam Fatet vs. John Jucker: Trials and Forgery in Egypt, Syria, and Tuscany (1739–1740)', *Quaderni storici*, 48, 2 (2013), p. 422.]
90. APF, SC, Maroniti, vol. 8, fols 492r–494r. [On Tommaso Diab (Diyāb), see Bellati Ceccoli, *Tra Toscana e Medioriente*, pp. 80–92. By the time of Nunziata's death (1768), Diab had been residing at the Dominican convent of Livorno for eight years. He was appointed as 'confessor of the Arabs' as soon as 1769. On Arsenio Diab, an important figure in the Maronite affairs, see Heyberger, *Hindiyya, Mystic and Criminal,* passim.]
91. APF, SC, Maroniti, vol. 1, fols 220–21. Acta, vol. 63, 6 April 1693, 18, *Stampa.*
92. APF, SC, Maroniti, vol. 1, fol. 240r (2 January 1695).
93. Ibid. fols 324r–325r (10 May 1704), 334r (2 August 1704).
94. APF, Acta, vol. 75, 22 June 1705, 9, *Maroniti* and *Stampa*. Acta, vol. 76, 14 June 1706, 24, *Maroniti*, and 5 October 1706, 25, *Maroniti.*
95. APF, Acta, vol. 78, 23 July 1708, 2, *Varie*; 2 October 1708, 29, *Varie*. Acta, vol. 79, 10 June 1709, 15, *Varie*; 22 November 1709, 40, *Varie*; 16 December 1709, 15, *Varie.*
96. APF, Acta, vol. 81, 1711, fols 268rv, 339r–343r, 573r–575v, 592rv. Acta, vol. 87, 1717, fols 318v, 323r.
97. APF, SC, Maroniti, vol. 4, fol. 170rv. Gemayel, *Les échanges culturels*, vol. 1, p. 123, has noted that he ran away from the Maronite college on 4 July 1724.

98. APF, SC, Greci Melchiti, vol. 1, fols 274r–278r (Italian translation), 280r–281v (Arabic). He must have made enemies in Malta as soon as he arrived: he denounced the Greeks to the local inquisitor as schismatics, asserting that he had found the schism at the heart of Christendom. He particularly accused them of using an anti-Latin Synaxarium (Book of Saints) that he had burnt while in Beirut!
99. APF, Acta, 26 February 1725, 15, *Melchiti*; 18 June 1725, 22, *Melchiti*; 31 July 1725, 28, *Melchiti*. SC, Greci Melchiti, vol. 2, fols 37r, 207r–208v; 257rv, 259r–260r, 287rv; vol. 3, fols 259r–263v. [After the accusations advanced while in Malta, in 1725 ibn Jubayr denounced also a Greek bishop residing in Rome for celebrating mass 'in a heretical way': Santus, 'Tra la chiesa di Sant'Atanasio e il Sant'Uffizio', p. 220.]
100. On François Picquet, see Ristelhueber, *Traditions françaises au Liban*, and Georges Goyau, *Un précurseur: François Picquet, consul de Louis XIV en Alep et évêque de Babylone* (Paris: Geuthner, 1942). Ilyās al-Mawṣilī met him in Lyon: *Il primo orientale nelle Americhe*, p. 28.
101. APF, SC, Greci Melchiti, vol. 1, fols 88r, 34r.
102. APF, SOCG, vol. 568, fol. 54rv (copy of the letter of P. Valeriano/Bulos).
103. Besides the use of the services of the Holy Land by Giovanni Shahīn, which has already been mentioned, one finds other disputes between the Friars Minor and Eastern Christians: Ḥannā Shalhūb Maʿūshī, a Maronite merchant from Jerusalem who apparently practised maritime trade on a large scale, came to Rome to plead an obscure cause opposing him to the '*Terra Santa*' (see above, note 39); Giovanni David, a Maronite from Acre, was in conflict with the Friars Minor concerning a deposit that his father had entrusted to the '*Terra Santa*': APF, SC, Maroniti, vol. 4, fols 166r–167v, 220rv, 297r–301r, 455r–459v. On the systems of aid from the '*Terra Santa*' in Palestine, see Heyberger, 'Terre Sainte et mission au XVIIe siècle', *Dimensioni e problemi della ricerca storica*, 2 (1994), pp. 140–45. See also the debt of 7,000 to 8,000 piasters contracted by Antonio Callimeri, 'procurator of the Holy Land' in Cyprus, from the Friars Minor: Heyberger, 'Les nouveaux horizons méditerranéens', p. 447.
104. APF, SOCG, vol. 519, fols 174rv, 176r. See Heyberger, *Les Chrétiens du Proche-Orient*, p. 217, where other actions by the Friars Minor against Eastern alms collectors have been mentioned.
105. Al-Mawṣilī, *Il primo orientale nelle Americhe*, pp. 32–33. He appears in ACU, *Registro*, under the name Giona Grazia, having arrived in 1661. On Grazia Zaccur, see Acta, vol. 82, 2 May 1712, 21, *Collegio Urbano*; 4 July 1712, 31, *Collegio Urbano*. The profession of his uncle appears in ACU, *Registro*.
106. APF, SC, Maroniti, vol. 3, fols 65r–66v (Arabic), 64r–65v (Italian translation). In an undated letter (fols 161r–162v), Giuseppe Assemani offered to take with him a young student from the Maronite college, Stefano Roselli (Ward), and recommended him for an allowance. At the time, the young man was employed copying Arabic manuscripts in a library in Bologna. But we know that he was to return to Lebanon later on.
107. APF, SC, Maroniti, vol. 4, fols 69r–78r.

108. APF, SC, Maroniti, vol. 2, fol. 174rv.
109. APF, SC, Maroniti, vol. 3, fols 463r–465v.
110. APF, Acta, vol. 86, fol. 283v, 9 June 1716. SC, Maroniti, vol. 3, fol. 172r: Metoscita said that he was in Rome to look after the patriarch's affairs and asked for a reference letter before returning to Malta.
111. APF, SC, Greci Melchiti, vol. 2, fols 45rv, 48r (Italian translation), 46r–47r (Arabic original).
112. Josée Balagna, *L'imprimerie arabe en Occident (XVIe, XVIIe et XVIIIe siècles)* (Paris: Maisonneuve and Larose, 1994), pp. 36–41. [On the Medici printing press, see now Sara Fani and Margherita Farina (eds), *Le vie delle lettere: La Tipografia Medicea tra Roma e l'Oriente* (Florence: Mandragora, 2012)]. The punches of the Medici typography were taken to France and have been at the Imprimerie Nationale since 1811.
113. Gemayel, *Les échanges culturels*, vol. 1, pp. 450–54.
114. He studied at the Maronite college at the same time as Mubārak: ibid. p. 111. He was in Rome as the patriarch's envoy together with Metoscita, in January 1695: APF, SC, Maroniti, vol. 1, fol. 239r.
115. APF, SC, Maroniti, vol. 3, fols 291rv, 389r–390r, 395rv, 397rv, 399r–401v, 404r–405v.
116. APF, SC, Maroniti, vol. 4, fols 200r–217v, 256r–257v. ARSI, *Gallia* 106, 22 December 1750: the Jesuit procurator of the seminary of Antoura wrote to the cardinals of the Propaganda about these typefaces, which had been given in 1712 by the three Maronites, on condition that they would be sent to the Levant to be used there. He noted that the material was in bad condition, that there was no hope of transferring them to the Orient; he offered to sell them and use the money for a better purpose.
117. APF, SOCG, vol. 528, fols 489r; SOCG, vol. 535, fols 178r–181v; SOCG, vol. 536, fols 421r–426v. Acta, vol. 68, 18 August 1698, 8, *Soria*.
118. APF, SOCG, vol. 568, fols 50r–51v, 56r (Arabic), 58r (Italian translation); 53rv (Italian translation), 56rv (Arabic); 54rv (copy of the letter from Fr. Valeriano/Bulos).
119. ARSI, *Gallia*, 96, III, fols 463r–465v.
120. Poumarède, *Pour en finir avec la croisade*, pp. 7, 129–34.
121. Bernard Heyberger, 'De l'image religieuse à l'image profane? L'essor de l'image chez les Chrétiens de Syrie et du Liban (XVIIe–XIXe siècle)', in Bernard Heyberger and Sylvia Naef (eds), *La multiplication des images en pays d'Islam: De l'estampe à la télévision (17e–21e siècle)* (Istanbul: Orient-Institut der DMG; Würzburg: Ergon, 2003), p. 38 [see the translation in Chapter 8 in this volume].
122. Heyberger, 'La carrière manquée'.
123. Al-Mawṣilī, *Il primo orientale nelle Americhe*, pp. 106, 111.
124. Abras, 'Le voyage de deux moines melkites', p. 64.
125. Roche, *Humeurs vagabondes*, p. 37.

CHAPTER 2

The Wasted Career of an Eastern Clergyman in Italy: Timothy Karnuk (Timoteo Agnellini), Syriac Catholic Archbishop of Mardin*

In the seventeenth and eighteenth centuries, visitors to Italy and Rome who belonged to the different Christian confessions from the Arab Middle East represented only a small proportion in relation to travellers from the states of Christian Europe. They formed none the less a significant group by virtue of their social status and their number, compared to the size of their original community.[1]

Only a few of this already small number left a written testimony of their stay. The travelogue genre, which was very popular in early modern Europe and still alive in the Muslim written tradition, only made a timid appearance in Arab Christian literature of this period, whereas the stereotyped formula of the 'pilgrim's guide', in which Rome occupied a secondary place behind Jerusalem and the Sinai, survived.[2] However, the Roman archives, and in particular the correspondence preserved at the Congregation *de Propaganda Fide*, partially compensate for this absence and make it possible to retrace some episodes of the lives of those who settled for a while in the capital of Catholicism, or elsewhere in Italy.

I have already mentioned those lay people, usually devoted to trade, who occasionally came to seek the protection of the Roman Church.[3] The clergy who came to Christian Europe were far more numerous. A certain number of them looked to establish themselves permanently in Europe, and the most famous succeeded in finding a biographer.[4] Some had successful careers in teaching and translating Eastern languages; others obtained an ecclesiastical living or casual income in exchange for offering pastoral care to Levantines in Malta,[5] Livorno,[6] or other Italian towns.[7] However, an ecclesiastical prebend was nearly always inaccessible to them, while the position of Orientalist scholar remained uncertain, dependent on a patron. Therefore, the recommendation of the cardinals of the Propaganda was often necessary to obtain or keep a stable job.

The most colourful character whose existence I was able to follow through the Congregation's records is also an exemplary case, in so far as, over the course of his long life, he explored all of the options available to an Eastern ecclesiastic in Europe: he tried to make a living using his regional and linguistic skills; he engaged in trade with his compatriots; and he sought the patronage of, or a pension from, the cardinals of the Propaganda. I am speaking of Ḥumaylī Ibn Daʿfī Karnuk, whose ecclesiastical name was Timothy ('Timoteo Carnuch' or 'Timoteo Agnellini' in Italian), originally from Diyarbakir.[8] A Syriac Orthodox priest converted to Catholicism by the Capuchins, he was elected archbishop of Mardin by the Catholic faithful of the town. He arrived in Marseille and travelled to Rome in the company of the Capuchin Jean François de Sevin, a missionary in Diyarbakir. The latter really wanted to give his protégé a proper Western-style education, to anchor him for good in Catholicism and to prepare him to lead his Church when the occasion arose.[9]

To be admitted to the Collegio Urbano (named after its founder, Pope Urban VIII), Timothy Karnuk first had to conceal his episcopal status (a bishop could not be admitted as a student), which was moreover marred by a secret breach of procedure, as it was a Chaldean (East Syriac Catholic) prelate who had consecrated him, even though he belonged to the West Syriac ('Jacobite') rite. This lack of legitimacy was to haunt him throughout his life, like a youthful mistake, and would render nearly impossible his return to the city of his see, which was not very receptive to Catholicism.[10]

Karnuk's main asset for an Italian career was his knowledge of Middle Eastern languages: when he arrived, he already knew Arabic, Syriac, Armenian, Persian, Turkish and some Italian, and he immediately set himself to learn Latin. He could therefore envisage a comfortable living in the service of European Orientalist scholarship.[11] Athanasius Kircher, the famous Jesuit scholar from the Roman College, on 7 August 1671 recommended him for a place at the Collegio Urbano, mentioning that he had examined his skills and used him as a copyist, in which role he had been very diligent.[12] Thanks to this prestigious intervention, Timothy was employed at the Propaganda for three years, for the sum of 6 *scudi* per month, and given the chance to study at the College.[13]

However, the Roman authorities were not generally keen on entertaining Eastern prelates in the city at their expense, faithful in this to the spirit of the Council of Trent, which had insisted on the duty of a bishop to reside in his own diocese and take care of his own flock. Thus, at the end of this period, in 1674, this Syriac Catholic bishop of Mardin was for the first time strongly encouraged by the cardinals to return home. To help him do so, they twice renewed the order to leave, without any result, and then deprived him of his income (the 'palace's share') and his accommodation at the College. To these pressing demands, he replied with a letter, saying that he had not started his journey back because the right conditions were not present. For his own security, he was asking for a safe conduct from the sultan (which could not be obtained without a payment), tools for educating his congregation and a missionary instructed in theology to accompany him. If he did not obtain all of this, so he stated, he would not be able to return home under any circumstances. The Secretary of the Congregation commented on his demands before the cardinals, saying that a *berat* from the Turks was not likely, but that they had written some good references for Timothy, and that they twice had given him 100 *scudi*, some liturgical objects and many books.[14]

Apparently, like many Eastern clerics who had come to Europe, Timothy thought it preferable to try his hand in Christian Europe, rather than to live the uncomfortable and politically unsafe life of a prelate in the service of the Catholic Church in the East. Instead of going back to his country, he went to France to collect alms.[15] The following year, the Syriac patriarch, surprisingly well informed, wrote from Aleppo to ask for his arrest, saying that he, together with a 'Nestorian' priest, was begging without the authorisation of his Church, or of Rome.[16]

The missionaries, Karnuk's former protectors, seemed less informed about the activities of their disciple in France. In 1676, when the same Syriac Catholic patriarch was on his deathbed, the Capuchin Jean-Baptiste de Saint-Aignan asked from Aleppo that Timothy be sent in haste to succeed the dying prelate. This was out of question for the Secretary of the Congregation, who recalled that Karnuk had been consecrated as a bishop by a Chaldean and that he had ignored letters sent to the nuncio in Paris and to the French cardinals, urging him to return to his seat. Finally, the Secretary asserted that the Propaganda was still trying to seize the money that he had collected, allegedly in the name of the Syriac Catholic Church.[17]

In 1678, the accusations against Karnuk became more serious. Despite the Propaganda's insistence *vis-à-vis* the French prelates, he stayed in Paris, where he was suspected of practising alchemy. It was rumoured that he had collected alms for a sum exceeding 3,000 *écus*, and it was feared that, if threatened, he would escape to England, as an archbishop from Samos had done the previous year.[18] We know, however, that he used his time in Paris to edit a 'Hymn to the Virgin', together with the seven Penitential Psalms in Arabic.[19]

While travelling through Western Europe, our archbishop was able to ally himself with Levantine merchants, whom he had no doubt met in Italy. Indeed, in 1680 the missionaries of Aleppo wrote to ask for money in favour of a debt-ridden Syriac Catholic patriarch who was living in the town. In relation to this, they mentioned that a sum had been consigned to the Levantine merchant ʿAbd al-Aḥād (Domenico), who was residing in Rome. This was the result of the alms collected by the '*monsignor vescovo Timoteo, per altro nome Carnuc*', through France and Italy. They specified that he was now in Spain, where he could still collect a good amount of money.[20] The following year, the same Domenico/ʿAbd al-Aḥād showed himself at the Roman offices, with his brothers Giovanni and Orazio (described as 'Levantines'). We do not know the reason why, but they said that they were the trustees of 290 *scudi* for the benefit of the Congregation of the Propaganda, from Timothy. Had the latter voluntarily entrusted this money to the Church? If so, he later regretted it, as he found himself in Naples with the firm intention of going back home (according to the three brothers' statements), but he was *scarsissimo di denari* (very short of money), especially since he had not received the donations he expected in Spain. He wanted 90 *scudi* from the tidy sum which he had entrusted to his compatriots to pay for his journey, the rest being for the Congregation. The cardinals decided not to respond to his request ('*lectum*').[21]

But Timothy Karnuk was not short of resources. In the following years, he found himself a powerful protector, Cardinal Gregorio Barbarigo, who used the former's skills in his Oriental printing business in Padua.[22] It was no doubt on the recommendation of the Orientalist Ludovico Marracci that Karnuk obtained this job. Marracci was the confessor of Innocent XI (who died in 1689), of whom Cardinal Barbarigo was a close collaborator. Marracci later was to teach Arabic at the seminary of Padua and there published a Qur'an, with a Latin translation and refutation (1698).[23]

In 1687, a second Syriac Catholic metropolitan from Mardin appeared, Athanasius Safar, who had carried out missions in Persia and later in Paris for François Picquet the former French consul in Aleppo and Latin bishop of Babylon. On 16 June 1687, Safar asked to be entrusted with the money collected by Timothy Karnuk. Confronted with this new difficulty of two bishops claiming to be from the same see, the Propaganda, embarrassed, wrote to Cardinal Barbarigo, asking him to question his *protégé*. The answer was in Karnuk's favour, stating that he could not go back home, as the Congregation suggested, because of the persecutions. To send him back would cost too much and would have been of little use.[24]

We again hear of 'Timoteo Carnuch' ten years later, in 1697, on the death of his protector. He apparently had made the mistake of wanting to improve his income by trading with the Levant, as others among his contemporaries living in Italy had done. Indeed, according to a new denunciation from the Catholic Syriac patriarch, he had sent his companion Isacco with goods from Naples to Aleppo and was preparing to do so a second time. However, the money from this commerce seems to have come from dishonest sources as, according to the accusing prelate, Timothy had ordained someone in Sicily two years earlier in a simoniacal way, collecting 5,000 *scudi*. An order was given to the papal nuncio to confiscate the money and use it to help the Syriac Church; if the man resisted, he would have to be sent to Rome.

Clearly, these accusations from the Syriac patriarch were not unfounded: other complaints had also arrived at the Roman offices, from the Grand Master of the Order of Malta, about the fact that in Messina Timothy had conferred ecclesiastical orders on some Maltese applicants. This time, the affair was serious, and a dossier on Karnuk was compiled, to be communicated to the Congregation of the Holy Office, in view of a trial. On 18 August 1698, Cardinal Cantelmo reported to the Propaganda on the case of 'Timoteo Agnellini', bishop of Mardin, accused on three main counts: of having ordained Maltese clerics in exchange for money; of having travelled around Europe begging, under the pretext of collecting money for his Church; and of having engaged in illicit business 'in the shops of the most disreputable artists' – that is to say, to have made loans with interest. He even had the naivety to address a report to the Cardinal Prefect of the Propaganda, asking him for the support of his authority in order to recuperate some outstanding sums he had lent to these artists and others. The Armenian merchant Isacco di Pietro, possibly the one with whom he had sent merchandise to Aleppo and who had been imprisoned in Naples at Karnuk's request, addressed the Propaganda. Timothy claimed to be owed 1,477 *zecchini* that he had apparently lent to Isacco at high interest in 1690, with the aim of investing them in trade in Venice. In another dossier, a deposition mentions a loan from Karnuk to a certain Antonio from Nineveh (Mosul) staying in Rome and to his companion, for the purchase of a herd of goats.[25]

The accused was then questioned on the various counts and denied them all. He swore that he had never been to Malta or Messina, but the archbishop of the town said he had hosted him and, seeing his certificates, had given him authorisation to say mass and hear the confessions of foreigners who did not know Italian. It was probably through this spiritual care that Karnuk began to build links with sailors. The archbishop was effectively able to establish that not only had Timothy in person conferred the tonsure on some of these disreputable people, but that even his servant had delivered false certificates of tonsure. The accused still denied the second charge against him, that of having unduly collected money around Europe. He recalled only his years spent in Rome, Padua and Naples, totally omitting his stays in Paris and Spain. He did, however, admit to having preached in several places, having said mass and collected money to survive and to print books. Nevertheless, the same dossier also contained references from some prestigious figures in favour of the accused, certifying to his religiosity and morality. In Naples, for example, he was said to have displayed great zeal in instructing the Eastern inhabitants of the city.[26]

This time, the case ended with a summons to Rome and a long imprisonment by order of the Holy Office.[27] In a petition presented to the Propaganda on 13 November 1702, Timothy stated that he had been confined in a convent, with only a small allowance insufficient to live on, with his brother and servant. He therefore asked for additional help, claiming that he knew fourteen languages and that he had edited several works in favour of the Catholic faith. The Secretary for his part recalled the negative records of the supplicant, and the cardinals directed him to another office of the pontifical administration.[28] Only a few months later, Timothy made a new effort, by informing the cardinals that he had been freed from the convent of Saints Cosmas and Damian where he had been held and asking on this occasion for financial help from the Propaganda.[29] This application to the ecclesiastical authorities, after all that he had experienced, may seem odd. In fact, after so many years, Karnuk doubtless saw no other possible course of action. In addition, he seemed to have been caught up in an attitude of welfare dependency, convinced that he was owed compensation for the injustice he had previously suffered.

In 1706, at his request, the typography of Propaganda provided Karnuk with gratis copies of fifteen works in Eastern languages.[30] That same year, he again addressed the Congregation to ask for the printing, by the same publisher, of a small book in Arabic and Italian dedicated to the Virgin Mary.[31] In 1708, he recalled in a letter his work in favour of his 'nation' and of other Easterners. He asserted that he heard confessions and catechised Muslims so that they could receive baptism, without being paid at all. He indeed appeared as godfather in the baptismal registers of Muslims in Rome.[32] He added that he had written various books, including a dictionary in twelve languages (six Western, six Eastern) and a summary of the lives of the saints. Unfortunately, he said, he did not have enough to pay the copyists or to publish these books, and the pension that he received was insufficient. He asked for a yearly allowance to be taken from the money of the Syriac Church. After all, he pointed out, the Chaldean patriarch, a refugee in Rome who had just died, had received an income of 5 *scudi* per month from these funds, even though he did not even belong to the Syriac Church, whereas he himself had been previously expropriated to the value of 600 *scudi* in favour of the patriarch of his own Church.[33]

Living in fairly shabby conditions, he attempted a somewhat pathetic deal in 1711. He addressed himself once again to the cardinals of the Propaganda to inform them that he had sent from Venice to the pontifical customs at Civitavecchia five cases of Arab, Armenian and Syriac printing types, which had cost him 200 *scudi* and which he wanted to donate to the Congregation. However, he asked to be compensated with 100 *scudi*, a sum that he would use to buy two more cases of these types. On this occasion, he could not help but remembering the 300 *scudi* that had been confiscated from him a long time ago by the Propaganda, which he now described as a voluntary donation. But the Secretary of the Congregation, who knew the entire story, took care to enlighten the cardinals on the subject.[34] Finally, after a valuation of these printing types, their value was estimated at barely 60 *scudi* in all and, as a note in the margin specified, Karnuk wanted to keep some of them, so that the remainder would only have been worth around 40 *scudi*. Thus, what had been presented as a gift was in reality a sale. In addition, the printing house of the Propaganda had no need for these types, which in any case were judged to be imperfect and insufficient. The experts decided that this 'gift' should be refused.[35] It was a shabby deal. However, other Eastern Christians also sought to cash in on the market of printing types.[36] Some, pretending missionary zeal, tried to deal in religious books, clearly a sought-after asset among the Levantine Christians.[37]

In 1710, the Propaganda again decided to send the Eastern bishops living in Rome back to their homeland, where they could be more useful. In answer, Karnuk, like the other Eastern prelates installed in 'Christendom', asked for dispensation from returning to Mardin, citing the persecutions suffered by Catholics, his great age (he was over seventy) and his public service in Rome at the Armenian church of Santa Maria Egiziaca.[38] In 1714, he again stated that he could not leave the city.[39] Faced with the persistence of the offices of the Propaganda, he went on the offensive in 1715. He reminded them of his public service, lamenting the fact that his allowance (the 'palace's share') had been abolished for a year to convince him to leave. At eighty, he said he was ready to undertake the journey, but asked for help and evoked the injustice that he suffered: Athanasius Safar, the 'intruder' bishop of his See, who was also living in Rome and no readier to return to his country, received a pension from the income of the Syriac Church. The cardinals eventually gave up, appraising that the old bishop was not in the shape for such a journey. They asked the Secretary to make sure that he was lodged at the pope's expense, so that he did not roam the town.[40]

This did not prevent Karnuk from putting himself forward as the Syriac Catholic patriarch in 1716. He explained to the Congregation the benefits that they would derive from such an appointment, claiming that he could get to his See at no expense. However, in an addendum, he specified that he needed 800 *scudi* to obtain a *berat* in Constantinople in his favour, a lower rate, he said, than that of the French Ambassador, who could not offer the same service for less than 1,000 *scudi*. Faced with this proposal, the Secretary drew the attention of the cardinals to the fact that the patriarch was elected by the clergy and the people and not designated by Rome; that they had but few positive reports on the supplicant; that he had refused to leave several times; and that, 'now that he can hardly stand up, he has had this idea and the zeal to be patriarch'.[41] This is the last trace of Timothy Karnuk I was able to find in the archives of the Propaganda. He finally died in Rome in a night-time fire in December 1724; he was buried in the church of Saint Luke, through the care of his rival, Athanasius Safar.[42]

This life-story raises the question of the social role and practices of young people from the Middle East brought up according to the norms of Western culture. They faced problems integrating in their home country; it would have been difficult for an Eastern Christian educated in Rome to return home. The persecutions that Timothy feared upon his return to Mardin were not just an excuse to remain in Europe. While Catholicism seems to have become established in Syria around 1670, the situation changed after the death of the Catholic patriarch of Aleppo, Andrew Akhijan (1677), who had only been accepted thanks to the energy and the fortune of the French consul François Picquet without ever obtaining the unanimous support of his people.[43]

The project to bring young Easterners to Europe to raise them in the principles of Tridentine Catholicism and of a 'good education', before sending them back to head their Churches, was one of the major ideas of the Propaganda, shared with the Latin missionaries.[44] But this project was fantastical and very often doomed to failure because, as in the case of Karnuk, these young people preferred to take their chances in Europe, or because, once back home, they were not accepted, stripped of their possessions and deprived of their office. In other cases, they aligned themselves with parties hostile to Rome, which they then helped with their knowledge and experience.[45]

For those who, like our archbishop, tried to make a career in Europe at any cost, integration was not easy. They remained second-rate clerics whose fate depended on a protector and who constantly lived at the limits of the legality and respectability inherent in their ecclesiastical status. One of the dangers of the missionary policy of the Roman authorities was to create a Christianity of dependants. In part, this is what happened, and it was to some extent recognised. Over the course of his long life, Timothy Karnuk became (in anachronistic terms) a 'charity case', dependent on the charitable services of the Church, which he tried to exploit as much as possible. On the institutional side, his 'case' was examined through a dossier and with a concern aimed primarily at social control, which shows that the papal state, at least in this respect, was a fully modern state.

Was Timothy Karnuk really looking for complete integration into his host society? His life sheds light on the importance of the networks put in place by Eastern Christians in the seventeenth and eighteenth centuries, formed by sodalities, associations and exchanges between those residing in Europe and those who had stayed behind in their country, or who had settled in Egypt and in Constantinople.[46] This explains why we are often surprised by the speed and accuracy with which certain pieces of information and gossip came to the ears of the patriarch of Aleppo, or of the Secretary of the Propaganda in Rome.[47] Ecclesiastical patronage was a major asset in this strategy. Italy appeared to Levantine Christians as an essential (but not exclusive) base for the circulations in which they took an increasing part, in a vision of the world whose horizon remained the Mediterranean.

NOTES

* This chapter is dedicated to social workers.

1. See especially the Eastern Christians educated in the Roman colleges: Bernard Heyberger, *Les chrétiens du Proche-Orient au temps de la Réforme catholique (Syrie, Liban, Palestine, XVIIe–XVIIIe siècles)* (Rome: École française de Rome, 1994), pp. 405–24. [Since 1995, the date of the original version of this article, numerous

publications concerning Eastern Christians in Western Europe have appeared; see the references in the updated notes of Chapter 1.]

2. Joseph Nasrallah, *Histoire du mouvement littéraire dans l'Église melchite du Ve au XXe siècle,* vol. IV, 1 (Louvain: Peeters, 1979), pp. 228–31; vol. IV, 2, pp. 300–4. Anton Baumstark, 'Eine arabische Palästinabeschreibung spätestens des 16. Jahrhunderts', *Oriens Christianus,* 6 (1906), pp. 238–99. Olga de Lébédew (ed.), *Codex 286 du Vatican: Récits de voyages d'un Arabe* (St Petersburg: s. n., 1902). [This assertion has to be corrected, since the travelogue became a main genre in the Arabic-speaking Christian literature during the eighteenth century. See some examples in Bernard Heyberger, 'Introduction', in Hanna Dyâb, *D'Alep à Paris: Les pérégrinations d'un jeune Syrien au temps de Louis XIV* (Arles: Actes Sud, 2015), pp. 12–13; Feras Krimsti, 'Arsāniyūs Shukrī al-Ḥakīm's Account of his Journey to France, the Iberian Peninsula, and Italy (1748–1757) from Travel Journal to Edition', *Philological Encounters,* 4 (2019), pp. 202–44.]
3. Bernard Heyberger, 'Sécurité et insécurité: Les Chrétiens de Syrie dans l'espace méditerranéen (XVIIe–XVIIIe siècles)', in Meropi Anastassiadou and Bernard Heyberger (eds), *Figures anonymes, figures d'élite: Pour une anatomie de l'Homo ottomanicus* (Istanbul: Isis Press, 1999), pp. 147–63 [see the English translation in Chapter 3 of this volume, as well as Chapter 1].
4. Nasser Gemayel, *Les échanges culturels entre les Maronites et l'Europe,* 2 vols. (Beirut: Imprimerie Gemayel, 1984); Pierre Raphael, *Le rôle du Collège maronite romain dans l'orientalisme aux XVIIe et XVIIIe siècles* (Beirut: Université Saint-Joseph, 1950); Eugène Tisserant, 'Notes pour servir à la biographie d'Étienne Évode Assémani', *Oriens Christianus,* 7 (1932), pp. 264–76. A Maronite, Carolus Rali Dadichi, managed to fool the German Orientalists at the beginning of the eighteenth century: Joseph Hajjar, 'La question religieuse en Orient au déclin de l'Empire ottoman (1683–1814)', *Istina,* 13, 2 (1968), p. 160. Nasrallah, *Histoire du mouvement littéraire,* has provided biographical notes on some of these individuals. [The literature on Eastern Christians settled in Europe has dramatically increased in volume in recent years: see Bernard Heyberger (ed.), *Orientalisme, science et controverse: Abraham Ecchellensis* (Turnhout: Brepols, 2010); Alastair Hamilton, 'An Egyptian Traveller in the Republic of Letters: Josephus Barbatus or Abudacnus the Copt', *Journal of the Warburg and Courtauld Institutes,* 57 (1994), pp. 123–50; Hilary Kilpatrick and Gerald J. Toomer, 'Niqūlāwus Al-Ḥalabī (c.1611–1661): A Greek Orthodox Syrian Copyist and His Letters to Pococke and Golius', *Lias,* 43, 1 (2016), pp. 1–159; John-Paul Ghobrial, 'The Life and Hard Times of Solomon Negri: An Arabic Teacher in Early Modern Europe', in Alastair Hamilton, Yan Loop and Charles Burnett (eds), *The Teaching and Learning of Arabic* (Leiden: Brill, 2017), pp. 310–32; Aurélien Girard, 'Was an Eastern Scholar Necessarily a Cultural Broker in Early-Modern Academic Europe? Faustus Naironus (1628–1711), the Christian East, and Oriental Studies', in Nicholas Hardy and Dmitri Levitin (eds), *Erudition and Confessionalisation: An Episode in the History of the Humanities* (Oxford: Oxford University Press, 2019), pp. 240–63.]

5. APF, SC, Maroniti, vol. 1, fols 324r–325r (10 May 1704) and 33rv (2 August 1704): Michele Metoscita, a Maronite, had been looking after slaves in Malta for four years. There was no question of letting him go. Acta, vol. 76, 14 June 1706, 24, *Maroniti* and 23 July 1708, 2, *Varie*: the same, from Malta, asked for his church back, having been dispossessed by the local bishop. A similar request can be found in Acta, vol. 79, 10 June 1709, 15, *Varie*. Ibid. 16 December 1709, 15, *Varie*: the Inquisitor of Malta wrote a long report on him, in his favour, at the request of the Propaganda. Acta, vol. 87, 25 January 1717, 14, *Greci*, and SC, Greci Melchiti, vol. 1, fols 274r–278r (Italian translation), 280r–281rv (original Arabic), May 1717: Nāwufītūs ibn Jubayr al-Ḥalabī (from Aleppo) had to flee Egypt and arrived in Malta, where he did not find many friends as he had denounced the Catholic Greeks on the island to the Inquisitor, on account of their liturgy; he asked to go to Rome. SC, Greci Melchiti, vol. 2, fols 207r–208v, 257rv: the same sums up his entire life. The order from Rome, in 1718, to pay him a salary from the income of the Greek Church in Malta was not executed. He thus lived on the island on alms, until 1725, at which date he asked the Propaganda for help. He could not be employed by the Greek parish on the pretext that he only knew Arabic, but he obtained a pension from Rome, which was nearly taken away from him in 1730. SC, Greci Melchiti, vol. 3, fols 259rv, 262r–263v (22 August 1735), a new threat emerged: the same Ibn Jubayr was accused by a Greek priest on Malta of 'latinising', of sending back home the 6 *scudi* he received monthly from Rome and of being useless and creating scandal, quite obviously in an attempt to take his place. SC, Maroniti, vol. 4, fol. 170rv (around 1730): Giovanni Gillal, a Maronite priest from Jerusalem who, after having studied in Rome, settled in Malta to (so he said) instruct the slaves, saw his activity challenged by the local bishop. [All of these figures are presented at length in Chapter 1 of this volume].
6. APF, SC, Greci Melchiti, vol. 2, fol. 60r (19 April 1727): the archbishop of Pisa authorised the Aleppine Melkite priest Graziano Salemi (a refugee in Italy, see fol. 56r) to conduct religious services in Livorno for two months, for the Arabs in the town, during Easter time. But there were already other Arab clerics present there, which caused problems. Ibid. fol. 76r: Arab tradesmen from the same town wrote to ask if the Maronite priest Giuseppe Georgi, on his way to France, could be authorised to hear their confessions [see also Chapter 1, note 88]. Butrus Fahd, *Ta'rīkh al-ruhbāniyya al-mārūniyya bi-far'ayhā al-Ḥalabī wa-l-Lubnānī*, vol. 2 (Jounieh: Matba'at al-Kraym, 1963), p. 260, has mentioned the monk Giranimus al-Ḥalabī, who had left his order and settled in Livorno, where he founded a chapel. Ibid. vol. 3, pp. 213–17: mention of the same, with two other fugitive monks [see also Chapter 1, note 89].
7. See the career of 'Abdallāh ibn Dawūd (Teodoro d'Aut, later David di San Carlo) in Heyberger, *Les chrétiens du Proche-Orient*, pp. 420–21. APF, Acta, vol. 74, 30 June 1704, 9, *Limosine*, *Soria*: mention of a Carmelite from Damascus, Giovanni Damasceno Della Natività, reader in Arabic at the San Pancrazio college. SOCG, vol. 502, fol. 502: Giorgio di Grazia, from Jerusalem, was for seven years a teacher of Arabic, Greek and Turkish in Naples, and he wanted to go to Spain. SC, Greci

Melchiti, vol. 2, fol. 559 (Florence, 1732): the Aleppine Lazzaro Aggiuri ('Ajjūrī) tried to obtain an ecclesiastical living in Tuscany for his brother. Acta, vol. 127, 8 March 1757, 16, *Terra Santa,* fols 89r–103r: mention of the 'runaway' Maronite monk Gabriel who, after having travelled all over Italy, returned to Aleppo.

8. [As is the case for other Eastern Christians travelling through Europe, the name of the archbishop appeared in various forms: Timoteo Carnuch or Carnug, Timothée de Carnuque, Timoteo Agnellini. Following Georg Graf, I chose to identify him by the Arabic form of his name, Ḥumaylī ibn Daʿfī Karnūk: Georg Graf, *Geschichte der Christlichen Arabischen Literatur*, vol. 4 (Vatican City: Biblioteca Apostolica Vaticana, 1951), pp. 54–55. Yet, looking for an Arabic origin of his name, I wrongly preferred Karnūsh to Karnūk. I ignored the Armenian origins of his name (Timotʻēos Gaṙnuk). In Armenian, 'gaṙnuk' (in Western pronunciation, 'karnug') means 'little lamb', as in the Italian 'agnellino' and in Arabic 'ḥumayl'. See Raymond Kévorkian, *Catalogue des 'incunables' arméniens, 1511–1695 ou Chronique de l'imprimerie arménienne* (Geneva: Cramer, 1986), pp. 169–70, and Cesare Santus, 'Wandering Lives: Eastern Christian Pilgrims, Alms-Collectors, and "Refugees" in Early Modern Rome', in Matthew Coneys Wainwright and Emily Michelson (eds), *A Companion to Religious Minorities in Early Modern Rome* (Leiden, Boston: Brill, 2021), p. 269 and note 88. In this volume, I have employed both Timoteo Agnellini and Timothy Karnuk.]
9. The Capuchins had settled in Diyarbakir in 1667. APF, SOCG, vol. 437, fol. 123rv (1672): the Capuchin Jean-Baptiste de Saint-Aignan asked that Karnuk be received at the College; ibid. fols 119r–120r: Jean François de Sevin, having come to Rome, asked that Karnuk be kept at the College for several months or that he be sent to Diyarbakir as bishop, in the see of the 'heretical' Patriarch Shukrallāh, who had just died. SOCG, vol. 438, fol. 16r (Rome, 22 December 1672): the same; ibid. fol. 17r: Karnuk asked to be allowed to celebrate mass according to his rite in the chapel of the College; ibid. fol. 19r: Cardinal Bona suggested he use the Maronite missal printed in Rome for this. See the biographical note devoted to 'Timotheus Karnūk' in Graf, *Geschichte der Christlichen Arabischen Literatur*, vol. 4, pp. 54–55. The author has presented him as someone with an unpleasant character ('eine ihrem Charakter nach unsympathische Persönlichkeit'). He has also mentioned that he collected alms in Italy and Austria but ignored his stay in France and Spain.
10. APF, SOCG, vol. 456, fols 120v–121r (1675, *Sommario*).
11. APF, SOCG, vol. 429, fol. 45r.
12. Ibid. fol. 46r (7 August 1671).
13. APF, Acta, vol. 41, fol. 204rv (1671).
14. APF, SOCG, vol. 445, fol. 43r (12 February 1674); the Secretary's comment is at fol. 42rv.
15. APF, SOCG, vol. 456, fol. 142r, *Sommario*. Details on this stay of Karnuk in France can be found in Kevorkian, *Catalogue des 'incunables' arméniens*, p. 169. We have other examples of clerics having gone to France when they should have returned home. Filippo Gailan (Ghaylān), from Damascus, had arrived in Rome in 1698: Acta, vol. 70, 24 May 1700, 14, *Greci*. First mention: Acta, vol. 69, 6

July 1699, 2, *Greci/Stampa*. SC, Melchiti, vol. 1, fol. 88r (undated, but 1699). He was supposed to go back home, helped by the Propaganda: ibid. fol. 34r (8 July 1700). In 1700, he preferred to go to France to collect alms that he then used to make more money: SOCG, vol. 568, fols 50r–51v, 58r. Theodore of Gelde, a cleric from Damascus, was robbed by corsairs on his return from France: SOCG, vol. 524, fol. 268r (July 1696). The Syrian Paolo Abdelnur had to go to Marseilles to hear confessions in Arabic and Turkish: SC, Siri, vol. 1, fol. 405rv (18 December 1706). The same returned to Aleppo after ten years in France: SC, Maroniti, vol. 3, fol. 126r (29 March 1716). Yuḥanna al-ʿUjaymī, expelled from the Collegio Urbano, left to live in France without the authorisation of the Propaganda: SOCG, vol. 743, fol. 16r (January-March 1750). This is not to mention those who, equipped with the necessary authorisations, went to France to collect money.

16. APF, SOCG, vol. 456, fol. 128r (1675); see a letter in Syriac from the Syrian patriarch, ibid. fols 125–26. The 'Nestorian' priest who accompanied him was called Elias. Indeed, we find an Elias, 'protector of the Church of Babylon, nephew of the patriarch of Nineveh', informing the Propaganda that he had been to Madrid to collect alms for his Church. The Queen gave him a note for 1,000 *scudi* for Naples, another for a similar sum for Sicily. But not having been paid in Naples, he asked the Congregation to intervene: SOCG, vol. 429, fol. 37rv (1671). [This Elias surely is to be identified with Ilyās al-Mawṣilī, the traveller who subsequently visited Spanish America: John-Paul Ghobrial, 'The Secret Life of Elias of Babylon and the Uses of Global Microhistory', *Past & Present*, 222 (2014), pp. 51–93.]
17. APF, SOCG, vol. 462, fols 599r–600r (Aleppo, 27 May 1676); ibid. fols 598rv, 602rv, *Sommario*.
18. APF, SOCG, vol. 471, fol. 17r, *Sommario*, and fol. 18r, copy of a letter from François Picquet. [According to Kévorkian, *Catalogue des 'incunables' arméniens*, p. 169, in February 1675 Timothy pretended to leave Paris to return to his see. But he was still in France in 1679, before crossing to Spain. On the bishop of Samos, see John-Paul Ghobrial, 'Moving Stories and What They Tell Us: Early Modern Mobility between Microhistory and Global History', *Past & Present*, 242 (2019), supplement n. 14, pp. 243–80.]
19. Graf, *Geschichte der Christlichen Arabischen Literatur*, vol. 4, pp. 54–55: *Sabʿ mazāmir al-tawba wa-madīḥa li-l-ʿadhrāʾ Maryām* (Paris, 1679).
20. APF, SOCG, vol. 481, fol. 5r–6r (Aleppo, 29 July 1680). The receipts for these funds were in the hands of the Jesuits of Marseilles, but they could be transferred to Rome. Same subject: ibid. fols 7rv, 12v (26 September 1680, François Picquet).
21. APF, SOCG, vol. 498, fol. 30r (2 September 1681).
22. On Cardinal Barbarigo, see Sebastiano Serena, 'Il cardinale Gregorio Barbarigo e l'Oriente', in *Società Italiana per il progresso delle scienze: Atti della XXVI riunione, Venezia, 12–18 settembre 1937* (Rome: Società Italiana per il progresso delle scienze, 1938), pp. 390–413, and Giacomo Poletto, 'Il Beato cardinale Gregorio Barbarigo, vescovo di Padova, e la riunione delle Chiese orientali alla romana', *Bessarione*, 1 (1906), pp. 14–31, 176–96, 305–33. APF, Acta, vol. 85,

26 March 1715, fols 128r–129v: Karnuk reported that he was for a long time 'superintendent of the Oriental languages printing-house' in Padua and that he worked for the conversion of the 'Turks', of whom he baptised twenty-eight in one go. Graf has mentioned several books published by Timothy in Padua between 1688 and 1693 (*Geschichte der Christlichen Arabischen Literatur*, vol. 4, pp. 54–55). [In Kévorkian, *Catalogue des 'incunables' arméniens*, p. 170, there is a description of the two books published in Armenian by Timothy in Padua. 'Timoteo Agnellini' appeared as a witness in the beatification process of Barbarigo: Maria Pia Pedani Fabris, 'Intorno alla questione della traduzione del Corano', in Liliana Billanovich and Pierantonio Gios (eds), *Gregorio Barbarigo patrizio veneto vescovo e cardinale nella tarda controriforma (1625–1697)* (Padua: Istituto per la storia ecclesiastica padovana, 1999), p. 361, quoting Sebastiano Serena, *S. Gregorio Barbarigo e la vita spirituale e culturale nel suo Seminario di Padova* (Padua: Antenore, 1963), p. 156.]

23. APF, SOCG, vol. 535, fols 178r–181v, *Ristretto* (synthetic report of the archives) of the Propaganda), 1700. This document mentions the fact that Marracci examined Timothy at the end of his studies and considered him sufficiently educated. On Marracci, see Gian Luca d'Errico (ed.), *Il Corano e il pontifice: Ludovico Marracci fra cultura islamica e Curia papale* (Rome: Carocci Editore, 2015).
24. APF, SOCG, vol. 497, fol. 337r; vol. 500, fols 200rv, 202rv; ibid. fol. 204rv (Padua, 16 October 1687).
25. APF, SOCG, vol. 528, fol. 489r (1697). An Armenian merchant, Isacco di Pietro, is mentioned as being in prison following Karnuk's intervention: SOCG, vol. 535, fols 178r–181v (1700), and in the report by Cardinal Cantelmo: Acta, vol. 68, 18 August 1698, 8, *Soria*. The originals examined at this plenary session are missing from the series SOCG. The testimony of Antonio of Nineveh is in SOCG, vol. 536, fols 421r–426v (19 July 1700): He asserted that he had served Timothy for five years in Naples and its kingdom, for 2 *zecchini* a month and a dress every two years, and he asked to be paid.
26. APF, SOCG vol. 536, fols 421r–426v, 19 July 1700. The documents concerning this affair were passed on to the Holy Office in 1695, but in July 1700 the Propaganda had still not received an answer.
27. APF, Acta, vol. 70, 14 June 1700, 1, *Soria*: Karnuk, back from Naples to defend himself, asked for the '*parte di palazzo*' and the right to celebrate mass.
28. APF, Acta, vol. 72, 13 November 1702, 10, *Soria*.
29. APF, Acta, vol. 73, 26 March 1703, 10, *Soria*.
30. APF, SC, Siri, vol. 1, fol. 400rv (15 December 1705), 402rv (24 May 1706): receipts for fifteen books from the Propaganda, in Armenian, Arabic, Hebrew, Greek, Syriac, Turkish and 'Egyptian' (Coptic).
31. APF, Acta, vol. 76, 22 November 1706, 12, *Stampa*.
32. Wipertus Rudt de Collenberg, 'Le baptême des musulmans esclaves à Rome aux XVIIe et XVIIIe siècles: Le XVIIIe siècle', *Mélanges de l'École française de Rome: Italie et Méditerranée*, 101, 2 (1989), p. 554, 'Timoteo Angellini' (sic) gave his name to two godsons, in 1708 and 1710.

33. APF, Acta, vol. 78, 27 March 1708, 18, *Soria.*
34. APF, Acta, vol. 81, 7 September 1711, 20, *Stampa*; ibid. 14 December 1711, 14, *Stampa.*
35. APF, Acta, vol. 82, 25 January 1712, 32, *Stampa.*
36. APF, SC, Maroniti, vol. 3, fols 389r–391v, 395rv, 397rv, 399r–401r, 404r–405v: dossier concerning the affairs of Michele Metoscita (see above, note 5) in 1724–25. Metoscita gathered in Malta all the materials necessary for a printing press, but with funds belonging to other donors. There was also question of 1,800 copies of three booklets printed at his expense which, at 1 *scudo* per booklet, would have been worth 600 Roman *scudi*, owed him by someone else. SC, Maroniti, vol. 4, fols 121r–123v (27 May 1730): on the death of Michele Metoscita, the Propaganda asked the Inquisitor in Malta to confiscate the types, a great number of books and other belongings of the deceased, for which an inventory was listed (ibid. fols 212r–215v, 26 June 1730).
37. APF, SOCG, vol. 568, fols 50r–51v, 58r (Italian translation), 56r (original Arabic), 53rv (original Arabic and Italian translation): Filippo Gailan (see note 15) in his turn settled at the seminary of Padua, and the protégé of Barbarigo's successor, Cardinal Cornaro, declared that his speculations were destined '*per profitarmi di qualche lucro per sostentarmi e per le spese di stampare in Padua li salmi di David in idioma Arabo*'. But a Jesuit from Damascus, Fr. Jean Barse, accused him of dealing in the books printed in Padua (ARSI, *Gallia*, vol. 96, III, fols 463–465). APF, Acta, vol. 89, 2 May 1719, fols 146r–147v: the French consul in Tripoli accused the Maronite patriarch of selling to priests at the highest price those books that the Propaganda sent him, to be distributed free of charge; the Maronite experts consulted by the Congregation did not deny this but tried to justify it: ibid. fols 229v–230r. [On this issue, see Bernard Heyberger, 'Livres et pratique de la lecture chez les chrétiens (Syrie, Liban), XVIIe–XVIIIe siècles', *Revue des mondes musulmans et de la Méditerranée*, 87–88 (1999), pp. 209–23.]
38. APF, Acta, vol. 80, 11 November 1710, 15, *Soria*; vol. 81, 23 March 1711, 29, *Soria.* A list of seven prelates who had been ordered to go back to the East and who asked to stay: ibid. 12 January 1711, 2, *Soria, Armeni.*
39. APF, Acta, vol. 84, 24 September 1714, 18, *Soria.*
40. APF, Acta, vol. 85, 26 March 1715, fols 128r–129v.
41. APF, Acta, vol. 86, 10 March 1716, fols 74v–75r ('et hora che appena si tiene in piedi, gli è entrato lo spirito e zelo d'esser patriarca').
42. Graf, *Geschichte der Christlichen Arabischen Literatur*, vol. 4, pp. 54–55.
43. Joseph Hajjar, *Les Chrétiens uniates du Proche-Orient* (Paris: Seuil, 1962), pp. 244–45; John Joseph, *Muslim-Christian Relations and Inter-Christian Rivalries in the Middle-East: The Case of the Jacobites in an Age of Transition* (Albany: SUNY Press, 1983), pp. 40–48.
44. See the report of the Secretary of the Propaganda Urbano Cerri, '*Informatione dello Stato della Religione cattolica in tutto il mondo . . .* ' (APF, Miscellanee Varie, vol. 4 and 13). French edition of the same text: Urbano Cerri, *État présent de l'Église romaine dans toutes les parties du monde écrit pour l'usage du Pape Innocent*

XI par Mgr Urbano Cerri, Secrétaire de la congrégation de Propaganda Fide (Amsterdam: Pierre Humbert, 1716).

45. Heyberger, *Les chrétiens du Proche-Orient*, pp. 417–24. In Gerhard Podskalsky, *Griechische Theologie in der Zeit der Türkenherrschaft (1453–1821)* (Munich: C. H. Beck Verlag, 1988), we find mention of several examples of Greeks educated in Italy who later became leaders of the anti-Latin reaction.
46. See Heyberger, 'Sécurité et insécurité' [see Chapter 3 in this volume], for some examples of lay people. As for ecclesiastical examples, Filippo Gailan sent a parcel of fine garments from Venice (worth 406 ducats), which he intended to sell for 600 ducats in Damascus, through the intermediary of his 'friends' and family (see above, note 37 of this chapter [see also Chapter 1 of this volume]. Michele Metoscita placed the money received as alms for a seminary to be settled in Mount Lebanon with some Eastern businessmen, who used it to pay for their court case against the privateers of Malta (see above, note 36). The same person was involved in a transaction, in which he refused to give the 1,000 *scudi* which he was supposed to lend to the Melkite traders of Egypt, through the intermediary of Name Facher (Niʿma Fakhr), settled in Livorno. On this occasion, the Propaganda informed him that these affairs were not compatible with the 'clerical state': APF, Acta, vol. 86, fols 183v–184r, 9 June 1723. Benigno (Lotfi) and Mosè di Nicola, Melkites from Aleppo, tried to recuperate the inheritance of their uncle, the Discalced Carmelite ʿAbdallāh ibn Dawūd (Teodoro d'Aut, see above, note 7), according to them unjustly usurped by the Parisian heirs of Cardinal de la Trémoille: SC, Greci Melchiti, vol. 2, fol. 33r (8 December 1725). Ibn Jubayr al-Ḥalabī (see note 5) settled in Malta and was asked by the Fakhr brothers to look after their business in the case against the Maltese privateers: SC, Greci Melchiti, vol. 2, fols 45rv, 48r (Italian translation: Niʿma Fakhr, Satalia, 28 May 1726), 46v, 47r (Arabic original). Bishop Athanasius Safar, Karnuk's direct competitor who brought back considerable sums of money from New Spain, was then able to live off his income in Rome and gave his heirs the benefit of it. See the accounts of his travels to America in SOCG, vol. 519, fols 174r–175r, 176r. Giovanni Domenico Safar, his nephew, who was living in Rome, received a regular pension from 1737 onwards. After his death in 1753, the cardinals extended the pension in favour of his widow and daughters: Acta, vol. 123, 15 January 1753, 16, *Soriani*. On the widow's death, a new request was made to the Propaganda in favour of a forty-year-old daughter, and it was granted: Acta, vol. 140, 2 April 1770, fols 71r–72r.
47. Bernard Heyberger, '*Pro nunc, nihil respondendum*: Recherche d'informations et prise de décision à la Propagande: L'exemple du Levant (XVIIIe siècle)', *Mélanges de l'École française de Rome: Italie et Méditerranée*, 109, 2 (1997), pp. 539–54.

CHAPTER 3

Security and Insecurity: Syrian Christians in the Mediterranean (Seventeenth and Eighteenth Centuries)

This chapter is the modest result of what Giovanni Levi has called an 'intensive technique for the reconstruction of the biographical events' of a number of Christians from Syria.[1] While some have questioned the validity of a method that starts on the level of the individual, such an approach has the advantage of enabling one to determine a certain coherence among individual attitudes, faced with events considered part of 'great history'. What appears from these analyses is the existence of a rationalisation of behaviour, a strategy on the personal or family level. But it is a strategy that aimed not solely at economic objectives. Returning to Giovanni Levi's analysis, we may say that it sought less the realisation of simple, predetermined economic concerns alone than the managing of uncertainty.[2] What no doubt obsessed the Christians of the Middle East, like men from *ancien régime* societies in general, was a guarantee of security in the face of unpredictable events.

Let us begin with an observation: there was a continuous circulation of people and goods between Italy and the Middle East. The enormous proportion of documents concerning Syrian Christians, and Eastern matters in general, in the archives of the Congregation *de Propaganda Fide* in Rome reveals the dominance of the Mediterranean in a Vatican ministry which might be expected to be more preoccupied by the missions of America or China during this period.

One should bear in mind that the religious, cultural, or even spiritual connections with the Catholic West were always accompanied by economic relations. Furthermore, the symbolic advantages gained from connecting with the Roman Church could be exploited financially and socially by those who benefitted from them. This is not surprising: the small Churches of the Middle East blended in with the confessional group (*ṭāʾifa*) that they defined, and local lay notables played a predominant role in their midst. One therefore must avoid trying to separate the socio-economic sphere from the religious one.

THE SEARCH FOR ALMS AND PROTECTION

The 'Persecutions'

In the registers of the Congregation *de Propaganda Fide*, there appear a certain number of people who, once in Rome, went to the cardinals to obtain financial support. They were not only Easterners: we can also find exiles from Protestant countries. The Catholics who came from the Ottoman Empire usually cited as the reason for their presence in Christian lands the fact that they had to flee persecution from both Orthodox and Muslims on account of their adherence to Catholicism, and that they had risked losing their life or their faith. In order to obtain help (always modest) or a recommendation to a potential sponsor, they had to show the Roman bureaucracy letters of introduction in their favour, signed by Latin missionaries or French consuls from their country of origin. Otherwise, as often seen in the records, they could meet with a negative response.

Thus, by a decree dated 14 October 1644, the Congregation welcomed in the Roman colleges a *Khūrī* from Aleppo and his son, who had come to Rome, sent by the Carmelites of their town, 'so that they not be perverted'.[3] A note that must date from 1662, meanwhile, evoked a certain Francesco di Paolo of Aleppo, who had fled with his two daughters, aged eighteen and fourteen, to avoid the danger of losing his life or his faith. Embarked on a Muslim ship, he was stripped of all his goods by Maltese corsairs and found himself in Rome with no means of support.[4] In 1724, Mosè and Benigno from Aleppo, sons of Nicola, stated that they had suffered prison, chains and beatings for their faith, and so they turned to Rome. They had suffered during the voyage on account of their great poverty and asked for a recommendation, to go to seek alms in Vienna and Germany.[5]

If we have to assess the veracity of these reasons, I would say that they are only half true. It is true that Christians in their affairs were not treated equally with Muslims (particularly in the courts) and that, if wealthy, their fortune could subject them to pressure to convert to Islam, to give their daughters in marriage to Muslims, or to renounce collecting their own credits. But the divisions between Christians of the same rite, even within the same family, often were the real origin of these 'persecutions' by the 'Turks'.[6]

Most often, these fugitives were in fact fleeing their creditors. The reason for what they called 'their persecution' was less their Catholic faith than their inability to honour their debts. It was certainly possible that their confessional commitment could be the cause of their material ruin, if an adjudicating qadi decided to exploit dissent between Christians for his own gain.[7] The children or wife of the fugitive were frequently referred to as being held by the creditors, and in these cases there certainly was a danger of forced conversion for these hostages, if the head of the family did not manage to pay back his debts.[8]

On 8 April 1680, for example, a certain Niʿmatallāh gave a detailed account of his life story. A native of Mardin, where he apparently led a comfortable existence, he operated as a merchant between Aleppo and Persia. But he suffered a setback that he attributed to the fact of his conversion to Catholicism which, he said, caused difficulties stirred up by the Nestorians. He therefore decided to leave Aleppo with his wife and children. Still too 'weak' to practise trade, 'I therefore bounced back and produced pure silk, woven with gold and silver, which gave me access to Turkish notables'. He lived in Aleppo for nearly twenty years and served Catholicism devotedly, but he found himself burdened with a considerable debt of 4,000 *scudi* to some 'Turks'. He then left his sons as hostages and joined François Picquet, former French consul in Aleppo, in Marseille. The latter wrote in his favour to the princes of the Church, but Niʿmatallāh, aged sixty at the time he wrote his account, found no help in Rome when he arrived.

How much truth is there in this narrative, and to what extent did François Picquet and the missionaries of Aleppo really plead the case of Niʿmatallāh before the cardinals? Whatever the case, two successive requests from him met with negative answers (*lectum*) on the part of the cardinals.[9]

The Insecurity of Maritime Trade[10]

Besides the landed notables in Lebanon and the clergy, whom we will leave aside, the supplications addressed to the Catholic Church most frequently came from merchants. Maritime exchanges were the principal reasons for resorting to Rome.

In some cases, the plaintiff had invested sums borrowed from Muslims in maritime trade. These deals were often founded on a system of partnerships called '*mudābara*', as described by Bruce Masters for Aleppo. This was a verbal agreement sworn before a judge and two witnesses, according to which the profit was to be shared following the terms of the agreement fixed beforehand, and a relative served as guarantor of the contract. According to the same author, the most typical situation was one where a Muslim provided the money, while the Christian made the voyage.[11]

This was the case of George, a Cypriot of the Greek rite, whose son was held as guarantee of a loan in 1676. His caique with its merchandise was captured by a knight of Malta, who promised to give back the ship and its load in exchange for a payment of 4,500 *scudi*. Eventually, the corsair did return the ship, but not its cargo. The Maronite patriarch asked for an intervention on George's behalf to free his son.[12]

As in this example, engaging in maritime trade involved facing great dangers, the main one being encounters with 'Frankish' corsairs. Once again according to Masters, the risk was assumed entirely by the provider of the capital. In fact, we need to imagine more complex types of contracts. Without a doubt, merchandise that belonged to Muslim traders was declared as belonging to Levantine

Christians and loaded onto ships whose *ra'īs* and sailors were Christians, to try to escape the *corso*. In such cases, Christians pillaged by Western corsairs might well be suspected by their Muslim associates of complicity with the attackers.

This is the explanation given in 1712 by the offices of Cosimo II, Duke of Etruria, to a request from the Propaganda asking that Tuscan ships not take the merchandise of Syrian Catholics. According to them, the 'Turks' had obliged the Catholic Melkite archbishop of Tyre and Sidon, Aftīmyūs Ṣayfī, as well as missionaries from these cities to counter-sign their own merchandise, so as to safeguard against attacks from Christian ships.[13] This is also what can be concluded from a detailed report, dating from the 1720s, on the subject of Ibrahīm Massad and Ibrahīm Massara, Christians from Aleppo settled in Cairo, who traded between Egypt and Syria on their ship, the *Saint George*. They held passports from the Holy See in due form, but had their merchandise confiscated by the Maltese, on the pretext that it belonged to Muslims. The two petitioners claimed that, on the contrary, it belonged to good Catholics and that the corsairs brutalised the *ra'īs*, who was a Greek Catholic from Candia, along with his sailors, to get them to sign a paper recognising that the merchandise belonged to 'Turks'. But at the same time, they asserted that the 'Turks' suspected them of being on the side of the 'Franks' and that their children (presumably serving as hostages) were in danger of renouncing their faith.[14]

The Christian *corso* in the Eastern Mediterranean, usually under a Maltese flag, was one of the main sources of problems for the Syrian Christians who turned to Rome at the end of the seventeenth century and in the first decades of the eighteenth century, or who went to Italy in order to obtain safe-conducts, or to demand justice after their merchandise or ships had been taken.

We know that the Christian *corso* of the seventeenth and eighteenth centuries had no other aim than to provide booty for the ship-owners, who could have obtained a patent from the Grand Master to this effect. Some business-minded Knights of Malta supplied the capital necessary to equip the great ships of the corsairs. The struggle against the infidel, which was not the real aim of this maritime activity, only existed as an alibi for official declarations. The private corsairs, acting with a patent from the Order of Malta, or in the name of another European sovereign, sometimes practised acts of pure piracy, particularly in the Eastern Mediterranean, at the beginning of the eighteenth century.[15]

This insecurity favoured Western maritime transport, and especially the French, for the Muslim traders could load 'Frankish' ships to escape the corsairs.[16] But trade within the Ottoman Empire, which was far from negligible, remained mostly in the hands of the Ottomans themselves. The fact that Catholic Ottoman Christians could count on pontifical safe-conducts to protect themselves from the corsairs helped to strengthen their role in maritime liaisons, particularly in the cabotage between the Syrian coast and Damietta.[17] In a detailed report from 1711 – concerning recent attacks by corsairs from Malta, Corsica and Livorno on the coasts of Palestine – the Guardian of the Holy Land, Lorenzo di San Lorenzo, explained that in the stretch of sea between Mount Carmel, Saint John of Acre and Jaffa they met no Muslim ships. Greek caiques transported the merchandise, of which only part belonged to Muslims.

Regardless, the corsairs seized all shipments on the pretext that they belonged to the 'infidels'. Thus, the *corso* was aimed directly at the Greeks, not the 'Turks', who had practically no ships, apart from a few crossings to Constantinople. The Guardian added further proof that the *corso* was directed against Christians: he wrote that there were never as many corsairs' ships as around Easter time, when pilgrims were coming and going. They were stripped of almost everything. Moreover, when Muslim merchandise was seized on a ship, the Friars of the Holy Land were held responsible, and the owners tried to extort repayment from them, with the complicity of the Turkish courts.[18]

We can thus see to what extent politics, economics and confessional belonging were intimately linked. That is why an Eastern Christian's being a Catholic, or a militant Orthodox, or refusing to decide between the two options was a reply to relatively complex strategies of security, making use of all these registers. This is illustrated by the case of the Ibn Fakhr family from Tripoli.[19]

MARITIME TRADE, SOCIAL COMPETITION AND CATHOLICISM

The Catholicism of the Fakhr Family[20]

In 1701, the Melkite archbishop of Tripoli in Syria promised obedience to the Catholic Church, sending a profession of faith to Rome, accompanied by the necessary certificates from missionaries and from a French consul.[21] In the following years, the same Bishop Makāryūs several times had occasion to send requests to the Propaganda, receiving books and liturgical objects in response. He told of the attacks that he had suffered from the Melkite patriarch of Damascus, Cyril al-Zaʿīm, who was hostile to Catholics at the time. To address this, he had to borrow large sums and pledge his church's wealth as a guarantee. In 1707 he asked the Congregation for help to be able to buy himself out.[22]

In 1705 and 1707, one of his nephews, Elia (Ilyās) Fakhr – approved by the French 'nation' in Tripoli and a zealous Catholic according to the information that reached the Secretary of the Propaganda – asked for and obtained from the cardinals, through the intermediary of French missionaries who were delegates in Rome, works printed on the multi-lingual presses of the Congregation, 'to conquer the errors of his schismatic compatriots'.[23] At the same time, Ilyās put his knowledge of languages and his culture at the service of the Catholic Reformation. He translated into Arabic Greek works that were favourable to Roman theses, particularly the very widely distributed *vade mecum* for a priest, composed by Neophytos Rhodinos (printed in Rome in 1628 and 1635), as well as a confessor's handbook in the form of questions and answers by the same author. In 1713, he was rewarded for his Catholic zeal with the title of Knight of the Golden Spur.[24]

In 1711, one of Ilyās's brothers, Michele Name (Mikhā'īl Niʿma) Fakhr, a merchant from Tripoli, settled in Livorno. Recommended to the Propaganda by his uncle, Bishop Makāryūs, for all his affairs in Rome and in Italy, he served as the former's proxy. It is he who, having come to the Christian capital, was given the job of obtaining from the cardinals and Pope Clement XI himself permission for his uncle the archbishop to grant plenary indulgences at the hour of death, to the faithful, or to members of his family.[25]

The same Niʿma rendered various services to the Catholic cause. In 1713, Sarufīm Ṭānās, nephew of the Catholic Melkite Archbishop Aftīmyūs Ṣayfī and future patriarch of his 'nation', recommended Niʿma to the Propaganda, describing him as a young man who was a missionary in Livorno and very devoted to the Church, given to reaching out to any schismatic, to try to convince him by force of reason or argument, just like his brother in Tripoli.[26]

It would be wrong to neglect this search for a good Catholic reputation in the life of the Fakhr family. For them, it was not merely a question of self-interested strategy to obtain the favour of the Roman protectors. The accumulation of 'symbolic capital' and the exchange of non-material goods (decorations and diplomas, books and devotional objects, and indulgences) that made up this symbolic capital were not negligible in the construction of their system of social relations in Tripoli and elsewhere. In general, the many requests for indulgences, the rise of devotional brotherhoods in the eighteenth century, the pious foundations (*waqfs*) to benefit Catholic monasteries in Lebanon, all went to show that the spiritual blessings generously spread by Rome were ardently sought-after by Eastern Christians who became Catholics and helped to inspire them with a feeling of security as regarded their future on earth and in Heaven.

The Affairs of the Fakhr Family

However, the presence of Niʿma Fakhr in Livorno (and briefly in Rome) also had less edifying reasons. In fact, he had come to Italy to try to obtain restitution or a refund for a 'large cargo' taken by Maltese and Livornese corsairs between the Archipelago and Syria.[27] During those years, attacks by corsairs on the Syrian coasts were particularly harmful to local Christian traders. In his above-mentioned report of November 1711, Lorenzo di San Lorenzo gave numerous details of these attacks, which for a while even prevented passage between Acre and Jaffa. Among the aggressors were Antonio Franceschi (or Franceschini) and one of his relatives, who remained in the region all year and plundered numerous caiques.[28] These were the same men who in 1710 had seized a ship belonging to the Greek Church of Saida and taken it to Livorno.

The Catholic Archbishop of the town, Aftīmyūs Ṣayfī, first applied to the Grand Master of Malta to obtain reparation, but the latter sent him away, saying he had no jurisdiction over the people from Livorno.[29] This was certainly splitting hairs: another document asserted that captain Franceschi was, in fact, 'of the religion of Malta'. While one could appeal against the judgements of the Maltese courts before the Church court, it was not the same for those of another jurisdiction: the Tuscan flag afforded better protection from findings that were too favourable to Christian victims.[30]

Ṣayfī then asked Rome to recommend his delegate (Niʿma Fakhr) in this affair, in order to have justice rendered in Livorno, while at the same time making energetic protests against the practices of the corsairs, whom he described as worse than the thieves and assassins to be found in Muslim lands and who prevented any progress of the Catholic faith by their crimes. Bishop Makāryūs of Tripoli and the 'Frankish' missionaries were mobilised to plead the affair in Europe, and delegates were sent to Italy.[31] The Propaganda intervened with the Tuscan and Maltese authorities but received only vague promises that attempted to discredit the Levantine Christians.

There is no doubt that the corsairs benefitted from the benevolent complicity of the courts, which were in no hurry to restore their goods to Eastern Christians, even if they were good Catholics and warmly supported by the Church. The Grand Duke of Tuscany, encouraged by Rome, intervened in favour of the Levantine Christians, and a document arrived at the Congregation from Livorno in June 1712, assuring the cardinals that the affair had been settled, that captain Franceschi would give back the ship and its cargo, and that he would only keep the merchandise that belonged to Muslims.[32] But a year later, nothing was settled. At the recommendation of the Propaganda, Niʿma Fakhr started legal proceedings against the captain, seeking restitution of his merchandise. In June he had received nothing, and the Fakhr family suffered another depredation from pirates, for which they began new proceedings.[33] Sarufīm Ṭānās – sent by his uncle, Bishop Aftīmyūs Ṣayfī – was received the same year by the Grand Duke of Tuscany, who demanded that the governor of Livorno see justice done. The captain again promised to return the merchandise but stalled the process further by contesting the validity of the documents that were presented to him. Sarufīm went back to the Levant, entrusting his interests to Niʿma Fakhr.[34]

In August of the same year (1713), an Observantine Franciscan who had returned from the Levant wrote from Livorno that Giuseppe Francesco, a relative of the Maronite patriarch who had come with authentic attestations 'clearer than the sun at midday' to reclaim merchandise which had been taken by the corsair Franceschini, had been threatened with punishment and prison. Unable to return to his country on account of his debts, or to stay in Livorno because of his poverty, he left, desperate, to 'become a Turk' (convert to Islam) in Algiers. Friar Giovanni Giuseppe added that Niʿma Fakhr and his proxy had acted, but obtained nothing, the *principali* of Livorno having a stake in the corsairs' armaments. He reported that the indignant Easterners came to see him, thundering that 'the French are dogs, that they only seek Catholics in the Levant to be able to eat them, and to keep them as slaves in their jurisdiction, without bringing them any relief from the hard slavery where they find themselves'.[35]

We do not know the outcome of these cases. However, Niʿma Fakhr did not spend all his time on court cases. In 1715, Jibrāʾīl ibn Ankārī al-Ḥalabī al-Mārūnī (a Maronite from Aleppo), an unhappy and freshly graduated pupil of a Roman college, recounted that among his recent misfortunes he had to forfeit books given to him by the Propaganda on his departure from Rome and to borrow from Fakhr 100 *scudi* ('with interest') at Livorno.[36]

At that time, Syrian Christians already had connections with Egypt. As previously stated, it was not persecution against Catholics (after the clash of 1724 in the Greek Antiochian Church) that were the basis of their first settlements in this country.[37] In 1716, Niʿma went to the Propaganda as 'proxy for the merchants of Egypt', asking the Propaganda to intervene with Michele Metoscita, a Maronite from Cyprus and former student of the Maronite college in Rome, who had settled in Malta and who, according to Niʿma, owed 1,000 *pezzi di otto*, which he refused to pay.[38]

The Fakhr family again appears in the sources a few years later. In 1725, the three brothers Giovanni, Elia (Ilyās) and Name (Niʿma) approached the Propaganda concerning their ships, which had been taken by the Maltese.[39] The following year, Niʿma, this time settled in Satalia, returned to the fray to complain about every day being manhandled by the Maltese, who had taken two of his ships in two years. The first, having left Damietta laden with merchandise for Satalia, was intercepted near Cyprus and taken to Malta. His brother and companion in business, Giovanni, who lived in Damietta, sent a representative to the island's courts. The corsairs confiscated the cargo and gave the ship back to the *raʾīs*, who returned to the Levant. But they gave no compensation for the merchandise, or for the goods, and stripped the ship of most of its equipment. When the representative asked for it back, he received the reply that the complaint, in order to be considered, had to be presented by the plaintiff in person. Another of the Fakhr family's ships, on its way from Damietta to Cyprus, was intercepted by the same captain Antonachi and loaded with soap at Tyre. Giovanni sent Niʿma a mandate so that he could go to Malta himself. But the latter did not want to leave Satalia, fearing that rivals ('heretics') would take advantage of this to seize his goods. Therefore, he delegated the job to the Melkite priest Neofito Giubair (Nāwufītūs ibn Jubayr al-Ḥalabī), the former Catholic priest of Damietta, who had settled in Malta. He asked the Propaganda to forward his dossier to the latter and to have the mandate accepted.[40]

Business, Confessional Choice, Local Solidarities

These examples have demonstrated the entanglement of Catholic zeal with commercial affairs. There existed a Mediterranean network of Melkite and Maronite Catholics whose security strategy passed via Rome. For them, Catholicism should have been a guarantee against the attacks of the corsairs, thus ensuring privilege in matters of trade. But we can see that this was not the case in so far as the Church was not obeyed in Malta or Livorno and that Eastern Christians felt a great sense of outrage when faced with the ineffectiveness of the Roman *raccomandazione*.

In 1726, at the time of Niʿma's letter, the Catholicism of the Fakhr family was already suspect in Rome. On 15 April 1725, Ilyās Fakhr, with his title of Roman knight, sought to justify himself in a note addressed to the cardinals of the Propaganda. In this, he presented himself, using arguments that were somewhat polemical, as 'still Catholic', a defender of the Catholic faith and the Roman primate, and he set out the reasons why he believed Catholicism did not flourish in the Levant.[41]

The attacks by the Maltese corsairs, as well as the difficulties of obtaining justice in the Christian tribunals, constituted one of the causes that Ilyās Fakhr put forward. He evoked the case of his brother Giovanni who, having lost 5,000 piastres' worth of goods this way, sent a proxy to Malta, with papers notarised by the French consul in Cairo, but who received no answer. These practices, he said, were the reason for the great hatred felt towards the Church by those schismatics who accused Rome of giving licence to plunder and theft. The argument was used again in the letter from Niʿma the following year.

But llyās' detachment from Catholicism had other reasons that originated in the Middle East itself. The Fakhrs found themselves associated with the Archbishop of Saida, Aftīmyūs Ṣayfī, and his family who, as we have seen, were also victims of the Maltese and Livorno *corso*. It is probable that Ilyās might temporarily have put his skills at Ṣayfī's service to write a controversial work in Arabic.[42] If there had once been links of friendship between the two families, this was no longer the case in 1723, when the tailor of Damascus, al-Usṭā Manṣūr, brother of Ṣayfī, wrote in a report to the Propaganda that, according to both himself and the Jesuit and Capuchin missionaries, Ilyās was a Catholic in name only, but not in reality, and that he was probably even hostile to the faith.[43] The same year, a Jesuit from Tripoli reported that Ilyās had been charged with the job of making copies of a book by the Englishman Sherman, which was 'a rhapsody for the strongest things that the sectarians had invented in Europe against the authority of the pope'.[44]

When Ilyās wrote to the Propaganda in 1725 to answer these accusations, he was living in Aleppo, where he was acting as dragoman to the English consul, a function he retained for many years. But one could be a good Catholic and at the same time serve the English honestly.[45] In fact, Ilyās Fakhr had joined the cause of the Patriarch Athanasius (Athanāsyūs) Dabbās. The latter, having been reinstated as head of the Melkite Church after the death of Cyril al-Zaʿīm in 1720, being fairly distrustful of the Latin believers and seeking to maintain good relations with Orthodoxy and with Rome, came up against some zealous Catholics, led by Aftīmyūs Ṣayfī and his nephew Sarufīm Ṭānās, who had set their hearts on the patriarchate for themselves. Athanasius Dabbās died in 1724; Sylvester the Cypriot, Constantinople's candidate for the see of Antioch, was supposed to succeed him. But instead, the Damascenes chose Sarufīm Ṭānās, under the name of Cyril.[46] This was the beginning of the schism among the Melkites, between Catholics and Orthodox. One must note that the people of Tripoli, unlike those of Damascus and Aleppo, aligned themselves under the banner of Orthodoxy. Sylvester stayed in their town and was painting icons there in 1726.

In 1725, Cyril Ṭānās still was not officially recognised in Rome as the Catholic patriarch. In his letter to the Propaganda, Ilyās opposed the attitude of past missionaries – who had shown respect and civility towards the Eastern clergy and had considered their masses and rites to be valid – to that of their successors who applied the prohibition of the *communicatio in divinis* pronounced in Rome, thus prohibiting Catholics from being associated with any liturgy and ceremony presided over by a non-united clergy. This accusation against the missionaries, as divisive trouble-makers attracting the faithful to the Latin rite, was constantly found during the eighteenth century, even among the most fervent Catholics.[47] However, Ilyās reproached Aftīmyūs Ṣayfī and his disciples for their disobedience towards the patriarchs and for the introduction on their own initiative of dogmatic and liturgical innovations, arguments towards which Rome was not insensitive and that both Cyril al-Zaʿīm and Athanasius Dabbās had put forward in their time. Finally, he contested the legitimacy of the election of Cyril Ṭānās, which was still not considered secure in the eyes of the Roman authorities.

In the ensuing years, when the action of the Orthodox Patriarch Sylvester, supported by Constantinople, and Rome's recognition of Cyril Ṭānās as legitimate Catholic patriarch obliged the Melkites to choose clearly between Catholicism and Orthodoxy, the ambivalent position of the Fakhr family became impossible to maintain. Ilyās' uncle, Bishop Makāryūs of Tripoli, after having received spiritual blessings in Rome, this time guaranteed his salvation for the next world by settling icons as donations (*waqf*), 'for the repose of his soul and those of his parents'.[48] Ilyās Fakhr, for many years, was to use his zeal for the benefit of the anti-Catholic controversy, attacking in particular the pillars of post-Tridentine dogma (namely, the primacy of Rome, the nature of transubstantiation, purgatory, the Immaculate Conception and the virginity of Saint Joseph).[49] His doctrinal turnabout was undoubtedly accompanied by social choices. In 1756, a new pasha was appointed at Aleppo, who arrived accompanied by a doctor of Greek origin from Constantinople. The latter came to an agreement with Ilyās to obtain a firman deporting the Catholic Melkite archbishop of the town, Maksīmūs al-Ḥakīm, to the citadel of Adana. But the protections for Catholics in Istanbul were also powerful. Through the mediation of the Maronite al-Khawāja Ḥannā ʿAsayla, the pasha-appointed representative (*wakīl*) of the four Christian *ṭāʾifa*s of Aleppo, whose brother was the sultan's doctor, the Catholics turned the situation around in their favour and had Maksīmūs brought back five months later. According to the same source, the English, considering Ilyās Fakhr to be guilty of a fault against them, sent him back to Tripoli shortly afterwards.[50]

To my mind, this range of biographical details of the Fakhr family points to the fact that, while the needs of the Mediterranean economy should not be ignored in understanding the strategies of Eastern Christians, their preoccupations cannot be reduced to just these alone. The internal local organisation of these small social groups, the Christian *ṭāʾifa*s, belonging to one solidarity network or another, was obviously taken into account by individuals such as Ilyās Fakhr, who aligned himself with the party of Athanasius Dabbās, then that of Sylvester the Cypriot, against the party of Ṣayfī and of Ṭānās.

We can thus appreciate that, from this point of view, it is not possible to establish a clear distinction between the purely material aims of survival or social success, on one hand, and identity issues at stake, on the other hand, which made Eastern Christians envy the indulgences and devotional techniques offered by the Roman Church or translate Greek works of anti-Latin controversy. We are thus in the presence of a more general search for security, both material and spiritual, as has been suggested by Jean Delumeau.[51]

Many Western observers of the period evoked the duplicity and deceit of the Eastern Christians and made it an ethnic characteristic.[52] Volney, more subtle than others, sought its origins in their education and in the government's attitude towards them.[53] These 'faults' were certainly not the prerogative of the Christians of the Levant, and without a doubt they were no more frequent among them than among other national, social and religious groups.[54] One could moreover consider commendable and legitimate the attitude of someone like Ilyās Fakhr, who still tried not to choose between Rome and Constantinople in 1725. But one should avoid going from historical analysis to moral judgement. Let us be content to underline that, for a security strategy to be efficient, for it to be able to manage the unexpected, it has to have several irons in the fire, to be able to play one against the other. Ambivalence was still encouraged by the complexities of the institutional position of these Christian minorities in the Ottoman Empire.

This study relies solely on sources preserved in the West. However, it is obvious that the Eastern Christians, in their search for economic and political security, did not confine themselves to a *tête-à-tête* with the Roman Church or

French diplomacy. Just as from the religious point of view they had a tendency to add Catholic and Orthodox imports to their own traditions, from an economic and political point of view, they knew well how to combine with their Western networks their good relations with Muslim notables or the Eastern Churches. Further articles, based on other sources, may help to clarify Christian security strategies in the Ottoman Empire.[55]

NOTES

1. Giovanni Levi, *Le pouvoir au village: Histoire d'un exorciste dans le Piémont du XVIIe siècle* (Paris: Gallimard, 1989), p. 12.
2. Levi, *Le pouvoir au village*, pp. 9–13, 51. See also the introduction 'L'histoire au ras du sol', by Jacques Revel, ibid. pp. xxii–xxiii.
3. APF, SOCG vol. 196, fol. 88r (14 October 1644).
4. APF, SOCG, vol. 235, fol. 123r (undated).
5. APF, SC, Greci Melchiti, vol. 2, fols 1r, 2v, 3r. See also SOCG, vol. 422, fol. 526r (1670): an Armenian from Jerusalem, a refugee in Rome for eight years, asked for money to return home. The answer: '*nihil*'. APF, SOCG, vol. 517, fol. 384r (1 February 1694): Abd Elrazzac Mesi, from Niniveh (Diyarbakir), who had to flee the persecutions of the 'Nestorians', was living in Rome, poor and sick, with his family, and asked for bread. The answer: '*lectum*'. APF, Acta, vol. 102, 16 March 1732, 1, *Maroniti*: Giuseppe Grazia, reduced to poverty due to Turkish tyranny, asked for letters of recommendation to collect money in Europe. The answer: '*lectum*'.
6. See the case of the Maronite Abū Rizq in Bernard Heyberger, *Les chrétiens du Proche-Orient au temps de la Réforme catholique* (Rome: École française de Rome, 1994), pp. 73–74. APF, SOCG, vol. 524, fol. 72r: Stefano Nacchi, former student of the Maronite college and secretary to the British consul of Aleppo, wrote from there to say that he wanted to become a Franciscan, explaining that he had been ruined by the 'Turks' while he was staying in Cyprus with his family. The Secretary of the Propaganda, having asked the Maronite college for information about him, learned that his brother and sister had made him flee Cyprus because he had wanted to seize his father's heritage (ibid. fol. 224r).
7. APF, SOCG, vol. 62, fol. 92r: in September 1644, Bruno de Saint Yves, a Discalced Carmelite missionary from Aleppo, notified the Propaganda of the case of the *shammās* Shahāde, a Maronite from his town who, burdened with debt, had left for Rome with letters of recommendation to try to get the money necessary for his reintegration. His certificates intended for the Roman authorities fell into the sea during his journey. Ibid. fol. 127r (22 September 1644): recommendation from the consul Lange Bonin for the same 'poor man'. Ibid. fol. 126r: the same thanked the Congregation for the reception of the Syrian Domenico and his family. Another case was evoked in SC, Greci Melchiti, vol. 2, fols 426r, 456rv (Italian translation), 458v (original Arabic): recommendation of Mosè Sisinio, priest of Zūq Mikhā'īl , a very zealous Catholic but burdened with debts on

account of the misfortunes he had suffered. He requested the right to celebrate mass in the Eastern rite at Livorno (fol. 594rv, 18 November 1733). Ibid. fol. 610r: he asked for this right to be extended until April 1733.

8. APF, SC, Greci Melchiti, vol. 2, fol. 80rv (10 April 1728): recommendation from Naples for a Greek Catholic from Mesopotamia, who had left a member of his family hostage with the 'Turks' to prevent the demolition of a church, dedicated to the Virgin, where he lived. SC, Greci Melchiti, vol. 4, fol. 127r and 135rv: letter from Muhalac or Mose Muchaila, a Melkite from Damascus, around 1740. Because of the role of his father in the promotion of the Catholic patriarch Cyril Ṭānās, he was apparently persecuted by the Orthodox patriarch Sylvester and deprived of his belongings. Burdened with debts towards the 'Turks', he left his wife and children and went to Christian Europe. He first asked for a letter of recommendation to go to settle in Venice, then for some financial aid. Acta, vol. 95, 22 January 1725, 9, *Greci Melchiti*: Giovanni Sciain, a Melkite priest from Jerusalem, left his son hostage with the 'Turks' and came with another son to Rome. He asked for letters of recommendation to collect alms in Christian Europe, which was refused by the Secretary. His son, Giorgio Harut, was accepted at the *Collegio Urbano*. Ibid. 7 May 1725, 3, *Greci Melchiti*: the same repeated his request and this time received letters of recommendation to the nuncios. SOCG, vol. 502, fol. 334r (5 October 1688): letter from Alduardo (ʿAṭallāh), whose sister was a widow and had three sons imprisoned and maltreated. He, a poor priest, came to ask for help to pay the ransom money. He was still in Rome two years later (SOCG, vol. 508, fol. 553r, 19 December 1690). SOCG, vol. 507, fol. 159r (12 June 1690): Michel from Bethlehem had two sons in prison. He was deprived of his goods, following a false testimony against him. In fact, all this happened because he was a true Christian.
9. APF, SOCG, vol. 478, fols 220r–221r, 222r (8 April 1680), in Latin: 'Surrexi ergo, et feci opera serica integra, et auro, argentoque contexta, qua de causa accessum habui apud magnates turcarum'. Acta, vol. 49, 11 September 1679, 12, *Soria*: previous request. SOCG, vol. 487, fol. 300r (1683): Giorgio Barbase, a Greek priest from Damascus, showed up with certificates from a Jesuit and the Franciscans: he had lost 600 piastres and asked for what he needed to survive. In Rome, he borrowed 15 *scudi* from a fellow countryman. He obtained 10 *scudi*. SC, Greci Melchiti, vol. 2, fol. 21r, 1725: Giorgio Abdalla, a Greek Catholic from Aleppo, had left his hometown for Greater Cairo, where he was accused ('by a libel', he said) of having made counterfeit money. He spent two years in prison there, then left everything to come to Rome.
10. [This chapter concerning piracy and Eastern Catholics has to be updated with Molly Greene, *Catholic Pirates and Greek Merchants: A Maritime History of the Mediterranean* (Princeton: Princeton University Press, 2010) and Cornel Zwierlein, 'Interaction and Boundary Work: Western Merchant Colonies in the Levant and the Eastern Churches, 1660–1800', *Journal of Modern European History*, 18, 2 (2020), pp. 156–76.]
11. Bruce Masters, *The Origins of Western Economic Dominance in the Middle East: Mercantilism and the Islamic Economy in Aleppo* (1600–1750) (New York: New York University Press, 1988), pp. 50, 63.

12. APF, SC, Maroniti, vol. 1, fols 174r–175v (Qannūbīn, 1 August 1676). Another case: Acta, vol. 78, 28 February 1708: Giorgi Sasi, a Greek from Damascus, borrowed 1,300 *pezzi* with interest from the 'Turks', to trade them on a boat, and lost everything. His creditors took his two sons hostage; they risked apostasy. He asked for money, recommended by a Maronite in Rome, but his request was refused. SC, Maroniti, vol. 1, fols 301r, 311r–314r, 318r–320v, 340r–341v: an obscure affair which opposed the Maronite merchant Scialub (Ḥannā Shalhūb Maʿūshī) from Jerusalem to the Friars of the Holy Land. What emerged from this was that Scialub had debts towards prominent Muslims in the town and that he came to Rome, leaving his wife and four children as a guarantee. He practised maritime trade on a large scale, for he was in correspondence with merchants in Aleppo, Damascus, Tripoli, Egypt and France, and the governors had confiscated cotton, gallnuts and three caiques, in the value of 18,000 *scudi*.
13. APF, SC, Greci Melchiti, vol. 1, fol. 131r, 19 February 1712
14. APF, SC, Maroniti, vol. 3, fols 463rv, 465r–466v; SOCG, vol. 579, fols 171r, 172r (29 May 1711): Lorenzo di San Lorenzo precisely evoked a French 'caravanier' that had picked up 120 Armenian pilgrims in Jaffa, as well as 1,100 piastres and some soap belonging to the qadi, many goods belonging to dervishes from Jerusalem and Jaffa, as well as three young 'Turks' travelling to Constantinople. The ship was attacked, and the passengers were stripped of their goods and disembarked at Haifa, while a young Muslim was drowned and two others taken as slaves. The merchandise was sold to the English consul in Haifa.
15. Michel Fontenay, 'Corsaires de la Foi ou rentiers du sol? Les chevaliers de Malte dans le "Corso" méditerranéen au XVIle siècle', *Revue d'histoire moderne et contemporaine*, 35 (1988), pp. 361–84; Michel Fontenay, 'L'Empire ottoman et le risque corsaire au XVIIe siècle', *Revue d'histoire moderne et contemporaine*, 32 (1985), pp. 185–208; Salvatore Bono, *Corsari nel Mediterraneo: Cristiani e musulmani fra guerra, schiavitû e commercio* (Milan: Mondadori, 1993), pp. 56–59. [On Christian privateers in the Mediterranean, see Anne Brogini, *Malte, frontière de Chrétienté (1530–1670)* (Rome: École française de Rome, 2006), pp. 253–331.]
16. André Raymond, *Artisans et commerçants au Caire au XVIIIe siècle*, vol. 1 (Damascus: Presses de l'IFPO, 1973), p. 170; Daniel Panzac, 'Commerce et commerçants des ports du Liban Sud et de Palestine (1756–1787)', *Revue du Monde Musulman et de la Mëditerranëe*, 55–56, 1–2 (1990), p. 91.
17. Panzac, 'Commerce et commerçants', pp. 87–92.
18. APF, SOCG, vol. 579, fols 171r–172r (29 May 1711). Daniel Panzac has noted the importance for maritime traffic of the pilgrimages made by Eastern Christians to the Holy Places ('Commerce et commerçants', p. 86). APF, SOCG, vol. 527, fols 259r–260r: in June 1697 Elia, Armenian bishop of Bethlehem, noted in detail the exemplary story of the pillage of an Armenian caravan, part of the pilgrimage from Constantinople to Jerusalem.
19. The writings of Robert M. Haddad have already partially analysed this entanglement, particularly concerning the conversion to Catholicism of the Melkite patriarch Cyril al-Zaʿīm: 'On Melkite Passage to the Unia: The Case of Patriarch Cyril al-Zaʿīm', in Benjamin Braude and Bernard Lewis (eds), *Christians*

and Jews in the Ottoman Empire: The Functioning of a Plural Society (New York, London: Holmes and Meier, 1982), vol. 2: *The Arabic-Speaking Lands*, pp. 67–90. By the same author, see also *Syrian Christians in Muslim Society: An Interpretation* (Princeton: Princeton University Press, 1970).

20. [On Ilyās Fakhr and his family, see Ronney El Gemayel, *Ḥāšiyah Waǧīzah of Ilyās Faḫr: An Arabic Byzantine Antiochian Ecclesiology Responding to Uniatism* (Rome: Pontificio Instituto Orientale, 2014), pp. 31–83.]
21. APF, SC, Greci Melchiti, vol. 1, fols 17r, 14v: profession of faith in Arabic of Makāryūs, '*muṭrān Ṭarābulus Al-Sharq*'; ibid. fols 9r–10v: criticism in Italian of this profession of faith, with testimonials from missionaries and the French consul in Tripoli; ibid. fols 18rv, 22rv: Latin translation of the profession of faith. Acta, vol. 82, 30 May 1712, 12, *Greci*: Makāryūs stated that he had been a Catholic since 1701.
22. APF, SC, Greci Melchiti, vol. 1, fols 42rv and 46r (Italian translation), 47rv (Arabic original), 50r (Italian translation), 51r (Arabic original): series of letters from Makāryūs, bishop of Tripoli. Other letters of the same: ibid. fols 70r (Italian translation), 72r–74r (January 1707). SOCG, vol. 554, fol. 522rv (26 April 1706): the same evoked the persecutions. SC, Maroniti, vol. 2, fol. 19r: 31 January 1708, receipt for the books, rosaries and other sacred objects sent to him by the Propaganda through the intermediary of the Carmelite Ferdinando di Santa Ludivina. SC, Greci Melchiti, vol. 1, fols 141v (Arabic original), 142rv (Italian translation): the same thanks for a letter received (25 January 1713).
23. APF, Acta, vol. 75, 27 January 1705, 1, *Stampa*: Bonaventura di Sant'Agata, a Friar Minor of the Observance from Tripoli, requested books for Elia, a Greek Catholic. SC, Greci Melchiti, vol. 1, fol. 78rv (25 January 1707): another request, through the intermediary of the Carmelite Ferdinando di Santa Ludivina. Acta, vol. 82, 30 May 1712, 12, *Greci*: the deacon 'Facri' was said to be 'molto benemerito de cattolici'. AN, AE, B/I, vol. 1114, fol. 11r: Ilyās Fakhr, 'Catholic, Apostolic and Roman', was cited in 1697 as an interpreter. However, Joseph Nasrallah, *Histoire du mouvement littéraire dans l'Église melchite du Ve au XXe siècle*, vol. IV, 2 (Louvain: Peeters, 1989), p. 203, has quoted the following colophon from ms. 1726 of the Greek Orthodox Patriarchate of Damascus: 'recopied on 24 December 1696 by the hand of the poorest of the universe, the sinning servant Ilyās ibn Fakhr, known (by the name of) Ibn Fakhr al-Ṭarābulsī of the Orthodox community'. This statement proves nothing, as the *rūm*s at this date were not yet divided into two communities, Catholic and Orthodox, rivals and separate.
24. Nasrallah, *Histoire*, vol. IV, 2, pp. 210–12, on the pro-Catholic work of controversy by Ilyās Fakhr. Ibid. p. 203, the author has mentioned the date of 1713 for the knighthood. On Neophytos Rhodinos and his works, see Gerhard Podskalsky, *Griechische Theologie in der Zeit der Türkenherrschaft, 1453–1821* (Munich: C. H. Beck 1988), pp. 201–5.
25. APF, SC, Greci Melchiti, vol. 1, fol. 120r (Italian translation), 121r–122v (Arabic original): Makāryūs to Cardinal Sacripante, 20 December 1711. Ibid. fol. 124r: letter by the same, on the same date, with the same request, to Pope Clement XI. Ibid. fol. 128r: same request, the same day, to the Propaganda. Ibid. fols 141v

(Arabic original), 142rv (Italian translation): Makāryūs thanked for the letter brought by Niʿma Fakhr and asked that he should be protected and helped in his affairs (25 January 1713). Acta, vol. 82, 30 May 1712, 12, *Greci*, and 2 August 1712, 7, *Stampa*: the same request mentioned the presence of Michel Grazia Facri (Mikhāʾīl Niʿma Fakhr) in Rome.

26. APF, SC, Greci Melchiti, vol. 1, fol. 169rv (Ṭānās). SC, Maroniti, vol. 2, fol. 262rv: letter from Niʿma Fakhr, from Livorno, 26 June 1713. We learn that he was charged by the Roman offices with a letter – sensitive because it concerned the deposition of the Maronite patriarch Yaʿqūb ʿAwwād – for the French consul in Saida, and that he hosted a Maronite priest, Daʿūd, who had come to Rome with a mission while waiting for a boat to take him back to Saida via Egypt.
27. APF, Acta, vol. 82, 4 July 1712, 23, *Greci*, and 2 August 1712, 7, *Stampa*; SOCG, vol. 582, fol. 424 (same case).
28. APF, SOCG, vol. 579, fols 171r–172r, 29 May 1711. See also ibid. fols 199r–200v. Bono, *Corsari nel Mediterraneo*, pp. 57–58.
29. APF, SOCG, vol. 580, fols 177rv (Arabic original), 178r (Italian translation), 14 March 1711. SC, Melchiti, vol. 1, fol. 153rv (Malta, 29 March 1711): document concerning the '*pezze quattro cento*' belonging to the church of Aftīmyūs . It was supposed that they had been taken by the Maltese captain Ascanio, but the latter had given up the *corso* and occupied honourable functions at the court of the Holy Office! Ibid. fol. 167r (Malta, 5 October 1713): same subject. Acta, 82, 10 May 1712, 10, *Terra Santa*: a caique taken by Franceschini, 'a corsair from Livorno', in sight of Mount Carmel, loaded mostly with merchandise belonging to Maronites, arrived in Malta. The Grand Master refused him the right to disembark but did not impose other sanctions out of 'respect for the flag of the Grand Duke'.
30. Bono, *Corsari nel Mediterraneo*, p. 57; APF, SOCG, vol. 582, fol. 431rv (6 June 1712): this document from Livorno presented Captain Antonio Franceschi as being 'of the religion of Malta'. His cousin Franceschi della Bocca was said to be the main party interested in the corsair vessels. SC, Maroniti, vol. 3, fol. 466r–469v, n. d. (probably later): '*Li nazionali greci orientali commoranti in Roma e Malta*' presented a note on the legal affairs concerning them. They notably explained the use of the various jurisdictions made by the corsairs. In 1712, the Grand Master of Malta stated that the owners who sailed under the Maltese flag could not approach the coast of Palestine and still less attack the pilgrims: the person in charge of the attacks on the pilgrimage was apparently a Corsican (Pietro Agostino), who did not sail under the Maltese flag and who moreover had the good idea to die. Acta, vol. 82, 15 February 1712, 15, *Terra Santa*: in 1723, Abramo Subani from Damascus lodged a complaint in Malta through the intermediary of the Propaganda. The Grand Master replied to the latter (28 June 1723) that the corsair vessel concerned, which belonged to his secretary's nephew, was under the Tuscan flag and that they should address their request to Livorno: SC, Greci Melchiti, vol. 1, fol. 475r and 477r. Recommendation for the same affair of Ṣayfī and the missionaries of Cairo ibid. fol. 431r (Italian translation), 432r (Arabic original), 433r (1722).

31. APF, SOCG vol. 580, fols 177rv (Italian translation), 178r (Arabic original): Ṣayfī to the pope, 14 March 1711. SC, Greci Melchiti, vol. 1, fol. 141v (Arabic original), 142rv (Italian translation): letter of Makāryūs, Archbishop of Tripoli, 25 January 1713. Ibid. fol. 463r: the deacon Stefano, sent by the archbishop of Sidon (undated).
32. APF, SOCG vol. 582, fol. 431rv (Livorno, 6 June 1712, copy).
33. APF, SC, Greci Melchiti vol. 1, fols 155r–156v (Livorno, 13 June 1713); SC, Maroniti, vol. 2, fol. 262rv (Livorno, 26 June 1713).
34. APF, SC, Melchiti, vol. 1, fols 159rv, 169rv (Sarufīm Ṭānās, 7 July 1713); ibid. fol. 165rv (Florence, 26 July 1713). Acta, vol. 83, 16 January 1713, fol. 4rv: Aftīmyūs Ṣayfī requested an intervention with the Grand Duke of Tuscany and the Grand Master of Malta. The Secretary reminded him of the latter's dilatory replies to the interventions of the Propaganda in 1710. Ibid. 3 April 1713, fol. 187rv, and 19 June 1713, fol. 387rv: further appeals from Ṣayfī on the same subject. Ibid. 13 May 1713, fol. 329rv: appeal by Niʿma Fakhr. Ibid. 24 July 1713, fol. 455v–456r: four Cigala brothers, one of the main Catholic families of Santorini, who traded in the Archipelago, requested a patent against the Corsairs. The Propaganda did not respond.
35. APF, SOCG vol. 589, fol. 255r–256r (Giovanni Giuseppe Mazet, Livorno, 21 August 1713): 'che li franchi sono cani, che non cercono cattolici in Levante, che per mangiarli, e tenerli come schiavi della loro giuriditione, senza portar loro nissun sollievo nella dura schiavitù in qual si ritrovano'.
36. APF, SC, Maroniti, vol. 3, fols 65r–66v (Arabic original), 64r–65v (Italian translation): Livorno, June 1715.
37. On the Syrians in Egypt, see Raymond, *Artisans et commerçants au* Caire, 477ff; Thomas Philipp, *The Syrians in Egypt, 1725–1975* (Stuttgart: Steiner-Verlag, 1985); André Bittar, 'La dynamique commerciale des Grecs catholiques en Égypte au XVIIIe siècle', *Annales Islamologiques*, 26 (1992), pp. 181–96; André Bittar, 'Les Juifs, les Grecs catholiques, et la ferme des douanes en Égypte sous Ali Bey al-Kabîr', *Annales Islamologiques*, 27 (1993), pp. 255–70. The Syrians of Egypt were not all Greek Catholics: the first Maronites in Cairo were mentioned in 1643 (Heyberger, *Les chrétiens du Proche-Orient*, p. 36).
38. APF, Acta vol. 86, 9 June 1716, *Varie*, fols 183v–184r: these affairs were not compatible with the clerical status of Metoscita. This individual had been kept by the Order in Malta since 1700, for the service of Eastern slaves, and he was praised for his work in this: SC, Maroniti, vol. 1, fols 324r–325r (10 May 1704). This did not stop him from misdeeds – see SC, Maroniti, vol. 3, fols 389r–390r, 391rv, 395rv, 397rv, 399rv, 404rv (1724), various documents concerning the financial affairs in which he was involved. He invested capital with some Easterners in Malta.
39. APF, Acta, vol. 95, 12 March 1725, 7, *Greci melchiti.*
40. APF, SC, Greci Melchiti, vol. 2, fol. 46v–47r (Arabic), fol. 45rv, 48r (Italian translation): 'Name Facher', Satalia, 28 May 1726. Bittar, 'La dynamique commerciale', and Bittar, 'Les Juifs, les Grecs catholiques', have mentioned the role of Mikhāʾīl Fakhr, customs officer at Damietta in 1748.

41. APF, CP, Greci Melchiti, vol. 76, fols 429rv, 431r (Italian translation), 430r (Arabic original): 'Elia Facher', Roman knight, Aleppo, 15 April 1725.
42. Qisṭanṭīn Bāshā, *Taʾrīkh ṭāʿifat al-Rūm al-malakiyya wa ruhbān al-mukhalliṣiyya* (Saida: Maṭbaʿa dayr al-Mukhālliṣ, 1938), pp. 196–201.
43. APF, CP, Greci Melchiti, vol. 75, fols 312rv, 315rv (Italian translation), 313r (Arabic original): Damascus, 13 January 1723.
44. Ibid. fol. 400v (Tripoli, 27 April 1723). [On Rowland Sherman and his proselytising, especially in Aleppo, see Simon Mills, *Commerce of Knowledge: Trade, Religion, and Scholarship between England and the Ottoman Empire, 1600–1760* (Oxford: Oxford University Press, 2020), pp. 229–48].
45. Heyberger, *Les chrétiens du Proche-Orient*, p. 258. It is true that in the years 1720–30 some English people were hostile towards Catholicism. Bittar, 'La dynamique commerciale', has mentioned the friendship between Mikhāʾīl Fakhr and Roben, the consul for England and for Holland in Egypt around 1750.
46. Heyberger, *Les chrétiens du Proche-Orient*, pp. 85–86, 89, 120–26, 393–400.
47. [On the development of Roman politics concerning *communicatio in sacris* during this period, see Cesare Santus, *Trasgressioni necessarie: Communicatio in sacris, coesistenza e conflitti tra le comunità cristiane orientali (Levante e Impero ottomano, XVII–XVIII secolo)* (Rome: École française de Rome, 2019).]
48. Virgil Cândea (ed.), *Icônes Melkites: Exposition organisée par le musée Nicolas Sursock du 16 mai au 15 juin 1969* (Beirut: Musée Nicolas Sursock, 1969), p. 182 (Archangel Saint Michael, n° 44, 1726), p. 186 (Saint Demetrius, n° 47, 1727). I suppose, without being sure, that Bishop Makāryūs was the same person. The formula of the donation, which mentioned 'the death of self', is new for the time and illustrates a Western influence.
49. Nasrallah, *Histoire du mouvement littéraire*, vol. IV, 2, pp. 204–9.
50. Nāwufītūs Idlibī (Edelby), *Asāqifa al-Rūm al-Malakiyyīn bi-Ḥalab* (Aleppo: Maṭbaʾat al-Iḥsān, 1983), p. 173; AGC, A.D. 106, journal of the Capuchins of Aleppo, pp. 68–70.
51. Jean Delumeau, *Rassurer et protéger: Le sentiment de sécurité dans l'Occident d'autrefois* (Paris: Fayard, 1989), p. 929. In the Rule of the Congregation of Melkite Celibates of Aleppo, the part that listed day by day the indulgences that its members could obtain makes one think of an account book, like those that these merchants kept for their business at the same time: Aleppo, Greek Catholic Archbishopric, ms. 518, *Sūra rusūm ʿakhawiyya al-ʿuzbān bī Ḥalab*.
52. AGC, A.D. 106, journal of the Capuchins, p. 163, quoted in Heyberger, *Les chrétiens du Proche-Orient*, pp. 128–29, concerning the Maronite dragoman Yūsuf Qarāʿalī (1799); see also APF, Missioni Miscellanee, vol. l, fol. 466v, report by a Franciscan custos, concerning the dragoman of Aleppo (1736). These negative moral judgements could be adopted by the Easterners themselves: Monsignor Joseph Nasrallah (Greek Catholic) suspected Ilyās Fakhr of hypocrisy and cupidity: 'Through interest, he took as his model his protector (Athanasius Dabbās) who, as we know, used both Catholicism and Orthodoxy according to the circumstances. [. . .] Finally he gave in to the solicitations of an English agent,

Chairman, who made him a redoubtable champion of Orthodoxy' (*Histoire du mouvement littéraire*, vol. IV, 2, pp. 203–4).

53. Constantin-François Volney, *Voyage en Égypte et en Syrie*, edited by Jean Gaulmier (Paris, The Hague: Mouton & Co., 1959), pp. 410–11.
54. Nathan Wachtel, 'L'acculturation', in Jacques Le Goff and Pierre Nora (eds), *Faire de l'histoire* (Paris: Gallimard 1986), vol. 1, pp. 184–85, has given this definition of 'cultural duality': 'These are the many cases of cultural duality where certain individuals conform to the rules and values of the dominant society when they are among representatives of the latter, but again adopt the traits and values of the dominated society when they return to their original milieu. Questions of acculturation show in this case, within a same social ensemble, a fundamental ambiguity'.
55. [See the other contributions in the volume where this chapter was originally published: Meropi Anastassiadou and Bernard Heyberger (eds), *Figures anonymes, figures d'élite: Pour une anatomie de l'Homo ottomanicus* (Istanbul: Isis, 1999).]

CHAPTER 4

A Border-crossing Ottoman Christian at the Beginning of the Eighteenth Century: Ḥannā Diyāb of Aleppo and his Account of his Travel to Paris

The source of this chapter is the travelogue of a Maronite Christian from Aleppo, called Ḥannā Diyāb.[1] He journeyed with the French traveller Paul Lucas, who hired him during his passage through Syria in 1707 and brought him to Paris, without ever mentioning Ḥannā in his published account of his journey.[2] Ḥannā made this peregrination when he was about twenty, but he wrote his account much later, beginning to compose it in 1763 and finally finishing his manuscript on 3 March 1764. Today, the sole copy of this manuscript is preserved at the Vatican Apostolic Library.[3]

In this text we find ourselves in the presence of an Ottoman Christian subject, whose mother language is Arabic and who supplies us with a very rich narration about his discovery of Europe (especially Paris) at the beginning of the eighteenth century. Nevertheless, one has to beware of the idea that this text introduces us directly into the problematic of the confrontation of an Eastern Christian with the West. Indeed, what Diyāb's travelogue reveals is that his perception of differences and borders did not fit with the common idea about them. Today, the categories 'West' or 'Christianity' are challenged by more recent research on 'diversity' and 'connectivity' in the Mediterranean of the early modern period.[4] Many historians have advocated a microhistorical approach to early globalisation, consisting in following an individual through the different stages of their biography, in order to observe not only their own connectedness to different *milieux* across multiple borders, but what their path points to for a more general understanding of the connections between different worlds which are usually assumed to be culturally distant.[5] Ḥannā belongs to this cast of 'border-crossing' characters who have been brought to light in recent years.[6]

Before we can answer the question of how an Easterner looked at the West through his testimony, we first must reflect on the nature of this narrative and on the position of the narrator.

THE TRAVEL STORY AND ITS AUTHOR

The story begins abruptly, because the first pages of the manuscript are missing. Diyāb probably said something here about his motivation to write down the story of his journey nearly sixty years after the fact, but we will never know the terms of the 'contract' he signed with his intended reader. It is unclear what kind of audience he addressed. The sole copy of his travelogue, which could be an autograph, has been conserved and read in his own family, as a footnote testifies.[7]

In comparison with other travelogues in Arabic or Turkish from the same time, that of Ḥannā Diyāb differs on several points. Firstly, the author is not immersed in a scholarly culture (*adab*) which he would seek to display in his account, with references, quotations and poetry, as it is usual among other travellers – such as the famous sheikh of Damascus 'Abd al-Ghānī al-Nābulusī, who wrote a number of accounts of his travels through Syria at the end of the seventeenth century,[8] or the Egyptian Sheikh Rifā'a al-Ṭahṭāwī, who left a very famous account of his stay in Paris in 1830.[9] The Christian Ilyās al-Mawṣūlī, who wrote a description of America around 1680, a copy of which certainly belonged to Ḥannā Diyāb, was immersed in a Christian clerical culture.[10] To some extent, Ḥannā Diyāb could be compared to Shihāb al-Dīn Ahmad ibn Budayr (known as Al-Budayrī), the barber of Damascus, who was his contemporary and wrote a chronicle between 1741 and 1762. Both were unusual writers, commoners exposed to the art of public story-telling in coffee shops, where they could listen to tales and epics and whose intellectual cosmos was formed and informed by the oral and the written.[11] It is possible that Ḥannā Diyāb, as well as Ibn Budayr, possessed a level of social ambition which they expressed through writing, in order to reach a level of authority through literacy. Moreover, both displayed an author-centric world and a kind of freedom and self-fashioning in their telling, which rarely appeared among other Syrian authors of the time.[12] Both wrote in a colloquial Arabic, demonstrating that they did not belong to the class of scholars (*'ulamā'*) and that they were addressing a lower audience of merchants and artisans, maybe through the oral transmission of their text.[13]

Generally, Ḥannā relied first on his own observations and records in his narrative. When he made reference to contextual knowledge outside of his own experience, he drew on what had been told to him, sometimes cross-referencing different oral sources in order to test their credibility. But the comparison with the barber of Damascus must stop here: Ibn Budayr followed the genre of the chronicle and strove after the Islamic *adab* of the *'ulamā'*, introducing classical forms such as poetic musings, rhymed prose and biographies into his chronicle, whereas Ḥannā intended to write a travel narrative without paying any homage at all to the traditional high literary culture in Arabic. When he did obviously refer to written sources, these were what we might call 'popular' literature.

However – and this is the most unusual aspect – these sources were almost exclusively European, not Arabic.[14] To give some examples, he told curious, very stereotyped general anecdotes, well-known in European literature, such as the story of the hanged man whose rope broke several times,[15] that of the woman buried alive,[16] that of the elixir of youth,[17] that of the shoe-maker who became a very famous painter through his love for a princess[18] and so on. He also told two stories very offensive to the Jews of Livorno.[19] In Paris, he discovered the exciting literary genre of death sentences (‘*al-santansa*’), loose printed sheets accounting the circumstances of the crime and death of those sentenced to capital punishment, which were sold in the streets on the occasion of public executions.[20] He told also hagiographic stories – for instance, that of the foundation of the sanctuary of the Madonna di Montenero in Livorno, or of Genevieve, the patron saint of Paris. In both cases, he followed well-known Western hagiographic traditions, which oddly did not fit at all with the genuine stories of Montenero or Saint Genevieve. This could be a clue to his indirect use of written sources, through memorisation and assimilation. He used written sources, but not directly, never quoting from a book or a text. When he drew from the Bible, his references were incorrect or vague, and once, on the stay of the Holy Family in Egypt, he may have been inspired by an Apocryphal Gospel diffused among the Copts.[21] If he had any link to written culture, it would have been an indirect one, through oral mediation.

Ḥannā did not travel with the mission of teaching his sovereign or his contemporaries, as was the case for al-Mawṣilī, al-Ṭahṭāwī, or Mehmed Efendi,[22] who headed an embassy of the Sublime Porte to Paris a few years after Ḥannā's travels. His journey was a kind of initiatory grand tour, of a young man who was seeking a path in life. He began by recounting his religious calling, which led him to become a novice among the Lebanese Monks, a new religious order recently founded in Mount Lebanon on the pattern of the Jesuits. But being ill and questioning his vocation, he turned back to Aleppo in order to reconsider it. Here, his first employer, a merchant from Marseille called Rémuzat, did not give him a new job. He therefore decided to leave home, without a very clear plan. At that moment he encountered Paul Lucas, who hired him as an aide on his travels to Beirut, Sidon, Cyprus, Egypt, Libya, Tunisia, Livorno, Genoa, Marseille and Paris. After that, he returned without Lucas, from Marseille to Smyrna, then to Constantinople, where he stayed for a long time, and then back to Aleppo through Anatolia.

If Paul Lucas' writings never mentioned Ḥannā, the latter said a lot about his master. He was young and needed somebody who could initiate him into life and the world. Paul Lucas fulfilled this function for him. When Lucas fell seriously ill in Tunis, Ḥannā described himself as feeling utterly distraught, imagining himself left to his own devices in a foreign country. When he in turn fell ill and Lucas was thinking of leaving Livorno for Genoa without him, he implored the Holy Virgin of Montenero, who helped to cure him and to take him on board with his master.[23] He had great admiration for Lucas' knowledge and expertise. He watched how he dealt in his trafficking to buy precious stones, manuscripts, or ancient coins, even a mummy in Egypt, through trickery. He learned also from him some basic knowledge of medicine, which would help him during his return journey through Anatolia, to be taken in turn for a Westerner, a *Franjī*, and as a *Franjī* to be taken for a physician.[24] And in Paris, at the suggestion of Antoine Galland, the famous translator and editor of the *Arabian Nights*, he began to imagine himself as a traveller, with an official mission from the French Minister to collect manuscripts and coins in the East for the Royal Academy and Library.

After Paul Lucas, Diyāb would search for other protectors and advisers. In Paris, Antoine Galland fulfilled this function for a time. On the ship from Marseille to Izmir and Istanbul, he struck up a friendship with a young man in the service of the French embassy, who guided and informed him in the Ottoman capital. And when he finally decided to return home from Istanbul, he followed the advice of a fellow countryman with whom he had travelled from Istanbul to Aleppo.

Diyāb wrote his narrative of this initiatory journey fifty years after his return. He stated that he was seventy-five years old at the time of writing,[25] and that he had had a long life as a woollen cloth merchant in the souk of Aleppo. He did not put his story on paper with the intention of offering an apology, enlightenment, or justification of himself. The leitmotif of his text was more a meditation on life. During his travels, when he was young, many opportunities offered themselves to him, but he was not sufficiently determined or able to catch them. He asserted that Paul Lucas promised to recommend him to the minister Pontchartrain or to the king himself in order to appoint him as librarian-interpreter for 'Oriental languages'. Antoine Galland, who might not have wanted competition in this field, may have promised him a mission as traveller, like those executed by Paul Lucas. Eventually, Ḥannā felt betrayed by both, at least as he tells it. He left France disappointed, with the sense that he had been misled.[26] In fact, the credibility of Eastern Christians as experts on academic Orientalism at that time was seriously challenged in Paris, and his chance to receive an official position was very low. If Ḥannā expressed dissatisfaction, it was not against Syrian society and its ruling classes, as in the case of the barber of Damascus, but against his French 'protectors'. His narrative was not coloured by social frustration, like that of Ibn Budayr.[27]

Recent publications have stressed the presence of self-consciousness in the documents produced in Syria and Mount Lebanon of this time.[28] The travelogue of Ḥannā Diyāb could be, after the writings of the pious Maronite Aleppine woman Hindiyya,[29] the most consciously autobiographical text written in Syria in the eighteenth century. He often introduced himself as 'the poor one',[30] to testify that he was an eyewitness to the events that he was recounting, or to report the trials he underwent and the emotions he felt. Not surprisingly, Hindiyya and Ḥannā belonged to the same Catholic circle of Aleppo, where the injunction to speak about the self and to confess oneself had been introduced as early as in the seventeenth century. Jarmānūs Farḥāt, the translator of the *Spiritual Exercises* of Saint Ignatius of Loyola into Arabic and future bishop of Aleppo, generally considered as a figure of the pre-*Nahda* (the Arab 'Renaissance' of the nineteenth century), was the superior of the monastery where Ḥannā had tried to become a monk, and he had subjected him to examinations of conscience.[31]

Historians looking for a perspective from the bottom up and listening to the point of view of the subalterns might be delighted to encounter Ḥannā Dyāb. As a servant, he paid attention to things that an ambassador, priest, or other literate traveller would not have noticed: when, for instance, he went to the opera in Paris, to see *Atys*, a '*tragédie lyrique*' by Lully, he explained how to book the tickets and what the different categories of seats were, with their respective prices.[32] However, according to his own testimony, even though he was confined to a domestic position with Paul Lucas and even though was young and inexperienced, he played a significant role and helped his master out of difficult situations. Antoine Galland wrote several times of Ḥannā in his journal, with rather affectionate words.[33] It is necessary to specify that this Maronite of Aleppo had been a valuable assistant to him. During several meetings he told the French scholar missing stories from the *Arabian Nights*, which resulted in Galland's famous edition and translation, guaranteeing the latter a place in posterity. It is worth underscoring that among the stories that Ḥannā told Galland were some of the most famous, including that of Ali Baba and Aladdin's lamp. For these tales, there exist no other known sources than the versions Ḥannā told to Galland.[34] It is an ongoing puzzle that, whenever sources for these tales can be identified, they are Western, not Arabic or 'Oriental', as is also the case for his travel narrative.[35] Unfortunately, when our author wrote his travelogue more than fifty years later, he was not aware that his tales had become so famous and that he himself had made a major contribution to European culture. He only mentioned his encounter with Galland in passing, without any consciousness that the *Arabian Nights*, and especially his tales, were becoming bestsellers in European literature.[36]

In any case, Diyāb was an energetic teller of stories, and the tales he recounted to Galland can help us to understand how he conceived his own narrative. He indisputably liked to regale and to captivate his audience. As in the tales, there is a framing story to his narrative, into which he inserted secondary tales, and he made transitions with comments such as: 'I only told a few parts of many, being afraid that it will be too long and that the reader will be bored'.[37]

One can imagine that Ḥannā spent his later life telling his story and, in the same way, memorised a narrative of his travels.[38] He complained of his failing memory, and he evidently confused some of the dates or the chronologic order of his trips: obviously, he had not kept a diary during his journey, to which he later could have referred. But he displayed a high capacity for precision in describing what he had observed as an eyewitness: the palace of Bardo in Tunis, the astronomical clock in Lyon, the executions in Paris.[39] Overall, he had a very strong memory of the impressions and feelings that he had experienced: wonder, curiosity, surprise, fear, perplexity. It is this which makes his narrative so lively and rich.

ḤANNĀ AND THE PERCEPTION OF DIFFERENCE

Ḥannā recounted the different stages of his journey in a kind of continuum. No obvious cultural gap appeared in his account, between a familiar world and a completely exotic one. A conscious and clear opposition between an Ottoman East and a Western Christianity, a common literary convention of similar travel accounts, did not appear in this travelogue. Instead, Diyāb often ascribed his astonishment or his trouble in awkward positions to his lack of experience and knowledge, not to a cultural opposition.

First, one must note that, even before he left Aleppo, Diyāb was already familiar with the Provencal merchants by whom he and his brothers were appointed, from the tradehouses of Marseille which had branches in the city. Working for these 'Franks', he learnt not only to speak, but (so he asserted) even to read and to write in French. He also mastered spoken Italian and perhaps read it. He understood and spoke Turkish, while the one language that gave him an impression of complete and hostile oddness was Greek, with which he was confronted in Ottoman Cyprus. There, he felt himself in a situation of the most radical impossibility of communication (as seen in the excerpt below).

Diyāb's familiarity with the Provencal traders settled in Aleppo also helped him to be welcomed in Marseille, where he could rely on the hospitality and the support of the kin of his Aleppine acquaintances.[40] Moreover, in Beirut, Livorno, Paris, and Istanbul, or in the Anatolian port of Payas he encountered fellow Syrians with whom he set up an almost spontaneous form of familiarity and solidarity.[41] For him, as for other travellers, like Paul Lucas, not only the recommendation letters, but also the rituals of drinking coffee and smoking a pipe with different persons wherever he stopped were important practices of sociability, which helped to build relationships and receive reliable information in distant cities.

As a Maronite Christian, Diyāb also considered himself as perfectly belonging to a Catholic culture, which in his time had been strongly instilled in the Christians of Aleppo.[42] As a very devout person, he felt at ease attending Catholic liturgical services during his travels and showed himself to be particularly attuned to forms of baroque religious expression such as the *Via Crucis* in Marseille, or the solemn procession of Saint Genevieve in Paris in May 1709, or the dramatised sermons he attended in several churches in Tunis and Paris.[43] In the cultural field of religion, Ḥannā did not feel any incommensurability,[44] and he also seemed completely at ease with questions related to trade and business.

When speaking of political institutions in Europe, he used the Ottoman terminology: the king of France is generally called sultan, not *malik*, whereas the Sultan of Istanbul in turn was often dubbed 'king' (*malik*) by him. The ushers of Versailles were called the equivalent of the Turkish term *kapıcı*, secretaries and stewards were called *kākhiyya*, the police and justice officers were *qādī* or *hukamā'*, and the Consul of the Sea in Marseille was a *shāh bandar* – a term which in Aleppo and elsewhere in the Ottoman Empire meant the head of the guilds. In Livorno, he mentioned boats whose crews he called 'janissaries'. The law was called 'sharia' by him. The founding incomes for churches or hospitals were called '*waqf*', which denoted the Islamic legal system of endowments for mosques and madrasas, although Christians and Jews also used the term for their churches and monasteries in the Islamic context.[45] The letters of the sovereign were '*firmans*'. Beyond these examples of vocabulary, one might assert that Ḥannā saw a commensurability of certain features of the political and social order between what he experienced at home and what he discovered in Tuscany or Paris, and that he had only one approach to political authority, whether Islamic or Christian, even if a mute hostility against the Ottoman governance is sometimes detectible in his account. Of course, this impression of commensurability was partly the result of misunderstanding, of his ignorance of the actual state machinery, in Versailles as well as in Istanbul. Political authority inspired him with both admiration and fear. He was at the same time fascinated and terrified by what he perceived of the practices of police and justice. He did not criticise the state's power, but he seemed only half relieved by what he learned of the politics of Louis XIV against the Protestants or the Jansenists.[46] He had personally experienced something of the methods of police and justice in Paris,and on one occasion feared that he himself would be handed over for torture.[47]

Ḥannā's narrative displayed a fascination with exhibitions of the strength of public authority. He meticulously described the military drilling in Livorno and emphasised the strong discipline of the troops. He stressed the good condition of the artillery and described how the weapons were maintained, which led him to a comparison with his home city, where weapons in the famous citadel were left in the sand to rust.[48] If there was a difference between the Western monarchies and the Ottoman Empire in this account, it would have been in their efficiency and their attention to public welfare. Like other Eastern travellers in Western Europe, Ḥannā displayed admiration for the stables at Versailles, or the scenography at the opera. Like them, he paid special attention to technological feats, such as the hydraulic engine of Marly, or the astronomical clock of Saint-Jean Church in Lyon. But, overall, he was fascinated by political and administrative organisation and its achievements: the guarding of the city walls in Livorno, the lighting and the cleaning up of the streets in Paris, the organisation of the stage-coach network between Paris and Marseille.[49] He devoted a long passage to a description of the hospitals and the general system of public assistance in Paris. He perceived clearly what, in the organisation of public charity and the repression of beggary, was completely new and very different from what he knew from Aleppo.[50]

Incontestably, there were forms of continuity between what Ḥannā perceived of the West and what he knew from Aleppo. However, exoticism and oddness were not exclusive to European Christianity. It was in the Ottoman province of Cyprus where Ḥannā experienced one of his strongest sensations when, for the first time in his life, he saw unveiled women on the streets; moreover, they were selling wine or pork! It is worth explaining that, in Aleppo, Christian women were veiled in the same manner as Muslims, that the clergy tried to forbid the manufacture and sale of alcohol, and that pork was considered haram among Christians as well as Muslims.[51] However, what shocked him the most was the hypocritical use of calling upon Islamic morality by a Greek neighbour, as a threat in a quarrel among Christians described in the excerpt below. Arriving in Livorno, 'the first city in the land of the Christians' he visited, he was 'stunned by what I never saw before': 'women in the shops, selling and buying as if they were men' and 'walking on the streets with the face uncovered, without a veil'. But this time he did not feel shocked: 'I felt like in a dream', he asserted.[52] Unlike the Damascene Muslim barber Ibn Budayr or his fellow countryman, the Greek Orthodox priest Mikhā'īl Burayk,[53] he did not view this more relaxed regimen for women as a sign of political disorder and decadence. Later, he unsuccessfully tried to help a Christian from Damascus, settled in Livorno, to convince his wife to leave her home unveiled. Diyāb said to her: 'If you want me to walk with you, remove this veil and dress like these women who are walking there. Nobody will turn around to give you a glance'. But the Damascene woman refused, and he concluded: 'I understood through this episode that the women from our countries cannot behave like those of these countries, because they have been educated to stay hidden'.[54]

In Versailles, Diyāb was filled with wonder at the appearance of the princesses and their public life. But in relation to women, he appeared rather more discreet than other Eastern travellers in Paris. However, his experience of European women perhaps inspired his 'Tale of Two Sisters', told to Antoine Galland, in which the princess Parizade knows how to read and write and 'in a short time [becomes] as skilled as the princes, her brothers, though she was younger than them'. She received a complete education in the 'fine arts', like her brothers, but she learned music 'during the breaks'. She knew horse riding and how to shoot weapons, and 'she often even overtook them in the races'. Eventually, she saved them, appearing more cold-blooded than them.

As a city dweller, Ḥannā appeared deeply shocked by the primitive nature of the rural populations in the Egyptian province of Fayum,[55] or in the desert of Sirt, in Libya, where his boat ran aground. Several times he spoke about men similar to devils. In the desert of Sirt, he encountered a man 'sitting, looking like a devil. His eyes were like those of a monkey. He was wrapped in a black blanket, and he was himself black. He was frightening'.[56]

The dress codes were more sophisticated than can be imagined today, and they changed as soon as the gates of Aleppo were crossed. In the city, Ḥannā wore a cap with a blue turban wound around it, called a '*shāsh*'. Blue was the colour that Islamic law imposed on Christians. But when he joined the caravan from Aleppo to Tripoli, he swapped his blue *shāsh* for a white one, so that during the journey he could not be distinguished from the other travellers as a Christian. Arriving in Beirut, he wanted to wind his blue turban again, but a friend who lived in the city praised the tolerance of the local society and asserted that he could wear a white turban, or even a green one, normally the exclusive privilege of the *sharifs* who claimed descent from the Prophet Muhammad. Finally, he preferred to wear his blue turban.[57] In contrast, in Tripoli (Maghreb), he was attacked by janissaries who would tear off his turban, because they regarded the headwear as a privilege reserved for Ottoman officers sent from Istanbul.[58]

Ḥannā even discovered different ways to be a Maronite. Near Beirut, he encountered a troupe of *aghas* armed to the teeth. In surprise, he realised that they were not Muslims, but Maronites like him! He also learned that the rules of fasting during Lent were stricter among the Maronites of Lebanon than those of Aleppo.[59] In Cyprus, he encountered an elderly man who spoke Greek, Turkish and Arabic and who belonged to the local Maronite community, present on the island since the twelfth century, as described in the excerpt below. Ḥannā had never heard of them before. In Versailles, his master, Paul Lucas, making his presentation to Pontchartrain, asserted that the Maronites were the only Eastern Christians who had always strictly adhered to Catholic orthodoxy and obedience to the pope.[60] In this way, travel helped Ḥannā to gain a broader consciousness of what it meant to be a Maronite in different contexts. Travelling and crossing borders thus had the potential to help the traveller to become not only more tolerant and pluralistic, but rather more conscious of his own identity; thus, it contributed to a sectarian consciousness of the self.

All this does not mean that Diyāb felt no difference between the Ottoman world and Christian Europe. First, during the period of his travels, the Western States were building up borders and beginning to monitor entrance to the territories under their jurisdiction. The first hurdle that Ḥannā encountered was that of the sanitary regime. He recalled his experience of the quarantine in Livorno. He described, for instance, precisely how a document had to be disinfected, or how passengers had to undergo a thorough medical examination at the end of their quarantine. After this, they had to cross the barrier of the customs inspection.

Ḥannā was afraid because he had concealed tobacco in his luggage. Smuggling tobacco was very strictly repressed in Tuscany in this period.[61] In Genoa, according to his account, a strict system of control was imposed on foreigners, who had to declare themselves to a judge before they could stay at a hotel and who had to renew their registration after a few days.

But what did it mean to be a foreigner? In Genoa, Paul Lucas declared to the judge that he was a 'French native' and that Ḥannā was an 'Oriental.'[62] This definition seemed very vague, but it was the most common and the most obvious, based on the physical appearance. Ḥannā presented his identity very strongly through his physical appearance and his clothes. After his quarantine in Livorno, he went to the barber:

> The barber, after washing my face and my beard, took the shaving knife and ran it through my beard, and he took half of my moustache off. When I felt that he shaved off half of my moustache, I screamed, frightening him. He stopped, alarmed, and asked me: 'What's wrong with you? You are not bleeding!' 'It would have been better if you had made me bleed, rather than shave my moustache!' I answered. 'Don't you know that the children of the East do not shave their moustache like you do?' Reluctantly, I let him shave the other half of my moustache. In these countries, all the men shave their beard and their moustache, even the priests, except the Capuchins, according to what I understood.[63]

This opposition between East and West concerning hairstyle and facial hair was a common stereotype among Western authors, but here Ḥannā felt himself injured in his physical integrity. He returned to the issue on several other occasions. When a French lady made an unpleasant comment about the beard of a Turkish diplomat coming out of the opera, Diyāb felt himself involved, too, and answered in French, criticising the lady for her insulting words.[64]

However, Diyāb also decided to make the journey back to Aleppo through Anatolia wearing his clothes and hair like a European, so that he would be thought of as a physician by the people he encountered on the way. But, upon returning to Aleppo, so he explained, he resumed his 'Oriental' identity: 'I dressed, I shaved the hair on my head, I wound a *shāsh* and dressed in a *qāwūq*. They sent somebody to ask for a safe-conduct. Only after that did I leave the home, and I went in my turn to greet my kin, my relatives and my friends'.[65]

While physical appearance was a significant element of identity, it was not sufficient. Everywhere it was very important for a stranger to not appear '*sans aveu*', without any recommendation and protection. At every stage of his travel, Ḥannā enjoyed the protection and support of French consuls or French merchants. He could also call on the network of Latin missionaries, like most of the Eastern Christians travelling through the Mediterranean at that time. The network of

Syrians settled in Europe also helped him. Ḥannā did not exactly belong to the so-called trading diasporas,[66] but the links based on trust and friendship in different Mediterranean ports appeared essential for travelling and trading. In Paris, Christophe Maunier, a member of a French-Syrian family, employed by the archbishop, in Diyāb's account surfaced as a key person for the reception and integration of Eastern Catholics within the city.[67] In Paris, too, Diyāb met an Armenian from Persia, who had reputedly stayed for some time in Aleppo. Ḥannā did not know him, but in order to win his trust, the man mentioned a number of persons in Aleppo. Finally, however, this man proved to be a swindler who had escaped the police of d'Argenson. Ḥannā, as an acquaintance of this man, was arrested and feared that he would be tortured. The intervention of his Syrian friend who had a famous coffee shop in the city, in his favour, proved insufficient. It was the testimony of Paul Lucas that finally delivered him. This experience induced Ḥannā Diyāb to leave Paris and return home.[68]

APPENDIX: THE EXPERIENCE OF DIFFERENCE IN CYPRUS

Extracts translated into English from: Hanna Dyâb, *D'Alep à Paris: Les pérégrinations d'un jeune Syrien au temps de Louis XIV*, translated and edited by Paule Fahmé-Thiéry, Bernard Heyberger and Jérôme Lentin, with a preface by Bernard Heyberger (Arles: Actes Sud, 2015), pp. 86–91.

Original Arabic manuscript: BAV, ms. Sbath 254, fols 14v–16v.

English Translation: Bernard Heyberger.

All their servants were Greeks, Orthodox,[69] who knew only Greek. I was among them like a deaf person in a bridal procession. I didn't understand their language, while they didn't understand mine. When I addressed them in the Frankish language (for they understood it), they answered me only mockingly in Greek, because they were filled with a stubborn hatred against the Catholic denomination. I felt hurt in company with them.

A few days thereafter, my master wanted to visit a city fourteen hours distant from Larnaca. This city is called Nicosia. It is the most important city of the island of Cyprus. [. . .] The muleteer hired out mounts for us, and we walked that day until the evening. Arriving in his village, we found accommodation in his home. After an hour, I heard a hubbub and a great racket coming from the countryside. I went out, and I saw herds of pigs coming back from their pasture. One of these herds headed for the house of the muleteer where we were staying. There was a surrounding wall outside, and the pigs entered this fence. They grunted so much that it wasn't possible to sleep that night.

At dawn we set off again. [. . .] At sunset, we arrived in Nicosia, and we went to stay at the monastery [of the Franciscan friars of Terra Santa]. We stayed there the whole day long because we found nobody who might show us the way [. . .].

There was an old man living there, who was unable to move. The Padre [the Franciscan] had put us in charge of feeding him with a part of our lunch and supper. He stayed in a small house in the courtyard of the convent. I brought him lunch and filled him a jug of water and made conversation with him. He started speaking in Greek. But when he became aware that I didn't understand Greek, he spoke Turkish and asked me about my origins.

– I am an Aleppine from the nation of the Maronites.

– Welcome to a son of my community, he answered in Arabic.

– Are you a Maronite? I asked.

– Yes, I am from the descent of the Maronites who lived on this island when it was under Venetian rule. There were more than five hundred families. There are some left, but they do not make themselves known, because they fear the Greek heretics. I took refuge with this Padre who gives me the alms of a bit of food for my subsistence, because I served this convent for a long time. Now I don't have any more strength. [. . .]

I saw a stone staircase, I climbed upstairs, and at the end of the terrace of the convent, I saw a parapet. I wanted to know what was behind it. I saw a courtyard where there were women and a man who seemed to be the master of the place. When he saw me, he started abusing me in Turkish and Greek. When I saw the women, I immediately turned around, while this man continued to shout and insult me. I came downstairs again and resumed my walk in the courtyard of the monastery. Suddenly, I heard that somebody was hitting the gate of the monastery with a stone. I headed for the door and asked:

– Who's knocking?

– Open, dirty dog, open, he answered me in Turkish. Then he went on to abuse me and to threaten me:

– If you don't open, I'll send for a bailiff from the pasha, to show him how you spoil people's women from above!

When I heard these words, I was overcome by a dreadful fear:

– Don't be angry with me, Mister, I said, I am a stranger, and I only arrived yesterday. I didn't know that there were women behind this parapet!

But the more I attempted to cajole him, the more he insulted and screamed and pelted the door of the monastery with stones.

At this moment, a Greek, but a Christian Catholic one, whom God had sent to deliver me from this nasty character, passed by. He started speaking with him in Greek and cajoling him. He calmed him down, and he succeeded in taking him away from the door. [. . .]

When the day ended, this young man came to visit me, comforting me and offering to entertain me. Considering the friendship that he had showed me, I asked him if he wanted to take me to visit the city before I left on the journey again. He agreed. We left the monastery, and he took me for a walk through the streets. It was a beautiful city, but most of its buildings were in ruins. We passed through a large place where I saw a mosque with vast arcades, surmounted by a high minaret and a large and wonderful dome. Marble statues of angels lined the whole perimeter of the dome. The gate of the mosque was in black and white marble. On each side of the gate stood a statue, one of Saint Peter, the other of Saint Paul, in white marble as well. Gazing at this beautiful building, I wondered and asked the young man what it could be:

– It's a mosque, he said.

– How could statues of angels and saints have been raised on a mosque? That is forbidden among the Muslims.

– There are also a lot of statues inside the building, he continued. They are embedded in a manner, that, if they wanted to remove them, they would have to destroy the whole church. Therefore, they kept them up for fear that the building would completely collapse.[70]

Then he took me to go around the town. I saw on the streets women who sold wine. Each one had a small wineskin in front of her, offering the wine for sale while praising its age and its quality. Each pot was sold for one *'uthmānī*.[71] Other women were selling pork meat and others had loaded a wineskin onto a donkey, going around the houses to sell it. All were with their face uncovered, without a veil. In front of such an immodest sight, I said to the young man I had with me:

– What about the words of that man who criticised me for glancing at his women? Now here are their women with their faces uncovered, without shame or modesty, sitting on the streets in full view of all the passers-by!

– You are right. However, as I have already explained to you, if this wicked man behaved in that way, it was not because you had looked at his women, but because he hates the *padre* and his monastery.

– How is it possible that the Muslims who live in this city allow wine and pork to be sold in the streets and alleys?

– They received the authorisation of the country's rulers, he replied, in order to be able to pay the *mīrī* tax which is imposed on them. This *mīrī* has remained the same they had to pay when the country was prosperous. Now it is almost ruined, but they continue to deduct it at the same level than before. Thus, numerous inhabitants of this island have been compelled to flee, because of the excessive injustice which overwhelms them.

NOTES

1. Bernard Heyberger, 'Introduction', in Hanna Dyâb, *D'Alep à Paris: Les pérégrinations d'un jeune Syrien au temps de Louis XIV*, translated and edited by Paule Fahmé-Thiéry, Bernard Heyberger and Jérôme Lentin, with a preface by Bernard Heyberger (Arles: Actes Sud, 2015), pp. 7–47.
2. Paul Lucas, *Deuxième voyage du Sieur Paul Lucas dans le Levant: Octobre 1704–septembre 1708*, new edition (Saint-Étienne: Publications de l'Université de

Saint-Étienne, 2002). [Lucile Haguet, 'Paul Lucas l'explorateur (1664–1737), ou la réhabilitation d'un affabulateur', in Christiane Demeulenaere (ed.), *Explorations et voyages scientifiques de l'Antiquité à nos jours* (Paris: CTHS, 2008), pp. 479–97.]

3. BAV, ms. Sbath 254. An Arabic version of the text, using references to our French translation without our agreement, was published in Beirut in 2017: Diyāb, Ḥannā, *Min Ḥalab ilā Bārīs: Riḥla ilā balāt Luwīs al-rābiʿ ʿashar* (Beirut: Manshūrāt al-Jamal, 2017). [An edition and translation into English, without any consultation with us, has been published in 2021: Ḥannā Diyāb, *The Book of Travels*, edited by Johannes Stephan, translated by Elias Muhanna, foreword by Yasmine Seale, afterword by Paolo Horta, 2 vol. (New York: New York University Press, 2021).]
4. E. Natalie Rothman, 'Interpreting Dragomans: Boundaries and Crossings in the Early Modern Mediterranean', *Comparative Studies in Society and History*, 51, 4 (2009), p. 772; E. Natalie Rothman, 'Afterword: Intermediaries, Mediation, and Cross-Confessional Diplomacy in the Early Modern Mediterranean', *Journal of Early Modern History*, 19 (2015), pp. 245–59. See also the reflection on continuity and discontinuity in the life of a 'border-crossing individual' by Jocelyne Dakhlia, 'Une archéologie du même et de l'autre: Thomas-Osman d'Arcos dans la Méditerranée du XVIIe siècle', in Jocelyne Dakhlia and Wolfgang Kaiser (eds), *Les musulmans dans l'histoire de l'Europe*, vol. 2: *Passages et contacts en Méditerranée* (Paris: Albin Michel, 2013), pp. 61–163. See also the comment on Ḥannā Diyāb's travelogue by Andrea Addobbati, 'Hanna Dyab, il mercante di storie', *Quaderni Storici*, 153, 3 (2016), pp. 830–42.
5. John-Paul Ghobrial, 'The Secret Life of Elias of Babylon and the Uses of Global Microhistory', *Past & Present*, 222 (2014), pp. 56–58. [John-Paul Ghobrial, 'Moving Stories and What They Tell Us: Early Modern Mobility between Microhistory and Global History,' *Past & Present*, 242 (2019), supplement n. 14, pp. 243–80.]
6. Natalie Zemon Davis, *Trickster Travels: A Sixteenth-Century Muslim between Worlds* (New York: Faber & Faber, 2006); Mercedes García-Arenal and Gerard Wiegers (eds), *Un hombre en tres mundos: Samuel Pallache, un judío marroquí en la Europa protestante y en la católica* (Madrid: Siglo XXI, 2006); Engl. transl. *A Man of Three Worlds: Samuel Pallache, a Moroccan Jew in Catholic and Protestant Europe* (Baltimore: Johns Hopkins University Press, 2007); L. Valensi, *Mardochée Naggiar: Enquête sur un inconnu* (Paris: Stock, 2008). See also various contributions in Jocelyne Dakhlia and Bernard Vincent (eds), *Les musulmans dans l'histoire de l'Europe*, vol. 1: *Une intégration invisible* (Paris: Albin Michel, 2011); Dakhlia and Kaiser (eds), *Les musulmans dans l'histoire de l'Europe*, vol. 2: *Passages et contacts en Méditerranée.*
7. Dyāb, *D'Alep à Paris*, pp. 9, 250, note 2 (fol. 90r of the manuscript): 'This travel account of my grandfather [added at the end of the line: 'father'] entered into the possession of Jibrāʾīl son of Dīdkūz Diyāb, from the Maronite community [*ṭāʾifa*], Nīsān 19th of the year 1840 of the Christian era'.
8. Ṣalāḥ-ad-Dīn al-Munağğid and Stefan Wild (eds), *Zwei Beschreibungen des Libanon: ʿAbd al-Ġānī an-Nābulusīs Reise durch die Biqāʿ und al-ʿUṭaifīs Reise nach*

Tripolis (Beirut: Orient Institut, 1979); Heribert Busse, *Die Reise 'Abd al-Ġānī an-Nābulusī durch den Libanon* (Beirut: Orient Institut, 2003).

9. Daniel L. Newman, *An Imam in Paris: Account of a Stay in France by an Egyptian Cleric (1826–1831)* (London: Saqi, 2011). [Rifā'a al-]Tahtāwī, *L'or de Paris: Relation de voyage 1826–1831*, translation from Arabic (Egypt) to French by Anouar Louca (Paris: Sindbad, 1988; new edition, Arles: Actes Sud, 2012).
10. Caesar E. Farah (ed.), *An Arab's Journey to Colonial Spanish America: The Travels of Elias al-Mûsili in the Seventeenth Century* (Syracuse: Syracuse University Press, 2003); Elias Al-Mawsilî, *Un Irakien en Amérique au XVIIe siècle*, edited by Nûrî al-Jarrâh and translated into French by Jean-Jacques Schmidt (Arles: Actes Sud, Sindbad, 2011). Arabic edition of the same text by Antoine Rabbath, 'Riḥlat 'awwal sharqī 'ilā 'Amrīkā', *Al-Machreq* 8 (1905), pp. 821–34, 875–86, 974–83, 1022–33, 1118–29. A good Italian translation: Iliyās ibn Ḥannā al-Mawṣilī, *Il primo Orientale nelle Americhe*, edited and translated by Marina Montanaro (Mazzara del Vallo: Liceo Ginnasio Gian Giacomo Adria, 1992). About this author and his travelogue, see Ghobrial, 'The Secret Life', pp. 51–93.
11. Dana Sajdi, *The Barber of Damascus: Nouveau Literacy in the Eighteenth-Century Levant* (Palo Alto: Stanford University Press, 2013), pp. 8–9, 43–45, 74–76.
12. Ibid. pp. 9–10, 145–62.
13. Ibid. pp. 108–14. Jérôme Lentin, 'Note sur la langue de Hanna Dyâb', in Dyâb, *D'Alep à Paris*, pp. 48–51.
14. Ruth B. Bottigheimer, 'Hanna Diyab and *The Thousand and One Nights*', *Marvel & Tales*, 28, 2 (2014), pp. 302–24. The same assertion could be made about the unpublished travelogue to the 'Christian lands' of the monks Yuḥannā Naqqāshsh and Tūmā Kurbāj (1775–77): Archives of the Basilian Aleppine Order, Monastery Saint-Sauveur of Ṣarbā, ms. Ṣarbā 261. See Michel Abras, 'Le voyage de deux moines melkites en France du nord en 1775', in Bernard Heyberger and Carsten Walbiner (eds), *Les Européens vus par les Libanais à l'époque ottomane* (Beirut: Orient-Institut der DMG; Würzburg: Ergon, 2002), pp. 59–65.
15. Dyâb, *D'Alep à Paris*, pp. 224–26.
16. Ibid. pp. 209–12. On the 'Mediterranean' sources of this story, see Régis Bertrand, *Mort et mémoire: Provence, XVIIIe–XXe siècles* (Marseille: La Thune, 2011), pp. 171–83.
17. Dyâb, *D'Alep à Paris*, pp. 181–84.
18. Ibid. pp. 276–80. On this tale, see also Addobbati, 'Hanna Dyab, il mercante di storie', pp. 836–40.
19. Dyâb, *D'Alep à Paris*, pp. 216–22. On this tale, see also Addobbati, 'Hanna Dyab, il mercante di storie', pp. 834–35.
20. Dyâb, *D'Alep à Paris*, pp. 314–23.
21. Ibid. pp. 107, 116; Lucette Valensi, *La fuite en Égypte: Histoires d'Orient et d'Occident* (Paris: Seuil, 2002), pp. 22–38.
22. Mehmed efendi, *Le paradis des infidèles: Un ambassadeur ottoman en France sous la Régence*, edited by Gilles Veinstein, translated by Julien-Claude Galland (Paris: Maspero, 1981). On this traveller, see Fatma Müge Göçek, *East Encounters*

West: France and the Ottoman Empire in the Eighteenth Century (Oxford: Oxford University Press, 1987).
23. Dyâb, *D'Alep à Paris*, pp. 180–81, 230–31.
24. Ibid. pp. 395–421.
25. Ibid. p. 231.
26. Ibid. pp. 345–54.
27. Sajdi, *The Barber of Damascus*, pp. 150–58.
28. Ibid. pp. 128–36. See also Ralf Elger and Yavuz Köse (eds), *Many Ways of Speaking about the Self: Middle Eastern Ego-Documents in Arabic, Persian, and Turkish (14th–20th Century)* (Wiesbaden: Harrassowitz, 2010); Stefan Reichmuth and Florian Schwarz (eds), *Zwischen Alltag und Schriftkultur: Horizonte des Individuellen in der arabischen Literatur des 17. und 18. Jahrhunderts* (Beirut: Orient-Institut, 2008).
29. Bernard Heyberger, *Hindiyya, Mystic and Criminal, 1720–1798: A Political and Religious Crisis in Lebanon*, translated by Renée Champion (Cambridge: James Clarke, 2013); Bernard Heyberger, 'Individualism and Political Modernity: Devout Catholic Women in Aleppo and Lebanon: Between the Seventeenth and the Nineteenth Centuries', in Amira Sonbol (ed.), *Beyond the Exotic: Women's Histories in Islamic Societies* (Syracuse: Syracuse University Press, 2005), pp. 71–85 [see Chapter 9 in this volume].
30. We decided to translate 'Anā al-fakīr' as 'Votre humble serviteur' or 'votre serviteur' in the French translation.
31. Dyâb, *D'Alep à Paris*, pp. 56–64. See also Ignatius Kratschkowsky and A. G. Karam, 'Farḥāt', in *Encyclopaedia of Islam, Second Edition*, online: <http://dx.doi.org/10.1163/1573-3912_islam_SIM_2282>.
32. Dyâb, *D'Alep à Paris*, pp. 300–1.
33. Ḥannā appeared several times in the journal of Antoine Galland between their first meeting arranged by Paul Lucas on 17 March and 6 June 1709: Frédéric Bauden and Richard Waller (eds), *Le journal d'Antoine Galland (1646–1715): La période parisienne*, vol. 1: *1708–1709* (Leuven, Paris: Peeters, 2011), pp. 286, 290–91, 320–33, 338–43, 346–47, 352–59, 363–67, 369–72, 373–76, 378. He was still mentioned when Galland received a letter he sent from Marseille, 25 October and 19 November: ibid. pp. 483, 504.
34. Richard van Leeuwen and Ulrich Marzolph, 'Hanna Diyab', in *The Arabian Nights Encyclopedia* (Santa Barbara: Abc-Clio, 2004), p. 582; Ulrich Marzolph, 'Les contes de Hannā', in *Les Mille et Une Nuits: Catalogue de l'exposition 'Mille et Une Nuits', Paris, Institut du monde arabe (27 novembre 2012–28 avril 2013)* (Paris: Éditions Hazan, Institut du monde arabe, 2012), pp. 87–91. The list of the sixteen tales told by Ḥannā is on p. 91.
35. Bottigheimer, *East Meets West*.
36. Dyâb, *D'Alep à Paris*, p. 334.
37. Ibid. p. 127.
38. These are exactly the skills that Ibn Budayr ascribed to 'his father, mentor and instructor' Sulaymān bin Hashīsh al-Hakawī (Sajdi, *The Barber of Damascus*, p. 75). See also the skills of the illiterate and the oral culture in Aleppo

through the testimony of a German traveller: Ulrich Jasper Seetzen, *Tagebuch des Aufenthalts in Aleppo (1803–1805)* (Zürich, New York: Georg Olms Verlag, 2011), pp. 148–50, 214.

39. Dyâb, *D'Alep à Paris*, pp. 73, 251–53, 314–25.
40. Ibid. pp. 247–48, 357–58.
41. Ibid. pp. 77, 204, 286, 336, 340, 375, 417, 429.
42. Heyberger, *Hindiyya, Mystic and Criminal.* See also Bernard Heyberger, *Les chrétiens du Proche-Orient au temps de la Réforme catholique*, 2nd ed. (Rome: École française de Rome, 2014).
43. Dyâb, *D'Alep à Paris*, pp. 179, 245–46, 325–27. See also his devotion to the Madonna of Montenero near Livorno, pp. 228–30.
44. For a reflection on (in)commensurability in the context of the early modern empires, see Sanjay Subrahmanyam, 'Par-delà l'incommensurabilité: Pour une histoire connectée des empires aux temps modernes', *Revue d'histoire moderne et contemporaine*, 54 (2007), pp. 34–53; Sanjay Subrahmanyam, *Courtly Encounters: Translating Gentleness and Violence in Early Modern Eurasia* (Cambridge, MA: Harvard University Press, 2012), p. xiv. In the Mediterranean context, see Guillaume Calafat, *Les interprètes de la diplomatie en Méditerranée: Traiter à Alger (1670–1680)*, in *Les musulmans dans l'histoire de l'Europe*, vol. 2, pp. 371–410. [See now also E. Natalie Rothman, *The Dragoman Renaissance: Diplomatic Interpreters and the Routes of Orientalism* (Ithaca: Cornell University Press, 2021).]
45. Sabine Mohasseb Saliba (ed.), *Les fondations pieuses waqfs chez les chrétiens et les juifs du Moyen Age à nos jours* (Paris: Geuthner, 2016).
46. Dyâb, *D'Alep à Paris*, pp. 292–97.
47. Ibid. pp. 343–45.
48. Ibid. pp. 212–16.
49. Ibid. pp. 255–57, 346–47.
50. Ibid. pp. 280–83, 288–91.
51. Bernard Heyberger, 'Morale et confession chez les melkites d'Alep d'après une liste de péchés (fin XVIIe siècle)', in Geneviève Gobillot and Marie-Thérèse Urvoy (eds), *L'Orient chrétien dans l'empire musulman: Hommage au professeur Gérard Troupeau* (Paris: Éditions de Paris, 2005), pp. 283–306.
52. Dyâb, *D'Alep à Paris*, p. 203.
53. Sajdi, *The Barber of Damascus*, pp. 30–31, 65–66.
54. Dyâb, *D'Alep à Paris*, pp. 207–9.
55. Ibid. pp. 124–27.
56. Ibid. p. 136.
57. Ibid. pp. 68, 77.
58. Ibid. pp. 155–59.
59. Ibid. pp. 76–78.
60. Ibid. p. 262. [On the construction of this official history of the Maronites in the seventeenth century, see Aurélien Girard, 'Was an Eastern Scholar Necessarily a Cultural Broker in Early Modern Europe? Faustus Naironus (1628–1711), the Christian East, and Oriental Studies', in Nicholas Hardy and Dmitri Levitin (eds), *Confessionalisation and Erudition in Early Modern Europe: An Episode in the*

History of the Humanities (Oxford: Oxford University Press, 2019), pp. 240–63; Aurélien Girard, 'La construction de l'identité confessionnelle maronite à l'époque ottomane (XVIe–XVIIe siècle)', in Bernard Heyberger (ed.), *Les chrétiens de tradition syriaque à l'époque ottomane* (Paris: Geuthner, 2020), pp. 153–200.]

61. Dyâb, *D'Alep à Paris*, pp. 196, 200–1.
62. Ibid. p. 232.
63. Ibid. p. 202.
64. Ibid. pp. 304–5.
65. Ibid. p. 433.
66. Philip D. Curtin, *Cross-Cultural Trade in World History* (Cambridge: Cambridge University Press, 1984); Bruce Masters, 'Trading Diasporas and "Nations": The Genesis of National Identities in Ottoman Aleppo', *International History Review*, 9 (1987), pp. 345–67.
67. Dyâb, *D'Alep à Paris*, pp. 283, 286, 341.
68. Ibid. pp. 336–44.
69. In Arabic, *Rūm Krīk*.
70. Ḥannā was very likely confusing two buildings established side by side: the Latin church of Saint Sophia, transformed into a mosque, adjoined with minarets, and the Greek church of Saint George, transformed into a market (*Bedestān*), surmounted by a dome and extensively decorated on its front. [The Eastern Christian Ḥannā Diyāb was not familiar with three-dimensional religious images, which do not exist in the Eastern Christian tradition.]
71. The '*uthmānī* is a small copper coin.

CHAPTER 5

The Migration of Middle Eastern Christians and European Protection: A Long History

INTRODUCTION

The history of the 'protection' of Christian minorities in the Middle East cannot be reduced to a diplomatic issue. 'Protection' in an anthropological approach is a universal rhetoric, shared by almost everybody in Mediterranean societies, and the notion of *dhimma*, which is the basic principle underlying relations between Muslims on one hand and Christians and Jews on the other means contract, pact, protection and guarantee. But beyond this, in segmented societies with a weak state, patronage and clientelism appear in various shapes.[1] Protection is an entangled issue, to which various players contribute on different scales: in this case, Eastern Christian individuals and congregations, local states and societies, Western opinion and Western States.

The history of protection first means one of circulations. From the sixteenth century onwards, a significant and increasing number of Eastern Christians, mainly members of the clergy, visited the 'Christian Lands' in order to claim support, collect alms and, sometimes, settle there. As a justification for their presence, they generally introduced themselves as victims of Islamic 'tyranny'. On another level, Western consuls, merchants and missionaries settling in the Levant belonged to networks in which they benefitted from local 'protections'. At the same time, they led complex systems of credit, advances on crops and tax-farming in which local Christians were involved.[2] Occasionally, as early as at the beginning of the seventeenth century, local leaders such as Emir Fakhraddīn in Mount Lebanon could claim political and military support from Europe. Especially from the eighteenth century onwards, the so-called *protégés* of the European nations, benefitting from the *berat* which gave them exemption from Ottoman law, were an important element in this system.[3]

Yet, 'protection' became an important diplomatic and ideological issue during the nineteenth century, when direct intervention by the European powers within the Ottoman Empire became heavier. At the same time, the ever-increasing anti-Christian tone of riots in the Ottoman cities and countries led to a mobilisation of international opinion through the press and to the first appearance of a humanitarian agenda for Mount Lebanon and Damascus after the massacres of 1860,[4] followed by those in Anatolia (1894–96)[5] and Crete (1897).[6]

CIRCULATION

The migration of Eastern Christians from the Middle East to Europe is not exclusively a contemporary issue. Indeed, we have evidence of 'Orientals', 'Greeks', 'Armenians', 'Maronites' and so on, circulating in Europe at least since the sixteenth century. They are not easy to spot in the sources, because they are not very numerous, and because they latinised their names: Ḥumaylī ibn Da'fī Karnuk, a Syriac ('Jacobite') priest originating from Diyarbakir, converted to Catholicism by the Capuchin Friars, was elected as archbishop of Mardin, then spent his long life in Europe under the name of Timoteo Agnellini;[7] Sulaymān ibn Ya'qūb had a complex career as an Arabic teacher and translator between Paris, Venice, Rome, London and Halle, under the rather common name of Salomone Negri/Salomon Niger.[8] The best-known of these travellers were monks or bishops, claiming to have an official mission for their churches. Travelling in order to collect money, in the Catholic countries as well as in Orthodox and Protestant states, became an intense activity and remains so until today. Belonging mostly to Eastern Catholic congregations, these travellers obtained a licence or recommendation from the Roman cardinals before visiting one or more countries. Arriving in a country, they had to obtain a visa, signifying permission to remain, by presenting their recommendations. After that, they needed the specific authorisation of the local bishop and the civil authorities to collect alms in their jurisdiction.[9] They often aroused great curiosity, as seen in the mentions of their stays in the newspapers.[10]

It is possible, for instance, to follow Maronite monks through the archives when, at the beginning of the eighteenth century, they visited Vienna and Prague, where they had to struggle against the strong opposition of the Franciscans, who feared competition from them. In 1730, in Madrid, they tried to obtain permission, without success, to go to America. After that, they were mentioned in Cologne, where they asked for a new recommendation for Vienna.[11]

We also know that some Greek Orthodox bishops or monks visited the territory of the tsars in order to collect financial support. The travelogue of the first journey of the Antiochian Patriarch Macarius (Makāryūs) al-Za'īm from Damascus to Moscow is famous. But this journey, as well as his second visit to Russia, is also documented in the Russian archives. Generally, Eastern monks or prelates presenting themselves at the borders of the Russian state first had to ask for a visa. It also happened that a monastery or a prelate was allowed by the

Russian authorities to collect alms every three or five years: in this way, the tsars won loyalty in the Ottoman Empire.[12]

These collectors generally did not begin their travel by chance. Like today, they prepared for their journey to Europe by using the networks of missionaries or diplomats that they had spun from their homeland before they left it. The priest Ilyās ibn Ḥannā al-Mawṣilī, who wrote an account of his travel to America, left Baghdad in 1668 with a Cretan artillery officer of the Ottoman army, who had close links to the Jesuits. In Rome, Ilyās met a nephew who was studying there and who joined him for part of his travels.[13] Arriving in Lyon, he met the previous French consul in Aleppo, François Picquet, a very devout man committed to Eastern Christianity.[14] In Paris, Louis XIV and his brother, the Duke of Orléans, greeted Ilyās, maybe thanks to a nephew of the Capuchin French missionary Jean-Baptiste de Saint-Aignan, who was the founder of the mission in Diyarbakir. Ilyās even used his knowledge of the Turkish language to approach the ambassador of the Sublime Porte, who was staying in Paris at the time.[15]

Most of these collectors, claiming to collect money in order to help their churches settle debts, actually did not distinguish between their own accounts and those of their congregation. Part of the money thus had a purely private destination. Athanāsyūs Safar, for instance, a Syriac Catholic bishop of Mardin, collected a very significant sum (46,000 *pezzi di otto*) in America, before being arrested after having been denounced by the Franciscans in Mexico in 1694. He was freed thanks to an intervention by the papal administration, which asked that the money be handed over to itself[16] and then used it to maintain the chapel and hospice of the Syriacs in Rome. Nevertheless, Bishop Athanāsyūs Safar enjoyed a quiet life in Rome for the rest of his days, free from financial worries, with a pension granted to him, using a part of the capital. These Eastern prelates settling in Rome generally brought a nephew or other relative with them. The nephew of Bishop Safar, Giovanni Domenico Safar, came to live with his uncle and in turn enjoyed a pension from 1736 until his death in 1753. After his death, his widow and his daughters continued to receive this living. As late as 1770, upon the death of his wife, it was granted to his unmarried forty-year-old daughter.[17]

In the nineteenth century, the confusion between private and institutional interests still appeared to have been the rule. In 1857, the Melkite bishop of Homs, Ghrīgūryūs ʿAtā, set out on a journey to Rome, Lyon and Paris, collecting gifts for rather ambiguous purposes. But after an interview with Alexandre Dumas, he benefitted from the publicity attracted by this popular writer who published an article on the attacks which had taken place against the village of Maʿalūla, belonging to ʿAtā's diocese, in 1850. At least a part of the collected money was used for the restoration of a church in this village.[18] After the massacres of 1860 in Syria, the same bishop returned to Europe in order to ask for financial support, but the papal representative in Beirut expressed doubts as to the effective use of the money collected and sought to take control of it.[19] At the same time, a Basilian Archimandrite called ʿIsā raised inquiries from the Irish clergy when he appeared in the very poor country of Ireland to collect alms for the relief of the Christians of Syria and Mount Lebanon, with a printed leaflet offering for sale palms directly imported from Syria.[20]

It was not only clergy who travelled to Europe asking for help. A number of laymen, single or with their families, came to Europe for a time or settled there indefinitely. Those who left personal testimonies about their journey or their lives far away from home generally expressed dissatisfaction and disillusion.[21] Several of them requested relief from the Christian authorities, arguing that they had escaped persecutions, either by Muslims, or by Orthodox Christians. Sometimes, this might have been true. However, looking at the stories they told when they asked for help, it appears that they were generally involved in complex business arrangements, in which they had ended heavily indebted to Muslim notables, who sometimes held their wife and children as a guarantee until they paid back their debts. However, if they were asking for relief from the Catholic Church, they would have had to display themselves as victims persecuted for their loyalty to the Catholic faith and the pope, and they would have had to produce written testimonies about their faithfulness from Latin missionaries.[22]

As early as 1660, the French traveller and consul Laurent d'Arvieux put the blame on the bishops who took France for 'their cash cow' (*vache à lait*) and knew how 'to counterfeit themselves to exhibite the poverty of their patriarch and of the Christians of the mountains in Lebanon and other places of the country'.[23] At the beginning of the eighteenth century, the number of Eastern Christians visiting Europe and asking for relief continued to increase. Not all of them had good reasons and genuine testimonies or recommendations, so the authorities took special measures to limit and control them. In 1751, the French consul in Tripoli informed the leaders of the Maronite nation in the city . . .

> . . . about the ill treatment those who would decide to go travelling the States of Christianity would expose themselves to, and that the intention of His Majesty was not to bear adventurers and tramps in the Kingdom. Several have already been arrested, and those belonging to their nation who would be found without testimonial of the consuls of France to justify their condition and the reasons for their trips would be arrested as well.[24]

In 1753, an official text published in France and aimed precisely at the 'Maronites and other Eastern Christians' obliged them to arrive in the country already provided with certificates from consuls of the French nation and legalised by the aldermen and commercial deputies in Marseille, on pain of imprisonment and being treated as tramps and disreputable people.[25]

We have evidence of some of these people who ended up in prison. But others did manage to succeed in their new lives. They played, for instance, a role in the introduction of coffee to Europe. The first coffee-sellers in Livorno were Eastern Christians. In Paris, the Maronite traveller Ḥannā Diyāb encountered during his stay in 1709 Isṭifān al-Shāmī, a café-owner in Paris, also mentioned in the treatise on coffee by Antoine Galland. According to the story told by Ḥannā Diyāb, al-Shāmī began in Paris as a beggar, and he obtained authorisation to beg at the door of Notre-Dame from an officer of the archbishop who himself was a native of Aleppo. With the money that he gathered from the alms, Isṭifān the Syrian began to sell coffee and swiftly made a fortune, opening one coffee shop in the *Quartier latin* and another in Versailles.[26] Virtually anywhere Ḥannā Diyāb passed through during his journey around the Mediterranean, he encountered Eastern Christians from Aleppo or Damascus, with whom he immediately felt at home. Not all of these people had migrated because of debts or other problems with the Ottoman authorities. In London, Malta, some Spanish ports and in Marseille, there was a presence of so-called 'Greeks' belonging to a modest category of seamen.

Best-known are those who settled in Europe in order to expand their businesses, who belonged to the so called 'trading diaspora', to networks dispersed to different places around the Mediterranean. The Armenians of New Julfa (Isfahan) – who spread their network as far as Livorno, Amsterdam and London – have already been studied and are well-known.[27] To give another example, Filippo Stamma, who published his *Essai sur le jeu des échecs* in Paris in 1737, moved to London in 1739, and there he published his famous *Noble Game of Chess* in 1745. He died in London in 1755, leaving behind two sons, William and Louis. He was related to an important Chaldean family settled in Aleppo since at least 1677, when ʿAbdallāh Shtamma was first mentioned there.[28] The family also seemed to maintain links with Diyarbakir. Francesco Namtalla Stamma was an important partner in the Smyrna branch of the Roux company from Marseille. He travelled throughout Europe and had strong links to Amsterdam. He often wrote his correspondence in Portuguese, which could indicate his previous activities in the Indian Ocean. He appears to have been involved in the colonial trade, sending an enormous quantity of woollen cloth, coffee, sugar and indigo to Smyrna between 1759 and 1762. In 1762, he brought a nephew, Antonio, into his business. Francesco must have been a brother of Filippo, the famous chess-player. When he died on 25 January 1763, a note in the archives of Marseille stated that he was a 'Chaldean, born in Aleppo, adopted French'. He belonged to the 'six Turks and Eastern Christians' who had been granted French 'naturality' by letters from Louis XV in 1760. Among the six names in this list appear 'Dom Francisco Nemetalla Stamma' and his cousin 'Cyriac Cazadour Chammas', a native of Diyarbakir, merchant-jeweller at the Palais-Royal.[29]

These migrants swiftly integrated into the host society, often becoming impossible to differentiate beyond the second generation of migrants. The absence of specific churches and parishes contributed to their assimilation.[30] As is often the case today, they had to worship in churches of other denominations. And where did they marry, or baptise their children? In London, where a small Greek community was settled, three Greek priests asked in 1675 to open their own church. A Greek bishop of Samos was then allowed to collect money in order to build this church, under certain conditions. But suspicions against this bishop and the other Greeks led to the confiscation of this building as early as 1682. At the beginning of the eighteenth century, Greeks instead came to pray at the Russian Chapel in London.[31]

In Rome, different Eastern denominations were allocated chapels and homes for sheltering their faithful during the seventeenth and eighteenth centuries. Little is known about the functioning of these places, which did not have a specific parish organisation.[32] Livorno was another place where Greeks and Armenians obtained a church, respectively, in the 1600s and 1700s. As within the small settlements of Eastern Christians in Western Europe today, the community appears when there is a priest who begins to gather the faithful and asks for an official acknowledgment of his role as a chaplain. From 1735 onwards, the Arabic-speaking Christians present in the city could enjoy the services of a Maronite priest who listened to confessions in Arabic, Turkish, or Armenian. But a specifically Maronite parish functioned there only between 1900 and 1939. In 1653, the Greek Church received official status with the approval of the archbishop of Pisa, and a brotherhood intended for the lay management of the church was then established. As is the case today, the members of the same denomination in the same city could be divided. The Greeks of Livorno were divided into individuals following the Latin rite, but sometimes they were considered as belonging to the Greek community; ethnic Greeks, who were Catholic, had settled in Livorno for several generations; Greek Orthodox who had settled more recently or were just passing through the city; and, finally, Arabic-speaking 'Greeks' (Melkites), who were generally Catholic. Only Catholics could worship freely; nevertheless, there is evidence that Orthodox Christians shared worship and sacraments with Catholics at least until 1757, when they obtained a church of their own. The landscape of the 'Greeks' in Livorno, as in other places around the Mediterranean, appeared rather complicated. Melkites used to worship in Arabic but were Catholics. During a conflict with the Greek-speaking clergy, some of them decided to become Latins. The Arabic-speaking 'Greeks' of Livorno experienced a long struggle before they were provided with their own Arabic-speaking priest in 1830. Before, they had attended the service by the Maronite priest.[33]

In France, the Eastern Christian presence was enhanced after Napoleon Bonaparte's expedition to Egypt (1798–1801), with a number of Melkites coming from Egypt to settle.[34] In 1821, the Melkite bishop Maksīmūs Maẓlūm opened the first Eastern Christian church in France, in Marseille, dedicated to Saint Nicholas, which still exists today. The archbishop of Marseille imposed a Western 'Restoration'-style architecture and decoration on this church. The same Maẓlūm also founded a church in Trieste, in the same period. Generally, in Catholic countries, until quite recently the Catholic branches of Eastern Christian Churches have been subject to the local Catholic bishop. Indeed, a very strong principle within the Roman Catholic Church is that only one ecclesiastical authority can have jurisdiction in one territory.[35]

In the last decades of the 1800s, the migration of Eastern Christians increased dramatically. The increasing population numbers in the rural districts, mainly in the mountains, pushed young people to emigrate. In Mount Lebanon, economic crisis and demographic growth caused the first massive departures to the Americas, while priests thundered from their pulpits against those who sought their fortune across the ocean.[36] Armenians and Assyrians from the borders of the Ottoman Empire, Persia and Russia also migrated, to the Americas or to the Russian Empire, especially Baku, where oil extraction had begun.[37] This important trend preceded the flow of the refugees from the ethnic cleansings of the First World War.

PROTECTION

Generally, when protection is discussed, the diplomatic agreements between the sultan and the Christian powers are mentioned. The first French 'capitulations' with the Sublime Porte (1536) actually did not mention the protection of the Ottoman Christians, nor did the renewal of these agreements. Capitulations (*ahdname*) officially granted to the French kings only the protection of those foreign Catholics present in the Ottoman Empire.

However, the different capitulations with the French, English, Dutch and other nations expressly foresaw the function of interpreter (dragoman) and the right of foreigners to be assisted by an official dragoman when they went to the court of the qadi. These dragomans, chosen from among the Eastern Christians or Jews, also fulfilled chancery functions at the consulates, registering commercial transactions and other documents in various Eastern languages, with a translation into Italian. Among these determined functions, they played a role as intermediary in many everyday situations. They had to be granted an official *berat*, a deed of appointment received from the Porte. In the 1700s, the number of these *berat*s increased and exceeded the number of interpreters needed by the embassies and consulates. The ambassadors began to sell *berat*s to wealthy Christians or Jews, who often worked in connection with foreign traders and thus became 'honorary dragomans'. Only about 300 of these *berat*s were in circulation in the entire Ottoman Empire at the end of the eighteenth century.

Nevertheless, every *berat* covered a man and his sons, or two of his other relatives. Thus, the number of *protégés* increased dramatically. The renewal of the capitulations in the 1600s introduced ambiguity with the idea that dragomans enjoyed the same fiscal status as foreigners – that is, exemption from the *jizya* or poll tax – although they clearly remained Ottoman subjects. In fact, they enjoyed a relatively favoured status as privileged subjects of the Porte.[38]

Generally, historians have described dragomans as privileged individuals released from communal solidarity, but a closer examination provides another insight. In Aleppo, Mikhā'īl Jarwah, who as a young man had been active in trade, was appointed bishop of the Suryani (Syriac Christians) on 23 February 1766 and became the Catholic patriarch of his denomination in 1782, remaining so until his death in 1800. He was protected by the *berat* of his father who was a dragoman of the Dutch consulate in the city. His brother Jibrā'īl enjoyed the same protection, but he received a *berat* of his own from the Austrian vice-consulate. He was appointed by Mikhā'īl as administrator (*wakīl*) of the Suryani community, with four other men, all Catholics and all enjoying the protection of the Dutch, English, or French consulates. These *beratlı* belonged to a new category of notables who took on responsibilities at the head of their community. Later, when the Ottoman Empire was reformed during the Tanzimat era (1839–76), they became the natural leaders of their *millets*, conceived as secular organisations, managing schools and hospitals.[39]

These men were involved in money-lending and -borrowing, not only with foreign merchants, but also with Muslim notables and Ottoman officers in the city. They were protected by the fiscal and jurisdictional privileges of *protégés*, but, thanks to their business and their networks within the Ottoman Empire, they controlled part of the trade at a regional level. Moreover, some of them were employed as *ṣarrāf* (treasury officials) or *kāhiyya* (secretaries) by the Ottoman governors or the local emirs and were involved in the tax-farming system (*'iqtā*). In this way, *protégés* could also become 'protectors': they had the power to help or threaten their European partners. Western merchants loaned money to Ottoman officials or to their Christian deputies and took control of cash crops in return, such as cotton or silk harvests. In 1750, the Maronite Lebanese monks were the biggest debtors to the French nation of Tripoli. Over two years, a French merchant managed to recoup part of his money by taking two silk gardens (*jardins à soie*) from them for two years and paying the taxes for the workers.[40] We know that this was an opportunity for the superior of the Lebanese Monks to travel to France and Spain in order to collect money, and he left an account of his travels. On his return, the monks decided to introduce the celebration of Saint Louis, whom they oddly called 'the first king of France', into their liturgical calendar.[41]

Interactions between foreigners and natives developed, mainly in the port-cities where European merchants were present and where local leaders favoured a more liberal environment. Jews and Christians took a central place in this system, acting as an interface. Christians of the Syrian coast, as well as those from the Greek islands, specialised in the transport of goods belonging to Muslim traders, who relied on this method to escape Christian Western corsairs. These Eastern Christians, claiming to be Catholics, asked for protection against pirates, with written recommendation obtained from the pope or Catholic state authorities. But it did not always help, and there were many trials and supplications before the courts in Malta, Tuscany, or Rome of these ship owners, asserting that they were good Catholics, in order to get their boats back, along with the cargo. In these cases, the networks of family and congregation between Aleppo, Cairo, Livorno, Rome and so on that appear so clearly in the sources are fascinating.[42] The same networking appears in private documents, when they are available, such as testaments or correspondence, until the twentieth century.[43] Matrimonial unions between Eastern Christians belonging to different denominations, or between Eastern Christians and Western Christians, which became more common from the 1700s onwards, can also be easily documented in the cosmopolitan cities of the Ottoman Empire, such as Alexandria, Beirut, Aleppo or Smyrna, as well as among the migrants settled in Europe.

Financial and political interactions were often muddled, especially in those districts where trade with European merchants granted good income to local political leaders. At the beginning of the 1600s, one of these local leaders, the Druze Emir Fakhraddīn of Mount Lebanon, like others after him, looked to enhance his power and his autonomy from Istanbul via the taxation of cash-crop exports. Politically, he hoped for an alliance with Tuscany and France, which was based on the religious links between Rome and the Maronites of Mount Lebanon, who were under his jurisdiction. But this vassal's rising power and the risk of an alliance with the Christian states and Persia led the Sublime Porte to launch a military expedition against the Emir, led by the governor of Damascus. Fakhraddīn decided to flee across the sea and took shelter in Tuscany from November 1613 to July 1615 and in the Spanish possessions of Southern Italy from July 1615 to August 1618. Thereafter, he returned to Mount Lebanon, and, taking advantage of Ottoman weakness, he enhanced and extended his power over Syria until a new Ottoman expedition was sent against him in summer 1633. Consequently, he was executed in Istanbul in April 1635.

Maronite prelates played an important role in Fakhraddīn's diplomacy, visiting the courts of Rome, Florence, Venice and Paris. They helped to plan a crusade in association with the army of the Emir and his Christian soldiers, which received some support from Tuscany as well as from France, but it came to nothing.[44] After this episode, Maronite representatives of the Church or of private interests often came to Versailles and Rome in order to ask for support. The French kings were not really interested in fighting the sultan, but they granted alms to these representatives and supported them with propaganda, such as letters claiming their traditional protection of the Maronites, or a portrait of Louis XIV which was displayed in the residence of the patriarch.[45]

In the 1800s – with the independence of Greece in 1830, the Egyptian occupation of Syria and Crete, and various national struggles for independence – a new kind of migrant appeared throughout the Mediterranean: political exiles. Political engineering by the Porte, with the support of Britain and Austria, was a common feature in the nineteenth century, in Europe as well as in the Ottoman Empire. Clergy visiting Europe, such as the Maronite bishop Nicolas Murad or Father ʿAzar, not only planned to collect alms. They also presented a political project and searched out support for it. They were especially committed to the struggle for a return of the Shihābī family as leaders in Mount Lebanon, following their dismissal, and for the interests of the landowning family of Khāzin, both targeted by the uprising of the Christian peasants in the Lebanese mountains in the previous years. ʿAzar and Murad were major contributors to the idea of 'France and the Maronites', consisting of a complex of representations which helped to shape Maronite identity, as well as French identity, in the colonial period.[46]

These Maronite representatives relied on a section of the French political leadership which argued that there was a French 'long tradition' of protection, going back to Charlemagne or Saint Louis. For instance, a famous 'letter of Saint Louis to the Maronites' is frequently quoted by both French and Maronite personalities as authentic to the present day, on any occasion when the issue of the French relationship to the Maronites and to Lebanon comes into question. This letter, dated 21 May 1250, from Saint-John of Acre for the first time appeared in the second edition of the travelogue of Alphonse de Lamartine, *Voyage en Orient* (1849).[47] It is probably an invention of Bishop Murad, who mentions it in his tract, asserting that 'it is drawn from a very ancient Arabic manuscript belonging to the archives of the Maronites, and the author of this manuscript states that he translated it from Latin into Arabic'. Yet, reading this text, it is quite easy to be convinced that it is a nineteenth-century forgery.[48]

The issue of 'protection of the Eastern Christians' was first directed towards French and Catholic public opinion, with the idea that Maronites and Eastern Catholics in exchange would support French expansion in the Mediterranean and help to tie the French presence into a narrative of the Crusades. The emancipation of Eastern Christians was thought of in the context of French and Catholic growth of influence in the Middle East. A colonisation of Syria by the French was even conceived (Lamartine had explained that the Maronites would be the community most able to improve Syria's prosperity under French rule), while projects to settle Maronites and Armenians as colonising farmers in Algeria were also mooted. The story of Emir Fakhraddīn was invoked as an episode of the traditional alliance between Eastern Christians and Crusaders, as well as a precedent in the European politics of 'civilising' the East.[49]

Beyond the specific Maronite case, it is worth exploring how the same topics were used in other local contexts. For instance, opening a French embassy in Tehran in 1854, Napoleon III evoked to the first ambassador the 'moral influence of France upon the Christians of Armenia and Persia, among whom the traditions and the records of the Crusades are deeply rooted'. And in 1867 the Chaldeans of Urmia (Persia) requested the opening of a French consulate in their city, imploring 'His Majesty the Emperor of the French to take us officially under his protection [. . .] We throw ourselves at the feet of France, protector of the Catholics throughout the world'.[50]

In the 1860s, the Maronite leader Yūsif Karam, who was seen as a romantic hero by a section of European Catholic opinion, was exiled from Mount Lebanon through an intervention by the French authorities, but continued to disseminate texts about fantastic political projects, for Mount Lebanon and beyond. Recent research has highlighted that migrants and exiles played a more important role in the construction of a national or sectarian consciousness in the nineteenth century than those people who remained in their homeland. In almost all communities, migrants living in the United States or in Europe, or those who had returned after a long stay in these countries, belonged to this important new category of intellectuals, journalists, physicians and engineers, who founded newspapers, wrote books, opened schools and launched political movements, thus contributing to the sectarian religious, ethnic and national awakening.[51]

In 1860, the social and political conflict between the Maronites and Druzes in Mount Lebanon led to violence generally interpreted as massacres of Christians. Following these events, a part of the Christians of Damascus was also the target of an uprising by Muslims, resulting in thousands who were killed or fled as refugees. These events provoked a strong movement of solidarity in European, mainly French, opinion, and not only among Catholics. They led to a French military expedition, which could be considered the first humanitarian intervention. They also led to the foundation of L'Œuvre d'Orient, which until today is the main Catholic organisation specialising in relief for Eastern Christians.[52]

After 1860, French and Catholic commitment to Eastern Christians thus became stronger, supported by an ideological discourse of 'the long tradition of protection' and of the 'regeneration' of Eastern Christians and Jews. Schools became heavily dependent on subventions from the French government, and school curricula were copies of the French. French became the main foreign language spoken among Christians and Jews, instead of Italian, which had been the previous *lingua franca* in the Eastern Mediterranean.[53] But this rise in the French and Catholic cultural presence, which has had consequences to the present day, was in competition with Russian official missions, especially with the activity of Protestant missionaries, mainly American, under British protection.

The French 'humanitarian' intervention of 1860 was used as a precedent for justifying other international military expeditions and for theorising the humanitarian right to intervention in the following decades. The Russo-Ottoman war of 1877 opened up the 'Armenian question', and the Treaty of San Stefano imposed reforms on behalf of the Armenians, under the control of the Russian army, which occupied the Eastern provinces of the Ottoman Empire. But only a few weeks later, at the Treaty of Berlin (1878), England imposed the Russian evacuation of Ottoman territory and obliged the sultan to take steps to protect Christian communities, under international control. At the same time, Britain took control of Cyprus as a guarantee that the treaty would be applied. In 1896, French, English, Russian, Italian and Austrian seamen landed in Crete, against Greece's attempt to take control of the island and in order to prevent new massacres among Christians and Muslims. The allied powers imposed autonomy on the island, but this favoured the Greeks against the Turks, who left Crete in large numbers, migrating to Turkey and thus paving the way for the annexation of the island by the kingdom of Greece in 1909.[54] There are further obvious examples of manipulating the question of Christian minorities by Russia, Britain and France, during and after the First World War.

CONCLUDING REMARKS

'Protection of the Eastern Christians (*chrétiens d'Orient*) is constitutive of our history, even of our identity, but also of the identities of the Middle East', asserted the French Foreign Minister Laurent Fabius in a newspaper interview in March 2015.[55] I believe that this assertion is true. However, the stereotypes which are constitutive of this concept have a history that needs to be questioned, especially today, when they are recalled by politicians and the media in a context in which the difference between Christian Syrian migrants and Muslim Syrian migrants, the opportunity of military humanitarian action of the Western forces in Iraq, Syria, or Libya, the possible alliance of European states with Russia and Bashar al-Assad for the 'rescue of civilisation' and the defence of Christian values against Islam are all yet again subjects of discussion.

What I have tried to describe here is an entangled history between French Catholics and Eastern Christians (mainly Catholics), which implied a long-term circulation of cultural representations between Europe and the Middle East. These representations on the one hand shaped the European perception of Eastern Christianity, but on the other hand contributed to the development of a specific self-consciousness on the part of Eastern Christians themselves. Victimisation, the fight against Islam, the concept of Christian solidarity, as well as political hope, manipulation and delusion all belong to this complex of representations. Perhaps the situations we are confronted with in countries where this history is less long and less entangled than in France offer opportunities for comparison with what I have described here.

May I finish with a personal anecdote? When I visited Jerusalem in spring 2012, I met in the streets a couple of Christians with a Swedish banner, who spoke Arabic. When I addressed them in Arabic, they answered that they were *Suryani Qadīm* from the region of Mosul, and that they had settled in Sweden in the 1980s. Knowing that I was French, they were proud to tell me that he was called Fabien and she Jeanne d'Arc! Belonging to the recent migration to Northern Europe, they came to reinforce their faith and their communal links in the Holy Land, like members of diaspora usually do (I met them when they were just leaving the *Suryani Qadīm* monastery of Saint Mark). But their names were also a testimony to a past gone by, that of the French 'protection' and 'civilising mission' through the French missionaries in the Christian surroundings of Mosul.

NOTES

1. [For a definition of 'protection', see Edmund Hayes and Eline Scheerlinck, 'Introduction', and Paul Jürgen, '*Ḥimāya* Revisited', in *Acts of Protection in Early Islamicate Societies*, monographic section of *Annales Islamologiques*, 54 (2020), online: <https://journals.openedition.org/anisl/7173>.]
2. Bernard Heyberger, 'Chrétiens orientaux dans l'Europe catholique (XVIIe–XVIIIe siècles)', in Bernard Heyberger and Chantal Verdeil (eds), *Hommes de l'entre-deux: Parcours individuels et portraits de groupe sur la frontière méditerranéenne* (Paris: Les Indes Savantes, 2009), pp. 61–94 [see the English translation in Chapter 1 of this volume]; Bernard Heyberger, 'Les nouveaux horizons méditerranéens des chrétiens du *bilād al-šām* (XVIIe–XVIIIe siècle)', *Arabica*, 51, 4 (2004), pp. 435–61; Maurits H. van den Boogert, *The Capitulations in the Ottoman Legal System: Consuls, Qadis and Beratlıs in the Eighteenth Century* (Leiden: Brill, 2005).
3. Van den Boogert, *The Capitulations*, pp. 19–115.
4. Leila Tarazi Fawaz, *An Occasion for War: Civil Conflict in Lebanon and Damascus in 1860* (London, New York: I. B. Tauris, 1994); Yann Bouyrat, *Devoir d'intervenir? L'expédition 'humanitaire' de la France au Liban, 1860* (Paris: Vendémiaire, 2013).
5. Vincent Duclert, *La France face au génocide des Arméniens: Une nation impériale et le devoir d'humanité* (Paris: Fayard, 2015), pp. 113–288.
6. Nikos Andriotis, 'Les querelles ethnoreligieuses en Crète et l'intervention des puissances européennes (seconde moitié du XIXe siècle)', in Anastassios Anastassiadis (ed.), *Voisinages fragiles: Les relations interconfessionnelles dans le Sud-Est européen et la Méditerranée orientale 1854–1923: Contraintes locales et enjeux internationaux* (Athens: École française d'Athènes, 2013), pp. 197–211.
7. Bernard Heyberger, 'La carrière manquée d'un ecclésiastique oriental en Italie: Timothée Karnûsh, archevêque syrien catholique de Mardin', in *L'Italie vue par les étrangers, Bulletin de la Faculté des Lettres de Mulhouse*, 19 (1995), pp. 31–47 [see the English translation in Chapter 2 of this volume].
8. John-Paul Ghobrial, 'The Life and Hard Times of Salomon Negri: An Arab Teacher in Early Modern Europe', in Jan Loop, Alastair Hamilton and Charles

Burnett (eds), *The Teaching and Learning of Arabic in Early Modern Europe* (Leiden, Boston: Brill, 2017), pp. 312–13. [Paula Manstetten, 'Solomon Negri: The Self-Fashioning of an Arab Christian in Early Modern Europe', in Cornel Zwierlein (ed.), *The Power of the Dispersed: Early Modern Global Travelers beyond Integration* (Leiden, Boston: Brill, 2022), pp. 240–84.]

9. Bernard Heyberger, 'Eastern Christians in Catholic Europe'; Tobias Mörike, 'Lebanese Travellers as Knowledge Brokers in Early Modern Europe 1725 to 1800' (paper presented at the international conference *The Middle East and Europe: Cross-Cultural, Diplomatic and Economic Exchanges in the Early Modern Period [1500–1820]*, Paris Sorbonne University Abu Dhabi, 4–7 March 2017). [Tobias P. Graf, 'Cheating the Habsburgs and Their Subjects? Eighteenth-Century "Arabian Princes" in Central Europe and the Question of Fraud', in Stefan Hanß and Dorothea Mcewan (eds), *The Habsburg Mediterranean* (Vienna: Austrian Academy of Sciences Press, 2021), pp. 229–54.]
10. [Graf, 'Cheating the Habsburgs']; Mörike, 'Lebanese Travellers'; *Le Journal de Paris* mentions the stay in Paris of 'M. Haun [ʿAwun], Abbé du Mont-Liban' (Superior of the Maronite Lebanese Monks): 2 January, 6 January, 18 January 1777. [See Ulrike Krampl, *Travailler avec les langues à Paris au XVIIIe siècle: La fabrique d'une ville plurilingue*, Mémoire inédit du dossier d'habilitation à diriger les recherches (Université de Paris: 2019), p. 352.]
11. Heyberger, *Les chrétiens du Proche-Orient*, pp. 216–17. APF, SC, Maroniti, vol. 3, fol. 305r; vol. 4, fols 156r–157r, 268r, 358r, 364r, 366r.
12. Vera Tchentsova, 'Les documents grecs du XVIIe siècle: Pièces authentiques et pièces fausses: 4. Le patriarche d'Antioche Athanase IV Dabbās et Moscou: En quête de subvention pour l'imprimerie arabe d'Alep', *Orientalia Christiana Periodica*, 79, 1 (2013), pp. 173–95.
13. Iliyās ibn Ḥannā al-Mawṣilī, *Il primo Orientale nelle Americhe*, translated by Marina Montanaro (Mazara del Vallo: G. G. Adria, 1992), 33; John-Paul Ghobrial, 'The Secret Life of Elias of Babylon and the Uses of Global Microhistory', *Past & Present*, 222 (2014), pp. 51–93.
14. Heyberger, *Les chrétiens du Proche-Orient*, p. 283. On François Picquet, ibid. pp. 252–61, 352–58, 421–25, and Georges Goyau, *Un précurseur: François Picquet, consul de Louis XIV en Alep et évêque de Babylone* (Paris: Geuthner, 1942).
15. Al-Mawṣilī, *Il primo orientale,* pp. 28–30. Salomon Negri also carried with him a recommendation letter of the Franciscan head of Aleppo (1688): Ghobrial, 'The Life and Hard Times', p. 317.
16. Heyberger, *Les chrétiens du Proche-Orient*, p. 217.
17. Heyberger, 'La carrière manquée', p. 46.
18. Frédéric Pichon, *Maaloula (XIXe–XXIe siècle): Du vieux avec du neuf: Histoire et identité d'un village chrétien de Syrie* (Beirut: Institut Français du Proche-Orient, 2010), p. 124.
19. AAV, Delegazione apostolica al Libano, busta 7, fols 24v–25r (Tripoli, 15 September 1861), 72r–73v (Beirut, 28 July 1863).
20. APF, SC, Siria, vol. 1 (1860–73), fols 241r–243r.

21. See the account by Ḥannā Diyāb of his travels from Aleppo to Paris, which gives some evidence of Syrians settled in Livorno, Marseille and Paris: Bernard Heyberger, 'A Border Crossing Ottoman Christian at the Beginning of the 18th Century: Hanna Dyâb of Aleppo and His Account of His Travel to Paris', *Studi e Materiali di Storia delle Religioni*, 84, 2 (2018), pp. 548–64; Hanna Dyâb, *D'Alep à Paris*. See also the disappointment of Salomon Negri: Ghobrial, 'The Life and Hard Times', pp. 311, 319.
22. Heyberger, 'Eastern Christians in Catholic Europe'.
23. Laurent d'Arvieux, *Mémoires du Chevalier d'Arvieux*, edited by Jean-Baptiste Labat (Paris: Charles-Jean-Baptiste Delespine, 1735), vol. 2, p. 370: 'qui savaient se contrefaire pour exposer la misère de leur patriarche et des chrétiens des montagnes du Liban et autres lieux du Païs'.
24. AN, AE, B/I, vol. 1118, fols 416r–418v, 10 December 1751: 'aux chefs de la nation maronite qui se trouvent en cette ville les mauvais traitements auxquels s'exposeroient ceux d'entre eux qui s'aviseroient d'aller inconsidérément parcourir les Etats de la Chrétienté, et que l'intention de Sa Majesté étant de ne point souffrir d'aventurier et vagabonds dans le Royaume, on en avoit déjà arrêté et qu'on continueroit d'arrêter comme tels ceux de leur nation que l'on trouveroit sans certificat des consuls de France pour justifier leur état et les raisons de leurs courses'.
25. *Ordonnance du roi, portant ce qui devra être observé par rapport aux Maronites & autres chrétiens orientaux, & aux esclaves rachetés, qui se trouveront dans le Royaume: Du 8 janvier 1753* (Paris: Imprimerie Nationale, 1753), Paris, Bibliothèque nationale de France, département Droit, économie, politique, F-21153 (2). Hélène Desmet-Grégoire, *Le divan magique: L'Orient turc en France au XVIIIe siècle* (Paris: L'Harmattan, 1994), pp. 48–49.
26. Hanna Dyâb, *D'Alep à Paris*, pp. 340–44; Antoine Galland, *De l'origine et du progrès du café: Extrait d'un manuscrit arabe de la Bibliothèque du Roi* (1699; new ed. Paris: La Bibliothèque, 1992), p. 88.
27. Olivier Raveux, 'Entre réseau communautaire intercontinental et intégration locale: La colonie marseillaise des marchands arméniens de la Nouvelle-Djoulfa (Ispahan), 1669–1695', *Revue d'histoire moderne et contemporaine*, 59, 1 (2012), pp. 83–102, provides a bibliography related to these subjects.
28. Information provided by Jean Fathi (KU Leuven), who has prepared an unpublished study on this family.
29. Sébastien Lupo, *Révolution(s) d'échelles: Le marché levantin et la crise du commerce marseillais au miroir des maisons Roux et de leurs relais à Smyrne (1740–1787)* (PhD dissertation, Université Aix-Marseille, 2015), vol. 2, pp. 450–54, 459–60.
30. Nevertheless, Angela Falcetta, *Ortodossi nel Mediterraneo cattolico: Frontiere, reti, comunità nel Regno di Napoli (1700–1821)* (Rome: Viella, 2016), pp. 200–1, has asserted that, even without symbolic institutions, a specific alterity could be preserved among the migrants.
31. [John-Paul Ghobrial, 'Moving Stories and What They Tell Us: Early Modern Mobility Between Microhistory and Global History', *Past & Present*, 242, Supplement n. 14 (2019) pp. 243–80].

32. Cesare Santus, 'Tra la chiesa di Sant'Atanasio e il Sant'Uffizio: Note sulla presenza greca a Roma in età moderna,' in Antal Molnár, Giovanni Pizzorusso and Matteo Sanfilippo (eds.), *Chiese e nationes a Roma: Dalla Scandinavia ai Balcani: Secoli XV-XVIII* (Roma: Viella, 2017), pp. 153–83; [Cesare Santus, 'Wandering Lives: Eastern Christian Pilgrims, Alms-Collectors, and "Refugees" in Early Modern Rome', in Matthew Coneys Wainwright and Emily Michelson (eds), *A Companion to Religious Minorities in Early Modern Rome* (Leiden: Brill, 2021) pp. 237–71.]
33. Falcetta, *Ortodossi nel Mediterraneo cattolico*, p. 222; Guido Bellatti Ceccoli, 'Voci dall'Oriente: Arabi cristiani e musulmani a Livorno in età moderna', in Adriano Prosperi (ed.), *Livorno 1606–1806: Luogo di incontro tra popoli e culture* (Turin: Umberto Allemandi, 2009), pp. 418–29; Guido Bellatti Ceccoli, *Tra Toscana e Medioriente: La storia degli Arabi cattolici a Livorno (sec. XVII-XX)* (Livorno: Editasca, 2008).
34. Ian Coller, *Arab France: Islam and the Making of Modern Europe, 1798–1831* (Berkeley: University of California Press, 2010).
35. Joseph Hajjar, *Un lutteur infatigable: Le patriarche Maximos III Mazloum* (Harissa: Imprimerie Saint Paul, 1957), pp. 50–54.
36. Akram Khater, *Inventing Home: Emigration, Gender and the Making of a Lebanese Middle Class, 1861–1921* (Berkeley, London: University of California Press, 2001).
37. Florence Hellot-Bellier, *Chroniques de massacres annoncés: Les Assyro-Chaldéens d'Iran et du Hakkari face aux ambitions des empires, 1896–1920* (Paris: Geuthner, 2014), pp. 258–74.
38. Van den Boogert, *The Capitulations*, pp. 19–115; Maurits H. van den Boogert, 'Intermediaries *par excellence?* Ottoman Dragomans in the Eighteenth Century', in Bernard Heyberger and Chantal Verdeil (eds), *Hommes de l'entre-deux: Parcours individuels et portraits de groupe sur la frontière méditerranéenne* (Paris: Les Indes Savantes, 2009), pp. 95–115.
39. Van den Boogert, 'Intermediaries *par excellence?*'
40. AN, AE, B/I, vol. 1120, fols 291r–293r.
41. Forschungs- und Landesbibliothek Gotha, ms. Orient A 1549: travel of Arsāniyūs Shukrī and Banyamīn ibn Zakhariyā [see Feras Krimsti, 'Arsāniyūs Shukrī al-Ḥakīm's Account of His Journey to France, the Iberian Peninsula, and Italy (1748–1757) from Travel Journal to Edition', *Philological Encounters*, 4, 2019, pp. 202–44]; Bernard Heyberger, *Hindiyya, Mystic and Criminal, 1720–1798: A Political and Religious Crisis in Lebanon* (Cambridge: James Clarke & Co., 2013), p. 89.
42. Bernard Heyberger, 'Sécurité et insécurité: Les chrétiens de Syrie dans l'espace méditerranéen (XVIIe–XVIIIe siècles),' in Meropi Anastassiadou and Bernard Heyberger (eds), *Figures anonymes, figures d'élite: Pour une anatomie de l'Homo ottomanicus* (Istanbul: Isis, 1999), pp. 147–63 [see the English translation in Chapter 3 of this volume]; Molly Greene, *Catholic Pirates and Greek Merchants: A Maritime History of the Mediterranean* (Princeton: Princeton University Press, 2010).

43. See, for instance, about the testament of Antonio Kair in Massimo Sanacore, 'Tra Livorno e l'Egitto: Vita e vicende commerciali di Antonio Kair,' *Nuovi Studi Livornesi*, 16 (2009), pp. 121–50.
44. Albrecht Fuess, 'An Instructive Experience: Fakhr al-Dîn's Journey to Italy, 1613–1618', in Bernard Heyberger and Carsten Walbiner (eds), *Les Européens vus par les Libanais à l'époque ottomane* (Beirut: Orient-Institut der DMG; Würzburg: Ergon, 2002), pp. 23–42; Abdul Rahim Abu-Husayn, *Provincial Leadership in Syria, 1575–1650* (Beirut: American University of Beirut, 1985); Khaled El Bibas, *L'Emiro e il Granduca: La vicenda dell'emiro Fakhr ad-Dīn II del Libano nel contesto delle relazioni fra la Toscana e l'Oriente* (Florence: Le Lettere, 2010).
45. René Ristelhueber, *Traditions françaises au Liban* (Paris: Librairie Alcan, 1918).
46. Carol Hakim, *The Origin of the Lebanese National Idea 1840–1920* (Berkeley: University of California Press, 2003); Bernard Heyberger, 'La France et la protection des chrétiens maronites: Généalogie d'une représentation', *Relations internationales*, 173, 1 (2018), pp. 13–30.
47. Alphonse de Lamartine, *Voyage en Orient*, edited by Sarga Moussa (Paris: Honoré Champion, 2000).
48. Nicolas Murad, *Notice historique sur l'origine de la nation maronite et sur ses rapports avec la France sur la nation druze et sur les diverses populations du Mont-Liban*, 2nd ed. (Paris: Librairie Adrien Le Clere, 1844), p. 25; Youssef Mouawad, 'Aux origines d'un mythe: La lettre de saint Louis aux maronites', in Bernard Heyberger and Carsten Walbiner (eds), *Les Européens vus par les Libanais à l'époque ottomane* (Beirut: Orient-Institut der DMG; Würzburg: Ergon, 2002), pp. 97–110.
49. Heyberger, 'La France et la protection'.
50. Hellot-Bellier, *Chroniques de massacres annoncés*, pp. 249–51.
51. See, for instance, Adam H. Becker, *Revival and Awakening: American Evangelical Missionaries in Iran and the Origins of Assyrian Nationalism* (Chicago: University of Chicago Press, 2015), pp. 299–338. For a different contribution, see Maurizio Isabella and Konstantina Zanou (eds), *Mediterranean Diasporas: Politics and Ideas in the Long 19th Century* (London, New York: Bloomsbury, 2016).
52. Hervé Legrand and Giuseppe Maria Croce (eds), *L'Œuvre d'Orient: Solidarités anciennes et nouveaux défis* (Paris: Cerf, 2010).
53. Patrick Cabanel (ed.), *Une France en Méditerranée: Ecoles, langues et cultures françaises, XIXe–XXe siècles* (Paris: Créaphis, 2006); Jean Riffier, *Les œuvres françaises en Syrie (1860–1923)* (Paris: L'Harmattan, 2000); Chantal Verdeil, *La Mission jésuite du Mont-Liban et de Syrie (1830–1864)* (Paris: Les Indes Savantes, 2011); Esther Möller, *Orte der Zivilisierungsmission: Französische Schulen im Libanon 1909–1943* (Göttingen: Vandenhoeck und Ruprecht, 2013).
54. Nikos Andriotis, 'Les querelles ethnoreligieuses en Crète et l'intervention des puissances européennes (seconde moitié du XIXe siècle)', in Anastassios Anastassiadis (ed.), *Voisinages fragiles: Les relations interconfessionnelles dans le Sud-Est européen et la Méditerranée orientale 1854–1923: Contraintes locales et enjeux internationaux* (Athens: École française d'Athènes, 2013), pp. 197–211; Sia Anagnostopoulou, 'Chrétiens, musulmans et l'arrivée du lion anglais: Les autorités

religieuses de Chypre face au pouvoir colonial britannique (1878–1884)', ibid. pp. 181–96.

55. Laurent Fabius, French Minister of Foreign Affairs, in *La Croix*, 27 March 2015. A similar declaration has been published by three previous Prime Ministers of France, François Fillon, Alain Juppé and Jean-Pierre Raffarin, in *Le Monde*, 13 August 2014.

PART II

Building Confessional Identities: Entangled Histories

CHAPTER 6

The Westernisation and Confessionalisation of Christians in the Middle East: An 'Entangled History' ('*Histoire Croisée*')[1]

For a long time, the culture of Eastern Christians was judged by placing them on a scale of civilisations, ahead of their Muslim environment but behind their Western counterparts. This was already Volney's method when in 1785 he mentioned the progress of writing and reading among Christians.[2] At the end of the nineteenth century, Eastern Christians themselves discussed their place on this scale, and they themselves used the European terminology of 'decadence' (*inḥiṭāṭ*) and 'renaissance' (*nahḍa*), which is still in use in some quarters today. In the 1950s and 1960s, during the period of decolonisation and the Second Vatican Council, voices were raised within Eastern Christianity (in particular by the Melkites) to protest against the imposition of the Latin model that deprived the Easterners of their roots; they demanded their autonomy, a return to their origins and a pursuit of authenticity.[3] This reaction was part of a broader movement that we can qualify as 'culturalist', the aim of which was to promote local specificity and to perfect the knowledge of the differentiated workings of societies and cultures. It was based on a dualist vision that assumed a clear opposition between Europeans and others and presented the latter as victims of Western aggression. In the specific case of the Middle East, however, it remained contained within a confessional tension that aimed to reaffirm the specific identity not only of the Christian minorities in Islam, but of one Christian denomination in relation to others. Today, however, we view the situation as incorporating more complex configurations that combine traits of varied origins in often unexpected ways. These include the effects that the encounter with the Other had on European civilisation. The latter can no longer be presented as a monolithic and timeless abstraction. By increasingly taking into account the diachronic dimension, we have become more sensitive to the dynamic of contact situations, in constant transformation. Here, I would like to present one approach from within this historiographical current, applying it to the Christians of the Middle East and their relationship to Catholicism. It is a '*histoire croisée*' in the sense that we are trying to connect stories that have been separated as a result of the compartmentalisation of twentieth-century historiographic production, and to highlight 'the dense tissue of intersections, based on the references effectively mobilised by one or the other in the establishing of their respective representations'.[4]

EASTERN CHRISTIANS AND SOCIETIES OF THE MIDDE EAST

Ethnology and colonial history made a point of making inventories and counting minority, ethnic, confessional and linguistic groups. This exhausting and permanently incomplete job has today been abandoned in favour of other methods more attentive to borders and to the performative declarations which generate identity by exclusion or opposition. This change in perspective has also made it possible to move away from essentialism and to historicise situations, observing that the relations between groups, their respective strategies and their discourse on tradition and authenticity were constantly being reorganised according to broad cultural and political contexts.[5]

However, in so far as Eastern Christians are concerned, we need to acknowledge that this change of perspective, despite recent remarkable historical works, has only partially succeeded in infiltrating the general narrative, including the one produced by academics.[6] Copts, Maronites, Armenians, Assyro-Chaldeans and Greeks felt the need to differentiate themselves not only from their Muslim environment, but also from Christians belonging to different denominations or confessions, starting with the Latins. Hence the quest for mythical origins and the affirmation of timeless and specific characters, and even of a destiny charged with specific eschatological meaning. I will give only two examples, both taken from the Maronites. Thus, a 'Letter' or 'Charter' from Saint Louis to the Maronites (dated 21 May 1250), clearly proven to be a nineteenth-century forgery, continues to be reproduced by some scholars, with the sole aim of demonstrating their ideological loyalty.[7] In another recent book, the author, after having evoked the fifteenth century as a 'golden age for the Maronites', has defended the role of the patriarch, in terms that to us seem directly inspired by the clerical and nationalist ideologies of the nineteenth century:

> It is the primacy of faith that made the whole Community's eyes converge towards one single person, the highest in ecclesiastical rank: the patriarch. It was he, the indisputable and undisputed leader. He was the father. He was the judge. This title of 'patriarch' gave the person bearing it all the honours and all the jurisdiction of one of the four patriarchal sees of the Eastern Church. He invested it, moreover, with all the prestige enjoyed by the patriarchs of the Old Testament, absolute masters of their tribes. The many bishops who helped him in the governance of his Community

were no more than his assistants and vicars. They had to answer to him for everything.[8]

This type of commentary presupposes the permanence of religious belief and practice as the basis of the social order. These supposedly permanent elements thus would seem to escape from the field of historical investigation, to remain unchanged throughout the ages. The group itself would be defined almost exclusively by its confessional belonging, which would distinguish it fundamentally from its environment, in particular from the Muslim majority. It would moreover form a hierarchically constituted entity, perpetually united.[9]

This confessional vision of Eastern Christians in reality is a modern construct, characteristic of the era of nationalism, which does not give a true account of the realities that preceded it. The confusion of the spiritual, temporal, even military roles in a sort of theocracy, far from being a remnant of previous centuries, as has so often been stated, was above all the consequence of nineteenth-century ideologies. In the same way, the outbreak of fanatical violence was not, as stated by one Lebanese historian in relation to the events of 1958, 'a deadly return to medieval history'.[10]

As a reaction to this confessional and essentialist reading of history, other historiographical currents tried to deny religion any role, or at least to reduce its significance, sometimes excluding it altogether from their analyses.[11] In fact, religion operated in the definition and discrimination between groups. The status of *dhimmī* defined Jews and Christians as different from Muslims. The constraints of collective responsibility in judicial and fiscal matters (*jizya*) imposed an internal structuring on the communities, at least locally.[12] In addition, the administration of the sacraments, the application of canon law in questions of marriage, the following of liturgical cycles and participation in collective rites made it possible to preserve the specific identity threatened by dissolution into Islam or into a rival Christian rite. However, in a society dominated by oral tradition, where writing was rare and varied, the norm could not be applied in a firm and invariable way, the more so as ecclesiastical authority was constantly placed in competition with other systems of authority, Islamic, Christian, or customary. Other factors were taken into account in the definition of the group. Christians of the same denomination lived scattered over vast discontinuous areas. Under these conditions, they adopted the way of life and values of the society into which they were integrated. Their perception of social order, their conception of hierarchy, lineage and alliances did not distinguish them from their Muslim – Sunni or 'unorthodox' – neighbours. Mountain-dwellers from Lebanon or Kurdistan and semi-nomads from the desert border of Transjordan shared an organisation and the common values of their tribes, regardless of their confessional affiliation. Melkites, Maronites, or Armenians from Aleppo likewise adhered to a social system founded on the Ottoman order and the sultan's sovereignty.[13] During his travels (1664–66), the Melkite patriarch Macarius III ibn al-Zaʿīm was horrified to discover the practice of infanticide among the Georgians ('things that make stones weep') and made this invocation: 'God, Praise be to Him, give help to our Sultan, and keep us safe in our homes!'[14] His son Būlus, visiting Kiev, shocked by the exactions of the Polish Catholics, cried out: 'May God make the Turkish Empire last forever!'[15] Christians not only participated in the dominant political culture, that of the Ottoman towns regulated by sharia law or that of the rural borders dominated by custom; they also for the most part shared the mentality of their fellow countrymen, including their perception of the sacred and their religious practices.[16]

A single confessional community often found itself deeply divided into factions that pitted the countryside against the town, or one town against another. The segmentation that characterised these societies worsened even more the divisions and rivalries within a single confession and Church.[17] This situation favoured external agents and the introduction of innovations, instrumentalised in local conflicts, according to a pattern that can be seen in many colonial situations. The discrepancies and tensions that divided local society laid the ground for the imposition of economic, political and cultural domination.[18] Frustrations, including within family groups, could make the cultural offer of the Western world seem attractive.

INDIVIDUALISATION, CONFESSIONALISATION AND THE 'PROCESS OF CIVILISATION'

It often happens that uninformed observers confuse Eastern Christianity with Christianity, full stop, even with Latin Catholicism. The latter followed its own trajectory in history, which is important to keep in mind if one wants to think about the phenomena of cultural transfers or, more correctly, of interrelation and interactivity, not only between Western and Eastern Christianity, but also between Christianity and Islam. We cannot, for example, characterise certain aspects of the spirituality of the Maronite mystic Hindiyya (science of the ignorant, abandonment of self in the presence of God) as being typically Islamic and assume in her the influence of Sufism, unless we completely ignore the developments of Catholic mysticism in the seventeenth century.[19] Outside these false structural analogies, an Islamic inspiration in Hindiyya's ideas still has to be proven, whereas that of Fénelon or of Saint Teresa of Avila is probable. Her Eastern sources, perhaps not written, are difficult to establish. If she quotes John Climacus, a mystic of Mount Sinai, one must not forget that this reference is shared with the Latin spirituality that inspired her.[20] Cultural movements are decidedly complex, and we are only at the beginning of the research to answer these questions!

The Catholicism that emerged from the Council of Trent, while at the same time reforming itself, engaged in an exploratory approach and an accumulation of knowledge about other Christians, in a spirit of dogmatic and intellectual competition with the Protestants. For those who delve into the missionary or Orientalist literature of the seventeenth century, what is most striking is the awareness of European authors of the distance that separates them from an Eastern Christian. This comes first of all from the application of a method of observation and ethnographic narrative developed in particular by the Jesuits, based on the advice of Ignatius of Loyola himself.[21] It also stems from an awareness of the gap between a culture founded on the widespread diffusion of printed material and a traditional culture in which writing was rare and verbal and where non-verbal forms of communication were dominant. On this basis, the ignorance and barbarity of the Easterners was not judged any more harshly than that of the Breton, Dauphinois or Corsican peasants of the same period.[22]

The discovery of the difference between 'we', the Europeans, and 'they', the Eastern Christians, allowed a well-educated Orientalist such as Richard Simon (1638–1712) to measure the considerable gap that had widened between modern Latin Catholicism and the original Christianity.[23] But the majority of Latins applied to the Easterners the post-Tridentine model of reading history, considering that the latter had distanced themselves from the true doctrine and true practice because of their separation from Rome, their ignorance, their negligence and the pernicious effects of their frequenting of 'infidels' and 'heretics'. It was therefore necessary to bring them back to an authentic Christianity by the reform of 'abuses', by the fight against 'superstition', by the restoration of ecclesiastical authority at different levels and by the instruction of the faithful. Thus, during the first legation of the Jesuits to the Maronites in 1579, Cardinal Carafa wrote to Patriarch Rizzī:

> We will be careful to bear in mind and put together everything that we deem useful for you, as much in doctrine, sound, integral and true, as in the rites and administration of the sacraments, so that everything be done according to the decency that is right for the ministers of Christ, all false doctrine and all superstitious abuses being banished.[24]

Sometimes, the Islamic dissidents (Druzes, Nuṣayrīs, Yazidīs) were also considered Christians whose faith had been corrupted due to their distance from the Church and whose conversion would be easier than that of Sunni Muslims. The method followed to achieve missionary goals was barely different from that which was applied elsewhere in Catholic lands. Only the deployment of public processions was impossible in *dār al-islām*, with some exceptions. The teaching of reading and catechism to Christians was one of the main missionary activities, wherever the presence of the 'Frankish' believers was tolerated in the Eastern Mediterranean. For young people beyond school age, it was the fraternities and the lay congregations that offered a place for training through their weekly meetings, where learning to read was one of the main activities.[25] The ideas and methods of the 'Catholic Reformation' were essentially shared and applied, in the wake of the missionaries, by the Eastern clergy united with Rome.[26]

Although we have some indication of the attendance at schools and the content of the teaching, more systematic research is yet to be done, in particular on the textbooks and devotional works translated from Western languages used in these instances, of which many copies have been preserved. It may be that some of these books were used to increase the standing of their author with no practical use. The quality of the language employed and the form given to the work might be indicative here. Translations are generally more like adaptations, and their differences from the originals can be significant. We should also compare the works by Catholics with those of the Orthodox, such as *The Very Useful Commandments That Every Christian Should Know and Respect, in order to Save His Soul* (*Waṣāyā nāfiʿa jiddan wa yajib ʿalā kull masīḥī biʾan yaʿrifahā wa yaḥfiẓahā likay yukhallaṣ nafsahu*), translated from the Greek by Patriarch Macarius III ibn al-Zaʿīm, which reveals a clear Latin influence, but takes great care to differ from Roman theology on certain points.[27]

The works available to literate Christians were intended for personal and silent reading. This reading should lead to the internalisation of new behaviours, encouraged by a daily examination of conscience and regular dialogue with the spiritual director (*murshid*). All of these readings and practices were aimed at rationalising the personal and social life of individuals. The introduction of new rules of sociability, based on the principles of politeness (*tartīb*) and decency (*iḥtishām*), formed the basis of a true 'civilising process' that tended to distance the Catholic faithful from their normal universe, shared with Muslims and other Christians.[28] Images, printed or painted, widely distributed in the same period, had the same educational goals.[29]

It is hard to measure the impact of this conditioning. One can at least note that individuals, especially women, started talking of their 'self' by borrowing for the most part the interpretative grids and terminology of Western psychology.[30] While Catholic education tended to an interiorisation of rules and thus an affirmation of the individual, it also took part in the bureaucratisation of social life, which was characterised by the reinforcement of institutional authority at the expense of primary ties and by the domination of legal norms imposed on all and implemented by a class of professionals, according to the Weberian pattern.[31] The path to salvation itself then moved from 'the contemplative escape from the world' to 'the transformation of the world' via an active ascetic lifestyle.[32]

Catholic influence resulted in a reinforcement and legitimation of ecclesiastical power, conceived of as a hierarchical pyramid, of which the pope was the undisputed summit. Eastern prelates united with Rome, or those who asked for confirmation after their election had to take an oath of obedience to the person of the Supreme Pontiff, which Rome would have been impossible to require of an eighteenth-century French bishop.[33] The Maronite patriarch Yūsuf Isṭifān, suspended by the Roman authorities following his role in the 'Hindiyya affair' had, in order to be reinstated, to sign a formula of retraction that he rejected. He had to declare that 'in the future' he only wanted 'to be a submissive child, obedient to the Roman and Apostolic Holy See and to his Holiness the Supreme Pontiff in place, Pius VI, to his successors and to the Congregation for the Propagation of the Holy Faith'.[34] This very hierarchical Catholic model probably inspired the communitarian or proto-nationalist constructions of the nineteenth century, deriving moreover from European clerical and counter-revolutionary ideologies: both the timeless confessionalist vision of the Maronite community, mentioned in the quote above, and the ideal type of the organisation of the *millet* as it is generally understood. According to this schema, each Christian confessional community would have been under the centralised authority of a patriarch, holding concurrently the powers that the sultan would have generously attributed to him.

At a lower level, the Catholicism that followed the Council of Trent insisted on the dignity and authority of the priestly function. By valuing the attendance of the sacraments, by placing the Eucharist and auricular Confession at the heart of Christian spirituality, it made the priest the favoured and exclusive mediator between the faithful and God. The collection of documents of the Lebanese synod of 1736, like other regulations or dogmatic texts, devoted most of its instructions to the sacraments and insisted on the practical, intellectual and spiritual qualities required of the priest who administered them.[35] The efforts to control and train the clergy in the nineteenth century led to a certain emancipation of the clergy *vis-à-vis* influential families. With recruitment from more modest origins, education received on the spot or in Europe, vast networks of information and aid, and their own more secure resources, the ecclesiastics (at least in Lebanon) aspired to play a more active role in society and public life.[36]

The new religious orders that were founded in the Eastern Christian communities united with Rome from the end of the seventeenth century onwards were all inspired by the Constitutions of the Society of Jesus or by those of the Visitandines, redacted by Saint Francis of Sales. The aim was to introduce into religious life a rationalisation of behaviour that had been totally absent from Eastern ascetism until then. Thus, the rule of the Congregation of the Sacred Heart of Jesus, dictated by Hindiyya, divided time in minute detail, took into account the architectural distribution of monastic buildings, fixed prescriptions for hygiene, formalised the election of the superior by a secret ballot and established a proportional coding of punishments. The intention to go beyond the traditional systems of relations founded on kinship and cronyism, to establish a homogenised group, guided the text. The same preoccupation is to be found in the rules of the fraternities intended for young Catholics of Aleppo and established by the Jesuits.[37]

At the same time, ecclesiastical justice asserted itself in its dealings with customary justice or the fairly frequent recourse to the justice of the qadi. The Maronite ʿAbdallāh Qarāʿalī, founder of the order of Lebanese Monks, originally from Aleppo, wrote legal handbooks inspired by Muslim legislation concerning different aspects of civil personal law. The Synod of Lebanon organised an ecclesiastical tribunal and ordered the patriarch to gift the bishops a compendium of canon and civil law. In 1744, the works of Qarāʿalī were adopted for this purpose.[38] In Aleppo, Catholic Melkites in 1753 established a tribunal presided over by a *wakīl* of the bishop, assisted by four priests and four lay people, which sat for two hours every morning to examine and deal with the spiritual and temporal matters brought to them. The aim was not only to avoid recourse to the sharia tribunals, but also to confront an Orthodox offensive.[39] Law thus became formalised. Acts were recorded, and the judge preferred written documents over oral testimony. The Maronite Synod of Lebanon insisted on the keeping of registers and organisation of archives by the bishops and patriarchs. At the end of the eighteenth century, Emir Bashīr entrusted the justice of the Mountain to the bishops, who applied sharia law in civil affairs, not without protest, when the latter contradicted Maronite practice in matters of succession.[40] Inside the Churches themselves, disciplinary questions took on a significant importance: thus the rhythm and the nature of fasting and abstinence imposed on the faithful during the liturgical year, or matrimonial prohibitions on the subject of consanguinity and affinity. The aim was to fix clear and universal rules where very often canon law had previously compromised with customary law or local power dynamics. The goal was the reinforcement and centralisation of ecclesiastical authority in each Church, as well as the distinction from Muslims and other rival Christian obediences, in a competitive atmosphere, not only between the Catholic and Orthodox, but also between Maronites, Melkites and Latins. The introduction of a Latin practice of dispensations concerning fasting as well as matrimonial affairs brought power and increased resources to the prelates who granted them.[41]

This evolution met that of the Ottoman authorities who were attempting to centralise and to formalise their own authority. Clericalisation and confessionalisation thus participated in a 'modernisation' of society, founded on the delegitimisation of custom and clannish or family solidarities. It is therefore true that this process had started in certain Christian communities of the empire long before it was put in place by the Ottoman state.[42]

PATTERNS OF EXCHANGE AND CONFRONTATION

The process described here is to be understood as taking place over an extremely long time period. If our attention, for practical reasons, is mainly focused on the seventeenth and eighteenth centuries, it is nevertheless quite clear that we should follow its evolution over a much longer time-scale, at least until the First

World War. On the whole, the nineteenth century continued and reinforced the work started in previous centuries.[43] Even the Protestant missionary enterprise in many ways acted in the same way as the Catholic one.

It was not, however, a linear evolution. Acculturation is never in one direction only, from indigenous culture to European culture, and it consists less in final, measurable results, than in an endless process, always incomplete.[44] It is the dynamics of exchange and confrontation that we must try to grasp, at the risk of appearing, like others, fascinated by 'the failures, the unexpected, the emotional'.[45]

Firstly, the West does not appear as a single entity. In the nineteenth century especially, competition between Catholics and Protestants was one of the main motors of missionary activity in the Ottoman Empire. Within Catholicism itself, the Roman Church and the main 'protecting' power (France) were far from sharing the same point of view or always aiming at the same objective; this also had repercussions for the activity of the religious orders, generally rivals of one another. While under the Ancien Régime, Jesuits and Capuchins were French and attached to French politics, it was not the same for the Friars Minor of the Holy Land, who were from Spain and Italy. 'National' rivalries between orders were exacerbated by quarrels over methods. It should also be pointed out that the missionaries of the end of the eighteenth century, in terms of motivation, number, age and training, were quite different from those of the first decades of the seventeenth century.[46] Let us add that the missionaries, who often had left behind their country of origin a long time ago, generally carried an out-of-date image of their own country and their own culture. The Church itself, with its Roman head, was not systematically the arrogant and unchanging institution that historians of Eastern Christianity enjoy depicting. It was traversed by crisis, by contradictions, by changes of direction. Thus, Benedict XIV (1740–58), attached to the *regolata devozione* at a time when Catholicism's break with the Enlightenment was not yet evident, proved to have reservations regarding a sentimental religiosity such as that expressed by the Maronites, with Hindiyya and her devotion to the Sacred Heart of Jesus. His successors were swept along by a current that characterised counter-revolutionary Catholicism from the trauma of the suppression of the Jesuits (1773) onwards. Furthermore, Roman bureaucracy generally found it hard to obtain reliable information and then apply its decisions firmly in the absence of a temporal on-the-spot power that would support it.[47]

In the East, the innovations briefly outlined above were not greeted without confrontation or opposition. Some of the regulations introduced by the Maronite Synod of Lebanon (1736), such as the regulation requiring the suppression of mixed monasteries, would take nearly a century to be applied. The hierarchical pyramid of authority – from the pope over the patriarch to the bishops and priests – was for a long time fragile and gave rise to endless conflicts between the Roman pontiff, the patriarch and the bishops, among the Maronites as much as the Melkites. The will to impose respect for principles such as the consent of girls and ecclesiastical control for matrimonial alliances raised opposition that was sometimes lively. The reform of the practice of fasting provoked violent quarrels among the Melkites. The rules of the new religious orders, tending to rationalise the individual and collective life of the believers, often fell on deaf ears in view of the quarrels that tore apart the monasteries, revealing the persistence of a patrimonial mentality and attachments to clients and family lineage. Thus, the congregation of the Sacred Heart of Jesus founded by Hindiyya was undermined almost from the start, because of opposition between the nuns originating from Aleppo and those originally from the Lebanese mountains, a division which also split the Lebanese Monks. It was moreover one of the major causes of the tragedy that finally played out at the Bkirki monastery.[48]

It is not, however, possible to see these conflicts simply as confrontations between traditionalists and innovators. Firstly, innovation was generally seen as the restoration of an antique tradition, the correction of an 'abuse' that had been introduced into the true doctrine or into good practice, according to the teaching of the Council of Trent. Thus, when Aftīmyūs Ṣayfī, Melkite bishop of Saida (1643–1723), lightened the rules of fasting for his faithful, he claimed to be doing away with bad habits brought into his Church by a few 'Manicheans' after the Schism of Photius. When Maksīmūs al-Ḥakīm, the Melkite archbishop of Aleppo, introduced the typically Latin feast of Corpus Domini, he gave it a Byzantine ritual and claimed to have unearthed an antique liturgy. And when the Maronite patriarch criticised the Lebanese Monks for taking off their hoods to say mass, contrary to tradition, ʿAbdallāh Qarāʿalī answered that the custom of celebrating with one's head covered was an 'abuse' introduced by 'the impious Dioscorus'.[49] On several occasions, the text of the Lebanese Synod referred to custom. For example, it stated:

> We also order, on pain of ecclesiastical sanctions, that the old custom be preserved, namely that the clerics bring the disputes arising between themselves and lay people before the bishop's tribunal. He who dares disregard the power of the bishop in order to appeal to the civilian judges [. . .] will *ipso facto* be excommunicated, as he will have infringed on ecclesiastical liberty.[50]

One must obviously see in this type of formula an idealised projection of the past rather than the attestation of an authentic 'old custom'. Confrontation with Western humanism brought the Easterners to a study of their own history, which they constructed mainly in a spirit of apologetics. This 'invention of tradition' later on contributed to the reinforcement of their own confessional identity.[51] Notably, the same phenomena are observable among the Orthodox, keen to condemn the Latin 'innovations' and 'deviations' by opposing them to their allegedly faithful respect of tradition.

The same group or the same person could, on the one hand, devote themselves to introducing an innovation and, on the other hand, be a defender of a custom or tradition. The Shuwayrite Melkite monks opposed the Patriarch Cyril Ṭānās and the Salvatorian monks, refusing all easing of fasting and abstinence on the model of the Latin Church. We cannot however qualify them as traditionalists: they contributed amply to the introduction of new ways of thinking and a new spirituality, notably through devotional works composed or printed by them.[52]

If we put ourselves on the level of individuals to try and understand the coherence of their behaviour, we have to recognise that they are often ambivalent and brought to some spectacular turnarounds due to circumstances. Hindiyya, taught by the Jesuits and promoted by them to a career of sainthood, ended by violently opposing her teachers, which did not stop her appealing for help from her brother, himself a Jesuit. Ilyās Fakhr, a Melkite from Tripoli, was recruited at a young age to serve the Latin missionaries and the Catholic cause, and for a while he played a double game before openly moving to Orthodoxy and becoming a passionate polemicist against Latin propaganda. This does not exclude the fact that he may have been reconciled with the Catholic Church at the end of his life.[53] Antūn Khabiyya (Kobié, Cubié), son and grandson of Melkite priests from Damascus, both fervent supporters of Catholicism, was admitted to the *Collegio Urbano* in Rome in 1725. He returned to his hometown in 1732, after having failed in his studies. Later on, he became violently hostile to the cardinals and missionaries, which did not stop him from being mixed up in religious affairs and looking after passing Europeans, earning his living by practising the painting skills he had acquired in Rome.[54]

In order to understand these attitudes, we must try to understand the whole system of relations of a person or a group, so as to reconstitute as far as possible its strategic action. For the most part, the above-mentioned processes must be understood at the most elementary level, that of the individual. We are then faced with 'an open system in constant transformation, determined by micro-social dynamics and mechanics of interactional type'.[55] This approach allows us to pay particular attention to the uncertain and unexpected dimensions of all behaviour. The significance of an institution or the value of a rule is then understood as part of a negotiation between actual social agents. We have already tried to reconstitute the system of relations and the strategic logic of an Aftīmyūs Ṣayfī, whose Catholic zeal is better understood when examining his social strategy as a whole.[56] If we look at the case of the Maronite patriarch Yūsuf Isṭifān, he certainly cannot be called 'conservative', even though the whole of his work deserves an attentive study.[57] His education in Rome, his acquaintances at the court of France, his active support for the new devotion to the Sacred Heart of

Jesus and his certain stance in favour of the power of bishops and the eminent authority of the Holy See meant that he could be seen as an 'innovator', to the point of being called a 'Frank' by his adversaries. From his stay at the Roman college he had acquired a taste for written communication, circulars and dissertations overloaded with learned references to canon law and history. As a young bishop, he took the side of the opposition to the patriarch Tūbiyā al-Khāzin who assumed the role of 'conservative' notable. But once he was patriarch, he in turn invoked tradition to justify his desire for innovation concerning the organisation of the liturgy and ecclesiastical discipline. He recalled the antiquity of the patriarchal throne of Antioch, of which he considered himself the only legitimate incumbent,as well as the perpetual faithfulness of the Maronites to the Catholic church, cornerstone of the confessional identity then being constructed, to claim full sovereignty over his people.

It is hard, however, to understand the person of Yūsuf Isṭifān and his subsequent evolution, if we do not take into account the fact that he belonged to an ecclesiastical dynasty that perpetuated patrimonial behaviour. Thus, very early on he inherited the family monastery of ʿAyn Warqa and at a very young was promoted to the head of the diocese of Beirut, following his uncle. Once a patriarch, he gathered a synod in his village of Ghūsṭā (1768), where it was stated that 'family links do not lead to the glory of God' and that the functions and ranks of the Church should not be inherited but allocated on the base of merit. This did not alter the fact that, during his reign (1766–93), six out of the fifteen bishops he ordained were from Ghūsṭā, where he resided most of the time. One of the six was his brother, and three others came from one family. His politic for the most part were dictated by his irrepressible hostility towards Mikhāʾīl al-Fāḍil who had followed a path similar to his own and in Rome had even been his master for a while. Fāḍil had obtained the diocese of Beirut against Isṭifān by relying on another network of solidarity.

An institutional innovation such as the confraternal structure was instrumentalised by the two adversaries to enlarge and organise the network of their followers. The patriarch encouraged the foundation and expansion of the Brotherhood of the Sacred Heart, founded by Hindiyya and linked to her by a vow required of its followers. Mikhāʾīl al-Fāḍil, the bishop of Beirut, answered by founding the Congregation of the Immaculate Conception of the Virgin with the approval of the General Superior of the Jesuits. He immediately exceeded the limits of his diocese, which provoked his official condemnation by Yūsuf Isṭifān. There are other examples of the instrumentalisation of these pious associations. Later on, a 'modern' procedure like that of confession – 'one of the most highly recommended techniques to produce the truth', according to Michel Foucault[58] – was used to reinforce the contested charisma of Hindiyya and the shaky authority of the patriarch.

Being a Catholic or adopting certain cultural or institutional innovations inspired by the West, as already stated above, offered new opportunities for power and action in an extremely unstable social context, in which networks of relations were endlessly recomposed. Aftīmyūs Ṣayfī, Yūsuf Isṭifān and Mikhā'īl al-Fāḍil, as in a lesser way the Latin missionaries and the Roman envoys themselves, were embedded in a clientelist system in which relationships between people and groups were founded on modes of domination of a patriarchal type: the personal connections and the solidarity of lineage or of the village behind the local leader definitely outweighed wider considerations of common interest, and this despite the declared intention to formalise and rationalise power. Hindiyya's charisma and the very strong link established between the prophetess and her followers could have made possible the foundation of a new pact between Maronites, going beyond the traditional social system. Instead, it ended up being subordinate to the latter. One may describe this functioning in the manner of the *'aṣabiyya* or 'tribal' loyalties that characterised Arab society, as described by Ibn Khaldun. But we are not very far from the mechanisms described in other contexts around the same period.[59] A society founded on lineage, clans, or clientelism should not appear to us as if it were frozen in archaic immobility. On the contrary, it had resources of dynamism and adaptation that allowed it to integrate new cultural or institutional elements, even if it was at the cost of crisis and conflicts, which were sometimes severe.

It is possible to argue that the processes discussed here concerned only a small minority of Christians open to the West. But we know that this minority occupied a specific place in exchanges with the 'Franks', as well as in the Arabic literary renaissance and in the construction of Arab, Egyptian, Syrian, or Lebanese identity.

Objects or practices in contact are not only interrelated but modify each other under the influence of their relationship.[60] The Orthodox should not escape our investigation, as they also belong to this 'entangled history' (*histoire croisée*). They themselves had to engage in confrontation and structure as a reaction to this 'Westernisation', often by using methods and arguments close to those of the Catholics. The attempts at Greek centralisation by the patriarchate of Constantinople in the eighteenth century were thus significant. It is moreover remarkable that many of the Greek Orthodox polemicists studied in the West or frequented the missionaries in the East. Historical research has suffered from an imbalance in favour of the Catholics, for one of the traits so characteristic of Catholic modernity was a taste for the written text and for the preservation of archives: we have at our disposal a much richer documentation concerning Catholic communities than other Christian denominations, which encourages one-sided research.

There has been a debate about modernisation in Islam from the eighteenth century onwards, in terms quite similar to those with which I have dealt here.[61] The question of reaction to Westernisation did not arise in the same way among Muslims as it did among Christians, but there may have been similarities in the processes of adaptation, rejection and compromise, especially at a microsocial level. It is moreover certain that the Islamic reformists of the early twentieth century were directly inspired by the methods of Christian missionary propaganda, and in many respects they fought battles similar to those of the Catholic clergy (modern education, the fight against 'superstitions', the reinforcement of confessional identity and the separation from 'infidels' and 'heretics/schismatics'). They were also led to reflect on their relationship with tradition and innovation in a process of identity construction that would merit comparison with the one discused in this chapter.[62]

NOTES

1. Michael Werner and Bénédicte Zimmermann, 'Penser l'histoire croisée: Entre empire et réflexivité', *Annales: Histoire, sciences sociales*, 58, 1 (2003), pp. 7–36; Michael Werner and Bénédicte Zimmermann, 'Beyond Comparison: *Histoire Croisée* and the Challenge of Reflexivity', *History and Theory*, 45 (2006), pp. 30–50. ['*Histoire croisée*' is not easily transposed into English. We decided to translate it as 'entangled history' throughout the entire essay].
2. Constantin-François Volney, *Voyage en Égypte et en Syrie*, edited by Jean Gaulmier (Paris, The Hague: Mouton & Co., 1959), pp. 227, 410–11.
3. Bernard Heyberger, 'Saint Charbel Makhlouf, ou la consécration de l'identité maronite', in Catherine Mayeur-Jaouen (ed.), *Saints et héros du Moyen-Orient contemporain* (Paris: Maisonneuve & Larose, 2002), pp. 139–59 [see the English version of the article in this volume, Chapter 10]. The Melkite Fr. Joseph Hajjar was representative of this way of looking at things: Joseph Hajjar, 'L'activité latinisante du lazariste Nicolas Gaudez en Syrie', *Revue d'histoire de l'Église*, 75, 1 (1980), pp. 40–83; Joseph Hajjar, 'La question religieuse en Orient au déclin de l'Empire Ottoman (1683–1814)', *Istina*, 2 (1968), pp. 152–236; Joseph Hajjar, *L'apostolat des missionnaires latins dans le Proche-Orient selon les directives romaines* (Jerusalem: Habesch, 1956).
4. Werner and Zimmermann, 'Penser l'histoire croisée', pp. 7–8 (the original quote is in French); Werner and Zimmermann, 'Beyond Comparison', pp. 31–3; Serge Gruzinski, 'Les mondes mêlés de la monarchie catholique et autres "connected histories"', *Annales: Histoire, sciences sociales*, 56, 1 (2001), pp. 86–87.
5. See the now classic Fredrik Barth (ed.), *Ethnic Groups and Boundaries: The Social Organization of Culture Difference* (Boston, Bergen, London: Universitets forlaget, Allen & Unwin, 1969). For a broader bibliographical discussion and an overview of this question, see Lucette Valensi, 'La tour de Babel: Groupes et relations ethniques au Moyen-Orient et en Afrique du Nord', *Annales: Économies, sociétés, civilisations*, 41, 4 (1986), pp. 817–38. For a solid clarification on the 'relational' approaches and a discussion of '*histoire croisée*' as regards comparativism, the study of cultural transfers and 'shared' or 'connected' history, see Werner and Zimmermann, 'Beyond Comparison'.
6. See the conscious defence of the essentialist method applied to the Druzes in the sixteenth century, with a quote from Hegel supporting it, by a historian of the

Lebanese University (Phanar): Jean Charaf, 'Introduction à l'histoire sociale du Mont-Liban au XVIe siècle', in Charles Chartouni (ed.), *Histoire sociétés et pouvoir aux Proche et Moyen Orients* (Paris: Geuthner, 2001), pp. 11–26. It is curious that, in the same volume, another author, a lecturer at the theology faculty at the Holy Spirit University (Kaslik), has analysed the historical birth of the myth of 'the eternal Maronite orthodoxy' between the sixteenth and seventeenth centuries: Paul Rouhana, 'Les versions des origines religieuses des Maronites entre le XVe et le XVIIIe siècles', in Charles Chartouni (ed.), *Histoire sociétés et pouvoir aux Proche et Moyen Orients* (Paris: Geuthner, 2001), pp. 191–211.

7. Elias Atallah, *Le Synode Libanais de 1736* (Antélias, Paris: CERO, Letouzey et Ané, 2001), vol. 1, p. 284. For a critique of this forgery and the conditions of its appearance, see Youssef Mouawad, 'Aux origines d'un mythe: La lettre de St Louis aux Maronites', in Bernard Heyberger and Carsten Walbiner (eds), *Les Européens vus par les Libanais à l'époque ottoman* (Beirut: Orient-Institut der DMG; Würzburg: Ergon, 2002), pp. 97–110.
8. Hector Douaihy, *Un théologien maronite: Gibra'il ibn al-Qalā'i: Évêque et moine franciscain* (Kaslik: Université Saint-Esprit de Kaslik, 1993), pp. 162–63.
9. Heyberger, 'Saint Charbel Makhlouf'.
10. Toufic Touma, *Paysans et institutions féodales chez les Druses et les Maronites du Liban du XVIIIe siècle à 1914* (Beirut: Librairie orientale, 1971), p. 29. For a critique of this view, see Ussama Makdisi, *The Culture of Sectarianism: Community, History, and Violence in Nineteenth-Century Ottoman Lebanon* (Berkeley, Los Angeles, London: Universiy of California Press, 2000).
11. This is one of the critiques that can be formulated concerning Ussama Makdisi's *The Culture of Sectarianism.* Concerning this attitude, see the historiographical introduction in Bruce Masters, *Christians and Jews in the Ottoman Arab World: The Roots of Sectarianism* (Cambridge: Cambridge University Press, 2001), pp. 1–5.
12. Bernard Heyberger, *Les chrétiens du Proche-Orient au temps de la Réforme catholique* (Rome: École française de Rome, 1994), pp. 39–62.
13. See the different contributions in Bernard Heyberger (ed.), *Chrétiens du monde arabe: Un archipel en terre d'Islam* (Paris: Autrement, 2003).
14. Carsten Walbiner, *Die Mitteilungen des griechisch-orthodoxen Patriarchen Makarius Ibn az-Za'īm von Antiochia (1647–1672) über Georgien nach dem arabischen Autograph von St. Petersburg* (PhD dissertation, Universität Leipzig, 1995), p. 166 (Arabic), p. 206 (German translation).
15. Heyberger, *Les chrétiens du Proche-Orient*, p. 394. For other manifestations of Ottoman legitimism in the diary of a Melkite Catholic notable from Aleppo, see Yūsuf bin Dimitrī bin Jirjis al-Khūrī 'Abbūd al-Ḥalabī, *Ḥawādith Ḥalab al-yawmiyya 1771–1805: Al-murtād fī ta'rīkh Ḥalab wa Baghdād*, edited by Fawāz Maḥmūd al-Fawāz (Aleppo: Sha'ār li-nashr wa-l-'ulūm, 2006), pp. 83, 198.
16. Heyberger, *Les chrétiens du Proche-Orient*, pp. 155–77; Bernard Heyberger, 'Frontières confessionnelles et conversions chez les chrétiens orientaux (XVIIe–XVIIIe siècles)', in Mercedes García-Arenal, *Islamic Conversions: Religious Identities in Mediterranean Islam* (Paris: Maisonneuve & Larose, European Science

Foundation, 2001), pp. 245–58. [For an updated study on this issue, see James Grehan, *Twilight of the Saints: Everyday Religion in Ottoman Syria and Palestine* (Oxford: Oxford University Press, 2014)].

17. Heyberger, *Les chrétiens du Proche-Orient*, pp. 63–107. [Bernard Heyberger, *Hindiyya, Mystic and Criminal, 1720–1798: A Political and Religious Crisis in Lebanon*, English translation by Renée Champion (Cambridge: James Clarke & Co., 2013), pp. 46–56, 157–218.]
18. Nathan Wachtel, 'L'acculturation', in Jacques Le Goff and Pierre Nora (eds), *Faire de l'histoire*, vol. 1 (Paris: Gallimard, 1986), p. 199.
19. Masters, *Christians and Jews in the Ottoman Arab World*, pp. 111–15.
20. [Heyberger, *Hindiyya*, p. 95]. Jad Hatem, *Hindiyyé d'Alep: Mystique de la chair et jalousie divine* (Paris: L'Harmattan, 2001).
21. Charlotte de Castelnau-L'Estoile, *Les Ouvriers d'une Vigne stérile: Les jésuites et la conversion des Indiens au Brésil 1580–1620* (Lisbon, Paris: Centre Culturel Calouste Gulbenkian, Commission nationale pour les commémorations des découvertes portugaises, 2000), pp. 58–81.
22. Heyberger, *Les chrétiens du Proche-Orient*, p. 140.
23. Girolamo Dandini, *Voyage du Mont Liban, traduit de l'italien du R. P. Jérôme Dandini, nonce en ce païs-là: Ou il est traité tant de la créance et des coutumes des Maronites, que de plusieurs particularitez touchant les Turcs, et de quelques lieux considérables de l'Orient; avec des remarques sur la Théologie des Chrétiens du Levant, et sur celle des Mahométans. Par R. S. P.* [Richard Simon, prêtre] (Paris: Louis Billaine, 1675). It was in fact the French translation, amply commented on by Richard Simon, of the book by the Jesuit Girolamo Dandini, *Missione apostolica al Patriarca e Maroniti del Monte Libano et Pellegrinazione a Gerusalemme di P. Jer. Dandini* (Cesena: per il Neri, 1656). See also Richard Simon, *Histoire critique de la Créance et des Coûtumes des Nations du Levant* (Frankfurt: Frédéric Arnaud, 1684).
24. Sami Kuri (ed.), *Monumenta Proximi-Orientis*, vol. 1: *Palestine-Liban-Syrie-Mésopotamie (1523–1583)* (Rome: Institutum historicum Societatis Iesu, 1989), p. 189.
25. Heyberger, *Les chrétiens du Proche-Orient*, pp. 453–509; Bernard Heyberger, 'Un nouveau modèle de conscience individuelle et de comportement social: Les confréries d'Alep (XVIIe–XVIIIe siècles)', *Parole de l'Orient*, 21 (1996), pp. 271–83; Bernard Heyberger, 'Entre Orient et Occident, la religion des dévotes d'Alep', in Louis Châtellier (ed.), *Religions en transition dans la seconde moitié du XVIIIe siècle* (Oxford: Voltaire Foundation, 2000), pp. 171–85; Bernard Heyberger, 'Individualism and Political Modernity: Devout Catholic Women in Aleppo and Lebanon: Between the Seventeenth and the Nineteenth Centuries', in Amira Sonbol (ed.), *Beyond the Exotic: Women's Histories in Islamic Societies* (New York: Syracuse University Press, 2005), pp. 71–85 [republished in Chapter 9 in this volume].
26. Heyberger, *Les chrétiens du Proche-Orient*, pp. 385–548. See the provisions of the Maronite Synod in 1736: Atallah, *Le Synode Libanais de 1736*, vol. 2, pp. 21–28, 357–77.

27. BAV, ms. Sbath 356, fols 192r–232v; Heyberger, *Les chrétiens du Proche-Orient*, p. 396. [On this issue, see also Vasileios Tsakiris, *Die gedruckten griechischen Beichtbücher zur Zeit der Türkenherrschaft: Ihr kirchenpolitischer Entstehungszusammenhang und ihre Quellen* (Berlin, New York: Walter de Gruyter, 2009)].
28. Heyberger, *Les chrétiens du Proche-Orient*, pp. 494–548; Heyberger, 'Un nouveau modèle de conscience individuelle'; [Heyberger, *Hindiyya*, pp. 32–36, 93–105]; Norbert Elias, *The Civilizing Process: Sociogenetic and Psychogenetic Investigations* (Oxford: Basil Blackwell, 2000).
29. Bernard Heyberger, 'De l'image religieuse à l'image profane? L'essor de l'image chez les chrétiens de Syrie et du Liban (XVIIe–XIXe siècles)', in Bernard Heyberger and Silvia Naef (eds), *La multiplication des images en pays d'Islam: De l'estampe à la télévision (17e–21e siècle)* (Istanbul: Orient-Institut der DMG; Würzburg: Ergon, 2003) [translated into English in Chapter 8 in this volume]; [Bernard Heyberger, 'Le renouveau de l'image de religion chez les chrétiens orientaux', *Archives des sciences sociales des religions*, 183 (2018), pp. 191–205].
30. [Heyberger, *Hindiyya*, pp. 23–46, 90–105]; Heyberger, 'Un nouveau modèle de conscience individuelle et de comportement social'.
31. Max Weber, *Sociologie des religions* (Paris: Gallimard, 1996), pp. 374–77.
32. Weber, *Sociologie des religions*, p. 363; Andreas Buss, 'The Individual in the Eastern Orthodox tradition', *Archives des sciences sociales des religions*, 91 (1995), pp. 259–75; Louis Dumont, *Essais sur l'individualisme: Une perspective anthropologique sur l'idéologie moderne* (Paris: Seuil, 1983).
33. Heyberger, *Les chrétiens du Proche-Orient*, p. 234.
34. [Heyberger, *Hindiyya*, pp. 190–91; Aurélien Girard, 'Comment reconnaître un chrétien oriental *vraiment* catholique? Elaboration et usages de la profession de foi pour les orientaux à Rome (XVIe–XVIIIe siècle)', in Marie-Hélène Blanchet and Frédéric Gabriel (eds), *L'union à l'épreuve du formulaire: Professions de foi entre Églises d'Orient et d'Occident (XIIIe–XVIIIe siècle)* (Leuven: Peeters, 2016), pp. 235–57.]
35. Atallah, *Le Synode Libanais de 1736*, vol. 2, pp. 39–195; see also the third part, 'Des diacres, des prêtres et des supérieurs', pp. 199–356.
36. John P. Spagnolo, *France and Ottoman Lebanon 1861–1914* (London: Ithaca Press, 1977), p. 17.
37. [Heyberger, *Hindiyya*, pp. 95–96]; Heyberger, *Les chrétiens du Proche-Orient*, p. 506.
38. Heyberger, *Les chrétiens du Proche-Orient*, pp. 70–71; Atallah, *Le Synode Libanais de 1736*, vol. 2, pp. 273–86.
39. Heyberger, *Les chrétiens du Proche-Orient*, p. 69.
40. Richard van Leeuwen, *Notables and Clergy in Mount Lebanon: The Khâzins Sheikhs and the Maronite Church (1736–1840)* (Leiden: Brill, 1994), pp. 198–202.
41. Heyberger, *Les chrétiens du Proche-Orient*.
42. Makdisi, *The Culture of Sectarianism*, passim; Selim Deringil, 'Conversion and Ideological Reinforcement: The Yezidi Kurds', in Mercedes García-Arenal, *Islamic Conversions: Religious Identities in Mediterranean Islam* (Paris: Maisonneuve & Larose, European Science Foundation, 2001), pp. 419–43.

43. Chantal Verdeil, 'Travailler à la renaissance de l'Orient chrétien: Les missions latines en Syrie (1830–1945)', *Proche-Orient Chrétien*, 51 (2001), pp. 267–316. [Verdeil, *La Mission jésuite du Mont-Liban et de Syrie (1830–1864)* (Paris: Les Indes Savantes, 2011).]
44. Wachtel, 'L'acculturation', pp. 184, 199.
45. Carmen Bernand and Serge Gruzinski, *Histoire du Nouveau Monde* (Paris: Fayard, 1991), vol. 1, p. 9.
46. Heyberger, *Les chrétiens du Proche-Orient*, pp. 241–71.
47. [Heyberger, *Hindiyya*, passim]; Bernard Heyberger, 'Pro nunc nihil respondendum: Recherches d'informations et prise de décision à la Propagande: L'exemple du Levant (XVIIIe siècle)', *Mélanges de l'École Française de Rome: Italie et Méditerranée*, 109, 2 (1997), pp. 539–54. [On Roman policy and missionaries, see Christian Windler, *Missionare in Persien: Kulturelle Diversität und Normenkonkurrenz im globalen Katholizismus (17–18. Jahrhundert)* (Cologne, Weimar, Vienna: Böhlau Verlag, 2018), pp. 31–153, 499–581].
48. [Heyberger, *Hindiyya*, pp. 47–56, 74–82, 118–43. On the introduction of new monastic rules among the Maronites, see Sabine Mohasseb Saliba, *Les monastères maronites doubles du Liban* (Paris: Geuthner; Jounieh: PUSEK, 2008), pp. 47–116.]
49. Heyberger, *Les chrétiens du Proche-Orient*, p. 239.
50. Atallah, *Le Synode Libanais de 1736*, vol. 2, p. 285.
51. Rouhana, 'Les versions des origines religieuses'; Mouawad, 'Aux origines d'un mythe'; [Aurélien Girard, 'La construction de l'identité confessionnelle maronite à l'époque ottomane (XVIe–XVIIIe siècle)', in Bernard Heyberger (ed.), *Les chrétiens de tradition syriaque à l'époque ottomane* (Paris: Geuthner, 2020), pp. 153–200; Lucy Parker, 'Yawsep I of Amida (d. 1707) and the Invention of the Chaldeans', ibid. pp. 121–52.]
52. [Carsten Walbiner, 'Monastic Reading and Learning in Eighteenth-Century *Bilād al-Šām*: Some Evidence from the Monastery of al-Šuwayr (Mount Lebanon)', *Arabica*, 51, 4 (2004), pp. 462–77].
53. Bernard Heyberger, 'Sécurité et insécurité: Les chrétiens de Syrie dans l'espace méditerranéen (XVIIe–XVIIIe siècles)', in Meropi Anastassiadou and Bernard Heyberger (eds), *Figures anonymes, figures d'élite: Pour une anatomie de l'Homo ottomanicus* (Istanbul: Isis, 1999), pp. 147–63 [see the English translation in Chapter 3 of this volume]; Masters, *Christians and Jews in the Ottoman Arab World*, p. 76.
54. Heyberger, *Les chrétiens du Proche-Orient*, pp. 418–19.
55. Maurizio Gribaudi, 'Echelle, pertinence, configuration', in Jacques Revel (ed.), *Jeux d'échelles: La micro-analyse à l'expérience* (Paris: Gallimard, Le Seuil, 1996), p. 113. See also Giovanni Levi, *Le pouvoir au village* (Paris: Gallimard, 1989).
56. Heyberger, *Les chrétiens du Proche-Orient*, pp. 120–26.
57. [Heyberger, *Hindiyya*, pp. 121–30, passim.]
58. Michel Foucault, *Histoire de la sexualité*, vol. 1: *La volonté de savoir* (Paris: Gallimard, 1976), pp. 79–84.
59. Levi, *Le pouvoir au village*; Christian Windler, 'Clientèles royales et clientèles seigneuriales vers la fin de l'Ancien Régime', *Annales: Histoire, sciences sociales*,

52, 2 (1997), pp. 293–319; Juan Luis Castellano and Jean-Pierre Dedieu (eds), *Réseaux, familles et pouvoirs dans le monde ibérique à la fin de l'Ancien Régime* (Paris: CNRS Éditions, 1998).

60. Werner and Zimmermann, 'Beyond Comparison', p. 35.
61. Reinhard Schulze, 'Das islamische 18. Jahrhundert: Versuch einer historiographischen Kritik', *Die Welt des Islam*, 30 (1990), pp. 140–59; Bern Radtke, 'Erleuchtung und Aufklärung: Islamische Mystik und europäischer Rationalismus', *Die Welt des Islam*, 34 (1994), pp. 46–66; Tilman Nagel, 'Autochtone Wurzeln des islamischen Modernismus: Bemerkungen zum Werk des Damazeners Ibn ʿAbîdîn 1784–1836', *Zeitschrift der Deutschen Morgenländischen Gesellschaft*, 146 (1996), pp. 92–111; Ira M. Lapidus, 'Islamic Revival and Modernity: The Contemporary Movements and the Historical Paradigms', *Journal of Economic and Social History of the Orient*, 40, 4 (1997), pp. 444–60.
62. Deringil, 'Conversion and Ideological Reinforcement'. See also several contributions in Anne-Laure Dupont and Catherine Mayeur-Jaouen (eds), *Débats intellectuels au Moyen-Orient dans l'entre-deux-guerres*, special issue of *Revue des mondes musulmans et de la Méditerranée*, 95–98 (2002).

CHAPTER 7

Polemic Dialogues between Christians and Muslims in the Seventeenth Century

The literary genre of dialogues between Christians and Muslims is ancient, going back to the first centuries of Islam, and it has roots in Islamic as well as Eastern Christian culture. In the time of the Abbasids, the Christian Arabic writers working in the court milieu and aspiring to equality with the Muslim *mutakallimūn* (theologians) devoted themselves to this type of literature.[1] It is difficult to determine to what extent these texts were linked to actual dialogues among Muslims and Christians. Nevertheless, there is evidence from this period on the practice of *majlis*, the sessions in which members of various religions were invited to explain their beliefs.

These sessions were no longer practised in the seventeenth century, in the Sunni surroundings of the Ottoman Empire, but we do have evidence of such meetings at the Mughal court in India and the Shiʿi Safavid court in Isfahan at that time.[2] Christian apologetics and disputations from the first centuries of Islam were then known only in part. The Catholic disputational dialogues against Islam in the sixteenth and seventeenth centuries were embedded in a more general practice of disputation in the Europe of this period.[3]

Here we will focus especially on the production of two French missionaries, both of whom lived in Aleppo in the 1670s. In 1679, Michel Febvre (alias Justinien de Neuvy) published a Latin pamphlet entitled *Praecipuae obiectiones quae vulgo solent fieri per modum interrogationis à Mahumeticae legis sectatoribus, Iudaeis, et Haereticis Orientalibus adversus Catholicos, earumque solutiones* (The Main Objections Commonly Made in an Interrogative Form by the Followers of the Law of Mahomet, the Jews and the Eastern Heretics against Catholics, and Their Solutions),[4] which appeared also in Arabic[5] and Armenian[6] translations. The same Capuchin, in two successive chapters of his *Théâtre de la Turquie* (1682), included a 'Method to Be Followed in order to Confute the Errors of the Turks, and the Abuses of Their Sect' and 'Another Method to Convince the Turks on Their Errors'.[7] Almost at the same time, in 1684, a Jesuit, Michel Nau, wrote *L'état présent de la religion mahométane* (The Present State of the Mahometan Religion), whose second tome added to the title . . . *contenant la vérité de la religion chrétienne défendüe et prouvée contre l'Alcoran, par l'Alcoran même* (. . . Which Contains the Truth of the Christian Religion Championed and Proven against the Qur'an by the Qur'an Itself), in the form of six conferences.[8] He also wrote a Latin apologetic treatise regarding Greek Christianity, *Ecclesiae Romanae Graecaeque vera effigies* (The True Portrait of the Roman and the Greek Church), followed by a dialogue titled *Religio christiana contra Alcoranum per Alcoranum pacifice defensa et probata* (The Christian Religion, Clearly Defended and Proven against the Qur'an, through the Qur'an).[9]

Having spent several years together in Aleppo, the two writers, members of rival religious orders but both natives of Touraine, were moved to compose a literary dialogue.[10] The books of Michel Nau apparently were part of a torrent of Jesuit publications in the period from 1689 to 1690, including handbooks, catechisms, dialogues and sermons, all intended for the conversion of Muslims.[11] The *Praecipuae obiectiones* by Michel Febvre and *L'état présent de la religion mahométane* by Michel Nau were published in a pocket edition, practical for travelling and for use in missions. The other two works, *Théâtre de la Turquie* and *Ecclesiae Romanae Graecaeque vera effigies*, were rather intended for libraries. Both authors claimed the utility of their handbooks for 'apostolic workers', but the literary features of their texts were also attractive to readers not directly concerned with proselytising. Michel Nau, for instance, asserted that he had adopted the vehicle of interviews because they 'teach with much more clarity, they represent more ingenuously the natural [disposition], the humour, and the manners of the persons, and they are more pleasant and entertaining than an uninterrupted narrative, which requires more industriousness from the reader'.[12] His texts are introduced with little stories and set in scenes that give the impression of exoticism and pre-Romantic picturesque, intended to create a realistic effect. In the dialogues of *L'état présent*, the use of transliterated Arabic for most of the Qur'anic quotations (even though almost incomprehensible) was designed to contribute to this realistic effect and to convince the reader of the accuracy of his method. In the Latin treatise, the Qur'anic quotations are in Arabic script. The author used short expressions only, for purposes of embellishment. He did the same in his *Protestation of the Holy Church of the Rūm, on the Rectitude of Their Faith*, written in Arabic and addressed to Arabic-speaking 'Greeks' but sprinkled with expressions in Greek, which they could neither read nor understand.[13]

Febvre's first work was divided into three parts, devoted to refuting the objections to Catholicism by the Muslims, by the Jews and by the Oriental 'heretics'. The eighteen objections by the Muslims with their answers covered only eighteen pages, while twenty are devoted to counter the five Jewish objections and 117 to the thirty-three objections of the 'Eastern heretics'. *Religio christiana contra Alcoranum per Alcoranum* by Michel Nau was a continuation of his *Ecclesiae Romanae Graecaeque vera effigies* in the same volume. Long passages of Febvre's *Théâtre de la Turquie* were also devoted to heretics in the Ottoman Empire. The Capuchin explained that he wrote against three kinds of men, united in one and the same 'army'. This association of heretics, Jews and Muslims belonged to a long disputational tradition, exemplified, for instance, by Ramon Llull's work.[14] The approach taken and the argumentation against all three are similar, but the objections against each religion and the answers provided are specific: Islam does not appear as a simple synthesis of Judaism and Christian heresy.

THE COMMON HABITUS APPROACH

Both Michel Febvre and Michel Nau opposed the notion, common since at least the sixteenth century, that discussing religion with Muslims was to be avoided, because it endangered the missionary presence in the Islamic countries, or because it was in vain.[15] Both argued from their own experience, enriched by conversations with Muslims. The Jesuit claimed that he wrote down the actual dialogues that he had held with Muslims and that these had never turned acrimonious. We know, however, that the French consul in Aleppo accused the two missionaries of causing confusion in the city with their misguided zeal. The departure of Michel Nau to Mesopotamia, in 1681, to found a mission in Mardin (which soon ended in failure), gave respite to the French consul in the city, who also wished to be rid of Justinien de Neuvy.[16] And although the Jesuit claimed that he wanted to debate with the 'Mahometans' peacefully, his text appears haunted by fear and images of martyrdom, which are also evident, though less intense, in Michel Febvre's dialogues. Nau's Papa (Father) Ephrem, in the role of Christian priest, continuously tooks oratorical precautions in order not to offend his Muslim hosts, who seemed to try to reassure him. Noureddin, one of the protagonists, declared: 'Speak fearlessly; there is no one in our company who does not give you complete permission [to speak].' Ephrem answered:

> I do it then because you want it [. . .] but I beg you, trust me, that all I want to say, I will say it only to justify my behaviour, or, to put it better, the behaviour of God with me. Because God, who is wise, good and fair in all things, having entrusted us to the Mahometans, who are our lords, we have to justify ourselves to them, when they wish [us to do] so, and especially when they are people [worthy] of your consideration and your esteem.[17]

After the meeting of the first day, the four Muslim friends with whom Papa Ephrem was debating decided to confront him with Abondaher, a substitute of the qadi, who had sent a servant for him. Immediately, the priest, 'reflecting on the liberty with which he had spoken the previous day about religious matters, suspected Ali and Noureddin of having accused him', and he prepared himself to suffer:[18]

> When he saw on the divan the four gentlemen with whom he had debated the previous day, with Abondaher sitting in the midst, he did not doubt that they would bring him to trial. Without seeming to take any notice, he kissed the hem of Abondaher's robe and greeted the rest of the company with respect. Abondaher ordered him to sit down and asked that a coffee be brought for him. At this moment he was surprised to see that he had, fortunately, been mistaken in suspecting them, because he passionately wished to spill his blood confessing his faith.[19]

Further, when the discussion moved towards the falsification of the Holy Scripture, Mustapha and Noureddin asked Abondaher to allow Ephrem to speak freely. Abondaher at this point ordered his servants to leave the room, because 'it is dangerous to have [them] as witnesses in this kind of conversation'.[20]

It is obvious that, for the missionaries, this type of dialogue was possible only with gentlemen, whom it was possible to trust. You must be careful with whom you speak, said Michel Febvre, 'because they are not all in the same mood, nor have the same feelings, even if they seem so outwardly – apart from the fact that most of them do not know what they believe'.[21]

The debate was supposed to be possible only with the educated elite class, with people who knew how to reason and how to discern and respect the intellectual and ethical qualities of the Latin friar with whom they were engaged in conversation. The underlying belief, already evident in some medieval treatises, was that the most learned and most reasonable among the Muslims could not possibly believe in the Qur'an to the best of their knowledge and faith and, therefore, could be touched by rational arguments.[22] It must also be said that a missionary yearned for opponents who could debate at the same level:

> One day, a European Christian, a man devoted to the propagation of Christ's faith, was sitting by the side of a Syrian Mahometan. And this Mahometan was as illustrious among his people for his reputation of scholarship and his glory of understanding the Qur'an as he was hostile to the Christian law and industrious in disparaging it and to holding it in contempt. When he knew that this man, sitting close to him, was a Christian and a priest, not ignorant, and considering that he was a good man and belonged to a higher social position [he spoke to him].[23]

The same notion is seen in the story in which Michel Nau introduces a dialogue with the Greeks. During a pilgrimage, two French friars had been induced by God to ask for lodging in a Greek monastery headed by an abbot called Nicolas, 'a man of singular virtue and not poorly educated in the doctrine, at least considering the condition of people and times'; when Nicolas saw from their face and dress that he had to deal with Latins, he offered them unaccustomed hospitality and urged them to share their knowledge. Once the missionaries had succeeded in being accepted, another monk, whose reputation of competence was higher but who was more hostile towards them, was then introduced to checkmate them. This monk, Methodius, was 'a middle-aged man, somewhat learned in the Greek letters, so that he could not only read, which was the general case of others, but he even understood what he read and explained it in the vernacular language'.[24]

In *L'état présent de la religion mahométane*, the four friends Ali, Aeumar, Noureddin and Mustapha, who opened the debate with the priest after having greeted him 'very civilly' and after having commended themselves to his prayers, wondered about him:

> From where, they said, do these people get their knowledge? Aren't you, added Mustapha, astonished that, being so learned, these people are so unpretentious and so humble: I do not see this kind of people among us. And as soon as we read the Qur'an a bit better than the others and know a bit of grammar, we are the learned ones, and we can hardly bear it when someone talks to us.[25]

They decided then that they would continue the discussion the next day, together with 'the most learned in their law who was staying in the city', whose name was Abondaher, the 'deputy to the qadi'.

As it appears in these discourses, equality in culture and education is, in fact, only a strategic fiction: the Christian priests were thoroughly convinced of their own intellectual superiority over their interlocutors, despite granting them some qualities. Their knowledge was always considered very limited, and it appeared all the more limited because the missionaries themselves were ignorant of Muslim theological and apologetic literature and unable to put in the mouths of their imaginary rivals any sophisticated arguments, although Michel Nau and Michel Febvre had a good knowledge of Arabic, both having written books in that language.

These exchanges, however, appeared to be made possible by the fact that each side was thought to share the same habitus distinguishing a specific social class. Our authors are not original in this: Riccoldo da Montecroce, who lived in Baghdad in the fourteenth century, was impressed by the taste for study, the devotion, the charitable work and the hospitality displayed by his Muslim acquaintances. The implicit idea that Christians and Muslims share the same values was already present in Western medieval literature.[26] In Nau's dialogue, Father Ephrem became friendly with a dervish living in a mausoleum (*turba*) on the outskirts of Aleppo, and when he visited him in order to continue their theological dialogue, the dervish took him by the hand and had him sit down on the divan. On other occasions, when Ephrem took the Gospel in his hands, he raised it over his head to mark his respect, as the Muslims do with the Qur'an, and he even began to quote the Qur'an by heart.[27]

In one of his dialogues, Febvre asserted that the partners had to be approached with subjects that were not controversial and that belonged to their common culture: such was the case with monotheism. Both of the authors under discussion acknowledged something not universally admitted in their time: that Muslims share with them one and the same God. Thus, they did not demonise Islam. Nau claimed that the Antichrist would be a Jew, not a Muslim, as previously believed.[28] Febvre began his conversations with the greatness of God, his attributes, his existence, the independence of his infinite being on whom all others depend and other such discourses 'that they enjoy a great deal'.[29] Nau made his Father Ephrem profess a monotheistic faith in order to attract his Muslim interlocutors:

> The positive sanctity [the kind of sanctity which, according to Thomas Aquinas, continues to perfect itself] means that, first of all, a Christian should enter into the depth of his nothingness [or non-being] and should acknowledge his infinite dependence on the sovereign and independent Being, who is God, and that he should be in boundless, total and perfect submission to Him; that he should be forever in His presence in the state of adoration, continuous annihilation of himself and blind devotion to His will.[30]

Elsewhere, to Ephrem's questions – 'What does it mean to believe? Isn't it to know the truth, to be convinced that it has been revealed by God, and thus to be subject to it and to profess it?' – Ali answered: 'That is it, indeed.'[31]

Febvre referred to the natural sciences as belonging to a culture common to both Christians and Muslims. But, at a time when scientific knowledge was growing in Europe, the natural sciences he referred to were completely embedded in a medieval mental context, with its categories inherited from classical Greek philosophy and largely shared with Muslims, such as the four elements and the four types of creatures in the world. His world was geocentric and anthropocentric, where planets exerted their influence on human spirits and where the same components present in the whole universe were present in human beings. Accordingly, the four humours of man (black bile, yellow bile, phlegm, blood) correlate with the four elements of nature (earth, water, air, fire). The human soul is said to be 'vegetative, sensitive and reasonable', inhabited by three powers (memory, will and intelligence).[32]

If there was a development in these dialogues with respect to the preceding centuries, it would be the manner in which these relations between Latin religious men and Muslim notables were staged in the texts. This evolution can already be seen, for instance, in the successive editions of the books of Filippo Guadagnoli, published by the Propaganda in 1637 and 1649.[33] The missionary experience led to a form of accommodation in human relations with the 'infidels', which presupposed the acknowledgment of some positive features in their culture, even if Christian and Western superiority was never questioned. It could be that the form of dialogue with the Muslims was influenced by the general evolution of the literary genre of dialogue, which required more realism and more picturesqueness. Eventually, the goodwill and desire to deal with Muslims peacefully must be understood in terms of a form of scepticism regarding religious controversies.[34] It is thus the rhetorical development of the dialogues and of controversy, rather than a change in the approach to Islam, that explains why relations with Muslims appear more positive in these texts. The approach of Nau to the 'Eastern heretics' was similar.

THE MISSIONARIES AND ISLAM

The accommodationist drive and the knowledge of the field were always confronted with the impossibility of approaching Islam as a specific object of scholarship, which could be studied on its own, free of controversy.

Both Nau and Febvre implicitly recognised the monotheism in Islam and the value of some of the devotional practices of the Muslims, but their goodwill towards the Muslims broke down in the face of ideologically insuperable obstacles. They continued, for instance, to call Muslims 'Mahometans' and Islam 'the Mahometan religion'. Nau used the word 'Muslim' once, but he made Noureddin say 'It is an article of the Mahometan faith, because the Prophet said it exactly in those terms',[35] and he made Ali say: 'You have been to blame, Papas, because you did not follow the movement God inspired to you for Mahometism'. In the Arabic version of Febvre's *Obiectiones*, the Muslims are called *Muslimīn* – and, oddly, *Islāmiyyīn* – which can be considered progress over Filippo Guadagnoli's book, printed by the Propaganda in 1637, in which the term *Muḥammadī*, inadmissible for a Muslim, had been used.[36]

The first question that arises – that is, how much our authors depended on the preceding Catholic controversialists – cannot be answered without a long and minute inquiry into their sources, which was not feasible for this article. The authors dealt with subjects that were neither original nor new and that concerned points that had been codified by the Qur'an: the falsification of the scriptures by Jews and Christians, and the denial of the divine nature of Christ, his divine filiation, his death on the cross and the Trinity. In opposition, the Christian offensive always concentrated on denying the prophetic nature of Mahomet, using the arguments of his immorality and the absence of miracles performed by him, and on the fact that Islam had been diffused by violent conquest or by its lax morals. These arguments were mostly part of a long apologetic tradition.[37] Indeed, the approach of our two authors appears less innovative than they pretended, and there is no proof of their use of original sources.

Michel Nau's approach was very close to that of Filippo Guadagnoli in the last version of his *Considerationes ad Mahomettanos* of 1649, which was censured by the Propaganda as soon as it was printed. This book was presented as using a peaceful argument, without contempt, in order to increase an interlocutor's curiosity and doubts before answering them with Christian theological arguments.[38] Nau had the same goal in his dialogues and wrote: 'Everyone returned home with less regard for the Mahometan religion and more prejudice against it, and more attachment for the Christian and for clerics such as Ephrem'.[39] Nau, like Guadagnoli, made ample use of Qur'anic quotations and strove to demonstrate that the Qur'an, in as much as it contained the truth, was in accordance with the Gospels.[40] What was the actual knowledge that our two missionaries had of Islam? It could be that, as was generally the case with Christian controversialists, they simply copied earlier treatises, without checking the original source. Let us only point out, for instance, that Nau made a frequent mistake, already corrected several times in earlier publications, of translating the expression *ahl al-kitāb* [People of the Book] as *possessores Alcorani*, which, it must be admitted, is very prejudicial to a correct understanding of the Qur'anic text.[41]

Comparing Michel Nau's Qur'anic translations with standard modern translations leads to an ambiguous conclusion. There is little discrepancy between the translation that Nau gives of The Cow (Q 2:219), concerning the wine, and a modern English version: 'Vous feres du vin de dattes et de raisins, qui a la force d'enivrer, et vous en tireres un profit honnête' (And from the fruit of the palm trees and vines you derive intoxicants as well as a goodly provision).[42]

The distortion is also not obvious in the quote from The Bees (Q 16:67): 'Ils vous interrogeront touchant le vin et les jeux de hazard: dites qu'en cela il y a beaucoup de péché, et d'utilité pour les hommes; mais que le péché l'emporte pardessus l'utilité' (They ask you about wine and gambling. Say: 'In them both lies grave sin, though some benefit, to mankind. But their sin is more grave than their benefit').[43]

There is only a small difference for Jonah (Q 10:94): 'Si vous avez quelque doute sur l'Alcoran que nous avons envoié, interrogés ceux qui lisent l'Ecriture Sainte avant vous' (If you are in doubt concerning what We revealed to you, ask those who have read the Book before you).[44]

The difference is more striking in the quote from The Women (Q 4:150–52):

> Les gens qui rejettent la parole de Dieu, et de ses apôtres, et qui veulent mettre de la différence entre l'un et l'autre, et tâchent de se faire par là un chemin; ces gens-là sont véritablement des infidèles et nous leur avons

> préparé d'épouvantables supplices. Mais ceux qui ont cru à Dieu, et à ses Apôtres, reçoivent également leur témoignage, et ils seront récompensés (As for those who disbelieve in God and His messengers, and seek to stir up division between God and His messengers, saying: 'We believe in some and disbelieve in others' and desire to adopt this as an in-between way – these are truly the unbelievers. For unbelievers We have readied an abasing torment. Those who believe in God and His messengers and do not distinguish between any of them – these He shall pay their wages, and God is All-Forgiving, Compassionate to each).[45]

This difference between the translations gives the impression that Nau remained close to the Qurʾanic text in his translation whenever it was in accordance with his Christian vision of ethics and his Christian views on Islam and that he tampered somewhat with the sense of the quote whenever the Qurʾan did not coincide with his views, in order to demonstrate the agreement between the Islamic message and the Gospel. The debate could begin only with misunderstanding when the meaning that the Christian attributed to a Qurʾanic quote was not the orthodox Sunni meaning.

The use of the Qurʾan in these dialogues may have provoked other misunderstandings. The authors used it as a source for arguments in favour of their own reasoning, without any understanding of the status that this text of revelation holds in Islamic culture. Nau wrote that 'this Mahometan, nodding his head in a religious movement regularly from right to left and with open admiring eyes, with a deep and suitable voice' began to recite the verse 2:136 (The Cow),[46] but he did not actually understand the significance of this posture. For our authors, the Qurʾan was only the 'Mahometan Law'. For a Muslim, however, the text is a prayer, which has to be recited or intoned in a form of liturgy called *tajwīd*. The sense of the text cannot be reduced to its rational dimension. It also belongs to a spiritual and symbolic order and therefore necessarily retains some mystery or unintelligibility.

The Qurʾan's unfathomable semantic depth, with its syntactic and narrative peculiarity, is the true source of its beauty and the proof of its truth and divinity for Muslims.[47] The *iʿjāz* doctrine, according to which the inimitable beauty of the Qurʾan testifies to its divine origin, was not ignored by Western scholars in the seventeenth century, but they worked desperately hard to refute it. While they were disposed to recognise that it was almost impossible to learn the Arabic language without referring to the Qurʾan, they were resolutely insensitive to the rhythm and meter of the text, which for them was far from perfect. It would only be during the eighteenth century that the Qurʾan's eloquence would be admitted as an element of Mahomet's 'genius'. The missionaries, of course, could not admit that the Qurʾan enjoyed the status of God's word. Here is how Nau twisted his argument: 'What the Qurʾan makes God say, speaking to

Mahomet', or 'Does he [Mahomet] not make God speak in the chapter Beni Israil or Eyra?'[48] But, more generally, the Jesuit made the Prophet speak directly. At the end of this dialogue, becoming overwrought about Mahomet's personality, he took no precautions, drawing an offensive portrait of him from the Qur'an ('he makes himself to stand above all the others') and ascribing to him the incoherencies of the text.

There was an incoherence in wanting to use the Qur'an in the way Nau did, in order to demonstrate Christian truth, while at the same time denying it any authority as a divine scripture. The points he intended to deal with were:

> According to the Qur'an, the Gospel is all from God; it has not been corrupted, and it could not be. The Qur'an, which fights the venerable mystery of Trinity, says things that prove it and make it easier to believe in. The Qur'an helps one believe in the mystery of Jesus Christ's divinity and his Incarnation. The Christian religion is justified, on several points, by the text of the Qur'an; Mahomet is not a Prophet, and the Qur'an is not a Book of God.[49]

Either one acknowledged the value and the authority of the book, allowing him to use it in order to argue before the Muslims, or one believed, as he mentioned in the Foreword, that it not only contained 'errors' and 'contradictions', but also 'thousands of absurdities and thousands of stupidities which make up the price of this mischievous book'; he wanted to demonstrate that 'it is not from God and that it is purely the work of impurity, ignorance, foolishness and Hell'. Under these conditions, it was impossible to imagine any kind of dialogue with a Muslim.

The absence of any reference to exegesis (*tafsīr*) in Nau's method brings out another problem. This absence may be self-conscious, because some of the Qur'anic commentaries were known by scholars in the second half of the seventeenth century and had first been used by some Christian controversialists and Orientalists.[50] In any case, Nau found them useless, because they were even more abstruse than the Qur'anic text itself. The only reference he gave in his two books was that of 'Jelaledin'. This probably refers to the famous Egyptian polygraph Jalāl al-Dīn al-Suyūṭī (d. 1505), who, in addition to hundreds of books, composed summaries of Qur'anic exegesis.[51] The use that the Jesuit made of this author is typical: on one of the more delicate points, regarding the prophetic nature of Mahomet, he cited two sensitive episodes in order to tackle the figure of the founder of Islam and to raise the problem of Qur'anic revelation. According to Jelaledin, so he wrote, Mahomet, carried off by a shameful passion, seduced his maid Maria in the home and in the bed of his wife Apsa [Ḥafsa] herself. And, he added: 'The interpreters of the Qur'an dispute together about the question, whether Mahomet was obliged to do what God had commanded in order to expiate this sin'.[52] The other episode in which Nau relied on al-Suyūṭī was that of the wife of Zayd. In the sura The Factions (Q 33:37), it is said that Mahomet married her only after she had been repudiated by his servant Zayd, but everybody knew that he obliged him to do so, 'as Gilaleldin explains in his commentaries'. This raises one of the more delicate points for the exegesis, because the text shows that the revelation came conveniently afterwards, to justify Mahomet's behaviour.[53]

The use of Qur'anic exegesis could make it more difficult to prove Christian truth from the Qur'an, as the Jesuit had set himself to demonstrate. The text of the Islamic revelation, with its numerous references to Torah and Gospels, from the very beginning raised the hermeneutic question of its dependence on – or, to the contrary, its radical difference from – the previous revelations, and this point escaped neither the Muslim apologists nor the earliest Christian protagonists. It is impossible to proceed, as our authors did, by extracting an expression or a verse from the Qur'an and attributing it a Christian meaning. It is impossible, for instance, as Nau and Febvre did, to infer from the fact that Jesus Christ is called *rūḥ Allāh* (Spirit of God) and *kalimat Allāh* (Word of God) that the Qur'an acknowledges his divinity. It is impossible also to select from the book the quotes that confirm the apologetic argument, while dismissing other verses that refute this reading.[54]

The use that the Jesuit and the Capuchin made of the Qur'an had to do with a broader conception, according to which Muslim gentlemen in their writings were susceptible to rational arguments, and the notion that the faculty of reason was on the side of Christianity. For the Latin Christians, they were the ones who had the correct reading of Islam, and its message was reduced to the Qur'an, or to those places in the Qur'an that were the most favourable to Christianity. The same idea – that it was the Latins who interpreted the texts correctly – was championed by Nau in his dialogue with the Greeks: there, the Latin friar explained the true religion of the Greeks to the Greeks themselves.

CONCLUSION

The dialogues studied here were not usable in the Christians' contacts with Muslims, and it is obvious that they were aimed primarily at European readers. Nevertheless, in their missionary approach to Muslims and to Islam they showed an undeniable change from that of the texts produced by Catholic missionaries in the previous decades.[55] What was actually new is their insistence on the context of the relationship with the protagonists, the belief of the missionaries that they shared a common habitus with them, defined by courtesy, the use of reason and monotheism.

It is possible that this approach was influenced by the accommodationist missionary culture that spread after Alessandro Valignano's arrival in Asia.[56] This approach rested on the idea of the rational strength of Christianity and its superiority over Islam. However, it clashed with the fact that the Islamic message cannot be reduced to the Christian, as well as with the incapacity of the missionaries to go beyond the most traditional Christian argumentation against Mahomet and his prophecy. These dialogues display the weakness of the Catholic missionaries' grasp of Islamic theology, which has to be explained by their intellectual incapacity to immerse themselves in it, more than by a lack of tools to understand it.

Islam – especially Mahomet and the Qur'an – became 'a tool that is good to think with' only in anti-Catholic surroundings, first for the libertines of the seventeenth century, then for the representatives of the Enlightenment in eighteenth-century Europe. It enabled a radical break with past Christian tradition, wholly removed from the apologetic approach of the Catholic missionaries of the seventeenth century.[57]

NOTES

1. Sidney H. Griffith, *The Church in the Shadow of the Mosque: Christians and Muslims in the World of Islam* (Princeton: Princeton University Press, 2008), pp. 75–84.
2. Muzaffar Alam and Sanjay Subrahmanyam, 'Frank Disputations: Catholics and Muslims in the Court of Jahangir (1608–1611)', *Indian Economic and Social History Review*, 46 (1999), pp. 457–511; Hugues Didier, 'Une mission chrétienne atypique auprès d'un souverain musulman atypique?' in Bernard Heyberger and Rémy Madinier (eds), *L'Islam des marges: Missionnaires chrétiens et espaces périphériques du monde musulman XVIe–XXe siècle* (Paris: IISMM; Karthala, 2011), pp. 17–43; Francis Richard, 'Trois conférences de controverse islamo-chrétienne en Géorgie vers 1665–1666', *Bedi Kartlisa*, 40 (1982), pp. 253–59; Richard, 'Catholicisme et Islam chiite au "Grand siècle": Autour de quelques documents concernant les missions catholiques en Perse au XVIIe siècle', *Euntes Docete*, 33, 3 (1980), pp. 339–40; Richard, *Raphaël du Mans missionnaire en Perse au XVIIe siècle* (Paris: L'Harmattan, 1995).
3. Giovanni Pizzorusso, 'La preparazione linguistica e controversistica dei missionari per l'Oriente islamico: Scuole, testi insegnanti a Roma e in Italia', in Bernard Heyberger, Mercedes García-Arenal, Emanuele Colombo and Paola Vismara (eds), *L'Islam visto da Occidente: Cultura e religione del Seicento europeo di fronte all'Islam* (Milan: Marietti 1820/2009), pp. 253–88.
4. Michel Febvre, *Praecipuae obiectiones quae vulgo solent fieri per modum interrogationis à Mahumeticae legis sectatoribus, Iudaeis, et Haereticis Orientalibus adversus Catholicos, earumque solutiones* (Rome: Typis Sacrae Congregationis De Propaganda Fide, 1679). [In this chapter, we adopt the archaic form 'Mahomet' used by the missionaries themselves.]
5. Michel Febvre, *Kitāb ijtamil ʿalā ajwāba ahl al-kanīsa al-muqaddassa al-qātūlīqiyya al-jāmiʿa al-rasūliyya li-iʿtirāḍāt al-muslimīn wa-l-yahūd wa-l-harātiqa ḍid al-qātūliqiyyīn* (Rome: Typis Sacrae Congregationis De Propaganda Fide, 1680).

6. In the copy of the Bibliothèque nationale de France, the Latin and the Armenian versions are bound with the *Dottrina christiana tradotta in lingua valacha dal padre Vito Pilutio da Vignanello Minore Conventuale di S. Francesco* (Rome: Sac. Cong. de Propaganda Fide, 1677).
7. Michel Febvre, *Théâtre de la Turquie, où sont représentées les choses les plus remarquables qui s'y passent aujourd'huy touchant les Mœurs, le Gouvernement, les Coutumes & la Religion des Turcs, & de treize autres sortes de Nations qui habitent dans l'Empire Ottoman* (Paris: Edme Couterot, 1682), pp. 47–54: 'Méthode qu'on doit garder pour réfuter les erreurs des Turcs, et les abus de leur secte', pp. 54–58: 'autre méthode pour convaincre les Turcs de leurs erreurs'. This is a French translation of *Teatro della Turchia, dove si rappresentano i disordini di essa, il genio, la natura, et i costumi di quattordici nationi, che l'habitano* (Milan: heredi di Antonio Malatesta, 1681).
8. Michel Nau, *L'état présent de la religion mahométane* (Paris: Veuve P. Bouillerot, 1684). The second tome of this work (published in the same volume) is titled *L'état présent de la religion mahométane contenant la vérité de la religion chrétienne défendüe et prouvée contre l'Alcoran, par l'Alcoran même.* [All the citations from this work come from the second tome.]
9. Michel Nau, *Ecclesiae Romanae Graecaeque vera effigies ex variis tum recentibus, tum antiquis monumentis singulari fide expressa romanis graecisque exhibita: Quo intelligant admirabilem utriusque consensionem et in tanta matrum concordia nefas esse pugnare et odisse inter sese ingenti damno liberos* (Paris: apud Gabrielem Martinum, 1680). This work was followed, in the same volume, by Michel Nau, *Religio christiana contra Alcoranum per Alcoranum pacifice defensa et probata.*
10. [Bernard Heyberger, 'Justinien de Neuvy, dit Michel Febvre', in David Thomas and John Chesworth (eds), *Christian-Muslim Relations: A Bibliographical History*, vol. 9: *Western and Southern Europe (1600–1700)* (Leiden: Brill, 2017), pp. 579–88; Heyberger, 'Michel Nau', ibid. pp. 602–9.]
11. Thomas Michel, 'Jesuit Writings on Islam in the Seventeenth Century', *Islamochristiana*, 15 (1989), pp. 57–85; Emanuele Colombo, 'Jesuits and Islam in Seventeenth-Century Europe: War, Preaching and Conversions', in Heyberger et al. (eds), *L'Islam visto da Occidente*, pp. 315–40; Colombo, *Convertire i musulmani: L'esperienza di un gesuita spagnolo nel seicento* (Milan: Mondadori, 2007).
12. Ces entretiens 'instruisent avec beaucoup plus de clarté, ils représentent plus naïvement le naturel, l'humeur et les manières des personnes et ils ont quelque chose de plus agréable et de plus divertissant qu'un discours de suite, qui demande du Lecteur davantage d'application' (Nau, *L'état présent de la religion mahométane*, 'avertissement').
13. *Ihtijāj kanīsat al-rūm al-muqaddasa fi istiqāma īmānihā*. Beirut, Bibliothèque Orientale, ms. 709. I am grateful to Aurélien Girard for this reference.
14. Norman Daniel, *Islam et Occident* (Paris: Cerf, 1993), pp. 256–57 (French translation; first English edition 1960).
15. Colombo, 'Jesuits and Islam', pp. 327–29.
16. Concerning Michel Nau, see AN, AE, B/I, vol. 76, fols 134–36, Aleppo, 1 July 1681. Laurent d'Arvieux, *Mémoires du Chevalier d'Arvieux*, edited by Jean-Baptiste

Labat (Paris: Charles-Jean-Baptiste Delespine, 1735), vol. 6, pp. 8–30, 70–81, 360–85. Concerning Justinien de Neuvy, see APF, SOCG, vol. 497, fols 445–46, 5 May 1687.

17. Nau, *L'état présent de la religion mahométane*, pp. 48–49: 'Parlés hardiment; il n'y a pas un de la compagnie qui ne vous donne toute permission. Je le ferai donc, puisque vous le désirés, réprit Ephrem, mais je vous conjure de croire que tout ce que je dirai, je le dirai uniquement pour justifier devant vous ma conduite ou pour mieux dire la conduite de Dieu sur moi. Car comme Dieu qui est sage, bon et juste en tout, nous a commis ici aux Mahométans, et qu'ils sont nos maîtres, nous devons leur rendre raison de nous-mêmes, quand ils le souhaitent, et que ce sont particulièrement des gens de votre considération et de votre mérite'.
18. Nau, *L'état présent de la religion mahométane*, p. 58: 'faisant réflexion à la liberté avec laquelle il avoit parlé le jour precedent des choses de la religion, il soupçonna Ali et Noureddin, de l'avoir accusé'.
19. Nau, *L'état présent de la religion mahométane*, p. 59: 'Quand il vit sur le Divan les quatre Messieurs, avec lesquels il avoit disputé le jour de devant, et Abondaher au milieu, il ne douta presque plus qu'on n'allât lui faire son procès. Il ne fit semblant de rien, il alla baiser le bas de la robe d'Abondaher, et il salua avec respect le reste de la compagnie. Abondaher lui ordonna de s'assoir, et il demanda qu'on lui apportât le café. Ce fut alors qu'il fût bien surpris se voïant si heureusement trompé dans le soupçon qu'il avoit eu; car il desiroit passionnément de répandre son sang pour la confession de sa foi'.
20. Nau, *L'état présent de la religion mahométane*, pp. 62–63.
21. Febvre, *Théâtre de la Turquie*, p. 47: 'Car comme j'ay dit, ils ne sont pas tous de mesme humeur, ny dans les mesmes sentimens, sinon à l'extérieur: outre que la plupart ne sçavent ce qu'ils croyent'.
22. Daniel, *Islam et Occident*, p. 98. Traditionally, Christian proselytisers held that it was necessary to provide purely rational demonstrations of Christianity to Muslims: Noel Malcolm, 'Comenius, the Conversion of the Turks, and the Muslim-Christian Debate, on the Corruption of Scripture', *Church History and Religious Culture*, 87 (2007), p. 492.
23. Nau, *Religio christiana contra Alcoranum pacifice defensa et probata*, p. 4: 'Assidebat aliquando Mahometano Syro Christianus Europaeus, vir propagandae Christi fidei studiosissimus. Et Mahometanus quidem, quam erat apud suos eruditionis fama, et intelligendi Alcorani gloria praeclarus, tam erat a Christiana lege aversus, in eaque vellicanda et despicienda assiduus. Is postquam agnovit assidentem sibi Christianum et sacerdotem esse et virum non indoctum, benigne illum, at non sine fastu, intuitus, Miror, inquit, vos Christianos . . .'
24. Nau, *Ecclesiae Romanae Graecaeque vera effigies*, pp. 1–2: 'Praeerat coenobio abbas nomine Nicolaus, vir tum singulari virtute, tum doctrina pro gentis ac temporum conditione non mediocriter instructus'. Ibid. p. 16: 'Vir erat aetate maturus, Graecis litteris nonnihil eruditus, ut non legere modo, quod solent alii, posset, sed intelligere lecta, eaque vernaculo idomate interpretari'.
25. Nau, *L'état présent de la religion mahométane*, pp. 53–54: 'Où, dirent-ils, ces gens-là vont-ils prendre cette science? Mais n'admirés-vous pas, ajoûta Mustapha,

qu'étant si sçavans, ils soient si modestes et si humbles: Je n'en vois point de cette sorte parmi nous. Et dès que nous lisons nôtre Alcoran un peu mieux que les autres, et que nous sçavons un peu de grammaire, nous faisons les docteurs, et à peine souffrons-nous qu'on parle devant nous'.

26. Daniel, *Islam et Occident*, pp. 262, 268–69. On Muslim virtues appreciated by Febvre and Nau in their non-dialogic writings, see Bernard Heyberger, *Les chrétiens du Proche-Orient*, p. 320. The same virtues were attributed to Muslims by Comenius (Malcolm, 'Comenius, the Conversion of the Turks', p. 489).
27. Nau, *L'état présent de la religion mahométane*, pp. 10, 149, passim.
28. Bernard Heyberger, *Les chrétiens du Proche-Orient au temps de la réforme catholique* (Rome: École française de Rome, 1994), pp. 197–202.
29. Febvre, *Théâtre de la Turquie*, p. 47. Daniel, *Islam et Occident*, p. 275. Riccoldo and other medieval authors wrote about the Muslim veneration of God's name. Malcolm, 'Comenius, the Conversion of the Turks', pp. 482, 485. Comenius insisted on the common ground of monotheism.
30. Nau, *L'état présent de la religion mahométane*, pp. 26–27: 'Celle qu'on nomme sainteté positive [. . .] veut que d'abord un Chrétien entre et pénètre dans toute la profondeur de son néant, et qu'il reconnaisse la dépendance infinie qu'il a en tout de l'Etre souverain et indépendant, qui est Dieu, qu'il ait pour luy une soumission immense totale et parfaite; qu'il soit toujours en sa présence dans un état d'adoration, d'anéantissement continuel de soi-même et de dévouement aveugle à sa volonté . . .'
31. Nau, *L'état présent de la religion mahométane*, pp. 30–31: 'Qu'est-ce que croire? N'est-ce pas connoître une vérité, être certain qu'elle a été révélée de Dieu, et par ce motif, s'y assujettir et la professer? C'est cela même, repartit Ali'.
32. Febvre, *Théâtre de la Turquie*, pp. 47–49.
33. Filippo Guadagnoli, *Pro christiana religione responsio ad obiectiones Ahmed filii Zin Alabedin, Persae Asphahanensis, Idjāba ilā Ahmad al-Sharīf Bin Zīn Al-ʿĀbidīn al-Fārisī al-Isbahānī* (Rome: Typis Sacrae Congregationis De Propaganda Fide, 1637). On this author and his work, see Giovanni Pizzorusso, 'Filippo Guadagnoli, i Caracciolini e lo studio delle lingue orientali e della controversia con l'Islam a Roma nel XVII secolo', in Irene Fosi and Giovanni Pizzorusso (eds), *L'ordine dei chierici regolari minori (Caracciolini): Religione e cultura in età postridentina, monographic issue of Studi Medievali e Moderni*, 14, 1 (2010), pp. 245–78; Andrea Trentini, 'Il Caracciolino Filippo Guadagnoli controversista e islamologo: Un'analisi dei suoi scritti apologetici contro l'Islam', ibid. pp. 297–314.
34. Bernard Dompnier, *Le venin de l'hérésie: Image du protestantisme et combat catholique au XVIIe siècle* (Paris: Le Centurion, 1985), pp. 169–97.
35. Nau, *L'état présent de la religion mahométane*, p. 19.
36. Trentini, 'Il Caracciolino Filippo Guadagnoli', pp. 309–10; Nathalie Zemon Davis, *Léon l'Africain: Un voyageur entre deux mondes* (Paris: Payot, 2006; original edition: *Trickster Travels: A Sixteenth-Century Muslim between Worlds*), p. 82, note 14 and 15. The term 'musulmano' was first used in Italian in 1557, but it became common only in the seventeenth century.

37. For example, see Trentini, 'Il Caracciolino Filippo Guadagnoli', and for the arguments in a Protestant context, Malcolm, 'Comenius, the Conversion of the Turks', pp. 485–88, 500–8.
38. Trentini, 'Il Caracciolino Filippo Guadagnoli', pp. 485–88. Guadagnoli was also used by Comenius: Malcolm, 'Comenius, the Conversion of the Turks', pp. 500–8.
39. Nau, *L'état présent de la religion mahométane*, pp. 216–17: 'Chacun se retira ches soi avec moins d'estime de la Religion Mahométane, et de grands préjugés contre elle, et avec beaucoup d'affection pour la Chrétienne, et pour les religieux semblables à Ephrem'.
40. The conviction that there is an *Arabica veritas* and that it is possible to rediscover a reflected light of the Gospel in the Qur'an can be detected in some Italian intellectual circles as early as the fifteenth century: Benoît Grévin and Giuseppe Mandalà, 'Le rôle des communautés juives siciliennes dans la transmission des savoirs arabes en Italie, XIIIe–XVe siècles', in Bernard Heyberger and Albrecht Fuess (eds), *La frontière méditerranéenne du XVe au XVIIe siècle: Conflits, circulations, échanges* (Turnhout: Brepols, 2013), pp. 283–99.
41. Nau, *Religio christiana contra Alcoranum per Alcoranum pacifice defensa et probata*, p. 19. On p. 4, for Christians he uses the expression *ahl al-kitāb* (People of the Book). On p. 6, he translates the expression: 'A vos quorum est divinus codex (sic Alcoranum dicimus)'. The expression *ahl al-kitāb* refers to Christians, Jews and Sabeans. The Protestant Orientalist Johann Heinrich Hottinger included Muslims (for instance, in his *Historia Orientalis*, 1651) and was corrected by the Catholic Orientalist Abraham Ecchellensis in his *De Origine nominis papae* (1661). See Loop, 'Johann Heinrich Hottinger', pp. 169–203; Bernard Heyberger, 'L'Islam dans la controverse entre catholiques et protestants: Le *De origine nominis papae* d'Abraham Ecchellensis (1661), réponse à l'*Historia Orientalis* de Johann Heinrich Hottinger (1651 et 1660)', in Chrystel Bernat and Hubert Bost (eds), *Énoncer/dénoncer l'autre: Discours et représentations du différend confessionnel à l'époque moderne* (Turnhout: Brepols, 2012), pp. 389–400. The mistake about the meaning of *ahl al-kitāb* was common. Trentini, 'Il Caracciolino Filippo Guadagnoli', pp. 304–5: Filippo Guadagnoli used the expression, sometimes correctly, sometimes not.
42. *The Qur'an: A New Translation*, translated by Tarif Khalidi (London: Penguin, 2008), p. 215.
43. Ibid. p. 29.
44. Ibid. p. 169.
45. Ibid. p. 79.
46. Nau, *Religio christiana contra Alcoranum per Alcoranum pacifice defensa et probata*, p. 6. 'Hic Mahometanus caput religioso motu dextrorum ac sinistrorum inflectens, et apertis admirantis in morem oculis, composita ad gravitatem voce subjunxit: [. . .] O! in Deo credimus, et fide omnia ea suscipimus, quae ipse nobis, et Abrahamo, et Isaaco, et Iacobo et tribulus docendo demisit, quaeque Mosi et Jesu et prophetis ab ipsorum Domino tradita sunt; nec quidam istos inter discriminis ponimus'.
47. Jan Loop, 'Divine Poetry? Early Modern European Orientalists on the Beauty of the Koran', *Church History and Religious Culture*, 89 (2009), pp. 455–88.

48. Nau, *L'état présent de la religion mahométane*, p. 33: 'ce que l'Alcoran fait dire à Dieu, parlant à Mahomet.' Ibid. p. 37: 'Ne fait-il pas encore parler Dieu dans le chapitre *Eyra* ou *Beni Asraïl*?'
49. Nau, *L'état présent de la religion mahométane*, 'Table des conférences': 'Que Selon l'Alcoran l'Evangile est tout de Dieu; qu'il n'est point corrompu et ne l'a pû être. [. . .] Que l'Alcoran qui combat le Mystère adorable de la Trinité, dit des choses qui l'établissent et en facilitent la créance. [. . .] Sur le Mystère de la Divinité de Jesus-Christ et de son incarnation, que l'Alcoran en favorise la créance. [. . .] La Religion chrétienne est justifiée sur plusieurs point, par les textes de l'Alcoran: que Mahomet n'est pas Prophète, et que l'Alcoran n'est pas un Livre de Dieu'.
50. On the first use of the Sunni *tafsīr* by the Judeo-Christian Guillelmus Raymundus de Moncata (alias Flavius Mithridates), see Grévin and Mandalà, 'Le rôle des communautés'.
51. Éric Vallet, '*Des grâces que Dieu m'a prodiguées* de Jalal al-Din al-Suyuti', in Patrick Boucheron (ed.), *Histoire du monde au XVe siècle* (Paris: Fayard, 2009), pp. 488–93.
52. Nau, *L'état présent de la religion mahométane*, p. 191: 'Les interprètes de l'Alcoran disputent entr'eux si Mahomet étoit obligé à ce que Dieu avoit commandé de faire pour l'expiation de ce péché'.
53. The same episode had been used for debate by Filippo Guadagnoli. See Trentini, 'Il Caracciolino Filippo Guadagnoli', pp. 302–3.
54. On the position of another Catholic Orientalist on these points, see Bernard Heyberger, 'L'Islam et les Arabes chez un érudit maronite au service de l'Église catholique (Abraham Ecchellensis),' *Al-Qantara*, 31, 2 (2010), p. 501. For a commentary on this passage of the Qur'an, see Michel Cuypers, *Le Festin: Une lecture de la sourate 'al-Mâ'ida'* (Paris: Lethielleux, 2007).
55. Bernard Heyberger, 'L'Islam dei missionari cattolici (Medio Oriente, Seicento)', in Heyberger et al. (eds), *L'Islam visto da Occidente*, pp. 289–314.
56. Ines G. Županov, 'Accommodation', in Régine Azria and Danièle Hervieu-Léger (eds), *Dictionnaire des faites religieux* (Paris: PUF, 2010), pp. 1–4; Ines G. Županov, '"One Civility, but Multiple Religions": Jesuit Mission among St Thomas Christians in India (16th–17th Centuries)', *Journal of Early Modern History*, 9, 3–4 (2005), pp. 283–325.
57. Loubna Khayati, 'Le statut de l'Islam dans la pensée libertine du premier XVIIe siècle', in Heyberger et al. (eds), *L'Islam visto da Occidente*, pp. 109–33; Ziad Elmarsafy, *The Enlightenment Qur'an: The Politics of Translation and the Construction of Islam* (Oxford: Oneworld, 2009), p. 122, passim; Martin Mulsow, 'Socinianism, Islam and the Radical Uses of Arabic Scholarship', *Al-Qantara*, 31, 2 (2010), pp. 549–86.

CHAPTER 8

From Religious to Secular Imagery? The Rise of the Image among Christians in Syria and Lebanon in the Seventeenth to Nineteenth Centuries

Eastern Christians, at least the Melkites and the Maronites from *bilād al-Shām* (Greater Syria), on whom this chapter focuses, had a tradition of images. This was, on the one hand, the art of the icon that expanded in the Byzantine Empire after the crisis of iconoclasm, with some local particularities.[1] On the other hand, it was the monumental decoration of churches and monasteries, which since ancient times had been covered with frescoes and mosaics.[2] It was also the art of the miniature in manuscripts. Images destined for the public were limited to sanctuaries where they formed part of the decoration, alongside lanterns, mirrors and ostrich eggs. Their place, the themes that they represented and the material figures chosen to appear in them followed very formal rules. They first of all helped to teach the people and to put the faithful in contact with the sacred, while at the same time narrating episodes from the life of Christ, the Virgin, or a saint. When an image was an icon, it had to be consecrated before being placed in a church.[3]

For unknown reasons, this traditional art of religious painting nearly died out in Syria, only surviving as miniatures in manuscripts. The painted décor of churches still visible around the eleventh century for the most part seems to have faded afterwards. In principle, the cult required icons. But these must have been extremely rare, and for the most part they were imported.[4]

From the seventeenth century onwards, there appeared a truly new phenomenon: an explosion of consumption, importation and production of images amongst Eastern Christians. It is this development, linked to the economic and cultural opening of Christian minorities towards Orthodox and Catholic Europe, that we will examine here. One can observe in particular an enormous distribution of religious images from, or inspired by, the West, which had consequences for local production and the use of figurative representations; this encouraged a significant evolution of attitudes, in the same manner as the growth of schools or the spreading consumption of printed books. As in other domains of cultural activity, Eastern Christians do not appear as passive consumers of imported images. They participated in the elaboration of a local synthesis of iconography and pictorial techniques, a synthesis that was characterised by a dialectic of modernity and authenticity.

THE SUDDEN ERUPTION OF IMAGES

In 1781, Father Étienne-Philippe Cuénot died in Antoura, Lebanon. He was the last of the ex-Jesuits of this missionary residence, which the French Consulate in Saida immediately sealed off, before shortly thereafter proceeding with an inventory of the property. This revealed a real muddle, from which emerged large quantities of books and images. It is the latter that interest us here.[5] The first thing that stands out was the overload of images in all the living spaces of the Jesuit residence, whether in public areas such as the church, or in private ones such as Cuénot's own bedroom. In the church, the inventory listed a picture of Saint Joseph with a golden frame at the high altar, one of the Virgin at the side altar, a large painting of Saint Francis Xavier and twenty-five other unspecified images. In the sacristy, there were 'an image of the Virgin painted on glass', two small pictures and five further small paintings. In the refectory: three old paintings. In the seminary: one large painting. In the bedroom of the deceased: a picture in a golden frame representing the Last Supper and another showing Saint Joseph. These images were destined for the Jesuits, but also for their Eastern pupils and visitors to their residence. They were not there by chance, or due to the personal taste of such and such a Jesuit; they corresponded to a very specific intention, to a function of the image already defined by Ignatius of Loyola.[6] That is not all. The inventory also revealed a practice confirmed elsewhere in the Latin missions in the East: the massive distribution of images to the indigenous Christians, who could put them up in their houses and even wear them. Indeed, we also find a mention of a small basket of pictures, of eight other unspecified images and of five of the Sacred Heart of Jesus. One may add to this the special images that were worn, the pious medals: the former Jesuit possessed a bag that contained forty-two and 'a small boxful' on top of that. Lastly, we note the presence of another modern image: a small map of Asia.

This inventory offers no surprises: it only confirms what other sources here and there have told us. On his second trip to Lebanon in 1580, Giovanni Battista Eliano, the first Jesuit sent to the Maronites, came bearing silver chalices, liturgical objects and large quantities of communion wafers, rosaries and images.[7] Later on, the Latin missionaries of all orders introduced Western iconography on a large scale, in the form of paintings, printed images, medals and even statues.[8] In their churches they carried out an iconographic programme in keeping with the taste of the Counter-Reformation, answering in particular to the criterion of 'decency' – that is to say, of a certain pomp in the ornamentation of altars and of sanctuaries, required by the Council of Trent in its twenty-fifth session.[9]

In Palestine, the decoration of the Holy Places, strategic as symbols and meeting places of communication, received particular attention. In Nazareth, the Friars Minor of the Holy Land completed their church on 7 May 1730.[10] They placed two altars on the western side, one dedicated to Saint Joseph, the other to Saint Francis, and two others on the eastern side, dedicated to Saint Anne and Saint Anthony of Padua. To the north, next to the high altar, was the Archangel Gabriel. In the middle of the church, one descended to the chapel of the Annunciation where the walls were covered with oil paintings by a French artist, representing the mysteries of the Virgin in frames inspired by grotesques, characteristic of the style of the period.

It was not only in churches and in the residences of the 'Franks' that images of European origin were displayed. Indeed, Westerners sometimes offered paintings to Eastern Christians to decorate their own sanctuaries. Thus, in 1757, three lay congregations in Aleppo, founded by the Jesuits for the Maronites and the Armenians, each received, with the approval of Rome, a painting created in Italy, which was solemnly displayed during a special celebration.[11]

As the inventory of Antoura suggested, the missionaries also distributed a large number of paper images that reached private homes. A 'report of what is sent each year to Fr. Fleuriau from Fr. Rigord of Marseille to be distributed to every mission house of the Levant', dating from the beginning of the eighteenth century, noted: 100 crosses and medals, 100 images of Saint Roch on sheets, fifty sheets of sixteen images, fifty images on lighter sheets and 200 small simple images.[12] At the start of their re-installation in Lebanon, in 1832, the Jesuits themselves took up hammer and nails to fix the images of the Virgin or crosses on the walls of the houses they visited. They encouraged Christians to pray before them morning and evening.[13]

In 1784, 'Isa Carus' ('Isā Kārūz?), a priest from Bethlehem, had engraved at his own expense, presumably in Rome, a 'Holy Family' in a Raphaelite style, accompanied by a Latin, Greek and Arabic dedication.[14] Prints were also imported from the Orthodox world. As early as 1650, some were made in Kiev. The deacon Būlus al-Za'īm, who kept a journal of the travels (1652–59) he made with his father, the Melkite patriarch Macarius III, stated that he had pictures of the Apostle Peter printed there in three different formats: a large size for the town notables, a medium size for the common people and a small one for women.[15] Between 1688 and 1700, a workshop that printed good-quality woodcuts was functioning in Lviv, financed by Hatzikyriakis, a Greek from Vurla in Asia Minor, who provided paper and ink and who saw to the distribution of the images. Based on his correspondence, one can estimate the production of this factory at more than 19,000 wood engravings between 1688 and

1709, sold over an area spreading from Moscow to Mount Sinai. They were destined particularly to popularise the latter, with its monastery of Saint Catherine, shown on the image, and to attract donations for it. They were sent there from Lviv in wooden crates, each containing a thousand copies.[16]

Eastern Christians sought to obtain paintings for their churches or engravings for their homes. In the Armenian church of Aleppo, for example, there was a painting brought back from Europe by an Armenian, showing a Carmelite in prayer in front of the Virgin, upon which a local painter had been invited to work.[17] The Melkite Ḥannā Darak, in a letter that he sent to Rome, commissioned a painting representing Saint Romanos, for the church he had founded in Ḥamānā.[18] In 1777, the Superior of the Aleppine Maronite monks wrote to one of his colleagues in Rome, asking him to find for his church in the monastery of Luwayza 'an image of the Assumption' of the Virgin and giving the desired dimensions, while specifying that the cost was of no importance, provided that it was good-quality work.[19] In fact, a large Assumption, which had been placed on the high altar of the church, today is in the museum of this monastery, which also has a collection of European paintings copied in the eighteenth century. But the painting is maybe somewhat more recent: it was given under *waqf* terms by the Vicar General and the Superior of the Aleppine monastery in Rome, in 1817 (Figure 8.1).

The Christians were no less fond of the printed pictures that were widely distributed to them by the missionaries during catechism sessions and visits to their homes, or that they received in exchange for alms during visits to sanctuaries. Ioannikos, the archbishop of Sinai, wrote to his correspondent in Lviv: 'Send us as many [images of] monasteries and saints as you have, as everyone outside has heard of them and begs the Fathers to obtain some for them'. We know these pictures because nine carved wooden blocks that were used to make them arrived at the Sinai monastery, where they have been preserved. But most of the European production printed before the nineteenth century escapes us, due to the fact that neither wood nor copper printing plates have been preserved.[20]

By the seventeenth century, the Eastern Christians generally were no longer content with imports. They themselves started to produce images locally, first turning to artists trained in Europe. The most famous case was no doubt that of the Persian Armenians who around 1650 had the decoration of their churches in New Julfa (Isfahan) carried out by European artists, according to an iconographic programme and techniques that combined Eastern tradition and Western influence.[21] In the same period, two Italian artists were apparently working in Aleppo and initiated the Armenians into painting.[22] More modestly, in Qannūbīn, in a rustic patriarchal Maronite church on Mount Lebanon, a monk from Cyprus painted a Coronation of the Virgin as a fresco in 1690; it seems to have been inspired by a printed European image, maybe an engraving by Dürer, but closer to Eastern taste than Jules Leroy has described it, both in the adaptation of the iconography and

Figure 8.1 Assumption of the Virgin Mary, Museum at Our Lady Monastery, Louaizeh (Luwayza), Zuk Mosbeh, Lebanon (Courtesy of Our Lady Monastery; acknowledgment to the Superior of the monastery). This large-size Baroque-style painting is a copy of an Italian work. It was first placed over the main altar of the monastery's church. An inscription at the bottom (under Saint Peter's foot) specifies that it was given as a *waqf* by the General Vicar and the General Superior of the Aleppine monks' monastery in Rome, 1817.

Figure 8.2 Coronation of the Virgin Mary by the Holy Trinity (1690), fresco, Monastery of Qannūbīn, Lebanon. Inscription in Garshūnī under the dove of the Holy Spirit: 'Come with me from Lebanon, my bride [*Song of Songs*, 4:8] and you will be coronated' (Courtesy of istockphoto).

in the choice of colours and the treatment of the borders (Figure 8.2).[23] When the Capuchins from Beirut wished to decorate their churches with images of Saint Peter and Saint Paul in 1705, they too called on a Maronite painter.[24]

Around the same time, the Maronites of Aleppo asked the patriarch Yaʿqūb ʿAwwād to send them the monks Buṭrus al-Qubruṣī (the Cypriot) al-Muṣawwir and Ibrāhīm Kurbāj al-Ḥalabī to decorate their church. They were then indeed authorised to go to work in the town.[25] We do not know where this Maronite from Cyprus acquired his training, but it was quite basic. We do know, however, that a number of Syrians studied painting in Rome, before returning to practise in their country. In 1647 Buṭrus Diyāb, a Greek from Aleppo, obtained permission from the cardinals of the Propaganda to follow a six-month training with a good Roman painter and to go with him to visit churches on Sundays and feast days, with a view to practising his art on his return to his own country. We do not know if he indeed put this into practice.[26] In any case, he ended up far from his hometown, as a teacher of Arabic at the Collège Royal (today the Collège de France) after 1667.[27]

Anṭūn Khabiyya, from a good Melkite clerical family from Damascus, entered the Collegio Urbano in Rome in 1723, at the age of thirteen. He failed in his studies, but his school report indicated that he was authorised to spend all his time painting 'to fix his hot-headedness'. Back home in 1732, we find him again in Aleppo in 1734, selling his paintings.[28]

Arsāniyūs Diyāb, a Maronite monk originally from Aleppo, also studied painting in the Christian capital. He was sent there in 1767, and he was apprenticed to a famous master, unfortunately not identified. Even though his superiors expressed doubts as to his capacity to learn, he practised his art later on in his country.[29] In 1769, when he was driven from the Bkirki monastery by his uncle, who was his superior, he found refuge with the Armenian Catholic patriarch, from Aleppo like himself, for whom he decorated the church and taught his art to the monks.[30] In 1789, the bishop of Aleppo authorised him to paint in the town.[31]

Without a doubt, one could find still more Easterners who studied painting in Italy at the time. The problem is that their work has so far not been identified. The direct impact of the West on the pictorial world of Eastern Christians still remains a mystery for the most part. We do know that throughout the Eastern Christian world there was an intensification of the local production of images in the eighteenth century. They adopted techniques, languages and themes that tended to be similar to Western painting, but the influence was not necessarily direct: it could have gone via the Byzantine world, itself open to some Italian innovations.[32] During the seventeenth and eighteenth centuries, an 'Aleppine school' of painting produced what has been called 'Melkite icons', characterised by their deep-rootedness in local taste, while at the same time being a synthesis of multiple inspirations.[33] These artists would have received their training in the workshops of Chios, of Crete, of the Lavra of Saint Sabbas near Jerusalem, or, more likely, they were influenced by the works that reached them. A certain taste for realism in their painting reveals an inspiration, direct or indirect, from Italian painting. One can observe a true professionalisation in them, marked particularly by the abundance of their production and the fact that they signed their work.[34] The latter trait is to be linked to a certain artistic freedom, controlled however by the requirements of their sponsors. Without wishing to deny the specificity of this dynasty of the 'Muṣawwir' from Aleppo, it seems to me that we cannot isolate it from the wider context of the production of images in the same region by the Maronites and the Armenians, maybe even by the Greeks and Georgians, as well as the flourishing import 'market' from Italy, France, Russia, or Greece.

Alongside painting, there also existed in the area a modest production of figures on paper. The monastery of Saint Catherine in the Sinai has preserved twenty or so basic wood carvings dating from the end of the seventeenth century, proof of the existence of a workshop there. One of them, representing views of the Sinai, warrants our attention in so far as it is signed. One side, carved in 1665, bears the name of Akakios; the other, from 1706, is signed by Matthaios from Crete. These are the most ancient wood carvings known from Orthodox sources.[35]

Later on, the establishment of printing presses in Aleppo and then in Lebanon made it possible to publish illustrated books. This is all the more remarkable since we know that few Arabic books printed before 1800 in the West had pictures. In the volumes consulted, one can sometimes find some decoration that does not go beyond a figure in a medallion, some border or, more generally, some *rinceaux* (foliated patterns). Catechisms from the eighteenth century had no images, which may be justified by the facts that at that time there was not one book per student and that reciting aloud was the main way of learning. It was only in the second half of the nineteenth century that illustrations appeared in schoolbooks. We do not know if the pictures in these locally produced books were printed separately, on loose sheets, following a practice attested elsewhere. Readers also often detached the pictures from their books in order to use them for something else, which further complicates our understanding of these images.

The *Kitāb al-Qaddāsāt al-thalāthat al-'ilāhiyyat* (Liturgikon), printed in Snagov in 1701 for the Melkite Church, features engravings on wood of people treated in a style close to Orthodox icons. The same is true of the *Kitāb al-bāraklītīkī* (The Paraclete), published in Aleppo in 1711.[36] The printing press of the Melkite monks of Shuwayr (which began its activity in 1734) published several illustrated works, sometimes in an unsophisticated manner.[37] The richest in images and doubtlessly the most original is the Book of Gospels of 1776, which ran to several editions. It contains four plates, each showing one of the four evangelists in a style that followed the conventions of Italian painting, even though the woodblocks used for the printing were probably made locally. Instead of writing with a dried reed (*qalam*), Saint Luke is depicted using a quill, a typically Western object. The same is true of the furniture shown (chair, table, hanging curtain), which was only gradually making its appearance in the bourgeois houses of Aleppo in this period. The effect of perspective (with the curtain pulled back and the window showing a landscape) in each of the four images was an imitation of Italian or Flemish paintings, although here the engraver betrayed his lack of technical mastery in his representation of chair and table (Figure 8.3). These images can give us an idea of the paper figures that the missionaries distributed and that probably served as models for the plates in this work. But what gives this book its originality is the combination of illustrations of Latin and Byzantine origins. Apart from the four evangelists, the book is decorated with grotesques, typical of rococo taste (Figure 8.4), as well as small icons of the Virgin in the Eastern tradition (Figure 8.5).

The juxtaposition of iconographic and stylistic traditions of different origins revealed in this Book of Gospels is a characteristic trait of the attitude of Eastern Christians towards imagery between the seventeenth and nineteenth centuries. Both paintings and engravings testify to this juxtaposition.[38]

Figure 8.3 Evangelist Saint Luke, woodcut, in *Kitāb al-Injil al-sharīf al-ṭāhir* (Khunshāra: Monastery of Saint John of Shuwayr, Lebanon, 1776). Inscription: *Al-Qiddīs Lūqā al-Injilī* (Bernard Heyberger, from the exemplar of the monastery of Saint John of Shuwayr; acknowledgment to the Superior of the monastery).

Figure 8.4 Woodcut in grotesque style, reproduced several times in *Kitāb al-Injil al-sharīf al-ṭāhir* (Khunshāra: Monastery of Saint John of Shuwayr, Lebanon, 1776). (Bernard Heyberger, from the exemplar of the monastery of Saint John of Shuwayr; acknowledgment to the Superior of the monastery).

Figure 8.5 Virgin Mary with the Child and Two Angels, woodcut in the style of a Byzantine icon, reproduced several times in *Kitāb al-Injil al-sharīf al-ṭāhir* (Khunshāra: monastery of Saint John of Shuwayr, Lebanon, 1776). (Bernard Heyberger, from the exemplar of the monastery of the monastery of Saint John of Shuwayr; acknowledgment to the Superior of the monastery.

FUNCTIONS OF THE MODERN IMAGE

We witness a veritable surge of sacred images among Eastern Christians from the seventeenth century onwards. Ancient frescos and icons of different origins and periods were already found side by side in sanctuaries, but in far fewer numbers. Many places of worship seem to have been totally bare of figurative representations.[39] It is certain that this quantitative change went together with changes in iconography and pictorial techniques, as well as in the uses of these pictures by the public.

All the examples given so far indicate the introduction of a number of significant transformations. Thus, alongside the traditional representations of the Virgin, a new Marian iconography spread, inspired by the Latin devotions that were becoming popular. As already mentioned above, the theme of the Assumption was added to that of the Dormition of the Virgin, without replacing it.[40] The Rosary and the Immaculate Conception, typical of modern Catholicism, could be treated as icons by an Aleppine painter, alongside the traditional *Hodigitria* (Virgin with Child).[41]

To the hieratic images of Christ in Majesty were added images imported from the West, whose representations seem more focused on the humanity of the incarnate God than on his divinity, in a conception entirely opposed to the Eastern tradition, reluctant to represent with realism the suffering human nature and seeking to translate in the image the imprint of divine nature and holiness.[42] In episodes of the life of Christ, modern images favour his childhood and his Passion. Thus, Sylvia Agemian has pointed out a *Descent from the Cross* printed in the Monastery of Saint Saviour during the reign of the Greek Catholic patriarch Agapius (Ajābyūs) II Maṭar (1796–1812); it is distinguishable 'by its composition and drama, even suffering that belonged to a conception totally different from the hieratic character and the sobriety of the Byzantine tradition'.[43]

We saw above a representation of the Last Supper in the room of the ex-Jesuit from Antoura. A book printed in Shuwayr featured a clumsy engraving representing the chalice.[44] A small icon was made by a Melkite painter to celebrate the miracle of the Eucharist that happened in Aleppo in 1737.[45] Here we are dealing with the favourite themes of baroque Catholicism. The insistence on the body of Christ present in the Eucharist (which also enhanced the priestly function) is found among the Maronites as well as the Melkites in the eighteenth century.

As the inventory of the belongings of Antoura and the description of the chapel of Nazareth have suggested, the 'Frankish' friars introduced into their churches and residences the saints linked to their orders: Saint Francis Xavier and Saint Ignatius for the Jesuits, Saint Francis of Assisi and Saint Anthony of Padua for the Friars Minor and the Capuchins, Saint Teresa of Avila for the Discalced Carmelites. The Latin female saints adopted by the Easterners probably had a deeper influence on devotions than their male counterparts, in competition with the indigenous saints rehabilitated by the clergy and local painters.[46]

If there was a massive Westernisation, it did not happen without a struggle, or without the necessary compromises. The realism of Italian-style painting may have caused some temporary difficulties of understanding to the Eastern Christians, because of the iconographic choices[47] or the figurative techniques.[48] But it seems that, on the whole, they rather allowed themselves to be fascinated by the living aspect of the people represented. In 1637, a Capuchin from Baghdad told how his church was invaded by a crowd, because the people, never having seen a painting, thought the figures represented were alive and came to ask which language they spoke and what they ate.[49] Būlus al-Zaʿīm expressed his enthusiasm for the realism of the Cossack painters whose works he discovered in Kiev.[50]

There existed a definite local taste, to which the Western religious leaders sometimes carefully tried to adapt the images that they distributed.[51] Still, in 1833, the Jesuit Paul Ricadonna gave this advice to potential candidates for the Lebanese missions: 'Those who want to bring images, only bring those with vivid colours and rather those of ancient and Eastern saints. Here the delicacy of the chisel as well as the modern European saints are unknown'.[52]

In fact, the preference for bright and contrasting colours in the locally produced works was noticed by other observers.[53] The traditional Byzantine themes did not disappear and were even the object of a certain revival. Eastern saints came back into fashion: a local saint, such as Saint Elian of Homs, was rescued from oblivion by iconography.[54]

Often artists attempted aesthetic and iconographic syntheses between the taste and the culture of local sponsors, on the one hand, and the Latin model they wanted to adopt, on the other. This was the case of the fresco of the Assumption in Qannūbīn. It was also the case in the commemoration of the miracle of the Eucharist in Aleppo, of the representation of the Rosary and the Immaculate Conception mentioned above. In the latter case, the painter Jirjis Ḥanania al-Muṣawwir in 1762 chose to illustrate a controversial Latin belief – the dogma of the Immaculate Conception would only be proclaimed in the Catholic Church in 1854 – and was not accepted in the Orthodox Church. But he interpreted the themes in a Byzantine context: the twelve medals around the Virgin carried symbols attributed to her in the Akathist Hymn. The themes treated at the bottom of the image also came from the Byzantine Marian tradition: the earthly paradise between two cypress trees, protected by a wall, and the earth blooming with fecundity. The aesthetic choices also remained faithful to the Orient: the face of the Virgin very obviously had a local character, and the background in gold leaf had nothing to do with baroque imagery, which usually represented the Immaculate Conception against a blue background with clouds of cherubs.[55]

These works, in fact, very precisely corresponded to the trend current among the Greek Catholics from the patriarchate of Antioch at the time, who thought that Latin and Byzantine devotions could be combined. They were not opposed to one another; rather, an attempt was made to have them coexist. The introduction of a liturgical or dogmatic novelty from the West was presented not as an innovation, but as the restoration of an authentic tradition that had been altered or forgotten.

But these attempts at merging were not without contradictions or conflicts. The realisation of iconographic programmes in churches gave place to real 'wars of images' between rival clergy, particularly in the Holy Places and also in other sanctuaries in the East. At Mount Carmel, the Greeks attacked a statue of Saint Elijah installed by the Carmelites.[56] In Mardin, the 'Nestorian' patriarch Elijah X, arriving from his monastery near Mosul, took down the images that the Christians of his rite, favourable to Catholicism, had put up in the church.[57]

Saint Joseph was a favourite saint of the Latin missionaries in the East, as everywhere in baroque Catholicism. Even though his presence is noted in churches as early as in the eighteenth century, he had some difficulty making a name for himself in the Eastern iconography.[58] The Western Saint Joseph, virginal and chaste, was difficult for Easterners to understand and accept; for them, he was a widower looking after children. Marriage for the Syrian Christians had to be fertile, whereas the Latin clergy promoted chastity even within marriage. The question gave rise to some rather lively debates.[59] In Aleppo, in 1725, the Orthodox patriarch Sylvester, who himself was a painter of icons, blinded and then destroyed an image of Saint Joseph that the Catholic Greeks had set up on the altar of their church.[60] The theme of the chastity of Saint Joseph, as well as that of the Holy Family, which was related to it, only became fully integrated into local iconography in the nineteenth century.[61] This was also true for the Virgin with Rose, a simple work in its expression, but in fact more complex in its references. It combines traditional Byzantine iconography (the Virgin with Child, the theme of the 'unfading rose') and the Western Marian devotion (the Virgin holding a lily, symbol of chastity; Saint Joseph, chaste spouse, also appears holding a lily).[62]

But these conflicts did not only oppose the Orthodox and the Catholics. The Greek Catholic patriarch was said to have torn up in public an image of Saint Maron, the great founding saint of the Maronites, considered a heretic by the Byzantines.[63] In 1937, a Capuchin reported having read on the stone of an altar in the Greek Catholic convent of Saint Saviour in South Lebanon an Arabic inscription from 1753, dedicated to Saint Anthony of Padua, while the image above it had been replaced by that of Saint Anthony of the Desert, more authentically Eastern.[64]

These examples show that the decoration of the sanctuaries was a tool in the powerplay between various rites or rival groups. One would be wrong, in trying to place anachronistic boundaries between the religious and the secular domains, to reduce these issues to simple clerical rivalries. It is the confessional identity of the different groups that is at stake, as well as their relations with the West. A proof of this is the introduction in the eighteenth century of the devotion to (and iconography of) the Sacred Heart, both strongly charged with political ideology (Figure 8.6).[65]

Moreover, a more directly political imagery became widespread at the same time. This was essentially the case of the portrait. At the time of Louis XIV, many portraits of the king were distributed in the Middle East, from the Maronite patriarchate of Mount Lebanon to Aleppo, Baghdad and Isfahan, for propaganda purposes.[66] But the practice of the portrait was also supposed to materialise local power among the Eastern Christians. In the sectarian system being put in place at that time, authority was concentrated mainly in the hands of the clerics. It was therefore natural that it should be they who were represented and shown in pictures in the churches and monasteries, the usual meeting places and true seats of power for Christians. The practice of painting the portrait of the patriarchs appeared at the end of the seventeenth century: we know how Macarius III ibn al-Zaʿīm discovered this practice in Ukraine before

Figure 8.6 Sacred Heart of Jesus with Eucharist, door lintel, Monastery of Mār Yūsaf al-Ḥuṣn, Ghosta (Ghūsṭā), Lebanon (Bernard Heyberger).

being painted himself.[67] In an Arabic Psalter printed in Vienna in 1792, its author, Anthimius, the Greek patriarch from Jerusalem, is shown in an engraving on the first page. He is depicted slightly from below, wearing sumptuous liturgical vestments, holding in his left hand a sacred book and giving a blessing with his right hand. An address in a cartouche praises him. Strictly speaking, it is less a portrait than an icon, highlighting the charisma of the patriarch and closely following the model of the ecclesiastical saint, distributed on paper in the Greek world of the nineteenth century.[68]

The new religious orders created on the strongly centralised Latin model adopted the Western tradition of representing their superior. We know the portraits of Nīqūlā al-Ṣā'igh, the superior of the Melkite monks of Shuwayr, as well as a writer and a poet, and of his companion ʿAbdallāh Zākhir, both from Aleppo.[69] In a letter, Tūmā ʿĀql, superior of the Aleppine Maronite monks, asked his representative in Rome for images (*qūna*) and . . .

> . . . an image of the bishop ʿAbdallāh, a true likeness, painted from the image made by Shukrallāh Ṣaqr; for it is important that you should know that he is very highly thought of and that many wish to see an authentic image of him.

The above-mentioned Bishop ʿAbdallāh Qarā'alī was the charismatic founder of this religious order.[70] The monastery of Luwayza has, in fact, kept a portrait of the dignitary, modeled in a slightly clumsy way on the images of the Roman prelates. He is wearing the vestments of a Western bishop. Behind him are rows of books on a shelf; reading and writing, not only the privileges but also the duty of the clergy, were the iconographic attributes of all these portraits of ecclesiastics. Only one of these works carries a recognisable title in Latin: *Biblia Sacra*. An Arabic text superimposed at the bottom of the picture enables the visitor to the monastery to identify the venerable founder. The original inscription, giving his names and titles in Latin in a banner, in the fashion used for Latin dignitaries, was no doubt more useful to legitimise him than to have him recognised by the public (Figure 8.7).[71]

But if the portrait functioned as a political image showing power, it was also natural to find caricatures, reactions to the official flattering portrait. Thus, Ibn Tūmā, Greek Orthodox trustee (*wakīl*) from Damascus, had apparently made a 'sacrilegious painting' to mock the pope, the Greek Catholic patriarch Cyril and the king of France.[72] The devout Maronite Hindiyya, founder of the Sacred Heart order and superior of the convent of Bkirki, was represented in an official portrait, maybe the work of the above-mentioned monk Arsāniyūs Diyāb.[73] Before that, the Jesuits, her first teachers and counsellors, had caricatured her when she had broken up with them. The image, on the model of the 'enigmatic figures' that the Fathers often used for popular instruction, represented the vices in the form of a tree and put in parallel the virtues and miracles attributed to Hindiyya, together with the discontent that she and her followers apparently caused. It is perhaps the novelty of the process of caricature that explains the intensity of the indignation that its spread caused, to the point that a protest petition against this picture was circulated in Aleppo.[74]

According to the classical schema of 'modernisation', the counterpart to this build-up of power is the development of individual conscience and internalisation, a process in which the image also participates. It is even the private use of the image that, in my opinion, constitutes the true novelty of this period. The struggles for the occupation of the visual public space that I have mentioned show that it was probably less in the painting and in the decoration of the sanctuaries than in the intimacy of the houses that modern iconography, notably in the form of printed pictures, was able to unfold. The rich merchants of Aleppo and elsewhere commissioned icons for their houses, or to give as *waqf* to the churches and monasteries of their respective *ṭāʾifas*.[75] Some paintings entered wealthy homes, like that of the Ḥawwā of Aleppo, who decorated a whole room with them. Shukrallāh ʿUjaymī, the father of Hindiyya, was very attached to a painting on canvas representing the Virgin and Child.[76] Later on, towards the end of the eighteenth century, the powerful Maronite merchant Yūsuf Qarāʿalī, connected to the French, had a representation of the Sacred Heart surmounted with the Seal of the Blessed Sacrament affixed on his house.[77] More modest images distributed by the missionaries, as we have seen, adorned bedrooms and found a place on bedheads.[78] In the brotherhoods of the lay people that they directed, the Jesuits also introduced the practice of the saint of the month: a representation of the saint was offered to each of the faithful, who had to take care to imitate for a month the person represented and could

Figure 8.7 Portrait of ʿAbdallāh Qarāʿalī (1672–1742), first Superior of the Lebanese Monks of Saint Anthony, from 1716 onwards bishop of Beirut. Anonymous painting, undated (eighteenth century?). Museum at Our Lady Monastery, Louaizeh (Luwayza), Zuk Mosbeh, Lebanon (Courtesy of Our Lady Monastery; acknowledgment to Father Walid Moussa and Father Joseph Moukarzel). Inscription in Latin in the band: *Abdallà Caralli Archiep[iscop]us Beryten[s]is Primus Ord[in]is S[anc]ti Antonij Congreg[ation]is Montis Libani Abbas G[e]n[er]alis.* Second inscription in Arabic, in red, over the band to the right, surely added later: *Al-Quds al-Ābātī ʿAbdallāh Qarāʿalī min sana 1700 ilā 1711.*

at the same time benefit from his protection. This practice, attested as early as 1640,[79] was still in use in 1858, when Father Paul Ricadonna mentioned it in Zahle and surrounding areas, specifying that he chose Eastern saints wherever possible and that each month more than 1,000 notes dedicated to these saints were selected at random.[80] As the inventory of Father Cuénot's possessions has revealed, the Jesuits of the old company, and then of the new one, had made themselves the disseminators of the cult of the Sacred Heart. At the beginning of the nineteenth century, images of this controversial devotion entered the homes of Aleppo. Part of the clergy of the town, who were hostile to it, went around the houses to confiscate and destroy them.[81]

The message that the Latin church leaders delivered through the mediation of these images was not unequivocal. The belief that one was in the presence of the sacred through a figurative representation was still alive. Prints were often treated by the faithful as 'paper icons' and revered in the same way, placed on a small altar, in a 'pretty spot' in the house, with a candle lit before them. On the image that he had printed in Rome, the priest Isa Carus had a consecration formula engraved, similar to those that were on painted icons. The 'Frankish' missionaries themselves, at least in the seventeenth century, sometimes had a magical relation to the image, to which they attributed supernatural or even therapeutic powers. Moreover, the image participated in a spirituality which in certain aspects was no different from that of an icon. Thus, through the image, the Virgin or a saint could profoundly touch the soul of the person who contemplated it and reveal to them hidden feelings.[82] A priest's manual published in Arabic by the Propaganda in Rome in 1844 opened with a sorrowful Crucifixion, typical of the Latin devotion. This time, the spiritual effects of the contemplation of the image were strictly set in the Latin system of indulgences granted by the popes, distributed with success among Eastern Catholics from the eighteenth century onwards. Indeed, a text opposite the frontispiece reminded the faithful that one could earn a plenary indulgence by reciting the prayer indicated before the representation of Christ on the cross. The illustrated book was a tool that allowed prayer and private and silent meditation outside the sanctuary. But the mediation of the Church was recalled for the person opening the book, based on the evocation of the indulgences granted by the pope, earned only by accompanying the prayer with confession and communion.[83]

On the Latin and Greek images printed in large numbers in Venice and Vienna, as on the engravings of the four evangelists in the Gospel Book printed in Shuwayr, the representation is less hieratic than on the Byzantine icons, which remained attached to a strict code, offering, for example, always a full-face image only. On the prints, however, the characters appear more alive and thus more human, closer to the person contemplating them. The transition from engraving on wood to engraving on copper in this respect constituted an innovation with great aesthetic consequences, as it gave more depth and plasticity to the image.[84] The faithful could then enter into a familiar, everyday dialogue with these paper figures, which previously had been unfeasible. This was even truer for women who, rarely going to church, had little contact with icons. From then on, they learned to meditate on an image that they carried with them, according to the recommendation of Saint Teresa, whose works were available in Arabic:

> You will find it very helpful if you can get an image or a picture of this Lord – one that you like – not to wear round your neck and never look at but to use regularly whenever you talk to Him, and He will tell you what to say.[85]

Hindiyya always kept with her a typical image of Western devotion, one entirely foreign to Eastern Christianity: that of Christ being scourged, which had already accompanied Saint Teresa.[86] This image sometimes came alive, and the Christ shown there started looking at her or talking to her. He also appeared in the guise of *Ecce Homo*, wearing a Crown of Thorns and covered in blood, another image popularised in the West from the seventeenth century onwards.[87] One day, when she was still very young, Hindiyya saw the Child Jesus carried by Saint Anthony of Padua on a painting owned by her Ḥawwā uncles smile and wink at her.[88]

In the baroque pedagogy of the image, the latter had to impress the soul of the believer. Thus, the Jesuits told us how they used these 'moral images', these 'enigmatical figures' invented in the Breton countryside in the seventeenth century and later employed them with the American First Nations, as well as with the Christians in Damascus and the Lebanese mountains.[89] They were not very inventive, being always a more or less faithful replica of a model. They were quite large (approximately 40 x 60 cm), so that they could be seen by a crowd. They represented the state of the human soul or 'man's end', shown according to an intended progression to bring the spectator, for fear of a bad death and damnation, to repent and to atone (attrition). A Jesuit recounted that he used them in the Lebanese mountains in the evening after supper, and that they provoked in the peasants an 'extraordinary terror'. They helped to draw the attention of the faithful to their 'internal being', what happened within their enclosed body and often provoked anxiety.[90] Hence, the image no longer established contact with an external sacred, as was the case with the icon, but became a mirror, helping to see within oneself. Following the new norms put in use by Catholic teaching, it helped to build oneself, at a time when the practice of the written confession or the private diary was equally encouraged. This was far from a simple narrative or decorative function.

The visual universe of the Christians of *bilād al-Shām* thus underwent a transformation between the seventeenth and nineteenth centuries. The rare and precious icon was succeeded by a plethora of images, the abundance of which must of course be put into perspective with respect to our present. The figurative representation left the sanctuaries, to be worn on one's person and to enter even the most modest homes. The individual, therefore, could appropriate the image and be involved in an intimate relationship with it, in a process similar to that which led from the reading aloud of liturgical texts to a personal and silent acquaintance with the book. At the same time, the iconography opened itself up to new themes, inspired by Roman Catholicism. The figurative representation itself became more realistic and livelier, insisting more on the humanity of the painted figures than on their role as intermediaries with the sacred, according to the tradition of the icon. This evolution did not happen without controversy, compromise and reinterpretations, as with any process of cultural appropriation; moreover, in order to be understood, it must be placed in a more general context of transformation of mentalities and society.

How did this relate to the emergence of 'modern art' in the East? This is still an open question. We cannot go along with the statement that 'art in its modern conception existed in Lebanon since the sixteenth century'.[91] It nonetheless remains true that the beginnings of a local dawning of visual arts were doubtlessly older than has been maintained until now.[92] In order to make a definitive judgement, more detailed studies on the production and consumption of images in the eighteenth and nineteenth centuries are needed, starting with an inventory of extant works, including copies of no artistic value. I am convinced, in any case, that the spread of religious images and the birth of the portrait in the seventeenth century prepared Eastern Christians to look at and appreciate secular images when they made their appearance in the East.

NOTES

1. Virgil Cândea, 'Introduction', in Virgil Cândea (ed.), *Icônes grecques, melkites, russes: Collection Abou Adal* (Geneva: Skira, 1993), pp. 34–35.
2. Joseph Nasrallah, 'La peinture monumentale des patriarcats melkites', in Virgil Cândea (ed.), *Icônes Melkites: Exposition organisée par le musée Nicolas Sursock du 16 mai au 15 juin 1969* (Beirut: Musée Nicolas Sursock, 1969), pp. 67–84.
3. See the commentaries of the patriarch Isṭifān al-Duwayhī, who combined Eastern and Tridentine discourses on images: 'Le candélabre des saints mystères', in Youakim Moubarac (ed.), *Pentalogie antiochienne/domaine maronite* (Beirut: Cénacle Libanais, 1984), vol. I, 1, pp. 67, 70, 91–94.
4. André Grabar, 'Les icônes melkites', in Cândea (ed.), *Icônes Melkites*, p. 22; Cândea, 'Introduction', ibid. p. 41. Similar observations concerning Egypt: Catherine Mayeur-Jaouen, 'La fonction sacrale de l'image dans l'Égypte contemporaine: De l'imagerie traditionnelle à la révolution photographique', in Bernard Heyberger and Silvia Naef (eds), *La multiplication des images en pays d'Islam: De l'estampe à la télévision (17e-21e siècle)* (Istanbul: Orient-Institut der DMG; Würzburg: Ergon, 2003), pp. 57–80.

5. AN, AE, B/I, vol. 1039, fols 145r–150v.
6. Anne Sauvy, *Le miroir du cœur: Quatre siècles d'images savantes et populaires* (Paris: Cerf, 1989), p. 157. The author has observed that in Jesuit retreat houses of the eighteenth century pictures were omnipresent: engravings and paintings in the common areas, as well as paper images hung in private rooms.
7. Isṭifān al-Duwayhī, *Taʾrīkh al-ṭāʾifa al-mārūniyya*, edited by Rashīd al-Shartūnī (Beirut: Imprimerie catholique, 1890), p. 444.
8. A statue of Saint Elijah at Mount Carmel: Giambattista di San Alessio, *Compendio istorico dello stato antico, e moderno del Carmelo* (Turin: nella stamperia d'Ignazio Soffietti, 1780), p. 372. A statue of the Virgin Mary at Alexandretta: Marcellino da Civezza, *Storia universale delle missioni francescane*, vol. 7 (Florence: Tipografia di E. Ariani, 1894), pp. 474, 476. In 1834, an image of the Sacred Heart in bas-relief decorated the Jesuit chapel in ʿAyn Trāz: Sami Kuri, *Une histoire du Liban à travers les archives des jésuites*, vol. 1: *1816–1845* (Beirut: Dar Al-Machreq, 1985), p. 144.
9. Giuseppe Alberigo (ed.), *Les Conciles œcuméniques* (Paris: Cerf, 1994), vol. II, 2, pp. 1572–77. Bernard Heyberger, 'Entre Byzance et Rome: L'image et le sacré au Proche-Orient au XVIIe siècle', *Histoire, économie et société*, 4 (1989), pp. 536–37.
10. Elzear Horn, *Iconographiae locorum et monumentorum veterum Terrae Sanctae . . . (1725–1744)*, edited by Girolamo Golubovich (Rome: typis Sallustianis, 1902), p. 167. For Bethlehem, see also Louis-Hugues Vincent and Félix-Marie Abel, *Bethléem: Le sanctuaire de la Nativité* (Paris: J. Gabalda, 1914).
11. Fardīnān Tawtal [Ferdinand Taoutel], 'Wathāʾiq tāʾrīkhiyya ʿan Ḥalab', *Al-Mashriq*, 42 (1948), pp. 231–33. Another example in Bernard Heyberger, 'Entre Byzance et Rome', p. 537.
12. ARSI, Gallia, vol. 96, III, fols 488r–489v: 'Mémoire de ce qui est envoyé chaque année au P. Fleuriau de la part du P. Rigord de Marseille pour être distribué à chaque mission du Levant'.
13. Sami Kuri, *Une histoire du Liban*, vol. 1, pp. 60, 62 (Letters of Fr. Planchet and Fr. Ricadonna).
14. Dory Papastratos, *Paper Icons: Greek Orthodox Religious Engravings, 1665–1899* (Athens: Papastratos Publications, 1990), vol. 1, n° 152, 154.
15. Būlus al-Ḥalabī, *Voyage du Patriarche Macaire d'Antioche*, Arabic edition and French translation (incomplete) by Basile Radu (Paris: Brepols, 1933), p. 699. Concerning the voyage of Makāryūs and the images, see Carsten Walbiner, '"Images Painted with Such Exalted Skill as to Ravish the Senses . . .": Pictures in the Eyes of Christian Arab Travellers of the 17th and 18th centuries', in Bernard Heyberger and Silvia Naef (eds), *La multiplication des images en pays d'Islam: De l'estampe à la télévision (17e–21e siècle)* (Istanbul: Orient-Institut der DMG; Würzburg: Ergon, 2003), pp. 15–30.
16. Papastratos, *Paper Icons*, vol. 1, p. 19.
17. Bernard Heyberger, *Les Chrétiens du Proche-Orient au temps de la Réforme catholique* (Rome: École Française, 1984), p. 449; Sylvia Agemian, 'Œuvres d'art melkite dans l'église arménienne des Quarante Martyrs d'Alep', *Revue des études arméniennes*, 1 (1973), pp. 91–113.

18. Buṭrus Fahd, *Taʾrīkh al-ruhbāniyya al-mārūniyya bi-farʿayhā al-Ḥalabī wa-l-Lubnānī* (Jounieh: Maṭābaʿ al-karīm al-ḥadītha, 1963–73), vol. 5, p. 519.
19. Fahd, *Taʾrīkh al-ruhbāniyya*, vol. 5, p. 219; Henri Guys, *Beyrouth et le Liban* (Beirut: Dar Lahad Khater, 1985, reprint of the original from 1850), vol. 2, p. 123, has noted 'the wealth of paintings' ('la richesse en tableaux') at Luwayza (around 1830).
20. Papastratos, *Paper Icons*, vol. 1, p. 19. The author has assembled a magnificent collection of 618 prints, dating from 1665 to 1899.
21. Otto Meinardus, 'The Last Judgements in the Armenian Churches of New Julfa', *Oriens Christianus*, 55 (1971), pp. 182–94; Otto Meinardus, 'The Iconography of the Eucharistic Christ in the Armenian Churches of New Julfa', *Oriens Christianus*, 58 (1974), pp. 132–37. [See now Amy S. Landau, 'European Religious Iconography in Safavid Iran: Decoration and Patronage of Meydani Betʿghehem (Bethlehem of the Maydan)', in Willem Floor and Edmund Herzig (eds), *Iran and the World in the Safavid Age* (London: I. B. Tauris, 2012), pp. 425–46].]
22. Ardavazt Surmeyan, *La vie et la culture arméniennes à Alep au XVIIe siècle* (Paris: Imprimerie Araxe, 1934), p. 35.
23. Heyberger, 'Entre Byzance et Rome', pp. 545–46; Jules Leroy, *Moines et monastères du Proche-Orient* (Paris: Horizons de France, 1958), p. 148.
24. Archives of the Capuchins of Paris, n° 1191: typed copy of the daily journal of the Capuchins of Beirut, p. 14.
25. Būlus Qarāʿalī, *'Al-laālīʿ fī ḥayāt al-muṭrān ʿAbdallāh Qarāʿalī'* (Bayt Shabāb: Matbaʿat al-ʿilm, 1932), part 1, p. 158.
26. Bernard Heyberger, 'Entre Byzance et Rome', p. 548.
27. Nasser Gemayel, *Les échanges culturels entre les Maronites et l'Europe* (Beirut: Imprimerie Gemayel, 1984), vol. 1, pp. 290–92.
28. Heyberger, *Les Chrétiens du Proche-Orient*, pp. 418–19.
29. Fahd, *Taʾrīkh al-ruhbāniyya*, vol. 4, p. 355.
30. Būlus ʿAbbūd al-Ghūstāwī, *Al-majālī al-taʿrīkhiyya fī tarjamat al-rāhiba al-shahīra Hindiyya* (Beirut: Al-Tawfīq, 1910), p. 169.
31. AGC, A.D. 106, Aleppo, 112. [On Arsānyūs Diyāb, see Bernard Heyberger, *Hindiyya, Mystic and Criminal, 1720–1798: A Political and Religious Crisis in Lebanon*, English translation by Renée Champion (Cambridge: James Clarke & Co., 2013), passim].
32. Paul Santi, *Miscellanées d'iconographies* (Beirut: n. p., 1966), p. 35; Meinardus, 'The Last Judgements'; Otto Meinardus, 'L'art copte au cours des trois derniers siècles', *Le Monde copte*, 18 (1990), pp. 89–99. [On this issue, with an updated bibliography, see Bernard Heyberger, 'Le renouveau de l'image de religion chez les chrétiens orientaux', *Archives de sciences sociales des religions*, 183 (2018), pp. 191–205.]
33. Concerning these icons, see Cândea (ed.), *Icônes Melkites*; Cândea (ed.), *Icônes grecques, melkites, russes*.
34. Sylvia Agemian, 'Les icônes melkites', in Cândea (ed.), *Icônes grecques, melkites, russes*, p. 176; Grabar, 'Les icônes melkites', pp. 23–25. This causes us to qualify

the opinion of Silvia Naef, *À la recherche d'une modernité arabe* (Genève: Slatkine, 1996), p. 129, on the origins of modern painting in Lebanon.

35. Papastratos, *Paper Icons*, vol. 1, p. 19. [The Sinai monks, expelled from Crete after the Ottoman conquest of the island (1669), transferred Western knowledge and technology, acquired through Venice, to Mount Sinai. See the case of vocal polyphony in Flora Kritikou, 'Les manuscrits musicaux post-byzantins d'origine crétoise comme témoins des échanges culturels entre Vénitiens et Grecs (XVIe–XVIIe s.)', in Aurélien Girard, Bernard Heyberger and Vassa Kontouma (eds), *Livres et confessions chrétiennes orientales: Histoire connectée entre Empire ottoman, monde slave et Occident (XVIe–XVIIIe siècles)* (Turnhout: Brepols, forthcoming).]
36. Nāwufītūs Idlibī (Edelby), *Asāqifa al-Rūm al-Malakiyyīn bi-Ḥalab* (Aleppo: Maṭbaʿat al-Iḥsān, 1983), pp. 115, 117. [Ioana Feodorov, 'Beginnings of Arabic Printing in Ottoman Syria (1706–1711): The Romanians' Part in Athanasius Dabbas's Achievements', *ARAM Periodical*, 25, 1–2 (2013), p. 240.]
37. Camille Aboussouan (ed.), *Le livre et le Liban jusqu'à 1900* (Paris: UNESCO, AGECOOP, 1982), p. 357, n° 194 (Epistles and Acts of the Apostles, 1756, 403 p. in 4°), p. 351, n° 190 (*Kitāb al-majmaʿ al-lubnānī*, 1788, 558 p. in 4°).
38. The collection completed by Dory Papastratos is characteristic in this sense, although the iconography is almost exclusively Orthodox: Papastratos, *Paper Icons*, vol. 1 and 2, passim.
39. Bernard Heyberger, 'Entre Byzance et Rome', pp. 528–32.
40. Dormition of the Mother of God: Cândea (ed.), *Icônes Melkites*, n° 17, 31, 78; Cândea (ed.), *Icônes grecques, melkites, russes*, pp. 266–67, n° 87.
41. Cândea (ed.), *Icônes Melkites*, n° 29 (*Rosary* of Jirjis Ḥanania Al-Muṣawwir, 1759), n° 30 (by the same, Immaculate Conception, 1762).
42. André Grabar, *Les voies de la création en iconographie chrétienne*, 2nd ed. (Paris: Flammarion, 1994), p. 260.
43. Sylvia Agemian, 'Introduction à l'étude des icônes melkites', in Cândea (ed.), *Icônes Melkites*, pp. 106–7. See ibid. n° 52, Crucifixion and Last Supper, treated in a very rigid style; Cândea (ed.), *Icônes grecques, melkites, russes*, pp. 224–5, n° 68 and 69, Crucifixions still in the Byzantine style. On the other hand, a print showing a Crucifixion, no doubt produced in Venice in 1782 for Chrysanthos of the Peloponnese, Protosyngelos of the Holy Sepulchre, visibly followed a baroque Latin model: Papastratos, *Paper Icons*, vol. 1, n° 31, pp. 69–70.
44. Aboussouan (ed.), *Le livre et le Liban*, p. 357, n° 194.
45. Cândea (ed.), *Icônes Melkites*, n° 28; Heyberger, *Les Chrétiens du Proche-Orient*, p. 527; Meinardus, 'The Iconography of the Eucharistic Christ in the Armenian Churches'.
46. Bernard Heyberger, 'Sainteté et chemins de la perfection chez les chrétiens du Proche- Orient', *Revue de l'histoire des religions*, 215, 1 (1998), pp. 117–37.
47. Interesting remark by Johann Michael Wansleben, in *Relazione dello Stato presente dell'Egitto* (Paris: A. Cramoizy, 1671), quote translated in Christine Chaillot, 'L'icône, sa vénération, son usage, d'après des récits de Wansleben au XVIIe siècle', *Le Monde copte*, 18 (1990), p. 83: 'Our missionaries in the Levant should do the same and not show images of the Blessed Virgin, with her breast uncovered, and

holding her naked child in front of us. For it scandalises the schismatics and even the Turks, who often enter churches and mock our religion, and our ecclesiastical discipline, when they see such images'. Kuri, *Une histoire du Liban*, vol. 1, p. 84: a large painting sent from Rome for the altar of the Jesuits in Beirut gave rise to disapproval ('this position of the Child Jesus does not please everyone. He is badly placed and too naked . . .', 1845). Ibid. vol. 2, p. 28: images showing the European princes were interpreted as images of saints ('They could not imagine that one could paint people other than saints', wrote a Jesuit in a letter from 1848).

48. Heyberger, *Les Chrétiens du Proche-Orient*, p. 449, concerning the incomprehension of an image in profile.
49. Letter of Michel-Ange de Nantes, 9 August 1637: Paris, Bibliothèque Nationale de France, ms. NAF 10220, pp. 205–7.
50. Walbiner, 'Images Painted with Such Exalted Skill as to Ravish the Senses . . .'; Heyberger, *Les Chrétiens du Proche-Orient*, p. 395. To be compared with the reactions of Jabartī to French painting: Naef, *À la recherche d'une modernité arabe*, pp. 42–43.
51. Bernard Heyberger, 'Entre Byzance et Rome', pp. 538–40.
52. Kuri, *Une histoire du Liban*, vol. 1, p. 131; Cândea (ed.), *Icônes grecques, melkites, russes*, p. 208: Martin, a typically Western saint, was exceptionally represented here on an icon.
53. Heyberger, 'Entre Byzance et Rome', p. 535.
54. Virgil Cândea, 'Une œuvre d'art melkite: L'icône de Saint Elian de Homs', *Syria* (1972), pp. 219–38; Cândea (ed.), *Icônes grecques, melkites, russes*, pp. 214–15, n° 64 and 65.
55. Cândea (ed.), *Icônes Melkites*, n° 30 (description and commentary on pp. 170–71). An Immaculate Conception, attributed to the school of Murillo (seventeenth century), has been preserved in the Maronite Museum of Luwayza.
56. Giambattista di San Alessio, *Compendio istorico dello stato antico*, p. 372.
57. Jean-Baptiste Chabot, 'Les origines du patriarcat chaldéen: Vie de Mar Youssef Ier (1681–1695)', *Revue de l'Orient Chrétien*, 1 (1896), p. 71.
58. Many images of Saint Joseph date from the mid-nineteenth century. One exception is Saint Joseph treated as the saint of an icon but carrying the infant and holding a lily (symbol of chastity): see Cândea (ed.), *Icônes Melkites*, n° 32. The icon was offered as *waqf* by a Melkite in 1774. The engraving representing the Holy Family evoked above only gave a small space to Saint Joseph, appearing behind the Virgin in the company of Anne, Elizabeth and Joachim: Papastratos, *Paper Icons*, vol. 1, n° 152 (p. 154).
59. Heyberger, *Les Chrétiens du Proche-Orient*, pp. 529–30, 541; Heyberger, 'Sainteté et chemins de la perfection chez les chrétiens du Proche-Orient', pp. 120–21.
60. Paul Bacel, 'La Congrégation des basiliens chouérites', *Échos d'Orient*, 6 (1903), pp. 174–83, 242–48; 7 (1904), pp. 156–63, 199–206: 7 (1904), p. 161; Idlibī, *Asāqifa al-Rūm al-Malakiyyīn bi-Ḥalab*, p. 143.
61. Kuri, *Une histoire du Liban*, vol. 2, p. 95: Fr. Billotet put forward some criticism concerning Fr. Ricadonna, who encouraged virginity and denigrated marriage

(1851). [On the complexity of crossing traditions concerning Saint Joseph and the Holy Family, see Lucette Valensi, *La fuite en Égypte: Histoires d'Orient et d'Occident* (Paris: Seuil, 2002).]

62. Cândea (ed.), *Icônes Melkites*, n° 88; Cândea (ed.), *Icônes grecques, melkites, russes*, n° 95, p. 282.
63. Joseph Nasrallah, *Histoire du mouvement littéraire dans l'Église melchite du Ve au XXe siècle*, vol. IV, 2 (Louvain: Peeters, 1979), p. 245. [On the controversial figure of Saint Maron, see Aurélien Girard, 'La construction de l'identité confessionnelle maronite à l'époque ottomane (XVIe–XVIIIe siècle)', in Bernard Heyberger (ed.), *Les chrétiens de tradition syriaque à l'époque ottoman* (Paris: Geuthner, 2020), pp. 157–66.]
64. Louis de Gonzague, O. F. M. Cap., 'Les anciens missionnaires capucins de Syrie et leurs écrits apostoliques de langue arabe', *Collectanea Franciscana*, 1, 3 (1931), pp. 319–59; 1, 4 (1931), pp. 457–91; 2, 1 (1932), pp. 35–71; 2, 2 (1932), 179–207: 2, 1 (1932), p. 47, note 1. Meinardus, 'L'art copte', p. 91, has indicated 'curious cultural transfers' of a similar type among the Copts. See also Otto Meinardus, 'A Critical Study on the Cult of Sitt Dimiana and Her 40 Virgins', *Orientalia Suecana*, 18 (1969), pp. 45–68.
65. [Heyberger, *Hindiyya, Mystic and Criminal*, passim]. A Christ showing his Sacred Heart radiant on his chest by a Roman painter of the eighteenth century has been kept at the Museum of Luwayza.
66. Heyberger, 'Entre Byzance et Rome', pp. 540–41; Francis Richard, *Raphaël du Mans missionnaire en Perse au XVIIe siècle* (Paris: L'Harmattan, 1995), vol. 1, p. 79.
67. Walbiner, 'Images Painted with Such Exalted Skill as to Ravish the Senses . . .'. [Vera Tchentsova, 'Portrait of the Patriarch of Antioch Makarius III Ibn al-Zaʿīm in the *Tituljarnik* of 1672' (in Russian), in Yulia Petrova and Ioana Feodorov (eds), *Europe in Arabic Sources: The Travel of Makarius Patriarch of Antioch* (Kiev: A. Krymsky Institute of Oriental Studies of the National Academy of Sciences of Ukraine, Institute for South-East European Studies of the Romanian Academy, 2016), pp. 160–74.]
68. Josée Balagna, *L'imprimerie arabe en Occident (XVIe, XVIIe, XVIIIe siècles)* (Paris: Maisonneuve et Larose, 1984), p. 122. To be compared with the icons of saints on paper published in Papastratos, *Paper Icons*, vol. 1, pp. 277, 284–88.
69. Portraits kept today in the monastery of Saint John of Shuwayr (Khinshāra, Lebanon).
70. Fahd, *Taʾrīkh al-ruhbānivva al-mārūniyva*, vol. 5, p. 222.
71. More original portraits of prelates have been attributed to the monk Mūsā Dīb: Mikhāʾīl Khāzin (1787) and Mikhāʾīl Fāḍil (1795), reproduced in *Lebanon – The Artist's View: 200 Years of Lebanese Painting: Catalogue of the Exhibition at the Barbican Centre* (London: British Lebanese Association, 1989). See the portraits of ecclesiastical dignitaries and lay-people in the nineteenth century in the same catalogue, pp. 59–63, 69, 78, 92, 99.
72. Leonhard Lemmens (ed.), *Collectanea Terrae Sanctae* (Quaracchi: Collegio di S. Bonaventura, 1933), p. 107 (1746).
73. Būlus Masʿad and Nasīb Wuhayba al-Khāzin (ed.), *Al-Uṣūl al-taʾrīkhiyya* (Achkouth: n. p., n. d.), vol. 1, p. 17. This image, very damaged, photographed at

the patriarchal monastery of Bkirki in the 1950s, is apparently lost today. [A copy of it has been published by Akram Fouad Khater, *Embrace the Divine: Passion and Politics in the Christian Middle East* (Syracuse: Syracuse University Press, 2011), frontispiece].

74. [Heyberger, *Hindiyya, Mystic and Criminal,* p. 70]; 'Interrogatoire de la Mère Hindyé', French translation in Moubarac, *Pentalogie antiochienne/domaine maronite*, vol. I, 1, p. 462; APF, CP, Maroniti, vol. 113, fol. 85rv (Arabic), fol. 84rv (Latin translation), 7 June 1752; ibid. fol. 235v, letter from the Jesuit Marc-Antoine Séguran, Aleppo, 23 July 1752; ibid. fol. 31r, 33v (Italian translation), 7 June 1752. The indignation provoked by this image was sufficiently great for a Melkite chronicler to mention it: Qusṭānṭīn Ṭarābulsī, *Taʾrīkh Nāfīshalla (Navicella) (1729–1772)* (Beirut, Bibliothèque Orientale, ms. 38). [A reproduction of this image, preserved at the Maronite Patriarchate at Bkirki, has been published by Khater, *Embrace the Divine*, p. 109.]
75. For the people who paid for them: Cândea (ed.), *Icônes Melkites*, pp. 129–220 passim; Cândea (ed.), *Icônes grecques, melkites, russes*, pp. 188, 258, 265, 272–73, 277, 279.
76. [Heyberger, *Hindiyya, Mystic and Criminal*, pp. 29–31]; APF, CP, Maroniti, vol. 118, 'Alcune notizie da servir al libro primo della vita della serva di Dio Hendie Ageimi . . .', fol. 132rv; 'Interrogatoire de la Mère Hindyé', pp. 433–35 (see above, note 74).
77. Jirjis Mannāsh (al-khūrī), 'Mustanadāt li-taʾrīkh al-muṭrān ʿAbdallāh Qarāʾalī', *La Revue Syrienne*, 1 (1926), p. 423.
78. Heyberger, 'Entre Byzance et Rome', pp. 542–43; 'Interrogatoire de la Mère Hindyé', p. 434.
79. On 5 August 1640, the Jesuit Jean Amieu asked for images to distribute to his companions and his congregation each month: ARSI, Gallia, vol. 95, I, fol. 494.
80. Kuri, *Une histoire du Liban*, vol. 2, p. 208.
81. APF, Acta, vol. 201 (1838), fols 137r, 171v; SOCG, vol. 954, fol. 290v (Aleppo, 1833): mention of hostility towards private images.
82. Heyberger, 'Entre Byzance et Rome', pp. 542–43, 532–33.
83. *Kitāb murshid al-kāhin . . .* (Rome: Sacra Congregatio de Propaganda Fide, 1844) (from the *Manuale Sacerdotum* by Paolo Segneri, translated into Arabic by a missionary from Aleppo, Fr. Pierre Fromage, in 1734).
84. See the crucial evolution in the representation of saints made by the passage from wooden engravings to engravings on copper at the beginning of the seventeenth century: Jean-Michel Sallmann, *Naples et ses saints à l'âge baroque* (Paris: PUF, 1994), pp. 43–49. In the Greek world, engravings on wood were discontinued in the first decades of the eighteenth century: Papastratos, *Paper Icons*, vol. 1, p. 20.
85. [Saint Teresa of Avila, *Book Called Way of Perfection*, in *The Complete Works of Saint Teresa of Jesus*, edited by E. Allison Peers (New York: Sheed & Ward, 1946), vol. 2, p. 109.]
86. [Heyberger, *Hindiyya, Mystic and Criminal*, p. 31]; 'Interrogatoire de la Mère Hindyé', p. 434.

87. [Heyberger, *Hindiyya, Mystic and Criminal*, p. 31]; *Sirr al-ittiḥād*, translated in French as 'Traité de l'union' in Moubarac (ed.), *Pentalogie antiochienne/domaine maronite*, vol. I, 1, p. 418. On the popularisation of the *Ecce Homo*: Sallmann, *Naples et ses saints*, p. 182. The theme was spread on prints in the Greek world in the mid-nineteenth century: Papastratos, *Paper Icons*, vol. 1, pp. 66–68, figures no. 27, 28, 29, 30.
88. [Heyberger, *Hindiyya, Mystic and Criminal*, p. 30]; APF, CP, Maroniti, vol. 118, 'Alcune notizie da servir al libro primo della vita della serva di Dio Hendie Ageimi . . .', fol. 132rv.
89. Heyberger, 'Entre Byzance et Rome', p. 538.
90. Anne Sauvy, *Le miroir du cœur*, pp. 183–84; Alain Croix, *La Bretagne aux XVIe et XVIIe siècles, la vie, la mort, la foi* (Paris: Maloine, 1980).
91. Quote from the Syrian art historian ʿAfīf Bahnasī, in Silvia Naef, *À la recherche d'une modernité arabe*, p. 122.
92. See the discussion on the origins of modern painting in Lebanon in Silvia Naef, *À la recherche d'une modernité arabe*, p. 122ff.

CHAPTER 9

Individualism and Political Modernity: Devout Catholic Women in Aleppo and Mount Lebanon between the Seventeenth and Nineteenth Centuries

Compared with the usual lack of documentation experienced by scholars studying the lives of Christian women in Islamic societies, the subject-matter treated here rests on a large amount of documents dating from the mid-seventeenth to mid-nineteenth centuries.[1] These documents deal with a group of Christian women, mainly from Aleppo, although some are from Lebanon.

This study begins with a presentation of these sources and the inevitable question regarding their authenticity and reliability. The fact that women's words have been delivered to us in written form means that they have been more or less reworked. The flood of words related by and about women, which could *a priori* be astonishing, might be easier to understand if it were put within the general modernisation and Westernisation process experienced by the Christian minorities in Lebanon and Syria (at least those who opted for the Roman Catholic Church and post-Tridentine Catholicism). As a result, the sincerity of these women's words is less important than what is learnt from them regarding the make-up of individual consciousness, the interiorisation of new social rules and the apparatus of power: the latter two not only offered public status to women, but even enjoined them to speak out.

The analysis of this process presented in this article was originally inspired by Max Weber who initiated the examination of the modernisation of post-sixteenth century European societies.

WRITINGS ABOUT WOMEN AND BY WOMEN

In the seventeenth and eighteenth centuries, Western travellers and missionaries quite frequently viewed Eastern Christian women as being in an unfortunate position, similar to Muslim women.[2] They never left their houses unless completely veiled in white calico, the colour and fabric alone distinguishing them from Muslim women. Married women also covered their faces in black crepe. This happened not only in towns where Muslims were in the majority, but even in villages wholly occupied by Christians.[3] Women were excluded from education and political life and had fewer occasions to leave their homes than did Muslim women; they scarcely even visited the church.[4] This picture must be corrected and nuanced by information about the role of women from judicial evidence, *waqf* and *maḥkama* documents. In the cities, at least, the position of women, as a whole, must have been less insignificant than outside observers of the time have led us to believe. Christian women made gifts or endowments to the church, the poor and the monks of their community.[5] One must not forget that observations made by Westerners also reflect their own culture. In Europe, at that time, for example, women belonged to those categories of persons whose ignorance and spiritual dereliction were regarded as a problem. As the Jesuit Joseph Besson wrote, . . .

> Besides, the lack of devotion of women, and their extreme ignorance, which is notably greater than that of men, in all that concerns the mysteries of our religion, is the cause of the perdition of the youth, which does not receive any instruction. We must confess that the mothers are to blame for the pitiful condition of the children [. . .] In this they are similar to the Mahometan women, who are banished from the mosques, and whom the Alcoran itself does not welcome in paradise.[6]

Thus, it was a prime task for the clergy to give these women access to religious services and the sacraments in order to ensure their salvation as well as to take control of their role as educators of their children. It is within this context that the discourse about women was constructed and that some women began to speak. These women were devoted to intense religious observances, mainly under the rule of Western missionary confessors. The first mention of them was in Aleppo during the 1660s. In 1672, there were about twenty of them who had renounced marriage and begun to lead a cloistered religious life in their parents' houses, teaching reading and catechism to the girls of their communities. It has been possible to follow them, up to the year 1707.[7]

Another group, formed by Melkite devotees from Aleppo, resolved in about 1730 to set up a convent in Mount Lebanon with their dowry money and to rely on the charity of the city's inhabitants. This initiative produced copious correspondence between these ten single women and their male protectors, some ecclesiastical, some not. As this affair gave rise to endless litigation lasting for more than fifteen years between Aleppo and various places in Mount Lebanon and Rome, the number of letters exchanged was prolific. There are also contracts, concluded and signed by these women.[8] Still, it would be easy to demonstrate that almost all these papers were not written by the women themselves, but that their parents or their ecclesiastical entourage held the pen in their stead. Even the signatures are not always authentic. Their declarations could be contradictory and often against the opinions dictated by their male protectors.[9]

But these features were not specific to this body of writing: a great bulk of eighteenth-century documents and witnesses are not reliable, as evidenced by the struggles among Eastern Christian groups at that time. It was rather easy for a leader of one of these groups to obtain signed declarations from people who often had not learned enough reading and writing to fully understand the meaning of their statements. Thus, the most important fact in this correspondence is the necessity felt by men to enjoin women to speak or, at least, to assert that they were speaking in their own names. In the end, the struggle with their protectors even gave these women a form of liberty that made it possible for them to oppose a decision that they considered unsuitable.[10]

The foundation of the religious order of the Sacred Heart of Jesus and of a convent in Bkirki, Mount Lebanon, in 1750 by a Maronite woman from Aleppo produced conflicts and documentation of the same kind. Hindiyya ʿUjaymī, the founder of this religious order, had created a reputation for holiness since her childhood. As proof of her vocation, she had to reveal obvious signs in accordance with the Latin pattern of female mystics, by adopting a body language easily recognisable by the people around her. The signs of her calling were displayed on her body: anorexia, mortification, stigmata, bleeding and a wedding ring (to prove her mystical marriage to Jesus).[11] Apart from this bodily discourse, so common in mystical women, Hindiyya claimed to have a prophetic mission that represented the only possible way within the Church for women to directly mediate with God.[12] Hindiyya asserted therefore that it was Jesus Christ in person who dictated the rules of her religious order to her, as well as the texts about her mystical union, prayers and lessons in ethics to be directed towards her entourage.[13]

Again, the authenticity of these documents can be questioned and their manipulation by the men around her seriously considered. Hindiyya's very ignorance of reading and writing was held up as a pledge of her honesty. Given this ignorance, she was judged unable to devise texts of such a high level or to plagiarise other mystical books.[14] Hindiyya herself was convinced that she was getting her knowledge from her inward subjective experience which she brought forth, speaking in the first person. Her autobiography, *Sirr al-ittiḥād* (Mystery of Union), began with these words: 'When I was a little girl, and I could not yet talk, I leaned on my elbows and looked to the sky, and I saw somebody'. She asserted that her discernment (*tamyīz*) had a nature quite different from that of scholars.[15] This theme, the wisdom of the simple, became a cliché within Christian literature.

It is true that Hindiyya did not write the contents of her revelations herself. The writing was done by her confessors (first a Jesuit, then Maronite bishops) and by a nun from Aleppo who recorded her visions, prophecies and exhortations.[16] This process, with all the manipulations that it may have afforded, was common concerning the output of women's spiritual texts. The reputation and glamour of Hindiyya were used by her entourage for social and political purposes, as it generally happens in cases of potential saints. Here, another source of documentation came into play: her male followers and confessors wrote hagiographic biographies in which they embellished her life from childhood onwards, with the aim of gathering evidence for her sanctity in order to spread her fame and to prepare for the probable formal consecration of her holiness by Church authorities after her death.[17]

The affirmation of divine inspiration and a direct link to the sacred, once recognised by her followers, gave a certain freedom to the female mystic, especially when rival institutions (as, in this case, the Jesuits and the Maronite clergy) fought for her exclusive control. The direct union of Hindiyya with God led her, in the name of a higher obedience to her heavenly husband, to disobey her earthly male authorities. Contestation of authority was common in eighteenth-century Catholicism, but in ways other than this call of 'obedience to the heavenly husband'.[18]

This claim to autonomy, justified by a preferential link with God, was common in female mystics, but it was quite unacceptable for the Roman ecclesiastical authority in the eighteenth century after censure against 'quietism'. As a result, Rome sent experts to Mount Lebanon on two occasions, once in 1753 and again in 1775, in order to evaluate the authenticity of Hindiyya's holiness. These inquiries, which produced documents of an inquisitorial nature, were directed at the mystic herself, along with women of her entourage who had to answer and sign very precise questions posed by these ecclesiastical investigators. They also signed written confessions that were supposed to be spontaneous, but at least part of them had actually been extracted by threats or violence.[19] These particular declarations were kept to the confines of the ecclesiastical courts. Thus, they were documents very different from the 'revelations' that were destined to be published. The precise questions, however, asked by the inquisitor in 1753 about, for instance, Hindiyya's childhood, could have inspired the autobiographical content of *Sirr al-ittiḥād*, which was dictated later.

At the beginning of the nineteenth century, another group of devout women who for more than thirty years had lived in Aleppo with their families (as opposed to having lived within the precincts of a religious order such as in cloisters), but who were directed by Latin and Eastern priests, was the centre of struggles between supporters and opponents of female mysticism with, again, frequent appeals to Rome. This struggle produced a body of writings that had the same features and problems as that concerning Hindiyya. Women, with the support of their spiritual directors, claimed independence from the Church and its social rules. This behaviour again gave rise to suspicion and hostility and, as a result, to a sequence of inquisitions, followed by dubitable female confessions.[20] For instance, in 1831, a certain Maria Hammoja came before the Apostolic Delegate Pietro Losana to declare that the written testimony attributed to her did not coincide exactly with her statements. She regretted that she was unable to write herself and thus had had to call upon a confessor, Giuseppe Hatem (Yūsif Hātim), an enemy of the devotees, in order to confess to that with which she did not agree in their observances. This priest, after plaguing her with questions, wrote an accusatory text that went beyond her intentions and that he induced her to sign.[21]

All this evidence proves that, if women began to speak publicly, they did so under the influence of powerful men who needed their confessions, testimonies and revelations. Yet, they were eager to keep these talks and their circulation under strict control, especially when set down in writing. This development was obviously part of a modernisation process, as it has been studied in the case of Western society. On one hand, the individuals asserted themselves as a subject (but according to a very conventional standard). On the other hand, the power became more rationalised and penetrated all areas of social life more and more deeply, including personal consciousness, interiorising a new ethics to be fully efficient.[22]

THE EMERGENCE OF THE WOMAN'S SELF

It had become a pressing necessity for the Catholic clergy to raise women from their ignorance. Like men, they had to learn to read in order to acquire the knowledge required for their own salvation and for the Christian education of their children. As early as the middle of the seventeenth century, there were in Aleppo Christian women who had access to the written word. Markings in some books from the eighteenth century are evidence that they belonged to women. Alexander Russell reported in about 1790 that Christian women of higher classes were known to read and write, although they rarely considered reading as entertainment.[23] In the rules of the Sisterhood of the Rosary intended for young women in Aleppo and founded by the Lazarists in 1794, article 1 required its members to possess spiritual books. Article 2 stated that the main purpose of the fellowship was the instruction of young women who must then report back to their individual homes on what they learned during the meetings. In addition, the devotees of the rosary had to meet on Sunday afternoons to repeat the catechism and to teach it to girls, especially those preparing for their first communion.[24] In these circles, reading was mostly a rather mechanical, oral and collective exercise (although the practice of silent and solitary reading was one of the goals stated by the rules).

What did these women read? They could read all the classics of baroque spirituality, widely available in Catholic Europe and translated into Arabic from the middle of the seventeenth century onwards. Thus, they could conform to the literary pattern of spiritual women as illustrated by many Western holy women, from Catherine of Siena to Marguerite-Marie Alacoque and, of course, Teresa of Avila, whose writings were available in Arabic as early as in the second part of the seventeenth century. The important role that a literary source may play in the forming of the style of narrating one's own life is well-known. Like most autobiographical documents, spiritual texts testify to the effort of their 'author' to follow a stereotyped standard and to reproduce a pre-existing pattern for the research of perfection or for a declaration of love. This striving for humility and conformity should prove more than anything one's divine inspiration and thus be the best means of obtaining social recognition.[25]

Most of the books translated into Arabic taught a way of life that broke with some of the most atavistic customs of everyday life. The handbooks analysed and commented on behaviour linked to a specific social condition, delivering judgment on good or sinful conduct according to each social situation: the duties of the mother, characteristic sins of youth, spiritual dangers incurred by merchants.[26] At every moment of the day, self-control must be maintained; nothing could be left to chance or escape the attention of the devout. For instance, the rule of the Sisterhood of the Rosary, intended for young women, specified that, in the evening, at bedtime, they must offer their heart to Jesus, their beloved. In the morning, they must wake up half an hour before sunrise, jump out of bed and begin to recite various prayers. They must not take more than three meals a day. They must show proof of temperance and decency (*iḥtishām*) while eating and not forget to rinse their mouth after the meal. They must keep their senses in check. They must not cast their glances around in every direction, must not stare at by-standers or passers-by and must not peep from behind windows out of curiosity. They must not walk swiftly, never joke together, never hold or touch one another and never shake a man's hand, even that of a priest. It was better to always hold work, a book, or a picture of Jesus Christ in their hands.[27]

Beyond these practical injunctions, the handbooks initiated the reader into a psychological self-consciousness, providing the necessary keys for telling oneself or one's confessor about the state of one's soul. Internalisation of this discourse was the best proof of its authenticity and truth. Eighteenth-century Catholicism advocated a culture of emotion as one of the main features of femininity as conceived at that time. Reading, writing, or gazing at a picture could then become acts that induced the presence of the heavenly husband, giving rise to excitement. Such was the 1837 testimony of Susana Daqur:

> With regard to those who are in possession of the union, they enjoy with their eyes the vision of the object, which appears to them in a pleasant shape. They have with it contacts and conversations, and other things continually and confidentially, as would have a married couple. They feel that it sleeps sensitively in their heart, it incites them with various requests

> like kisses, embraces and all that the Book of the Canticles points out, regarding gestures, words and flirtation. And on these occasions, they feel even sensitively that the object pricks the will of his heart in themselves. That is the main substance of the spiritual wedding; since the object, the deed and the soul receive the operation, the subject gives, and the soul receives what is flowing out of it.[28]

Such a declaration shows to what extent this female mysticism mainly consisted of questioning the Present and the Absent, the core of the Christian mystery of the Incarnation.

The handbooks taught that even temptation could become a sin; thus, one must gain conscious awareness of it and express it through self-confession. Paolo Segneri, whose books were available in Arabic translation, explained, for instance, how temptation moved from the object to the senses, then towards understanding and to the will. In order for temptation to become a sin, it must reach the will. It could eventually lead to sin in two different ways: through desire (ardently desiring the realisation of the temptation), or by complacency (when pleasure is derived from the realisation of the temptation, without nonetheless having wished it).[29]

In 1836, the ecclesiastical investigator Jean-Baptiste d'Auvergne described these sessions of 'conscience revelation' between penitent and confessor secretly in use in Aleppo:

> She explains the alleged operations of the Holy Ghost within herself during her mental prayer, the apparitions and inspirations she enjoyed, then she comes to the temptations, and she has to explain the origin, the sequence and the effects of temptation, and all that an impure temptation has generated within her.

He then added:

> And what is much worse is that almost every devotee has, in addition to this kind of spiritual Director, a female Director to whom she makes the same confessions, or rather overtures. It is unbearable, even horrible, to think that a woman, under pretext of devotion and improving, speaks to another woman about her temptations, about all that temptations produce within her.[30]

In the way in which Michel Foucault has perceived it, this game of confession and secrecy and of veiling and unveiling that came about especially between penitent and confessor did not lead to hiding sex but, on the contrary, emphasised it by putting it continually into words; it was always accompanied by guilty feelings that may even cause suffering. One can find some rather detailed erotic elicitations in the *Sirr al-ittiḥād*:

> As I said these words, I saw him embrace me with an infinite sweetness. By this embrace, he penetrated my soul and my body with his divinised body. It was as if I had plunged into him in amazement, I was perplexed and stunned, dreading the form of his efficiency. For by his penetration of me, I still see him with my weak understanding (and I perceive) that he is high of an unlimited height. He holds my soul and my body by his penetration into me, and without being touched in his motion, I distinguish the parts of his body, which are of perfect delicacy and lightness in this penetration.[31]

In 1777, some nuns from Hindiyya's cloister had to confess in writing to copulating with priests (the enemies of the 'saint') and even with Satan, as well as having had abortions. In this case, these confessions clearly concerned the usual figure of inversion, something customary in witchcraft charges. The same women declared themselves guilty of committing homicide by poison, of gluttony, of insubordination and so on.[32] Later (in the 1830s), several Aleppine devotees confessed to having experienced orgasm in auto-suggestion and masturbation sessions that took place within the context of initiation in mystical union.[33] It does not matter whether these charges were made up or were half-true. What was really new in these declarations was the fact that such discourses were expressed and even written down by Eastern Christian women and then sent to Rome and read by cardinals of the Propaganda.

Moreover, it is beyond question that, in the course of the evolution that had begun in the West at the end of the Middle Ages, confession became more important than the deed itself. On one hand, it alone gave a feeling of relief and even of enjoyment to the one who submitted to confession; on the other hand, confession legitimated the power and competence of the one who received it. Additionally, it exemplified the power structure to which the subject was submitted. The Aleppine devotees of the 1830s were charged with wishing too often for confession, remaining too long in the confessional every time and monopolising the confessor's time, making him unable to attend to his other parishioners. A rule had to be issued to set strict limits to the practice of their confession.[34]

We have seen that Hindiyya dictated her *Sirr al-ittiḥād* to male scribes. In the nineteenth century, confessors directed the Aleppine devotees to write down their state of mind on paper, to keep a secret diary that could be used within collective reading sessions to generate suggestions from others, to control if necessary the orthodoxy of their revelations and to build up and spread the fame of their divine inspiration and communication with the sacred.[35] In talking about themselves, their deepest feelings, the love they felt – including the love for God – these women touched upon the borders of modern literature with its sphere of subjectivity characterising diary, autobiographical and romance writing.[36]

CHANGING THE WORLD?

Modernisation or *Westernisation*: the use of either of these words relates to the problem of a terminology conceived by Europeans for an extra-European society. How can this pattern, usually considered a Western one, be applied to the Christian societies of Aleppo and Mount Lebanon? Why did this new power structure and this new position of the individual in relation to authority meet with such favour? These devotees were, after all, but a small group of holy women. Nevertheless, they embodied a widespread model in Christian society, especially among women.

The condition of women, at least among the leading families linked to Rome, actually improved between the middle of the seventeenth and the middle of the nineteenth century. But this change in social standing gave birth to new problems. For instance, the devotees' choice of virginity, either assumed within the cloister or in their parents' houses, was not part of common tradition. Female celibacy was almost impossible in the Christian society of that time. As with Muslim customs, girls were promised for marriage at a very early age, in the cities as well as in the Lebanese mountains. The new discourse valorised virginity and chastity, thereby offering an option other than marriage and childbirth to women, outside the social norms of alliance and succession. Even women who did not eventually follow a religious calling might have interiorised these new ethics that they could have imparted to their children.[37] The above-mentioned rules of the Sisterhood of the Rosary taught a standard of life intended for wives and mothers that was similar to a nun's. They advised these women to let themselves be touched by the overflowing love of their holy husband and to show an outward image of a respected spouse.[38] Helena Ḥawwā, Hindiyya's mother, for instance, is described as a model of Christian motherhood: she was chaste, pious and fertile.[39]

It can be hypothesised, although not statistically proven, that this society saw the beginning of an evolution similar to the important Malthusian changes in the West in modern times, with its increase in life-long female celibacy and a postponement of marriage age. This process may have had its origins in the demographic growth and economic prosperity of these Christian minorities, coinciding with the introduction of Western ethics in their society, ethics that encouraged stricter control over individual behaviour, especially sexuality, thereby ensuring the best conditions for inheritance within the family.

Nevertheless, the decision of a woman to remain unmarried was not necessarily the result of a straightforward inheritance strategy on the part of her family. One can even find evidence to the contrary. In 1669, a Capuchin of Aleppo related that a young woman named Catherine had found shelter within a rich family because her father 'had become a Turk' (had converted to Islam). She cut off her plaits and threw them, laughing, into the middle of the women assembled in order to get her mother's and her benefactress's assent to become a nun. She was eventually thrown out of her adopted home, charged with having prompted one of the family's daughters, already promised in marriage, to commit the same irreparable act.[40]

An interiorised ideal can often be more compelling than direct pressure from relatives. It could happen that the choice of a religious life was freely taken up by a woman because it might be the only way for her to gain autonomy and authority. This situation was true for Hindiyya and for Theresa al-Khāzin, who belonged to the most prominent family of Maronite sheikhs in the district of Kisruwān. Already promised in marriage, around 1750 she suddenly opted for the convent.[41] Family opposition and potential hostility from the parents concerning their daughters' religious calling was not very strong in these two cases. They themselves knew and revered the ideal of the consecrated virgin, even if they had not wished it for their own daughters.

According to the rules of the Catholicism of that day, the improvement of girls' education encountered, nevertheless, opposition and controversy from the male side. As early as 1711, the representatives of four Aleppine *ṭā'ifas* (confessional groups) challenged the intentions of missionaries who were involved in attracting women to education. Armenian leaders sent a protest letter also undersigned by Maronites, Melkites and Chaldeans to the Guardian of Jerusalem, objecting to the Jesuits and Capuchins who visited women's houses '[w]here they go to deceive women and boys, giving them medals, crosses, pictures, and money; and the Turks use this pretext against us'.[42]

Women fell under men's suspicion because of their preferential links with their spiritual directors and their lack of obedience toward their own family leaders.[43] In 1801, several Eastern bishops signed a common declaration challenging the false doctrines of a Lazarist. They asserted that he had spread unrest among the faithful, gathering men and women together in his church for the purpose of instructing them. He had taught that a husband could not approach his wife as soon as he knew that she was pregnant or sterile. He had asserted that putting kohl on women's eyes was a sin, even though Eastern women were convinced that it protected them from certain ailments.[44] Devotees were repeatedly accused of refusing to receive the sacraments or to attend mass held by priests other than those of their choice, of meeting in secret at night and of denying obedience to their parish priest, bishop and even Rome. It is said that they saluted one another using unusual and proud greetings and ran from one church to another, from one meeting to another, and in this way disturbed family life.[45]

Ideal devotion encouraged breaking away from traditional systems of authority within the family and larger group in order to concentrate on the relationship between the spouse of Christ and her divine husband or, at least, between the penitent and her spiritual director. Thus, traditional rules for the education of girls, promoting alliance and solidarity, could lose their legitimacy. Hence, the auto-domestication process, as previously stated, coincided with an attempt at modernising power among the Christians. One can observe the formalisation of some social rules under the control of the clergy and a will to centralise each Church and confessional group according to local powers founded on clientelism.

Different synods introduced Western discipline in matters of the sacraments, fasting, marriage rules, religious vocation, religious instruction and the like. Confessional justice dispensed by bishops extended its role, trying to unify the practice within the same *ṭā'ifa* or within the political entity of the Shihābī emirate in the Lebanese mountains. This justice placed written text above oral testimony and sought to lay down ecclesiastical discipline in matters such as interest-bearing loans, inheritance, free assent of young women to marriage and alliances between close consanguine or collateral relatives.[46]

This type of modernity was well represented in Eastern religious orders founded at the end of the seventeenth and the beginning of the eighteenth centuries within the different *ṭā'ifa*s, whose rules rather closely followed the constitutions of the Company of Jesus.[47] The ideology of the efficiency of actions in the world and upon the world, a belief that had progressively developed in Latin Christianity, began to overlap the more spiritual Arab Christianity. In this second pattern, an ecclesiastical non-temporal hierarchy did not have worldly claims but rather adhered to a 'natural' political order.[48] These new religious orders, on the contrary, tried to create a network of persons, goods and institutions for the purpose of passing beyond regional, local and familial solidarities. These orders attempted to include all members of a *ṭā'ifa* from Egypt to Mount Lebanon, from Aleppo to Istanbul, Livorno, Rome, or Marseilles. At the same time, the most powerful Eastern Christian bourgeois families were also widening their world to these broader horizons.[49] This practice could have contributed to the beginning of a nation-making process.

The devout women were involved in this process and became stakes in the power struggles among different religious orders. Hindiyya was a disciple of the Jesuits. The Jesuit Antonio Venturi, her spiritual director, once declared to Hindiyya: 'You are the daughter of our religious order. You must remain among us'.[50] In the eighteenth century, the Jesuits tried to build a female congregation under their own authority, with women from different *ṭā'ifa*s. They eventually failed because of opposition from the Maronites and the Melkites who therein sensed a danger to their own identity, fearing the risk of dissolution into 'Latinism'. But the Oriental orders, such as the Melkite Shuwayrites and Salvatorians, as well as the Maronite Lebanese monks, mainly followed Western rules.

After breaking with her Jesuit masters, Hindiyya founded a female congregation of the Sacred Heart for Maronite women. The rules of this order clearly showed the will of the founder to direct the entire life of her nuns according to a new rationality. Even the architecture of the convent was conceived in accordance with the rules of cloistered life. Hygiene was a part of the nuns' daily routine. Each responsibility inside the convent was carefully defined. Punishments were, for the most part, foreseen in the rules and in proportion to the faults. Traditionally, nuns maintained relationships with their relatives and with the lay protectors of their convent. Here, on the contrary, these ties had to be severed, and the young women had to submit completely to the institution and the authority of the mother superior. The order's text, directed to the novices, asserted:

> Let them make every effort regarding impiety of the spirit, and especially regarding their own opinion and their own will. And they must detest them completely and behave no more with them. They will have no opinion and no will but the opinion and the will of the [mother] superior. They must behave with the requisite holy obedience by all their actions. Let them know with all their pledge that the monastic life in brief is only obedience. And whoever lacks obedience lacks the whole monastic condition.[51]

Questioning according to the analysis of modern state-building within Western societies, especially in France, cannot be completely followed through in the case of the Orient, considering the mere fact of the weakness of its state institutions.[52] For example, the intensifying of justice by Christians led not to secularisation, but rather to confessionalisation and clericalisation. This development was not a revolution, but a reallocation of power within the churches and *ṭā'ifas*. In these social dynamics, personal loyalties and ancestral customs continued to play their role. It is impossible to distinguish between supporters of innovation and followers of tradition, because one can opt for change in one matter and claim regard for custom in another.[53]

In the eighteenth and at the beginning of the nineteenth centuries, all the ecclesiastic hierarchies and new religious orders were deeply divided by rifts between different authority levels (patriarchs, bishops, parish priests and friars), as well as between different geographical and lineage networks. For instance, the Melkite Shuwayrite monks, who mostly came from Aleppo, struggled against the Salvatorians who were linked to the Damascenes. At the same time, a group of 'Aleppines' fought against a group of 'highlanders' or 'countrymen' within the Maronite order of the Lebanese Monks (although this partition may hide more tenuous divisions). In the Sacred Heart order founded by Hindiyya and in its convent in Bkirki, the conflict between 'Aleppines' and 'Lebanese' women gradually increased. As a result, doubt and suspicion concerning divine inspiration and the legitimacy of the founder mother's authority arose in the minds of some of the nuns. Through testimonies, evidence came to light about the new interchange between the nuns and outsiders, the rekindling of links with their relatives (*ahl*) and claims on convent property – all in breach of the rules.[54]

In this specific context, the gruesome events involving the nuns of Bkirki between 1770 and 1779 point to a crisis in the social consensus as well as in the development of reason, in a way reminiscent of the large-scale witch hunts that covered Europe with stakes between 1580 and 1640. The struggles inside the religious community run by Hindiyya and inside the whole Maronite *ṭāʾifa* were solved this time, not in the traditional way, but with a ruthless demonstration of power: the use of torture and even murder in order to give credit to the idea of a duel between good and evil. Each side tried to demonstrate the diabolical inspiration of their enemy, employing inquisitorial procedures introduced by the Roman representatives and producing confessions as their main proof. The documents immerse the reader in an atmosphere recalling the witch trials, the possession incidents that occurred in female convents at the beginning of the seventeenth century and the more contemporary narrative of Diderot's *La Religieuse*.[55] Eventually, the spiritual authority of Rome was reinstituted, overcoming the warring factions with the help of the worldly power of the Shihābī emirs who at the same time attempted to unify the Lebanese mountains under their authority.

At the conclusion of this incident, those authorities in charge of institutions that had attempted to use the glamour and influence of Hindiyya to establish their own power escaped unscathed. Their escape was possible because the official argument transformed the mystic into the guilty one: she was a female devil who knew how to cheat patriarchs, bishops and many others among the clergy and the faithful; all of them were cast purely as victims of her evil intrigues.[56]

From the sixteenth century onwards, Catholic teaching introduced to the East the idea of 'changing the world' or changing the self in order to change the world. This idea was rejected by most traditional societies that tried, or at least claimed, to perpetuate an old natural order. This 'modern madness' most likely came from the Western perception of the divine Incarnation and the cross of Jesus Christ.[57] Women had played an important role in the development of this concept of divinity.[58] However, the introduction of this pattern of modernity among Eastern Christians did not result in a modern political contract, or the emergence of the state and the nation, as was the case in Europe after the French Revolution. The evolution of attitudes and power relationships as depicted here led to greater divisions between Christians and non-Christians, and to a strengthening of confessional structures. It did not lead to a religiously neutral state where individuals would be free in their beliefs and ethics. On the contrary, Eastern Christianity of the nineteenth and twentieth centuries became permeated with the integralist and antimodernist ideologies of Roman Catholicism and of Russian and Greek Orthodoxy.

These problems cannot, of course, be analysed in depth in this study, as doing so would require extensive research into more contemporary periods. Questions about the incursion of this pattern and of its adaptation and transformation within Christian Eastern society must remain unanswered for the time being.[59] It must be linked with a questioning of society as a whole. This study does not claim to put forward a diffusionist theory, nor to suggest that the model described could be applied to Muslim society. Rather, it is a study about a part of Ottoman society that could perhaps be used for a more generic reflection on Mediterranean societies with a Muslim majority.

NOTES

1. [I am grateful to Mark Bean and Stuart Barber for their help in the correction of this English version.]
2. See, for instance, Joseph Besson, *La Syrie Sainte ou la mission de Jésus et des pères de la Compagnie de Jésus en Syrie* (Paris: Jean Henault, 1660), part II, pp. 116–22; Michel Febvre, *Théâtre de la Turquie* (Paris: Edme Couterot, 1682); and Alexander Russell, *The Natural History of Aleppo* (London: G. G. and J. Robinson, 1794), vol. 2, pp. 39–44, 55–56.
3. Russell, *Natural History*, vol. 1, p. 114; vol. 2, pp. 43–44. Concerning the black crepe veil, see Laurent d'Arvieux, *Mémoires du Chevalier d'Arvieux*, edited by Jean-Baptiste Labat (Paris: Charles-Jean-Baptiste Delespine, 1735), vol. 6, pp. 425–26; and Besson, *La Syrie Sainte*, II, p. 114.
4. Russell, *Natural History*, vol. 2, p. 44, note 23. The footnote has restored remarks of a previous edition on this subject. On ecclesiastical provisions against the free movement of women in Aleppo, see AAV, *Missioni*, vol. 52, Sidon, 17 September 1764, unnumbered; and Bernard Heyberger, *Les chrétiens du Proche-Orient au temps de la réforme catholique* (Rome: École française de Rome, 1994), p. 522.
5. Fardīnān Tawtal [Ferdinand Taoutel], *Wathā'iq ta'rīkhiyya 'an Ḥalab*, vol. 1 (Beirut: al-Maṭba'a al-kāthūlīkiyya, 1958), pp. 50, 119. Icon offered as a *waqf* (religious endowment) by Sara 'Aida in Mount Lebanon: Virgil Cândea (ed.), *Icônes Melkites: Exposition organisée par le musée Nicolas Sursock du 16 mai au 15 juin 1969* (Beirut: Musée Nicolas Sursock, 1969), pp. 173–74. Maryam bint Bashāra b. Ni'matallāh Sā'igh appeared in a *hijja shar'iyya* (legal document) concerning the purchase of two houses (1786): see 'Abbūd al-Ḥalabī Yūsif b. Dīmītrī b. Jirjis al-Khūrī, *Al-Murtād fī ta'rīkh Ḥalab wa-Baghdād*, edited by Fawāz Maḥmūd al-Fawāz (MA thesis, University of Damascus, n. d.), p. 67. See also Dror Ze'evi, 'Women in Seventeenth-Century Jerusalem: Western and Indigenous Perspectives', *International Journal of Middle East Studies*, 27 (1995), pp. 157–73; and Hedda Reindl-Kiel, '*Damet ismetüha* – immer wahre ihre Sittsamkeit: Frau and Gesellschaft im Osmanischen Reich', *Orientierungen*, 1 (1989), pp. 37–81.
6. 'Au reste, l'indévotion des femmes, et leur extrême ignorance, qui est notablement plus grande que celle des hommes, en tout ce qui regarde les mystères de notre

religion, causent la perte de la jeunesse, qui ne reçoit de ses parents aucune instruction. Il faut avouer que la condition des enfants est pitoyable par la faute des mères [. . .] en cela elles sont semblables aux femmes mahométanes qu'on bannit des mosquées, et que l'Alcoran même ne recoit point dans le paradis' (Besson, *La Syrie Sainte*, II, p. 118). All translations are my own unless otherwise noted.

7. AGC, A.D. 106, 25; APF, SOCG, vol. 536, fol. 301v; SC, Francia, vol. 3, fols 16r–18r, 54r, 56v–57r. See also fols 16r, 113r, 118r.
8. Timothée Jock, *Jésuites et chouéirites, ou la fondation des religieuses basiliennes chouéirites de Notre Dame de l'Annonciation à Zouq-Mikaïl (Liban), 1730–1746* (Central Falls, USA: self-published, 1936), pp. 19, 27, 29, 50–52, 81, 83–85, 88, 93, 96, 99, 102, 105, 112, 131, 141, 147, 153, 155, 156, 160, 162, 164, 180, 187, 197, 203, 228, 236, 239, 249, 260, 276, 278. This aggressively misogynistic and not very reliable book has given most of the letters in French translation, without referring to the originals. The latter are preserved in Lebanon, archives of the Shuwayr convent; or in APF, CP, Greci Melchiti. The contracts were published in Italian by Ioannes Dominicus Mansi (ed.), *Sacrorum Conciliorum nova et amplissima collection*, vol. 46: *Sinodi Melchitarum, 1716–1902* (Paris: expensis Huberti Welter, Bibliopolae, 1911), cols 322–23. See also the judicial evidence left by the superiors (*khādima*) of the Maronite convent of Dayr Sayyidat al-Bizāz: Richard Van Leeuwen, *Notables and Clergy in Mount Lebanon: The Khazin Sheikhs and the Maronite Church (1736–1840)* (Leiden, New York, Cologne: Brill, 1994), p. 159.
9. Jock, *Jésuites et chouéirites*, pp. 19, 180, passim; Mansi, *Sacrorum Conciliorum*, cols. 309–20, and Report of the Apostolic Delegate Emmanuel a Sancto Spirito, cols 345–79 (especially cols 355, 364), 419–26, 430.
10. See the letters of the devotees that the editor-translator has called 'insolent' or 'abominable' (Jock, *Jésuites et chouéirites*, pp. 180, 197, 228, 278). Testimony of their resistance is in Mansi (ed.), *Sacrorum Conciliorum*, vol. 46, cols. 353–56, 365–67.
11. [Bernard Heyberger, *Hindiyya, Mystic and Criminal, 1720–1798: A Political and Religious Crisis in Lebanon*, English translation by Renée Champion (Cambridge: James Clarke, 2013), passim]; 'Interrogatoire de la Mère Hindiyé', French translation in Youakim Moubarac (ed.), *Pentalogie antiochienne/domaine Maronite* (Beirut: Cénacle libanais, 1984), vol. I, 1, pp. 430–67: pp. 438, 442–43, 445–50. This translation is the one referred to in this article (the original is in Latin and Italian). See also APF, CP, Maroniti, vol. 118, fols 115r–376r (Antonio Venturi, S. J., 'Alcune notizie da servir al libro Primo della vita della serva di Dio Hendie Ageimi'): fol. 127r.
12. Jean-Pierre Albert, *Le sang et le Ciel: Les saintes mystiques dans le monde chrétien* (Paris: Aubier, 1997), pp. 84–85.
13. The works of Hindiyya have been published by Michel al-Ḥā'ik [Hayek], 'Al-Rāhiba Hindiyya: Āmālīhā wa-rahbanatuhā', *Al-Mashriq* (1965), pp. 525–646, 685–734; (1966), pp. 273–332, 519–52. Moubarac (ed.), *Pentalogie antiochienne/domaine maronite*, has given a French translation of *Sirr al-ittiḥād*, the main spiritual treatise of Hindiyya, under the title 'Traité de l'union'. Here I refer to this translation (vol. I, 1, pp. 395, 396).

14. This opinion was by her brother, Nicolas: [Heyberger, *Hindiyya*, pp. 92–93, 150–51]; APF, CP, Maroniti, vol. 135, fol. 155r, interrogatory of 12 July 1775.
15. 'Lorsque j'etais une petite fille et que je ne pouvais pas parler, je m'accoudais pour regarder le ciel, et je voyais quelqu'un' ('Traité de l'union', in Moubarac (ed.), *Pentalogie antiochienne/domaine maronite*, vol. I, 1, p. 394). See also al-Ḥā'ik [Hayek], 'Al-Rāhiba Hindiyya' (1965), pp. 288, 542–45. Jesus Christ himself, in a revelation, criticised the lack of discernment by the doctors ('Traité de l'union,' p. 398).
16. [Heyberger, *Hindiyya*, p. 93]; al-Ḥā'ik [Hayek], 'Al-Rāhiba Hindiyya' (1965), pp. 528–48; APF, CP, Maroniti, vol. 135, fol. 155r, interrogatory of 12 July 1775.
17. [Heyberger, *Hindiyya*, pp. 39, 60–61]; APF, CP, Maroniti, vol. 118, fols 115r–376r ('Alcune notizie'): fols 349r–367r, 'Ristretto della Vita della Figlia Endia, menata da lei doppo la partenza del P. Antonio Venturi . . .,' by Bishop Jarmanus Saqr (1748). APF, CP, Maroniti, vol. 113, fols 114v–104r (Arabic), 128r–142v (Italian), testimony of Mikhā'īl Fāḍil on Hindiyya's behalf, alleged to have been spread in Aleppo.
18. 'Traité de l'union', pp. 399, 405–6, 409–12, 415, 422–23.
19. [Heyberger, *Hindiyya*, pp. 74–88]. There is an enormous file of interrogations of Hindiyya's companions and of herself in APF, CP, Maroniti, vol. 118 (1753). The questions are in Latin, with the answers in Italian. Much evidence (spontaneous or not) is in vols 135–36 (1775–77). Commenting on these documents, Lentin wrote: 'Bien que visiblement imposés, ces récits, qui accablent ou au contraire disculpent Hindiyya, sont des documents de premier ordre sur les dialectes de l'époque. Ce sont les documents les plus dialectisants de notre corpus' (Though these tales, which overwhelm or on the contrary exonerate Hindiyya, are obviously forced, they are first-rank documents on dialects at that time. They are the most dialectological documents in our corpus): Jérôme Lentin, *Recherches sur l'histoire de la langue arabe au Proche-Orient à l'époque moderne* (PhD dissertation, Université Paris 3, 1997), vol. 1, p. 50.
20. Bernard Heyberger, 'Entre Orient et Occident: La religion des dévotes d'Alep', in Louis Châtellier (ed.), *Religions en transition dans la seconde moitié du XVIIIe siècle* (Oxford: Oxford University Press, 2000), pp. 171–85. It was impossible for me to examine the entire enormous documentation concerning this affair in APF. See SC, Melchiti, vols. 11, 19; SOCG, vol. 946 (1831), vol. 954 (1838); and Acta, vol. 194 (1831), vol. 201 (1838). This list is not exhaustive.
21. APF, Acta, vol. 194 (1831), fol. 501r.
22. Michel Foucault, *Histoire de la sexualité*, vol. 1: *La volonté de savoir* (Paris: Gallimard, 1976), English translation by Robert Husley, *The History of Sexuality* (New York: Vintage Books, 1988); Michel de Certeau, *La fable mystique XVIe–XVIIe siècle* (Paris: Gallimard, 1982), English translation by Michael B. Smith, *Mystic Fable*, vol. 1 (Chicago: University of Chicago Press, 1995); Alois Hahn, 'Contribution à la sociologie de la confession et autres formes institutionnalisées d'aveu', *Actes de la recherche en Sciences Sociales*, 62, 3 (1986), pp. 54–68.
23. Russell, *Natural History*, vol. 2, p. 45.
24. Aleppo, Greek Catholic Archbishopric, ms. 508. An exemplar of the same rule at Aleppo, Georges and Mathilde Salem Foundation, ms. 829.

25. Albert, *Le sang et le ciel*, pp. 364–73; Philippe Lejeune, *Le moi des demoiselles: Enquête sur le journal de jeune fille* (Paris: Seuil, 1993).
26. See, for instance, the famous *Il penitente istruito a ben confessarsi* by Paolo Segneri (Venice: Biagio Maldura, 1669). French translation: Paul Segneri, *L'instruction du pénitent, ou la méthode pratique pour se bien confesser* (Paris: chez Jean-Baptiste Coignard, 1695). This book was translated into Arabic and condensed with *Il confessore istruito* of the same author (1672) by the Aleppine Maronite Yūsuf al-Bānī (*Kitāb al-mu'arrif wa-l-mu'tarif*) at the beginning of the eighteenth century: see Georg Graf, *Geschichte der christlichen arabischen Literatur*, vol. 3 (Vatican City: Biblioteca Apostolica Vaticana, 1949), pp. 384–85. It was printed in Dayr Yuḥannā of Shuwayr in 1747.
27. Aleppo, Greek Catholic Archbishopric, ms. 508, passim. See also Heyberger, *Les chrétiens du Proche-Orient*, pp. 515–16. The same prescriptions can be seen in the rule of the congregation of the Sacred Heart founded by Hindiyya but intended for cloistered nuns: al-Ḥā'ik [Hayek], 'Al-rāhiba Hindiyya' (1965), pp. 573–75, 582–83.
28. 'Riguardo poi a quelle che sono in possesso della unione, elle godono la visione dell'oggetto ocularmente, perché comparisce loro in figura amena, e fanno con lui pratiche, conversazioni, ed altre cose in modo continuo e confidenziale, come farebbe uno sposo verso la sua sposa, e si sentono che egli dorme sensibilmente nel loro cuore, egli le fa incite diverse domande, tra le quali baci, abbracciamenti, e tutto quello di cui indica il libro dei cantici riguardo ai cenni, alle parole, ed agli amoreggiamenti, ed elle in queste circonstanze si sentono in modo anche sensibile, che l'oggetto punge la voglia del suo cuore in loro, ed in questo modo consiste la principale sostanza del matrimonio spirituale; poiché l'oggetto, l'opera, e l'anima riceve l'operazione, l'oggetto dà, e l'anima riceve ciò che esce da lui' (APF, Acta, vol. 201, fol. 154v). The document's original with its translation in Italian was ordered in SOCG, vol. 954, fol. 192r (Arabic), fols 187r–191v (Italian translation), 24 February 1837. For the effects of reading and suggestion, see ibid. fols 287r–293r, copy of the deposition of Maria Maẓlūm, 20 August 1833.
29. Segneri, *L'instruction du pénitent*, pp. 77–79; Būlus Mas'ad and Nasīb al-Wuhayba al-Khāzin (eds), *Al-Uṣūl al-ta'rīkhiyya*, vol. 1 (Achkouth, Lebanon: n. d.), pp. 569, 570. The rule of the Brotherhood of the Sacred Heart for laymen founded by Hindiyya emphasised temptation.
30. 'Elle lui expose les prétendues opérations de S. Esprit en elle pendant l'oraison mentale, les apparitions, les illuminations dont elle a été favorisée; viennent ensuite les tentations, et là elle doit exposer le principe, les suites, les effets de la tentation, et tout ce qu'une tentation impure a produit dans elle. [. . .] Et ce qu'il y a de pire, c'est que presque chaque Dévote outre cette espèce de Directeur a encore une Directrice à qui elle va faire les mêmes aveux, ou plutôt les mêmes ouvertures, et c'est une chose insoutenable, horrible même, de penser que sous prétexte de dévotion et de perfection une femme va parler à une autre femme de ses tentations, de tout ce que ces tentations produisent en elle' (APF, Acta, vol. 201, 1838, fol. 158rv, letter of 19 June 1836).
31. 'Comme je disais ces paroles et d'autres, je le vis m'embrasser avec une infinie douceur. Par cet embrassement, il pénétra mon âme et mon corps par son corps

divinisé. C'est comme si j'avais plongé en lui dans la stupéfaction, perplexe, stupéfaite, redoutant la forme de son efficacité. Car par sa pénétration de moi, je le vois encore avec mon faible entendement (et je m'aperçois) qu'il est élevé d'une élévation illimitée. Il tient mon âme et mon corps par sa pénétration de moi et sans qu'il soit touché dans ses mouvements, je distingue les parties de son corps qui sont d'une parfaite subtilité et légèreté dans la pénétration' ('Traité de l'union', p. 425).

32. [Heyberger, *Hindiyya*, pp. 167–78]; APF, CP, Maroniti, vol. 136, confession of Warda (Arabic), fols 452r, 449v; confession of Ruzāliyya (Arabic), fols 587r–588r. The embarrassed denials of Maryam concerning homosexual relations with Catherine, the inseparable companion of Hindiyya, are disconcerting (fol. 533r).
33. APF, SOCG, vol. 954, fols 287r–299v, deposition of Maria Maẓlūm, copy of the Italian translation; Acta, vol. 194 (1831), fol. 498rv, 489v, Italian copy of the depositions of Margarita Dier Arotini; fol. 499v, Italian copy of the deposition of Maria Passis. See also in SOCG, vol. 946, fols 132r–133v, copy of the letter of Maria, widow of Anṭūn Buṭrus Diyāb, to the patriarch Ḥubaysh, in which she confesses to intercourse with a priest (134rv, complementary note).
34. Heyberger, 'Entre Orient et Occident,' pp. 171–75; APF, Acta, vol. 194 (1831), fol. 486, deposition of Angelico da Genova, superior of the Capuchins.
35. APF, Acta, vol. 194 (1831), fols 477v, 480r.
36. Lejeune, *Le moi des demoiselles*, pp. 25–27; Hahn, 'Contribution à la sociologie'. It would be interesting to compare it with the origin and development of the autobiographical genre in the Muslim world. See Elisabeth Siedel, 'Die türkische Autobiographie: Versuch einer Problematisierung', *Die Welt des Islams*, 31 (1991), pp. 246–54.
37. Albert, *Le sang et le ciel*, pp. 140–41; [Heyberger, *Hindiyya*, pp. 18–19, 76].
38. Aleppo, Greek Catholic Archbishopric, ms. 508, chap. 1, no. 4.
39. [Heyberger, *Hindiyya*, pp. 18–19]; 'Interrogatoire de la Mère Hindiyé', in Moubarac (ed.), *Pentalogie antiochienne/domaine maronite*, vol. I, 1, p. 432; APF, CP, Maroniti, vol. 118, 'Alcune notizie . . .', fol. 117v.
40. APF, SC, Francia, vol. 3, fols 16r–18r, 54r, 56v–57r. See also fols 113r, 118r, and 16r.
41. [Heyberger, *Hindiyya*, pp. 80–81 (translation from an original Italian ms.)]; APF, CP, Maroniti, vol. 118, fol. 514rv, interrogatory of Sister Theresa, 17 June 1753.
42. 'Dove vanno ingannando Donne e figlioli, dandoli medaglie, croci, figure e Denari, e con questo li Turchi si fanno forti contro di noi altri' (APF, SOCG, vol. 578, fol. 233r [Armenian], fol. 232rv [Italian translation]; see also Heyberger, *Les chrétiens du Proche-Orient*, p. 369).
43. See APF, CP, Greci Melchiti, vol. 75, summary, point 9, fols 64v–86v, about the behaviour of the Franciscan friar Tommaso Campaja towards women in Damascus; and Heyberger, *Les chrétiens du Proche-Orient*, p. 489 (1757), p. 522 (1768, 1772). The English Protestant physician Russell also criticised the relations between Latin friars and women (*Natural History*, vol. 2, p. 39).
44. APF, SC, Melchiti, vol. 11, fols 335v–335r (Arabic), 337r–340r (Italian translation). The Lazarist Nicolas Gaudez justified his gathering of men and

women in his church an hour before midday. He reported that he was suspected of holding his meetings on purpose when the men were not at home (APF, Acta, vol. 194, fols 481v–482r).

45. APF, Acta, vol. 201 (1838), fol. 145r (archive note referring to the congregation of 6 December 1817). In 1836, the apostolic delegate d'Auvergne asserted that he had received 'des plaintes amères des pères de famille, qui se plaignaient hautement que leurs filles dévotes refusaient obéissance à leur père et mère pour n'obéir qu'au Directeur des Dévotes' (bitter complaints from the family fathers, who complained strongly that their devout daughters refused obedience to their father and their mother, obeying only the Directors of the Devotees): ibid. fol. 157r, letter to the Prefect of Propaganda (19 June 1836). Scide Abdad reported that her confessor penalised her after she came late to church because her parents had made her finish some sewing work (fol. 500r).
46. Van Leeuwen, *Notables and Clergy*, pp. 107–48, 198–233; Randi Deguilhem (ed.), *Le waqf dans l'espace islamique: Outil de pouvoir sociopolitique* (Damascus: IFEA, 1995), pp. 259–75; Heyberger, *Les chrétiens du Proche-Orient*, pp. 69–72, 522–48.
47. Van Leeuwen, *Notables and Clergy*, pp. 174–97; van Leeuwen, 'The Maronite *Waqf* of Dayr Sayyidat Bkirki in Mount Lebanon during the 18th century', in Randi Deguilhem (ed.), *Le waqf dans l'espace islamique*, pp. 259–75; Heyberger, *Les chrétiens du Proche-Orient*, pp. 433–51.
48. Andreas Buss, 'The Individual in the Eastern Orthodox Tradition', *Archives de sciences sociales des Religions*, 91 (1995), pp. 41–64. Buss has followed the questioning of Louis Dumont in *Essays on Individualism.*
49. Van Leeuwen, *Notables and Clergy*, pp. 174–97. About the Shuwayrite friars and their economic organisation, see Souad Abou El Rousse Slim, *Le métayage et l'impôt au Mont-Liban, XVIIIe–XIXe siècles* (Beirut: Dar el-Machreq, 1987); and Joseph Abou Nohra, *Contribution à l'étude du rôle des monastères dans l'histoire rurale du Liban* (PhD dissertation, Université de Strasbourg, 1983).
50. 'Interrogatoire de la Mère Hindiyé', in Moubarac (ed.), *Pentalogie antiochienne/domaine maronite*, vol. I, 1, p. 452. Antonio Venturi sent a letter to a Jesuit superior on 11 May 1746, in which he clearly explained his strategy: [Heyberger, *Hindiyya*, pp. 44–45]; copy in ACPF, CP, Maroniti, vol. 118, fol. 638rv.
51. Translated from al-Ḥā'ik [Hayek], 'Al-Rāhiba Hindiyya' (1965), pp. 570–635 (in Arabic) by the author. [Heyberger, *Hindiyya*, pp. 92–93].
52. See, for instance, the assertions of Robert Muchembled in *Le roi et la sorcière: L'Europe des bûchers XVe–XVIIIe siècle* (Paris: Desclée, 1993) ('Rien ne se fait sans Etat') and *Le temps des supplices: De l'obéissance sous les rois absolus, XVe–XVIIIe siècle* (Paris: Colin, 1992).
53. Christian Windler, 'Clientèles et État en Espagne au 18e siècle', *Annales: Histoire, sciences sociales*, 52, 2 (1997), pp. 293–319. Windler, in discussing the dynamics of the Spanish case, has given us a good critical and methodological framework.
54. [Heyberger, *Hindiyya*, pp. 135–43]. For the confession of Ruzāliyya, see APF, CP, Maroniti, vol. 136, fol. 587r; for Warda's, see ibid. fols 452r, 449v; for Khādimat al-Qalb's, see fols 474v–475v; and for Maryam's, see fol. 534v.

55. [Heyberger, *Hindiyya*, pp. 131–66]; APF, CP, Maroniti, vol. 136, fol. 587r. For a summary of the whole affair by Cardinal Boschi, 25 June 1779, see ibid. fols 3r–48r. For overwhelming and undeniable statements by Nicolas Agemi (ʿUjaymī), see APF, CP, Maroniti, vol. 135, fols 154r–175r; and by Ignace Giamati (Jamātī), vol. 136, fols 251r–254v. About correspondence concerning witchcraft, sec Muchembled, *Le roi et la sorcière*.
56. This outrageously misogynistic interpretation is given as early as 1779 by Cardinal Boschi in his summary (see note above). The same interpretation was resumed in an archive note (APF, Acta, vol. 194 [1831], fols 467rv, 468rv) that called Hindiyya 'quella femina scellerata e scaltra' (this wicked and evil female), in a manuscript treatise by Būlus Ḥātim in 1839 (*Kitāb yusamma dakhd al-adālil al-Batishtawiyya al-atiyya ʿan dalalat taʿalim Hindiyya . . .*) and in Cyrille Charon [Korolevskij], *Histoire des patriarcats melkites*, vol. 2: *La période moderne (1833–1855)* (Rome: M. Bretschneider, 1910), pp. 344–82, re-edited in Moubarac (ed.), *Pentalogie antiochienne/domaine maronite*, vol. I, 1, pp. 351–81.
57. Louis Dumont, *Essais sur l'individualisme: Une perspective anthropologique sur l'idéologie moderne* (Paris: Seuil, 1983), pp. 11–19. English translation: *Essays on Individualism: Modern Ideology in an Anthropological Perspective* (Chicago: University of Chicago Press, 1986).
58. Caroline Walker Bynum, *Holy Feast and Holy Fast: The Religious Significance of Food to Medieval Women* (Berkeley: University of California Press, 1987).
59. An ethnological study such as Jacqueline des Villettes, *La vie des femmes dans un village maronite libanais: Aïn el Kharoubé* (Tunis: Institut des Belles Lettres Arabes, 1964) has given a picture of women's conditions in the Lebanese mountains that seems in contradiction with the developments that I have suggested here.

CHAPTER 10

Saint Charbel Makhlouf, or the Consecration of Maronite Identity

Saint Charbel Makhlouf (Sharbal Makhlūf), the subject of this chapter, was a nineteenth-century monk belonging to the Maronite community, the most significant Christian community in Lebanon in terms of numbers and political influence. This community, with its own rites and an autonomous hierarchy under the authority of a patriarch whose seat is in Bkirki (Lebanon), is nonetheless a full member of the Roman Catholic Church, whose authority it recognises.

Our study will not focus principally on the period of Charbel's life (1828–98), as there is in fact not much to say about the man himself during his lifetime. What is, in fact, more pertinent and more coherent with the theme of this collection is an analysis of the discourse triggered about him when he was at the height of his saintly fame, more than half a century after his death, in a period stretching from Vatican II and the first inter-community difficulties in constitutional Lebanon to his canonisation in 1977, when the country was exiting the first violent phase of the war. The 'creation' of this Christian hero thus coincided with similar phenomena in the emergence of charismatic figures in other communities and countries of the Islamic world during the same period. Saint Charbel is certainly original in an Arab-Muslim pantheon, especially on account of his Catholic character, rubber-stamped by Rome. But his consecration lies within a context which was probably not specific to the Maronite community: the search for local authenticity (as opposed to Western influence) and the constitution of a 'national' community narrative, all this not without some element of paradox.

Charbel Makhlouf did not write anything and left practically no trace of his time on Earth, which made him quite a convenient saint for the hagiographers. Michel Hayek has stated in the introduction to a book that is dedicated to him and that manages to extend to 187 pages: 'His greatest miracle was that his silence could give rise to so many words. [. . .] As a consequence, to write his life-story is not possible, as there was no history where one could research and find sufficient elements to "make" a book'.[1]

It was precisely this gap that facilitated the construction of a stereotyped discourse, loaded with identitarian indicators on the one hand Catholic and on the other 'national'. It was no doubt this synthesis that allowed Charbel Makhlouf to be set solemnly on the altar for the devotion of the faithful.

THE LIFE AND POSTHUMOUS WORKS OF SAINT CHARBEL

Charbel Makhlouf was born in 1828 in Biqaʿ Kafrā, on Mount Lebanon.[2] Christened Yūsif, he was the youngest in a family of five children. He spent a rural childhood and youth in a mountain village, about which we know very little. He was still very young when his father Antūn was required to go down to the coast to work on transport duty with his beast of burden, according to the writers, either on behalf of Emir Bashir II Shihāb for the construction of his palace in Beiteddine, or to carry supplies to the Egyptian troops during Ibrahim Pasha's occupation of Syria.[3] On the road back from this corvée labour, he fell ill and died. His wife Brigitte, after having been a widow for two years, remarried in October 1833, to Lahūd Ibrāhīm, a man from the same village, who was ordained and became the parish priest shortly after. Young Yūsif was placed under the tutelage of his uncle Tanios, who was a deacon.[4]

Yūsif also had two maternal uncles who were monks in the monastery close to Quzḥayyā. Following the tradition and the Rule of Lebanese Monks, they had been authorised, after a requisite number of years of proving their devotion, to live as hermits close to the monastery. Hagiographers have cited them as a probable influence on the young man, of whom it is said that at the age of sixteen he liked to withdraw to a cave where he had set up a shrine to the Virgin. At the age of twenty-three, he left his house at dawn, with no warning for fear of opposition from his mother and his uncle, and set off towards the monastery of Mayfūq, a day's walk away.[5] From then on, he took the name of Charbel (Sharbal) and led a simple life as monk in the Antonine Lebanese Order, the main Maronite religious community. He carried out his novitiate in Kfīfān, where Niʿmatallāh al-Hardīnī was teaching at the time. The cause of Ḥardīnī, later proclaimed Blessed, has often been linked to that of Charbel.[6] The latter was ordained priest at the age of thirty-one. At forty-seven he was granted the right to withdraw to live as hermit in ʿAnnāyā, with links to the nearby monastery of Saint Maroun, on a 1,200m-high promontory overlooking the sea and the town of Jbayl (Byblos). There he led an edifying life of devotions, asceticism and mortification. On Friday, 16 December 1898, he was struck by paralysis at the altar, at the moment of the elevation of the host and the chalice, the holy consecrated species. He died on Christmas Eve, 24 December.[7]

The Superior wrote the following commentary, which was to become prophetic, in the register where he noted Charbel's death: 'What he will achieve after his death dispenses me from having to give more details of his life. Faithful to his vows, of exemplary obedience, his conduct was more that of an angel than of a man'.[8]

Indeed, stories about Charbel truly started with his death. Emblematic of this is that a book by Paul Daher (Būlus Ḍāhir) opens with his burial, before retracing with the reader the story of his life.[9] This way of presenting events is in accordance with the modern Catholic vision, which is wary of emphasising living saintliness and only consecrates Christian heroes long after their deaths. Well before the burial, while a monk was guarding the body of Charbel in the chapel, he saw a light come from the tabernacle and illuminate the dead man's remains. He was buried without a coffin, as is the rule with monks, in a pit filled with mud, during a season of rain and snow. A few weeks later, some local people, including several Turkish soldiers, saw lights rise from the tomb; hence, four months after his burial, on 15 April 1899, they proceeded to exhume his body. Preserved in the mud, it had remained intact. The body was then placed in a closed and remote place to remove him from the devotions of the faithful, but it started to exude a reddish liquid. The news of this new wonder brought a surge of visitors asking to see Charbel. The body was laid to rest in a shrine, where it went on exuding until 1927. In 1925, the Superior General of the Lebanese Monks went to Rome to ask Pope Pius XI to start the beatification process. A commission was formed, and an investigation was opened, according to canonical procedure.[10] It was during this time that the monks began to collect testimonials of the life and miracles of Charbel; although this represented a fairly small collection, it constitutes the basic outline of all the works that were devoted to him afterwards. At the end of the investigation in July 1927, the remains of the holy monk were placed in a new wooden coffin, secured in a zinc sarcophagus, officially sealed and cemented in a wall.[11]

Although Charbel's reputation for saintliness had grown, it seemed to be limited to Lebanon. Many, even among the Maronites, were apparently unaware of his existence until 1950. At the beginning of that year, a viscous liquid exuded from the wall that contained the coffin, which provoked a genuine mass movement, followed by miracles, and popular devotion reached unprecedented proportions. On 25 February, it was decided to re-open the tomb, and the body was found to be still intact. A second investigation was carried out and new reports made. In the register kept since 22 April 1950, 2,200 miraculous events were recorded over a two-year period. In 1955, 'Annāyā apparently received more than 300,000 letters, of which 23,000 came from France and 18,000 from the United States.[12] Unlike in earlier periods, the development of air and road transport facilitated the influx of pilgrims. In addition, the wonders of Charbel were passed on by a veritable editorial campaign, which involved most of the works quoted here, with books, newspapers and photos sharing the miracles of 'Annāyā throughout the Christian world. Thus, in the issue of the weekly *Ici Paris* dated 16 September 1951, it was reported that a woman from La

Rochelle, suffering from a breast tumour, was cured by relics brought back from 'Annāyā.[13] This keen interest, inspired by the press, activated the case for beatification in Rome, which had been put aside since 1927. In 1954 the 'apostolic process' started, a procedure which was accelerated by Pope John XXIII after his accession in 1958. Charbel was declared Blessed by Paul VI on 5 December 1965, then canonised by the same pope on 9 October 1977.

THE MAKING OF A SAINT: BETWEEN LATIN SOURCES AND THE QUEST FOR AUTHENTICITY

The biographical itinerary of Charbel was, in many respects, typical of a career of sainthood in modern Catholicism. That career, ever since the final establishment of the canonisation process in the seventeenth century, required a complex dialectic between popular acknowledgment and institutional control, with meticulous verification, not only of the veracity of the miracles attributed to the candidate for sainthood, but also mainly of the heroic nature of the virtues that he or she practised during their lifetime. This is why we find warnings in most hagiographic books dedicated to Charbel, where the authors only credit a 'human belief' in the wonders that they recount, and they use the terms 'saint' or 'miracle' only in the common meaning, without prejudging the decision that the Holy See would make based on the facts.[14] Gathering testimonials that might convince the Roman jury, while at the same time organising popular devotion without infringing on the ban on an unapproved cult, was the difficult task incumbent on those who wanted to raise their champion onto the altar.[15] Very often it is a religious order that takes charge of this, as was the case for Charbel, since the Order of Lebanese Monks to whom he belonged put together the dossier for his beatification, then for his canonisation. It was also the Order of Lebanese Monks that would be the first to benefit from the material and symbolic profits of this consecration. In the main, the biographies dedicated to Saint Charbel are apologia for the monastic life of which he was a paragon, carrying to perfection the practice of its virtues.[16] But the construction of Charbel's sainthood was not possible without the approval of the higher ecclesiastical authority, the patriarch and the pope, at each step. For him to have a chance of reaching canonisation it was necessary that the narratives and depositions concerning the virtual saint conformed to the Roman definition of saintliness, while at the same time being confirmed in their legitimacy. As Michel Hayek has reminded us, Charbel was the first Eastern saint canonised by a pope since Alexander III in 1170, and this was done according to the rules established by the Catholic Church between the end of the Middle Ages and the eighteenth century. In this context, all the works dedicated to Charbel had a pedagogical aim, or more precisely an edifying one. All the stories of the saint's life and the wonders worked after his death answer the question: what meaning does this have for Christians?

A first answer is given by the whole of the hagiography that insists on the Eastern character of Saint Charbel. It is true that in his history one can find typical elements of the Christian Lebanese society in which he was born and raised, including his membership of a clerical dynasty that had given several priests and monks to the Maronite Church. There are other examples since the sixteenth century, of families in which hermits succeeded each other from uncle to nephew.[17] The traits of a saintly charisma identifiable by his circle after his death also refer us to an Eastern perception of sanctity, as we are reminded in an article from the *Irenikon* review in 1965:

> After the death of Father Charbel, the classic phenomenon of the preservation of the body, surrounded by a fluorescent glow, which Eastern people found so important, then the flowing of a health-giving balm, brought countless Christian and Muslim pilgrims come to his tomb at ʿAnnāyā. [. . .] According to the tradition of the Eastern Church, saints are glorified 'not only in their soul but also in their body. This glorification starts during their earthly life and after their death their bodily remains stay filled with the spirit that moved them. They are not corpses but bodies that have started to be glorified, which will be completed at the resurrection'.[18]

But it was not so much this 'Eastern' aspect of Charbel's sainthood that was put forward in the texts. Indeed, during the 1950s, when the fame of the ascetic Maronite was spreading, Catholicism was beginning to rediscover the 'desert saints' of the first centuries, and it is against this model of 'Eastern sainthood' that he was constantly measured and identified.[19] In an introductory text to Michel Hayek's book, Louis Boyer, an Oratorian who spent most of his life studying 'the Eastern Fathers', has stated that while reading this work he felt a shock, something like that of a pre-historian meeting a Cro-Magnon man, a sort of confirmation that the ideal he was studying corresponded to reality.[20]

This rediscovery of desert asceticism, the tradition of which was preserved by the Maronites, also constituted a sort of revenge of Eastern Christianity over Latinism. Vatican II recognised the value of the Eastern Churches and their tradition in the Church's history, and the beatification of Charbel in 1965, at the end of the Council, was a consecration of this recognition. Paul VI, in the speech proclaiming the Lebanese monk Blessed, recalled the 'ancient Eastern monastic traditions'.[21] In this way, some people expected to make of the newly Blessed a symbol of the ecumenical tendency of the Church that had been inaugurated during the Council. Lebanon, a junction of several different Christian denominations, as well as a place of contact with Islam and Judaism, was one day to be called upon to play a pivotal, even providential, role in this new religious state of affairs.[22] It was also a time when Rome insisted on simplicity, on a return to the spirit of the first centuries of Christianity, and when a renewal of the hermit's life was seriously considered.[23] That a man such as Charbel was beatified between the two votes of the Council approving 'Schema XIII' (dedicated to 'The Church in the Modern World') was 'almost nonsense', wrote *Irenikon*. But, so the review added, 'several Eastern people put forward the fact, on the occasion of Schema XIII, that discarding this world to live already in the other has not been sufficiently taken into consideration by the Council as being a true value of Christian life'.[24] Father Hayek contrasted Eastern Christian spirituality, embodied by Charbel, with Western spirituality. The former, according to him, valued matter by making it part of the 'religion of the soul', whereas the latter seemed to be 'strongly dominated by Augustinian psychology':

> Thus, Western spirituality is constantly tempted to place itself on a psychological level, whereas Eastern spirituality is of a cosmic nature; it considers the being as a whole, body and soul, in its context that supports it, with all the information that defines and conditions it.

Thus, Eastern spirituality was supposed to be 'the expression of a religious emotion both spiritual and physical'.[25] This is indeed not only a rehabilitation of Eastern Christian spirituality, but also an attempt to give room again to the body and the environment in spiritual practices, a precursor of the charismatic movement in later years. It is also possible that this apologia for mysticism rebelling against the primacy of the rational was inspired by Maurice Barrès' thinking, as we find it in *La colline inspirée*, or in certain passages of *Une enquête aux pays du Levant*.[26] Further on, Father Hayek complained about the Superior of the monastery in ʿAnnāyā, who subjected Charbel's remains to physical treatments to stop them from leaking. He called him stubborn, knowing only the rules of religious life and moral theology.[27] Another recurring theme of the relevant hagiographic literature was the failure of science confronted with faith, modern medicine's helplessness when faced with the case of the holy monk.[28]

As we can see, Charbel's claim to be the incarnation of an authentic spiritual and aesthetic Eastern tradition owed a lot to the movements that stirred Catholicism as a whole from the beginning of the century and particularly in the 1950s and1960s. Charbel's silence, fasting, exposure to the elements, his energy at work and his humility as told in the narratives about him remind us of Saint Anthony, the other Desert Fathers, or Maronite hermits. Nevertheless, we must agree that for the most part, and despite what the hagiographers say, what we learn about him shows us the existing stereotypes of sainthood that were current within nineteenth- and early-twentieth-century Catholicism.[29] The search for action in the world through isolation, silence, interiority, as attributed to Charbel, doubtlessly owed more to contemporary models (such as Charles de Foucauld and Thérèse of Lisieux) than to the Egyptian and Syrian ascetics.[30] Tales of Charbel's life, especially those that came directly from the Lebanese Order, insisted on his meticulous respect of the monastic vows to foolish extremes, in particular the vow of obedience. Paul Daher has stated, in relation to the ascetics of the desert, 'that it is fortunate to know that this way of life of the anchorites has been replaced by well-organised religious orders', and he has reminded us that in the Order of the Lebanese Monks the hermit was subject to a very strict rule that did not leave him alone and free with his imagination.[31] 'Luckily, not everyone who wants to gets to go to the desert!' Daher has said.[32] In fact, Charbel embodied the ideal of the monk. To take just one example, even though for poverty he wore completely worn, patched clothes which may remind us of the desert ascetics, the hagiographers specified that his garments were always scrupulously clean, which would certainly have differentiated him from the earlier saints.[33]

Charbel also suited the definition of the 'good priest'. Following early conditioning by his environment, he experienced God's call to become a monk, then a priest, at the age of sixteen, in accordance with the Catholic Church's idea of 'vocation'. According to the Latin spirituality of the priesthood, the Maronite monk had to have a very great devotion to the Eucharist and meticulous application in his way of saying mass. Like the Curé d'Ars (Saint John Vianney, canonised in 1925), Charbel was apparently a sought-after confessor. He 'would read the heart of the penitent' and imposed harsh penances, but these pleased the faithful.[34] A fundamental source of his spirituality, according to our authors, was *The Imitation of Christ*, a reference book if ever there was one of Latin Christianity since the period of *devotio moderna*. He also showed a very strong devotion to the Virgin, a nineteenth-century trait, associated with the contemplation of an image of the Rosary, which he never stopped reciting.[35] The tale of Charbel's youth followed the near-universal stereotype in Christianity, of a saintly childhood, or of the learning of sainthood. But it further implied an idealisation of rural life, typical of contemporary Catholicism. His parents were depicted as good Christian models, illiterate but fervent peasant-farmers:

> His father, a small farmer, only possessed a modest piece of land and a small number of livestock. But he was rich with a double treasure: his love of work and his faith more solid than the thousand-year-old cedar trees that he contemplated every day.[36]

The fact that his mother married again presented a few problems for hagiographers, who would have preferred her to remain a widow, raising her children alone. Even so, she has been depicted as an exemplary woman. She fasted every day and made a vow not to eat meat but was freed from this vow by her confessor who asked her to replace this with a daily rosary; here again, an Eastern ascetic practice was replaced by a Latin devotion.[37] The texts insisted on the mother's role in Christian education:

> This brave mother was uncompromising on the duty of family prayer. When the time came, all her children would kneel down around her and recite the evening prayer in front of an icon of the Virgin, while the aroma of incense rose to the heavens from a simple saucer. When the church bell rang, Brigitta abandoned her pots and pans and, baby in arms, answered its call. To be present at mass was the basis of her devotion for this farmer's wife.[38]

Of course, nothing distinguished the young Yūsif from the other village children, 'only a greater piety'.[39] The modest schooling took place under the oak tree in summer. The teacher was often the priest himself. There was little risk of secular teaching, which would exceed what was useful to make a good Christian: 'The only diploma that one could dream of attaining was the priest certifying that the pupil could read Syriac with no mistakes and serve the church'.[40]

It is easy to recognise the whole Sulpician folklore there, which has nothing typically 'Eastern', 'Lebanese', or 'Maronite', but surely refers back to the conservative Catholicism of the early twentieth century. However, it was upon these stereotypes belonging to a very Westernised culture that the discourse on Maronite identity, supposedly embodied by Charbel, was built.

CHARBEL AND THE CELEBRATION OF THE LEBANESE/MARONITE FATHERLAND

These images appear less mawkish if we put them back into context. The praise of the pious Maronite peasant sets up an evocation of the geography, history and politics of Lebanon, which gave Charbel's story a strong symbolic dimension. We recognise in it a part of the 'national' Maronite narrative, progressively developed since the end of the Middle Ages. Already in the nineteenth century Maronite authors tried to link their own history to that of a romantic, Catholic and counter-revolutionary France. They showed their people as 'backward', 'ignorant' and 'wretched', making this a virtue, since in this way they remained attached to their land, their religion and the natural hierarchy, which even predisposed them to receive civilisation thanks to colonial occupation.[41] At the beginning of the twentieth century, the stories produced by the Jesuits and published in their review, *Al-Mashriq*, in particular the plays, emphasised the value of the nation, the family and religion as pillars of morality. Particularly the texts by Henri Lammens SJ were full 'of nostalgic descriptions of country life and of mountainous settings to take your breath away'. At the sound of the bells, the hero, returning from foreign lands where he had earned a good living, fell to his knees to give thanks to his country and gave praise to the Church for this idyllic country life.[42] Emigration, already discussed in these evocative dramas, certainly played an important role in the mythologisation of Lebanese soil, as in the propagation of the cult of Saint Charbel. The ideology of Maurice Barrès – in particular, his nationalism of the earth and the dead – was later added to an older, more conservative and reactionary influence.[43]

As Father Hayek has stated, Charbel was 'the saint of his people'. Not an excrescence, but a product of his environment, he said. Hayek volunteered, moreover, to show his readers the history and the geography of Lebanon, 'one of the most modern and most ancient countries of the East'.[44] Indeed, all the authors mentioned Lebanon, and their remarks were generally illustrated with photos of mountains. A work by Paul Daher started with a description of the country as seen from the sea, such as we find in the tales of Western travellers. It was the Orientalist image *par excellence*, accompanied by a quotation from Barrès: 'We go on the unchanging sea, at the foothills of the mountains, which, under the eternal sun, dressed in the same shadows and the same lights, are always full of divine invocations'.[45]

The idea expressed here, which in fact came from Ernest Renan, was that in this landscape there has been a determinism that inspired the sacred in Man, from all eternity, that there has been a continuity in the religious soul of Lebanon. This idea has largely been revisited by our authors. Nasri Riscallah, following Barrès, has evoked 'Adonis's soul' near Byblos (Jbayl), not far from ʿAnnāyā, and added: 'So many thousands of adorers have cherished all these marvels, that we can wonder if they have not left something of their soul in this nature that continues to live and to sing'.[46]

The continuity with paganism could not be so bluntly expressed by the monk Daher. He linked Lebanon's history to Church history, seeing similarities between Biqaʿ Kafrā and Bethlehem, then between ʿAnnāyā and the Holy Places, making several comparisons.[47] Charbel was not a child of mixed Lebanese districts such as Beirut, Matn or Shūf, not even from Kisruwān, a land of recent Maronite colonisation. He came from the historical heart of the Maronite mountain, of Mount Lebanon. Biqaʿ Kafrā is the highest village in Lebanon, at 1,600 metres, and very close to the Cedars, as our authors liked to make clear.[48] There was a symbol here. This region, the *Wādī qadīsha*, the Holy Valley, has been recalled in epic terms, with a Barresian flavour. Father Hayek has written: 'A whole nation lived in this Valley. It is there too that she lays down to die and to germinate again, watered by the blood, periodically refreshed, of her martyrs'.[49] And he has suggested that the case of Lebanon is unique, through this alliance in blood between the peasant-farmer and his land. The latter, who lives close to nature, but wears himself out trying to get his land to be productive, has been celebrated in all the texts, with a touch of nostalgia, however, as the Lebanon of the 1950s was already experiencing a strong rural exodus and as our authors personally were very far from this mountain life that they extolled.

The evocation of the earth and the dead, like Barresian nationalism, was strongly charged with aggression. The theme of a continuous and thousand-year-long struggle against a hostile environment was largely exploited in these writings. Daher went back to the origins of Maronite history, recalling the story of how 350 monks from Mar Maroun shed their blood in defence of the Council of Chalcedon in 517, before the resettlement of the community in the mountains, where they became 'the defenders of a Christian bastion that neither the centuries, nor the constant unleashing of persecutions and heresies, were able to shatter'.[50]

All the books have mentioned the past, in particular the Phoenicians, Christian Antiquity and the Crusades.[51] However, the Muslim presence in Lebanon appears as if erased from history. We get the sense that they are only foreign invaders who oppress the true owners of the land. Several hagiographers have insisted on the fact that, in his youth, Saint Charbel had studied Syriac more than Arabic in his village school and again in the seminary of the Lebanese Monks.[52] He lived through the massacres of 1860 and other events of Lebanese history, apparently without it interfering in his personal life in the least. However, the villages of Qadīsha have been described as bastions of liberty engaged in resistance, while Turkish oppression hung over the towns. The death of Charbel's father coming back from corvée labour, although it was due to illness, became a sort of martyrdom:

> This drama was for him in keeping with the storyline of the whole history of the Maronites, who had always been a people in danger of martyrdom. Constantly threatened in their liberty and their faith [. . .] From his earliest childhood the orphan had heard told this long list of martyrs in which his young years were cruelly involved.[53]

Every evening, according to Michel Hayek, his mother told him of these 'distressing stories', before ending with the recital of the rosary.[54] The hagiography of Charbel was thus enriched with the myth of the martyr, and even of the fighting saint, two traditional forms of sainthood valued in the East and essential for any national construction. The first name that he chose when entering the order, 'Charbel', recalls an ancient martyr from Edessa.[55] The hermitage at ʿAnnāyā became a sort of bunker during the First World War, in the description that Michel Hayek has given of it when, having recalled the modesty of the place, he exclaimed: 'We cannot ask for more in trench warfare'.[56]

It was certainly a metaphorical war. But ʿAnnāyā was a recent post for Christian re-conquest, bordered by Shiʿite villages. Daher went back to the thirteenth century, a time when, according to him, the Crusaders, who had taken refuge with the Maronites, were defeated despite fierce resistance, while the patriarch was horribly martyred. Then, so he has said, 'the conquerors decided to exterminate the Maronites and fetched Shiʿites from Iraq and Persia to populate Lebanon'.

These new arrivals, however, were welcomed with charity and fraternity, which of course led them to convert.[57] The rebuilding of ʿAnnāyā as a Christian site, at the beginning of the nineteenth century, after having passed through Shiʿism, was presented as natural in the plans of Providence. 'This new Golgotha seemed, for centuries, to be waiting for a man who would come there to live and die raising the Host . . .'[58] The narratives have all insisted on the fact that both Muslims and Christians benefitted, and still benefit, from Saint Charbel's favours.[59] This fact has come to the help of those who have attributed an ecumenical mission and interreligious dialogue specific to Lebanon. But upon looking more closely, the favours of the Maronite saint towards the Muslims and the fervour of the latter towards him are, above all, proof that the miracle is on the Christian side and, thus, a confirmation of the truth of the Christian faith. '[Father Charbel] will show us, by his favours towards the Muslim people, that we must understand more fully the love of Christ, who died for the salvation of all men created in the image of God'. This statement could be seen as universalist, tolerant, open to non-Christians, if it were not situated in the midst of musings on the restoration of ʿAnnāyā as a source of pride for Christianity.[60] Charbel must, of course, become the saint of all the Lebanese. But Lebanon, in this version, is primarily a Christian creation, a land where the history of the Maronite people is rooted. They benefit from a precedence in the occupation of the place and from an intimate relationship with the earth, formed of sweat and blood, which gives it a special legitimacy.

The hagiographic discourse has generally been characterised by a confusion in time, a refusal of historicity, that attempts to abolish the distance between past and present, to underline the continuity and faithfulness of identity. Our narratives have not contradicted this rule. Among the publications of the 1950s, only the work by Nasri Riscallah explicitly referred to the political realities of the time when, before a crowd of pilgrims clogging the roads to ʿAnnāyā, he remembered another exodus, that of the Palestinians.[61] The other narratives have distanced themselves from the burning reality, but nonetheless kept alive elements of the above-mentioned 'national' Maronite/Lebanese identity, this 'maronitude' or 'political Maronitism' that characterised the discourse of the Lebanese Forces in later years.[62] The works written in French seem more heavily weighted with ideological content than those published in Arabic, which are generally more restrained.

The festivities around the canonisation of Saint Charbel in 1977 took place while the first extremely violent phase of the civil war (1975–76) had given way to a truce, in a divided country where the Syrian army was encamped. Paul Daher at the time put together a souvenir album, based on press articles, which he titled

'*Liban, patrie ivre de Charbel*' (Lebanon, a Homeland Inebriated with Charbel).[63] Texts and declarations from politicians collected in the volume mentioned the war but, in the irenic atmosphere created by the festivities of the canonisation, called for an appeasement, hoping that Lebanon, once reconciled, would regain its unity.[64] Father Charbel Qassīs, Superior General of the Lebanese Monks and ideologist of the Christian faction, expressed the opinion that Lebanon was dying, or already dead, in order to affirm on the contrary its perpetuation and future, in a new and exemplary form, because it had been founded on a pluralist society.[65] In a published letter addressed to the members of his order on the occasion of Charbel's canonisation, he made a vow that 'Lebanon [would] remain a land of encounters, of democracy and plurality'. He implored the intercession of Saint Charbel so that the three great religions would keep meeting there and complementing each other, thus preserving a civilisation in which East and West would meet and complement each other, within a political system both democratic and pluralist.[66] Without saying it explicitly, it was the Christian militia alone whom he considered able to guarantee this future.

This collection also constituted a celebration of the classic themes of 'maronitude'. The link between the saint and the country has been underlined. Religion (*dīn*) and fatherland (*waṭan*) form an inseparable pair. Maronite identity and Lebanese identity blend into one another. This is true of an article by Yūsif Ibrāhīm Yazbak, dedicated to the period of Charbel, which coincides with the moment of fixation of this political-religious ideology. The author has insisted on religious continuity, despite the political upheavals of the nineteenth century:

> [The faith of the Lebanese or Maronite] became a part of his national identity (*juz'an min kiyānihi al-waṭanī*). Or, more precisely: this identity was founded on the religious faith of this Lebanese person. And the Maronite continued to satisfy his devotional duties at all times, day and night, since he became a Maronite. And he accomplished them in accordance with the manner in which Christianity had practiced them since its origins.[67]

Thus, discourse can become a factor for integration, when it states and aspires to democracy and plurality, and for discrimination when it establishes the Maronites and their monks as the perpetual guardians and watchmen of a Lebanon bearing a particular 'civilisation' embodied by Charbel:

> *Lubnānī, Anā Lubnān al-ḥubb wa-l-jamāl, Lubnān Allāh . . . fa-man laysa min al-ḥubb wa-l-jamāl, man laysa min Allāh, fa-laysa min Lubnānī, wa laysa bi-l-khamra sharbaliyya yaskar . . .* (Lebanese, I am the Lebanon of Love and Beauty, the Lebanon of God . . . whoever is not on the side

of Love and Beauty, whoever is not on the side of God, is not Lebanese, and he cannot become inebriated with the wine of Charbel).[68]

Charbel's story lies entirely within a providential vision of the history of Lebanon, a Lebanon that is predominantly Christian. The Maronites have benefitted from a specific legitimacy in embodying this Lebanon, in that they are portrayed as its oldest occupiers, the jealous guardians of its heritage, in that they have tilled the earth with perseverance, and in that they have constantly spilled their blood on it, resisting invasion and persecution. A man of the refuge huts in the mountains and of the defensive promontory, a tireless worker of the earth, Charbel, about whose life we know very little, embodied this nationalism of the Earth and the Dead, which no doubt owes a lot to Maurice Barrès. Even his spirituality, as it is interpreted by his hagiographers, shared the Barresian idea of the inherent Sacred, linked to place and to history. Charbel's image, repeated endlessly on the roadside in the Christian zones of present-day Lebanon and associated with that of Saint Elias annihilating the infidels, has materialised this political spirituality, aggressive or defensive (even when posing as a bastion of pluralism and of democracy), as expressed through his hagiography.

The 'nationalist' discourse centred on Lebanon does not contradict the one that makes Saint Charbel a true heir of the desert saints, who kept alive or gave new life to authentic Syrian or Egyptian asceticism in the middle of the twentieth century. Within Catholicism, the Maronites would become the heirs to this tradition of the Desert Fathers, its value having been officially recognised by Rome at the end of Vatican II. In fact, since Jibrāʾīl ibn al-Qilāʿī at the end of the fifteenth century, the Maronite consciousness has needed this Western recognition in order to feel legitimate. The unflinching resistance of this small people taking refuge in its mountains has become meaningful in an eternal faithfulness to Rome and the West, despite the persecutions it has endured. This everlasting struggle gives it a specific mission (not always recognised and often misunderstood) in the heart of the East, of the Church and of all Christianity.

NOTES

1. Michel Hayek, *Le chemin du désert: Le Père Charbel moine d'Orient* (Le Puy, Lyon: Xavier Mappus, 1962), p. 14: 'Son plus grand miracle reste que son silence ait pu susciter tant de paroles. [. . .] Dès lors, écrire son histoire devient une vaine tentative, puisque il n'y a pas eu d'histoire où l'on puisse rechercher et trouver assez d'éléments pour "fabriquer" un livre'. This is a new edition of Michel Hayek, *Le père Charbel ou la voix du silence* (Paris: La Colombe, 1956). In 1996, the author 'disavowed' this book written 'in three weeks in the Foyer libanais' in Paris; see the interview given to Charlotte Michelet, *Le culte d'un saint chrétien dans la montagne libanaise* (Mémoire de maîtrise: Université Paris X-Nanterre, 1997), pp. 115–17.

See also Paul Daher, *Vie, survie et prodiges de l'ermite Charbel Makhlouf* (Paris: Spes, 1953), p. 16. Another work by the same author is devoted to the 'paroles de Charbel', which in fact consists of a few short expressions that the author has commented on in a specific chapter: Būlus Dāhir, *Kalimāt Sharbal*, 2nd ed. (Harissa, Lebanon: Al-tib'a al-būlusiyya, 1995).

2. Pierre Saadé, *Charbel: El gran santo del siglo XX (1830–1898)*, vol. 1 (Mendoza, Argentina: s. n., 1998), p. 72, has discussed the date of birth between 1828 and 1833 and retained 1830.
3. The first explanation has been given by Antūnyūs Shiblī, *Al-Āb Sharbal Makhlūf biqa'kafra min ibnā' al-ruhbāniyya al-baladiyya al-lubnāniyya al-mārūniyya habīs mahbasa dayr 'Annāyā*, 2nd ed. (Jounieh: Dakāsh, 1999), p. 10. The second version came from Daher, *Vie, survie et prodiges de l'ermite Charbel Makhlouf*, p. 22. On this point, as on others, Michel Hayek has followed Daher: Hayek, *Le chemin du désert*, p. 35.
4. Shiblī, *Al-Āb Sharbal Makhlūf*, p. 11; Hayek, *Le chemin du désert*, p. 36.
5. Daher, *Vie, survie et prodiges*, p. 26; Shiblī, *Al-Āb Sharbal Makhlūf*, pp. 12–13. The second author has evoked the same episodes taken from the first, but without all these details.
6. Shiblī, *Al-Āb Sharbal Makhlūf*, p. 14; Yūsuf Khashān, *Al-kawākib al-khamsa*, 3rd enriched ed. (Jounieh: Dakāsh, 1996), pp. 23–48 (Charbel was the first star), 115–44 (Ḥardīnī was the third). Charbel, Ḥardīnī and Sister Rafqa have also been associated in Manṣūr 'Awwād, *Baraka 'an Qabr al-Qadīs Sharbal*, 1st part ('Annāyā, s. n.: 1952), later re-edited without a date. [Ni'matallāh Kassāb al-Ḥardīnī was canonised by John-Paul II in 2004. On Sister Rafqa, canonised in 2001, see Chantal Verdeil, 'Le corps souffrant de Rifqâ, sainte maronite du XIXe siècle', in *Le corps et le sacré en Orient musulman*, special issue of *Revue des mondes musulmans et de la Méditerranée*, 113–14 (2006), pp. 247–64].
7. Shiblī, *Al-Āb Sharbal Makhlūf*, pp. 7, 15–25; Daher, *Vie,survie et prodiges*, pp. 54–92.
8. Paul Daher, *Charbel: Un homme ivre de Dieu 1828–1898*, 2nd ed. (Annaya, Liban: Monastère Saint-Maron, 1993), p. 9: 'Ce qu'il accomplira après sa mort me dispense de donner plus de détails sur sa vie. Fidèle à ses vœux, d'une obéissance exemplaire, sa conduite fut plus angélique qu'humaine'. Approximate translation of an Arabic text given by Shiblī, *Al-Āb Sharbal Makhlūf*, p. 26, note 1.
9. Daher, *Charbel: Un homme ivre de Dieu*, pp. 7–35.
10. Daher, *Vie, survie et prodiges*, pp. 93–108; Shiblī, *Al-Āb Sharbal Makhlūf*, pp. 27–28.
11. The first publications date from this period: Antūnyūs Shiblī had a biography published with the first elements of the investigation: 'Al-Āb Sharbal, habīs 'Annāyā al-qadīs', *Al-Mashriq* (1922), pp. 289–97. The same elements were used and completed in his book of 1950, *Al-Āb Sharbal Makhlūf*. See also Joseph Carame (ed.), *Deux religieux maronites: Le P. Nemattalla Alhardini et le Père Charbel* (Paris: Letouzey et Ané, 1923): this was a translation of a life of Fr. Ḥardīnī written by Fr. Ni'matallāh Al-Kafrī and a life of Fr. Charbel by the same Tanūs Shiblī.
12. Daher, *Vie, survie et prodiges*, pp. 111–36; Hayek, *Le chemin du désert*, pp. 153–62. Nasri Riscallah and Gilles Phabrey, *Charbel Makhlouf* (Paris: Spes, 1950), pp. 9–34, 151–81, has borne witness to the atmosphere in Lebanon and the Lebanese

diaspora in 1950. There was a new edition of this work (Paris: A. D. L. P., 1954) with minor modifications. It was plagiarised by Jean-Pierre Haddad, *Charbel: Un saint du Liban* (Paris: Adrien Maisonneuve, 1978), with an introduction by René de Castries, of the Académie Française.

13. Daher, *Vie, survie et prodiges*, p. 136. See also ibid. p. 103 (articles published in *La Revue Nouvelle*, April 1951) and p. 138 (articles published in *Témoignage Chrétien* and *Vie Spirituelle*, April 1951, and in *La Croix*, March 1953). Riscallah and Phabrey have mentioned articles from *Le Soir* of Beirut, the *Revue du Liban* and the *Figaro* (concerning a miracle at Lourdes, at the same time): *Charbel Makhlouf*, pp. 26, 88.
14. Shiblī, *Al-Āb Sharbal Makhlūf*, p. 2; Riscallah and Phabrey, *Charbel Makhlouf*, introductory note; Hayek, *Le chemin du désert*, pp. 15–17, 138–39; Daher, *Vie, survie et prodiges*, p. 101.
15. André Vauchez, *La sainteté en Occident aux derniers siècles du Moyen Age, d'après les procès de canonisation et les documents hagiographiques* (Rome: École française de Rome, 1981); Jean-Michel Sallmann, *Naples et ses saints à l'âge baroque 1540–1750* (Paris: PUF, 1994); [Bernard Heyberger, *Hindiyya, Mystic and Criminal, 1720–1798: A Political and Religious Crisis in Lebanon* (Cambridge: James Clarke & Co., 2013)].
16. According to his hagiographers, Saint Charbel distinguished himself particularly by his absolute respect for the monastic vows (poverty, chastity, obedience), which gave rise to detailed developments in almost all the books: Shiblī, *Al-Āb Sharbal Makhlūf*, pp. 18–19; Carame (ed.), *Deux religieux Maronites*, pp. 31–32; Daher, *Vie, survie et prodiges*, pp. 47–71; Daher, *Charbel: Un homme ivre de Dieu*, pp. 80–84 (on pp. 55–58, there is a flattering presentation of the order of Lebanese monks, as the heirs of the Maronite monastic tradition); Saadé, *Charbel: El gran santo del siglo XX*, pp. 111–40; Hayek, *Le chemin du désert*, pp. 89–97.
17. Paul Sfeir, *Les ermites dans l'Église maronite: Histoire et spiritualité* (Kaslik: Université Saint-Esprit, 1986), pp. 121–81.
18. 'Dans ou hors de la perspective du schéma XIII: La béatification du P. Charbel Makhlouf', *Irenikon*, 38 (1965), pp. 547–48. Quote taken from Elisabeth Behr-Sigel, *Prière et sainteté dans l'Église russe* (Paris: Cerf, 1950), p. 32.
19. Paul Daher, 'A Testimony to the Interior Life of Father Charbel Makhlouf, Monk of the Order of St Anthony the Great of the M. Monks in the Lebanon', *Eastern Churches Review*, 10, 1–2 (1978), 106; 'Dans ou hors de la perspective du schéma XIII'; Arthur Vööbus, *History of Asceticism: Early Monasticism in Persia* (Louvain: Secrétariat du CSCO, 1958); André-Jean Festugière, *Les moines d'Orient*, 4 volumes in 7 tomes (Paris: Cerf, 1961–65); Jacques Lacarrière, *Les hommes ivres de Dieu* (Paris: Arthaud, 1961); Jules Leroy, *Moines et monastères du Proche-Orient* (Paris: Horizons de France, 1958). Daher, *Charbel: Un homme ivre de Dieu*, appeared for the first time in 1965, with a new edition in 1993. To be compared also with the contemporary hagiographic activity of the Copts: Brigitte Voile, 'Hagiographie et communauté coptes au XXe siècle: Naissance d'un courant editorial', in Rachida Chih and Denis Gril (eds), *Le saint et son milieu ou comment lire les sources hagiographiques* (Cairo: Ifao, 2000), pp. 187–201.

20. Hayek, *Le chemin du désert*, pp. 9–10; for ancient monasticism, see pp. 61–70, 108, 111–14.
21. 'Allocution de Sa Sainteté le Pape Paul VI, lors de la béatification de Charbel Makhlouf' appeared in *L'Osservatore Romano*, 5–6 December 1965, published in *Collectanea Cisterciensia*, 28 (1966), pp. 73–74. The expression was used again in 1977, at the canonisation: 'Allocution de Sa Sainteté le Pape Paul VI lors de la canonisation de Saint Charbel Makhlouf', *L'Osservatore Romano*, 10–11 October 1977, quoted by Sfeir, *Les ermites dans l'Église maronite*, p. xiv.
22. Daher, *Vie, survie et prodiges*, p. 103, quote from Father Youakim Moubarac, appeared in the *Revue Nouvelle*, April 1951; Hayek, *Le chemin du désert*, pp. 152–53.
23. See Paul VI's homily at the canonisation, on 9 October 1977, in Daher, *Charbel: Un homme ivre de Dieu*, pp. 167–70.
24. 'Dans ou hors de la perspective du schéma XIII'.
25. Hayek, *Le chemin du désert*, pp. 112–14.
26. Maurice Barrès, *Une enquête aux pays du Levant*, in *L'œuvre de Maurice Barrès*, vol. 11 (Paris: Plon, 1923): see the dedication 'À Monsieur l'abbé Henri Bremond', pp. 101–3, and the chapter on Hindiyya, 'La religieuse du Liban', pp. 177–87.
27. Hayek, *Le chemin du désert*, pp. 143–45.
28. The introduction of the Maronite bishop of Mexico to the most recent book in our corpus, that of Saadé, *Charbel: El gran santo del siglo XX*, pp. 11–12, has warned against the '*mercadotecnica*' based on writings that make Charbel '*un prestigioso exhibidor de milagros*' and congratulated the author, who was writing especially for Latin America, for remedying this situation by favouring 'the ascensional movement' in the life of the saint.
29. The 'latinised' character of Charbel, associated with a 'mode of life' in accordance with the Eastern monastic tradition, has clearly been emphasised by D. Bede Winslow, as quoted in Allen Maloof, 'A New Maronite Saint: Fr. Charbel Makhlouf', *Eastern Churches Review*, 10, 1–2 (1978), p. 101.
30. Hayek, *Le chemin du désert*, has referred to Thérèse several times: pp. 47, 131, 171. Mention of Charles de Foucauld in Daher, *Vie, survie et prodiges*, pp. 68, 138; Daher, *Charbel: Un homme ivre de Dieu*, pp. 70, 109, 116; Carame (ed.), *Deux religieux maronites*, p. 6. The year in which the first article on Charbel appeared, the review *Al-Mashriq* also published a text on Monsieur de Chasteuil, a French hermit in Lebanon (1634–44) and on Charles de Foucauld: Butrus Sāra, 'Habīs fransawī fī Lubnān: al-masyū Franswā dī Shastuwīl (1634–1644)', *Al-Mashriq* (1922), pp. 571–76, 649–59; Fardīnān Tawtal [Ferdinand Taoutel], 'Rasūl al-Sahrā', al-āb Sharl dī Fūkū', *Al-Mashriq* (1922), pp. 991–1006.
31. Daher, *Vie, survie et prodiges*, p. 27.
32. Daher, *Charbel: Un homme ivre de Dieu*, p. 102.
33. Shiblī, *Al-Āb Sharbal Makhlūf*, p. 18; Carame (ed.), *Deux religieux maronites*, p. 31; Daher, *Vie, survie et prodiges*, p. 76; Riscallah and Phabrey, *Charbel Makhlouf*, p. 107.
34. Daher, *Vie, survie et prodiges*, pp. 65–66; Philippe Boutry, *Prêtres et paroisses au pays du curé d'Ars* (Paris: Cerf, 1986); Marcel Launay, *Le bon prêtre: Le clergé rural au XIXe siècle* (Paris: Aubier, 1986).

35. Shiblī, *Al-Āb Sharbal Makhlūf,* p. 17. See ibid. p. 176, a copy of the image of the Virgin of the Rosary before which Charbel used to kneel in his hermitage: the image bears an inscription in French. Daher, *Vie, survie et prodiges,* pp. 56, 63–64; Daher, *Charbel: Un homme ivre de Dieu,* pp. 44–45, 76, 88–89; Hayek, *Le chemin du désert,* pp. 50–51, 108, 122. Concerning Marian devotion, the authors have based their remarks on Joseph Goudard, *La Sainte Vierge au Liban* (Paris: 1908).
36. Daher, *Charbel: Un homme ivre de Dieu,* p. 37; Saadé, *Charbel: El gran santo del siglo XX,* pp. 39–41, 44. This idyllic image of rural life was put into pictures in the naïve style by the painter Joseph Alam, in the saint's birthplace in Biqaʿkafrā. These pictures have often been copied. Concerning the idealisation of the countryside, see Pierre Pierrard, *La vie quotidienne du prêtre français au XIXe siècle 1801–1905* (Paris: Hachette, 1986), pp. 193–95.
37. Hayek, *Le chemin du désert,* p. 45.
38. Daher, *Charbel: Un homme ivre de Dieu,* p. 37. A strong insistence on the role of the mother in Saadé, *Charbel: El gran santo del siglo XX,* pp. 46, 81–82. Concerning the role of the mother and the clerical uncles in the awakening of his vocation, Charbel's case can be related to a more general case: Boutry, *Prêtres et paroisses,* pp. 192–98; like the Curé d'Ars, he refused to kiss his mother.
39. Hayek, *Le chemin du désert,* p. 47.
40. Daher, *Charbel: Un homme ivre de Dieu,* p. 42. The author has explicitly referred to the lack of knowledge of the Curé d'Ars (p. 100). But the layman Nasri Riscallah was more attached to the quality of the studies and has thus suggested a different version of Charbel's education: Riscallah and Phabrey, *Charbel Makhlouf,* pp. 39, 98–101.
41. [Chrétien Dehaisnes (ed.)], *Les Marounites, d'après le manuscrit arabe du R. P. Azar, Vicaire-Général de Saïda (Terre Sainte), délégué du patriarche d'Antioche et de la Nation Marounite* (Cambrai: F. Deligne et E. Lesne, 1852), pp. 79–87. See also Nicolas Murad, *Notice historique sur l'origine de la nation maronite et sur ses rapports avec la France, sur la nation druze et sur les diverses populations du Mont Liban,* translated into Arabic and edited by Joseph Moawad and Antoine Kawal (Paris: Cariscript, 1988); the French text was first published in 1844. [On this issue, see Bernard Heyberger, 'La France et la protection des chrétiens maronites: Généalogie d'une représentation', *Relations internationales,* 173, 1 (2018), pp. 13–30].
42. Robert B. Campbell, 'The Devil and Devilry in Some Arabic Fiction at the Turn of the Century', in Angelika Neuwirth, Birgit Embalo, Sebastian Günther and Maher Jarrar (eds), *Myths, Historical Archetypes and Symbolic Figures in Arabic Literature: Towards a New Hermeneutic Approach* (Stuttgart: Steiner in Komm., 1999), pp. 295–99.
43. Zeev Sternhell, *Maurice Barrès et le nationalisme français* (Paris: Fayard, 2000).
44. Hayek, *Le chemin du désert,* pp. 47, 18. The book by Saadé, *Charbel: El gran santo del siglo XX,* which was aimed at emigrants who had maybe never seen Lebanon, devoted passion-filled pages to the country; see pp. 34–43.
45. Daher, *Vie, survie et prodigies,* p. 12: 'Nous allons sur la mer inchangée, au pied des montagnes, qui, sous le soleil éternel, vêtues des mêmes ombres et des mêmes lumières, sont toujours pleines d'invocations divines . . .' Barrès' quote

is associated with one by Michel Chiha concerning the Phoenicians. The same reference to Barrès has appeared in Hayek, *Le chemin du désert*, p. 21. Ernest Renan has been recalled in the following pages.

46. Riscallah and Phabrey, *Charbel Makhlouf*, p. 79: 'Tant de milliers d'adorateurs ont caressé de leurs regards toutes ces merveilles, qu'on peut se demander s'ils n'ont pas laissé un peu de leur âme dans cette nature qui continue à vivre et à chanter'. [On Barrès and Lebanon, see Heyberger, *Hindiyya, Mystic and Criminal*, pp. 216–18.] A 'scientific' explanation of this theory of the continuity of the sacred in a place is provided by Charles Velay, *Le culte et les fêtes d'Adônis-Thammouz dans l'Orient antique* (Paris: Ernest Leroux, 1904). The author has quoted Renan, but also Jules Soury, proponent of physiological determinism and one of Barrès' mentors.
47. Daher, *Vie, survie et prodiges*, pp. 19, 45; Daher, *Charbel: Un homme ivre de Dieu*, p. 101. The comparison with Bethlehem was used again by Saadé, *Charbel: El gran santo del siglo XX*, p. 38.
48. Daher, *Charbel: Un homme ivre de Dieu*, p. 36; Hayek, *Le chemin du désert*, p. 30; Saadé, *Charbel: El gran santo del siglo XX*, p. 38.
49. Hayek, *Le chemin du désert*, pp. 39–41.
50. Daher, *Charbel: Un homme ivre de Dieu*, p. 57. Hayek, *Le chemin du désert*, pp. 50–51, has recalled the massacre of Qadīsha in the thirteenth century, then that of Dayr Al-Qamar in 1860.
51. Hayek, *Le chemin du désert*, p. 45; Daher, *Charbel: Un homme ivre de Dieu*, p. 57; Daher, *Vie, survie et prodiges*, pp. 1, 33, 44; Riscallah and Phabrey, *Charbel Makhlouf*, pp. 78–79.
52. Daher, *Vie, survie et prodiges*, p. 23; Daher, *Charbel: Un homme ivre de Dieu*, p. 42; Riscallah and Phabrey, *Charbel Makhlouf*, pp. 100–1; Hayek, *Le chemin du désert*, pp. 48, 72. ʿAwwād, *Baraka ʿan Qabr al-Qadīs Sharbal*, p. 15, is an exception, as he has specified that Charbel, as the first in his village and then in the seminary, had been taught in Arabic and in Syriac. [On the issue of language among the Maronites, see Aurélien Girard, 'La construction de l'identité confessionnelle maronite à l'époque ottoman (XVIe–XVIIIe siècle)', in Bernard Heyberger (ed.), *Les chrétiens de tradition syriaque à l'époque ottomane* (Paris: Geuthner, 2020), pp. 153–200.]
53. Hayek, *Le chemin du désert*, p. 37.
54. Ibid. pp. 37–38. This time the remarks refer to Charles Péguy.
55. Daher, *Charbel: Un homme ivre de Dieu*, p. 61; Saadé, *Charbel: El gran santo del siglo XX*, p. 149; Maloof, 'A new Maronite saint: Fr. Charbel Makhlouf', pp. 101–3; Būlus Ḍāhir [Paul Daher], *Lubnān watan sukrān bi-Sharbal* (ʿAnnāyā: 1978), p. 14.
56. Hayek, *Le chemin du désert*, p. 101; Daher, *Charbel: Un homme ivre de Dieu*, p. 68, has recalled the monastery of ʿAnnāyā as a fortress.
57. Daher, *Vie, survie et prodiges*, p. 44.
58. Ibid. p. 45.
59. Ibid. pp. 102, 123, 137; Riscallah and Phabrey, *Charbel Makhlouf*, pp. 16–18, 88; Ḍāhir, *Lubnān watan sukrān bi-Sharbal*, p. 16.
60. Daher, *Vie, survie et prodiges*, pp. 44–45.

61. Riscallah and Phabrey, *Charbel Makhlouf*, pp. 75–76. The book has also mentioned the fact that the Syrian authorities tried to stop their citizens from crossing the border and that the pilgrims forced their way through the roadblocks (p. 23).
62. One finds them, for example, in the speeches of Bachir Gemayel, which often referred to historical identity: Selim Abou, *Béchir Gemayel ou l'esprit d'un peuple* (Paris: Anthropos, 1984), passim. See especially Bachir's last speech (Monastery of the Holy Cross, 14 September 1982), pp. 407–15. I have borrowed his expression 'political maronitism' (p. 412). See also Saadé, *Charbel: El gran santo del siglo XX*, p. 110: 'la Marunidad es artífice de tesoros inmensos de civilización humana, de cultura y, sobre todo, de santidad'.
63. Ḍāhir, *Lubnān watan sukrān bi-Sharbal.*
64. Ibid. pp. 27, 70, 114, 185–86, 188, 192.
65. Ibid. p. 195.
66. Ibid. p. 30.
67. Ibid. p. 9. [For a thorough analysis of the historical thought of Yūsif Ibrahīm Yazbak, see Ahmed Beydoun, *Identité confessionnelle et temps social chez les historiens maronites contemporains* (Beirut: Librairie orientale, 1984), pp. 387–401.]
68. Ḍāhir, *Lubnān watan sukrān bi-Sharbal*, p. 7.

EPILOGUE

The Maestro and his Music

At first glance, Colmar seems an unlikely place for thinking about the Middle East. Mostly spared the violence of the French Revolution, its colourful homes, cobblestone streets and picturesque shops were allegedly the basis for Disney's version of *Beauty and the Beast*. Similarly, its museums and attractions all speak to the local circulation that connects Colmar to the region of Alsace and places further afield in Germany – for example, the Unterlinden Museum with its evocation of the Issenheim Altarpiece, as well as stunning works by Holbein, Cranach and Schongauer. Locals also celebrate the quaint, folkloric work of the artist 'Hansi', Jean-Jacques Waltz, whose characterful depictions of everyday life in Alsace are another reminder, if any was needed, of the distinctly local, regional spirits that animate the city of Colmar today.

It is perhaps strange, therefore, that Colmar has also gained for itself a certain global notoriety in recent years. Consider, for instance, that the city provided the setting for a widely popular Chinese reality show called *Chinese Restaurant*. With over 200 million viewers, the show offered an occasion for droves of tourists to visit Colmar, bringing with it the arrival – likely for the first time in the city's history – of the bilingual French-Chinese menus that one finds in some of its restaurants today. The city also hosts the annual Colmar International Festival, a celebration of classical music that gathers performers and audiences from around the world. Rich and varied therefore are the afterlives of a one-time provincial town in a supposedly 'global' age, with connections to the world that owe much to digital communications, the growing ease of transport and international fashions and patterns of consumption.

On a casual walk through Colmar, one might not suspect that the city's relevance also extends to the international role that it has played as a site for incredible transformations in the writing of Middle Eastern history, in particular the history of Christianity in the Middle East. For over the past three decades, Colmar has proven a *lieu de retour* for Bernard Heyberger, the scholar whose writings fill the pages of this volume. During a career that has carried him East and West, through Europe, the Middle East and America, to Paris and back over and over again, Heyberger's perambulations have always carried him eventually back home to Colmar. For this reason, the city unknowingly preserves a hidden history intimately linked to the career of a scholar who has spent much of his life writing and rewriting the local, connected and global histories of Eastern Christianity.

If the writings of a historian can be likened to the music of a composer, this volume stands as a testament to the creative and scholarly fruits of a lifetime of movement – intellectually, personally, geographically. Above all, it speaks to the refinement of a certain historical imagination and the development of a distinct, coherent and personal view of a period of Middle Eastern history that stretches from the fifteenth to the twenty-first century. Looking beyond the lengthy bibliography of works published by Heyberger, anyone who knows him understands that the metaphor of historian-as-composer actually falls short of capturing the way in which his works were never simply the product of a lone scholar who was content to publish and be read by his colleagues and students. Rather, his is a body of work that has effectively redirected the energies, agenda and efforts of an entire field of scholarship over three decades. In quiet, subtle ways, Heyberger has come to occupy a central role – the *bona fide* maestro of Colmar – busy for decades conducting, coordinating and setting the tone for an entire field of scholarship. This is clear to anyone who has witnessed for themselves the seminar over which he presided for so many years – the spirit of which is captured so beautifully in Heather Sharkey's preface to this volume – wherein the energies of one speaker after another seem time and time again to develop a set of themes, methods and histories, all of which were already present in Heyberger's 1993 doctoral thesis, *Les chrétiens du Proche-Orient au temps de la Réforme catholique*. In this way, his work has served as both a catalyst and an example to an entire community of scholars whose work he has touched and influenced in profound ways.

This volume itself stands as a sort of microhistory of the history of scholarship. On the one hand, the volume tells a general story of how a single individual scholar can transform an entire field of knowledge: through collaboration with colleagues and students, through the widest possible engagement with the historical record and through perseverance, patience and a discerning level of reflexivity about his own methodological approaches and theoretical frameworks. On the other hand, the volume offers a snapshot of the specific ways in which Heyberger's work in particular has come to shape how an entire field conceptualises and approaches the study of Middle Eastern Christianity today. Although it is impossible (and indeed undesirable) ever to impose any sort of contrived coherence on a set of works written across such a long period of time, in the short space that remains of this epilogue I want to identify a handful of distinctive qualities that provide a sort of continuity of interests, methods and preoccupations stretching across the entire body of Heyberger's work.

First, in the earliest publications included in this volume, we can already witness the distinctive way in which Heyberger sought to give shape to the lived experiences of Eastern Christians in the early modern world. Of course, there has long been an awareness of the various trajectories that carried different Eastern Christians to Europe, for example, as merchants, ecclesiastics and even scholarly Orientalists. However, what is so striking in his 1998 article on Timothy Agnellini is the extent to which he sought already early on in his work to get beyond facile typologies of these individuals. Instead, Heyberger's deft study of the faint traces that survive about Agnellini has demonstrated how multiple modes of belonging could assemble around the life of a single individual. In practice, this means recognising that what became both plausible and possible in the past – for example, in terms of Agnellini's experiences in Europe – can only be understood by exploring the intersection of several spheres of activity, ranging from religious networks to merchant interactions, from alms-collecting to academic Orientalism. As evoked in Agnellini's life – as well as in that of Ecchellensis, Ḥannā Diyāb, Hindiyya and many more – these practices fed off one another in dynamic and often unpredictable ways.

This is not to say that Heyberger's actors lacked agency. On the contrary, Heyberger's depiction of Eastern Christians in Europe have brought to life the extent to which contemporaries themselves were aware of and reacted to the variety of contexts and situations in which they found themselves. This approach retains particular relevance for a much larger body of work being produced today on dissimulation and identity formation. In contrast to binary constructions of identity as being either fixed or fluid, Heyberger's studies have placed the emphasis on larger themes, such as the quest for security, rootedness and survival. In this way, Heyberger's earliest contributions in this volume foreshadowed the skill with which his later works would bring to life the 'multiple possibilities' that lay at the heart of the lived experiences of Eastern Christians in early modern Europe. While tales of fraudsters and impostors may continue to delight readers today, Heyberger's work has consistently defied the facile, one-dimensional caricatures sometimes used to describe Eastern Christians in the early modern world, by contemporaries as much as some modern historians.

A second aspect of Heyberger's method that comes clearly across many of the works in this volume is his firm rejection of any simplistic views that religion could be the primary, or in some cases the only category of analysis used to understand Middle Eastern Christians. We might think of this approach as a sort of 'desacralisation', or an attempt to push back against the fetishisation of religion in the arsenal of tools used by historians to study the Middle East. Such a critical approach to religion may seem an obvious route today, but it cannot be underestimated how powerful and ahead of its time it was for Heyberger to warn, as he did in 1994, that 'we must avoid trying to separate the socio-economic sphere from the religious one'. This was the very moment when a wide range of scholars were placing religion at the forefront of their analysis of Middle Eastern societies, whether in the mournful accounts of 'what went wrong' by Bernard Lewis, or in area studies approaches that too quickly sought to explain all sorts of developments in the Middle Eastern past and present with reference to religious belief, whether in Islam or Christianity. In the context of decolonisation, such attempts to see religion as the primary agent of historical change sometimes appealed to and resonated with the sectarian claims of certain Middle Eastern governments who saw in a retreat to religion a useful way of advancing their own political and nationalist agendas. In place of these scholarly and political efforts, Heyberger's fine-grained studies (especially of 'security and insecurity') have rejected the fetishisation of religion and instead sought to recover a better sense of the ways in which confessional identity was often purposefully deployed by individuals across a range of social, economic and political spheres. This sensitivity to the indivisibility of religious, economic and political spheres in Heyberger's early work has become the hallmark of some of the most sophisticated studies of Ottoman and Middle Eastern history to date, many of which explicitly mention their debt to Heyberger for a vision of confessional identity that extends far beyond the boundaries of religion.

Thirdly, the vision of total history that emerges in this volume also manages to excavate a vision of Middle Eastern Christianity that is local, specific and rooted in the distinctive world of the multi-sited Ottoman Empire. Heyberger has always eschewed any superficial ideas of a monolithic 'Eastern Christianity', not least because of the way in which this idea – useful as it is in some contexts – also risks ignoring diversity across geography and change over time. Instead, Heyberger's method has reflected the practices of 'connected history' *avant la lettre*, particularly in its attention to the multiple contexts in which Eastern Christianity was thriving. This method achieved its finest fulfilment in his ground-breaking 2001 study *Hindiyya: Mystique et criminelle, 1720–1798*, which tells the story of an eighteenth-century charismatic Maronite nun. What stands out is the intricate way in which he placed Hindiyya in multiple contexts at once – that is, in close interaction with a wide variety of 'protagonists in this drama'. She is not simply a representative of 'Eastern Christianity' in the eighteenth century. Rather, he positioned her expertly and simultaneously within the social and political contexts of the Ottoman world and the complicated histories of families in Aleppo and Beirut, the mountainous geography of the Maronites, as well as in conversation with genres and traditions emerging within both Latin Christianity and Ottoman Syria. For Heyberger, the history of community identity in Eastern Christianity writ large is a hyper-local story of family, of kin, of geography and of economics, one that goes far beyond the theological boundaries that are so often the focus of an older generation of histories of Eastern Christianity.

Taken together, these three aspects combine to create a distinctive conceptual framework that connects all of Heyberger's writings. However, those who know this work well equally know that it is not only his method but also his materials that have transformed our understanding of the Eastern Christianity. Across this entire volume, one is struck by the combination of a rigorous, philological study of Eastern Christian sources in Arabic with the deep mining of European archives, especially the command of Catholic archives and the archives of the Propaganda Fide. Indeed, his first encounter with the Catholic archives for his 1993 dissertation shaped the vast tableau on which his subsequent writings would continue to add further texture, colour and shape, with new images of the past coming to the surface in the manner of a pointillist painting. It would be wrong to see in this method something as simple as a quest for documentary comprehensiveness; rather, the capacious archive of sources under study speaks to an attempt to capture a truly three-dimensional perspective on early modern Eastern Christians, as refracted through the multiple sites in which they lived.

The outcome of this approach to sources has had important implications for both the geography and chronology of Eastern Christianity that emerged in Heyberger's work. First, the wide range of sources at his disposal has transformed our understanding of the geographical frontiers of Eastern Christianity, taking us far from major centres such as Aleppo, Rome, or Paris and outwards to an uncharted and often surprising series of local spaces that have proven themselves vital to our understanding of Middle Eastern Christianity. Who could have dreamed that the history of Eastern Christianity would really carry us to the scene of a prison cell in Granada where Giovanni Sciain sat alone, worried and armed with little hope but his pile of forty-six patents? As a result, Heyberger's approach has paved the way for the unleashing of Eastern Christianity far beyond its traditional borders in the Middle East, as a whole generation of scholars knock on the doors of archives scattered around the world: a Swiss canton, a court in Malta, or a ship in Buenos Aires. These are the new spaces of Eastern Christianity that have emerged in the wake of Heyberger's scholarship.

Secondly, the immense set of sources under study by Heyberger has enabled him to paint a compelling vision of a 'long history' of Eastern Christianity, one that transcends the periodisation of late medieval, early modern and modern history. These period divisions are perhaps less pronounced in French scholarship, but even so the tendency towards specialisation has meant that most scholars of the nineteenth or twentieth century have tended not to consider the ways in which their subjects saw themselves in conversation with their seventeenth- and eighteenth-century ancestors. In contrast, this volume offers a compelling case for rejecting the periodisation inherited from a previous generation of Ottoman and Middle Eastern fields of scholarship. Moreover, the volume engages deeply with wider questions about modernity, the rise of the self and the ruptures of modernisation, in a way that serves as an antidote to some of the legacies of Orientalism which continue to slumber in some corners of Middle Eastern history.

Finally, this volume makes clear that a deep engagement with the global archives of Christianity and the close philological study of these sources need not detract from a close engagement with a range of theoretical frameworks. In fact, Heyberger's work has offered some of the finest (and pleasingly subtle) examples of microhistory, certainly in the field of Middle Eastern history. It is striking to note here that, when Heyberger does refer explicitly to the Italian school of *microstoria*, rather than Carlo Ginzburg, it tends to be Giovanni Levi whom he has conjured up in his own work. This is no surprise: Levi's is a form of microhistory that remains deeply rooted in social and economic history, less interested in a playful flirtation with clues and epistemology than with the task of reconstructing the social history of multiple possibilities of the past. Combine this microhistorical inclination with an interest in historical anthropology, and the extent to which Heyberger's research has sought to recover webs of meaning in the past becomes clear. In other words, in this volume we are presented over and over again with a vision of Eastern Christianity as seen on its own terms. These are terms created not in reference to social science theories or fashionable waves of cultural studies; rather, these terms are infused by the views of contemporaries. Reading his work is to feel as if in conversation with the dead – Michel Febvre, Laurent Arvieux, Hindiyya, Ḥannā Diyāb – a testament to how in the hands of a good historian even the silence of sources cannot stop us from hearing the voices of the past clearly and vividly.

Stepping back from these individual voices, we hear three distinct sounds coming through from the maestro of Colmar. First, his research offers an example of an empathetic scholarship that remains as acceptable, affirming and enriching to members of the community of Eastern Christianity as it is rigorous, stimulating and inspiring to academics working outside of these communities. It is a rare scholar who can be embraced in such a wide network of workshops and conferences – university, Church and media. This is also what makes him a unique historian of Middle Eastern Christianity who, even in discussions aimed at popular audiences, manages to steer clear of any lachrymose narratives of Middle Eastern history that are often so desired by the public. Second, long before the advent of interest in what some scholars have called 'place-based research', Heyberger's scholarship has offered an example of how to be deeply rooted in the region and how to ensure attention to issues of place in the writing of history. It is also a testament to the possibility of writing about a community in a way that engages with local scholars and community historians with respect, civility and in good faith. Finally, his work stands as an example of religious history that avoids the extremes of either apology or skepticism and, in doing so, facilitates a conversation about religion that is open to both believers and non-believers. It sees the Middle East not as some sort of museum where old faiths stand like dinosaurs in a world of reason. Rather, his work has brought to life the processes whereby Middle Eastern individuals, groups and families *became* religious in a way that was meaningful to them in the times and worlds in which they lived.

It is tempting to wonder whether the good folk of seventeenth-century Colmar ever set their sights on an Eastern Christian alms-collector. Until we find out, we can take some satisfaction in knowing that Colmar did play an important role in the history of Eastern Christianity in as much as Heyberger's work has quite simply set the agenda for the next generation of scholars. He has also managed to excavate a good deal of the raw material from which the future versions of this history will be written. For all that he has written of the limitation of sources, he has in fact managed from the silence of the sources to resurrect the cacophony of lived experiences, religious meanings and human emotions that animated the lives of a segment of people who – much like him – lived in constant movement. It is good that this volume should finally make his work available to a larger circle of readers in English. In this way, the maestro of Colmar and his music will continue to delight all those who encounter it, whether these audiences be new listeners, devoted fans, or simply neophytes in search of inspiration.

John-Paul Ghobrial
Holywell Manor, Oxford

Complete Bibliography of Bernard Heyberger (December 2021)

BOOKS

1. *Les chrétiens du Proche-Orient au temps de la Réforme catholique* (Rome: École française de Rome, **1994**), 665 p. (Bibliothèque des Écoles françaises d'Athènes et de Rome, 284).

1b. Second Edition: *Les chrétiens du Proche-Orient au temps de la Réforme catholique* (Rome: École Française de Rome, **2014**), xxix, 665 p. (Classiques-École française de Rome).

2. *Hindiyya, mystique et criminelle (1720–1798)* (Paris: Aubier, **2001**), 456 p. (Collection Historique).

2b. Arabic translation: *Hindiyya al-ṣufiyya al-āthima, 1720–1798: Azma dīniyya wa siyāsiyya fī Jabal Lubnān fī al-qarn al-thāmin ʿashar*, translated by Jān Hāshim (Beirut: Dar al-Nahār, **2010**).

2c. English translation: *Hindiyya, Mystic and Criminal, 1720–1798: A Political and Religious Crisis in Lebanon*, translated by Renée Champion (Cambridge: James Clarke & Co., **2013**), 322 p.

3. *Les chrétiens au Proche-Orient: De la compassion à la compréhension* (Paris: Payot, **2013**), 153 p. (Manuels Payot).

4. *Les chrétiens d'Orient* (Paris: PUF, **2017**), 128 p. (Que sais-je? 4050)

4b. Second Edition: *Les chrétiens d'Orient* (Paris: PUF, **2020**), 128 p. (Que sais-je? 4050)

4c. Romanian translation: *Creştinii din Orient*, translated by Aniela Siladi, edited by Ioana Feodorov (Cluj-Napoca: Editura Renaşterea, **2020**), 171 p.

EDITED VOLUMES

5. Bernard Heyberger (ed.), *L'Italie vue par les étrangers*, monographic issue of the *Bulletin de la Faculté des Lettres de Mulhouse*, 19 (**1995**), 217 p.
6. Meropi Anastassiadou and Bernard Heyberger (eds), *Figures anonymes, figures d'élite: Pour une anatomie de l'Homo ottomanicus* (Istanbul: Isis, **1999**), 212 p. (Travaux du CeRATO, 4).
7. Bernard Heyberger and Carsten Walbiner (eds), *Les Européens vus par les Libanais à l'époque ottomane* (Beirut: Orient-Institut der DMG; Würzburg: Ergon, **2002**), 244 p. (Beiruter Texte und Studien, 74).
8. Bernard Heyberger (ed.), *Chrétiens du monde arabe: Un archipel en terre d'Islam* (Paris: Autrement, **2003**), 271 p. (Collection Mémoires, 94).
9. Bernard Heyberger and Silvia Naef (eds), *La multiplication des images en pays d'Islam: De l'estampe à la télévision (17e-21e siècle)* (Istanbul: Orient-Institut der DMG; Würzburg: Ergon, **2003**), 328 p. (Istanbuler Texte und Studien, 2) [Republished in 2016].
10. Catherine Mayeur-Jaouen and Bernard Heyberger (eds), *Le corps et le sacré en Orient musulman,* monographic issue of the *Revue des mondes musulmans et de la Méditerranée*, 113–14 (**2006**), 383 p.
11. Bernard Heyberger and Chantal Verdeil (eds), *Hommes de l'entre-deux: Parcours individuels et portraits de groupe sur la frontière méditerranéenne* (Paris: Les Indes Savantes, **2009**), 349 p. (Rivages des Xantons).
12. Bernard Heyberger, Mercedes García-Arenal, Emanuele Colombo and Paola Vismara (eds), *L'Islam visto da Occidente: Cultura e religione del Seicento europeo di fronte all'Islam* (Milan: Marietti 1820, **2009**), xix, 356 p.
13. Bernard Heyberger (ed.), *Orientalisme, science et controverse: Abraham Ecchellensis (1605–1664)* (Turnhout: Brepols, **2010**), 240 p. (Bibliothèque de l'École des Hautes Études, Sciences Religieuses, 143).
14. Bernard Heyberger and Rémy Madinier (eds), *L'Islam des marges: Mission chrétienne et espaces périphériques du monde musulman XVIe–XXe siècles* (Paris: IISMM; Karthala, **2011**), 288 p. (Terres et gens d'Islam).
15. Bernard Heyberger and Albrecht Fuess (eds), *La frontière méditerranéenne du XVe au XVIIe siècle: Conflits, circulations, échanges* (Turnhout: Brepols, **2013**), 412 p. (Études Renaissantes, 12).
16. Hanna Dyâb, *D'Alep à Paris: Les pérégrinations d'un jeune Syrien au temps de Louis XIV*, translated and edited by Paule Fahmé-Thiéry, Bernard Heyberger and Jérôme Lentin, with a preface by Bernard Heyberger (Arles: Actes Sud, **2015**), 440 p. (Sindbad).
17. Bernard Heyberger and Aurélien Girard (eds), *Chrétiens au Proche-Orient*, monographic section of *Archives de sciences sociales des religions*, 171 (**2015**), pp. 11–208.

18. Bernard Heyberger, Valérie Assan and Jakob Vogel (eds), *Minorités en Méditerranée au XIXe siècle: Identités, identifications, circulations* (Rennes: Presses Universitaires de Rennes, **2019**), 284 p. (Histoire).
19. Bernard Heyberger (ed.), *Les chrétiens de tradition syriaque à l'époque ottomane* (Paris: Geuthner, **2020**), 262 p. (Études Syriaques, 17).
20. Nadine Amsler, Andreea Badea, Bernard Heyberger and Christian Windler (eds), *Catholic Missionaries in Early Modern Asia: Patterns of Localization* (London, New York: Routledge, **2020**), 280 p.
21. Ioana Feodorov, Bernard Heyberger and Samuel Noble (eds.), *Arabic Christians between Ottoman Levant and Eastern Europe* (Leiden: Brill, **2021**), 381 p. (Arabic Christianity, 3).

ARTICLES IN ACADEMIC JOURNALS

22. 'Les chrétiens d'Alep (Syrie) à travers les récits des conversions des missionnaires carmes déchaux (1657–1681)', *Mélanges de l'École française de Rome: Moyen-Âge, temps modernes*, 100, 1 (**1988**), pp. 461–99.
23. 'Entre Byzance et Rome: L'image et le sacré au Proche-Orient au XVIIe siècle', *Histoire, économie et société*, 4 (**1989**), pp. 527–50.
24. 'Le catholicisme tridentin au Levant (XVIIe–XVIIIe siècles)', *Mélanges de l'École française de Rome: Italie et Méditerranée*, 101, 2 (**1989**), pp. 897–909.
25. 'Terre Sainte et mission au XVIIe siècle', *Dimensioni e problemi della ricerca storica*, 2 (**1994**), pp. 127–53.
26. 'Se convertir à l'Islam chez les chrétiens de Syrie', in Lucetta Scaraffia and Anna Foa (eds), *Conversioni nel Mediterraneo,* special issue of *Dimensioni e problemi della ricerca storica*, 2 (**1996**), pp. 133–52.
27. 'Un nouveau modèle de conscience individuelle et de comportement social: Les confréries d'Alep (XVIIIe–XIXe siècle)', *Parole de l'Orient*, 21 (**1996**), pp. 271–83.
28. '*Pro nunc, nihil respondendum*: Recherche d'informations et prise de décision à la Propagande: L'exemple du Levant (XVIIIe siècle)', special issue of *Mélanges de l'École française de Rome: Italie et Méditerranée*, 109, 2 (**1997**), pp. 539–54.
29. 'Sainteté et chemins de la perfection chez les chrétiens du Proche-Orient (XVIIe–XVIIIe siècles)', *Revue de l'histoire des religions*, 215, 1 (**1998**), pp. 117–37.
30. 'Livres et pratique de la lecture chez les chrétiens (Syrie, Liban), XVIIe–XVIIIe siècles', in Frédéric Hitzel (ed.), *Livres et lecture dans le monde ottoman*, monographic issue of *Revue des mondes musulmans et de la Méditerranée*, 87–88 (**1999**), pp. 209–23.

31. 'La carrière manquée d'un ecclésiastique oriental en Italie: Timothée Karnûsh, archevêque syrien catholique de Mardin', in Bernard Heyberger (ed.), *L'Italie vue par les étrangers*, monographic issue of *Bulletin de la Faculté des Lettres de Mulhouse*, 19 (**1995**), pp. 31–47.
31b. Italian translation: 'La carriera mancata di un ecclesiastico orientale in Italia: Timoteo Karnush, arcivescovo siriano cattolico di Mardîn', *Incontri Mediterranei*, 2, 1–2 (**2001**), pp. 9–16.
32. 'Le Gymnase de Strasbourg à travers ses commémorations: Quatre siècles et demi sur une frontière politique et culturelle (1538–1988)', *Histoire de l'éducation*, 97 (**2003**), pp. 3–36.
33. 'Pour une "histoire croisée" de l'occidentalisation et de la confessionnalisation chez les chrétiens du Proche-Orient', *The MIT Electronic Journal of Middle Eastern Studies* 3 (**2003**), pp. 36–49.
34. 'Les nouveaux horizons méditerranéens des chrétiens du *bilād al-šām* (XVIIe–XVIIIe siècle)', *Arabica*, 51, 4 (**2004**), pp. 435–61.
35. 'Les transformations du jeûne chez les chrétiens orientaux', in Catherine Mayeur-Jaouen and Bernard Heyberger (eds), *Le corps et le sacré en Orient musulman*, monographic issue of the *Revue des mondes musulmans et de la Méditerranée*, 113–14 (**2006**), pp. 267–85.
36. 'Les relations entre chrétiens et musulmans: Chassés-croisés d'images', *Bulletin de la Société Suisse Moyen Orient et Civilisation islamique*, 26 (**2008**), pp. 14–19.
37. 'Pratiques religieuses et lieux de culte partagés entre islam et christianisme (autour de la Méditerranée)', *Archives de sciences sociales des religions*, 149 (**2010**), pp. 273–83.
38. 'Eastern Christians, Islam and the West: A Connected History', *International Journal of Middle Eastern Studies* 42 (**2010**), pp. 475–78.
39. 'Conclusions: Raison et volonté, contrainte et accommodement dans les conceptions catholiques de la conversion', in Marina Caffiero (ed.), *Forzare le anime: Conversioni tra libertà e costrizione in età moderna*, monographic issue of *Rivista di Storia del Cristianesimo*, 7, 1 (**2010**), pp. 139–48.
40. 'L'islam et les Arabes chez un apologiste catholique du XVIIe siècle', *Al-Qantara*, 31, 2 (**2010**), pp. 481–512.
41. 'Dhimmî-s dans la société ottomane (XVIe–XIXe siècles)', *Diasporas: Histoire et sociétés*, 16 (**2010**), pp. 45–50.
42. 'Préface', in Karène Sanchez-Summerer (ed.), *Langue française, identité(s) et école(s): Le cas de la minorité catholique au Levant (milieu XIXe–XXe siècles)*, monographic issue of *Documents pour l'histoire du français langue étrangère ou seconde*, 45 (**2010**), pp. 9–14.
43. 'Partage du sacré et compétition confessionnelle entre chrétiens et musulmans (Méditerranée orientale)', *Giornale di Storia*, 7 (**2011**), online journal: <https://www.giornaledistoria.net/saggi/articoli/partage-

du-sacre-et-competition-confessionnelle-entre-chretiens-et-musulmans-mediterranee-orientale/>.

44. 'Polemic Dialogues between Christians and Muslims in the Seventeenth Century', *Journal of the Economic and Social History of the Orient*, 55 (**2012**), pp. 495–516.

45. 'De l'ambiguïté en Islam: Notes critiques (à propos de Thomas Bauer, *Die Kultur der Ambiguität: Eine andere Geschichte des Islams*, Berlin, Verlag der Weltreligionen, 2011, 462 p.)', *Revue de l'histoire des religions*, 229, 3 (**2012**), pp. 403–12

45b. English translation: 'On Ambiguity in Islam – Critical Notes', *Revue de l'histoire des religions*, 229, 3 (**2012**), online: <https://www.cairn-int.info/journal-revue-de-l-histoire-des-religions-2012-3-page-403.htm>.

46. 'De l'histoire ecclésiastique à l'histoire connectée: Les chrétiens orientaux, l'Islam et l'Occident', in Noureddine Amara, Candice Raymond and Jihane Sfeir (eds), *Écritures historiennes du Maghreb et du Machrek: Approches critiques*, special issue of *NAQD*, Hors-série 3, 2 (**2014**), pp. 173–90.
46b. Arabic translation: 'Min al-taʾrīkh al-kanisī ilā al-taʾrīkh al-mutarābiṭ: Al-masīḥiyyūn al-sharqiyyūn wa-l-Islām wa-l-Mashriq [*sic*]', *NAQD*, Hors-série 3, 2 (**2014**), pp. 149–58.

47. 'L'Orient et l'islam dans l'érudition européenne du XVIIe siècle', *XVIIe siècle*, 268, 3 (**2015**), pp. 495–508.

48. [with Aurélien Girard] 'Chrétiens au Proche-Orient: Les nouvelles conditions d'une présence', *Archives de sciences sociales des religions*, 171 (**2015**), pp. 11–35.

49. 'La France et la protection des chrétiens maronites: Généalogie d'une représentation', *Relations internationales*, 173, 1 (**2018**), pp. 12–30.

50. 'Le renouveau de l'image de religion chez les chrétiens orientaux', *Archives de sciences sociales des religions*, 183 (**2018**), pp. 191–205.

51. 'A Border Crossing Ottoman Christian at the Beginning of the 18th Century: Hanna Dyâb of Aleppo and his Account of his Travel to Paris', in Serena Di Nepi and Felicita Tramontana (eds), *Contacts on the Move*, monographic section of *Studi e Materiali di Storia delle Religioni*, 84, 2 (**2018**), pp. 548–64.

52. 'De L'Europe des dévots à la Syrie des dévots: Un parcours', in *L'histoire en héritage: Louis Châtellier, François Roth: Hommages*, monographic issue of *Annales de l'Est*, 1 (**2018**), pp. 17–29.

53. 'Préface: Un retour en scène des "Chrétiens d'Orient" (1980–2020)', in Jérôme Bocquet (ed.), *La France et les 'chrétiens d'Orient': Écrire une histoire dépassionnée*, monographic issue of *Cahiers d'EMAM*, 32 (**2020**), online: <https://journals.openedition.org/emam/2364>.

54. 'Le christianisme oriental à l'époque ottomane: Du postcolonial au global (1960–2020)', *Annales: Histoire, sciences sociales*, 76, 2 (**2021**), pp. 301–37.

55. 'Les frères mineurs de la Terre sainte entre régime ottoman et Réforme catholique (XVIIe-début XIXe siècle)', in *1219–2019: Saint-François et le Sultan: Fécondité d'une rencontre?* monographic issue of *Études franciscaines*, 14, 2 (**2021**), pp. 309–28.

BOOK CHAPTERS

56. 'Missions (époque moderne)', in *Dictionnaire Historique de la Papauté* (Paris: Fayard, **1994**), pp. 1115–20.
57. 'Eudistes', in Lucien Bely (ed.), *Dictionnaire de l'Ancien Régime* (Paris: PUF, **1996**), p. 522.
58. 'Missions', in Lucien Bely (ed.), *Dictionnaire de l'Ancien Régime* (Paris: PUF, **1996**), pp. 839–41.
59. 'Pèlerinages', in Lucien Bely (ed.), *Dictionnaire de l'Ancien Régime* (Paris: PUF, **1996**), p. 980.
60. 'Réforme catholique et union des Églises orientales (XVIe–XVIIIe siècles)', *Homo religiosus: Autour de Jean Delumeau* (Paris: Fayard, **1997**), pp. 292–98.
61. 'Les chrétientés du Proche-Orient', in Jean-Marie Mayeur, Charles and Luce Pietri, André Vauchez and Marc Venard (eds), *Histoire du christianisme*, vol. 10: Bernard Plongeron (ed.), *Le défi de la modernité (1750–1840)* (Paris: Desclée, **1997**), pp. 150–62.
62. 'Les chrétiens arabes et l'idéologie de la croisade (XVIIe–XVIIIe siècles)', in Edgar Weber (ed.), *De Toulouse à Tripoli: Itinéraires de cultures croisées* (Toulouse: AMAM, **1997**), pp. 221–36.
63. 'Sécurité et insécurité: Les chrétiens de Syrie dans l'espace méditerranéen (XVIIe–XVIIIe siècles)', in Meropi Anastassiadou and Bernard Heyberger (eds), *Figures anonymes, figures d'élite: Pour une anatomie de l'Homo ottomanicus* (Istanbul: Isis, **1999**), pp. 147–63.
64. 'La place des non-musulmans: Les chrétiens", in Jean-Claude Garcin (ed.), *États, sociétés et cultures du monde musulman médiéval (Xe–XVe siècle)*, vol. 3: *Problèmes et perspectives de recherche* (Paris: PUF, **1999**), pp. 145–63.
65. 'Entre Orient et Occident: La religion des dévotes d'Alep', in Louis Châtellier (ed.), *Religions en transition dans la seconde moitié du XVIIIe siècle* (Oxford: Voltaire Foundation, **2000**), pp. 171–85.
66. 'Taṭawur Kathlaka fī al-Sharq (Al-Qarn al-sādis ʿashar–al-qarn al-tāsi ʿashar)' [The Development of Catholicism in the East (16th–19th centuries)], in Habīb Badr, Suʿād Slim and Jūzīf Abū Nuhra (eds), *Al-Masīḥiyya ʿabr taʾrīkhihā fī al-Mashriq* [Christianity through its History in the West] (Beirut: Majlis Kanāʾis al-Sharq al-Awṣat, **2001**), pp. 631–54.
67. 'Frontières confessionnelles et conversions chez les chrétiens orientaux', in Mercedes García-Arenal (ed.), *Conversions islamiques: Identités religieuses en*

Islam méditerranéen/Islamic Conversions: Religious Identities in Mediterranean Islam (Paris: Maisonneuve & Larose; European Science Foundation, **2001**), pp. 245–58.

68. 'Les Européens vus par les Libanais à l'époque ottomane', in Bernard Heyberger and Carsten Walbiner (eds), *Les Européens vus par les Libanais à l'époque ottomane* (Beirut: Orient-Institut der DMG; Würzburg: Ergon, **2002**), pp. 1–22.
69. 'Saint Charbel Makhlouf, ou la consécration de l'identité Maronite', in Catherine Mayeur-Jaouen (ed.), *Saints et héros du Moyen-Orient contemporain* (Paris: Maisonneuve & Larose, **2002**), pp. 139–59.
70. 'Clercs et ascètes chrétiens du Proche-Orient', in Gilles Veinstein and Dominique Iogna-Prat (eds), *Histoires des hommes de Dieu dans l'islam et le christianisme* (Paris: Flammarion, **2003**), pp. 203–30.
71. 'Introduction', in Bernard Heyberger (ed.), *Chrétiens du monde arabe: Un archipel en terre d'Islam* (Paris: Autrement, **2003**), pp. 3–28.
72. 'Alep, capitale chrétienne (XVIIe–XIXe siècle)', in Bernard Heyberger (ed.), *Chrétiens du monde arabe: Un archipel en terre d'Islam* (Paris: Autrement, **2003**), pp. 49–67.
73. 'Un nouveau modèle: La dévote catholique?' in Bernard Heyberger (ed.), *Chrétiens du monde arabe: Un archipel en terre d'Islam* (Paris: Autrement, **2003**), pp. 187–207.
74. 'De l'image religieuse à l'image profane? L'essor de l'image chez les chrétiens de Syrie et du Liban', in Bernard Heyberger and Silvia Naef (eds.), *La multiplication des images en pays d'Islam (XVIIe–XXIe s.)* (Istanbul: Orient Institut der DMG, Würzburg: Egon, **2003**), pp. 31–56.
75. 'L'envie au couvent', in Fabrice Wilhelm (ed.), *L'envie et ses figurations littéraires: Colloque interdisciplinaire Littérature et psychanalyse, Mulhouse, 7–8 juin 2002* (Dijon: Éditions Universitaires de Dijon, **2005**), pp. 71–83.
76. 'L'écriture prophétique au service du charisme: Hindiyya 'Ujaymî, mystique maronite', in Louis Châtellier and Philippe Martin (eds), *L'Écriture du croyant* (Turnhout: Brepols, **2005**), pp. 151–62.
77. 'Politique et spiritualité du "Sacré-Cœur" en Syrie et au Liban (XVIIIe siècle)', in Marc Vénard and Dominique Julia (eds), *Sacralités, culture et dévotion: Bouquet offert à Marie-Hélène Froeschlé-Chopard* (Marseille: La Thune, **2005**), pp. 93–106.
78. 'Morale et confession chez les melkites d'Alep d'après une liste de péchés (fin XVIIe siècle)', in Geneviève Gobillot and Marie-Thérèse Urvoy (eds), *L'Orient chrétien dans l'empire musulman: Hommage au professeur Gérard Troupeau* (Paris: Éditions de Paris, **2005**), pp. 283–306.
79. 'Individualism and Political Modernity: Devout Catholic Women in Aleppo and Lebanon between the Seventeenth and the Nineteenth Centuries', in

Amira Sonbol (ed.), *Beyond the Exotic: Women's Histories in Islamic Societies* (New York: Syracuse University Press, **2005**), pp. 71–85.

80. 'The Development of Catholicism in the Middle East (16th–19th Century)', in Habib Badr, Souad Slim and Joseph Abou Nohra (eds), *Christianity: A History in the Middle East* (Beirut: Middle East Council of Churches, **2005**), pp. 631–54.
81. 'Die Rolle der orientalischen Christen bei der Vermittlung antisemitischer Stereotypen in die arabische Welt', in Dirk Ansorge (ed.), *Antisemitismus in Europa und in der arabischen Welt* (Paderborn: Bonifatius; Frankfurt am Main: Lembeck, **2006**), pp. 183–99.
82. [with Chantal Verdeil] 'Spirituality and Scholarship: The Holy Land in Jesuit Eyes (Seventeenth to Nineteenth Centuries)', in Heleen Murre-Van Den Berg (ed.), *New Faith in Ancient Lands: Western Missions in the Middle East in the Nineteenth and Early Twentieth Centuries* (Leiden: Brill, **2006**), pp. 19–41.
83. 'Charisme et politique chez les maronites (Liban, XVIIIe siècle)', in Henri Bresc, George Dagher and Christiane Veauvy (eds), *Politique et Religion en Méditerranée: Moyen âge et époque contemporaine* (Paris: Bouchène, **2008**), pp. 197–212.
84. 'Confréries, dévotions et société chez les chrétiens orientaux', in Bernard Dompnier and Paola Vismara (eds), *Confréries et dévotions dans la catholicité moderne (mi XVe–début XIXe siècle)* (Rome: École française de Rome, **2008**), pp. 225–41.
85. 'Barrès Maurice', in François Pouillon (ed.), *Dictionnaire des orientalistes de langue française* (Paris: IISMM; Karthala, **2008**), pp. 50–52.
85b. Second edition: 'Barrès Maurice', in François Pouillon (ed.), *Dictionnaire des orientalistes de langue française: Nouvelle édition revue et augmentée* (Paris: IISMM; Karthala, **2012**), pp. 57–58.
86. 'Du Mans Raphaël, Jacques Dutertre dit', in François Pouillon (ed.), *Dictionnaire des orientalistes de langue française* (Paris: IISMM; Karthala, **2008**), pp. 326–27.
86b. Second edition: 'Du Mans Raphaël, Jacques Dutertre dit', in François Pouillon (ed.), *Dictionnaire des orientalistes de langue française: Nouvelle édition revue et augmentée* (Paris: IISMM; Karthala, **2012**), pp. 348–50.
87. 'Febvre (ou Le Febvre, ou Lefebure) Michel, Justinien de Neuvy dit', in François Pouillon (ed.), *Dictionnaire des orientalistes de langue française* (Paris: IISMM; Karthala, **2008**), pp. 377–78.
87b. Second edition: 'Febvre (ou Le Febvre, ou Lefebure) Michel, Justinien de Neuvy dit', in François Pouillon (ed.), *Dictionnaire des orientalistes de langue française: Nouvelle édition revue et augmentée* (Paris: IISMM; Karthala, **2012**), pp. 401–2.

88. 'Jaussen Antonin', in François Pouillon (ed.), *Dictionnaire des orientalistes de langue française* (Paris: IISMM; Karthala, **2008**), pp. 515–17.
88b. Second edition: 'Jaussen Antonin', in François Pouillon (ed.), *Dictionnaire des orientalistes de langue française: Nouvelle édition revue et augmentée* (Paris: IISMM; Karthala, **2012**), pp. 548–50.

89. 'Nau Michel', in François Pouillon (ed.), *Dictionnaire des orientalistes de langue française* (Paris: IISMM; Karthala, **2008**), pp. 717–18.
89b. Second edition: 'Nau Michel', in François Pouillon (ed.), *Dictionnaire des orientalistes de langue française: Nouvelle édition revue et augmentée* (Paris: IISMM; Karthala, **2012**), pp. 761–62.

90. [with Sylvette Larzul] 'Simon Richard', in François Pouillon (ed.), *Dictionnaire des orientalistes de langue française* (Paris: IISMM; Karthala, **2008**), pp. 900–2.
90b. Second edition: [with Sylvette Larzul] 'Simon Richard', in François Pouillon (ed.), *Dictionnaire des orientalistes de langue française: Nouvelle édition revue et augmentée* (Paris: IISMM; Karthala, **2012**), pp. 957–59.

91. 'Inschriften und Malereien des Aleppo-Zimmers: Zeugnisse von Kulturangehörigkeit und konfessionneller Abgrenzung in Aleppo', in Julia Gonnella and Jens Kröger (eds), *Angels, Peonies, and Fabulous Creatures: The Aleppo Room in Berlin: International Symposium of the Museum für Islamische Kunst, Staatliche Museen zu Berlin 12.–14. April 2002* (Berlin: Museum für Islamische Kunst, **2008**), pp. 87–90.

92. 'Préface', in Laure Guirguis (ed.), *Conversions religieuses et mutations politiques en Égypte* (Paris: Non Lieu, **2008**), pp. 9–18.

93. 'L'islam dei missionari cattolici (Medio Oriente, Seicento)', in Bernard Heyberger, Mercedes García-Arenal, Emanuele Colombo and Paola Vismara (eds), *L'Islam visto da Occidente: Cultura e religione del Seicento europeo di fronte all'Islam* (Milan: Marietti 1820, **2009**), pp. 289–314.

94. 'Chrétiens orientaux dans l'Europe catholique (XVIIe–XVIIIe siècles)', in Bernard Heyberger and Chantal Verdeil (eds), *Hommes de l'entre-deux: Parcours individuels et portraits de groupe sur la frontière méditerranéenne* (Paris: Les Indes Savantes, **2009**), pp. 61–94.

95. 'Presentazione', in Paolo Pieraccini (ed.), *Acta S. Congregationis de Propaganda Fide pro Terra Sancta: Parte III (1847–1851)* (Milan: Edizioni Terra Santa, **2009**), pp. vii–x.

96. 'La rencontre problématique de l'Islam avec les Lumières', in Louis Châtellier, Claude Langlois and Jean-Paul Willaime (eds), *Lumières, Religions et Laïcité: Rencontres historiques de Nancy, novembre 2005* (Paris: Riveneuve, **2009**), pp. 101–13.

97. 'Lieux saints', in André Vauchez (ed.), *Christianisme: Dictionnaire des temps, des lieux et des figures* (Paris: Seuil, **2010**), pp. 347–49.

98. 'Orientales (Églises)', in André Vauchez (ed.), *Christianisme: Dictionnaire des temps, des lieux et des figures* (Paris: Seuil, **2010**), pp. 417–20.

99. 'Abramo Ecchellense (1605–1664): I Maroniti, Livorno e la Toscana', in Adriano Prosperi (ed.), *Livorno 1606–1806: Luogo di incontro tra popoli e culture* (Turin: Umberto Allemandi, **2010**), pp. 430–37.
100. 'Abraham Ecchellensis dans la République des Lettres', in Bernard Heyberger (ed.), *Orientalisme, science et controverse: Abraham Ecchellensis* (Turnhout: Brepols, **2010**), pp. 9–51.
101. [with Hélène Bellosta] 'Abraham Ecchellensis et *Les Coniques* d'Apollonius: Les enjeux d'une traduction', in Bernard Heyberger (ed.), *Orientalisme, science et controverse: Abraham Ecchellensis* (Turnhout: Brepols, **2010**), pp. 191–201.
102. 'Ecrire l'histoire des chrétiens dans les villes de Syrie avant les réformes ottomanes', in Peter Sluglett (ed.), *Syria and Bilad al-Sham under Ottoman Rule: Essays in Honour of Abdul-Karim Rafeq* (Leiden: Brill, **2010**), pp. 443–54.
103. 'Préface', in Frédéric Pichon, *Maaloula (XIXe–XXIe siècle): Du vieux avec du neuf: Histoire et identité d'un village chrétien de Syrie* (Beirut: Institut français du Proche-Orient, **2010**), pp. 11–13.
104. 'Préface', in Jérôme Bocquet (ed.), *L'enseignement français en Méditerranée: Les missionnaires et l'Alliance israélite universelle* (Rennes: Presses Universitaires de Rennes, **2010**), pp. 9–12.
105. 'Christianismes orientaux', in Danièle Hervieu-Léger and Régine Azria (eds), *Dictionnaire des faits religieux* (Paris: PUF, **2010**), pp. 145–52.
106. 'Peuples "sans loi, sans foi, ni prêtre": Druzes et nusayrîs de Syrie découverts par les missionnaires catholiques (XVIIe–XVIIIe siècles)', in Bernard Heyberger and Rémy Madinier (eds), *L'Islam des marges: Mission chrétienne et espaces périphériques du monde musulman XVIe–XXe siècles* (Paris: IISMM; Karthala, **2011**), pp. 45–80.
107. 'I cristiani orientali e il mondo musulmano', in Alessandro Barbero (ed.), *Storia d'Europa e del Mediterraneo*, vol. 11: Roberto Bizzocchi (ed.), *L'età moderna (secoli XVI–XVIII): Culture, religioni, saperi* (Rome: Salerno, **2011**), pp. 239–78.
108. 'Frontières et circulations en Méditerranée', in Michel Vergé-Franceschi (ed.), *La Corse, la Méditerranée et le monde musulman: Douzièmes Journées Universitaires d'Histoire Maritime de Bonifacio* (Ajaccio: Alain Piazzola, **2011**), pp. 19–36.
109. 'L'autorité cléricale chez les Maronites: Mythe politique et dispositif social', in Denise Aigle (ed.), *Les autorités religieuses entre charisme et hiérarchie: Approches comparatives* (Turnhout: Brepols, **2011**), pp. 87–98.
110. 'L'Islam dans la controverse entre catholiques et protestants: Le *De origine nominis papae* d'Abraham Ecchellensis (1661), réponse à *l'Historia orientalis* de Johann Heinrich Hottinger (1651 et 1660)', in Chrystel

Bernat and Hubert Bost (eds), *Enoncer/dénoncer l'autre: Discours et représentations du différend confessionnel à l'époque moderne* (Turnhout: Brepols, **2012**), pp. 389–400.

111. 'Monachisme oriental, catholicisme et érudition (XVIIe–XXe siècles)', in Florence Jullien and Marie-Joseph Pierre (eds), *Monachismes d'Orient: Images, échanges, influences: Hommage à Antoine Guillemont* (Turnhout: Brepols, **2012**), pp. 165–83.

112. 'Les partenaires syriens', in *Les mille et une nuits*, catalogue of the exhibition at the Institut du Monde Arabe, 27 November 2012–28 April 2013 (Paris: Institut du Monde Arabe; Hazan, **2012**), cols. 68–73.

113. 'Missions catholiques en Syrie à l'époque moderne', in Chantal Verdeil (ed.), *Missions chrétiennes en terre d'Islam: Anthologie de textes missionnaires* (Turnhout: Brepols, **2013**), pp. 61–94.

114. [with Rachid Benzine, François Clément and John Tolan] '718/719–1797: Histoires croisées', in Pascal Blanchard, Naïma Yahi, Yvan Gastaut and Nicolas Bancel (eds), *La France arabo-orientale: Treize siècles de présences* (Paris: La Découverte, **2013**), pp. 24–37.

115. 'Catholicisme et construction des frontières confessionnelles dans l'Orient ottoman', in Francisco Bethencourt and Denis Crouzet (eds), *Frontières religieuses à l'époque moderne* (Paris: Presses Universitaires de la Sorbonne, **2013**), pp. 123–42.

116. 'La frontière méditerranéenne du XVe au XVIIe siècle: Introductionì', in Albrecht Fuess and Bernard Heyberger (eds), *La frontière méditerranéenne du XVe au XVIIe siècle: Échanges, circulations et affrontements* (Turnhout: Brepols, **2013**), pp. 9–27.

117. 'I Cristiani orientali e l'Occidente', in Luciano Vaccaro and Cesare Alzati (eds), *Da Costantinopoli al Caucaso: Imperi e popoli tra Cristianesimo e Islam* (Vatican City: Libreria Editrice Vaticana; Gazzada: Fondazione Ambrosiana Paolo VI, **2014**), pp. 233–48.

118. 'Afrique du Nord et Moyen-Orient: Vers la disparition? Introduction', in Jean-Michel Di Falco, Timothy Radcliffe and Andrea Riccardi (eds), *Le livre noir de la condition des chrétiens dans le monde* (Paris: XO Éditions, **2014**), pp. 165–84.

118b. Italian translation: 'Nordafrica e Medio Oriente: Verso la scomparsa? Introduzione', in Jean-Michel Di Falco, Timothy Radcliffe and Andrea Riccardi (eds), *Il libro nero della condizione dei cristiani nel mondo* (Milan: Mondadori, **2014**).

119. 'Introduction', in Hanna Dyâb, *D'Alep à Paris: Les pérégrinations d'un jeune Syrien au temps de Louis XIV*, translated and edited by Paule Fahmé-Thiéry, Bernard Heyberger and Jérôme Lentin, with a preface by Bernard Heyberger (Arles: Actes Sud, **2015**), pp. 7–47.

120. 'Histoire et usages mémoriels d'un conflit', in Dima de Clerck, Carla Eddé, Naila Kaidbey and Souad Slim (eds), *1860: Histoires et mémoires d'un conflit* (Beirut: Presses de l'IFPO, **2015**), pp. 467–75.
121. 'Préface', in Sabine Mohasseb Saliba (ed.), *Les fondations pieuses waqfs chez les chrétiens et les juifs du Moyen Âge à nos jours* (Paris: Geuthner, **2016**), pp. 9–12.
122. 'Uniates', in François Georgeon, Nicolas Vatin and Gilles Veinstein (eds), *Dictionnaire de l'empire ottoman* (Paris: Fayard, **2016**), pp. 1183–84.
123. 'Missions XVIe–XVIIIe siècles', in François Georgeon, Nicolas Vatin and Gilles Veinstein (eds), *Dictionnaire de l'empire ottoman* (Paris: Fayard, **2016**), pp. 801–2.
124. 'Saints chrétiens', in François Georgeon, Nicolas Vatin and Gilles Veinstein (eds), *Dictionnaire de l'empire ottoman* (Paris: Fayard, **2016**), pp. 1038–39.
125. 'Conversion et confessionalisation au Proche-Orient (XVIe–XXIe siècles)', in Philippe Gelez and Gilles Grivaud (eds), *Les conversions en Asie mineure dans les Balkans et dans le monde musulman: Comparaisons et perspectives* (Athens: École française d'Athènes, **2016**), pp. 191–210.
126. 'Clôture féminine, violences, rapports de genre et crise de l'autorité: La congrégation des religieuses du Sacré-Cœur (Mont Liban, 1750–1786)', in Isabelle Heullant-Donat, Julie Claustre, Élisabeth Lusset and Falk Bretschneider (eds), *Enfermements III: Le genre enfermé: Hommes et femmes en milieux clos (XIIIe–XXe siècle)* (Paris: Publications de la Sorbonne, **2017**), pp. 87–102.
127. 'Abraham Ecchellensis ou les Arabes expliqués en latin', in Mireille Issa (ed.), *Le latin des Maronites* (Paris: Geuthner, **2017**), pp. 77–84.
128. 'Les minorités chrétiennes du Proche-Orient', in Alain Dieckhoff and Philippe Portier (eds), *L'Enjeu mondial: Religion et politique* (Paris: Sciences Po Les Presses, **2017**), pp. 311–21.
129. 'Eugène Roger', in David Thomas and John Chesworth (eds), *Christian-Muslim Relations: A Bibliographical History*, vol. 9: *Western and Southern Europe (1600–1700)* (Leiden: Brill, **2017**), pp. 447–52.
130. 'Justinien de Neuvy, dit Michel Febvre', in David Thomas and John Chesworth (eds), *Christian-Muslim Relations: A Bibliographical History*, vol. 9: *Western and Southern Europe (1600–1700)* (Leiden: Brill, **2017**), pp. 579–88.
131. 'Michel Nau', in David Thomas and John Chesworth (eds), *Christian-Muslim Relations: A Bibliographical History*, vol. 9: *Western and Southern Europe (1600–1700)* (Leiden: Brill, **2017**), pp. 602–9.
132. 'Transformations religieuses et culturelles à l'époque ottomane (XVIe–XIXe siècle)', in Raphaëlle Ziadé (ed.), *Chrétiens d'Orient: 2000 ans d'histoire*, catalogue of the exhibition at the Institut du Monde Arabe (Paris: Gallimard, **2017**), pp. 116–25.

133. 'Prefazione', in Alessia Melcangi, *I copti nell'Egitto di Nasser: Tra politica e religione (1952–1970)* (Rome: Carocci, **2017**), pp. 15–20.
134. 'Migration of the Middle Eastern Christians and European Protection: A Long History', in Andreas Schmoller (ed.), *Middle Eastern Christians and Europe: Historical Legacies and Present Challenges* (Vienna: LIT, **2018**), pp. 23–42.
135. 'Pour une histoire des notions de "minorités" et de "protection"', in Valérie Assan, Bernard Heyberger and Jakob Vogel (eds), *Minorités en Méditerranée au XIXe siècle: Identités, identifications, circulations* (Rennes: Presses Universitaires de Rennes, **2019**), pp. 243–62.
136. '1709: Un Syrien à Paris: Le "Grand Hyver" d'Ḥannā Diyāb', in Romain Bertrand (ed.), *L'exploration du monde: Une autre histoire des Grandes Découvertes* (Paris: Seuil, **2019**), pp. 293–97.
137. 'Missionaries and Women: Domestic Catholicism in the Middle East', in Nadine Amsler, Andreea Badea, Bernard Heyberger and Christian Windler (eds), *Catholic Missionaries in Early Modern Asia: Patterns of Localization* (London, New York: Routledge, **2020**), pp. 190–203.
138. 'Le regard exceptionnel d'un homme "ordinaire": Paris en 1709 vu par Ḥannā Diyāb, chrétien syrien et informateur d'Antoine Galland', in Frédéric Bauden and Richard Waller (eds), *Antoine Galland (1646–1715) et son journal: Actes du colloque international organisé à l'Université de Liège (16–18 février 2015) à l'occasion du tricentenaire de sa mort* (Louvain, Paris, Bristol: Peeters, **2020**), pp. 31–49.
139. 'Les chrétiens de tradition syriaque à l'époque ottomane: Systèmes de connaissance et transferts culturels', in Bernard Heyberger (ed.), *Les chrétiens de tradition syriaque à l'époque ottomane* (Paris: Geuthner, **2020**), pp. 1–33.
140. 'Fasting: The Limits of Catholic confessionalization in Eastern Christianity in the eighteenth century', in Jan Loop and Jill Kraye (eds), *Scholarship between Europe and the Levant: Essays in Honour of Alastair Hamilton* (Leiden, Boston: Brill, **2020**), pp. 217–35.
141. 'Préface', in Anastassios Anastassiadis, *La Réforme orthodoxe: Église, État et société en Grèce à l'époque de la confessionnalisation post-ottomane (1833–1940)* (Athens: École française d'Athènes, **2020**), pp. xi–xiv.
142. 'Christianity within the Ottoman Empire', in Mitri Raheb and Mark Lamport (eds), *The Rowman & Littlefield Handbook of Christianity in the Middle East* (Lanham: Rowman & Littlefield, **2020**), pp. 77–87.
143. 'East and West: A Connected History of Eastern Christianity', in Ioana Feodorov, Bernard Heyberger and Samuel Noble (eds), *Arabic Christians between Ottoman Levant and Eastern Europe* (Leiden: Brill, **2021**), pp. 3–29.
144. 'Les chrétiens en Syrie', in *Minorités en Islam, Islam en minorité* (Paris: IISMM; Diacritiques Éditions, **2021**), pp. 59–77.

BOOK REVIEWS

145. Review of Francis Richard, *Raphaël du Mans missionnaire en Perse au XVIIe siècle* (Paris: L'Harmattan, 1995): *Revue d'histoire de l'Église de France*, 82, 209 (**1996**), pp. 403–4.
146. Review of Giovanni Pizzorusso, *Roma nei Caraibi: L'organizzazione delle missioni cattoliche nelle Antille e in Guyana (1635–1675)* (Rome: École française de Rome, 1995): *Revue d'histoire de l'Église de France*, 83, 210 (**1997**), pp. 295–96.
147. Review of Sami Kuri, *Une histoire du Liban à travers les archives des jésuites*, 3 vols (Beirut: Dar Al-Machreq, 1985–96): *Annales d'histoire et d'archéologie de l'Université Saint-Joseph*, 8–9 (**1997–98**), pp. 75–85.
148. Review of Silvia Naef, *A la recherche d'une modernité arabe: L'évolution des arts plastiques en Égypte, au Liban et en Irak* (Genève: Slatkine, 1996): *Arabica*, 45, 3 (**1998**), pp. 293–95.
149. Review of Yoram Shalit, *Nicht-Muslime und Fremde in Aleppo und Damaskus im 18. und in der ersten Hälfte des 19. Jahrhunderts* (Berlin: Klaus Schwartz Verlag, 1996): *Orientalistische Literaturzeitschrift*, 93, 1 (**1998**), pp. 61–66.
150. Review of Ronnie Po-Chia Hsia, *The World of Catholic Renewal, 1540–1770* (Cambridge: Cambridge University Press, 1998): *Annales: Histoire, sciences sociales*, 55, 2 (**2000**), pp. 447–49.
151. Review of Hans-Lukas Kieser, *Der verpasste Friede: Mission, Ethnie und Staat in den Ostprovinzen der Türkei (1830–1930)* (Zurich: Chronos, 2000): *Archives de sciences sociales des religions*, 116 (**2001**), pp. 132–35.
152. Review of Meropi Anastassiadou, *Salonique, 1830–1912: Une ville ottomane à l'âge des Réformes* (Leiden: Brill, 1997): *Atti e memorie della Società Dalmata di Storia Patria*, 3, 23 (**2001**), pp. 188–90.
153. Review of Maria Antonietta Visceglia and Catherine Brice (eds), *Cérémonies et rituel à Rome (XVIe–XIXe siècle)* (Rome: École française de Rome, 1997): *Annales: Histoire, sciences sociales*, 57, 2 (**2002**), pp. 471–73.
154. Review of Bernard Dompnier and Marie-Hélène Froeschle-Chopard (eds), *Les religieux et leurs livres à l'époque moderne* (Clermont-Ferrand: Presses Universitaires Blaise-Pascal, 2000): *Bulletin du bibliophile*, 1 (**2002**), pp. 188–91.
155. Review of Lucette Valensi, *La fuite en Égypte: Histoires d'Occident et d'Orient* (Paris: Seuil, 2002): *Rivista di Storia e Letteratura religiosa*, 1 (**2003**), pp. 158–61.
156. Review of Thomas Philipp, *Acre: The Rise and Fall of a Palestinian City, 1730–1831* (New York: Columbia University Press, 2001): *Annales: Histoire, sciences sociales*, 58, 5 (**2003**), pp. 1187–89.
157. Review of Dominique Trimbur and Ran Aaronsohn (eds), *De Bonaparte à Balfour: La France, l'Europe occidentale et la Palestine 1799–1917*

(Paris: CNRS, 2001): *Rivista di storia e letteratura religiosa*, 39, 2 (**2003**), pp. 407–8.

158. Review of Géraldine Châtelard, *Briser la mosaïque: Les tribus chrétiennes de Madaba, Jordanie (XIXe–XXe siècle)* (Paris: CNRS, 2004): *Annales: Histoire, sciences sociales*, 60, 1 (**2005**), pp. 155–56.

159. Review of Ussama Makdisi, *The Culture of Sectarianism: Community, History, and Violence in Nineteenth-Century Ottoman Lebanon* (Berkeley, Los Angeles, London: University of California Press, 2000): *Annales: Histoire, sciences sociales*, 60, 2 (**2005**), pp. 891–94.

160. Review of Hervé Pennec, *Des Jésuites au Royaume du Prêtre Jean (Ethiopie)* (Paris: Centre Culturel Calouste Gulbenkian, 2003): *Annales: Histoire, sciences sociales*, 60, 4 (**2005**), pp. 887–88.

161. Review of Marie-Thérèse Urvoy (ed.), *En hommage au Père Jacques Jomier, o.p.* (Paris: Cerf, 2002): *Bulletin critique des annales islamologiques*, 21 (**2005**), pp. 16–17.

162. Review of Méropi Anastassiadou (ed.), *Identités confessionnelles et espace urbain en terres d'Islam*, monographic issue of *Revue des mondes musulmans et de la Méditerranée*, 107–10 (2005): *Bulletin critique des annales islamologiques*, 22 (**2006**), pp. 55–57.

163. Review of Catherine Mayeur-Jaouen, *Pèlerinages d'Égypte: Histoire de la piété copte et musulmane, XVe–XXe siècle* (Paris: Éditions de l'EHESS, 2005): *Bulletin critique des annales islamologiques*, 22 (**2006**), pp. 92–93.

164. Review of Sara Cabibbo, *Santa Rosalia tra terra e cielo* (Palermo: Sellerio, 2004): *Rivista di storia del Cristianesimo*, 1 (**2006**), pp. 268–71.

165. Review of Dalal Arsuzi-Elamir, *Arabischer Nationalismus in Syrien: Zakî al-Arsûzî und die arabisch-nationale Bewegung an der Peripherie, Alexandretta/Antakya 1930–1938* (Münster: LIT, 2003): *Revue des mondes musulmans et de la Méditerranée*, 115–16 (**2006**), pp. 285–88.

166. Review of Alastair Hamilton, *The Copts and the West, 1439–1822: The European Discovery of the Egyptian Church* (Oxford: Oxford University Press, 2006): *Archives de sciences sociales des religions*, 138 (**2007**), pp. 174–75.

167. Review of Dimitrie Cantemir, *The Salvation of the Wise Man and the Ruin of the Sinful World: Ṣalāḥ al-ḥakīm wa-fasād al-ʿālam al-dhamīm*, edited and translated by Ioana Feodorov, with introduction and commentaries by Virgil Cândea (Bucarest: Editura Academiei Române, 2006): *Revue d'histoire ecclésiastique*, 103, 2 (**2008**), pp. 664–67.

168. Review of Dominique Avon, *Les Frères prêcheurs en Orient: Les dominicains du Caire (années 1910–années 1960)* (Paris: Cerf Histoire, 2005): *Annales: Histoire, sciences sociales*, 63, 4 (**2008**), pp. 922–25.

169. Review of Magdi Guirguis, *An Armenian Artist in Ottoman Egypt: Yuhanna Al-Armani and His Coptic Icons*, translated by Amina Elbendary

(Cairo: The American University in Cairo Press, 2008): *Arabica*, 56, 4–5 (**2009**), pp. 466–68.

170. Review of Roger Botte, *Esclavages et abolitions en terres d'Islam* (Bruxelles: André Versaille, 2010): IISMM website (**2010**), <http://iismm.ehess.fr/docannexe/file/1147/botte.pdf>.
171. Review of Vasileios Tsakiris, *Die gedruckten griechischen Beichtbücher zur Zeit der Türkenherrschaft: Ihr kirchenpolitischer Entstehungzusammenhang und ihre Quellen* (Berlin, New York: De Gruyter, 2009): *Revue d'histoire ecclésiastique*, 105, 2 (**2010**), pp. 504–7.
172. Review of Hervé Legrand and Giuseppe Maria Croce (eds), *L'Œuvre d'Orient: Solidarités anciennes et nouveaux défis* (Paris: Cerf, 2010): *Archives de sciences sociales des religions*, 156 (**2011**), pp. 196–97.
173. Review of Charlotte de Castelnau-L'Estoile, Marie-Lucie Copete, Aliocha Maldavsky and Ines G. Županov (eds), *Missions d'évangélisation et circulation des savoirs, XVIe–XVIIIe siècle* (Madrid: Casa de Velázquez, 2011): *Annales: Histoire, sciences sociales*, 68, 1 (**2013**), pp. 222–24.
174. Review of Anh Nga Longva and Anne Sofie Roald (eds), *Religious Minorities in the Middle East: Domination, Self-Empowerment, Accommodation* (Leiden: Brill, 2012): *Revue des mondes musulmans et de la Méditerranée*, 134 (**2013**), online: <http://journals.openedition.org/remmm/7962>.
175. Review of *Timotheos I., Ostsyrischer Patriarch: Disputation mit dem Kalifen Al-Mahdi*, edited by Martin Heimgartner, 2 vols (Leuven: Peeters, 2011): *Revue d'histoire ecclésiastique*, 108, 1 (**2013**), pp. 397–99.
176. Review of Guillaume Dye and Fabien Nobilio (eds), *Figures bibliques en Islam* (Bruxelles: EME, 2011): *Archives de sciences sociales des religions*, 168 (**2014**), pp. 177–78.
177. Review of Natalia Muchnik, *De paroles et de gestes: Constructions marranes en terre d'Inquisition* (Paris: Éditions de l'EHESS, 2014): *Archive de sciences sociales des religions*, 172 (**2015**), pp. 336–38.
178. Review of Anastassos Anastassiadis (ed.), *Voisinages fragiles: Les relations interconfessionnelles dans le Sud-Est européen et la Méditerranée orientale 1854–1923: Contraintes locales et enjeux internationaux* (Athens: École française d'Athènes, 2013): *Archives de sciences sociales des religions*, 172 (**2015**), pp. 241–44.
179. Review of Francine Costet-Tardieu, *Les minorités chrétiennes dans la construction de l'Égypte moderne, 1922–1952* (Paris: Karthala, 2016): *Archives de sciences sociales des religions*, 176 (**2016**), pp. 295–96.
180. Review of Georges Koutzakiotis, *Attendre la fin du monde au XVIIe siècle: Le messie juif et le grand drogman* (Paris: Association Pierre Belon, 2014): *Archives de sciences sociales des religions*, 176 (**2016**), pp. 341–42.

181. Review of Dionigi Albera, Maryline Crivello and Mohamed Tozy (eds), *Dictionnaire de la Méditerranée* (Arles: Actes Sud, 2016): *Cahiers de la Méditerranée*, 95 (**2017**), pp. 315–17.
182. Review of Sasha Goldstein-Sabbah and Heleen Murre-Van den Berg (eds), *Modernity, Minority and the Public Sphere: Jews and Christians in the Middle East* (Leiden, Boston: Brill, 2016): *Archives de sciences sociales des religions*, 180 (**2017**), pp. 350–52.
183. Review of Reinhold F. Glei and Roberto Tottoli, *Ludovico Marracci at Work: The Evolution of his Latin Translation of the Qur'ān in the Light of His Newly Discovered Manuscripts, with an Edition and a Comparative Linguistic Analysis of Sura 18* (Wiesbaden: Harrassowitz, 2016): *XVIIe siècle*, 274, 1 (**2017**), pp. 171–72.
184. Review of Aline Schlaepfer, *Les intellectuels juifs de Bagdad: Discours et allégeances (1908–1951)* (Leiden, Boston: Brill, 2016): *Annales: Histoire, sciences sociales*, 72, 4 (**2017**), pp. 1229–31.
185. Review of Anna Poujeau, *Des monastères en partage: Sainteté et pouvoir chez les chrétiens de Syrie* (Nanterre: Société d'ethnologie, 2014): *Annales, Histoire sciences sociales*, 72, 4 (**2017**), pp. 1244–46.
186. Review of Marie-Hélène Blanchet and Frédéric Gabriel (eds), *Réduire le schisme? Ecclésiologies et politiques de l'union entre Orient et Occident (XIIIe–XVIIIe siècle)* (Paris: Association des amis du Centre d'histoire et civilisation de Byzance, 2013): *XVIIe siècle*, 278, 1 (**2018**), pp. 165–68.
187. Review of Marie-Hélène Blanchet and Frédéric Gabriel (eds), *L'union à l'épreuve du formulaire: Professions de foi entre Églises d'Orient et d'Occident (XIIIe–XVIIIe siècle)* (Leuven, Paris, Bristol: Peeters; Paris: Centre de recherche d'histoire et civilisations de Byzance, 2016): *XVIIe siècle*, 281, 4 (**2018**), pp. 769–71.
188. Review of Vasile-Octavian Mihoc, *Christliche Bilderverehrung im Kontext islamischer Bilderlosigkeit: Der Traktat über die Bilderverehrung von Theodor Abū Qurrah (ca. 755 bis ca. 830)* (Wiesbaden: Harrassowitz, 2017): *Orientalistische Literaturzeitung*, 114, 3 (**2019**), pp. 59–60.
189. Review of Christian Windler, *Missionare in Persien: Kulturelle Diversität und Normenkonkurrenz im globalen Katholizismus (17–18. Jahrhundert)* (Cologne, Weimar, Vienna: Böhlau Verlag, 2018): *Archives de sciences sociales des religions*, 188 (**2019**), pp. 432–36.
190. Review of Alain Blondy, *Le monde méditerranéen: 15 000 ans d'histoire* (Paris: Perrin, 2018): *Cahiers de la Méditerranée*, 99 (**2019**), pp. 199–200.
191. Review of Alastair Hamilton (ed.), *Johann Michael Wansleben's Travels in the Levant 1671–1674: An Annotated Edition of His Italian Report* (Leiden, Boston: Brill, 2018): *Revue des mondes musulmans et de la Méditerranée*, 147 (**2020**), online: <http://journals.openedition.org/remmm/13067>.

192. Review of Stefan Winter, *A History of the 'Alawis: From Medieval Aleppo to the Turkish Republic* (Princeton: Princeton University Press, 2016): *International Journal of Middle East Studies*, 52, 3 (**2020**), pp. 594–96.
193. Review of Peter Hill, *Utopia and Civilisation in the Arab Nahda* (Cambridge: Cambridge University Press, 2020): *Revue des mondes musulmans et de la Méditerranée*, 150 (**2021**), online: <http://journals.openedition.org/remmm/16324>.
194. Review of Dominique Avon, *La liberté de conscience: Histoire d'une notion et d'un droit* (Rennes: Presses universitaires de Rennes, 2020): *Archives de sciences sociales des religions*, 196 (**2021**), pp. 169–72.

DISSEMINATION ARTICLES

195. 'Chrétiens d'Orient et archives de la congrégation "De Propaganda Fide"', *Dirāsāt fī al-ādāb wa-l-'ulūm al-insāniyya*, special issue of *Al-arshīf ta'rīkh Lubnān*, 26, 2 (**1997**), pp. 909–16.
196. 'L'identité plurielle des Églises d'Orient', *Qantara* [Journal of the Institut du Monde Arabe, Paris], 55 (**2005**), pp. 36–41.
197. 'Les chrétiens arabes aujourd'hui', in *L'Arabie chrétienne*, monographic issue of *Archéologie & sciences des origines*, 309 (**2005–6**), pp. 108–17.
198. 'L'Europe dans le regard des Libanais (XVIIe–XIXe siècle)', *Le Détour*, 4 (**2004**), pp. 153–69.
199. 'Le "bon temps" des Ottomans', in *Les Chrétiens d'Orient*, monographic section of *L'Histoire*, 337 (December **2008**), pp. 56–61.
200. 'Les chrétiens d'Orient entre le passé et l'avenir', *Les Cahiers de l'Orient*, 93 (**2008**), pp. 9–21.
201. 'Les chrétiens et l'Occident', *Qantara*, 74 (**2010**), pp. 29–32.
202. 'Des chrétiens d'Orient au service de l'orientalisme chrétien', *Qantara*, 80 (**2011**), pp. 31–37.
203. 'Le mythe du dhimmî', in *L'Islam: Faits et mythes*, special issue of *Le Point Références* (March–April **2013**), pp. 50–53.
204. 'Les chrétiens orientaux et l'Occident', *L'Œuvre d'Orient: Perspectives et réflexions*, 2 (**2014**), pp. 65–80.
205. 'Les chrétiens orientaux, entre l'Islam et l'Occident', *Les cahiers de l'Orient*, 118, 2 (**2015**), pp. 11–21.

205b. Published also in *Chrétiens d'Orient: Les oubliés*, monographic section of *Revue des deux mondes* (February **2015**), pp. 9–19.

206. 'Qui sont les chrétiens d'Orient ?' in *Les monothéismes: Des origines à aujourd'hui*, special issue of *Sciences humaines*, Hors série 5 (December **2016**–January/February **2017**), pp. 44–45.

207. ‘Un chrétien d’Alep à la cour de Versailles’, *L’Histoire*, 432 (February **2017**), pp. 88–93.
208. ‘Églises d’Orient’, in *Bibliothèques d’Orient* (Bibliothèque Nationale de France: **2017**), online: <https://heritage.bnf.fr/bibliothequesorient/fr/eglises-orient-article>.
209. ‘Lieux saints’, in *Bibliothèques d’Orient* (Bibliothèque Nationale de France: **2017**), online: <https://heritage.bnf.fr/bibliothequesorient/fr/lieux-saints-article>.
210. ‘Le Liban, refuge et carrefour’, *Le monde de la Bible*, 239 (December **2021**), pp. 30–36.

INTERVIEWS IN THE MEDIA (SELECTION, AFTER 2011)

Newspapers, Magazines, Websites

Interview with Antoine Ajoury, ‘Le printemps arabe, un salut pour les chrétiens autant que pour les musulmans’, *L’Orient-Le Jour* (10 October **2011**), online: <https://www.lorientlejour.com/article/726161/Le_printemps_arabe%252C_un_salut_pour_les_chretiens_autant_que_pour_les_musulmans.html>.

Interview, ‘Les trois pistes de la modernité maronite contemporaine’, *L’Orient-Le Jour* (3 December **2011**), online: <https://www.lorientlejour.com/article/734577/Les_trois_pistes_de_la_modernite__maronite_contemporaine.html>.

Interview with Daniele Zappalà, ‘Cristiani d’Oriente tra fuga e speranza’, *Avvenire* (30 July **2013**), online: <https://www.avvenire.it/agora/pagine/cristiano-di-oriente-tra-fuga-e-speranza>.

Interview with Thomas Wild, ‘Bernard Heyberger: “Le clash des civilisations n’est pas une fatalité”’, *Réforme* (30 May **2013**), online: <https://www.reforme.net/chretiens-dorient/2013/05/30/journal-05302013-3515-acces-payant-clash-civilisations-est-fatalite/>.

Interview with Louis Fraysse, ‘Bernard Heyberger: “Les chrétiens d’Orient ont un lien complexe vis-à-vis de l’Occident”’, *Réforme* (4 September **2014**), online: <https://www.reforme.net/chretiens-dorient/2014/09/04/journal-evenement-enjeu-memoriel-est-essentiel/>.

Interview with Anne-Bénédicte Hoffner, ‘La longue tragédie des chrétiens d’Orient’, *La Croix* (18 February **2015**), online: <https://www.la-croix.com/Archives/2015-02-18/La-longue-tragedie-des-chretiens-d-Orient-ENTRETIEN.-Bernard-Heyberger-historien-directeur-d-etudes-a-l-Ecole-des-hautes-etudes-en-sciences-sociales-1-Il-n-y-a-pas-un-plan-d-eradication-concertee-2015-02-18-1282439>.

Interview, *Les clés pour le Moyen-Orient* (11 May **2015**), online: <https://www.lesclesdumoyenorient.com/Entretien-avec-Bernard-Heyberger.html>.

Interview with Agnès Rotivel, 'À Alep, "les chrétiens ont dû négocier un espace vital avec le regime"', *La Croix* (6 July **2015**), online: <https://www.la-croix.com/Actualite/Monde/A-Alep-les-chretiens-ont-du-negocier-un-espace-vital-avec-le-regime-2015-07-06-1331847>.

Interview, *Courrier de l'ACAT*, 334 (**2015**), pp. 6–7.

Interview, 'Alep: Une cité syrienne "au passé historique glorieux"', *L'Histoire* (10 March **2016**), online: <https://www.lhistoire.fr/entretien/alep-une-cit%C3%A9-syrienne-au-pass%C3%A9-historique-glorieux>.

Interview with Isabelle Demangeat, 'Que peut faire la France pour les chrétiens d'Orient?' *La Croix* (18 August **2016**), online: <https://www.la-croix.com/Debats/Forum-et-debats/Que-peut-faire-France-pour-chretiens-dOrient-2016-08-18-1200783107>.

Interview, *Chrétiens d'Orient: 2000 ans de civilisation*, special issue of *La Vie*, Hors-Série *Histoire*, 30 (23 November **2017**), pp. 6–11.

Interview, 'Les minorités chrétiennes d'Orient au cœur des tensions liées à la question nationale', *Diplomatie*, 93 (July–August **2018**), pp. 58–61.

Interview with Augustine Passilly, 'En Irak, Noël devient un jour férié', *Réforme* (22 December **2020**), online: https://www.reforme.net/gratuit/2020/12/22/en-irak-noel-devient-un-jour-ferie/.

Interview with Louis Fraysse, 'La France, traditionnelle protectrice des chrétiens d'Orient?' *Réforme* (3 March **2021**), online: <https://www.reforme.net/chretiens-dorient/2021/03/13/la-france-traditionnelle-protectrice-des-chretiens-dorient/>.

Interview with Louis Fraysse, 'Assyriens, chaldéens, syriaques . . . Qui sont les chrétiens d'Irak?' *Réforme* (11 March **2021**), online: <https://www.reforme.net/chretiens-dorient/2021/03/11/qui-sont-les-chretiens-dirak-entretien-avec-bernard-heyberger/>.

Interview with Louis Fraysse, 'Maronites, Grecs-orthodoxes, Arméniens . . . qui sont les chrétiens de Syrie?' *Réforme* (12 March **2021**), online: <https://www.reforme.net/chretiens-dorient/2021/03/12/maronites-grecs-orthodoxes-armeniens-qui-sont-les-chretiens-de-syrie/>.

Radio

'Orientalisme, science et controverse: Abraham Ecchellensis (1605–1664)', *Foi et traditions des chrétiens d'Orient*, France Culture (15 May **2011**).

'Être chrétien dans le monde arabe', *Culture Monde*, France Culture (17 October **2011**).

'Les Chrétiens d'Orient: Permanence et précarité', *Concordance des temps, France Culture* (24 December **2011**).

'Les Maronites du Liban', *La marche de l'histoire*, France Inter (17 September **2012**).

'Les chrétiens au Proche Orient: De la compassion à la compréhension', *Chrétiens d'Orient*, France Culture (10 November **2013**).
Interview, *Le débat du jour*, RFI (24 January **2014**).
'Connaissez-vous Hanna Dyâb?' *Cultures d'Islam*, France Culture (25 October **2015**).
'Le voyage rocambolesque d'un jeune Syrien vers Paris au temps de Louis XIV', *Traversées du monde*, Fréquence Protestante (6 January **2016**).
'Les pérégrinations d'un drapier d'Alep', *La marche de l'histoire*, France Inter (2 March **2016**).
'Hannah Dyab, d'Alep à Paris', *Chrétiens d'Orient*, France Culture (20 November **2016**).
'Livres et confessions', *Orthodoxie*, France Culture (5 March **2017**).
'Chrétiens d'Orient, un archipel planétaire', *Tout un monde*, France Culture (29 April **2017**).
Interview, Vatican Radio (29 August **2017**).
'Minorités et empires', *Chrétiens d'Orient*, France Culture (23 February **2020**).

Television

Interview, 'Le printemps noir des coptes', documentary directed by Daniel Grandclément, broadcast on Public Sénat (June **2013**).
Interview, 'Actualités orientales', *Chrétiens orientaux: Foi, espérance et traditions*, France 2 (18 August **2013**).
Maghreb Orient Express, TV5 Monde (13 September **2015**).
Journal, TV5 Monde (29 October **2015**).
Interview, *La gerboise et les 1001 nuits* (CRAL, CNRS-EHESS: **2015**), documentary directed by Momoko Seko (25 minutes), first broadcast on 18 March 2016, online: <https://www.youtube.com/watch?v=Eimvzr2F5vw>.
Interview, 'Chrétiens en monde arabe: L'histoire', *Chrétiens orientaux: Foi, espérance et traditions*, France 2 (4 July **2021**).

Bibliography

The works cited in the volume are listed here, with the exception of those contained in the previous section.

ʿAbbūd al-Ghūstāwī, Būlus, *Al-majālī al-taʿrīkhiyya fī tarjamat al-rāhiba al-shahīra Hindiyya* (Beirut: Al-Tawfīq, 1910).

ʿAbbūd al-Ḥalabī, Yūsuf bin Dimitrī bin Jirjis al-Khūrī, *Ḥawādith Ḥalab al-yawmiyya 1771–1805: Al-murtād fī taʾrīkh Ḥalab wa Baghdād*, edited by Fawāz Maḥmūd al-Fawâz (Aleppo: shaʿār li-nashr wa-l-ʿulūm, 2006).

ʿAbbūd al-Ḥalabī, Yūsuf bin Dimitrī bin Jirjis al-Khūrī, *Al-Murtād fī taʾrīkh Ḥalab wa-Baghdād*, edited by Fawāz Maḥmūd al-Fawāz (Master's thesis, University of Damascus, s. d.).

Abdel Nour, Antoine, *Introduction à l'histoire urbaine de la Syrie ottomane (XVIe–XVIIIe siècle)* (Beirut: Publications de l'Université libanaise, 1982).

Abou Nohra, Joseph, *Contribution à l'étude du rôle des monastères dans l'histoire rurale du Liban* (PhD dissertation, Université de Strasbourg, 1983).

Abou, Selim, *Béchir Gemayel ou l'esprit d'un peuple* (Paris: Anthropos, 1984).

Aboussouan, Camille (ed.), *Le livre et le Liban jusqu'en 1900* (Paris: UNESCO, AGECOOP, 1982).

Abras, Michel, 'Le voyage de deux moines melkites en Italie du Nord en 1775', in Bernard Heyberger and Carsten Walbiner (eds), *Les Européens vus par les Libanais à l'époque ottomane* (Beirut: Orient-Institut der DMG; Würzburg: Ergon, 2002), pp. 59–65.

Abu-Husayn, Abdul-Rahim, *Provincial Leadership in Syria, 1575–1650* (Beirut: American University of Beirut, 1985).

Addobbati, Andrea, 'Hanna Dyab, il mercante di storie', *Quaderni storici,* 153, 3 (2016), pp. 830–42.

Agemian, Sylvia, 'Introduction à l'étude des icônes melkites', in Virgil Cândea (ed.), *Icônes Melkites: Exposition organisée par le musée Nicolas Sursock du 16 mai au 15 juin 1969* (Beirut: Musée Nicolas Sursock, 1969), pp. 95–126.

Agemian, Sylvia, 'Les icônes melkites', in Virgil Cândea (ed.), *Icônes grecques, melkites, russes. Collection Abou Adal* (Geneva: Skira, 1993), pp. 171–85.

Agemian, Sylvia, 'Œuvres d'art melkite dans l'église arménienne des Quarante Martyrs d'Alep', *Revue des études arméniennes*, 1 (1973), pp. 91–113.

Alam, Muzaffar, and Sanjay Subrahmanyam, 'Frank Disputations: Catholics and Muslims in the Court of Jahangir (1608–1611)', *Indian Economic and Social History Review*, 46 (1999), pp. 457–511.

Albera, Dionigi and Maria Couroucli (eds), *Religions traversées: Lieux saints partagés entre chrétiens, musulmans et juifs en Méditerranée* (Arles: Actes Sud, 2009).

Alberigo, Giuseppe (ed.), *Les Conciles œcuméniques*, 3 vols (Paris: Cerf, 1994).

Albert, Jean-Pierre, *Le sang et le Ciel: Les saintes mystiques dans le monde chrétien* (Paris: Aubier, 1997).

Alleaume, Ghislaine, 'Un "Ottoman Turn"? L'historiographie des provinces arabes de l'Empire ottoman', in Eberhard Kienle (ed.), *Les sciences sociales en voyage: L'Afrique du Nord et le Moyen-Orient vus d'Europe, d'Amérique et de l'Intérieur* (Aix-en-Provence: IREMAM; Karthala, 2010), pp. 23–39.

'Allocution de Sa Sainteté le Pape Paul VI lors de la canonisation de Saint Charbel Makhlouf', *L'Osservatore Romano*, 10–11 October 1977.

'Allocution de Sa Sainteté le Pape Paul VI, lors de la béatification de Charbel Makhlouf' (*L'Osservatore Romano*, 5–6 December 1965), *Collectanea Cisterciensia*, 28 (1966), pp. 73–74.

Alois Hahn, 'Contribution à la sociologie de la confession et autres formes institutionnalisées d'aveu', *Actes de la recherche en sciences sociales*, 62, 3 (1986), pp. 54–68.

Al-Qattan, Najwa, 'Dhimmīs in the Muslim Court: Legal Autonomy and Religious Discrimination', *International Journal of Middle East Studies*, 31, 1999, pp. 429–44.

Al-Qattan, Najwa, 'Across the Courtyard: Residential Space and Sectarian Boundaries in Ottoman Damascus', in Molly Greene (ed.), *Minorities in the Ottoman Empire* (Princeton: Markus Wiener, 2005), pp. 13–45.

Anagnostopoulou, Sia, 'Chrétiens, musulmans et l'arrivée du lion anglais: Les autorités religieuses de Chypre face au pouvoir colonial britannique (1878–1884)', in Anastassios Anastassiadis (ed.), *Voisinages fragiles: Les relations interconfessionnelles dans le Sud-Est européen et la Méditerranée orientale 1854–1923: Contraintes locales et enjeux internationaux* (Athens: École française d'Athènes, 2013), pp. 181–96.

Anastasopoulos, Antonis, 'Non-Muslims and Ottoman Justice(s?)', in Jeroen Duindam, Jill Diana Harries, Caroline Humfress and Hurvitz Nimrod (eds), *Law and Empire: Ideas, Practices, Actors* (Leiden, Boston: Brill, 2013), pp. 275–92.

Anderson, Benedict, *Imagined Communities: Reflections on the Origin and Spread of Nationalism*, revised 2nd edition (London: Verso, 1991).

Andrade, Tonio, 'A Chinese Farmer, Two African Boys, and a Warlord: Toward a Global Microhistory', *Journal of World History*, 21, 4 (2010), pp. 573–91.

Andriotis, Nikos, 'Les querelles ethnoreligieuses en Crète et l'intervention des puissances européennes (seconde moitié du XIXe siècle)', in Anastassios Anastassiadis (ed.), *Voisinages fragiles: Les relations interconfessionnelles dans le Sud-Est européen et la Méditerranée orientale 1854–1923: Contraintes locales et enjeux internationaux* (Athens: École française d'Athènes, 2013), pp. 197–211.

Armanios, Febe, *Coptic Christianity in Ottoman Egypt* (Oxford: Oxford University Press, 2011).

Arvieux, Laurent Chevalier d', *Mémoires du Chevalier d'Arvieux, envoyé extraordinaire à la Porte, Consul d'Alep, d'Alger, de Tripoli et autres Échelles du Levant*, edited by Jean-Baptiste Labat, 7 vols (Paris: Charles-Jean-Baptiste Delespine, 1735).

Aslanian, Sebouh D., '"A Ship with Two Rudders"? Gregorio di Girach-Mirman of Venice, Global Armenian Trade Networks, and Religious Ambiguity in the Age of Confessionalization', in Helen C. Evans (ed.), *Art and Religion in Medieval Armenia* (New York: Metropolitan Museum of Art, 2021), pp. 85–108.

Aslanian, Sebouh D., '"Many Have Come Here and Have Deceived Us": Some Notes on Asateur Vardapet (1644–1728), an Itinerant Armenian Monk in Europe,' *Handēs amsōreay*, 1–12 (2019), pp. 133–94.

Aslanian, Sebouh D., 'The "Quintessential Locus of Brokerage": Letters of Recommendation, Networks, and Mobility in the Life of Thomas Vanandets'i, an Armenian Printer in Amsterdam, 1677–1707', *Journal of World History*, 31, 4 (2020), pp. 655–92.

Aslanian, Sebouh D., *Early Modernity and Mobility: Port Cities and Printers across the Armenian Diaspora, 1512–1800* (New Haven: Yale University Press, forthcoming).

Atallah, Elias, *Le Synode Libanais de 1736*, 2 vols (Antélias-Paris: CERO-Letouzey et Ané, 2001).

Auber, Julien, *Yūḥannā al-Armanī et le renouveau de l'art de l'icône en Égypte ottomane* (PhD dissertation, Université de recherche Paris Sciences et Lettres, 2018).

ʿAwwād, Manṣūr, *Baraka ʿan Qabr al-Qadīs Sharbal*, 1st part (Annāyā, s. n.: 1952).

Bacel, Paul, 'La Congrégation des basiliens chouérites', *Échos d'Orient*, 6 (1903), pp. 174–83, 242–48; 7 (1904), pp. 156–63, 199–206.

Bakhit, Muhammad A., 'The Christian Population of the Province of Damascus in the Sixteenth Century', in Benjamin Braude and Bernard Lewis (eds), *Christians and Jews in the Ottoman Empire: The Functioning of a Plural* Society, vol. 2: *The Arabic-Speaking Lands* (New York, London: Holmes & Meier, 1982), pp. 19–66.

Bakhkhāsh, Naʿūm, *Akhbār Ḥalab*, edited by Yūsuf Qūshaqjī, 3 vols (Aleppo: Maṭbaʿat al-Iḥsān, 1985–92).

Balagna, Josée, *L'imprimerie arabe en Occident (XVIe, XVIIe et XVIIIe siècles)* (Paris: Maisonneuve and Larose, 1994).

Bardakjian, Kevork B., 'The Rise of the Armenian Patriarchate', in Benjamin Braude and Bernard Lewis (eds), *Christians and Jews in the Ottoman Empire: The Functioning of a Plural Society*, vol. 1: *The Central Lands* (New York, London: Holmes & Meier, 1982), pp. 89–100.

Barrès, Maurice, *Une enquête aux pays du Levant*, in *L'œuvre de Maurice Barrès*, vol. 11 (Paris: Plon, 1923).

Barth, Fredrik (ed.), *Ethnic Groups and Boundaries: The Social Organization of Culture Difference* (Boston, Bergen, London: Universitets forlaget-Allen & Unwin, 1969).

Bāshā, Qisṭanṭīn, *Taʾrīkh ṭāʾifat al-Rūm al-malakiyya wa ruhbān al-mukhalliṣiyya* (Saida: Maṭbaʿa dayr al-Mukhālliṣ, 1938).

Bauden, Frédéric, and Richard Waller (eds), *Le journal d'Antoine Galland (1646–1715): La période parisienne*, vol. 1: *1708–1709* (Leuven, Paris: Peeters, 2011).

Baumstark, Anton, 'Eine arabische Palästinabeschreibung spätestens des 16. Jahrhunderts', *Oriens Christianus*, 6 (1906), pp. 238–99.

Bayraktar Tellan, Elif, *The Patriarch and the Sultan: The Struggle for Authority and the Quest for Order in the Eighteenth-Century Ottoman Empire* (PhD dissertation, Bilkent University, 2011).

Becker, Adam H., *Revival and Awakening: American Evangelical Missionaries in Iran and the Origins of Assyrian Nationalism* (Chicago: University of Chicago Press, 2015).

Bellati Ceccoli, Guido, *Tra Toscana e Medioriente: La storia degli Arabi cattolici a Livorno (Sec. XVII–XX)* (Livorno: Editasca, 2008).

Bellatti Ceccoli, Guido, 'Voci dall'Oriente: Arabi cristiani e musulmani a Livorno in età moderna', in Adriano Prosperi (ed.), *Livorno 1606–1806: Luogo di incontro tra popoli e culture* (Turin: Umberto Allemandi, 2009), pp. 418–29.

Bernand, Carmen, and Serge Gruzinski, *Histoire du Nouveau Monde*, 2 vols (Paris: Fayard, 1991–93).

Bertrand, Gilles, 'Pour une approche comparée des modes de contrôle exercés aux frontières des anciens États italiens', in Claudia Moatti (ed.), *La mobilité des personnes en Méditerranée de l'Antiquité à l'époque moderne: Procédures de contrôle et documents d'identification* (Rome: École Française de Rome, 2004), pp. 253–303.

Bertrand, Régis, *Mort et mémoire: Provence, XVIIIe–XXe siècles* (Marseille: La Thune, 2011).

Bertrand, Romain, and Guillaume Calafat, 'La microhistoire globale: Affaire(s) à suivre', *Annales: Histoire, sciences sociales*, 73, 1 (2018), pp. 3–18.

Besson, Joseph, *La Syrie Sainte ou la mission de Jésus et des pères de la Compagnie de Jésus en Syrie* (Paris: Jean Henault, 1660).

Bevilacqua, Alexander, 'Beyond East and West', in Ann Blair and Nicholas Popper (eds), *New Horizons for Early Modern European Scholarship* (Baltimore: Johns Hopkins University Press, 2021), pp. 72–91.

Beydoun, Ahmed, *Identité confessionnelle et temps social chez les historiens maronites contemporains* (Beirut: Librairie orientale, 1984).

Bittar, André, 'La dynamique commerciale des Grecs catholiques en Égypte au XVIIIe siècle', *Annales Islamologiques*, 26 (1992), pp. 181–96.

Bittar, André, 'Les Juifs, les Grecs catholiques, et la ferme des douanes en Égypte sous Ali Bey al-Kabîr', *Annales Islamologiques*, 27 (1993), pp. 255–70.

Bono, Salvatore, *Corsari nel Mediterraneo: Cristiani e musulmani fra guerra, schiavitù e commercio* (Milan: Mondadori, 1993).

Boogert, Maurits H. van den, 'Intermediaries *par excellence?* Ottoman Dragomans in the Eighteenth Century', in Bernard Heyberger and Chantal Verdeil (eds), *Hommes de l'entre-deux: Parcours individuels et portraits de groupe sur la frontière méditerranéenne* (Paris: Les Indes Savantes, 2009), pp. 95–115.

Boogert, Maurits H. van den, *The Capitulations in the Ottoman Legal System: Consuls, Qadis and Beratlıs in the Eighteenth Century* (Leiden: Brill, 2005).

Bottigheimer, Ruth B., 'Hanna Diyab and *The Thousand and One Nights*', *Marvel & Tales*, 28, 2 (2014), pp. 302–24.

Boutry, Philippe, and Dominique Julia (eds), *Pèlerins et pèlerinages dans l'Europe moderne* (Rome: École Française de Rome, 2000).

Boutry, Philippe, *Prêtres et paroisses au pays du curé d'Ars* (Paris: Cerf, 1986).

Bouyrat, Yann, *Devoir d'intervenir? L'expédition 'humanitaire' de la France au Liban, 1860* (Paris: Vendémiaire, 2013).

Braude, Benjamin, 'Foundation Myths of the *Millet* System', in Benjamin Braude and Bernard Lewis (eds), *Christians and Jews in the Ottoman Empire: The Functioning of a Plural Society*, vol. 1: *The Central Lands* (New York, London: Holmes & Meier, 1982), pp. 69–88.

Braudel, Fernand, *La Méditerranée et le Monde méditerranéen à l'époque de Philippe II*, 3 vols (Paris: A. Colin, 1949).

Brockelmann, Carl, *Geschichte der arabischen Litteratur*, 2 vols (Weimar, Berlin: Felber, 1898–1902).

Brogini, Anne, 'Un cosmopolitisme de frontière: Les étrangers à Malte (fin XVIe–XVIIe siècles)', *Cahiers de la Méditerranée*, 67 (2003), pp. 15–32.

Brogini, Anne, *Malte, frontière de Chrétienté (1530–1670)* (Rome: École française de Rome, 2006), pp. 253–331.

Būlus al-Ḥalabī, *Voyage du Patriarche Macaire d'Antioche*, Arabic edition and French translation by Basile Radu (Paris: Brepols, 1933).

Buss, Andreas, 'The Individual in the Eastern Orthodox Tradition', *Archives des sciences sociales des religions*, 91 (1995), pp. 259–75.

Busse, Heribert, *Die Reise 'Abd al-Ġānī an-Nābulusī durch den Libanon* (Beirut: Orient Institut, 2003).

Cabanel, Patrick (ed.), *Une France en Méditerranée: Ecoles, langues et cultures françaises, XIXe–XXe siècles* (Paris: Créaphis, 2006).

Calafat, Guillaume, 'Ramadam Fatet vs. John Jucker: Trials and Forgery in Egypt, Syria, and Tuscany (1739–1740)', *Quaderni storici*, 48, 2 (2013), pp. 419–40.

Calafat, Guillaume, *Les interprètes de la diplomatie en Méditerranée: Traiter à Alger (1670–1680)*, in Jocelyne Dakhlia and Wolfgang Kaiser (eds), *Les musulmans dans l'histoire de l'Europe*, vol. 2: *Passages et contacts en Méditerranée* (Paris: Albin Michel, 2013), pp. 371–410.

Campbell, Robert B., 'The Devil and Devilry in Some Arabic Fiction at the Turn of the Century', in Angelika Neuwirth, Birgit Embalo, Sebastian Günther and Maher Jarrar (eds), *Myths, Historical Archetypes and Symbolic Figures in Arabic Literature: Towards a New Hermeneutic Approach* (Stuttgart: Steiner in Komm., 1999), pp. 291–300.

Cândea, Virgil (ed.), *Icônes grecques, melkites, russes: Collection Abou Adal* (Geneva: Skira, 1993).

Cândea, Virgil (ed.), *Icônes Melkites: Exposition organisée par le musée Nicolas Sursock du 16 mai au 15 juin 1969* (Beirut: Musée Nicolas Sursock, 1969).

Cândea, Virgil, 'Une œuvre d'art melkite: L'icône de Saint Elian de Homs', *Syria* (1972), pp. 219–38.

Carame, Joseph (ed.), *Deux religieux maronites: Le P. Nemattalla Alhardini et le Père Charbel* (Paris: Letouzey et Ané, 1923).

Castellano, Juan Luis, and Jean-Pierre Dedieu (eds), *Réseaux, familles et pouvoirs dans le monde ibérique à la fin de l'Ancien Régime* (Paris: CNRS Éditions, 1998).

Castelnau-L'Estoile, Charlotte de, *Les Ouvriers d'une Vigne stérile: Les jésuites et la conversion des Indiens au Brésil 1580–1620* (Lisbon, Paris: Centre Culturel Calouste Gulbenkian, Commission nationale pour les commémorations des découvertes portugaises, 2000).

Cerri, Urbano, *État présent de l'Église romaine dans toutes les parties du monde écrit pour l'usage du Pape Innocent XI par Mgr Urbano Cerri, Secrétaire de la congrégation de Propaganda Fide* (Amsterdam: Pierre Humbert, 1716).

Certeau, Michel de, *La fable mystique XVIe–XVIIe siècle* (Paris: Gallimard, 1982); English translation by Michael B. Smith, *Mystic Fable*, vol. 1 (Chicago: University of Chicago Press, 1995).

Chabot, Jean-Baptiste, 'Les origines du patriarcat chaldéen: Vie de Mar Youssef Ier (1681–1695)', *Revue de l'Orient Chrétien*, 1 (1896), pp. 66–90.

Chaillot, Christine, 'L'icône, sa vénération, son usage, d'après des récits de Wansleben au XVIIe siècle', *Le monde copte*, 18 (1990), pp. 81–88.

Charaf, Jean, 'Introduction à l'histoire sociale du Mont-Liban au XVIe siècle', in Charles Chartouni (ed.), *Histoire sociétés et pouvoir aux Proche et Moyen Orients* (Paris: Geuthner, 2001), pp. 11–26.

Charles-Roux, François, *France et chrétiens d'Orient* (Paris: Flammarion, 1939).

Charon [Korolevskij], Cyrille, *Histoire des patriarcats melkites (Alexandrie, Antioche, Jérusalem), depuis le schisme monophysite du VIe siècle jusqu'à nos jours*, vol. 2: *La période moderne (1833–1855)* (Rome: M. Bretschneider, 1910).

Charon, Cyrille, 'L'Église grecque catholique de Livourne', *Échos d'Orient*, 11 (1908), pp. 227–37.

Cohen, Mark R., *Under Crescent and Cross: The Jews in the Middle Ages*, with a new introduction and foreword (Princeton: Princeton University Press, 2008).

Çolak, Hasan, and Elif Bayraktar Tellan, *The Orthodox Church as an Ottoman Institution: A Study of Early Modern Patriarchal Berats* (Istanbul: The Isis Press, 2019).

Çolak, Hasan, *The Orthodox Church in the Early Modern Middle East: Relations between the Ottoman Central Administration and the Patriarchates of Antioch, Jerusalem and Alexandria* (Ankara: Türk Tarih Kurumu, 2015).

Coller, Ian, *Arab France: Islam and the Making of Modern Europe, 1798–1831* (Berkeley: University of California Press, 2010).

Colombo, Emanuele, 'Jesuits and Islam in Seventeenth-Century Europe: War, Preaching and Conversions', in Bernard Heyberger, Mercedes García-Arenal, Emanuele Colombo and Paola Vismara (eds), *L'Islam visto da Occidente: Cultura e religione del Seicento europeo di fronte all'Islam* (Milan: Marietti 1820, 2009), pp. 315–40.

Colombo, Emanuele, *Convertire i musulmani: L'esperienza di un gesuita spagnolo nel seicento* (Milan: Mondadori, 2007).

Croix, Alain, *La Bretagne aux XVIe et XVIIe siècles, la vie, la mort, la foi* (Paris: Maloine, 1980).

Curtin, Philip D., *Cross-Cultural Trade in World History* (Cambridge: Cambridge University Press, 1984).

Cuypers, Michel, *Le Festin: Une lecture de la sourate 'al-Mâ'ida'* (Paris: Lethielleux, 2007).

d'Errico, Gian Luca (ed.), *Il Corano e il pontifice: Ludovico Marracci fra cultura islamica e Curia papale* (Rome: Carocci Editore, 2015).

Daher, Paul, 'A Testimony to the Interior Life of Father Charbel Makhlouf, Monk of the Order of St Anthony the Great of the M. Monks in the Lebanon', *Eastern Churches Review*, 10, 1–2 (1978), pp. 104–7.

Daher, Paul, *Charbel: Un homme ivre de Dieu 1828–1898*, 2nd ed. (Annaya, Liban: Monastère Saint-Maron, 1993).

Daher, Paul, *Vie, survie et prodiges de l'ermite Charbel Makhlouf* (Paris: Spes, 1953).

Ḍāhir, Būlus [Paul Daher], *Lubnān watan sukrān bi-Sharbal* (ʿAnnāyā: n. p., 1978).
Dāhir, Būlus, *Kalimāt Sharbal*, 2nd ed. (Harissa, Lebanon: Al-tibʿa al-būlusiyya, 1995).
Dakhlia, Jocelyne, 'Une archéologie du même et de l'autre: Thomas-Osman d'Arcos dans la Méditerranée du XVIIe siècle', in Jocelyne Dakhlia and Wolfgang Kaiser (eds), *Les musulmans dans l'histoire de l'Europe*, vol. 2: *Passages et contacts en Méditerranée* (Paris: Albin Michel, 2013), pp. 61–163.
Dakhlia, Jocelyne, and Bernard Vincent (eds), *Les musulmans dans l'histoire de l'Europe*, vol. 1: *Une intégration invisible* (Paris: Albin Michel, 2011).
Dakhlia, Jocelyne, and Wolfgang Kaiser (eds), *Les musulmans dans l'histoire de l'Europe*, vol. 2: *Passages et contacts en Méditerranée* (Paris: Albin Michel, 2013).
Dandini, Girolamo, *Missione apostolica al Patriarca e Maroniti del Monte Libano et Pellegrinazione a Gerusalemme di P. Jer. Dandini* (Cesena: per il Neri, 1656).
Dandini, Girolamo, *Voyage du Mont Liban, traduit de l'italien du R. P. Jérôme Dandini, nonce en ce païs-là: Ou il est traité tant de la créance et des coutumes des Maronites, que de plusieurs particularitez touchant les Turcs, et de quelques lieux considérables de l'Orient; avec des remarques sur la Théologie des Chrétiens du Levant, et sur celle des Mahométans. Par R. S. P.* [Richard Simon, prêtre] (Paris: Louis Billaine, 1675).
Daniel, Norman, *Islam et Occident* (Paris: Cerf, 1993).
'Dans ou hors de la perspective du schéma XIII: La béatification du P. Charbel Makhlouf', *Irenikon*, 38 (1965), pp. 547–48.
Davie, May, *Le millat grecque-orthodoxe de Beyrouth, 1800–1940: Structuration interne et rapport à la cité* (PhD dissertation, Université Paris 3, 1993).
Deguilhem, Randi (ed.), *Le waqf dans l'espace islamique: Outil de pouvoir sociopolitique* (Damascus: IFEA, 1995).
[Dehaisnes, Chrétien (ed.)], *Les Marounites, d'après le manuscrit arabe du R. P. Azar, Vicaire-Général de Saïda (Terre Sainte), délégué du patriarche d'Antioche et de la Nation Marounite* (Cambrai: F. Deligne et E. Lesne, 1852).
Delumeau, Jean, *La peur en Occident (XIVe–XVIIIe siècles): Une cité assiégée* (Paris: Fayard, 1978).
Delumeau, Jean, *Rassurer et protéger: Le sentiment de sécurité dans l'Occident d'autrefois* (Paris: Fayard, 1989).
Demacopoulos, George E., and Aristotle Papanikolaou (eds), *Orthodox Constructions of the West* (New York: Fordham University Press, 2013).
Denoix, Sylvie, 'Hommages à André Raymond (1925–2011): Un chercheur infatigable', *Revue des mondes musulmans et de la Méditerranée*, 131 (2012), online: <https://journals.openedition.org/remmm/7945>.
Deringil, Selim, 'Conversion and Ideological Reinforcement: The Yezidi Kurds', in Mercedes García-Arenal (ed.), *Islamic Conversions: Religious Identities in Mediterranean Islam* (Paris: Maisonneuve & Larose, European Science Foundation, 2001), pp. 419–43.

Desmet-Grégoire, Hélène, *Le divan magique: L'Orient turc en France au XVIIIe siècle*, 2nd ed. (Paris: L'Harmattan, 1994).

Dib, Pierre, *Joseph Simon Assémani et ses deux neveux: Leurs testaments* (Paris: G. P. Maisonneuve, 1939).

Didier, Hugues, 'Une mission chrétienne atypique auprès d'un souverain musulman atypique?' in Bernard Heyberger and Rémy Madinier (eds), *L'Islam des marges: Missionnaires chrétiens et espaces périphériques du monde musulman XVIe–XXe siècle* (Paris: IISMM; Karthala, 2011), pp. 17–43.

Diyāb, Ḥannā, *Min Ḥalab ilā Bārīs: Rihla ilā balāt Luwīs al-rābiʿ ʿashar*, edited by Muḥammad Muṣṭafā al-Jārūsh and Ṣafāʾ Abū Shahlā Jubrān (Beirut: Manshūrāt al-Jamal, 2017).

Diyāb, Ḥannā, *The Book of Travels*, edited by Johannes Stephan, translated by Elias Muhanna, foreword by Yasmine Seale, 2 vols (New York: New York University Press, 2021).

Diyāb, Hanna, *Von Aleppo nach Paris: Die Reise eines jungen Syrers bis an den Hof Ludwigs XIV*, translated from French by Gennaro Ghirardelli (Berlin: Die andere Bibliothek, 2016).

Dominique Chevallier, *La société du mont Liban à l'époque de la révolution industrielle en Europe* (Paris: Geuthner, 1951).

Dompnier, Bernard, *Le venin de l'hérésie: Image du protestantisme et combat catholique au XVIIe siècle* (Paris: Le Centurion, 1985).

Dottrina christiana tradotta in lingua valacha dal padre Vito Pilutio da Vignanello Minore Conventuale di S. Francesco (Rome: Sac. Cong. de Propaganda Fide, 1677).

Douaihy, Hector, *Un théologien maronite: Gibraʿil ibn al-Qalāʿi: Évêque et moine franciscain* (Kaslik: Université Saint-Esprit de Kaslik, 1993).

Duclert, Vincent, *La France face au génocide des Arméniens: Une nation impériale et le devoir d'humanité* (Paris: Fayard, 2015).

Dumont, Louis, *Essais sur l'individualisme: Une perspective anthropologique sur l'idéologie moderne* (Paris: Seuil, 1983); English translation: *Essays on Individualism: Modern Ideology in an Anthropological Perspective* (Chicago: University of Chicago Press, 1986).

Dupont, Anne-Laure, and Catherine Mayeur-Jaouen (eds), *Débats intellectuels au Moyen-Orient dans l'entre-deux-guerres*, special issue of *Revue des mondes musulmans et de la Méditerranée*, 95–98 (2002).

Dursteler, Eric R., *Venetians in Constantinople: Nation, Identity and Coexistence in the Early Modern Mediterranean* (Baltimore: Johns Hopkins University Press, 2006).

Duverdier, Gérald, 'Propagande protestante en langues orientales aux XVIIe et XVIIIe siècles', in Gérald Duverdier, *Européens en Orient au XVIIIe siècle* (Paris: L'Harmattan, 1994), pp. 1–33.

Duwayhī, Iṣṭifān al-, 'Le candélabre des saints mystères', in Youakim Moubarac (ed.), *Pentalogie antiochienne/domaine maronite* (Beirut: Cénacle Libanais, 1984), vol. I, 1, pp. 23–106.

Duwayhī, Isṭifān al-, *Ta'rīkh al-ṭā'ifa al-mārūniyya*, edited by Rashīd al-Shartūnī (Beirut: Imprimerie catholique, 1890).

Dyâb, Hanna, *D'Alep à Paris: Les pérégrinations d'un jeune Syrien au temps de Louis XIV*, translated and edited by Paule Fahmé-Thiéry, Bernard Heyberger and Jérôme Lentin, with a preface by Bernard Heyberger (Arles: Actes Sud, 2015).

El Bibas, Khaled, *L'Emiro e il Granduca: La vicenda dell'emiro Fakhr ad-Dīn II del Libano nel contesto delle relazioni fra la Toscana e l'Oriente* (Florence: Le Lettere, 2010).

El Gemayel, Ronney, *Ḥāšiyah Wağīzah of Ilyās Faḫr: An Arabic Byzantine Antiochian Ecclesiology Responding to Uniatism* (Rome: Pontificio Instituto Orientale, 2014), pp. 31–83.

Elger, Ralf, and Yavuz Köse (eds), *Many Ways of Speaking about the Self: Middle Eastern Ego-Documents in Arabic, Persian, and Turkish (14th–20th Century)* (Wiesbaden: Harrassowitz, 2010).

Elmarsafy, Ziad, *The Enlightenment Qur'an: The Politics of Translation and the Construction of Islam* (Oxford: Oneworld, 2009).

Fahd, Butrus, *Ta'rīkh al-ruhbāniyya al-mārūniyya bi-far'ayhā al-Ḥalabī wa-l-Lubnānī*, 6 vols (Jounieh: Matba'at al-Kraym, 1963–73).

Falcetta, Angela, *Ortodossi nel Mediterraneo cattolico: Frontiere, reti, comunità nel Regno di Napoli (1700–1821)* (Rome: Viella, 2016).

Fani, Sara, and Margherita Farina (eds), *Le vie delle lettere: La Tipografia Medicea tra Roma e l'Oriente* (Florence: Mandragora, 2012).

Farah, Caesar E. (ed.), *An Arab's Journey to Colonial Spanish America: The Travels of Elias al-Mûsili in the Seventeenth Century* (Syracuse: Syracuse University Press, 2003).

Febvre, Michel, *Kitāb ijtamil 'alā ajwāba ahl al-kanīsa al-muqaddassa al-qātūlīqiyya al-jāmi'a al-rasūliyya li-i'tirāḍāt al-muslimīn wa-l-yahūd wa-l-harātiqa ḍid al-qātūliqiyyīn* (Rome: Typis Sacrae Congregationis De Propaganda Fide, 1680).

Febvre, Michel, *Praecipuae obiectiones quae vulgo solent fieri per modum interrogationis à Mahumeticae legis sectatoribus, Iudaeis, et Haereticis Orientalibus adversus Catholicos, earumque solutiones* (Rome: Typis Sacrae Congregationis De Propaganda Fide, 1679).

Febvre, Michel, *Teatro della Turchia, dove si rappresentano i disordini di essa, il genio, la natura, et i costumi di quattordici nationi, che l'habitano* (Milan: heredi di Antonio Malatesta, 1681).

Febvre, Michel, *Théâtre de la Turquie, où sont représentées les choses les plus remarquables qui s'y passent aujourd'huy touchant les Mœurs, le Gouvernement, les Coutumes & la Religion des Turcs, & de treize autres sortes de Nations qui habitent dans l'Empire Ottoman* (Paris: Edme Couterot, 1682).

Feodorov, Ioana, 'Beginnings of Arabic Printing in Ottoman Syria (1706–1711): The Romanian's Part in Athanasius Dabbas's Achievements', *ARAM Periodical*, 25, 1–2 (2013), pp. 231–60.

Festugière, André-Jean, *Les moines d'Orient*, 4 vols in 7 tomes (Paris: Cerf, 1961–65).

Fettah, Samuel, 'Le cosmopolitisme livournais: Représentations et institutions (XVIIe–XVIIIe s.)', *Cahiers de la Méditerranée*, 67 (2003), pp. 51–60.

Filippo Guadagnoli, *Pro christiana religione responsio ad obiectiones Ahmed filii Zin Alabedin, Persae Asphahanensis, Idjāba ilā Ahmad al-Sharīf Bin Zīn Al-ʿĀbidīn al-Fārisī al-Isbahānī* (Rome: Typis Sacrae Congregationis De Propaganda Fide, 1637).

Fontenay, Michel, 'Corsaires de la foi ou rentiers du sol? Les chevaliers de Malte dans le "Corso" méditerranéen au XVIle siëcle', *Revue d'histoire moderne et contemporaine*, 35 (1988), pp. 361–84.

Fontenay, Michel, 'L'Empire ottoman et le risque corsaire au XVIIe siècle', *Revue d'histoire moderne et contemporaine*, 32 (1985), pp. 185–208.

Foucault, Michel, *Histoire de la sexualité*, vol. 1: *La volonté de savoir* (Paris: Gallimard, 1976); English translation by Robert Husley, *The History of Sexuality* (New York: Vintage Books, 1988).

Frazee, Charles A., *Catholics and Sultans: The Church and the Ottoman Empire (1453–1923)* (Cambridge: Cambridge University Press, 1983).

Fuess, Albrecht, 'An Instructive Experience: Fakhr al-Dîn's Journey to Italy, 1613–1618', in Bernard Heyberger and Carsten Walbiner (eds), *Les Européens vus par les Libanais à l'époque ottomane* (Beirut: Orient-Institut der DMG; Würzburg: Ergon, 2002), pp. 23–42.

García-Arenal, Mercedes, and Gerard Wiegers (eds), *Un hombre en tres mundos: Samuel Pallache, un judío marroquí en la Europa protestante y en la católica* (Madrid: Siglo XXI, 2006); English translation: *A Man of Three Worlds: Samuel Pallache, a Moroccan Jew in Catholic and Protestant Europe* (Baltimore: Johns Hopkins University Press, 2007).

Gemayel, Nasser, *Les échanges culturels entre les Maronites et l'Europe*, 2 vols (Beirut: Imprimerie Gemayel, 1984).

Gerd, Lora, *Russian Policy in the Orthodox East: The Patriarchate of Constantinople* (Warsaw: De Gruyter Open, 2014).

Gernet, Jacques, *Chine et christianisme: Action et réaction* (Paris: Gallimard, 1982).

Ghobrial, John-Paul A. (ed.), *Global History and Microhistory*, monographic issue of *Past & Present*, 242 (2019), suppl. n° 14.

Ghobrial, John-Paul A., 'Moving Stories and What They Tell Us: Early Modern Mobility between Microhistory and Global History', *Past & Present*, 242 (2019), suppl. n° 14, pp. 243–80.

Ghobrial, John-Paul A., 'The Life and Hard Times of Solomon Negri: An Arabic Teacher in Early Modern Europe', in Alastair Hamilton, Jan Loop and Charles Burnett (eds), *The Teaching and Learning of Arabic in Early Modern Europe* (Leiden: Brill, 2017), pp. 310–31.

Ghobrial, John-Paul A., 'The Secret Life of Elias of Babylon and the Uses of Global Microhistory', *Past & Present*, 222 (2014), pp. 51–93.

Ghobrial, John-Paul, 'The Archives of Orientalism and Its Keepers: Reimagining the Histories of Arabic Manuscripts in Early Modern Europe,' *Past & Present*, 230 (2016), suppl. n° 11, pp. 90–111.

Giambattista di San Alessio, *Compendio istorico dello stato antico, e moderno del Carmelo* (Turin: nella stamperia d'Ignazio Soffietti, 1780).

Gibb, Hamilton A. R., and Harold Bowen, *Islamic Society and the West: A Study of the Impact of Western Civilization on Moslem Culture in the Near East*, 2 vols (London, New York, Toronto: Oxford University Press, 1950–57).

Ginzburg, Carlo, and Carlo Poni, 'Il nome e il come: Scambio ineguale e mercato storiografico', *Quaderni storici*, 40 (1979), pp. 181–90; English translation: 'The Name and the Game: Unequal Exchange and the Historiographical Marketplace', in Edward Muir and Guido Ruggiero (eds), *Microhistory and the Lost Peoples of Europe* (Baltimore: Johns Hopkins University Press, 1991).

Girard, Aurélien (ed.), *Connaître l'Orient en Europe au XVIIe siècle*, special issue of *XVIIe siècle*, 268 (2015), pp. 385–508.

Girard, Aurélien, 'Comment reconnaître un chrétien oriental *vraiment* catholique? Elaboration et usages de la profession de foi pour les orientaux à Rome (XVIe–XVIIIe siècle)', in Marie-Hélène Blanchet and Frédéric Gabriel (eds), *L'union à l'épreuve du formulaire: Professions de foi entre Églises d'Orient et d'Occident (XIIIe–XVIIIe siècle)* (Leuven: Peeters, 2016), pp. 235–57.

Girard, Aurélien, 'La construction de l'identité confessionnelle maronite à l'époque ottomane (XVIe–XVIIe siècle)', in Bernard Heyberger (ed.), *Les chrétiens de tradition syriaque à l'époque ottomane* (Paris: Geuthner, 2020), pp. 153–200.

Girard, Aurélien, 'Was an Eastern Scholar Necessarily a Cultural Broker in Early Modern Europe? Faustus Naironus (1628–1711), the Christian East, and Oriental Studies', in Nicholas Hardy and Dmitri Levitin (eds), *Confessionalisation and Erudition in Early Modern Europe* (Oxford: Oxford University Press, 2019), pp. 240–63.

Girard, Aurélien, and Giovanni Pizzorusso, 'The Maronite College in Early Modern Rome: Between the Ottoman Empire and the Republic of Letters', in Liam Chambers and Thomas O'Connor (eds), *College Communities Abroad: Education, Migration and Catholicism in Early Modern Europe* (Manchester: Manchester University Press, 2017), pp. 174–97.

Girard, Aurélien, Bernard Heyberger and Vassa Kontouma (eds), *Livres et confessions chrétiennes orientales: Histoire connectée entre Empire ottoman, monde slave et Occident (XVIe–XVIIIe siècles)* (Turnhout: Brepols, forthcoming).

Glesener, Thomas, 'Gouverner la langue arabe: Miguel Casiri et les arabisants du roi d'Espagne au siècle des Lumières', *Annales: Histoire, sciences sociales*, 76, 2 (2021), pp. 227–67.

Göçek, Fatma Müge, *East Encounters West: France and the Ottoman Empire in the Eighteenth Century* (Oxford: Oxford University Press, 1987).

Goudard, Joseph, *La Sainte Vierge au Liban* (Paris: n. p., 1908).

Goyau, Georges, *Un précurseur: François Picquet, consul de Louis XIV en Alep et évêque de Babylone* (Paris: Geuthner, 1942).

Grabar, André, 'Les icônes melkites', in Virgil Cândea (ed.), *Icônes Melkites: Exposition organisée par le musée Nicolas Sursock du 16 mai au 15 juin 1969* (Beirut: Musée Nicolas Sursock, 1969), pp. 19–26.

Grabar, André, *Les voies de la création en iconographie chrétienne*, 2nd ed. (Paris: Flammarion, 1994).

Gradeva, Rossitsa, 'Orthodox Christians in the Kadı Courts: The Practice of the Sofia Sheriat Court, Seventeenth Century', *Islamic Law and Society*, 4, 1 (1997), pp. 37–69.

Graf, Georg, *Geschichte der christlichen arabischen Literatur*, 5 vols (Vatican City: Biblioteca Apostolica Vaticana, 1944–53).

Graf, Tobias P., 'Cheating the Habsburgs and Their Subjects? Eighteenth-Century "Arabian Princes" in Central Europe and the Question of Fraud', in Stefan Hanß and Dorothea McEwan (eds), *The Habsburg Mediterranean* (Vienna: Austrian Academy of Sciences Press, 2021), pp. 229–54.

Greene, Molly, *A Shared World: Christians and Muslims in the Early Modern Mediterranean* (Princeton: Princeton University Press, 2000).

Greene, Molly, *Catholic Pirates and Greek Merchants: A Maritime History of the Mediterranean* (Princeton: Princeton University Press, 2010).

Grehan, James, *Twilight of the Saints: Everyday Religion in Ottoman Syria and Palestine* (New York: Oxford University Press, 2014).

Grendi, Edoardo, 'Micro-analisi e storia sociale', *Quaderni storici*, 35 (1977), pp. 506–20.

Grene, Clement, review of Bernard Heyberger, *Hindiyya, Mystic and Criminal (1720–1798)* (London: James Clarke & Co., 2013), in *The Expository Times*, 127, 6 (2016), pp. 303–4.

Grévin, Benoît, and Giuseppe Mandalà, 'Le rôle des communautés juives siciliennes dans la transmission des savoirs arabes en Italie, XIIIe–XVe siècles', in Bernard Heyberger and Albrecht Fuess (eds), *La frontière méditerranéenne du XVe au XVIIe siècle: Conflits, circulations, échanges* (Turnhout: Brepols, 2013), pp. 283–99.

Gribaudi, Maurizio, 'Echelle, pertinence, configuration', in Jacques Revel (ed.), *Jeux d'échelles: La micro-analyse à l'expérience* (Paris: Gallimard, Le Seuil, 1996), pp. 113–39.

Griffith, Sidney H., *The Church in the Shadow of the Mosque: Christians and Muslims in the World of Islam* (Princeton: Princeton University Press, 2008).

Gruzinski, Serge, 'Christianisation ou occidentalisation? Les sources romaines d'une anthropologie historique', *Mélanges de l'École française de Rome: Italie et Méditerranée*, 101, 2 (1989), pp. 733–50.

Gruzinski, Serge, *La colonisation de l'imaginaire: Sociétés indigènes et occidentalisation dans le Mexique espagnol, XVIe–XVIIIe siècle* (Paris: Gallimard, 1988).

Gruzinski, Serge, 'Les mondes mêlés de la monarchie catholique et autres "connected histories"', *Annales: Histoire, sciences sociales*, 56, 1 (2001), pp. 85–117.

Guirguis, Magdi, *An Armenian Artist in Ottoman Egypt: Yuhanna al-Armani and His Coptic Icons* (Cairo: American University in Cairo Press, 2008).

Guys, Henri, *Beyrouth et le Liban*, 2 vols (Beirut: Dar Lahad Khater, 1985).

Haddad, Jean-Pierre, *Charbel: Un saint du Liban* (Paris: Adrien Maisonneuve, 1978).

Haddad, Robert M., 'On Melkite Passage to the Unia: The Case of Patriarch Cyril al-Za'îm', in Benjamin Braude and Bernard Lewis (eds), *Christians and Jews in the Ottoman Empire: The Functioning of a Plural Society*, vol. 2: *The Arabic-Speaking Lands* (New York, London: Holmes and Meier, 1982), pp. 67–90.

Haddad, Robert M., *Syrian Christians in Muslim Society: An Interpretation* (Princeton: Princeton University Press, 1970).

Haddad, Robert M., *The Orthodox Patriarchate of Antioch and the Origins of the Melkite Schism* (PhD dissertation, Harvard University, 1965).

Haguet, Lucile, 'Paul Lucas l'explorateur (1664–1737), ou la réhabilitation d'un affabulateur', in Christiane Demeulenaere (ed.), *Explorations et voyages scientifiques de l'Antiquité à nos jours* (Paris: CTHS, 2008), pp. 479–97.

Hajjar, Joseph, 'L'activité latinisante du lazariste Nicolas Gaudez en Syrie', *Revue d'histoire de l'Église*, 75, 1 (1980), pp. 40–83.

Hajjar, Joseph, 'La question religieuse en Orient au déclin de l'Empire ottoman (1683–1814)', *Istina*, 13, 2 (1968), pp. 153–236.

Hajjar, Joseph, *L'apostolat des missionnaires latins dans le Proche-Orient selon les directives romaines* (Jerusalem: Habesch, 1956).

Hajjar, Joseph, *Les Chrétiens uniates du Proche-Orient* (Paris: Seuil, 1962).

Hajjar, Joseph, *Un lutteur infatigable: Le patriarche Maximos III Mazloum* (Harissa: Imprimerie Saint Paul, 1957).

Hakim, Carol, *The Origin of the Lebanese National Idea 1840–1920* (Berkeley: University of California Press, 2003).

Hamilton, Alastair, 'An Egyptian Traveller in the Republic of Letters: Josephus Barbatus or Abudagnus the Copt', *Journal of the Warburg and Courtauld Institutes*, 57 (1994), pp. 123–50.

Hamilton, Alastair, and Francis Richard, *André Du Ryer and Oriental Studies in Seventeenth-Century France* (London, Oxford: The Arcadian Library, Oxford University Press, 2004).

Hamilton, Alastair, Maurits. H. van den Boogert and Bart Westerweel (eds), *The Republic of Letters and the Levant* (Leiden: Brill, 2005).

Hamilton, Alastair, *The Copts and the West, 1439–1822: The European Discovery of the Egyptian Church* (Oxford: Oxford University Press, 2006).

Hamilton, Alastair, *William Bedwell the Arabist, 1563–1632* (Leiden: Brill, 1985).

Hanna, Nelly, and Raouf Abbas (ed.), *Society and Economy in Egypt and the Eastern Mediterranean 1600–1900: Essays in Honor of André Raymond* (Cairo: The American University in Cairo Press, 2005).

Hardy, Nicholas, and Dmitri Levitin (eds), *Faith and History: Confessionalisation and Erudition in Early Modern Europe* (Oxford: Oxford University Press, 2019).

Harik, Iliya F., *Politics and Change in a Traditional Society: Lebanon 1711–1845* (Princeton: Princeton University Press, 1968).

Hatem, Jad, *Hindiyyé d'Alep: Mystique de la chair et jalousie divine* (Paris: L'Harmattan, 2001).

Hayek, Michel, *Le chemin du désert: Le Père Charbel moine d'Orient* (Le Puy, Lyon: Xavier Mappus, 1962).

Hayek, Michel, *Le père Charbel ou la voix du silence* (Paris: La Colombe, 1956).

Ḥāʾik [Hayek], Michel al-, 'Al-Rāhiba Hindiyya: Āmālīhā wa-rahbanatuhā', *Al-Mashriq* (1965), pp. 525–646, 685–734; (1966), pp. 273–332, 519–52.

Hayes, Edmund, and Eline Scheerlinck, 'Introduction', and Paul Jürgen, '*Ḥimāya* Revisited', in *Acts of Protection in Early Islamicate Societies*, monographic section of *Annales Islamologiques,* 54 (2020), online: <https://journals.openedition.org/anisl/7173>.

Hellot-Bellier, Florence, *Chroniques de massacres annoncés: Les Assyro-Chaldéens d'Iran et du Hakkari face aux ambitions des empires, 1896–1920* (Paris: Geuthner, 2014).

Henny, Sundar, 'Nathanael of Leukas and the Hottinger Circle: The Wanderings of a Seventeenth-Century Greek archbishop,' *International Journal of the Classical Tradition*, 27 (2020), pp. 449–72.

Horn, Elzear, *Iconographiae locorum et monumentorum veterum Terrae Sanctae accurate delineatae et descriptae a P. Elzeario Horn Ordinis Minorum Provinciae Thuringiae (1725–44)*, edited by Girolamo Golubovich (Rome: typis Sallustianis, 1902).

Idlibī (Edelby), Nāwufītūs, *Asāqifa al-Rūm al-Malakiyyīn bi-Ḥalab* (Aleppo: Maṭbaʾat al-Iḥsān, 1983).

İnalcik, Halil, 'Ottoman Archival Materials on *Millets*', in Benjamin Braude and Bernard Lewis (eds), *Christians and Jews in the Ottoman Empire: The Functioning of a Plural* Society, vol. 1: *The Central Lands* (New York, London: Holmes & Meier, 1982), pp. 69–88.

İnalcik, Halil, 'The Status of the Greek Orthodox Patriarch under the Ottomans', *Turcica*, 21–23 (1991), pp. 407–36.

Isabella, Maurizio, and Konstantina Zanou (eds), *Mediterranean Diasporas: Politics and Ideas in the long 19th Century* (London, New York: Bloomsbury, 2016).

Jennings, Ronald C., *Christians and Muslims in Ottoman Cyprus and the Mediterranean World, 1571–1640* (New York: New York University Press, 1993).

Jock, Timothée, *Jésuites et chouéirites ou la fondation des religieuses basiliennes chouéirites de Notre-Dame de l'Annonciation à Zouq-Mikaïl (Liban), 1730–1746* (Central Falls, USA: self-published, 1936).

Joseph, John, *Muslim-Christian Relations and Inter-Christian Rivalries in the Middle-East: The Case of the Jacobites in an Age of Transition* (Albany: SUNY Press, 1983).

Kenanoğlu, Macit, *Osmanlı Millet Sistemi: Mit ve Gerçek* (Istanbul: Klasik, 2004).

Kévorkian, Raymond H., *Catalogue des 'incunables' arméniens, 1511–1695 ou Chronique de l'imprimerie arménienne* (Geneva: Cramer, 1986).

Khashān, Yūsuf, *Al-kawākib al-khamsa*, 3rd enriched ed. (Jounieh: Dakāsh, 1996).

Khater, Akram Fouad, *Embrace the Divine: Passion and Politics in the Christian Middle East* (Syracuse: Syracuse University Press, 2011).

Khater, Akram (ed.), 'How Does New Scholarship on Christians and Christianity in the Middle East Shape How We View the History of the Region and Its Current Issues?' *International Journal of Middle East Studies*, 42, 3 (2010), pp. 471–88.

Khater, Akram, *Inventing Home: Emigration, Gender and the Making of a Lebanese Middle Class, 1861–1921* (Berkeley, London: University of California Press, 2001).

Khayati, Loubna, 'Le statut de l'Islam dans la pensée libertine du premier XVIIe siècle', in Bernard Heyberger, Mercedes García-Arenal, Emanuele Colombo and Paola Vismara (eds), *L'Islam visto da Occidente: Cultura e religione del Seicento europeo di fronte all'Islam* (Milan: Marietti 1820, 2009), pp. 109–33.

Kilpatrick, Hilary, 'Brockelmann, Kaḥḥâla & Co: Reference Works on the Arabic Literature of Early Ottoman Syria', *Middle Eastern Literatures*, 7, 1 (2004), pp. 33–51.

Kilpatrick, Hilary, and Gerald J. Toomer, 'Niqūlāwus Al-Ḥalabī (c.1611–1661): A Greek Orthodox Syrian Copyist and his Letters to Pococke and Golius', *Lias*, 43, 1 (2016), pp. 1–159.

Kitāb murshid al-kāhin . . . (Rome: Sacra Congregatio de Propaganda Fide, 1844).

Konortas, Paraskevas, *Othōmanikes theōrēseis gia to Oikoumeniko Patriarcheio: Beratia gia tous prokathēmenous tēs Megalēs Ekklēsias, 17os-arches tou 20ou aiōna* (Athens: Alexandreia, 1998).

Köse, Ensar, 'İstanbul Ermeni Patrikliği'nin Osmanlı Hükümeti'yle Münasebetlerine Tesir Eden Dinamikler (18. Yüzyılın İlk Yarısı)', *Osmanlı Medeniyeti Arastırmaları Dergisi*, 3–5 (2017), pp. 1–24.

Krampl, Ulrike, *Travailler avec les langues à Paris au XVIIIe siècle: La fabrique d'une ville plurilingue*, Mémoire inédit du dossier d'habilitation à diriger les recherches (Université de Paris, 2019).

Kratschkowsky, Ignatius, and A. G. Karam, 'Farḥāt', in *Encyclopaedia of Islam, Second Edition*, online: <http://dx.doi.org/10.1163/1573-3912_islam_SIM_2282>.

Krimsti, Feras, 'Arsāniyūs Shukrī al-Ḥakīm's Account of his Journey to France, the Iberian Peninsula, and Italy (1748–1757) from Travel Journal to Edition', *Philological Encounters*, 4 (2019), pp. 202–44.

Kritikou, Flora, 'Les manuscrits musicaux post-byzantins d'origine crétoise comme témoins des échanges culturels entre Vénitiens et Grecs (XVIe–XVIIe s.)', in Aurélien Girard, Bernard Heyberger and Vassa Kontouma (eds), *Livres et confessions chrétiennes orientales: Histoire connectée entre Empire ottoman, monde slave et Occident (XVIe–XVIIIe siècles)* (Turnhout: Brepols, forthcoming).

Krstić, Tijana, and Derin Terzioğlu (eds), *Entangled Confessionalizations? Dialogic Perspectives on the Politics of Piety and Community Building in the Ottoman Empire, 15th–18th Centuries* (Piscataway: Gorgias Press, 2022).

Kuri, Sami, *Une histoire du Liban à travers les archives des jésuites*, 3 vols (Beirut: Dar Al-Machreq, 1985–96).

Lacarrière, Jacques, *Les hommes ivres de Dieu* (Paris: Arthaud, 1961).

Laiou, Sophia, 'Christian Women in an Ottoman World: Interpersonal and Family Cases Brought before the Shariʿa Courts during the Seventeenth and Eighteenth Centuries', in Amila Buturovic and Irvin C. Schick (eds), *Women in the Ottoman Balkans: Gender, Culture and History* (London: I. B. Tauris, 2007), pp. 243–71.

Lamartine, Alphonse de, *Voyage en Orient*, edited by Sarga Moussa (Paris: Honoré Champion, 2000).

Landau, Amy S., 'European Religious Iconography in Safavid Iran: Decoration and Patronage of Meydani Bet'ghehem (Bethlehem of the Maydan)', in Willem Floor and Edmund Herzig (eds), *Iran and the World in the Safavid Age* (London: I. B. Tauris, 2012), pp. 425–46.

Lapidus, Ira M., 'Islamic Revival and Modernity: The Contemporary Movements and the Historical Paradigms', *Journal of Economic and Social History of the Orient*, 40, 4 (1997), pp. 444–60.

Launay, Marcel, *Le bon prêtre: Le clergé rural au XIXe siècle* (Paris: Aubier, 1986).

Le Behr-Sigel, Elisabeth, *Prière et sainteté dans l'Église russe* (Paris: Cerf, 1950).

Lebanon – The Artist's View: 200 Years of Lebanese Painting: Catalogue of the Exhibition at the Barbican Centre (London: British Lebanese Association, 1989).

Lébédew, Olga de (ed.), *Codex 286 du Vatican: Récits de voyages d'un Arabe* (St Petersburg : s. n., 1902).

Leeuwen, Richard van, *Notables and Clergy in Mount Lebanon: The Khāzin Sheikhs and the Maronite Church, 1736–1840* (Leiden: Brill, 1994).

Leeuwen, Richard van, 'The Maronite *Waqf* of Dayr Sayyidat Bkirki in Mount Lebanon during the 18th century', in Randi Deguilhem (ed.), *Le waqf dans l'espace islamique: Outil de pouvoir sociopolitique* (Damascus: IFEA, 1995), pp. 259–75.

Leeuwen, Richard van, and Ulrich Marzolph, 'Hanna Diyab', in *The Arabian Nights Encyclopedia* (Santa Barbara: Abc-Clio, 2004), p. 582.

Legrand, Hervé, and Giuseppe Maria Croce (eds), *L'Œuvre d'Orient: Solidarités anciennes et nouveaux défis* (Paris: Cerf, 2010).

Lejeune, Philippe, *Le moi des demoiselles: Enquête sur le journal de jeune fille* (Paris: Seuil, 1993).

Lemmens, Leonhard (ed.), *Collectanea Terrae Sanctae ex archivio Hierosolymitano deprompta* (Quaracchi: Collegio di S. Bonaventura, 1933).

Lemos Horta, Paulo, *Marvellous Thieves: Secret Authors of the Arabian Nights* (Cambridge: Harvard University Press, 2017).

Lentin, Jérôme, *Recherches sur l'histoire de la langue arabe au Proche-Orient à l'époque moderne* (PhD dissertation, Université Paris 3, 1997).

Lepetit, Bernard, 'Histoire des pratiques, pratique de l'histoire', in Bernard Lepetit (ed.), *Les formes de l'expérience: Une autre histoire sociale* (Paris: Albin Michel), pp. 13–15.

Leroy-Ladurie, Emmanuel, *Montaillou, village occitan de 1294 à 1324* (Paris: Gallimard, 1975).

Leroy, Jules, *Moines et monastères du Proche-Orient* (Paris: Horizons de France, 1958).

Levi, Giovanni, *Le pouvoir au village: Histoire d'un exorciste dans le Piémont du XVIIe siècle* (Paris: Gallimard, 1989).

Loop, Jan, 'Divine Poetry? Early Modern European Orientalists on the Beauty of the Koran', *Church History and Religious Culture*, 89 (2009), pp. 455–88.

Loop, Jan, Alastair Hamilton and Charles Burnett (eds), *The Learning and Teaching of Arabic in Early Modern Europe* (Leiden: Brill, 2017).

Louis de Gonzague, O. F. M. Cap., 'Les anciens missionnaires capucins de Syrie et leurs écrits apostoliques de langue arabe', *Collectanea Franciscana*, 1, 3 (1931), pp. 319–59; 1, 4 (1931), pp. 457–91; 2, 1 (1932), pp. 35–71; 2, 2 (1932), pp. 179–207.

Lucas, Paul, *Deuxième voyage du Sieur Paul Lucas dans le Levant: Octobre 1704–septembre 1708*, new ed. (Saint-Étienne: Publications de l'Université de Saint-Étienne, 2002).

Lupo, Sébastien, *Révolution(s) d'échelles: Le marché levantin et la crise du commerce marseillais au miroir des maisons Roux et de leurs relais à Smyrne (1740–1787)*, 2 vols (PhD dissertation, Université Aix-Marseille, 2015).

Lyon-Caen, Nicolas, and Raphaël Morera, *À vos poubelles citoyens! Environnement urbain, salubrité publique et investissement civique (Paris, XVIe–XVIIIe siècle)* (Paris: Champ Vallon, 2020).

Makdisi, Ussama, *The Culture of Sectarianism: Community, History, and Violence in Nineteenth-Century Ottoman Lebanon* (Berkeley, Los Angeles, London: University of California Press, 2000).

Malcolm, Noel, 'Comenius, the Conversion of the Turks, and the Muslim-Christian Debate, on the Corruption of Scripture', *Church History and Religious Culture*, 87 (2007), pp. 477–508.

Maloof, Allen, 'A New Maronite Saint: Fr. Charbel Makhlouf', *Eastern Churches Review*, 10, 1–2 (1978), pp. 101–3.

Mannāsh (al-khūrī), Jirjis, 'Mustanadāt li-taʾrīkh al-muṭrān ʿAbdallāh Qarāʾalī', *La Revue Syrienne*, 1 (1926), pp. 415–25.

Mansi, Ioannes Dominicus (ed.), *Sacrorum Conciliorum nova et amplissima collectio*, vol. 46: *Sinodi Melchitarum, 1716–1902* (Paris: expensis Huberti Welter, Bibliopolae, 1911).

Manstetten, Paula, 'Kultureller Vermittler, *homme de lettres*, Vagabund? Zur Selbstdarstellung arabischer Christen in Europa am Beispiel Salomon Negris (1665–1727)', in Regina Toepfer *et al.* (eds), *Übersetzen in der Frühen Neuzeit: Konzepte und Methoden/Concepts and Practices of Translation in the Early Modern Period* (Stuttgart: Springer-Metzler, 2021), pp. 427–53.

Manstetten, Paula, 'Solomon Negri: The Self-Fashioning of an Arab Christian in Early Modern Europe', in Cornel Zwierlein (ed.), *The Power of the Dispersed: Early Modern Global Travelers beyond Integration* (Leiden, Boston: Brill, 2022), pp. 240–84.

Marcellino da Civezza, *Storia universale delle missioni francescane*, vol. 7 (Florence: Tipografia di E. Ariani, 1894).

Marcus, Abraham, *The Middle East on the Eve of Modernity: Aleppo in the Eighteenth Century* (New York: Columbia University Press, 1989).

Marino, Brigitte, *Le faubourg de Mīdān à Damas à l'époque ottomane, 1742–1830* (Damas: Institut français de Damas, 1997).

Marino, Brigitte, 'Le "Quartier des Chrétiens" (Maḥallat al-Naṣārā) de Damas au milieu du XVIIIe siècle (1150–1170/1737–1757)', *Revue des mondes musulmans et de la Méditerranée*, 107–10 (2005), pp. 323–51.

Marzolph, Ulrich, 'Les contes de Hannā', in *Les Mille et Une Nuits: Catalogue de l'exposition 'Mille et Une Nuits', Paris, Institut du monde arabe (27 novembre 2012–28 avril 2013)* (Paris: Éditions Hazan, Institut du monde arabe, 2012), pp. 87–91.

Masters, Bruce, *Christians and Jews in the Ottoman Arab World: The Roots of Sectarianism* (Cambridge: Cambridge University Press, 2001).

Masters, Bruce, *The Origins of Western Economic Dominance in the Middle East: Mercantilism and the Islamic Economy in Aleppo, 1600–1750* (New York: New York University Press, 1988).

Masters, Bruce, 'Trading Diasporas and "Nations": The Genesis of National Identities in Ottoman Aleppo', *International History Review*, 9 (1987), pp. 345–67.

Mas'ad, Būlus, and Nasīb Wuhayba al-Khāzin (ed.), *Al-Uṣūl al-ta'rīkhiyya* (Achkouth: n. p., n. d.).

Mawsilî, Elias al-, *Un Irakien en Amérique au XVIIe siècle*, edited by Nûrî al-Jarrâh and translated into French by Jean-Jacques Schmidt (Arles: Actes Sud/Sindbad, 2011).

Mawṣilī, Iliyās ibn Ḥannā al-, *Il primo Orientale nelle Americhe*, edited and translated by Marina Montanaro (Mazzara del Vallo: Liceo Ginnasio Gian Giacomo Adria, 1992).

Mayeur-Jaouen, Catherine, 'La fonction sacrale de l'image dans l'Égypte contemporaine: De l'imagerie traditionnelle à la révolution photographique', in Bernard Heyberger and Silvia Naef (eds), *La multiplication des images en pays d'Islam: De l'estampe à la télévision (17e–21e siècle)* (Istanbul: Orient-Institut der DMG; Würzburg: Ergon, 2003), pp. 57–80.

Mayeur-Jaouen, Catherine, *Pèlerinages d'Égypte: Histoire de la piété copte et musulmane, XVe–XXe siècles* (Paris: Éd. de l'EHESS, 2005).

McCallum, Fiona, 'Christians in the Middle East: A New Subfield?' *International Journal of Middle East Studies*, 42, 3 (2010), pp. 486–88.

Mehmed efendi, *Le paradis des infidèles: Un ambassadeur ottoman en France sous la Régence*, edited by Gilles Veinstein, translated by Julien-Claude Galland (Paris: Maspero, 1981).

Meinardus, Otto, 'A Critical Study on the Cult of Sitt Dimiana and her 40 Virgins', *Orientalia Suecana*, 18 (1969), pp. 45–68.

Meinardus, Otto, 'L'art copte au cours des trois derniers siècles', *Le monde copte*, 18 (1990), pp. 89–99.

Meinardus, Otto, 'The Iconography of the Eucharistic Christ in the Armenian Churches of New Julfa', *Oriens Christianus*, 58 (1974), pp. 132–37.

Meinardus, Otto, 'The Last Judgements in the Armenian Churches of New Julfa', *Oriens Christianus*, 55 (1971), pp. 182–94.

Michel, Thomas, 'Jesuit Writings on Islam in the Seventeenth Century', *Islamochristiana*, 15 (1989), pp. 57–85.

Michelet, Charlotte, *Le culte d'un saint chrétien dans la montagne libanaise* (Mémoire de maîtrise: Université Paris X-Nanterre, 1997).

Mills, Simon, *A Commerce of Knowledge: Trade, Religion, and Scholarship between England and the Ottoman Empire, 1600–1760* (Oxford: Oxford University Press, 2020).

Mohasseb Saliba, Sabine (ed.), *Les fondations pieuses waqfs chez les chrétiens et les juifs du Moyen Âge à nos jours* (Paris: Geuthner, 2016).

Mohasseb Saliba, Sabine, *Les monastères maronites doubles du Liban: Entre Rome et l'Empire ottoman, XVIIe–XIXe siècles* (Paris: Geuthner; Jounieh: PUSEK, 2008).

Möller, Esther, *Orte der Zivilisierungsmission: Französische Schulen im Libanon 1909–1943* (Göttingen: Vandenhoeck und Ruprecht, 2013).

Monge, Mathilde, and Natalia Muchnik (eds.), *Early Modern Diasporas: A European History* (London: Routledge, 2022).

Mörike, Tobias, 'Lebanese Travellers as Knowledge Brokers in Early Modern Europe 1725 to 1800' (paper presented at the international conference *The Middle East and Europe: Cross-Cultural, Diplomatic and Economic Exchanges in the Early Modern Period [1500–1820]*, Paris Sorbonne University Abu Dhabi, 4–7 March 2017).

Mouawad, Youssef, 'Aux origines d'un mythe: La lettre de Saint Louis aux maronites', in Bernard Heyberger and Carsten Walbiner (eds), *Les Européens vus par les Libanais à l'époque ottomane* (Beirut: Orient-Institut der DMG; Würzburg: Ergon, 2002), pp. 97–110.

Moubarac, Youakim (ed.), *Pentalogie antiochienne/domaine Maronite*, 7 vols (Beirut: Cénacle libanais, 1984).

Muchembled, Robert, *Le roi et la sorcière: L'Europe des bûchers XVe–XVIIIe siècle* (Paris: Desclée, 1993).

Muchembled, Robert, *Le temps des supplices: De l'obéissance sous les rois absolus, XVe–XVIIIe siècle* (Paris: Colin, 1992).

Mulsow, Martin, 'Socinianism, Islam and the Radical Uses of Arabic Scholarship', *Al-Qantara*, 31, 2 (2010), pp. 549–86.

Munağğid, Salāḥ-ad-Dīn al-, and Stefan Wild (eds), *Zwei Beschreibungen des Libanon: 'Abd al-Ġānī an- Nābulusīs Reise durch die Biqā' und al-'Uṭaifīs Reise nach Tripolis* (Beirut: Orient Institut, 1979).

Murad, Nicolas, *Notice historique sur l'origine de la nation maronite et sur ses rapports avec la France sur la nation druze et sur les diverses populations du Mont-Liban*, 2nd ed. (Paris: Librairie Adrien Le Clere, 1844).

Murad, Nicolas, *Notice historique sur l'origine de la nation maronite et sur ses rapports avec la France, sur la nation druze et sur les diverses populations du Mont Liban*, translated into Arabic and edited by Joseph Moawad and Antoine Kawal (Paris: Cariscript, 1988).

Murre-van den Berg, Heleen, *Scribes and Scriptures: The Church of the East in the Eastern Ottoman Provinces (1500–1850)* (Leuven, Paris, Bristol: Peeters, 2015).

Murre-van den Berg, Heleen, 'The Unexpected Popularity of the Study of Middle Eastern Christianity', in Sidney Harrison Griffith and Sven Grebenstein (eds), *Christsein in der islamischen Welt: Festschrift für Martin Tamcke zum 60. Geburstag* (Wiesbaden: Harrassowitz, 2015), pp. 1–12

Naef, Silvia, *À la recherche d'une modernité arabe* (Genève: Slatkine, 1996).

Nagel, Tilman, 'Autochtone Wurzeln des islamischen Modernismus: Bemerkungen zum Werk des Damaszeners Ibn 'Abîdîn 1784–1836', *Zeitschrift der Deutschen Morgenländischen Gesellschaft*, 146 (1996), pp. 92–111.

Nasrallah, Joseph, 'La peinture monumentale des patriarcats melkites', in Virgil Cândea (ed.), *Icônes Melkites: Exposition organisée par le musée Nicolas Sursock du 16 mai au 15 juin 1969* (Beirut: Musée Nicolas Sursock, 1969), pp. 67–84.

Nasrallah, Joseph, *Histoire du mouvement littéraire dans l'Église melchite du Ve au XXe siècle*, 8 tomes in 5 vols (Louvain: Peeters, 1979–2017).

Nau, Michel, *Ecclesiae Romanae Graecaeque vera effigies ex variis tum recentibus, tum antiquis monumentis singulari fide expressa romanis graecisque exhibita. Quo intelligant admirabilem utriusque consensionem et in tanta matrum concordia nefas esse pugnare et odisse inter sese ingenti damno liberos. Accessit Religio christiana contra Alcoranum per Alcoranum pacifice defensa et probata* (Paris: apud Gabrielem Martinum, 1680).

Nau, Michel, *L'état présent de la religion mahométane* (Paris: Veuve P. Bouillerot, 1684).

Newman, Daniel L., *An Imam in Paris: Account of a Stay in France by an Egyptian Cleric (1826–1831)* (London: Saqi, 2011).

Noble, Samuel, and Alexander Treiger (eds), *The Orthodox Church in the Arab World, 700–1700: An Anthology of Sources* (DeKalb: NIU Press, 2014).

Panchenko, Constantin, *Arab Orthodox Christians under the Ottomans: 1516–1831* (Jordanville: Holy Trinity Seminary Press, 2016).

Panzac, Daniel, 'Commerce et commerçants des ports du Liban Sud et de Palestine (1756–1787)', *Revue du monde Musulman et de la Méditerranée*, 55–56, 1–2 (1990), pp. 75–93.

Papademetriou, Tom, *Render unto the Sultan: Power, Authority, and the Greek Orthodox Church in the Early Ottoman Centuries* (Oxford: Oxford University Press, 2015).

Papastratos, Dory, *Paper Icons: Greek Orthodox Religious Engravings, 1665–1899*, 2 vols (Athens: Papastratos Publications, 1990).

Parker, Lucy, 'The Interconnected Histories of the Syriac Churches in the Sixteenth Century', *The Journal of Ecclesiastical History*, 72, 3 (2021), pp. 509–32.

Parker, Lucy, 'Yawsep I of Amida (D. 1707) and the Invention of the Chaldeans', in Bernard Heyberger (ed.), *Les chrétiens de tradition syriaque à l'époque ottomane* (Paris: Geuthner, 2020), pp. 121–52.

Pedani Fabris, Maria Pia, 'Intorno alla questione della traduzione del Corano', in Liliana Billanovich and Pierantonio Gios (eds), *Gregorio Barbarigo patrizio veneto vescovo e cardinale nella tarda controriforma (1625–1697)* (Padua: Istituto per la storia ecclesiastica padovana, 1999), pp. 353–65.

Philipp, Thomas, *Acre: The Rise and Fall of a Palestinian City 1730–1831* (New York: Columbia University Press, 2001).

Philipp, Thomas, *The Syrians in Egypt, 1725–1975* (Stuttgart: Steiner, 1985).

Pichon, Frédéric, *Maaloula (XIXe–XXIe siècle): Du vieux avec du neuf: Histoire et identité d'un village chrétien de Syrie* (Beirut: Institut Français du Proche-Orient, 2010).

Pierrard, Pierre, *La vie quotidienne du prêtre français au XIXe siècle 1801–1905* (Paris: Hachette, 1986).

Pizzorusso, Giovanni, 'Filippo Guadagnoli, i Caracciolini e lo studio delle lingue orientali e della controversia con l'Islam a Roma nel XVII secolo', in Irene Fosi and Giovanni Pizzorusso (eds), *L'ordine dei chierici regolari minori (Caracciolini): Religione e cultura in età postridentina, monographic issue of Studi Medievali e Moderni*, 14, 1 [2010]), pp. 245–78.

Pizzorusso, Giovanni, 'La preparazione linguistica e controversistica dei missionari per l'Oriente islamico: Scuole, testi insegnanti a Roma e in Italia', in Bernard Heyberger, Mercedes García-Arenal, Emanuele Colombo and

Paola Vismara (eds), *L'Islam visto da Occidente: Cultura e religione del Seicento europeo di fronte all'Islam* (Milan: Marietti 1820, 2009), pp. 253–88.
Pizzorusso, Giovanni, *Propaganda fide, I. La Congregazione pontificia e la giurisdizione sulle missioni* (Rome: Edizioni di Storia e Letteratura, 2022).
Podskalsky, Gerhard, *Griechische Theologie in der Zeit der Türkenherrschaft (1453–1821)* (Munich: C. H. Beck Verlag, 1988).
Poletto, Giacomo, 'Il Beato cardinale Gregorio Barbarigo, vescovo di Padova, e la riunione delle Chiese orientali alla romana', *Bessarione*, 1 (1906), pp. 14–31, 176–96, 305–33.
Poumarède, Géraud, *Pour en finir avec la croisade: Mythes et réalités de la lutte contre les Turcs aux XVIe et XVIIe siècles* (Paris: PUF, 2004).
Qarāʿalī, Būlus, *'Al-laāliʾ fī ḥayāt al-muṭrān ʿAbdallāh Qarāʿalī'* (Bayt Shabāb: Matbaʿat al-ʿilm, 1932).
Rabbath, Antoine, *Documents inédits pour servir à l'histoire du christianisme en Orient*, 3 vols (Paris: A. Picard, 1907–11).
Rabbath, Antoine, 'Riḥlat 'awwal sharqī 'ilā 'Amrīkā', *Al-Machreq* 8 (1905), pp. 821–34, 875–86, 974–83, 1022–33, 1118–29.
Radtke, Bern, 'Erleuchtung und Aufklärung: Islamische Mystik und europäischer Rationalismus', *Die Welt des Islam*, 34 (1994), pp. 46–66.
Rafeq, Abdul-Karim, 'Craft Organizations and Religious Communities in Ottoman Syria (XVI–XIX Centuries)', in *La Shīʾa nell'impero ottomano* (Rome: Accademia Nazionale Dei Lincei, 1993), pp. 25–55.
Rafeq, Abdul-Karim, review of Bernard Heyberger, *Les chrétiens du Proche-Orient au temps de la Réforme catholique* (1994), in *Journal of the Economic and Social History of the Orient*, 42, 1 (1999), pp. 120–22.
Raphael, Pierre, *Le rôle du Collège maronite romain dans l'orientalisme aux XVIIe et XVIIIe siècles* (Beirut: Université Saint-Joseph, 1950).
Raveux, Olivier, 'Entre réseau communautaire intercontinental et intégration locale: La colonie marseillaise des marchands arméniens de la Nouvelle-Djoulfa (Ispahan), 1669–1695', *Revue d'histoire moderne et contemporaine*, 59, 1 (2012), pp. 83–102.
Raymond, André, *Artisans et commerçants au Caire au XVIIIe siècle*, 2 vols (Damascus: Institut français de Damas, 1973).
Raymond, André, 'The Population of Aleppo in the Sixteenth and Seventeenth Centuries According to Ottoman Census Documents', *International Journal of Middle Eastern Studies*, 16, 4 (1984), pp. 447–60.
Raymond, André, 'Une communauté en expansion: Les chrétiens d'Alep à l'époque ottomane (XVIe–XVIIe siècles)', in André Raymond, *La ville arabe: Alep, à l'époque ottomane (XVIe–XVIIIe siècles)* (Damascus: Institut français de Damas, 1998), pp. 353–72.
Raymond, Candice, 'Beyrouth avant Beyrouth: Historiographies contemporaines d'une "ville arabe ottomane" (XVIe–XVIIIe siècles)', *Revue des mondes musulmans et de la Méditerranée*, 148 (2020), pp. 131–48.

Raymond, Candice, 'Les Annales à Beyrouth: Circulations savantes et appropriations historiographiques entre la France et le Liban', *Revue d'histoire des sciences humaines*, 34 (2019), pp. 17–34.

Raymond, Candice, 'L'historiographie du Liban ottoman entre conflits idéologiques et renouveau disciplinaire', *NAQD*, Hors-série 3, 2 (2014), pp. 95–120.

Reichmuth, Stefan, and Florian Schwarz (eds), *Zwischen Alltag und Schriftkultur: Horizonte des Individuellen in der arabischen Literatur des 17. und 18. Jahrhunderts* (Beirut: Orient-Institut, 2008).

Reindl-Kiel, Hedda, '*Damet ismetüha* – immer wahre ihre Sittsamkeit: Frau and Gesellschaft im Osmanischen Reich', *Orientierungen*, 1 (1989), pp. 37–81.

Ricci, Giovanni, *Ossessione turca: In una retrovia Cristiana dell'Europa moderna* (Bologna: Il Mulino, 2002).

Richard, Francis, 'Catholicisme et Islam chiite au "Grand siècle": Autour de quelques documents concernant les missions catholiques en Perse au XVIIe siècle', *Euntes Docete*, 33, 3 (1980), pp. 339–403.

Richard, Francis, *Raphaël du Mans missionnaire en Perse au XVIIe siècle* (Paris: L'Harmattan, 1995).

Richard, Francis, 'Trois conférences de controverse islamo-chrétienne en Géorgie vers 1665–1666', *Bedi Kartlisa*, 40 (1982), pp. 253–59.

Richard, Francis, 'Un érudit à la recherche de textes religieux venus d'Orient: Le docteur Louis Picques (1637–1699)', in Emmanuel Bury and Bernard Meunier (eds), *Les Pères de l'Église au XVIIe siècle* (Paris: Cerf, 1993), pp. 253–76.

Riffier, Jean, *Les œuvres françaises en Syrie (1860–1923)* (Paris: L'Harmattan, 2000).

Riscallah, Nasri, and Gilles Phabrey, *Charbel Makhlouf* (Paris: Spes, 1950).

Ristelhueber, René, *Les traditions françaises au Liban* (Paris: Felix Alcan, 1918).

Robson, Laura, 'Recent Perspectives on Christianity in the Modern Arab World', *History Compass*, 9, 4 (2011), pp. 312–25.

Roche, Daniel, *Humeurs vagabondes: De la circulation des hommes et de l'utilité des voyages* (Paris: Fayard, 2003), pp. 394–419.

Rondot, Pierre, *Les Chrétiens d'Orient* (Paris: Peyronnet, 1955).

Rothman, E. Natalie, 'Afterword: Intermediaries, Mediation, and Cross-Confessional Diplomacy in the Early Modern Mediterranean', *Journal of Early Modern History*, 19 (2015), pp. 245–59.

Rothman, E. Natalie, *Brokering Empire: Trans-Imperial Subjects between Venice and Istanbul* (Ithaca: Cornell University Press, 2011).

Rothman, E. Natalie, 'Interpreting Dragomans: Boundaries and Crossings in the Early Modern Mediterranean', *Comparative Studies in Society and History*, 51, 4 (2009), pp. 771–800.

Rothman, E. Natalie, *The Dragoman Renaissance: Diplomatic Interpreters and the Routes of Orientalism* (Ithaca: Cornell University Press, 2021).

Rouhana, Paul, 'Les versions des origines religieuses des Maronites entre le XVe et le XVIIIe siècles', in Charles Chartouni (ed.), *Histoire sociétés et pouvoir aux Proche et Moyen Orients* (Paris: Geuthner, 2001), pp. 191–211.

Rowell, Geoffrey, review of Bernard Heyberger, *Hindiyya, Mystic and Criminal (1720–1798)* (London: James Clarke & Co., 2013), in *Church Times*, 11 October 2013.

Rudt de Collenberg, Wipertus, 'Le baptême des musulmans esclaves à Rome aux XVIIe et XVIIIe siècles: Le XVIIIe siècle', *Mélanges de l'École française de Rome. Italie et Méditerranée*, 101, 2 (1989), pp. 519–670.

Runciman, Steven, *The Great Church in Captivity: A Study of the Patriarchate of Constantinople from the Eve of the Turkish Conquest to the Greek War of Independence* (Cambridge: Cambridge University Press, 1968).

Russell, Alexander, *The Natural History of Aleppo* (London: G. G. and J. Robinson, 1794).

Saadé, Pierre, *Charbel: El gran santo del siglo XX (1830–1898)*, vol. 1 (Mendoza, Argentina: s. n., 1998).

Sajdi, Dana, *The Barber of Damascus: Nouveau Literacy in the Eighteenth-Century Levant* (Palo Alto: Stanford University Press, 2013).

Salibi, Kamal, *A House of Many Mansions: The History of Lebanon Reconsidered* (London: I. B. Tauris, 1988).

Salibi, Kamal, *Maronite Historians of Medieval Lebanon* (Beirut: American University of Beirut, 1959).

Sallmann, Jean-Michel, *Naples et ses saints à l'âge baroque* (Paris: PUF, 1994).

Salvadore, Matteo, '"I Was Not Born to Obey, But Rather to Command": The Self-Fashioning of Ṣägga Krəstos, an Ethiopian Traveller in Seventeenth-Century Europe', *Journal of Early Modern History*, 25, 2 (2021), pp. 1–33.

Sami Kuri (ed.), *Monumenta Proximi-Orientis*, vol. 1: *Palestine – Liban – Syrie – Mésopotamie (1523–1583)* (Rome: Institutum historicum Societatis Iesu, 1989).

Sanacore, Massimo, 'Tra Livorno e l'Egitto: Vita e vicende commerciali di Antonio Kair,' *Nuovi studi Livornesi*, 16 (2009), pp. 121–50.

Sanjian, Avedis K., *The Armenian Communities in Syria under the Ottoman Dominion* (Cambridge, MA: Harvard University Press, 1965).

Santi, Paul, *Miscellanées d'iconographies* (Beirut: n. p., 1966).

Santus, Cesare, 'The Great Imposture: Eastern Christian Rogues and Counterfeiters in Rome, c. 17th–19th Centuries', in Cornel Zwierlein (ed.), *The Power of the Dispersed: Early Modern Global Travelers beyond Integration* (Leiden: Brill, 2022), pp. 98–130.

Santus, Cesare, 'Tra la chiesa di Sant'Atanasio e il Sant'Uffizio: Note sulla presenza greca a Roma in età moderna', in Antal Molnár, Giovanni Pizzorusso and Matteo Sanfilippo (eds), *Chiese e nationes a Roma: Dalla Scandinavia ai Balcani, secoli XV–XVIII* (Rome: Viella, 2017), pp. 193–223.

Santus, Cesare, *Trasgressioni necessarie: Communicatio in sacris, coesistenza e conflitti tra le comunità cristiane orientali (Levante e Impero ottomano, XVII–XVIII secolo)* (Rome: École française de Rome, 2019).
Santus, Cesare, 'Wandering Lives: Eastern Christian Pilgrims, Alms-Collectors and "Refugees" in Early Modern Rome', in Emily Michelson and Matthew Coneys Wainwright (eds), *A Companion to Religious Minorities in Early Modern Rome* (Leiden, Boston: Brill, 2021), pp. 237–71.
Sāra, Butrus, 'Habīs fransawī fī Lubnān: Al-masyū Franswā dī Shastuwīl (1634–1644)', *Al-Mashriq* (1922), pp. 571–76, 649–59.
Saracino, Stefano, 'Griechisch-orthodoxe Almosenfahrer im Heiligen Römischen Reich und ihre wissensgeschichtliche Bedeutung (1650–1750)', in Markus Friedrich and Jacob Schilling (eds), *Praktiken frühneuzeitlicher Historiographie* (Berlin, Boston: De Gruyter, 2019), pp. 141–73.
Sauvy, Anne, *Le miroir du cœur: Quatre siècles d'images savantes et populaires* (Paris: Cerf, 1989).
Schulze, Reinhard, 'Das islamische 18. Jahrhundert: Versuch einer historiographischen Kritik', *Die Welt des Islam*, 30 (1990), pp. 140–59.
Seetzen, Ulrich Jasper, *Tagebuch des Aufenthalts in Aleppo (1803–1805)* (Zürich, New York: Georg Olms Verlag, 2011).
Segneri, Paolo, *Il confessore istruito* (Venice: per Gio. Antonio Remondini, 1672).
Segneri, Paolo, *Il penitente istruito a ben confessarsi* (Venice: Biagio Maldura, 1669).
Segneri, Paul, *L'instruction du pénitent, ou la méthode pratique pour se bien confesser* (Paris: chez Jean-Baptiste Coignard, 1695).
Semerdijan, Elyse, 'Naked Anxiety: Bathhouses, Nudity, and the *Dhimmī* Woman in 18th-Century Aleppo', *International Journal of Middle East Studies*, 45 (2013), pp. 651–76.
Semerdijan, Elyse, *'Off the Straight Path': Illicit Sex, Law and Community* (Syracuse: Syracuse University Press, 2008).
Semerdijan, Elyse, 'Sinful Professions: Illegal Occupations of Women in Ottoman Aleppo, Syria', *Hawwa*, 1, 2003, pp. 60–85.
Semerdijan, Elyse, 'Women and the Politics of Conversion in Early Modern Ottoman Aleppo', *The Journal of Middle Eastern Women's Studies*, 12 (2016), pp. 2–30.
Serena, Sebastiano, 'Il cardinale Gregorio Barbarigo e l'Oriente', in *Società Italiana per il progresso delle scienze: Atti della XXVI riunione. Venezia, 12–18 settembre 1937* (Rome: Società Italiana per il progresso delle scienze, 1938), pp. 390–413.
Serena, Sebastiano, *S. Gregorio Barbarigo e la vita spirituale e culturale nel suo Seminario di Padova* (Padua: Antenore, 1963).
Sfeir, Paul, *Les ermites dans l'Église maronite: Histoire et spiritualité* (Kaslik: Université Saint-Esprit, 1986).

Sharkey, Heather J., *A History of Muslims, Christians, and Jews in the Middle East* (Cambridge: Cambridge University Press, 2017).

Sharkey, Heather J., review of Bernard Heyberger, *Les Chrétiens d'Orient* (Paris: Presses universitaires de France, 2017), in *Islam and Christian-Muslim Relations*, 29, 1 (2018), pp. 111–13.

Shiblī, Antūnyūs, 'Al-Āb Sharbal, habīs 'Annāyā al-qadīs', *Al-Mashriq*, 25 (1922), pp. 289–97.

Shiblī, Antūnyūs, *Al-Āb Sharbal Makhlūf biqa'kafra min ibnā' al-ruhbāniyya al-baladiyya al-lubnāniyya al-mārūniyya habīs mahbasa dayr 'Annāyā*, 2nd ed. (Jounieh: Dakāsh, 1999).

Siedel, Elisabeth, 'Die türkische Autobiographie: Versuch einer Problematisierung', *Die Welt des Islams*, 31 (1991), pp. 246–54.

Simon, Richard, *Histoire critique de la Créance et des Coûtumes des Nations du Levant* (Frankfurt: Frédéric Arnaud, 1684).

Slim, Souad Abou el-Rousse, *Le métayage et l'impôt au Mont-Liban aux XVIIIe et XIXe siècles* (Beirut: Dar el-Machreq, 1993).

Slim, Souad Abou el-Rousse, *The Greek Orthodox Waqf in Lebanon during the Ottoman Period* (Würzburg: Ergon Verlag, 2007).

Sluglett, Peter, and Stefan Weber (eds), *Syria and Bilad al-Sham under Ottoman Rule: Essays in Honour of Abdul-Karim Rafeq* (Leiden: Brill, 2010).

Spagnolo, John P., *France and Ottoman Lebanon 1861–1914* (London: Ithaca Press, 1977).

Stannek, Antje, 'Migration confessionnelle ou pèlerinage? Rapport sur le fonds d'un hospice pour les nouveaux convertis dans les Archives secrètes du Vatican', in Philippe Boutry, Pierre-Antoine Fabre and Dominique Julia (eds), *Rendre ses vœux: Les identités pèlerines dans l'Europe moderne (XVIe–XVIIIe siècle)* (Paris: Éditions de l'EHESS, 2000), pp. 57–74.

Sternhell, Zeev, *Maurice Barrès et le nationalisme français* (Paris: Fayard, 2000).

Strauss, Johann, 'Is Karamanli Literature Part of a 'Christian-Turkish (Turco-Christian) Literature?' in Evangelia Balta and Matthias Kappler (eds), *Cries and Whispers in Karamanlidika Books* (Wiesbaden: Harrassowitz, 2010), pp. 153–200.

Subrahmanyam, Sanjay, *Courtly Encounters: Translating Gentleness and Violence in Early Modern Eurasia* (Cambridge, MA: Harvard University Press, 2012).

Subrahmanyam, Sanjay, 'Par-delà l'incommensurabilité: Pour une histoire connectée des empires aux temps modernes', *Revue d'histoire moderne et contemporaine*, 54 (2007), pp. 34–53.

Surmeyan, Ardavazt, *La vie et la culture arméniennes à Alep au XVIIe siècle* (Paris: Imprimerie Araxe, 1934).

Tahtāwī, [Rifā'a al-], *L'or de Paris: Relation de voyage 1826–1831*, translated from Arabic by Anouar Louca (Paris: Sindbad, 1988; new edition: Arles: Actes Sud, 2012).

Tarazi Fawaz, Leila, *An Occasion for War: Civil Conflict in Lebanon and Damascus in 1860* (London, New York: I. B. Tauris, 1994).

Tawtal, Fardīnān [Ferdinand Taoutel], 'Rasūl al-Sahrā', al-āb Sharl dī Fūkū', *Al-Mashriq* 25 (1922), pp. 991–1006.

Tawtal, Fardīnān [Ferdinand Taoutel], 'Wathā'iq tā'rīkhiyya 'an Ḥalab', *Al-Mashriq*, 42 (1948), pp. 215–41, 371–412.

Tawtal, Fardīnān [Ferdinand Taoutel], *Wathā'iq ta'rīkhiyya 'an Ḥalab*, vol. 1 (Beirut: al-Maṭba'a al-kāthūlīkiyya, 1958).

Tchentsova, Vera G., 'Le premier voyage du patriarche d'Antioche Macaire III Ibn al-Za'îm à Moscou et dans les Pays roumains: 1652–1659', in Ioana Feodorov (ed.), *Relations entre les peuples de l'Europe Orientale et les chrétiens arabes au XVIIe siècle* (Bucarest: Bucureşti, Editura Academiei Române, 2012), pp. 69–122.

Tchentsova, Vera, 'Les documents grecs du XVIIe siècle: Pièces authentiques et pièces fausses: 4. Le patriarche d'Antioche Athanase IV Dabbās et Moscou: En quête de subvention pour l'imprimerie arabe d'Alep', *Orientalia Christiana Periodica*, 79, 1 (2013), pp. 173–95.

Tchentsova, Vera, 'Portrait of the Patriarch of Antioch Makarius III Ibn al-Za'īm in the *Tituljarnik* of 1672' [in Russian], in Yulia Petrova and Ioana Feodorov (eds), *Europe in Arabic Sources: The Travel of Makarius Patriarch of Antioch* (Kiev: A. Krymsky Institute of Oriental Studies of the National Academy of Sciences of Ukraine, Institute for South-East European Studies of the Romanian Academy, 2016), pp. 160–74.

Teresa of Avila, Saint, *Book Called Way of Perfection*, in *The Complete Works of Saint Teresa of Jesus*, vol. 2, edited by E. Allison Peers (New York: Sheed & Ward, 1946).

The Qur'an: A New Translation, translated by Tarif Khalidi (London: Penguin, 2008).

Thomas, David (ed.), *Christian-Muslim Relations: A Bibliographical History*, 20 vols, in progress (Leiden: Brill, 2009–).

Tisserant, Eugène, 'Notes pour servir à la biographie d'Étienne Évode Assémani', *Oriens Christianus*, 7 (1932), pp. 264–76.

Touma, Toufic, *Paysans et institutions féodales chez les Druses et les Maronites du Liban du XVIIIe siècle à 1914* (Beirut: Librairie orientale, 1971).

Trentini, Andrea, 'Il Caracciolino Filippo Guadagnoli controversista e islamologo: Un'analisi dei suoi scritti apologetici contro l'Islam', in Irene Fosi and Giovanni Pizzorusso (eds), *L'ordine dei chierici regolari minori (Caracciolini): Religione e cultura in età postridentina, monographic issue of Studi Medievali e Moderni*, 14, 1 (2010), pp. 297–314.

Trivellato, Francesca, 'Is There a Future for Italian Microhistory in the Age of Global History?' *California Italian Studies*, 2, 1 (2011), online: <http://dx.doi.org/10.5070/C321009025>.

Tsakiris, Vasileios, *Die gedruckten griechischen Beichtbücher zur Zeit der Türkenherrschaft: Ihr kirchenpolitischer Entstehungszusammenhang und ihre Quellen* (Berlin, New York: Walter de Gruyter, 2009).

Tyrrell, Ian, *Reforming the World: The Creation of America's Moral Empire* (Princeton: Princeton University Press, 2010).

Ursinus, Michael, 'Millet', *Encyclopaedia of Islam, Second Edition* (Leiden, New York: Brill, 1993), vol. 7, pp. 61–64.

Valensi, Lucette, 'Le choix des Annales', *Annales: Histoire, sciences sociales*, 50, 5 (1995), p. ii.

Valensi, Lucette, *La fuite en Égypte: Histoires d'Orient et d'Occident* (Paris: Seuil, 2002).

Valensi, Lucette, 'La tour de Babel: Groupes et relations ethniques au Moyen-Orient et en Afrique du Nord', *Annales: Économies, sociétés, civilisation*, 41, 4 (1986), pp. 817–38.

Valensi, Lucette, *Mardochée Naggiar: Enquête sur un inconnu* (Paris: Stock, 2008).

Vallet, Éric, '*Des grâces que Dieu m'a prodiguées* de Jalal al-Din al-Suyuti', in Patrick Boucheron (ed.), *Histoire du monde au XVe siècle* (Paris: Fayard, 2009), pp. 488–93.

Valognes, Jean-Pierre, *Vie et mort des chrétiens d'Orient: Des origines à nos jours* (Paris: Fayard, 1994).

Vauchez, André, *La sainteté en Occident aux derniers siècles du Moyen Age, d'après les procès de canonisation et les documents hagiographiques* (Rome: École française de Rome, 1981).

Velay, Charles, *Le culte et les fêtes d'Adônis-Thammouz dans l'Orient antique* (Paris: Ernest Leroux, 1904).

Verdeil, Chantal, *La Mission jésuite du Mont-Liban et de Syrie (1830–1864)* (Paris: Les Indes Savantes, 2011).

Verdeil, Chantal, 'Le corps souffrant de Rifqâ, sainte maronite du XIXe siècle', in *Le corps et le sacré en Orient musulman*, special issue of *Revue des mondes musulmans et de la Méditerranée*, 113–14 (2006), pp. 247–64.

Verdeil, Chantal, 'Travailler à la renaissance de l'Orient chrétien: Les missions latines en Syrie (1830–1945)', *Proche-Orient Chrétien*, 51 (2001), pp. 267–316.

Villettes, Jacqueline des, *La vie des femmes dans un village maronite libanais: Aïn el Kharoubé* (Tunis: Institut des Belles Lettres Arabes, 1964).

Vincent, Louis-Hugues, and Félix-Marie Abel, *Bethléem: Le sanctuaire de la Nativité* (Paris: J. Gabalda, 1914).

Voile, Brigitte, 'Hagiographie et communauté coptes au XXe siècle: Naissance d'un courant editorial', in Rachida Chih and Denis Gril (eds), *Le saint et son milieu ou comment lire les sources hagiographiques* (Cairo: Ifao, 2000), pp. 187–201.

Volney, Constantin-François, *Voyage en Égypte et en Syrie*, edited by Jean Gaulmier (Paris, The Hague: Mouton & Co., 1959).

Vööbus, Arthur, *History of Asceticism: Early Monasticism in Persia* (Louvain: Secrétariat du CSCO, 1958).

Wachtel, Nathan, 'L'acculturation', in Jacques Le Goff and Pierre Nora (eds), *Faire de l'histoire* (Paris: Gallimard 1986), vol. 1, pp. 184–85.

Wagner, Esther-Miriam (ed.), *A Handbook and Reader of Ottoman Arabic* (Cambridge: University of Cambridge, Open Book Publishers, 2021).

Walbiner, Carsten, *Die Mitteilungen des griechisch-orthodoxen Patriarchen Makarius Ibn az-Za'īm von Antiochia (1647–1672) über Georgien nach dem arabischen Autograph von St. Petersburg* (PhD dissertation, Universität Leipzig, 1995).

Walbiner, Carsten, '"Images Painted with Such Exalted Skill as to Ravish the Senses . . .": Pictures in the Eyes of Christian Arab Travellers of the 17th and 18th Centuries', in Bernard Heyberger and Silvia Naef (eds), *La multiplication des images en pays d'Islam: De l'estampe à la télévision (17e-21e siècle)* (Istanbul: Orient-Institut der DMG; Würzburg: Ergon, 2003), pp. 15–30.

Walbiner, Carsten, 'Monastic Reading and Learning in Eighteenth-Century *Bilād al-Šām*: Some Evidence from the Monastery of al-Šuwayr (Mount Lebanon)', *Arabica*, 51, 4 (2004), pp. 462–77.

Walker Bynum, Caroline, *Holy Feast and Holy Fast: The Religious Significance of Food to Medieval Women* (Berkeley: University of California Press, 1987).

Walters, J. Edward, *Eastern Christianity: A Reader* (Grand Rapids: Eerdmans, 2021).

Wansleben, Johann Michael, *Relazione dello Stato presente dell'Egitto* (Paris: A. Cramoizy, 1671).

Weber, Max, *Sociologie des religions* (Paris: Gallimard, 1996).

Werner, Michael, and Bénédicte Zimmermann, 'Beyond Comparison: *Histoire croisée* and the Challenge of Reflexivity', *History and Theory*, 45 (2006), pp. 30–50.

Werner, Michael, and Bénédicte Zimmermann, 'Penser l'histoire croisée: Entre empire et réflexivité', *Annales: Histoire, sciences sociales*, 58, 1 (2003), pp. 7–36.

Windler, Christian, 'Clientèles royales et clientèles seigneuriales vers la fin de l'Ancien Régime', *Annales: Histoire, sciences sociales*, 52, 2 (1997), pp. 293–319.

Windler, Christian, *Missionare in Persien: Kulturelle Diversität und Normenkonkurrenz im globalen Katholizismus (17–18. Jahrhundert)* (Cologne, Weimar, Vienna: Böhlau Verlag, 2018).

Windler, Christian, 'Clientèles et État en Espagne au 18e siècle', *Annales: Histoire, sciences sociales*, 52, 2 (1997), pp. 293–319.

Winet, Monica, 'Religious Education on the Road: An Anonymous Christian Arabic Diary', *Parole de l'Orient*, 39 (2014), pp. 297–312.

Winter, Stefan, review of Bernard Heyberger, *Hindiyya, mystique et criminelle (1720–1798)* (Paris: Aubier, 2001), in *MIT Electronic Journal of Middle East Studies*, 4 (2004), pp. 77–79.

Womack, Deanna, 'Christian Communities in the Contemporary Middle East: An Introduction', *Exchange*, 49 (2020), pp. 189–213.

Zachariadou, Elisabeth A., *Deka tourkika eggrafa gia tēn Megalē Ekklēsia* (Athens: Ethniko Idryma Erevnon, 1996).

Ze'evi, Dror, 'Women in Seventeenth-Century Jerusalem: Western and Indigenous Perspectives', *International Journal of Middle East Studies,* 27 (1995), pp. 157–73.

Zemon Davis, Nathalie, *Léon l'Africain: Un voyageur entre deux mondes* (Paris: Payot, 2006).

Zemon Davis, Natalie, *Trickster Travels: A Sixteenth-Century Muslim between Worlds* (New York: Faber & Faber, 2006).

Županov, Ines G., 'Accommodation', in Régine Azria and Danièle Hervieu-Léger (eds), *Dictionnaire des faites religieux* (Paris: PUF, 2010), pp. 1–4.

Županov, Ines G., '"One Civility, But Multiple Religions": Jesuit Mission among St Thomas Christians in India (16th–17th Centuries)', *Journal of Early Modern History*, 9, 3–4 (2005), pp. 283–325.

Zwierlein, Cornel, 'Interaction and Boundary Work: Western Merchant Colonies in the Levant and the Eastern Churches, 1660–1800', *Journal of Modern European History*, 18, 2 (2020), pp. 156–76.

Tabula Gratulatoria

Abi Younes, Alexandre, Université Libanaise
Ade, Mafalda, Koç University, Istanbul
Aigle, Denise, EPHE-CNRS, UMR 'Orient et Méditerranée'
Alichoran, Joseph, INALCO, Paris
Ambrosio, Alberto Fabio, Luxembourg School of Religion & Society
Amir-Moezzi, Mohammad Ali, EPHE/PSL/LEM, Paris
Amsler, Nadine, Université de Fribourg
Anastassiadis, Tassos, McGill University, Montréal
Anastassiadou-Dumont, Méropi, INALCO
Ancel, Stéphane, CNRS, CéSor-EHESS
Armogathe, Jean-Robert, Institut de France-EPHE
Aslanian, Sebouh, UCLA
Assan Valérie, EPHE-CNRS, PSL
Astafieva, Elena, CNRS-EHESS-CEFR, Moscow
Auber de Lapierre, Julien, Collège de France
Aubin-Boltanski, Emma, CNRS
Aydın, Mustafa Cenap, International Jacques Maritain Institute, Rome
Bayle, Marie-Hélène, Paris
Bercé, Yves-Marie, Académie des inscriptions et belles lettres
Berezhnaya, Liliya, University of Amsterdam-KU Leuven
Bernard-Maugiron, Nathalie, IRD/CEPED/Université de Paris
Bevilacqua, Alexander, Williams College
Blanc, Julien, Université Gustave Eiffel
Boëx, Cécile, EHESS
Bost, Hubert, EPHE-PSL, LEM, Paris
Bouquet, Olivier, CESSMA, Université de Paris

Bourmaud, Philippe, Université Jean Moulin Lyon 3-LARHRA
Boutier, Jean, EHESS
Boutry, Philippe, Université Paris 1 Panthéon-Sorbonne, EHESS
Bozarslan, Hamit, EHESS
Bras, Jean-Philippe, Université de Rouen
Briquel Chatonnet, Françoise, CNRS
Brogini, Anne, Université Côte d'Azur, CMMC
Buresi, Pascal, CNRS-EHESS
Buskens, Léon, NIMAR-Leiden University in Rabat
Caffiero, Marina, Sapienza-Università di Roma
Calafat, Guillaume, Université Paris 1 Panthéon-Sorbonne-IHMC
Cannuyer, Christian, Université catholique de Lille
Caporal, Jacques, Louveciennes
Casale, Giancarlo, EUI, Florence
Castelnau L'Estoile de, Charlotte, Université de Paris
Chauvard, Jean-François, Université Paris 1 Panthéon-Sorbonne-IHMC
Chrissidis, Nikolaos, Southern Connecticut State University
Clayer, Nathalie, CNRS-EHESS
de Clerck, Dima, IFPO-Université Saint-Joseph, Beirut
Codignola Bo, Luca, University of Notre Dame, Saint Mary's University
Çolak, Hasan, ERC AdG 2019 Typarabic/TOBB University of Economics & Technology, Ankara
Colombo, Emanuele, DePaul University, Chicago
Cresti, Federico, Università di Catania
Croce, Giuseppe M., Vatican Archives
Dakhlia, Jocelyne, CRH-EHESS
Dalachanis, Angelos, CNRS
Debié, Muriel, EPHE, PSL
Dermarkar, Salim, Saint Jean de Moirans
Der Haroutiounian, Haïk, INALCO
Di Pietrantonio, Stefano, Université catholique de Louvain
Dompnier, Bernard, Université Clermont Auvergne
D'Ottone Rambach, Arianna, Sapienza-Università di Roma
Dubois, Olivier, ancien bibliothécaire scientifique de l'Institut français d'études arabes de Damas
Dupont, Anne-Laure, Sorbonne Université
du Roy, Gaétan, Universiteit Radboud, Nijmegen
El Gemayel, Maroun-Nasser, Bishop, Maronite Catholic Eparchy of Notre-Dame du Liban, Paris
El Gemayel, Ronney, CEDRAC-Université Saint-Joseph, Beirut
Elmarsafy, Ziad, King's College London
Erol, Su, İstanbul

Fabre, Pierre Antoine, CéSor-EHESS
Fahmé-Thiéry, Paule, Rochecolombe, France
Farina, Margherita, CNRS/Université de Paris – Histoire des théories linguistiques
Farra-Haddad, Nour, CEDIFR/Université Saint-Joseph de Beyrouth – Université Libanaise
Feodorov, Ioana, Institut d'Etudes Sud-Est Européennes, Académie Roumaine, Bucarest
Ferrand, Antoinette, Sorbonne-Université
Ficquet, Éloi, EHESS, CéSor
Fuess, Albrecht, Philipps-Universität, Marburg
Gaboreau, Werner, Université Sorbonne Nouvelle
Gabriel, Frédéric, CNRS
Gabry-Thienpont, Séverine, CNRS
García-Arenal, Mercedes, CSIC, Madrid
Garzaniti, Marcello, Università degli Studi di Firenze
de Gayffier-Bonneville, Anne-Claire, INALCO
Georgelin, Hervé, National University of Athens
Gerd, Lora, Institut d'Histoire, St Petersburg
Ghobrial, John-Paul, University of Oxford
Girard, Aurélien, Université de Reims Champagne-Ardenne
Glesener, Thomas, Aix-Marseille Université
Grenet, Mathieu, INU Champollion, Albi
Guirguis, Laure, IREMAM, Aix-Marseille
Hager, Anna, Universität Wien
Hamilton, Alastair, Warburg Institute, University of London
Harrak, Amir, University of Toronto
Henny, Sundar, Université de Berne
Hill, Peter, Northumbria University, Newcastle-upon-Tyne
Hitzel, Frédéric, CNRS-EHESS, Paris
Hurel, Daniel-Odon, CNRS-PSL, LEM, Paris
Jabbour, Pierre, USJ-Beyrouth
Jalloul, Maïssa, Paris
Jobert, Nathan, Université Paris 1 Panthéon-Sorbonne
Jomier, Augustin, INALCO, Paris
Jullien, Christelle, CNRS
Jullien, Florence, CNRS, Centre de recherche sur le monde iranien (CeRMI)
Kaiser, Wolfgang, Université Paris 1 Panthéon Sorbonne / EHESS Paris
Katerji, Nader, INRAE
Kaufhold, Hubert, Universität München
Khater, Akram, North Carolina State University
Kieser, Hans-Lukas, Basel
Kilpatrick, Hilary, Lausanne

Knost, Stefan, Martin-Luther-Universität Halle-Wittenberg
Kontouma, Vassa, EPHE-PSL
Krampl, Ulrike, Université de Tours
Krimsti, Feras, Gotha Research Library of the University of Erfurt
Krstić, Tijana, Central European University, Vienna
Larcher, Pierre, Aix-Marseille Université
La Spisa, Paolo, Università degli Studi di Firenze
Lentin, Jérôme, INALCO
Lory, Pierre, EPHE-PSL, LEM
Madinier, Rémy, CNRS
Maggiolini, Paolo, Università Cattolica di Milano
Makdisi, Ussama, Rice University
Makrides, Vasilios, Universität Erfurt
Mallat, Chibli, University of Utah
Malsagne, Stéphane, Université de Paris I
Marino, Brigitte, CNRS/AMU, IREMAM
Martin, Philippe, Université Lumière Lyon 2
Massot, Anais, CéSor-EHESS
Mayeur-Jaouen, Catherine, Sorbonne Université
Meier, Astrid, Martin-Luther-Universität Halle-Wittenberg
Messaoudi, Alain, Nantes Université
Meyer, Guy, Université Paris 4 Sorbonne
Micheau, Françoise, Université Paris1 Panthéon-Sorbonne
Moennig, Ulrich, Universität Hamburg
Mohasseb Saliba, Sabine, CéSor-CNRS
Möller, Esther, Universität der Bundeswehr München
Molnár, Antal, Research Centre for the Humanities, Institute of History, Budapest
Morel, Teymour, Université de Genève
Mouawad, Youssef, Beirut
Moukarzel, Joseph, Université Saint-Esprit de Kaslik
Muchnik, Natalia, EHESS
Murre-van den Berg, Heleen, Radboud University
Naef, Silvia, Université de Genève
Naïli, Falestin, IFPO-Universität Basel
Najm, Simon, University of Balamand
Nassif, Charbel, Institut d'Études Sud-Est Européennes – Bucarest, CEDRAC-USJ Beyrouth
Neveu, Norig, CNRS/AMU, IREMAM
Ohanian, Daniel, University of California, Los Angeles (UCLA)
Olar, Ovidiu, Austrian Academy of Sciences, Vienna
Ollivry, Florence, EPHE/Université de Montréal
O'Mahony, Anthony, Blackfriars, University of Oxford

Oualdi, M'hamed, Sciences Po-Paris
Panchenko, Constantin, Moscow State University
Parker, Lucy, University of Oxford
Paša, Željko, Pontifical Oriental Institute
Păun, Radu G., CERCEC, CNRS-EHESS, Paris
Pettinaroli, Laura, École française de Rome
Pichon, Frédéric, Nantes
Pieraccini, Paolo, Rome-Florence
Pierre, Benoist, CESR, Université de Tours
Pizzo, Paola, Università G. d'Annunzio Chieti-Pescara
Pizzorusso, Giovanni, Università G.d'Annunzio Chieti-Pescara
Planès, Hugo, Université de Toulouse Jean Jaurès
Portier, Philippe, EPHE-LEM
Poujeau, Anna, CNRS
Poumarède, Géraud, Université Bordeaux Montaigne
Prudhomme, Claude, Université de Lyon
Rafeq, Abdul-Karim, William and Annie Bickers Professor of Arab Middle Eastern Studies, Emeritus, College of William and Mary, Williamsburg, Virginia
Richard, Elisabeth, EPHE
Richard, Francis, BULAC
Richard, Nicolas, Sorbonne Université
Robert, Jean-Noël, Collège de France, EPHE, Paris
Romano, Antonella, CAK-EHESS, Paris
del Río Sánchez, Francisco, Universidad Complutense de Madrid
Ruiz de Elvira, Laura, IRD
Salem, Ketty, Université d'Alep
Saracino, Stefano, Universität Jena
Sanchez Summerer, Karène, Groningen University
Sanfilippo, Matteo, Università della Tuscia (Viterbo)
Santus, Cesare, Università degli Studi di Trieste
Schlaepfer, Aline, Universität Basel
Schmoller, Andreas, Katholische Universität Linz
Schneidleder, Adoram, Marseille
Seri-Hersch, Iris, Aix-Marseille Université
Sharkey, Heather, University of Pennsylvania
Simon, Fabien, Université de Paris
Skordi, Maria, EPHE
Sleiman, André, Alumnus EHESS, Democracy Reporting International, Beirut
Slim, Souad, Université de Balamand
Smyrnelis, Marie-Carmen, Institut Catholique de Paris
Strauss, Johann, Rottenburg
Strotsau, Andrei, EHESS Paris

Szuppe, Maria, CNRS
Szurek, Emmanuel, École des Hautes Études en Sciences Sociales, Paris
Tamdoğan, Işık, CNRS-Cetobac, Paris
de Tapia, Aude Aylin, Albert-Ludwigs-Universität Freiburg
de Tapia, Stéphane, Université de Strasbourg
Tatarenko, Laurent, CNRS
Tchentsova, Vera, ERC AdG 2019 Typarabic/ESSEE, EPHE-PSL
Teule, Herman, Université de Nimègue, Université de Louvain
Torbay, Joseph/Youssef, Président de l'Association des Amis d'Abraham Ecchellensis, France-Liban
Tottoli, Roberto, Università di Napoli L'Orientale
Tramontana, Felicita, Università Roma Tre
Trentacoste, Davide, Florence
Trimbur, Dominique, Centre de Recherche français à Jérusalem
Uginet, François-Charles, Rome
Valensi, Lucette, EHESS/Paris
van den Boogert, Maurits, Brill
Verdeil, Chantal, INALCO
Vincent, Bernard, École des Hautes Études en Sciences Sociales, Paris
Visceglia, Maria Antonietta, Sapienza-Università di Roma
Vivier-Muresan, Anne-Sophie, Institut Catholique de Paris
Voile, Brigitte, Paris
Volait, Mercedes, CNRS
Walbiner, Carsten, Cairo
Windler, Christian, Historisches Institut der Universität Bern
Winet, Monika, Universität Basel
Winter, Stephan, Koç University, Istanbul
Youssef, Soueif, Maronite Archbishop of Tripoli (Liban)
Ziadé, Raphaëlle, Petit Palais, Paris
Županov, Ines G., CNRS, Paris
Zwierlein, Cornel, Freie Universität Berlin

Index

Note: page references in **bold** indicate a more in-depth treatment of the subject

Abbasids, 182
'Abd al-Aḥād (Domenico, merchant), 92–3
Abdallah, Giorgio, 83n, 117n
'Abdallāh ibn Dawūd (Teodoro d'Aut/David di San Carlo), 62, 99n, 104n
Abdelnur, Paolo, 68, 101n
Abd Elrazzac Mesi, 116n
Abondaher (deputy to qadi), 184–5, 186
Abramo (Maronite priest), 85n
abstinence, 170, 173
Abū Rizq, Yūsif, 62–3
Acchar, Giuseppe, 59
acculturation, 24, 123n, 171
Acre, 88n, 110
Adana (Turkey), 115
Agapius II Maṭar (Melkite Greek Catholic Patriarch), 209
Agemian, Sylvia, 209
Agemi, Giovanni, 78n
Aggiuri, Lazzaro, 55, 61, 65, 85n, 100n
Aggiuri, Thecla, 85n
Agnellini, Timoteo *see* Karnuk, Timothy
Agostino, Pietro, 120n
Aix-en-Provence, 57
Akhijan, Andreas *see* Andreas Akhijan
Alacoque, Saint Marguerite-Marie, 230
'Aladdin and the Wonderful Lamp', 5, 30, 128
Alam, Joseph, 261n
alchemy, 56, 92
alcohol, 131, 136
Aleppian Maronite Monks, 212
Aleppo, 131, 267, 268
  book printing, 206
  Catholic women in, 5, 26, **225–38**
  co-existence of Muslims and Christians, 16–17
  Eastern Christians from/in, 51, 55, 56, 61, 75, 76, 106–7, 108, 146, 169: Armenians, 68, 74, 134, 201, 202; Chaldeans, 146; Greeks, 117n, 204; Maronites, 30, 66, 68, 73, 124, 126, 127, 131, 132, 133, 165, 170, 201, 202, 212; Melkites, 60, 62, 65, 68, 70, 85n, 113, 114, 170, 172, 212; Syriacs, 67, 72, 92, 149
  family and congregation networks, 150
  French consul/consulate, 56, 61, 71, 93, 144
  French missionaries in, 182, 183, 184
  Heyberger in, 33
  merchants from/in, 73, 118n, 129, 149, 213
  Muslims in, 186
  painters in, 202, 205
Alexander III (Pope, r. 1159–81), 248
Alexandria, 150
Algeria, 151
Algiers, 52
'Ali Baba', 5, 30, 128
alms collection, 71
  in America, 144
  in Europe, 55, 59, 59–60, 92, 100n, 106, 142, 143
  licences/authorisation, 51, 117n, 143
  political interests and, 151
  private vs institutional interests, 144
  in Russia, 144

alms collection (*cont.*)
unauthorised/false, 56, 58, 59, 64, 72, 92, 94, 104n, 144–5
see also begging/beggars
Alsace, 20, 21, 33, 264
Amasi, Giorgio, 57
America, 265
alms collection in, 67, 144
travel/travelogues, 76, 125, 143, 144
American missions/missionaries, 105, 152
American University of Beirut, 15
Americas, 148
Aminione, Giovanni, 57, 58
Amsterdam, 146
Anastasio (Maltese corsair), 73
Anastassiadou, Méropi, 24
Anatolia, 12, 126, 127, 129, 133, 143
Ancari, Gabriele (Jibrā'īl ibn al-Ankārī al-Ḥalabī al-Marūnī), 72, 112
Anderson, Benedict, 2
Andrade, Tonio, 19
Andreas Akhijan (Syriac Catholic Patriarch), 13, 96
Annales. Histoire, Sciences Sociales (previously *Annales, Économies, Sociétés, Civilisations*), 7, 15, 25
'Annāyā (Lebanon), 246, 247–8, 249, 250, 253, 254–5, 262n
Anne, Saint, 201
Antalya (Satalia), 73, 112
Anthimius (Greek Patriarch of Jerusalem, r. 1788–1808), 212
Anthony of the Desert, Saint, 211, 251
Anthony of Padua, Saint, 209
images of, 201, 211, 216
Antichrist, 187
Antioch, 12; *see also* Melkite Church/Melkites
Antonachi (Maltese corsair), 73, 112
Antonio of Nineveh, 94, 102n
Antoura, 89n, 200, 201, 209
apologetics/apologetic literature, 14, 15, 172, 182, 183, 186, 189, 192, 193, 248, 250, 269
apostasy, 61, 62, 63, 113, 118n
'Aql, Tūmā, 212
The Arabian Nights, 5, 30, 127, 128
Arabic (language)
Christian literature in, 14–15, 26, 57, 67, 74, 76, 95, 109, 128, 182, 212, 215, 216, 229–30
religious services and sacraments in, 55, 67, 68
teaching and studying of, 66, 67, 69, 70, 73–4, 93, 99n, 143, 204, 254, 262n
Arabic literature, 14, 206
Arab renaissance (*nahḍa*), 128, 163
archives
Catholic, 21, 22, 175, 268
Ottoman, 16
travellers and migrants in Roman, **50–5**, 90, 105
see also Propaganda Fide
Aretin, Giovanni, 59
Argenson, Marc-René, Marquis d' (lieutenant-general of police), 134
Ariès, Philippe, 22
al-Armanī, Yūḥannā, 36n
Armenian Catholic Church, 13, 15, 56, 202, 205
Armenian (language)
Christian literature in, 102n, 182
Armenian Apostolic Church, 11
Armenian question (1878), 153
Armenians, 15, 56, 84n, 118n, 151, 164
from/in Aleppo, 68, 74, 134, 165, 201, 202, 205
church decoration/religious images, 202, 205
in/from Europe, 52: France, 67, 134; Italy, 52, 59, 67, 68, 74–5, 79n, 116, 147
from/in Lebanon, 13
merchants, 86–7n, 93, 94, 146
Arvieux, Laurent d', 145, 269
'Asayla, al-Khawāja Ḥannā, 115
Ascanio (corsair), 120n
asceticism, 168, 169, 249–50, 251, 252; *see also* dervishes; Desert Fathers/Saints
Asia, 192, 200
al-Assad, Bashar, 153
Assemani, Elia, 62, 63, 84n
Assemani, Giuseppe Simone (Yūsif al-Sam'ānī), 51, 60, 65, 72–3, 74, 88n
Assyrian Church *see* Church of the East; Nestorians
'Atā, Ghrīgūryūs (Melkite Bishop of Homs), 144–5
Atallah, Odoardo, 83n
Athanasius III Dabbās (Melkite Patriarch of Antioch, d. 1724), 114, 115, 122n
Auber, Julien, 36n
Austria, 100n
authority, 130, 165; *see also* ecclesiastical authority/power; Islamic authority
autobiographies
of women, 227, 228, 232
autonomous communities *see millets*
Auvergne, Jean-Baptiste d', 231, 243n

Avignon, 57
ʿAwwād, Yaʿqūb (Maronite Patriarch), 120n, 204
ʿAyn Warqa (monastery, Mount Lebanon), 174
ʿAzar, Father, 151

Babylon, 71
Baghdad, 51, 61, 144, 186, 209
Baietto, Gianbattista, 73
Bakhkhāsh, Naʿum, 22
Baku, 148
Baladites *see* Lebanese Maronite Order
Balkans, 12
baptism, 59, 80n, 147
of Muslims, 95, 102n
Barakat, Salim, 21
Barbarigo, Cardinal Gregorio, 66, 85n, 93, 102n, 103n
Barbase, Giorgio, 117n
Bardo palace (Tunis), 129
Baroco, Domenico, 55–6
Barrès, Maurice, 250, 253–4, 257, 261–2n
Barse, Jean, 75, 103n
Bashir Shihab II (Emir of Mount Lebanon, r. 1789–1840), 246
Basilians, 81n, 145
begging/beggars
permission to beg, 57, 59, 146
repression of beggary, 51, 131
unauthorised/false begging, 58, 64, 72, 92, 93–4
see also alms collection
Beirut, 51, 60, 64, 88n, 126, 129, 132, 145, 150, 174, 253, 267
Beiteddine (Lebanon), 246
bells/bell ringing, 4, 12, 252
Belluga, Cardinal Luigi, 85n
Benedetti, Pietro (Buṭrus Mubārak), 73, 74, 89n
Benedict XIV (Pope, r. 1740–58), 171
Benigno (Lotfi) di Nicola, 60–1, 104n, 106
*berat*s (deeds of appointment), 148–9
Berlin, Treaty of (1878), 153
Besson, Joseph, 226
Bestros, Ḥabīb, 74
Bethlehem, 51, 58, 117n, 201, 253
biographies/biographers, 6, 19, 25, 49, 62, 85n, 90, 105, 125, 228, 248
Biqaʿ Kafrā (Mount Lebanon), 246, 253, 261n
bishops
obligation of residence, 66, 91
ordination of, 11, 174
power of, 174
travelling, 143
see also Karnuk, Timothy
Bkirki (Maronite monastery, Mount Lebanon), 172, 205, 213, 223n, 227, 236, 245; *see also* Hindiyya; Sacred Heart of Jesus
Bona, Cardinal, 100n
Bonaventura di Sant'Agata, 119n
Bonici, Fabrizio, 70
Book of Gospels (*Kitāb al-Injīl*), 206, 207–8*ill.*
books
requests for/dissemination of European, 26, 57, 59, 64, 68, 71, 92, 95, 103n, 109, 119n
see also Christian literature; printing/printing press
Boutry, Philippe, 22
Bowen, Harold, 17
Boyer, Louis, 249
Braude, Benjamin, 17
Braudel, Fernand, 18
Britain, 152, 153; *see also* England
Brockelmann, Carl, 14
Bruno de Saint Yves, 116n
al-Budayrī, Shihāb al-Dīn Ahmad *see* Ibn Budayr
Buenos Aires, 268
Buktī, Yuḥannā, 68
Buktī, Yūsif, 68
Būlus (Paul of Aleppo, son of Macarius III) *see* al-Zaʿīm, Būlus,
Burayk, Mikhāʾīl, 131
business
relation between protection and, **71–5**
see also commercial affairs/interests; merchants; trade
Byblos (Jbayl, Lebanon), 253
Byzantine Empire/Byzantines, 11, 210, 211
Byzantine iconography, 211, 215, 220

Cairo, 13, 16–17, 60, 62, 73, 83n, 108, 113, 117n, 150
Callimeri, Antonio, 88n
Campaja, Tommaso, 58
canonisation, 5, 27, 245, 247, 248, 251, 255–6, 258n, 260n
Cantelmo, Cardinal, 94, 102n
capital punishment, 62, 126
Capuchin missions/missionaries, 113, 144, 182, 184; *see also* Febvre, Michel; Saint-Aignan, Jean-Baptiste

Capuchins, 61, 71, 91, 92, 100n, 133, 143, 171, 209, 211
  decoration of churches, 204, 209
Carafa, Cardinal, 167
caricatures, 213, 266
Carmelites *see* Discalced Carmelites
Carnuch, Timothy *see* Karnuk, Timothy
Carus, Isa (ʿIsā Kārūz), 201, 215
cash crops, 149, 150
Castel Sant'Angelo (Rome), 56
catechisms, 24, 167, 183, 202, 206, 226, 229
Catherina of Siena, Saint, 230
Catholic Church/Catholics, 3, 6, 10, 11, 169
  certificates of Catholicism, 51, 58, 60, 65, 73, 74, 83n, 94, 109, 116n, 117n, 145
  counter-revolutionary Catholicism, 169, 171, 252
  detachment from/objections to, 113, 114, 122n, 183; *see also* Fakhr family
  entanglement with commercial affairs, 74, 113; *see also* maritime trade; merchants
  modernity, 175
  mysticism, 166
  Orthodox vs Catholic, 13, 60, 106, 168, 170, 172–3; *see also* Melkite Church/ Melkites
  Protestantism vs Catholicism, 167, 171
  relation with Eastern Christians, 23, 151, 163, 183, 188
  see also conversion; Roman Catholic Church
'Catholic connection', 75; *see also* protection; recommendation
Catholic missions/missionaries, 6, 7, 12, 13, 50, 59
  (knowledge of) Islam and, 186, **188–92**, 193
  see also Febvre, Michel; Nau, Michel
Catholic Reformation, 22, 109, 167, 168
Cazadour, Cyriac, chammas, 146
celibacy
  female, 233
Certeau, Michel de, 25
Chalcedon, Council of (451), 11, 254
Chalcedonian Christians *see* Melkite Church/ Melkites
Chaldean Catholic Church/Chaldeans, 52, 71, 86n, 91, 92, 146, 152, 164
charitable endowments (*waqf*), 17
Charlemagne (King of the Franks, r. 768–814), 151
Chartier, Roger, 22
chastity, 211, 221n, 233, 259n
Châtellier, Louis, 20, 21, 22
Chevallier, Dominique, 15–16, 23
Chiarelli, Meletio, 74
Chiha, Michel, 262n
Chinese missions/missionaries, 105
Chios (Greece), 205
Christ
  divine nature of, 188, 191, 192
  images of, 209, 215, 216, 220n, 220–1n
Christianity/Christians
  Eastern Christianity and/vs Western, **129–36**, 149–50, 163, 166, 167, 188, 235, 250
  Muslim–Christian coexistence/relations, 6–7, 12, 16–17, 29, 166, **182–93**, 255
  original Christianity vs Roman Catholicism, 167
  role in Middle Eastern history, 28
Christian missions/missionaries, 2, 7, 171
Christoforo, Dimitri, 59
Chrysanthos (Greek Orthodox Patriarch of Jerusalem, r. 1707–31), 58
Chrysanthos of the Peloponnese, 220n
Church of the East, 11, 13, 15; *see also* Chaldean Catholic Church; Nestorians
churches
  alms collection for, 144, 147
  bell ringing, 4, 12, 252
  decoration of, 199, 201, 202–4, 205, 209, 210
  shared vs own, 147, 148
  transformed into mosques, 136, 141n
Cigala family, 121n
circulation, 19, 31, 53*ill.*, 98, 105, 142, **143–8**, 153, 229; *see also* migration; travels/ travellers; wanderings/wanderers
Cittadini, Ortola, 74
civilisation/civilising missions, 151, 154, 163, 168
Civitavecchia, 95
Clement XI (Pope, r. 1700–21), 110, 119n
clergy/clerics
  disputes/rivalry, 166, 171–2, 211, 235, 236
  motivation for migration, 55, 60, 90, 143, 144
  portraits of, 211–13, 214*ill.*
  role in society and public life, 17–18, 61, 149, 169
  see also bishops; patriarchs
clericalisation, 170, 236
Climacus, John, 166
Cobbié, Abramo (Ibrahīm Khubiyya), 62
Codignola, Luca, 22

coexistence, 249–50
of Christians and Muslims, 5, 7, 12, 16–17, 255
coffee/coffee-sellers, 72, 73, 125, 129, 134, 146
Collège Royal/Collège de France (Paris), 204
College of Saint Athanasius (Rome), 51
Collegio Urbano (Rome), 58, 100n
admission/admission requirements, 56, 57, 60, 61, 65, 68, 82n, 91, 117n, 173, 204
alumni, 51, 55, 58, 62, 64, 67, 68
expulsion from, 72, 101n
teachers, 66
Colmar, 264–5, 269, 270
Cologne, 52, 143
commercial affairs/interests
entanglement with Catholicism/religion, 74, 105, 113, 266–7
relation between business and protection, **71–5**
see also merchants; trade
communitarianism, 15, 16, 169
confessionalisation, 18, 23, 26, **166–70**, 236, 237
confessional justice, 235
confessions, 169, 232
'conscience revelation', 231
female, 228, 229, 231–2, 237, 242n
hearing of, 58, 67, 68, 101n
confiscation of goods, 60, 61, 62, 65, 73, 75, 82n, 103n, 106, 107, 108, 118n; *see also* corsairs
conflicts
between/within religious orders, 166, 171, 172, 211, 235, 236–7
Congregation of the Holy Office, 56, 79n, 81–2n, 94, 102n; *see also* Inquisition
Congregation of the Immaculate Conception of the Virgin, 174
Congregation of Melkite Celibates, 122n
Congregation *de Propaganda Fide see* Propaganda Fide
Congregation for the Propagation of the Holy Faith *see* Propaganda Fide
connected history, 26, 31, 267
transnational vs, 3, 20
Constantinople, 17, 60, 62, 63, 65, 66, 80n, 97, 109, 118n, 175
Constantinople, Council of (680–1), 11
convents
set up by women, 226, 227; *see also* Bkirki; Sacred Heart of Jesus
conversion, 83n, 107
forced, 61, 62, 106, 108
of Muslims, 62, 67–8, 69, 70, 102n, 167, 183, 255
of Orthodoxy to Catholicism, 91, 118n
to Islam, 56, 57, 61, 62, 106, 108, 111, 234
to Protestantism, 56
copper engravings, 202, 215, 223n
Coptic Orthodox Church/Copts, 11, 13, 164
copyists, 66, 85n, 88n, 91, 95
Corbagi, Elia (Kurbājī), 61
Cornaro, Cardinal, 103n
Corpus Domini (Latin feast), 172
correspondence *see* letters
corsairs, 31, 63, 67, 82n, 101n, **107–9**, 111–12, 118n, 121n, 150
Barbary, 67
court cases against, 104n, 110–12, 113, 150
French, 63
Italian, 73
Livornese, 60, 110, 120n
Maltese, 60, 63, 73, 104n, 106, 107–8, 110, 112, 113, 120n
Corsica, 108, 167
Cosimo II (Duke of Tuscany, r. 1609–21), 108
cotton trade, 118n, 149
Counter-Reformation, 201
counter-revolution (Catholicism), 169, 171, 252
courts
ecclesiastical vs courts of the *qadi*, 17, 148, 170
creditors
Muslim, 61, 106, 107–8, 117n, 118n, 142, 145, 149
Crete, 143, 151, 153, 205, 220n
Crucifixion, 215, 220n
Crusades, 150, 151–2, 254
Cuénot, Étienne-Philippe, 200, 201, 209, 215
cultural differences
observed by Eastern Christian travellers, 124, **129–36**
Curé d'Ars (John Vianney), 251, 261n
customs, 166, 172
Cyprus, 56, 112, 153
Eastern Christians from/in, 66, 69, 112, 116n, 126, 129, 132: women, 135, 136
perception of differences between Western and Eastern Christianity in, 134–6
Cyril VI Ṭānās (Melkite Greek Catholic Patriarch of Antioch, r. 1724–60), 57, 110, 111, 114, 117n, 173, 213
Cyril V al-Zaʿīm (Melkite Patriarch of Antioch, d. 1720), 60, 71, 109, 114

Dabbās, Athanasius *see* Athanasius III Dabbās
Daher, Paul (Būlus Ḍāhir), 247, 251, 253, 254–5, 255–6
Damascus
1860 massacre, 143
Eastern Christians from/in, 12, 51, 62, 68, 85n, 114, 117n, 143, 146: Greeks, 118n; Jesuits, 66, 75, 103n; Melkites, 57, 60, 61, 68, 71, 74, 109, 204
merchants from/in, 118n
Damietta (Egypt), 60, 64, 112
Daniele (Basilian monk), 81n
Daqur, Susana, 230–1
Darak, Ḥannā, 202
Daʿūd (Maronite priest), 120n
David di San Carlo *see* ʿAbdallāh ibn Dawūd
David, Giovanni, 88n
Dāwūd (Melkite martyr), 62
Dayr al-Qamar, 262n
Debray, Régis, 28
debts/debtors, 61, 83n, 88n, 116n, 149
Muslims creditors, 61, 106, 107–8, 117n, 118n, 142, 145, 149
decadence (*inḥiṭāṭ*), 163
decolonisation, 163, 267
Del Giudice, Giovanni Battista (Shidyāq Ḥannā al-Muḥāsīb), 64
Delumeau, Jean, 20, 22, 115
De Marchis, Bartolomeo, 63, 84n
denunciations, 62, 64, 71, 73, 80n, 84n, 93
dervishes, 118n, 186–7
Desert Fathers/Saints, 249–50, 251, 257
detention, 55, 56–7, 58, 63, 64, 66, 69, 71, 83n, 94, 102n, 117n, 145–6
*dhimmī*s (protected subordinates), 7, 12, 142, 165
Diab, Arsenio *see* Diyāb, Arsāniyūs
Diab, Tommaso, 68–9, 87n
dialogues
between Catholics and Greeks, 185
between Christians and Muslims, **182–93**
diaspora studies, 19
Dick, Ignace, 22
Diderot, Denis, 237
dioceses, 11
duty of bishops to reside in own, 66, 91
Dioscorus, 172
Discalced Carmelites, 21, 62, 69–71, 104, 106, 116n, 119n, 202, 209, 210
disputations, 172, 182, 184
divinity
of Christ, 188, 191, 192, 237
Diyāb, Antūn Buṭrus, 242n
Diyāb, Arsāniyūs, 69, 76, 87n, 205, 213
Diyāb, Buṭrus, 204
Diyāb, Ḥannā, 5, 25, 266, 269
background/career, 30, 126, 127
in Cyprus, 134–6
linguistic skills, 129
in Paris, 124, 126, 127, 128, 129, 130, 131, 134, 146
perception of cultural differences, 124, **129–36**
protectors of, 127
tales of *Arabian Nights*, 5, 30–1, 128
travelogue, 30, 77n, 124, 125–6, 127
writing style, sources and audience, 125–6
Diyarbakir (Mesopotamia),
Eastern Christians from/in, 52, 61, 71, 80n, 86n, 91, 100n, 116n, 143, 144
merchants from/in, 61, 146
domestication, 235
dowries, 226
dragomans, 148–9; *see also* interpreters
dress codes, 132, 133
Druzes, 29, 150, 152, 167, 176n
Ducal printing press (Parma), 76
Dumas, Alexandre, 144
Dupront, Alphonse, 22
Dürer, Albrecht, 202
al-Duwayhī, Isṭifān *see* Isṭifān al-Duwayhī

Eastern/Middle Eastern Christianity/Christians
employment of (in Europe), **65–70**, 85n, 88n, 90–1
fragmentation, 11–13, 166
history of, 7, 10–13, 23, 264–5, 268
mediating role between Ottoman Empire and Europe, 50, 75–6, 149–50
relation with (Roman) Catholicism, 23, 75, 151, 163, 166, 167, 183, 188
reputation/image and physical appearance, 115, 133
scholarship on, 1, 2, 7, 10, **13–20**, 268
Western Christianity and/vs, 124, **129–36**, 149–50, 163, 166, 167, 188, 235, 250
East Syriac Church, 11; *see also* Chaldean Catholic Church/Chaldeans
Ecce Homo images, 216
Ecchellensis, Abraham, 25, 29, 266
ecclesiastical authority/power, 167
centralisation, 170
hierarchy, 13, 165, 168–9, 171, 174, 175, 235, 236, 245

importance of portraits in showing, 211
jurisdiction, 148
other systems of authority and, 12, 18, 165, 170, 235
power struggles/conflicts, 13, 24, 171–2, 174, 235, 236, 237
Western vs Eastern Christianity, 11–12
women, 228, 235, 236–7
ecclesiastics *see* bishops; clergy/clerics; patriarchs
École des Hautes Études en Sciences Sociales (EHESS), 27, 29, 31
École française de Rome, 21, 22
École pratique des Hautes Études (EPHE, Paris), 27, 28, 29, 31
economy
relation between religion, politics and, 105, 267
see also commercial affairs/interests; trade
Edessa (Urfa, Đanlıurfa), 254
education, 60, 97, 104n, 168, 169
of women/girls, 229, 234, 235
see also Collegio Urbano; Maronite College of Rome
Efendi, Mehmed, 126
Egypt, 120n, 126, 151
Eastern Christians from/in, 97, 99n: Maronites, 66, 121n; Melkites, 70, 104n; Syrian Christians, 112
merchants from/in, 75, 104n, 112, 118n
Egyptian asceticism, 251, 257
Elia (Armenian Archbishop of Bethlehem), 63
Elia Giacinto di Santa Maria, 69, 71
Elian of Homs, Saint, 210
Eliano, Giovanni Battista, 200
Elias/Elijah, Saint, 210, 257
Elijah X (Patriarch of the Church of the East), 210
endowments (*waqf*), 17
England, 56, 66, 92, 114, 122n, 148; *see also* Britain
Enlightenment, 171
entangled history (*histoire croisée*), 153, 163, 175
Ephesus, Council of (431), 11
erotic elicitations, 232
Ethiopian Church, 11; *see also* Coptic Orthodox Church
Eucharist, 169, 209, 210, 212*ill.*, 251
Europe
alms collection in, 55, 59, 59–60, 92, 100n, 106, 142, 143
control and repression of Eastern Christians, **55–9**
evolution of number of Eastern Christians in, 145, 147–8
exile in, 63, 65, 106, 151, 152
intervention in Ottoman Empire, 142–3
mediatory role of Eastern Christians between Ottoman Empire and, 50, 75–6, 149–50
motivations for coming to, 55, 60, 64, 90, 143, 144
travel to, 19, 31, **49–55**, 53–4*ill.*, 59, 71
European merchants *see* Western merchants
Eva, Gabriele *see* Ḥawwā, Jibrā'īl
Eva, Tommaso *see* Ḥawwā, Tūmā
exile/exiles, 63, 65, 106, 151, 152

Fabius, Laurent, 153
Facher, Name *see* Fakhr, Mikhā'īl Ni'ma
Facri, Michel Grazia *see* Fakhr, Mikhā'īl Ni'ma
al-Fāḍīl, Mikhā'īl (Bishop of Beirut), 174, 175
Fahmé-Thiery, Paule, 30
Fakhraddīn (Druze Emir of Mount Lebanon, r. 1592–1606), 29, 142, 150, 151
Fakhr family, 104n, **109–15**
Catholic reputation, 109–10, 113–14
Fakhr, Giovanni, 112, 113
Fakhr, Ilyās/Elia, 109–10, 112, 113–15, 119n, 122n, 173
Fakhr, Mikhā'īl Ni'ma, 68, 73, 104n, 110–13, 120n, 122n
Fargialla/Fargellà/Farjallāh family, 81n
Fargialla, Nicola, 58, 81n
Farḥāt, Jarmānūs, 128
fasting, 26, 132, 170, 172
Fayum (province, Egypt), 132
Febvre, Michel (Justinien de Neuvy), 182, 183–4, 185, 186, 187, 188, 192, 269
female emancipation/feminisation, 5, 6, 25
female mysticism, 25, 227, 228–9, 231; *see also* Hindiyya
female sainthood, 27, 251
Fénelon, François (Archbishop of Cambrai), 166
Fernando di Santa Ludivina, 119n
Ferrara, 80n
financial support
from Propaganda Fide, 59, 61, 95, 106, 109, 117n, 145
from Russia, 143
First Nations, 216
First World War, 148, 153, 170–1, 254
Fleuriau, Thomas Charles d'Armenonville, 201, 218n
Florence, 51, 52, 58, 63, 64, 73, 150
Foucauld, Saint Charles de, 251

Foucault, Michel, 25, 174, 231
France, 28, 116, 118n, 150, 153, 205, 247
alms collection in, 64, 92, 100n
Eastern Christians in/from, 7, 51, 52, 58, 62, 65, 71, 74, 101n, 147; Maronites, 51, 62, 77n, 127, 150–1, 164, 252; Melkites, 58, 147–8; Syriac Catholics, 67–8, 76
Heyberger in, 24–9
protection by, 14, 23, 31, 61, 62, 71, 133–4, 150–1, 152, 171
Roman Catholic Church vs, 171
state-building, 236
see also Marseille; Paris
Franceschi, Antonio (corsair), 110–11, 120n
Franceschi della Bocca (cousin of Antonio Franceschi), 120n
Francesco Antonio da Rimini, 80n
Francesco di Paolo, 61, 106
Francis of Assisi, Saint, 201, 209
Franciscans of the Holy Land *see* Friars Minor of the Holy Land
Franciscans (Mexico), 144
Francis of Sales, Saint, 169
Francis Xavier, Saint, 200, 209
'Franks', 71, 108, 129, 174, 175, 201
fraternities
rules, 169
Sisterhood of the Rosary (Aleppo), 229, 230, 233
Fraternity of the Guardian Angel (Rome), 58
fraudulous activities, 58, 74, 81n, 83n, 94, 103, 104n, 116n; *see also* alms collection; begging/beggars
Freijate, Faèz, 22
French Catholics
entangled history between Eastern Christians and, 153
French consulates/consuls, 152, 184; *see also* Picquet, François
French missionaries, 109, 182; *see also* Febvre, Michel; Nau, Michel
French Revolution (1789–99), 264
French scholarship, 268
frescoes, 199, 202, 204*ill.*, 208, 210
Friars Minor of the Holy Land, 13, 52, 56, 68, 116n, 117n, 119n, 171, 185
church decoration, 201, 209
disputes/fraudulous activities, 57–8, 72, 81n, 88n, 109, 118n
Friars Minor of the Observance *see* Friars Minor of the Holy Land
fundraising *see* alms collection; begging/beggars
Gabriel (Archangel), 201
Gabriele di Salomone (Greek archpriest), 81n
Gailan, Filippo (Fīlībus Ghaylān), 71–2, 74–5, 76, 103n, 104n
Galioparsi, Giorgio, 74
Galland, Antoine, 5, 30, 127, 128, 139n, 146
Garcin, Jean-Claude, 41n
Gaudez, Nicolas, 242–3n
Gaziro, Abramo, 74
Gemayel, Bachir, 263n
Genevieve, Saint, 126, 130
Genoa, 52, 57, 126, 133
George (Cypriot merchant), 107
Georges and Mathilde Salem Foundation (Aleppo), 22
Georgians, 166, 205
Georgi, Giuseppe, 68, 99n
Gerach, Gregorio, 86–7n
Germany, 28, 60, 63, 106
Gernet, Jacques, 23
Ghosta/Ghūsṭā (Lebanon), 174, 212*ill.*
Giacomo of Marash (Armenian Archbishop), 56
Giallali, Pietro, 58
Gibb, Hamilton A. R., 17
Gibraltar, 57
Gillal, Giuseppe, 52, 70, 99n
Ginzburg, Carlo, 269
Giorgio di Grazia, 67, 99n
Giovanni Felice da Barga, 68
Giovanni of Jerusalem (Syrian suffragan bishop), 83n
Girolamo Nonziata/Girolamo of Aleppo (Maronite monk), 68, 87n
Giubair, Neofito (Nāwufītūs ibn Jubayr al-Ḥalabī), 60, 70, 71, 73, 88n, 99n, 104n, 112
Giuseppe Grazia, 116n
Giuseppe Michele, 64
global history, 19, 31, 124
global microhistory, 4, 25, 31
goods
circulation between Italy and Middle East, 75, 105
confiscation of, **60–3**, 65, 73, 75, 82n, 103n, 106, 107, 108, 118n; *see also* corsairs
see also trade
Gospel, 187
Qur'an vs, 185, 187, 189, 190, 191, 192, 197n
Graf, Georg, 14, 102n
Granada, 57, 268
Greece, 151, 205
merchants from/in, 107, 109, 201

Greek Catholic Church/Catholics, 15, 51, 175, 210, 211
church decoration/images, 211
in Livorno, 147, 104n
in Malta, 70, 99n
in Venice, 58, 83n
see also Melkite Church/Melkites
Greek (language), 70, 134, 135
Greek Orthodox Church/Christians, 11–12, 143, 147, 175, 192, 237
1724 schism, 13, 15; *see also* Melkite Church/Melkites
dialogues between Catholics and, 185–6
in Italy/Livorno, 68, 104n, 147
in London, 147
in Russia, 143–4, 147
Gruzinski, Serge, 21, 23
Guadagnoli, Filippo, 188, 189
Guirguis, Magdi, 36n
Guiseppe Francesco (Maronite), 111

Habaisci (Ḥubaysh) sheikhs, 59, 64, 73
Habaisci, Taleb (Ṭālib Ḥubaysh), 64
Haddad, Robert M., 15
hagiographies/hagiographers, 27, 126, 228, 245, 246, 248, 249, 250, 251, 254, 255, 257
Haifa, 118n
al-Hakawī, Sulaymān bin Hashīsh, 139n
al-Ḥakīm, Maksīmūs (Melkite Archbishop of Aleppo), 115, 172
Halle (Germany), 66
Ḥamānā (Lebanon), 202
Hammoja, Maria, 229
al-Ḥardīnī, Saint Niʿmatallāh Kassāb, 246, 258n
Harik, Iliya F., 15
Harut, Giorgio, 117n
Hatem, Giuseppe (Yūsuf Hātim), 229
Hatzikyriakis (Greek from Vurla), 201
Ḥawwā (Hawā) family, 213
Ḥawwā, Helena (mother of Hindiyya), 233
Ḥawwā, Jibrāʾīl (Gabriele Eva, Archbishop of Cyprus), 66
Ḥawwā, Tūmā (Tommaso Eva), 66, 213, 216
Hayek, Michel, 245, 248, 249, 250, 253, 254
Herabied, Tommaso, 67
heresy/heretics, 24, 57, 112, 135, 167, 176, 183–4, 188
Heyberger, Bernard
conferences/seminars, 1–2, 25–6, 27–8, 29, 31–2
educational background, 20–1
scholarship, 2, 3, 13, 18, **20–33**, 265: research approach, 3–5, 7, 13, 23, 31, 49, **265–8**, 269–70; sources used, 4, 268–9
works, 5–7, 18, 23–4, 24–6, 26–7, 32, 265
hierarchy *see* ecclesiastical authority/power
Hill Museum & Manuscript Library (HMML), 15
Hindiyya (al-ʿUjaymī, Maronite nun, d. 1798), 169, 171, 266, 267, 269
autobiography, 127, 227, 228, 232
background/education, 24, 128, 228
bodily discourse, 227
condemnation/interrogations, 6, 24, 213, 237, 240n
foundation of order, 24, 172, 174, 213, 227, **236**
hagiographic biographies on, 228
holiness/authority, 24, 175, 227, 228, 234, 236–7
imprisonment, 24
Islamic inspiration, 166
Jesuit masters of, 6, 24, 173, 213, 235
mystical marriage/bond, 25, 227, 228
portrait of, 213
revelations/spiritual texts, 227–8
use of images, 216
see also Sacred Heart of Jesus
histoire croisée (entangled history), 153, 163, 175
Holy Valley *see* Qadīsha, Wādī
homeland
ties with/return to, 66, 73, 92–3, 96–7, 101n
Homs, 144
honorific titles, 55, 65, 74
hostage
by Muslims creditors, 61, 106, 107, 108, 117n, 118n, 145
Ḥubaysh family *see* Habaisci
Hungary, 77n

Ibn Budayr (Shihāb al-Dīn Ahmad al-Budayrī), 125, 127, 131, 139n
Ibn Jubayr *see* Giubair, Neofito
Ibn Khaldun, 175
Ibn Munqidh, Usāma, 21
Ibn Tūmā (Greek Orthodox from Damascus), 213
Ibn Yaʿqūb, Sulaymān *see* Negri, Salomone
Ibrāhīm, Lahūd, 246
Ibrahim Pasha of Egypt (r. 1848), 246
iconoclasm, 199

icons/iconography, 25–6, 199, 210, 212
contradictions/conflicts around, 210–11, 215, 217
Eastern, 202, 204*ill.*, 210
Greek icons, 205, 215
Melkite icons, 205
Orthodox, 206
transformation/evolution of role of, 216–17
Western, 200
see also images
identity/identity formation, 175, 266
by exclusion or opposition, 164
of Middle Eastern Christians, 32, 50, 163
of various Christian denominations, 163, 164, 165
see also confessional identity; religious identity
Ignatius of Loyola, Saint, 128, 167, 200, 209
i'jāz (doctrine of the inimitable beauty of the Qur'an), 190
images, 25–6, 199
in Arabic books, 206
distribution by missionaries, 200, 201, 206, 209–10, 213, 216
Eastern Christian: evolution, 208; importation/(own) production, 199–200, 202, 204–5; taste, 209–10; Western influence, 205, 206, 207–8*ill.*, 208–10, 216, 217
educational goal of, 168
Greek, 205, 215
meditation on, 215, 216
moral, 216
printed images vs icons, 215, 217
in private homes, 200, 201, 202, 213, 215, 218n
religious vs political/secular, 211–13, 217
transformation/evolution of role of, 216–17
Western, 200, 201, 202, 215
see also icons/iconography; Marian images/iconography
Immaculate Conception
representation of, 208, 210
imprisonment *see* detention
income, 66, 70, 71, 83n, 90, 91, 93, 95, 104n, 130, 150; *see also* pensions; salaries; stipends
India, 182
individualisation, 168, 213; *see also* self-consciousness
infanticide, 166
infidels, 57, 59, 67, 108, 109, 167, 176, 188, 257
inheritance, 174, 233, 235
inḥiṭāṭ (decadence), 163
Innocent XI (Pope, r. 1676–89), 93
innovation
liturgical, 114, 172, 174, 210
tradition vs, 172–5, 236
Inquisition
Inquisitorial inquiry about Hindiyya, 228–9, 237
in Malta, 57, 69–70, 74, 88n, 99n, 103n, 120n
Roman, 58, 80n; *see also* Congregation of the Holy Office
Spanish, 57–8, 64, 80n
Institut d'études de l'Islam et des sociétés du monde musulman (IISMM), 28–9
Institut du Monde Arabe (Paris), 28
Institut français d'études arabes (IFEAD, Damascus), 21–2
Institut universitaire de France, 27
integration, 16, 31, 58, 63, 96, 97, 134, 147, 256
intermediaries
(Middle) Eastern Christians as, 50, 75–6, 149–50
interpreters, 30, 63, 65, 66, 69, 70, 127, 148–9; *see also* translators
Ioannikos (Archbishop of Sinai), 202
Iraq, 28, 153, 255
Ireland, 145
Isaac (Archbishop of Niniveh), 86n
'Isā (Basilian Archimandrite), 145
Isacco di Pietro, 93, 94, 102n
Isdrael, Paolo, 67
Isfahan, 146, 182, 202
Islam, 249
Christianity and/vs, 166, 189, 191, 193
Christian-Muslim dialogues, **182–93**
(forced) conversion to, 56, 57, 61, 62, 106, 108, 111, 234
immorality of, 188–9
miracles in, 188
missionaries' knowledge of, 186, **188–92**, 193
modernisation, 175
Islamic authority, 23, 190–1
persecution of Eastern Christians, 60–2, 75, 142
subordination to, 7, 12
see also millets

Islamic law, 166, 170
community vs, 17
Issenheimer Altarpiece (Colmar), 264
Istanbul, 115, 127, 129, 132
Isṭifān al-Duwayhī (Maronite Patriarch), 57, 217n, 218n
Isṭifān, Yūsuf *see* Yūsuf Isṭifān
Italian (language)
as *lingua franca* for Eastern Christians and Jews, 152
Italy
circulation of people and goods between Middle East and, 97, 105
Eastern Christians in/from, 90, 97: Maronites, 100n; Melkites, 58, 77n
immigration formalities, 132–3
missionaries from, 171
paintings from, 205
see also Livorno; Rome
Izmir, 127

Jacobites *see* Syriac Orthodox Church
Jaffa, 108, 110, 118n
al-Jāḥiẓ (d. 869), 21
Jansenists, 130
Jarwah, Mikhā'īl *see* Mikhā'īl Jarwah
Jbayl (Byblos, Lebanon), 246
Jean François de Sevin, 71, 91
Jelaledin *see* [al-]Suyūṭī, Jalāl al-Dīn
Jerusalem,
Eastern Christians from/in, 52, 61, 67, 117n, 118n: Armenians, 63, 118n; Maronites, 88n, 99n, 118n; Melkites, 57, 58, 60
merchants from/in, 88n, 118n
pilgrimages to, 90, 118n
Jesuits/Jesuit missionaries, 3, 71, 113, 117n, 126, 144, 167, 169, 171
from/in Aleppo, 85n
archives, 21
from/in Damascus, 66, 75, 103n
distribution of religious images, 200, 201, 202, 209–10, 213, 216
from/in Marseille, 101n
masters of Hindiyya, 6, 24, 173, 213, 235
publications, 182–3, 252
saints, 209, 213, 215
scholars, 66, 91
suppression of, 171
on women, 226
see also Nau, Michel
Jews, 2, 130, 149, 249
Christian–Jewish relations, 183, 184, 187
dragomans, 148
in Livorno, 126
Muslim–Jewish relations, 142, 165, 188
regeneration of, 152
jizya (poll tax), 149, 165
John XXIII (Pope, r. 1958–63), 248
Joseph (Chaldean Patriarch), 86n
Joseph, Saint, 200, 201, 210–11, 221n
Josue, Gregory (Syrian Archbishop of Jerusalem), 86n
Julfa (Isfahan), 202
justice
confessional, 235
ecclesiastical vs justice of *qadi*, 17, 148, 170
Justinien de Neuvy *see* Febvre, Michel

Kaiser, Wolfgang, 31
Karam, Yūsif (Maronite leader), 152
Karnuk, Ḥumaylī ibn Da'fī *see* Karnuk, Timothy
Karnuk, Timothy (Timoteo Agnellini, Syriac Catholic Archbishop of Mardin), 71, 84n
background/career, 4, 31, 66, 67, 85n, 91, 94, 96, 102n, 143, 266
death, 96
editing/printing activities, 76, 92, 93, 94, 95, 102n
name, 100n
order/request to return to homeland, 64, 91–2, 93, 96, 97
simoniacal ordination of clerics by, 93–4
trading activities/merchant interactions, 91, 92, 93, 94, 95, 266
trial and detention, 56, 93–4, 94–5
unauthorised alms collection/begging by, 56, 64, 74, 92, 94, 100n, 266
Kfīfān (Lebanon), 246
Khabiyya, Anṭūn (Kobié, Cubié), 173, 204
Khalīl, Father, 74–5
Khāzin family/sheiks, 17, 64, 151
al-Khāzin, Theresa, 234
al-Khāzīn, Tūbiyā *see* Tūbiyā al-Khāzīn
Kieser, Hans-Lukas, 24
Kiev, 166, 201, 209
Kircher, Athanasius, 66, 91
Kisruwān (district, Lebanon), 253
Kontouma, Vassa, 31
Kurbāj al-Ḥalabī, Ibrāhīm, 204
Kurbāj, Tūmā, 76, 77n, 138n
Kurdistan, 165

Lamartine, Alphonse de, 151
Lammens, Henri, 252
language/language skills, 13, 50, **65–6**, **67–70**, 91, 134, 152, 186, 254
Larnaca (Cyprus), 134
La Rochelle (France), 247
Latakia (Syria), 51, 82n
Latin Church/Catholicism *see* Roman Catholic Church
Latin missions/missionaries *see* Roman Catholic/Latin missions/missionaries
Lavra of Saint Sabbas (near Jerusalem), 205
law *see* community law; Islamic law
laymen, 59, 145, 241n
Lazarists, 229, 234, 242–3n
Lebanese Civil War (1975–90), 25, 27, 245, 255–6
Lebanese Maronite Order, 126, 170, 172, 214, 236, 246, 248, 251, 256; *see also* Makhlouf, Saint Charbel
Lebanon, 14, 33, 110, 217, 253
  book printing in, 206
  Catholic women in, 5, 26, 225–38
  co-existence in, 249, 255
  Eastern Christians from/in, 31, 65, 76, 249: Armenians, 13, 56; Maronites, 15, 17, 25, 74, 132, 170, 171, 245, 253, 255–6
  history/historiography, 253, 254, 257
  interreligious dialogues, 249, 255
  Lebanese identity, 255–6
  missionaries in, 200
  mountain-dwellers from, 165
  Muslims in, 254–5
  nationalism, 253, 254, 255
  role of clergy in society and public life, 169
  see also Maronite Church/Maronites
Leeuwen, Richard van, 17
Lentin, Jérôme, 15, 30
Leroy, Jules, 202
Leroy-Ladurie, Emmanuel, 20
letters, 63, 72–3, 76, 81n, 91, 92, 95, 113, 120n, 130, 144, 146, 234, 247, 256
  between and with women, 226–7
  of credit, 63
  of naturality/protection, 146, 150, 151, 164
  of recommendation, 58, 62, 63, 71, 72, 79n, 83n, 88n, 106, 110, 116n, 117n, 129, 150, 155n
  requests for images, 202, 212
Levant, 12, 50, 51, 52, 69, 93, 111, 112, 113, 115, 142, 201, 220n
Levantine Christians, 28, 59, 63, 74, 90, 96, 97, 107–8, 111
  merchants, 68, 92
Levi, Giovanni, 105, 269
Lewis, Bernard, 17, 267
librarians, 30, 65, 66, 72, 127
Libya, 132, 153
Limassol, 82n
linguistic skills *see* language/language skills
Lisbon, 52, 58
literacy, 26
  of women, 226–7, 229–30
liturgical innovation, 114, 172, 174, 210
liturgical objects, 92, 109, 119n, 200
Livorno, 52, 126, 130–1
  churches/places of worship, 147
  corsairs, 60, 108, 110, 112, 120n
  Eastern Christians in/from, 62, 68–9, 76, 90, 110, 117n, 150: Armenians, 63, 67, 68, 86–7n, 147; Greeks, 68, 147; Maronites, 87, 126, 129, 130–1; Melkites, 57–8, 73, 99n, 147; Syriacs, 72
  Jews in, 126
  merchants in, 68, 73, 146
  quarantine and customs inspection, 132–3
Llull, Ramon, 184
loans *see* creditors
London
  Eastern Christians in, 52, 66, 146, 147
  merchants in, 146
  places of worship for Eastern Christians, 147
Lorenzo di San Lorenzo, 58, 108, 110, 118n
Losana, Pietro, 229
Louaizeh/Luwayza (monastery, Zuk Mosbeh, Lebanon), 202, 203*ill.*, 212, 214*ill.*
Louis IX (King of France/Saint Louis, r. 1226–70), 151, 164
Louis XIV (King of France, r. 1643–1715), 130, 144, 151, 211
Louis XV (King of France, r. 1715–74), 146
Lucas, Paul, 30, 77n, 124, 126–7, 128, 129, 132, 133, 139n
Ludolf, Heinrich Wilhelm, 66
Luke, Saint, 206, 207*ill.*
Lutheranism, 56
Luwayza *see* Louaizeh/Luwayza
Lviv, 201–2, 202
Lyon, 72, 129, 131, 144

Maʿalūla (Syria), 144
Macarius III ibn al-Zaʿīm (Melkite Patriarch of Antioch, r. 1647–72), 143, 166, 168, 201, 211–12
Madeleine (partner of Giovanni Sciain), 57
Madinier, Rémy, 28
Madonna di Montenero (Livorno), 126, 127
Madrid, 52, 58, 63, 64, 143
Mahomet *see* Muhammad, the Prophet
'Mahometans' (term/name), 188
majlis (sessions between members of various religions), 182
Makāryūs (Bishop of Tripoli), 109, 110, 111, 114, 119n, 120n, 122n
Makhlouf, Antūn, 246, 252, 254
Makhlouf, Brigitta, 246, 251–2, 254
Makhlouf, Saint Charbel (Sharbal Makhlūf, Maronite monk, d. 1898),
  asceticism of, 250–1
  biographies/hagiographies, 248–9, 250, 254, 257
  canonisation/sainthood, 5, 27, 245, 247, 248, 249, 253, 255–6
  career, 246
  childhood/youth, 246, 251–2, 254
  death and burial, 246–7
  education/skills, 254, 261n, 262n
  miracles, 245, 247–8, 249
  monastic vows, 259n
  origins, 253
Malta
  corsairs/confiscation of goods, 60, 73, 103n, 104n, 106, 107–8, 110, 112, 113, 120n, 150
  court archives, 268
  Eastern Christians in/from, 52, 59, 60: Greeks, 70, 99n, 146; Maronites, 52, 69–70, 74, 99n, 112, 120n, 121n; Melkites, 57, 73, 88n, 112; Syriac Catholics, 90, 93–4
  pastoral care in, 90, 94, 99n, 121n
Manṣūr, al-Usṭā, 113
manuscripts
  collection/purchase of, 127
  digitisation of, 15
  miniatures in, 199
  revival of, 26
maps, 200
Marash (Turkey), 56
Marcus, Abraham, 16, 23
Mardin (Mesopotamia/Turkey)
  Eastern Christians from/in, 52, 106–7: Nestorians, 210; Syrian Catholics, 56, 84n, 91, 93, 96, 143, 144
  Jesuits in, 184
  see also Karnuk, Timothy
Marian images/iconography, 200, 201, 202, 203*ill.*, 208, 208*ill.*, 210, 211, 213, 220–1n, 252, 261n
maritime trade, 50, 61, 88n, 109, 118n
  insecurity of, 107–8; *see also* corsairs
  mudābara (agreements between Christians and Muslims), 107
Maronite Church/Maronites, 6, 17, 19
  from/in Aleppo, 30, 66, 68, 73, 77n, 124, 126, 127, 131, 132, 133, 165, 170, 201, 202, 212
  ascetism, 249
  autonomy/differentiation from other denominations, 151, 164–5, 170, 245
  conflicts: with Druzes, 152; on ecclesiastical authority, 172, 174
  in/from Cyprus, 135
  in/from Egypt, 73, 121n
  in/from Europe, 151: Austria, 143; France, 29, 30, 51, 62, 77n, **124–36**, 150–1, 164, 252; Germany, 143; Italy, 52, 62–3, 85n, 150; Livorno, 87, 126, 129, 130–1; Malta, 52, 69–70, 74, 99n, 112, 120n, 121n; Rome, 29, 51, 59, 66, 67, 68, 69, 72, 73, 77n, 84n, 88n, 89n, 120n, 147, 150, 205; Spain, 143
  history/origins, 11, 12, 15, 174, 249, 252, 254, 255
  images, 199, 201, 202, 209
  from/in Jerusalem, 52, 88n
  from/in Lebanon, 15, 17, 25, 74, 132, 170, 171, 245, 253, 255–6
  Maronite/national identity, 151, 235, **245–57**, 252, 255
  mediatory role between Ottoman Empire and Europe, 150
  missions to, 200
  nuns, 234; *see also* Hindiyya
  painters, 204, 205
  persecution/martyrdom, 254–5
  political Maronitism/involvement, 245, 255, 256, 263n
  protection by/relation with France, 150–1, 164
  Roman Catholic Church attitude towards, 171
  social system, 165
  from/in Tripoli, 103n, 149
  see also Diyāb, Ḥannā; Lebanese Maronite Order; Makhlouf, Saint Charbel
Maronite College of Rome, 51, 66, 68, 69, 73, 88n, 112, 116n
Maron, Saint, 211

Marracci, Ludovico, 93, 102n
marriage, 165, 170, 172, 221n
 arranged, 172, 233, 234
 fertility vs chastity, 211
 mixed, 12, 106, 150
 mystical, 227, 228, 230–1, 232, 235; *see also* Hindiyya
 of the Prophet, 192
Marseille, 72
 Eastern Christians in/from, 52, 64–5: Armenians, 63, 67; Chaldeans, 146; Maronites, 126, 127; Melkites, 57, 58, 148; Syriacs, 68, 71, 91; Syrians, 55, 57, 62, 107
 merchants/trade in, 55, 64–5, 126, 129, 146
 pastoral care in, 101n
martyrdom/martyrs, 62, 63, 184, 254–5
Mār Yūsaf al-Ḥuṣn (monastery, Ghosta, Lebanon), 212*ill.*
Masbani, Michele, 51
massacres, 143, 144, 152, 254, 262n
Massad, Abramo/Ibrahīm, 73, 108
Massaica, Fatallah, 61
Massara, Ibrahīm, 108
Massara, Saʿāda, 68
Masters, Bruce, 16, 23, 107
Matn (district, Lebanon), 253
Maunier, Christophe, 134
Maʿūshī, Ḥannā Shalhūb *see* Scilhub/Scialup, Giovanni
al-Mawṣilī, Ilyās, 71, 72, 76, 101n, 125, 126, 144
al-Mawṣilī, Yunān, 72
Mayeur-Jaouen, Catherine, 26
Mayfūq (monastery), 246
Mazet, Giuseppe Giovanni, 111–12, 121n
Maẓlūm, Maksīmūs (Melkite Bishop and Patriarch), 148
Medici printing press, 73, 74, 89n
Mediterranean, 30, 49–50
 Syrian Christians in, **105–15**
 trading diaspora/trading networks, 134, 146
Mediterranean ports, 30, 49, 50
 Eastern Christians settling/working in, 52, 71, 75
 see also Livorno; Marseille
Mehmed II (Sultan of the Ottoman Empire, r. 1444–6/1451–81), 12, 17
Melkite Church/Melkites, 6, 19, 108, 109, 112
 from/in Aleppo, 60, 62, 68, 85n, 104n, 113, 114, 170, 172, 212
 archives, 22
 book printing, 206
 from/in Cairo, 83n
 conflicts, 172
 from/in Damascus, 57, 60, 61, 68, 71, 74, 109, 204
 differentiation from other denominations, 170
 in/from Egypt, 104n
 in/from Europe, 52: France, 58, 147–8; Livorno, 57–8, 73, 99n, 147; Malta, 57, 73, 88n, 112; Rome, 51, 57, 58, 60, 62, 68, 71, 77n, 85n, 117n, 144; Spain, 58, 64, 77n; Venice, 57, 62
 history/origins, 11, 12, 163
 identity, 235
 images/iconography, 199, 202, 205, 209
 merchants, 104n
 monks, 173, 206, 212
 painters, 209
 Patriarch of Antioch, 12–13, 114, 174, 210
 schism (1724), 13, 15, 114, 170, 173
 social system, 165–6
 women, 226
 see also Greek Catholic Church/Catholics
merchandise *see* goods
merchants, 90, 107, 134, 266
 in/from Aleppo, 73, 118n, 129, 149, 213
 Armenian, 86–7n, 93, 94, 146
 in/from Egypt, 75, 104n, 112, 118n
 Greek, 107, 109, 201
 in/from Jerusalem, 88n, 118n
 Levantine, 68, 92
 in/from Livorno, 68, 73, 146
 in/from Marseille, 55, 64–5, 126, 129, 146
 Syrian, 55, 106–7, 110
 Western, 149, 150
Mervin, Sabrina, 41n
Mesopotamia, 52, 184
Messina (Italy), 94
Methodius (Greek monk), 186
Metoscita, Michele, 69–70, 71, 73–4, 76, 89n, 99n, 103n, 104n, 112, 121n
Mexico, 72, 144, 260n
microhistory, 4, 18, 19, 25, 31, 124, 265, 269
Middle Eastern Christianity/Christians *see* Eastern/Middle Eastern Christianity/ Christians
migration/migrants, 253
 careers/skills, **65–70**, 90
 motivation for coming to Europe, 31, 55, 60, 90, 143, 144, 148
 national/sectarian consciousness and, 152

origins and destinations, 52, 54*ill.*
preparation for/planned, 64–5, 72, 144
successful, 146–8
supporting networks, 49, 57, 58, 71, 72, 73; *see also* networks for protection and recommendation
ties with/return to homeland, 66, 73, 92–3, 96–7
travellers vs migrants, 63–5
see also circulation; travels/travellers
Mikhāʾīl al-Rizzī (Maronite Patriarch, r. 1567–81), 167
Mikhāʾīl Jarwah (Syriac Catholic Patriarch, r. 1783–1800), 149
military, 130
military expeditions/interventions, 50, 150, 152, 153
millets (religious communities), 17–18, 149, 169
miniatures, 199
miracles, 188, 247–8, 249
missionary literature, 167
missionary schools, 167–8
missions/missionaries, 167–8; *see also* Catholic missions/missionaries; Christian missions/missionaries; Jesuits/Jesuit missionaries; Lazarists; Protestant missions/missionaries; Roman Catholic/Latin missions/missionaries
mobility, 10
of Eastern Christians, 11, 19, 49, 53–4*ill.*
mobility studies, 30–3
see also migration; travels/travellers
modernisation/modernity, 225, 235, 268
Catholic, 175
in Islam, 175
of Ottoman society, 170
of women, 136, 233, 235, 237
see also Westernisation
Mogailes, Rafaele (Mughaylaṣ), 82n
monasteries, 65, 174, 246
decoration of/images in, 199, 202, 203*ill.*, 204*ill.*, 205, 207–8*ill.*, 210, 212, 212*ill.*
mixed, 171
see also ʿAyn Warqa; Bkirki; Louaizeh/Luwayza; Mār Yūsaf al-Ḥuṣn; Mayfūq; Qannūbin; Saint Catherine; Saint John of Shuwayr; Saint Maroun/Mar Maroun
Monastery of the Annunciation (Zūq Mikhāʾīl), 85n
monastic vows, 259n; *see also* chastity; obedience; poverty
money lending- and borrowing *see* creditors; debts/debtors
monks
gifts/endowments to, 226
Greek, 143, 186
Maronite, 143, 149, 170, 172, 202, 204, 205, 212, 213, 235, 236; *see also* Makhluf, Saint Charbel
Melkite, 173, 206, 212
travelling, 19, 56, 143
see also religious orders
monotheism, 187, 188, 192, 196n, 267
monothelitism, 11
Morea (Peloponnese), 63
Moscow, 143, 201
Mosè di Nicola, 60–1, 104n, 106
Mosè (Syrian cleric in Marseille), 57
mosques
churches transformed into, 136, 141n
Mosul, 210; *see also* Nineveh
mountain-dwellers, 165
Mount Carmel, 108, 120n, 210
Mount Lebanon, 15, 24, 51, 59, 69, 83n, 126, 246
1860 massacre, 143, 254
alms collection for, 104n, 145
Catholic women in Aleppo and, 5, 26, **225–38**
church decorations, 202
documents produced in, 127
economic crisis, 148
geography, 76, 253
political system/conflicts, 6, 11, 142, 150, 151, 152, 170
see also Lebanese Maronite Order; Maronite Church/Maronites; Sacred Heart of Jesus
Mount Sinai, 166, 201, 220n
Mubārak, Buṭrus *see* Benedetti, Pietro
Muchalla, Mosè, 82–3n, 117n
Mughal court (India), 182
Mughaylaṣ, Nicolas and Ḥabīb, 64–5
Muhammad, the Prophet, 132
immorality/sins of, 191–2
prophecy of, 188, 191, 193
wives of, 191–2
al-Muḥāsīb, Shidyāq Ḥannā *see* Del Giudice, Giovanni Battista
Murad, Nicolas (Maronite Bishop), 151
Murcia (Spain), 57
Murre-van den Berg, Heleen, 13
al-Muṣawwir, Buṭrus al-Qubruṣī, 204
al-Muṣawwir, Jirjis Ḥanania, 210

Muslims, 2, 11, 238
Christian–Muslim coexistence/relations, 5, 7, 12, 16–17, 29, **182–93**, 255
conversion to Christianity, 62, 67–8, 69, 70, 102n, 167, 183, 255
creditors, 61, 106, 107–8, 117n, 118n, 142, 145, 149
differentiation from, 164, 165, 170
in Lebanon, 254–5
persecution of Eastern Christians by, 60–2, 75, 83n, 106–7, 142, 145
term/name, 188
women, 225–6
see also Turks
al-Mutanabbī (d. 965), 21
mystical marriage/union, 227, 228, 230–1, 232, 235
mysticism, 166
female, 25, 227, 228–9, 231; *see also* Hindiyya
rationalism vs, 250

al-Nābulusī, ʿAbd al-Ghānī, 125
Nacchi, Stefano, 116n
Nachet, Grazia, 67
Naef, Silvia, 24, 25
Naim, Lazzaro, 59
Nancy II University, 21
Naples
Eastern Christians in/from, 52, 59, 64, 67, 72, 99n: Armenians, 63–4, 74, 94; Maronites, 63, 67; Syriac Catholics, 56, 93, 94, 102n
Napoleon Bonaparte (Emperor of the French, r. 1804–14/1815), 147
Napoleon III (Emperor of the French, r. 1852–70), 152
Naqqāsh, Yuḥannā, 76, 77n, 138n
Nasrallah, Joseph, 14, 122n
nationalism, 165
Maronites, 245, 246, 252, 253, 254, 255, 256, 257
natural sciences, 187
Nau, Michel, 182–3, 184, 186, 187, 188, 189, 190, 191, 192
Nazareth, 201
Neeme di Kuri, (Niʿma ibn al-Khūrī), 82n
Negri, Salomone (Sulaymān ibn Yaʿqūb), 66, 143
Nestorians, 107, 116, 210; *see also* Church of the East
Nestorius (Patriarch of Constantinople, r. 428–31), 11
Netherlands, the, 28, 52, 148
networks for protection and recommendation, 50, 52, 58, 75, 97, 133, 150
New Julfa (Armenian quarter of Isfahan), 19, 146
Nicosia, 134
Niʿmatallāh, 106–7
Nineveh (Mesopotamia), 86n, 94, 101n, 116n
Nonziata, Girolamo *see* Girolamo Nonziata
North Africa, 77n
Notre-Dame (cathedral of Paris), 146
Nunciatures, 52
nuns, 234
confessions of, 231–2, 242n
obedience of, 228, 234, 236, 243n
opposition between, 172
rules for, 230, 233, 236
see also female mysticism; Hindiyya; Sacred Heart of Jesus
Nuṣayrīs, 167

obedience, 247, 251, 259n
to pope, 132, 169
of women/nuns, 228, 234, 236, 243n
L'Œuvre d'Orient (French Catholic relief organisation), 152
oral testimony
written text vs, 235
Order of Saint John of Malta, 69, 70, 108
Order of the Visitation of Holy Mary (Visitandines), 169
Orientalism/Orientalists, 14, 19, 22, 29, 90, 91, 127, 167, 266
stereotyping, 16, 75, 253, 268
Oriental press (Padua), 74, 93, 102n
Orthodox Church/Orthodox, 7
conversion to Catholicism, 91, 118n
identity, 18
images/iconography, 201–2, 205, 206
polemics, 173
(Roman) Catholic Church vs, 13, 60, 106, 114, 168, 170, 172–3, 210, 211
see also Greek Orthodox Church/Christians; Melkite Church/Melkites
Ottoman Empire/Period, 10
archives, 16
European interventions in, 142–3
modernisation, 170; *see also* Westernisation
position of non-Muslim subjects in, 12, 16, 49, 60–2, 170: mediatory role of Eastern Christians with West, 50, 75–7, 149–50;

role of clergy in society and public life, 17–18, 61, 149, 169; *see also* Islamic authority; *millets*
trade, 108
urban society, 16
Western Christianity vs Ottoman East, 124, **129–36**
Ottoman terminology, 130

Paci, Balthazar, 74
Padua, 66, 74, 76, 85n, 93, 102n
paganism, 253
paintings/painters, 202, 204–5, 209; *see also* al-Muṣawwir
Palermo, 72
Palestine/Palestinians, 51, 109, 120n, 201, 255
Panzac, Daniel, 118n
Paris, 265, 268
Eastern Christians in/from, 52, 62, 64, 66, 94, 143, 144: Armenians, 134; Chaldeans, 71; Maronites, 29, 30, **124–36**, 150; Melkites, 57; Syriac Catholics, 56, 92, 93
opera, 128, 130
'poison affairs', 56
police, 130
public executions, 126, 129
Quartier Latin, 146
Parma, 76
pastoral care, 90, 94, 99n, 101n, 121n; *see also* confessions
Patriarchate of Antioch *see* Melkite Church/ Melkites
patriarchs, 151
authority and role, 18, 164–5, 169, 174
portraits of, 211–13
patronage, 90–1, 97, 142; *see also* protection; recommendation
Paul, Saint, 204
Paul VI (Pope, r. 1963–78), 248, 249
Paun, Radu, 31
Payas (Anatolia), 129
peasants, 151, 167, 252–3
Pécout, Gilles, 31
Péguy, Charles, 262n
pensions, 56, 65, 66, 70, 84n, 91, 95, 96, 99n, 104n, 144
persecution, 49
by creditors *see* hostage
by ecclesiastical opponents, 60–1, 68, 71, 72, 82–3n, 96–7, 106, 109, 116, 117n, 145
by Muslims/Islamic authorities, 60–2, 75, 83n, 106–7, 142, 145
Persia/Persians, 107, 150
Byzantines vs Persians, 11
migration from, 134, 148, 255
missions to, 67, 93
Peter, Saint, 201, 204
Phabrey, Gilles, 259n
Philipp, Thomas, 23
Photian Schism (863–7), 172
Picques, Louis, 66, 85n
Picquet, François (French consul/Latin Bishop of Babylon), 56, 61, 67, 71, 93, 97, 107, 144
pilgrimage/pilgrims, 19, 59, 90, 109, 118n, 120n, 247, 263n
piracy *see* corsairs
Pisa, 74, 147
Pistoia, 57
Pius VI (Pope, r. 1775–99), 169
Pius XI (Pope, r. 1922–39), 247
Pizzorusso, Giovanni, 22
places of worship *see* churches
plurality, 11, 132, 256, 257
'poison affairs' (Paris), 56
Poland, 83n
polemics
Christian-Muslim dialogues, **182–93**
Orthodox, 173
police (Paris), 130
Polish Catholics, 166
political authority/leadership, 130, 150, 235
political exiles, 151, 152
political images
religious vs, 211–13, 221n
politics/political interests, 74, 166
alms collection and, 151
political involvement, 151, 245, 255, 255–6, 256, 263n
political organisation, 131
relation between religion, economy and, 105, 267
Pontchartrain, Jérôme Phélypeaux, Count of (Minister of the Navy and State Secretary of France), 132
Ponte Sisto (ecclesiastical college, Rome), 68
popes
obedience to, 132, 169
pork, 131, 136
portraits, 211–13, 214*ill.*
ports *see* Mediterranean ports
Portugal, 64, 77n
power *see* ecclesiastical authority/power

printing/printing presses, 67, 76, 85n, 94, 102n
  censorship, 57, 189
  collaboration and power struggles, 26, 69
  fraudulous activities, 74, 95, 103n
  image printing, 206, 215
  trade in printing types, 95–6, 103n
  see also books; Propaganda Fide
privateers *see* corsairs
propaganda, 150, 173, 176
Propaganda Fide, 55, 57, 169
  archives, 21, 22, 49, 50–1, 90, 105, 106, 268
  book printing/publications, 29, 68, 109, 188, 189, 215
  policy of, 97
  recruitment and employment of migrants, 66, 72, 91
  sending clergy back to homeland, 66, 91–2, 96
  support/endorsement from, **59–63**, 64, 67, 95, 99n, 106, 109, 111, 112, 117n, 145
prophecy
  of Muhammad, the Prophet, 188, 191, 193
protection, 65, 68, 75, 90, 108, 115, **148–53**
  by France, 14, 23, 31, 61, 62, 71, 133–4, 150–1, 152, 171
  history of, 142–3
  of/by lay people/merchants, 90, 108, 133–4
  networks for recommendation and, 50, 52, 58, 75, 97, 133, 150
  relation between business and, **71–5**
Protestantism/Protestants
  Catholicism vs/competition amongst missionaries, 167, 171
  conversion to Protestantism, 56
  in France, 130
Protestant missions/missionaries, 2, 3, 7, 12, 13, 66, 152
Protestant states
  travel to, 79n, 143
public executions, 126, 129
public welfare, 130, 131

qadi
  ecclesiastical justice vs justice of, 17, 148, 170
Qadīsha, Wādī (Holy Valley, Lebanon), 253, 254, 262n
Qannūbīn (monastery, Mount Lebanon), 202, 204*ill.*, 210
Qarāʿalī, ʿAbdallāh (Bishop of Beirut), 170, 172, 212–13, 214*ill.*
Qarāʿalī, Yūsuf, 213
Qassīs, Charbel, 256
al-Qassīs, Yūsif, 65
Qattā, Ḥannā ibn, 85n
al-Qilāʿī, Jibrāʿīl ibn, 257
quarantine, 132–3
al-Qubruṣī, Silfāstrūs *see* Sylvester al-Qubruṣī
Qurʾan, 186
  authority of, 190–1
  eloquence of, 190
  Gospel vs, 185, 187, 189, 190, 191, 192, 197n
  translations of, 93, 189–90
Qurʾanic exegesis (*tafsīr*), 191, 192
Qurʾanic quotations/verses, 183, 189
  Q 2 (*The Cow*): 2:136, 190; 2:219, 189
  Q 4 (*The Women*): 4:150–2, 189–90
  Q 10 (*Jonah*): 10:94, 189
  Q 16 (*The Bees*): 16:67, 189
  Q 33 (*The Factions*): 33:37, 192
Qurʾanic revelation, 190, 191, 192
Qūshaqjī, Yūsuf, 22

Rafeq, Abdul-Karim, 16, 23
Raqfa, Saint, 258n
rationalism
  mysticism vs, 250
Raymond, André, 16, 16–17, 23
reading, 26, 167–8
reason, 185, 192
recommendation, 55, 65, 113, 143
  letters of, 58, 62, 63, 71, 72, 79n, 83n, 88n, 106, 110, 116n, 117n, 129, 150, 155n
  networks for protection and, 50, 52, 58, 75, 97, 133, 150
refutations, 183, 190
religion
  entanglement with commercial affairs, 74, 105, 113, 266–7
  to advance political interests, 267
religious belief
  social order and, 165–6
religious identity, 164, 235
  Maronites, 151, 235, **245–57**, 252, 255
religious images *see* images
religious orders
  rivalry/conflicts between, 166, 171–2, 211, 235, 236–7
  set up by women, 227
  see also Lebanese Maronite Order; Order of Saint John of Malta; Sacred Heart of Jesus
Rémuzat (French merchant in Aleppo), 126
Renan, Ernest, 253, 262n

Rennes, 71
repression
of Eastern Christians in Europe, **55–9**
Republic of Letters, 29
revelation
Qur'anic, 190, 191, 192
Rhodinos, Neophytos, 109
Ricadonna, Paul, 209, 215
Riccoldo da Montecroce, 186
Rigord, Fr., 201
Rimini, 55
Riscallah, Nasri, 253, 255, 259n, 261n
rivalry
between/within religious orders, 166, 171–2, 211, 235, 236–7
robbery *see* corsairs
Roben (consul for England and Holland), 122n
Roman Catholic Church, 3, 267
antimodernist ideologies, 237
ecclesiastical power/authority of, 168–9, 171, 234, 237, 245
France vs, 171
imagers, 215
original Christianity vs, 167
Orthodox vs, 13, 60, 114, 168, 170, 172–3, 210, 211; *see also* Melkite Church/Melkites
relation with Eastern Christianity, 75, 166, 167, 188
see also Catholic Church/Catholics
Roman Catholic/Latin missions/missionaries, 66, 167–8, 175
approach/methods of, 23–4
(distribution of) religious images, 200, 201, 202, 209–10, 213, 215
female emancipation and, 6
Islam and, **188–92**
recommendations from, 71, 133, 145
scholarship on, 2
see also Capuchin missions/missionaries; Catholic missions/missionaries; Jesuits/Jesuit missionaries; Lazarists
Roman College (Rome), 91
Roman Empire, 11
Romanos, Saint, 202
Rome, 268
court cases against corsairs, 150
Eastern Christians in/from, 33, 52, 55, 59, 60, 61, 65, 144: Armenians, 52, 59, 79n; Greeks, 117n; Maronites, 29, 51, 59, 66, 67, 68, 69, 72, 73, 77n, 84n, 88n, 89n, 120n, 147, 150, 205; Melkites, 51, 57, 58, 60, 62, 68, 71, 77n, 85n, 117n, 144; Syriacs, 55–6, 66, 68, 86n, 91, 94, 144; Syrian Christians, 106
Eastern vs European Christians visiting, 90
Heyberger in, 22–3
primacy of, 114
schooling in, 76, 99n; *see also* College of Saint Athanasius; Collegio Urbano; Maronite College of Rome
Roque, Jean de la, 62
Rosary
Sisterhood of the Rosary (Aleppo), 229, 230, 233
Rosary images, 208, 210, 251
Roselli, Stefano, 88n
Roux (company, Marseille), 146
Russell, Alexander, 229
Russian Chapel (London), 147
Russian missions/missionaries, 152
Russian Orthodox Church, 237
Russia/Russian Empire, 7, 153
Greek Orthodox in, 143–4
migration to, 148
paintings from, 205
Russo-Ottoman War (1877–8), 153

sacraments, 55, 57, 67, 68, 169
Sacred Heart of Jesus (cult), 215
images/iconography, 211, 212*ill.*
Sacred Heart of Jesus (religious order, Bkirki),
foundation, 24, 213, 236
images, 213
opposition and power struggles, 24, 171, 172, 236–7
rule, 169, 236, 241n
support for, 74, 173–4
see also Hindiyya
Safar, Athanasius (Syriac Archbishop of Mardin), 66–7, 67, 72, 93, 96, 104n, 144
Safar, Giovanni Domenico, 104n, 144
Safavid court (Isfahan), 182
Saida (Sidon, Lebanon), 51, 62, 64, 84n, 108, 110n, 120n, 126
al-Ṣā'igh, Nīqūlā, 212
Saint-Aignan, Jean-Baptiste de, 71, 92, 100n, 144
Saint-Aignan, 'prince' de (nephew of Jean-Baptiste Saint-Aignan), 71
Saint Catherine (monastery, Mount Sinai), 201, 205

Saint George Church (Nicosia), 136, 141n
sainthood/sanctity, 27, 248, 249
  desert saints, 249–50, 251, 257
  female saints, 27, 209, 251
  'saint of the month' (Jesuits), 213, 215
Saint-Jean Church (Lyon), 131
Saint John of Acre (Israel), 109, 151
Saint John of Shuwayr (monastery, Khunshāra, Lebanon), 65, 207–8*ill.*; *see also* Shuwayrite Melkites/monks
Saint Luke Church (Rome), 96
Saint Maroun/Mar Maroun (monastery, Lebanon), 246, 254
Saint Saviour (convent, Lebanon), 62, 211
Saints Cosmas and Damian (convent, Rome), 95
Saint Sophia Cathedral (Nicosia), 136, 141n
Sakkakīnī, Farjallāh, 81n
Sakkakīnī, Niqūla, 81n
salaries, 26, 66, 67, 70, 91, 99n
Saleb, Elia, 83n
Salemi, Graziano, 68, 82n, 99n
Saliba, Sabine Mohasseb, 17
Salibi, Kamal, 15
salvation, 114, 168, 226, 229, 255
Salvatorians/Salvatorian monks, 173, 235, 236
al-Sam'ānī, Yūsif *see* Assemani, Giuseppe Simone
Samir, Samir Khalil, 14
Samos, 147
Sanfilippo, Matteo, 22
San Giovanni hospital (Rome), 67
Sanjian, Avedis K., 15
San Leo (fortress, Italy), 55, 56
San Stefano, Treaty of (1878), 153
Santa Maria in Aquiro (orphanage, Rome), 82n
Santa Maria Egiziaca (Armenian Church, Rome), 67, 96
Santi Pietro e Marcellino (Maronite hospice), 66
Santorini, 121n
Sapienza (University of Rome), 29, 66
Ṣaqr, Shukrallāh, 212
Sasi, Giorgio, 61
Satalia (Antalya), 73, 112
Saxony, 66
Ṣayfī, Aftīmyūs (Melkite Archbishop of Saida), 64, 84n, 108, 110, 111, 113, 114, 120n, 121n, 172, 173, 175
Sbath collection, 30
Sbat, Souheil, 21
scholarship
  Anglophone vs Francophone, 2–3
  evolution of scholarship on Middle Eastern Christianity, 1, 2, 7, 10, **13–33**, 268
  knowledge transfer between Eastern and European, 19
  see also Heyberger, Bernard
Sciain, Anastasia, 58
Sciain, Giovanni (Shahīn, Melkite priest), 57–9, 60, 63, 64, 72, 88n, 117n, 268
Scilhub/Scialup, Giovanni (Ḥannā Shalhūb Ma'ūshī), 81n, 88n, 118n
Sciocrallah, Stefano (Shukrallāh), 65
scriptures
  falsification of, 188
Second Vatican Council *see* Vatican II
secularisation, 14, 236
Segneri, Paolo, 231
segregation, 16
self-consciousness, 132, 153
  of women, 127, 225, 229, 230
Selim I (Sultan of the Ottoman Empire, r. 1512–20), 12
Seville, 57
Shahīn *see* Sciain, Giovanni
al-Shāmī, Isṭifān, 146
Shāmī, Sulayman ibn Būlātiyya, 85n
sharī'a law, 17, 166, 170
Sharkey, Heather, 265
Shediak, Francesco (Shidyāq), 59
Sherman, Rowland (Englishman), 113
Shihābī family/emirate, 151, 235, 237
Shi'ism/Shi'a Muslims, 182, 254–5
ships
  confiscation of, 60, 112, 150
  see also corsairs
Shtamma, 'Abdallāh, 146; *see also* Stamma family
Shūf (Lebanon), 253
Shukrallāh (Patriarch of the Church of the East), 100n
Shukrallāh (Stefano Sciocrallah), 65
Shuwayrite Melkites/monks, 173, 212, 235, 236; *see also* Saint John of Shuwayr
Shuwayr (Mount Lebanon), 209
Sicily, 93
Sidon *see* Saida
silk trade, 29, 67, 107, 149
Simon, Richard, 167
simony, 57
Sinai, 90; *see also* Mount Sinai
Sirt (desert, Libya), 132

Sisinio, Mosè, 116n
slaves, 29, 57, 62, 67, 69, 70, 75, 99n5, 121n
Slim, Souad, 17
Smyrna, 62, 126, 146, 150
Snagov (Romania), 206
sociability/social rules, 168, 235
social class/status, 32, 50, 55, 163, 186
social order, 130, 165–6
Society of Jesus *see* Jesuits
Society for Promoting Christian Knowledge (London), 66
Soury, Jules, 262n
Spain
  alms collection in, 59, 100n
  Eastern Christians in/from, 52, 59, 99n: Greeks, 146; Maronites, 143; Melkites, 58, 64, 77n; Syriac Catholics, 92, 93, 94, 101n, 104n
  missionaries from, 171
spiritual marriage *see* mystical marriage/union
Stamma family, 146
  Antonio Stamma, 146
  Filippo Stamma, 146
  Francesco Namtalla Stamma, 146
state-building, 235, 236
statues, 136, 141n
status *see* social class/status
Stefano (deacon), 84n
Stefano Pietro *see* Iṣṭifān al-Duwayhī
stipends, 68, 70
storytellers, 128; *see also* Diyāb, Ḥannā
Strauss, Johann, 24
Subani, Abramo, 120n
Sufism, 166
Sunnism/Sunni Muslims, 165, 167, 182
Suryani *see* Syriac Christians
al-Suyūṭī, Jalāl al-Dīn (d. 1505), 191–2
Sweden, 154
Sylvester (Silfāstrūs al-Qubruṣī, Greek Orthodox Patriarch of Antioch), 60–1, 68, 114, 115, 117n, 211
Synod of (Mount) Lebanon (1736), 51, 171, 172
Syria, 3, 18, 28, 267
  1860 massacre, 143, 144
  documents produced in, 127
  Eastern Christians from/in, 31, 51, 105: Melkites, 74
  Greater Syria, 2, 3, 199
  Heyberger in, 21–2
  missions to, 66
  occupation/colonisation/intervention, 151, 153
  persecution in, 68, 96–7, 106–7
  religious painting in, 199
  travels through, 124, 125
  see also Aleppo
Syriac Catholic Church/Catholics, 149
  alms collection for, 93, 94, 144
  in Europe, 52: France, 67, 92; Italy, 55, 94, 95; Malta, 90, 93–4; Paris, 56, 92, 93; Rome, 55–6, 66, 68, 86n, 94, 144; Spain, 92, 93, 94, 101n, 104n
  see also Karnuk, Timothy; Safar, Athanāsyūs
Syriac Christianity/Christians, 154
  from/in Aleppo, 67, 72, 92, 149
  in/from Livorno, 72
  in/from Marseille, 68, 71, 91
  in/from Rome, 55–6, 66, 68, 86n, 91, 94, 144
  see also Maronite Church/Maronites
Syriac (language), 254, 262n
Syriac Orthodox Church/Syriac Orthodox, 11, 12, 13, 91
Syrian asceticism, 251, 257
Syrian Catholic Church/Catholics, 108
Syrian Christians
  connections with Egypt, 112
  in Mediterranean, 55, **105–15**
  protection of/by, 133–4
  Syrian Muslims vs, 153
  see also Fakhr family

tafsīr (Qur'anic exegesis), 191, 192
al-Tahtāwī, Rifā'a, 125, 126
ṭā'ifas (social groups, specifically: Christian congregations), 115, 235, 236
tajwīd (method of recital/intonation of Qur'an), 190
tales, 5, 30
'Tale of Two Sisters', 131
Ṭānās, Sarufim *see* Cyril VI Ṭānās
Tanios (uncle of Charbel Makhlouf), 246
Tanzimat (Ottoman reforms), 149
Taoutel, Ferdinand, 21
Tarsus (Turkey), 56
Tatarenko, Laurent, 31
taxation/tax-farming, 18, 136, 142, 149, 165
teaching/teachers, 65, 75, 90, 252
  of Arabic language, 66, 67, 69, 70, 73–4, 93, 99n, 143, 204, 254, 262n
Tehran, 152
temptation, 231

Teodoro d'Aut *see* ʿAbdallāh ibn Dawūd
Teresa of Avila, Saint, 166, 209, 216, 230
Terra Santa (Franciscan province), 72, 88n, 134
Thérèse of Lisieux, Saint, 251
Thomas Aquinas, Saint, 187
Tissan, Gabriele, 64
tobacco, 133
Torah, 192
Toulon, 63
Touraine, 183
trade, 61, 72, 91, 104n
  in printing types, 95–6, 103n
  protection of/by traders/merchants, 134
  trading diaspora/trading networks, 134, 146
  see also commercial affairs/interests; cotton trade; maritime trade; merchants; silk trade
tradition
  innovation vs, 172–5, 236
Transjordan, 165
translators, 109, 128, 143; *see also* interpreters
transnational history
  connected vs, 3
travelogues, 31, 90, 124, 127, 143, 151; *see also* Diyāb, Ḥannā
travels/travellers, 19, 33, **49–55**, 53–4*ill.*, 58–9
  migration vs, 63–5
  motivation for coming to Europe, 55, 60, 90, 143, 144
  origins and destinations, 54*ill.*
  preparation of journey, 144
  to Paris, **124–36**
  wanderings vs, 56
  see also alms collection; circulation; migration
Treaty of Berlin (1878), 153
Treaty of San Stefano (1878), 153
Trémoille, Cardinal de la, 104n
Trent, Council of (1545–63), 51, 91, 167, 169, 172, 201
tribes, 165, 175
Trieste, 148
Trinity, 188, 191
Tripoli (Maghreb), 132
Tripoli (Syria)
  Eastern Christians from/in, 51, 61, 68, 115: Melkites, 109; Orthodox, 114
  merchants from/in, 110, 118n
  missionaries in, 74
Trivellato, Francesca, 4, 19
tsars, 143–4
Tūbiyā al-Khāzin (Maronite Patriarch of Antioch, r. 1756–66), 174
Tunis, 126, 129, 130
Tunisia, 126
Turkey, 153
Turkish (language)
  knowledge of, 66, 70, 135, 144
  religious services and sacraments in, 67, 68, 70
  teaching of, 67, 99n
Turks
  conversion of, 67, 69, 70, 102n
  in Europe, 67, 153
  persecution by, 60–1, 83n, 106, 107
  slaves, 57, 67, 69, 70
  Western representation of, 75–6
  see also Muslims
Tuscany, 52, 63, 65, 150
Tyre (Lebanon), 108, 112

ʿUjaymī, Hindiyya *see* Hindiyya
ʿUjaymi, Shukrallāh, 213
al-ʿUjaymī, Yuḥanna, 101n
Ukraine, 212
al-ʿUmar, Zāhir, 65
Umbria, 55
United Kingdom, 7
United States, 3, 15, 152, 247
University of Haute-Alsace (Mulhouse), 24
University of Strasburg, 20, 21
Unterlinden Museum (Colmar), 264
Urban VIII (Pope, r. 1623–44), 91

vagrants/vagrancy, 51, 56, 59
Valenci, Lucette, 23
Valérien (Capuchin missionary), 71–2, 74
Valignano, Alessandro, 192–3
Valletta, 70
Vatican II, Council (1962–5), 27, 163, 249, 257
Vatican Library, 30, 51, 72, 124
veiling, 131, 136, 225–6, 231
Venice
  Eastern Christians in/from, 52, 83n, 117n: Armenians, 67, 74–5; Greeks, 58, 83n; Maronites, 62–3, 150; Melkites, 57, 62; Syriac Catholics, 94, 95
  image printing in, 215, 220n
Venturi, Antonio, 235
Versailles, 130, 131, 132, 146, 150
Via Crucis (Marseille), 129
Vianney, Saint John (Curé d'Ars), 251, 261n

Vienna
alms collection in, 106
Eastern Christians in/from, 52, 56, 61, 65, 106, 143
image printing in, 212, 215
Vincent, Bernard, 31
virginity, 233
Virgin Mary, 251; *see also* Marian images/iconography
Visitandines (Order of the Visitation of Holy Mary), 169
Volney, Constantin-François, 115, 163
Vurla (Asia Minor), 201

Wādī Qadīsha *see* Qadīsha, Wādī
Wagner, Esther-Miriam, 15
Waltz, Jean-Jacques (Hansi), 264
wanderings/wanderers, 64
travels vs, 56
see also circulation; migration; travels/travellers
waqf (charitable endowments), 17
Weber, Max, 225
West
perception by European Christians of, 124, **129–36**
Western Christianity/Christians
Eastern and/vs, 124, **129–36**, 149–50, 163, 166, 167, 188, 235, 250
Western imperialism, 7
Westernisation, 14, 25, 26, 174, 175, 225, 233, 235
Western merchants, 149, 150
Western spirituality
Eastern vs, 250
Western 'superiority', 188
West Syriac rite, 91
Windler, Christian, 24
witchcraft, 232
witch hunts/trials, 237
women
autobiographies, 227, 228, 232
autonomy of, 228, 234
Catholic women (Aleppo/Mount Lebanon), 5, 26, **225–38**
chastity and celibacy, 233
confessions of, 228, 229, 231–2, 237, 242n
in Cyprus, 135, 136
divinity/sainthood, 27, 209, 237, 251
education of, 229, 234, 235
female mysticism, 25, 227, 228–9, 231
literacy, 226–7, 229–30
modernisation and Westernisation, 136, 233, 235, 237
religious observances by, 226
self-consciousness/individualisation, 127, 168, 225, 229, 230
sexual acts/erotic elicitations, 75, 191, 231–2, 242n
single, 226, 234
veiling, 131, 136, 225–6, 231
Western perception of Eastern/Muslim, 225–6
women's history, 6
writings about and by Eastern Christian, **225–9**
see also marriage; nuns
wood carvings, 205
woodcuts, 201–2, 206, 207–8*ill.*, 215
writers/writings
Christian Arabic writers, 182
oral testimony vs, 226–7, 229, 235
women, 226–7, 229
see also Christian literature

Ximenes, Gianbattista, 74

Yazbak, Yūsif Ibrāhīm, 256
Yazidīs, 167
Yūsuf Istifān (Maronite Patriarch of Antioch, r. 1766–93), 169, 173–4, 175

Zaccur, Grazia, 72
Zahle (Libanon), 215
al-Zaʿīm, Būlus, 201, 209
al-Zaʿīm, Makāryūs *see* Macarius III ibn al-Zaʿīm
Zākhir ʿAbdallāh, 212
Zarur, Agostino, 62
Zaydān, Jurjī, 15
Zayd (servant of Muhammad, the Prophet), 192
Zūq Mikhaʾīl (Lebanon), 85n, 116–17n

EU representative:
Easy Access System Europe
Mustamäe tee 50, 10621 Tallinn, Estonia
Gpsr.requests@easproject.com

www.ingramcontent.com/pod-product-compliance
Lightning Source LLC
Chambersburg PA
CBHW050200240426
43671CB00013B/2190
* 9 7 8 1 3 9 9 5 0 3 5 4 9 *